L M Kendall

PSYCHOLOGICAL PRINCIPLES
IN SYSTEM DEVELOPMENT

CONTRIBUTORS

RICHARD A. BEHAN · System Development Corporation

PAUL C. BERRY · Psychological Research Associates

WILLIAM C. BIEL · System Development Corporation

ROBERT BOGUSLAW · System Development Corporation

MEREDITH P. CRAWFORD · George Washington University, Human Resources Research Office

ROBERT H. DAVIS · System Development Corporation

WARD EDWARDS · University of Michigan

JOHN L. FINAN · California Department of Public Health

ROBERT M. GAGNÉ · Princeton University

ROBERT GLASER · University of Pittsburgh

PAUL HORST · University of Washington

JOHN L. KENNEDY · Princeton University

J. S. KIDD · System Science Affiliates

DAVID J. KLAUS · American Institute for Research

ROBERT B. MILLER · IBM Corporation

ELIAS H. PORTER · System Development Corporation

JOSEPH W. WULFECK · Dunlap and Associates

J. JEPSON WULFF · Psychological Research Associates

LAWRENCE R. ZEITLIN · Dunlap and Associates

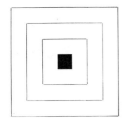

PSYCHOLOGICAL PRINCIPLES IN SYSTEM DEVELOPMENT

Edited by ROBERT M. GAGNÉ

Princeton University

Foreword by ARTHUR W. MELTON

University of Michigan

HOLT, RINEHART AND WINSTON

NEW YORK

FOREWORD

THIS BOOK has the distinction of being the first of its kind, and a very significant first indeed. It marks the coming of age of a systematic conception of the application of psychological principles to the invention, development, and use of complex man-machine systems. As such it has many of the properties of a *theory* of psychotechnology—and a very broad-based theory, at that, when one considers the wide range of basic psychological knowledge that it focuses on the many issues that relate to the human component or components in a system. As a theory of the psychotechnology of man-machine systems, it achieves integration of what has heretofore been variously called "human engineering," "human factors engineering," or "engineering psychology" on the one hand and "personnel psychology" or "personnel and training research" on the other hand. This union comes easily and naturally once the concept of *system* is examined and once the full implications of the concept of the human being as a *component* of a man-machine system are recognized. For it immediately becomes clear that the available properties or functions of man must be considered in planning the mating of man and machine components to achieve the desired system function; that the desired properties and functions of man must be exactly specified (and sometimes revised) as system development progresses; that the desired characteristics of man must be achieved through selection and/or training techniques of high precision and efficiency; and that the functional efficiency of the human component must be maintained and tested within the system context not only on installation but also continuously or at least periodically thereafter.

The student or practitioner in engineering, psychology, personnel management, or system design and development who reads this lucid, well-organized, and completely reasonable exposition of the interrelations and interdependencies of psychological principles in the design of systems may not realize the difficulties and misunderstandings that had somehow to be resolved before such an integrated statement could be presented. The psychotechnologies appropriate to personnel selection, training, and equipment design and use developed more or less in isolation from one another. In part this was because different specialties and specialists within the science of psychology were involved in them, in part because the users of the technologies placed the management of personnel matters, training, equipment design, and system design in more or less isolated compartments of the over-all management system.

By far the most important factor producing resistance to the integration of these psychotechnologies has been the management system commonly employed by the military establishment and industry for the development and use of systems. During World War II, the technology of personnel selection and the technology of personnel training were insulated from one another in the Army Air Forces because these personnel subsystem functions were the responsibilities of different staff agencies. The schism was bridged only during the last year or so of the war by psychologists who *knew* that selection and training were but two aspects of a personnel management "package" or system and could not be properly specified in isolation. During this same time the "human engineers" concerned with equipment design were moving in the direction of integration of equipment design and training considerations, but again with very limited success because they had the resistance of an inappropriate management system.

After World War II and before about 1953, only limited progress was made toward unification of the psychotechnologies. In the Air Force, the unification of personnel selection and training, at least in research, was achieved in 1949 by the Air Training Command through the creation of the Human Resources Research Center (later to become the Air Force Personnel and Training Research Center), but the isolation of personnel and training technologies from the technology of human factors in equipment design persisted, since the latter was the management function of the Air Materiel Command (and later the Air Research and Development Command).

Then, in the early 1950's, two events of great significance for the development of the ideas in the present book took place. First, the Air Force formalized the concept of the weapon system, its subsystems and components. Secondly, it drew together within the Air Research and Development Command the research and development agencies concerned with systems, their equipment components, and their human components. While this still left the critical features of personnel management—selection, training, and maintenance of men—in managerial isolation from the research and development aspects of those problems in systems, a large net gain for the concept of a unified psychotechnology of man in man-machine systems was to occur. Within the Air Research and Development Command, the personnel selection, training, and equipment-design psychologists collaborated in promoting and demonstrating the—to them—obvious truth that there must be an integrated application of these technologies at every stage of man-machine system development from conception to operational obsolescence. Comparable developments were taking place in the Navy, and perhaps occurred there even earlier in time in the case of certain major systems.

At the present time there is widespread acceptance of the unified psychotechnology of man-machine system design by the Air Force, Navy, and Army, and perforce by their contractors. Human-factors scientists and specialists are attached to design teams, system project offices, development groups, and system tests. Other specialists prepare detailed documents in which qualitative and quantitative predictions are made regarding the personnel required to operate and maintain systems under development, and they make statements about training and training-equipment requirements. And all this effort directed toward the human component of a future system explicitly recognizes the necessity of a "doctrine of concurrency"—that is, that the human components and the remainder of the system must be programmed to arrive at a man-machine assembly point at the same moment in time. Finally, much psychological research and development effort, both in-house and on contract, recognizes the obvious need for basic and applied research in support of this unification of the several originally disparate psychotechnologies in the context of man-machine system design, development, and utilization.

Nevertheless, the idea that was born at least a decade ago, and that has grown steadily since then in spite of some temporary reversals, does not have the full acceptance and implementation that a casual examination of regulations, mission assignments, contract clauses, and research and development project statements might imply. In part this is because the management systems of the users of the technology have adapted only slightly to the idea of a personnel management system within which the unified technology can operate continuously on all aspects of the problem of the human component of complex systems. In part it is because only a portion of the human-factors scientists and specialists have had the time or opportunity to explore the integrated conception of psychological principles in system development. Thus it may be confidently asserted that this first presentation of this conception in book form will be the best of all possible kinds of milestones—it will serve as a synoptic and hence available and referenceable statement of the idea that has guided the most exciting and important advances in psychotechnology of the past decade; it will serve as the schema for the instruction of psychologists, engineers, and planners in the broad conception as well as the minutiae of this new psychotechnology; it will guide the definition of new basic and applied research and will assist in locating the points of impact of both old and new scientific knowledge; and if the managerial users of man-machine systems can be seduced into reading it, it may even participate in the correction of management obstacles to the efficient employment of the unified technology of man in man-machine systems.

The editor of this important book, Professor Gagné, is eminently qualified to be the driving force and filter in this first effort to present an integrated psychotechnology of system development. No single person within psychology can claim to be the originator of this systematic conceptualization of psychotechnology; it is the product of many minds—of some basic scientists, some applied scientists, some professional military men. Among them are some who may have contributed much to the notion but may also have delayed its realization by overemphasis on the importance, or ontogenetic priority, of one component technology or another. However that may be, all who know the intimate history of this idea over the last decade recognize Professor Gagné as one of the chief architects of the idea, one of the most persistent and critical originators of propositions and techniques for the transformation of the idea into procedural practice, and—as a consequence of his position as Technical Director of the Maintenance Personnel Laboratory of the Air Force Personnel and Training Research Center—one of the leaders in the actual implementation of the idea in the case of airborne fire-control systems and the early ballistic missile weapon systems. His leadership is attested by the outstanding and widely representative authors of the chapters of this book.

ARTHUR W. MELTON

Ann Arbor, Michigan
October 1961

ACKNOWLEDGMENTS

IT SEEMS FITTING, first of all, for the editor of this book to express his gratitude to those of his colleagues and associates who provided him with initial encouragement in this undertaking—who share his belief that a sizable area of scientific technology and its related fundamental knowledge has been until now inadequately represented in literature available to students, as well as to interested scientists. It is fervently hoped that this volume will accomplish some small degree of fulfillment of their expectations; at the very least, perhaps, in demonstrating that there is indeed a body of knowledge which can be entitled *Psychological Principles in System Development.*

The general conception and design of contents for the book are due in large part to the editor's experience in a formerly existing organization called the Air Force Personnel and Training Research Center, of the USAF Air Research and Development Command. It was during this period of time that he shared with others in the development, first, of a realization of the existence of a yawning cavern of technological ignorance in what came to be called "human factors engineering" relating to military systems; second, of the general nature of the contributions that might be made to this technology by the science of psychology; and third, the need for constructing conceptual bridges to this technology which are firmly based upon the findings of experimental behavioral science. During this period, he came to know many talented and devoted people, working in both government and industrial organizations, who shared his conception of the tremendous potentialities of such a scientifically based technology, and who were unselfishly engaged in expanding the boundaries of its frontier. This constantly growing group of people, who have no single professional name or affiliation, have made innumerable contributions to the knowledge that can now be reflected, in some measure, in this book. Were the book to have a formal dedication, it should be to these individuals, whose daily concern has been, and is, with the job of improving the human aspects of system development and use.

Authors of individual chapters include the following acknowledgments:

Introduction. This has benefited in several places from comments made by William C. Biel, on the basis of a critical reading.

Chapter 2. Gratitude is expressed in particular for the extensive and most helpful critical comments contributed by Ward Edwards and by Robert B. Miller, as well as for suggestions by several authors of other chapters in this book. The author also desires to pay special tribute to the pioneering work of Dr. Miller in this general area.

Chapter 3. The author is grateful to B. F. Green, Jr., J. H. Holland, A. Newell, R. F. Rosin, and D. H. Wilson for wise and informed criticism, and to Rosin also for preparing Table 3.1.

Chapter 4. The authors are indebted to associates who co-authored with Wulfeck the report entitled *Vision in Military Aviation* (see Chapter 4 reference, Wulfeck, Weisz, and Raben, 1958). They participated intimately in developing the framework within which sensory data have been presented in this chapter. M. W. Raben and A. Z. Weisz wrote the detailed example of visual data applied to an operational problem which has been adapted for use here.

Chapter 8. Many of the ideas expressed in this chapter have evolved in the course of research supported by the Office of Naval Research, Personnel and Training Branch, and by the American Institute for Research.

Chapter 9. Many of the concepts and most of the research cited in this chapter have come from the work of the George Washington University Human Resources Research Office (HumRRO). The author expresses his appreciation to his colleagues in HumRRO for the selected samples of their research cited, and for their stimulating discussion and criticisms of drafts of the chapter.

Chapter 14. The writer wishes to express his appreciation to Eugene A. Cogan and S. James Goffard for their helpful criticism of various drafts of the chapter, as well as to Meredith P. Crawford for encouragement and support in its preparation.

Specific acknowledgment of the sources of quoted passages and figures is made in connection with each as it appears in the text. Thanks are recorded here, in general, to those authors, publishers, and copyright owners who have extended permission to reprint these materials.

R.M.G.

Princeton, N. J.
October 1961

CONTENTS

PSYCHOLOGICAL PRINCIPLES
IN SYSTEM DEVELOPMENT

INTRODUCTION

Robert M. Gagné

In our society, some of the most important and spectacular developments of the current age are *systems*. Although the invention of individual machines is still taking place, we tend to think of this kind of invention as being characteristic of a previous "golden age," often associated with what historians call the industrial revolution. In a general sense, machines were conceived as extensions of man's capacity for perceiving and manipulating the environment. They were tools which helped him to see in the dark, to lift heavier loads, to move objects around more rapidly, to perform delicate operations more precisely, to record and retrieve quantities of words, pictures, and sounds, and to do many other things. But as time went on, it became apparent that the social potentialities of machines as tools was far overshadowed by the possibilities exhibited when machines of somewhat different design were embedded within a complex organization, or system. Thus the electric light soon came to be, not simply a tool (a lamp), but a complex "lighting system" which later evolved into a "power distribution system." The telephone became not simply a tool for transmitting and amplifying the human voice but a communication system. Such has been the trend of history for a great many inventions which began as machines.

To progress from a simple machine like the telephone to a complex communication system required many additional inventions, including among others such devices as central switchboards, methods of multiple transmission in single wires, and, in more modern times, the dial system. Such inventions had initially to be conceived, as well as designed and developed, within a total conception of a *system*. A similar picture can be drawn of the development of most military systems. The airplane was initially conceived as a tool which

1

enabled a man to overcome the force of gravity and propel himself and other bodies through the air. Fitted with another kind of tool, a machine gun, it was capable of directing fire at targets on the ground or at other aircraft in the air. But it was not many years before the requirements for increased speed, altitude, and maneuverability of the fighter aircraft forced the design and development of something quite different and more highly sophisticated— an *interceptor aircraft system*. The "tools" were, in effect, taken out of man's hands, and they as well as the man himself became only parts of a complex system of radar detection, communication, and control. In such a system, all of the parts had to be conceived and built to fit together and function as a total organized whole.

Although it is evident that many systems in the past evolved by steps, nowadays it has become quite commonplace for designers to take from the very outset the deliberate course of deriving from some originally stated purposes the characteristics of a total organized system. With such a conception, the various parts of the system can no longer be thought of as tools for the extension of man's capacities but instead must be designed in such a way as to integrate their functions with other parts of the system in the accomplishment of system purposes. As an example, an oscilloscope cannot appropriately be conceived in a systems framework as merely a tool for displaying wave forms to man; rather it must be looked upon as a link in a communication chain whose function is to transform one variety of information coding into another. The determining ideas in such a conception are the system's goals, in relation to which any part, whether man or machine, has a subordinate, albeit essential, function. As a consequence, both kinds of system components—man and machine—must be planned from the very outset with specific reference to the system's goals. The designers of a system must not only choose the most desirable characteristics of machines to perform functions which "fit together" to accomplish these goals; they need also to make similar kinds of decisions, throughout the development process, with respect to the characteristics of the men who become parts of the system.

Planning for the design and development of human components of systems is not an activity which has been performed, over a long period of years, in an entirely systematic way. Rather, such systematic planning is something which has evolved in quite recent years. Up until the early 1950s at the latest, the human components of systems were still being fitted into existing systems, drawn from a pool of manpower which had been selected, trained, and prepared either for quite different jobs or in a manner which gave them only general capabilities for the specific activities they were expected to perform. The idea of planning for human components of systems arises from the same need as does planning for machine components: the desire to eliminate the costly and wasteful modifications and "retrofittings" that delay the time at which a system can be placed in full operation. In brief, the need for systematic planning of human components is based upon the desire to achieve maximal efficiency of system development.

▣ PLANNING FOR HUMAN COMPONENTS
IN SYSTEM DEVELOPMENT

As our previous discussion implies, planning the development process for human components of a system must be thoroughly integrated with the planning for machine development. Of course one does not acquire human beings by constructing them, as one does machines. Nevertheless, the processes by means of which human components are "developed" is just as orderly, in its way, as is the process of machine development. Development pertaining to human components has its own techniques, procedures, and tools. It also takes time, and therefore must be integrated with the planning of system and subsystem from the very earliest stages, in order that delays be avoided or ineffective compromise be eliminated.

The Design Stage

System design begins with a statement of purposes for the system, one or more "missions" the system is expected to perform. The purposes set the stage for the derivation of what the system's characteristics will be. Before going any further, systematic *plans* must be made for how the system is to work, and this means not only that the machines must be conceived functionally, but that there must also be a *design for operations*. More and more frequently in modern systems, the conduct of "advanced design" studies is coming to be an enterprise of increasing importance and thoroughness, with the recognition that some of the most crucial decisions affecting the system's ultimate usefulness are made at this point. Furthermore, it is recognized that human capabilities and human functioning constitute essential factors in the statement of planned operations which results from these decisions. "Operations," after all, must be conceived as prospective events that human beings do with and to machines.

From these plans for operations, together with the knowledge that system designers possess of the current state of technological knowledge, are derived decisions about the functions of subsystems, the major parts of the total system, and the ways in which they may be connected together to fulfill the system goals. At this stage, too, some highly important judgments are made with regard to human beings, and often some entirely crucial ones. Whether explicitly or not, designers at this stage are engaged in decisions that determine what kinds of *human functions* will be employed as well as what machine functions are to be used. If costly mistakes are to be avoided, con-

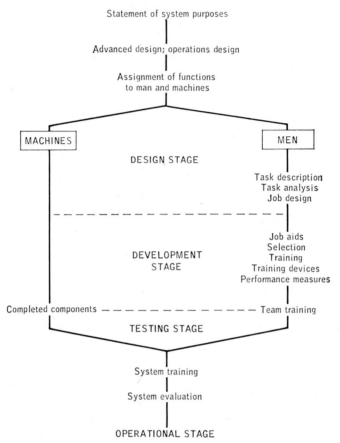

Figure 0.1. The procedures used in the development of human components of systems, and their order of initiation, in relation to the stages of system development. Procedures used for equipment development are not shown in detail.

sideration must be given to the kinds of human functions that are being contemplated: are these the sorts of activities that human beings do well, badly, or perhaps not at all? Are functions being assigned to machines which human beings can perform better, and vice versa? Does the proposed design, in short, exploit to the fullest possible extent the *capacities* of man and machine in combination? It is difficult to overemphasize the importance of such choices in determining the progress of system development, as well as the ultimate success of the system in use.

Assuming that wise decisions have been made at this early stage of planning, the process of design and development is now ready to follow two parallel paths: machine components and human components. They are not independent, of course; rather, they interact at many points as development proceeds. But they use different techniques. Here we shall follow the line of human component development, and indicate how and at what points such interactions occur.

Once the purpose and function of a subsystem has been stated, the designer of human components can proceed to describe in specific terms the nature of the human functions being utilized. This is the job of *task description,* whose basic role in the unfolding process of development is easy to understand. The description of tasks provides the kind of information to which all subsequent plans for human beings in the system must constantly be referred. These are the statements which specify exactly what it is that the man-machine combinations comprising the subsystem are doing. Although begun at this early stage of system development, such descriptions, it is apparent, must be continually revised and refined, to reflect changes in machine design, throughout the development process.

Initially, task descriptions make it possible for the psychological designer to perform the two activities that underlie all the rest of his work: to *design jobs* and to undertake the *task analysis* which makes possible decisions about the techniques to be used in achieving the human behavior required for these jobs. Job design may be considered to be primarily a matter of determining how individual tasks may best be put together ("packaged") so that they can most efficiently be performed by single individuals. Consideration has to be given to the number of tasks, their length, and their physical location within the subsystem. In addition, the attempt is made to combine into single jobs tasks which require similar human capabilities, so that more or less specialization of human functioning will result. The *analysis* of tasks is undertaken to determine to what extent each kind of human behavior required can be achieved with the use of the various techniques available: by providing job aids (job "supports"), by selection, by training.

At this point the designer of human components has considerable basic knowledge of what kinds of behavior are required within the system. He now knows what human beings will be required to do, and in a general way what procedures will need to be followed to insure that people can meet these requirements. It is now time for another set of decisions which make demands upon the technology derived from psychological science. Can the required behaviors be achieved by providing *job aids* to facilitate human performance? Can they be obtained by *selection* of people with the right kinds of fundamental abilities? To what extent must the capabilities needed be established by *training?* The result of these decisions may be a set of requirements which specify the goals of each of these sets of procedures. Obviously, such decisions must be made together, since they mutually influence each other: if the human tasks can be simplified by job aids, less stringent selection and training may have to be done; the more precise and specialized selection can be made, the less training will be needed; and so on. Just as obviously, these decisions, if they are to be wisely made, demand the most careful and thoroughgoing use of the facts and theories of the science of psychology.

The Development Stage

The actual development of the procedures needed to carry out these processes can now be undertaken, once their requirements have been established. *Job aids* can be developed to provide for storage of information beyond the capacity of the human memory, or to serve as external cues for the instigation of behavior required in system tasks. Most commonly, these additions to the system take the form of check lists and instructional manuals. Aptitude tests can be developed or chosen from existing stocks to measure the basic abilities that have been identified, within programs of *personnel selection and classification*. And procedures can be designed for *individual training*, based upon psychological principles of learning relevant to the kinds of performances needed.

A variety of purposes must be served by procedures of *training*. First of all is the need to establish skills which pertain to the performance of a man in relation to a machne or to a set of tools; this is the province of *individual training*. But still a different kind of technique is needed to bring about the effective functioning of various human interactions which take place within the subsystem or between subsystems. Men must not only acquire the capabilities of operating machines, but also of communicating with other men in ways which will bring about the most efficient attainment of system goals under a wide variety of conditions. At the level of the subsystem, the procedures required to bring about such effective functioning comprise what is known as *team training*. A further extension of the idea of having the human beings acquire and refine their competence in interactive and communicative techniques brings us to the functioning of the system as a whole, and to the concept of *system training*. Systematic training of entire system groups is an extremely important enterprise, having the aim of improving the efficiency of operation of systems by making it possible for people to discover and use the most effective techniques of man-man and man-machine interaction to bring about the attainment of system objectives. It will be apparent that training of these three different sorts ordinarily takes place at different times with relation to the total system development. Individual training is usually begun, at least, months before the first equipment is available, in order that crews will be ready to take their places in the system when machines have been built. Team training is usually undertaken at a subsequent time, since it is assumed that individual skills have already been established. System training is the last, and often the longest-lasting as well. It requires the simulation of total system operation, which often makes use of completed equipment components. Actually, system training is sometimes conceived as a part of the operation called the "system test," and may occur over a period of years during which a system attains a steadily increasing degree of operational efficiency.

One of the particular techniques that has achieved considerable success in the conduct of training is the use of *training devices.* Such devices, of course, have an equipment development cycle of their own, which must be keyed in with the development of system equipment. Training devices have an important role to play, not only in establishing the specific skills of machine operation, but also, in the form of simulators, for the conduct of team training as well as system training.

The purpose of training of any and all sorts is to bring about in human beings a capability of some kind of performance of which they were formerly incapable. This being the case, it is evident that a means must be provided to measure the results of training—to determine whether the desired capability has in fact been established. This circumstance calls for the development of *performance measures,* a general name for a set of techniques used to assess human performance. The results of this kind of behavioral measurement provide, first of all, a criterion for performance based upon skills established in individual training, as well as a means of testing the efficacy of selection and individual training techniques. But performance measurement does not stop here. Assessment is also needed of the performance of the teams that operate subsystems, as well as of the performance of the total "team" which operates the system as a whole. For this reason, performance measurement takes on an additional essential role in the later stages of system development, particularly in the *system test.*

Although we have described the events of the design and development stages for human components as occurring in order, two other characteristics of the development process should not be overlooked. The first is the fact that interactions between the lines of development for machine and for man occur all along the way. As the design for hardware becomes progressively defined in detail, changes may be required in the description of tasks which are based upon this equipment; these in turn occasion changes or refinements in the task analysis, and consequently in the requirements for selection, training, and performance measurement. The interaction can also work the other way. It is not at all uncommon, as the operational uses of the system become more firmly described, for some undesirable or infeasible assumption concerning job design, selection, or training to be revealed. Such an occurrence may lead to alterations in the design of the equipment or to the development of additional equipment to perform some previously neglected function. Although Figure 0.1 does not show these interactions, they are nevertheless an important aspect of the system development process.

The second general point to be remarked upon is the occurrence of "testing" throughout every stage of development. Many aspects of the design of jobs, for example, depend upon a test to prove their effectiveness in terms of human performance; this is often referred to as a "human engineering evaluation." Similarly, job aids must often be tried out in a systematic manner before their form can be finally decided upon. The testing of selection techniques is a well-known procedure; the evaluation of training and performance measures are also conducted according to well-established methods. It is apparent, therefore, that the process of development is a dynamic one, a matter of continuous decision making, testing, and revision, and the simplified step-by-step illustration of it contained in Figure 0.1 should not hide this fact.

System Testing and Operation

Once the various developmental activities have been carried out to provide the men required for the system, it is time to bring together the products of this effort and those of the parallel machine-development sequence. The system as a whole may now be assembled with completed components of hardware and men, and "put into operation."

The process of putting a system into operation is seldom done all at once. Rather, this process itself is composed of several stages which are carried out more or less systematically for any given system. These stages are given various names, including "system integration," "shake-down," "system test," and "operational test," among others. Actually, two major kinds of effort can be distinguished; they usually proceed simultaneously, and are mutually interdependent. The first of these is the *exercise* of the system, to establish and refine the interrelationships of its subsystems by means of communication and other forms of human interaction; in other words, to accomplish *system training*. The second comprises the set of procedures used to determine what the system can do and how well it performs the operations implied by its purposes; this is system testing or, more generally, *system evaluation*.

It is sometimes supposed that system testing can be accomplished on the equipment alone, but the complexity of modern systems makes it more and more obvious that this is a fallacious view. Actually, the equipment may be put together and operated during the initial phases of a system test by highly trained and expert personnel. Even under such circumstances, there are many examples of "test failures" that are directly traceable to human error and failing. If the test is to be useful, the occurrence of each failure must be traced back to a deficiency which may turn out to be primarily of a hardware sort, or primarily human. Thus it is essential in all cases to know what it is that human beings are supposed to be doing, as well as what they can do, even if they are highly skilled. This means that standards of human performance and measures of human performance must enter crucially into the decisions that are made during the testing of a system.

But more than this, the testing of a system with highly skilled personnel leaves a major question yet unanswered. How well will the system work *in operation?* Such a question implies the need to know the level of the system's performance when in a "normal" environment, including the social environment created by the kinds of people who will, over a period of some years, be selected and trained to operate the system. *System evaluation* must therefore be conducted under as realistic conditions as possible, as well as under conditions that permit the taking of analytical measures of its performance. For this reason, the final stages of system testing frequently go on for a number of years during which the system may actually be said to be "in operational use." There is usually no hard and fast line that can be drawn between the stage of "system test" and "operational use"; instead, one suffuses imperceptibly into the other. Accordingly, it is to be expected that system training, by means of which increasing efficiency of operation is obtained, and system evaluation, which measures the system's performance, will both extend into the period of actual usage of the system.

▣ PLAN OF THE BOOK

The purpose of the book is to provide an account of the various procedures of psychotechnology used in the development of systems and the principles of psychological science on which they are based. In general, each chapter provides a description of the technology employed at a particular stage of development of the "man" section of the man-machine system, some examples of these techniques, and a discussion of their relation to relevant aspects of the science of human behavior. The chapters are arranged in the order in which problems of development of human components and teams are ordinarily encountered during the entire cycle of system development. A brief stage-setting introduction has been provided for each chapter, the purpose of which is to relate the information among chapters, as well as to the process of system development as a whole.

In an initial chapter, the nature of psychological effort in the systems framework is described, including the ways used to apply psychological knowledge to the process of system development, and the potentialities of systems as vehicles for psychological research. Following this, there are three chapters dealing with psychological principles of specific relevance to system design and, more basically, to the whole process of development of human components of systems. Chapter 2 describes the nature of human functioning as seen by the psychologist. Chapter 3 relates the capabilities of man to that most important modern equipment component, the computer. Chapter 4 discusses the capacities and limitations of human functioning. Related to these in its relevance to the design stage is Chapter 5, which describes the kinds of psychological knowledge that enter into the design of equipment components for a system, and the consequent design requirements for such components.

The stage of development proper is represented by a set of chapters which follow. These begin with Chapter 6, dealing with the topics of task description and task analysis. The logic of procedures used in the selection and classification of personnel for systems is discussed in Chapter 7. Chapter 8 gives an account of the development of aids to job performance, and the rationale on which they are based. Chapter 9 considers the important subject of training, and Chapter 10 provides an account of the requirements for training devices generated by training programs. Progressing in time to the latter end of the phase of system development, we come to a consideration of team functions and training in Chapter 11 and of techniques for assessing human performance in Chapter 12.

Consideration is given in two final chapters to the problems encountered in using psychological principles and methodology in situations involving the testing of total systems. The subject of evaluating system performance is considered in Chapter 13. Chapter 14 discusses generally the nature of psychotechnology as an approach to system research and development.

System development is an enterprise of growing importance in our society, and of rapidly expanding interest to the psychologist. Psychology as a science has a tremendous amount to offer as the basis of an organized technology of human behavior. The psychologist is constantly challenged by questions arising during system development, many of which he can answer only in approximate and incomplete ways. It is the intention of this volume to collect together current knowledge of the most evident relevance to system development, to show its origins in psychological research, and to indicate the aspects of psychological science which may be expected to yield additional facts and principles as the development of the science of behavior proceeds. It is hoped that the student who uses this book will come to recognize what it is that we as psychologists know which can be applied to the design and development of systems, as well as what it is we need to discover in the future prosecution of psychological research.

NOW THAT WE HAVE INTRODUCED THE reader to the kinds of activities that take place in system development and given some idea of the sequence of these activities, it is appropriate to set the stage for the unfolding of the details of the whole enterprise in which psychological scientists engage. This is the purpose of Chapter 1.

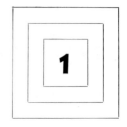

What is the nature of a system? When one engages in the development of technology, the application of psychological principles to developing systems, how can these in fact be conceived as "influencing development"? Is it possible that this process of development is itself something that can become the object of scientific inquiry? The attempt to answer questions such as these leads in this chapter to a consideration of some of the rationale for systems and to a view of their essential nature. Systems are described as man-made "synthetic" organisms, whose components, subsystems, and interactive mechanisms have analogous functions to those of biological organisms, as well as a definite life cycle. Men and the organizations they establish as part of the total system create the characteristics of stability and continuity which are a prominent feature of systems.

Within this organismic framework, it is possible to conceive of the specific activities that form a part of system development—and that are to be discussed more fully in subsequent chapters—as interventions which are made by system developers initially, and later by system managers, in the on-going life processes of the synthetic organism. The effects of such interventions as selection of human components, their individual and team training, and the provision of suitable supports and job environments, can be studied and evaluated as a part of the development enterprise. But there is also an additional possibility. Because of the nature of a synthetic organism, the functioning of its parts and subsystems may be studied directly, thus providing a means of developing systematic accounts of the processes of interaction within the system, as well as their effects on total system functioning. Although the scientific study of systems in this sense has been going on for only a relatively few years, it provides at present the lively promise of the development of an orderly body of "system theory" which will illuminate the operation of a great variety of human organizational enterprises, as well as the activities of the individual organism.

In the sense that it relates the concepts of system and system development to the aims of psychology as a science, this chapter is intended to provide a setting against which the process of developing the "man" part of man-machine systems can be viewed in broad perspective. But the chapter has another purpose too: it provides the opportunity for the student of psychology to appreciate some of the future possibilities of the system as a point of view for the development and use of scientific knowledge about human behavior.

PSYCHOLOGY AND
SYSTEM DEVELOPMENT

John L. Kennedy

"Man"—what does the word really mean? To me it suggests no mere primeval ape-like creature that walked erect and had hands. To be truly human, he must have had the power to reason and the ability to fashion crude tools to do his work.

There is the key, the ability to make tools, as distinct from merely using the pointed sticks or sharp stones that lay readily at hand. Such a being, who set about shaping the raw materials of nature in a regular pattern to suit his needs, was the one worthy to be considered the earliest human. And at last we have found him.

I call him Zinjanthropus, or East Africa Man. He lived more than 600,000 years ago.[1] (LEAKEY, *1960*)

Zinjanthropus and the stones that he fashioned into crude choppers, enabling him to add meat to his diet, formed the first simple man-machine system. The shaped stones extended his ability to perform the task of skinning an animal—a task that he could not accomplish without them. Why *system?* Because the goal is achieved by an interaction between man and device. When we add the stones to the man, we design a different organism, man-in-relation-to-stones—indeed, a "synthetic" organism. In the ensuing 600,000 years, man has created an ever-more complex series of synthetic organisms by the process of physical and social invention. He has found ways of extending his individual natural abilities in every direction, so that modern man-machine systems

---

[1] Quoted by permission of *National Geographic Magazine.* Copyright 1960, National Geographic Magazine.

may now consist of hundreds of men and machines covering thousands of square miles.

The Development of Systems

The synthetic organisms we call man-machine systems appear to be relatively unstable, *ad hoc,* and contrived when compared to natural organisms, but they go through processes of development akin to biological evolution on the one hand and to the life cycle of a single organism on the other. The developmental process similar to biological evolution is that of design and redesign of families of man-machine systems, such as has occurred in the "evolution" of the jet aircraft, the atomic submarine, or the high-speed digital computer. Possibly the term "design evolution," as opposed to biological evolution, might assist in keeping the analogy within bounds.

When men and machines are assembled into a particular operational system, the assembly exhibits development, involving stages similar to birth (test in the operational environment), infancy (initial operational capability), maturity (full operation in relation to other systems), and senescence (phasing out for obsolescence). Possibly the term "system life cycle" might help in distinguishing these developmental processes in man-machine systems from their analogs in the individual biological organism.

Bonner (1960) points to the trilogy of evolution, genetics, and development in describing biological organisms. It is difficult to conceive of an exact analogue for the genetics of synthetic organisms, but an analogous process might be found in the sets of plans and decisions resulting in changes in system design during the life of a particular design configuration. Thus, in the family of piloted aircraft, the progressive changes from B-17 to B-36 could be viewed as genetic modifications on the same general design configuration, while the shift from piloted aircraft to missiles could be viewed as a major evolutionary change. In any case, design evolution and system genetics are now occurring at such a rapid rate, as compared to the biological process, that they may be indistinguishable. This book is primarily devoted to problems of system development during the system life cycle, taking the machine components as given.

It should be noted that the *men* provide the stability and continuity of the synthetic organism. The organization of men and machines creates an entity different from, although dependent upon, individual men. Thus, commanding officers come and go, but the aircraft carrier and its crew create a synthetic organism that has a life cycle relatively independent of who happens to be in command at any particular time.

What is a System?

We have discussed complex man-machine systems in a general way, but we have not given either a definition or examples. What are systems, and how would one recognize such an entity? Synthetic organisms are not as easily defined, specified, or recognized as natural organisms because they are not bounded by a generally accepted interface, such as the skin. And they have the property of being embedded in ever-larger systems. This is not a new problem in science, but it warrants some discussion. Astronomers, for example, seem to have little conceptual difficulty in defining a solar system, even though it is obvious now that a particular solar system is embedded in a larger system such as a galaxy, which is embedded in the Milky Way, which is embedded in the universe. The definition of system is in a sense arbitrary and depends heavily on *a priori* definition of a task or problem. If the problem is to account for the behavior of the planets in the solar system, it is possible, at one level of explanation, to consider the interactions between the sun and the planets only. It turns out that the concept of gravity will account for many of the major phenomena observed. Another problem or task may require the definition of a larger system to discover the essential laws to account for the observed phenomena.

If the problem is to describe, predict, and control individual human behavior, it may suffice to treat the individual organism as an entity. But there is much human behavior, such as the work humans perform, that cannot be described, predicted, or controlled without reference to the machines men use or to the social organization in which individual humans perform these tasks. The concept of system, then, implies a *goal* or *purpose,* and it implies *interaction* and *communication* between components or parts. For the individual human organism, the components are cells and the subsystems are the organs of the body. In the case of complex man-machine systems, the components are individual humans and the machines they control and by which they are controlled.

Automobile and driver make up a system, a drive-in restaurant is a system, a factory is a system, the United States government is a system and the United Nations General Assembly is a system, all of them man-made, and thus synthetic, organisms. In these examples it should be noted that the progression is from the man-machine system to the organism composed almost entirely of men, the human organization. Thus, man-machine systems represent a subclass of human organizations.

In the case of the solar system, the regularities or laws governing the interactions of the components are sufficiently well known to make a great deal of accurate prediction possible. Many of the regularities in the behavior of man-machine systems remain to be discovered; but, as this book will demonstrate, the process of development is being studied. Complex man-machine systems are designed and developed to meet the ever-expanding tasks that technology and organization make possible, on the one hand, and that the aspirations of man to describe, predict, and control nature and other men demand, on the other. System development is characterized by continuous compromise between the desired and the possible; each new system stretches physical science and technology and our capacity to organize to the limit.

This discussion of the origins of man-machine systems may be summarized with a working definition as follows: *A man-machine system is an organization whose components are men and machines, working together to achieve a common goal and tied together by a communication network.*

As systems have become larger and more complex, they have created serious economic, political, social, psychological, and even moral problems in addition to technological problems of engineering design and feasibility. But the most important psychological problem relating to systems arises from the necessity to organize people, to acquire them as system components, to select and classify them, to train them, to keep them working for *system* goals and to bring their performance to a peak to achieve the system goals.

What Psychologists Do in System Development

Psychologists carry out research and development on the human components, subsystems, and total system interactions of man-machine systems. They give advice, based upon psychological facts and principles, about design interventions in systems, about measuring the performance of man-machine systems, and about improving the performance of systems. In rare instances, they may actually manage the process of development of man-machine systems. They are specialists in "human engineering," personnel selection, training, "human factors," and other applied arts connected with the development of systems. The next section of this chapter contains a brief discussion of these activities in relation to the concept of systems as developing organisms.

All these activities lead to the conception of an even more fundamental and important enterprise, that of utilizing the concept of man-machine system as a framework for the organization and definition of problems of basic research on human behavior. The design and conduct of fundamental research to extend our understanding of system development is an activity which exhibits great promise for the understanding of human behavior as it occurs in socially important and productive situations. These possibilities are discussed in the latter portion of this chapter, where we consider the man-machine system and its development as an arena for psychological research, and give an account of the methods employed in such research. Some of the major implications of this approach for the definition of psychological problems are also considered.

▣ APPLICATION OF PSYCHOLOGICAL KNOWLEDGE TO SYSTEM DEVELOPMENT

The concept of organismic development has considerable influence on the selection and application of interventions in the system life cycle. Interventions are the means by which the system psychologist gives effective advice to the system manager. Interventions may range all the way from advice to wait for the next developmental stage to the design and application of a particular reinforcement procedure at a particular time in the system life cycle. The methods developed by psychologists for effective intervention will be discussed in a later section. The timing of their application to get maximum benefit is still an unsolved problem. In this section we shall relate the kinds of intervention used by the psychologist to the stages of system development.

Designing Equipment

As machines and devices are more frequently used to extend man's performance capabilities in systems, the problem of matching men and machines arises, particularly in relation to the informational displays and controls of machines. Man, as an operator of equipment, is not infinitely adaptable. He has inherent limitations as an information processer and as a manipulator of equipment (see Chapter 4). These limitations pertain to a wide range of human tasks, from simple reaction time to complex decision making.

The psychological specialty of "human engineering," or engineering psychology, emerged during World War II to assist engineering designers in the development and choice of displays and controls which would optimize the man-machine relationship. Thus, many alternative designs of knobs, hand-wheels, joysticks, and the like, for adjusting and manipulating machines have been subjected to comparative psychological evaluation by measuring performance with them under standardized conditions. Similarly, comparative psychological evaluations have been conducted on the design of numerals, letters, maps, scales, dials, and so forth, by measuring performance under similar and controlled conditions. A *Handbook of Human Engineering Data for Design Engineers* (Kennedy, 1949) is available to assist in the application of psychological information and method to the design stage of system development. Excellent reviews of the engineering psychology literature have been provided by Fitts (1958) and by McCormick (1957).

Division of Functions

One important consequence of engineering psychology studies has been a growing concern over the assignment of functions in systems to men or machines during the design stage. Such a concern arises because mistakes can limit the performance of the system throughout its life cycle or require expensive design modifications (retrofit) during the system life cycle. Decisions about division of functions also interact with the problem of the design of tasks for the human components. The functions that men perform best are the nonroutine, problem-solving, "troubleshooting," programming, inventing, goal seeking, and integrating functions. Machines perform best when called upon to *extend* human capabilities, such as seeing, hearing, moving rapidly, lifting, manipulating, memorizing, and the like. Humans in systems have been described as "the glue that holds the system together," but proper allocation of functions during the design stage may substantially assist rapid system development. The most important point to be made is this: the design problem is not how to design a machine—it is how to design an organism.

Job design for human components is done in several stages. The system designer does a rough translation of functions into jobs in estimating numbers and categories of people required to man the system. It will be the task of the system manager to actually fit the human components provided him by the personnel subsystem (see the next section) into operating jobs. Psychological research on job design is still in a relatively early stage of development, and much of the technology of placing men in jobs is carried out by consultation and advice based on experience with other systems or with previous evolutionary versions of the same system.

The Personnel Subsystem

Man-machine systems are developed by three interrelated and interacting subsystems of a higher-order system or organization of planners. The first of these subsystems is that of machine design, procurement, logistics, and supply: the *"hardware" subsystem*. The second subsystem has to do with the procurement, selection, classification, training, promotion, and the like, of men: the *personnel subsystem*. The third consists of the operational managers of man-machine systems: the *management subsystem*.

From the point of view of the higher-order planning system, individual men are considered to be rather independent components who might, at one time or another, be required to operate in *any* man-machine system. The personnel subsystem concept is based upon certain practical human life-cycle considerations. Human life cycles include death, retirement, resignation, obsolescence, and forced termination of employment at the exit end of the stream. The concept first of all assumes a stream of people flowing into and out of the condition of availability to be organized into operating man-machine systems. Secondly, it assumes different lengths of time of availability, ranging from the "career" to the "short hitch." Thirdly, it assumes large and important individual differences between the human components. Psychologists, for the past half-century, have been investigating the range and nature of differences between people by devising, administering, and interpreting tests. Chapter 7 describes the procedures used and the problems encountered in the psychological study of individual differences. Many psychologists are engaged in these studies. The practical outcome is information of use to managers—that is, to the developers of the system's operations—who are making decisions about people in relation to the system's mission.

Let us consider the decisions as exemplified in a military personnel subsystem and the nature of the information supplied by psychologists. The first decision about a new human component is whether or not he should be acquired as a component. The range of general aptitude for military service is so wide that some men are eliminated as possible components in any military system. The psychological contributions to this decision are the general classification test battery, interviews, special aptitude tests, and other screening devices. These contributions are validated against some criterion of success or failure in performance during military service.

If the decision is in favor of acquiring the new human component, the next decision is whether to put him directly into an operating man-machine unit or to send him to a school for specialized training. The psychological contributions to this decision again are classification test batteries, interview techniques, and special aptitude measures, validated against pass-fail and grades in the schools.

The next decision concerns the kind of training, and again scores on special aptitude tests plus interview information assist the system developer in making wise decisions about personnel allocations. An important decision is whether or not the component should be trained to become a manager or officer, and again psychological tests of general and special aptitude are involved.

If the individual is to be given specialized training, he is again managed by procedures to which psychologists make important contributions (Chapter 9). The arrangement of experience for most rapid and efficient learning (the curriculum) is influenced by psychological research on human learning and training. The tests of proficiency which measure success or failure following training are designed by psychological methods (see Chapter 12).

As the new component gains experience in the military service, many additional managerial decisions are required. Considerations of promotion, pay, and assignment are influenced by scores on qualification tests designed by psychological methods, as well as by years of experience and kinds of experience. Psychologists are assisting military managers at all levels of the personnel subsystem in the most efficient utilization of the human raw material at their disposal.

Training for Operations

After people are assorted into jobs, the designer of operations must give consideration to the criteria of system performance. How well will it accomplish the task it was designed for? Will performance be at a satisfactory level? If not, what interventions are needed? Psychologists may assist at every step in this decision process, beginning with the problem of evaluating system performance (see Chapter 13). If performance is judged to be inadequate (and it usually is in the early stages of development), a variety of psychological remedial techniques are available, depending upon the particular diagnosis of this deficiency.

Individual Training

If the diagnosis points to an inadequate level of individual knowledge and skill (a common diagnosis in the early stages of a system life cycle), individual training devices and procedures (Chapter 10) have been designed for improving the system-related performance of individual components. Psychological research on human learning and training has contributed heavily to the design and utilization of such devices and procedures. The Link Trainer for developing skill in piloting aircraft is an example of an individual skill-training device. A training device for trouble shooting in the maintenance of electronic equipment is another example. Training devices at the level of the individual may be used to maintain a given level of individual proficiency, as well as to achieve it.

Environmental Supports

In addition to individual training devices and procedures, individual system-related performance may be improved by providing job aids (Chapter 8), such as manuals, check lists, procedural outlines. Very often, individual performance can be aided effectively by the provision of external sources of systematized knowledge about the effects of certain decisions or actions on other parts of the system. Job aids may also break complex jobs down into step-by-step operations, so that the learner does not become completely confused in performing the job initially.

Team Training

A common diagnosis in the early stages of system development is that system performance may be potentially inadequate because of poor teamwork in the operating subsystems. Successful performance of the mission of the system depends upon the ability of two or more individuals to act in cooperation as a group. Thus, the psychological techniques arising from research on small groups and teams may be applied to system performance by the design and use of team training devices and procedures (see Chapters 10 and 11). Examples of such devices are the gunnery team trainers and combat-information-center trainers on naval vessels and in shore stations.

System Training

Finally, the diagnosis may point to the necessity for coordinated procedural training of the whole operating crew, so-called system training (see Chapter 11), in which the complete man-machine system is exercised in the operating environment or in a simulation of the operating environment. Examples of such system training are fleet exercises, air-defense exercises in which friendly aircraft simulate hostile raids, and the "packaged" synthetic system-training exercises prepared by simulating operational problems with computers. Several hundred psychologists are involved in the latter program alone.

Psychological research on man-machine system training and evaluation and on crew development has not kept pace with the applications of these techniques, in no small part due to the expense and difficulty of such research. Since complete physical simulation is often impractical, a continuing question concerns what needs to be simulated and how faithfully the operational environment must be matched in order to permit generalization from the simulated environment to the operational environment.

▣ PSYCHOLOGICAL RESEARCH ON MAN-MACHINE SYSTEM DEVELOPMENT

The modern trend toward the replacement of men and machines for many tasks and the consequent requirement for organizing and coordinating the work of man has created new demands on psychological knowledge and methods. Raben's (1960) recent and excellent survey of operations and systems research literature lists nearly 1000 references to particular research contributions ranging from mathematical analysis to empirical studies of systems. As psychologists continue to make important contributions to the man-machine design and development problem, they are learning how to place the individual in suitable interaction with other individuals and components of the system and how to develop criterion measures arising from the system as a whole in addition to the more familiar component criteria of performance.

Let us take some examples. The invention of radar makes possible a tremendous extension of the individual's capability to detect at a distance. This increased capability is, however, achieved at a cost. Instead of an "object," with all its information content, the individual man now works with a cathode ray tube display in which the object is translated into a dot or "blip," moving against a grid of geographical coordinates. The blip may be produced by a variety of circumstances—it is no longer an object but a symbol, and the object-properties (such as size, shape, number, markings, identification, and intent) must be *added* to the symbol by a complicated process of inference, involving communication with other people and organizations. Systematic use of redundancy available in the system is required for checking facts and inferences, and a complex chain of decision-making organizes the work of many individuals. Good distance vision on the part of the individual man is thus replaced by a complex man-machine system—it replaces one kind of human performance capability, on which there are severe limitations because of the structure and function of the eyes and nervous system, with another kind of performance capability that the organization of the task now requires. The new capability demands new information to be supplied by other men and it demands the managerial skills of scheduling and planning. It may, in the latest systems, require the construction of complex computer programs, and it may put excessive demands on the exercise of good human judgment in making decisions about variables not included in computer programs. But the most important consequence for psychology of the man-machine system is that the criteria for evaluating performance now go beyond measures of individual performance. A high correlation may be found between the visual acuity of the squirrel hunter and his success in shooting squirrels, but the possibility of a significant correlation between the individual visual acuity of the radar operators with success of the system in defense against an attack by intercontinental ballistic missiles seems unlikely. Other human functions are substituted for visual acuity as primary determining variables, and the performance of the system is now the result of the coordinated action of many men and many machines.

The search for simple, individual variables is further complicated by the nature of system tasks. It is possible to maximize the performance of one component to the detriment of performance of the whole system. ("The operation was successful, but the patient died.") A possible measure of the performance of a radar operator might be to report movements on every blip on his screen as rapidly as possible. It becomes clear that he contributes most effectively to system performance if he can be trained to do "filtering," to exercise "judgment" about the requirements of the rest of the system in pacing his reporting. In order to do the filtering job effectively, he needs to be kept in communication with and reinforced by information about the criteria of system performance.

Criteria of System Performance

The tasks of systems are often stated in such broad and general terms that the psychologist encounters difficulty in task definition and measurement. The primary task of the living organism, to stay alive, illustrates the problem. Are there measurable degrees of "aliveness"? Is the concept "alive" sufficiently operational to provide hardheaded measures of performance? Clinical psychologists work with the concept of "adjustment," a mysterious balance between organism and environment. For many industrial man-machine systems, profit-making is often the system criterion, and economists have laid down the rules for the computation of the criterion measure as a continuous variable using the unit of money. For military and government systems, the variables and the units in which task performance may be measured have not been well defined. "Military worth" and "governmental efficiency" are concepts that continue to elude the criterion measurer in much the same way that "adjustment" eludes the clinician.

It may be that the ultimate system performance criterion for many large systems will remain a matter for the judgment of experts—the interactions may be too complex to measure in any other way than by psychological rating methods similar to those used in estimating the popular vote in national elections, or by the decisions of the Joint Chiefs of Staff.

One possible route for the psychologists in search of system criterion measures is to define and work with measurable subcriteria. Such a procedure requires task analysis and the careful selection of subsystems that will reflect the essential interactions of the system. Cost in dollars is such a subsystem variable—it cuts across many of the system interactions. The subcriteria of system performance are more difficult to specify. New measures that have many of the aggregative properties of cost need to be discovered. Aggregated measures of output in relation to input, as in the case of the metabolism of the living organism, may provide operating criteria for psychological study of system performance. Thus Chapman, Kennedy, Newell and Biel (1959) were able to measure the "filtering" of information passing through a 30-to-40 man air defense crew by comparing input information with information formally acquired by the system; and they were able to measure distribution of effort by comparing the number of responses made to important and unimportant information by the system as a whole. Such measures are only examples of subsystem variables that may be developed as criteria of performance.

Systems or Components?

The fracturing of systems into manageable components is the standard way of dealing with the entity. As we have seen, a popular method has been to separate men and machine components and to define a personnel subsystem and a machine or hardware subsystem. Such a procedure begs the question of total system performance, permitting the psychologist to concentrate on people and their properties and the engineer to concentrate on machines and their properties. The problem of integration of men and machines is left to the skill and ingenuity of the system manager. Criterion measures for the personnel subsystem tend to be grades in special schools or training programs, while criterion measures for machine subsystems tend to be the subgoals of "flying higher and faster."

By defining a personnel subsystem, psychologists are often able to pursue such problems as the measurement of individual aptitudes, capacities and skills, motivation, and personality variables quite independently of the question of operational system performance. There are many advantages to such a procedure. The primary advantage is the easy accessibility of a criterion measure such as the performance of people judged in training, against which to validate individual test scores. A tremendous amount of research has been done by this means (see Chapter 7). A second advantage is that psychologists are not required to understand the equipment environment provided by the operational system. The principal method for improving system performance is selection and classification of the human components into aptitude categories on the one hand and the development of skill and experience categories on the other. Thus the new human system component is placed in a general aptitude category by psychological tests and then given specialized training (if his general aptitude is sufficiently high) to prepare him for a skill category. Operational systems are manned by a "table of organization" which attempts to specify the numbers and skills of people required to achieve the system goal. The system managers are left with the task of fitting these components into "jobs," organizing their efforts, defining and reinforcing the system goal, evaluating performance; in short, the integrating task. The science of psychology can better assist the manager with the integrating task when psychologists begin to study man-machine systems as developing, interacting organisms.

Why should psychologists study man-machine system development? Development or directed change of behavior in time is the most characteristic property of systems, as it is of living organisms. The study of development in living organisms has shown that it follows an orderly sequence or pattern, the developmental schedule (Carmichael, 1951). In the prenatal period, structure and function unfold in a predictable sequence under the control of growth processes, hormones, and environmental influences. The variables influencing the rate of growth are becoming known and the growth rate may be changed by manipulating these variables. After birth, the variables of the environment become more active determiners of behavior, but gene-determined growth processes continue to create the inevitable stages of infancy, childhood, adolescence, maturity, and senescence. The managers of man-machine systems deal with a growth process analogous to that of the living organism. Systems go through a design and assembly stage resembling the period of gestation. Systems are "born" when they become operational in the environment for which they were designed. They go through stages like infancy, childhood, adolescence, maturity, and old age. Weiner (1960) has described rough developmental stages for a particular man-machine system.

An answer to the question of why system development should be studied is that similar principles, laws, and rules may be discovered for the design and management of man-machine systems to those which have appeared from the study of biological development. Characteristic managerial problems appear to have their biological analogues. For example, the manager may be concerned with a high rate of personnel turnover and its effect on the development and maintenance of operational capability of the man-machine system. This is a problem like that posed by the biological grafting procedure, in which it has been demonstrated that the success of the graft of new tissue depends, among many other variables, on the stage of development of the organism. Or the manager may be concerned with the problem of a slow rate of growth in performance capability and may wish for some technique for speeding it up. The biological counterpart, of course, is the technique of injection of hormones to speed up biological growth. The psychological methods for influencing rate of psychological growth consist of the design and application of interventions, such as special training techniques, reinforcement procedures, and motivational procedures. The manager may be forced to recognize that techniques appropriate to an early developmental stage of the system are no longer desirable or effective at a later stage. A managerial art, related to the science of development and growth, may very well replace "scientific management," which tends to be based upon simple component measures of "efficiency."

The research psychologist who is involved with systems must also recognize the overwhelming importance of development in choosing performance criteria and in measuring performance. Performance measures taken at a given stage of development should not be viewed as necessarily representative of the "potential" of the system. Without some indication of the developmental stage, such performance measures are most difficult to interpret. Possibly a measure of "system IQ" would help to solve this problem! The IQ does have the property of relating present performance to a developmental measure, chronological age.

System Theory

Although much theoretical work has been done on biological systems, no really comprehensive "map" for describing the growth of synthetic organisms, for determining how to combine human capabilities with machine capabilities to achieve system goals, is now available.

> Of particular difficulty to system theory are the many criteria which are necessarily used in evaluating system effectiveness. Typical criteria in current use are system accuracy and reliability, flexibility, autonomy, reaction time, and rate of response, resources utilized, enemy resources neutralized, resistance to obsolescence, safety, ability to recover from catastrophe, and so forth. Even ethical and political criteria must somehow be taken into account. Although it may be difficult to find common denominators for these multiple criteria, some method is needed to deal conceptually with their interrelationships. And research on human performance must be at least guided, perhaps controlled, by known or expected relationships between system criteria and the sub-criteria of human performance.[2] (Research Group in Psychology and the Social Sciences, 1960.)

Of possibly more direct and immediate benefit to the man-machine system manager is research on the conditions under which the human components of systems invent ways of improving system performance, on how to make the system as a whole learn to use its resources, both human and machine, more effectively. Much more research needs to be done on a general hypothesis about speeding up system development in its later stages toward maturity. The hypothesis or principle is: *Train the team as a whole in an adequately simulated environment and give it immediate knowledge of results.*

[2] Quoted by permission of the Research Group in Psychology and the Social Sciences.

▣ METHODS USED IN RESEARCH ON SYSTEM DEVELOPMENT

The methods used by psychologists in studying system development do not differ in any fundamental way, except possibly in scope, from those used in the study of other psychological problems involving human behavior. Let us consider how these methods are applied at the several stages of system development, beginning with the "prenatal" stage. At this stage, a man-machine system consists of all the individuals who *might* become components of an operating system.

As we have seen, the psychometric procedures of selection and classification on the basis of aptitude are applied to sort individuals into aptitude, skill, and knowledge categories. A standard methodology for selection of test items, test administration, recording of behavior, and analysis of data is available and generally agreed upon. The methods of selecting and classifying on the basis of skill often involve the development and use of special apparatus. Knowledge classification again returns to the psychometric procedures of design, administration, and interpretation of achievement tests of performance.

Psychological methods for providing individual knowledge instruction and training at the general level are also well established, if not well understood. Classroom instruction tends to be evaluated by the verbal or written performance test of "memory" for the material studied. These procedures are thought to "condition" or prepare the individual for his eventual role in system operations but the criteria of performance appear to be either excessively subjective, based upon ratings of instructors, or excessively objective, like scores on multiple-choice tests, the connection of which to system performance is often remote.

When the man-machine system is born, it encounters the operational environment with a relatively fixed set of human components and a relatively fixed set of machine components. The problem now becomes one of development of the operational crew against measures of system performance. What psychological methods should now be used?

It seems clear that *crews* (see Chapters 10 and 11) need to be studied over long periods of time under a variety of environmental conditions, ranging from routine operations to times of maximum stress. The appropriate methods shift from those characteristic of the field of psychometrics and traditional experimental psychology of the individual (aptitude, skill, and knowledge testing) to the methods developed by social psychologists for the study of groups and organizations. The organism under investigation changes and the traditional methodology of individual psychology must accommodate to the change.

We may observe, however, that psychological methods of experimentation are applicable to the synthetic organism by reference to a particular set of experiments on system development (Chapman and Kennedy, 1956) performed in a laboratory which was specially designed to permit the application of these methods. The general hypothesis tested by these experiments was that the psychological techniques used so successfully in inducing rapid and efficient learning and adaptation in individual living organisms would transfer successfully to guide the rapid development of synthetic organisms. This hypothesis was essentially confirmed, although adaptations of standard psychological methods were required. Let us use the categories of methods in psychology devised by Andrews (1948) in describing them.

1. *Methods of selecting the individuals to be studied.* Four crews were selected to operate a simulated man-machine system requiring 30 to 40 men. A first "shakedown" run was conducted with a paid crew of college students, selected on the basis of availability, some aptitude test scores, and willingness to work part time in the laboratory for a school term. The remaining crews were obtained through the Air Force personnel subsystem from operating Air Defense sites and were released for six-week periods of temporary duty at the laboratory. Air Force rank, skill-category, and aptitude level information were available, but the problem of job design and assignment was turned over to the commanding officer or manager of the crew. The experimenters wished to observe the changes in job assignment as a function of crew development and environmental "stress" applied in the experiments. Such crew selection procedures ensured that new crews would be under developmental study with a minimum of interference from the experimenters.

2. *Methods of controlling extraneous stimulation during the investigation.* These experiments were performed in a special laboratory where a good deal of the working environment was under the control of the experimenters. For example, telephone calls to subjects, except those of emergency nature, were excluded. Interaction between the crew and experimenters was kept to a bare minimum and was conducted through formal channels.

3. *Methods of instructing or directing the attention of individuals under investigation.* Since "set" is such an important determiner of human behavior, many special techniques were devised to establish the appropriate level of information about the purpose of the experiments, to explain the nature of the system goal, and to foster a developmental point of view. Special lectures, instruction sheets, and memoranda were devised to create the desired conditions.

4. *Methods of presenting the stimuli.* In these experiments, the stimuli were presented as a total air picture to a variety of simulated radar scopes. In addition, written and verbal channels were used to convey related information to complete the total operational environment of the crew. Stimulus presentation was controlled by automatic timing devices and by a written "script" for the verbal inputs.

5. *Methods of registering intermediate bodily change.* A major reason for choosing the air-defense direction center as an example of man-machine system is that its internal workings are open to the "measurement of intermediate bodily changes"—that is, the "intervening variables" of the organism are accessible. By strategic placement of microphones and recorders and by

requiring the synthetic organism to keep records of its internal actions, it is theoretically possible to follow each item of input information through the system to output without serious interaction between recording method and data. Observers may also record crucial data about internal variables because the organism is spread out and accessible.

6. *Methods of observing and recording overt responses to stimulation.* The flow of verbal interaction at many points was recorded on voice recorders for later analysis. Observers with headphones could also listen to verbal behavior at almost any place in the system. A method of coding verbal data into punched cards was worked out, so that specially trained observers could code input, internal actions, and output data during operations.

7. *Methods of analyzing and synthesizing the data from an investigation.* Two phases of data analysis and synthesis were utilized. The first concerned the information about performance which was routinely furnished to the commanding officer for discussion with the crew immediately after a period of operations. Rapid data analysis methods, involving the punched cards described above and a computer, were designed to give immediate knowledge of results to the crew. The second phase of data analysis involved listening to and taking information from recordings and relating this information to input and output data.

The major problem encountered in applying these methods was the sheer volume of information—some 12,000 hours of recordings of verbal data and some 60 file drawers full of supporting information. With the increasing availability and lower cost of high-speed computers for psychological research (compare Chapter 3), however, such mountains of data will not in the future represent as serious a problem as is currently the case.

This rather lengthy example illustrates the feasibility of applying the methods of psychology to the problem of system development at all stages. What kinds of outcomes and implications can be perceived for conducting psychological research on the development of man-machine systems? What psychological variables are given importance from the system development point of view? What new insights for psychological theory may emerge from such studies? Let us turn to these questions in the following section.

▣ AN EVALUATION OF SYSTEM DEVELOPMENT AS A PSYCHOLOGICAL PROBLEM

A proper evaluation of system development cannot be made without reference to its relatively short and stormy history. World War I started psychologists on a long and profitable development of psychological testing as a tool for assisting personnel managers in making decisions about the aptitudes, capabilities, and limitations of people to perform in *any* organization or system. World War II created the psychological problem of the design of equipment for maximum efficiency of human use. Some of the equipment invented and utilized during World War II began to require complex and coordinated behavior on the part of large groups of men. With the invention of radar, for example, new levels of intelligence could be achieved concerning enemy plans and actions if only the information could be collected and interpreted rapidly enough. This requirement resulted in the invention of special information-collecting and -processing centers, variously known as combat information centers, air defense control centers, and the like. Psychological study of large interacting man-machine systems really began with problems of equipment design for human use and the layout of these information-processing centers during and after World War II. The managerial problem of organizing the human components and developing their performance to satisfy the many criteria described above has only gradually emerged as a problem for psychological research.

The initial reaction to the problem on the part of both psychologists and managers was hostility. The managers of these new organisms were hostile to the notion of research on system development, because it seemed to call into question traditional management methods. The psychologists were hostile because such research seemed to go beyond the boundaries of "accepted" psychological investigation and methodology. Many false starts were made, laboratories and research teams were established, only to discover that the problems of system development were difficult, the cost in relation to traditional psychological research was astronomic, and gains in understanding system development were slow in coming.

But the rapid development of machines demanding more and more organization of the human components of systems continues to pose the system development problem—new systems demand new managerial insights and methods, and psychology is the source of such methods. The practical outcomes of better system performance sooner and at lower cost, both in people and machines, are too important to ignore.

The major implication of the system development point of view for psychology seems to be that psychological methods and techniques must be expanded to encompass the managerial problems encountered when men and machines are organized into complex systems. The traditional way of dealing with people in systems by means of an externally organized "personnel subsystem" does not force the psychologist to confront the criteria of total system performance and the developmental processes involved in achieving system goals.

The kinds of human behavior given importance by the system development problem may be listed as follows:

1. *Learning,* and the *transfer of skills* acquired in one situation to other situations. Much research on learning has been done on the individual human learner. This research needs to be expanded to include the learning and adaptation of human groups and organizations, using system measures of performance.

2. *Planning and programming.* These managerial skills involve the

ability to anticipate, forecast and take corrective action on situations before they arise. Planning and programming represent one of the highest levels of human functioning.

   3. *Inventing and problem solving*. The technological revolution has put a premium on invention of machines and machine processes. Invention in the area of management techniques and methods has lagged far behind. The hypothesis may be entertained that every human individual possesses the capacity to invent at some useful level. Man-machine systems, by managerial techniques, might be able to "improve themselves" if this inventive ability could be brought to bear on system problems of coordination and development.

   4. *Communicating*. At the heart of the problem of coordination and successful group effort lies the process of communication, the skill of when to say what to whom. Complex man-machine systems live on a stream of communication, both formal and informal. Studies of rates, timing, and the content of communication that characterize "successful," rapidly developing systems as opposed to unsuccessful systems would represent a first attack on the function of communicating in man-machine systems.

   The question was raised earlier about possible implications for psychological theory arising from the study of system development. In many theoretical formulations of behavior, assumptions about "intervening variables" or hypothetical constructs of one kind or another seem to be necessary. These mysterious entities arise because the individual living organism presents problems of access to its internal workings. By defining and working with synthetic organisms, the problem of access is ameliorated, if not solved, since the synthetic organism is "spread out" and its boundaries are not as definite as the skin. The possibility exists that the study of the internal workings of synthetic organisms may give us hints about the mechanisms underlying the behavior of individual living organisms.

▣ SYSTEM DEVELOPMENT AS AN ARENA
FOR PSYCHOLOGICAL RESEARCH

   As we have seen, man's behavior plays a part in all phases of system development, both in design evolution and in the system life cycle, where man functions as planner, designer, manager, and operator. System development provides a "rich" environment in which to study human behavior, from basic sensory processes to the most complex skills (see Chapter 2). Because system development is an important social and economic problem, the psychologist may find resources available to support kinds and levels of investigation extremely difficult to perform in other settings.

   It is often possible, with some ingenuity, to establish experimental laboratories, already rather fully equipped, in the field installations of operating man-machine systems. Thus, an air traffic control center, an air defense center, a submarine, a destroyer, a computing center, and a factory, are all laboratories in which interesting human behavior is taking place. Simulation methods, such as those described in Chapter 11, now enable the psychologist to gain enough control of many operational environments so that the field installation does in fact become a laboratory.

These "field laboratories" differ from the standard academic psychological laboratories in a number of important ways. In the first place, the field installation has a mission of its own, to which psychological experimentation must be accommodated. Quite often, however, mission and experiment are not in conflict, particularly when the experiment is designed to study the performance of the mission. The psychologist working in such field laboratories must expect frustrations if he aspires to elegance of experimental designs and must exercise considerable ingenuity in "working around" the mission. The main offsetting advantage is, of course, the relative ease in obtaining subjects or observers, particularly when the research is related to the particular mission. Such field-laboratory work makes possible the extension of academic research, using the college undergraduate as subject, to greater ranges of aptitude, skill, age and motivation.

The psychologist working in the field laboratory is often required to "stretch" standard scientific methodology to encompass the problems he finds. Very often he is unable to define an independent variable and a dependent variable and hold all other variables constant, as he may have been taught to do, and he may therefore be driven to the growing field of multivariate analysis to find methodology suited to the problem.

In addition to the field laboratory, several more traditional psychological laboratories for the study of system development have been in operation for some years. The former Systems Research Laboratory at the RAND Corporation, the Logistics Simulation Laboratory of the RAND Corporation, the Human Factors Laboratory of the System Development Corporation, and the System Simulation Research Laboratory of the System Development Corporation are examples of such special laboratories.

In these installations the machine aspects of man-machine systems or components of systems are often represented by programming a computer to present operational problems to individuals or groups of men. These special laboratories generally concentrate on the performance of people and the ways in which their performance in achieving system goals with machines may be improved.

REFERENCES

Andrews, T. G. 1948. *Methods of psychology.* New York: Wiley.
Bonner, J. T. 1960. The unsolved problem of development: An appraisal of where we stand. *Amer. Sci., 48,* 514–527.
Carmichael, L. 1951. Ontogenetic development. In S. S. Stevens (ed.), *Handbook of experimental psychology.* New York: Wiley, 281–303.

Chapman, R. L., and Kennedy, J. L. 1956. The background and implications of the systems research laboratory studies. In G. Finch and F. Cameron (ed.), *Symposium on Air Force human engineering, personnel, and training research.* Washington, D. C.: National Research Council.

Chapman, R. L., Kennedy, J. L., Newell, A., and Biel, W. C. 1959. The systems research laboratory's air defense experiments. *Mgmt. Sci., 5,* 250–269.

Fitts, P. M. 1958. Engineering psychology. In P. M. Farnsworth and Q. McNemar (eds.), *Annual review of psychology.* Palo Alto, Calif.: Annual Reviews, Inc., 267–294.

Kennedy, J. L. (ed.) 1949. *Handbook of human engineering data for design engineers.* Port Washington, N. Y.: Special Devices Center, Office of Naval Research. Report SDC 199–1.

Leakey, L. S. B. 1960. Finding the world's earliest man. *Nat. Geogr., 118,* 420–435.

McCormick, E. J. 1957. *Human engineering.* New York: McGraw-Hill.

Raben, M. W. 1960. *A survey of operations and systems research literature.* Medford, Mass.: Institute for Applied Experimental Psychology, Tufts University.

Research group in psychology and the social sciences. 1960. *The technology of human behavior.* Washington, D. C.: Smithsonian Institution.

Weiner, M. G. 1960. Observations on the growth of information-processing centers. In A. H. Rubenstein, and C. H. Haberstroh (ed.), *Some theories of organization.* Homewood, Ill.: Dorsey, 147–156.

PLANNING FOR THE DEVELOPMENT OF A system begins with a series of decisions regarding the functions to be performed by various parts of the system in their subordinate contributions to a total complex which will accomplish system goals. On the side of equipment, these decisions are based upon current hardware technology and upon estimates of the feasibility of new combinations of machine functions. To a considerable degree, also, they are founded upon estimates of what man can do, since the subsystems which result from these plans almost invariably include human operators. Assumptions are made and conclusions are drawn about *human functions* in systems, which ideally involve thorough and orderly considerations of the comparative capabilities of man and machine.

The chapter which follows attempts to describe and categorize the basic types of human functions which are known and differentiated by psychologists. These are the "information-processing" functions of man, which are generally agreed to divide themselves into the three major categories of sensing, perceiving, and thinking. These are here given the names of *sensing, identifying,* and *interpreting,* in order to more certainly imply their operational definitions. The attempt is made to represent these human functions and their interrelationships by means of flow diagrams, and to provide a rationale for doing so. Using such a representation, it becomes possible to consider the bases for limitations in human functioning and to draw some instructive comparisons and contrasts between the functions of man and machine.

The early decisions which assign functions to man and to machine can be seen to affect the entire course of development of the "man" portion of a man-machine system. The functions required of man are reflected immediately in the description of the specific tasks he must perform, and in the design of jobs he must fill. These in turn determine what criteria will be used to select suitable human beings for system operation, to provide them with proper training, and to furnish the necessary supports for their efficient performance. Later still, the choice of functions for man may be seen to have a determining effect on the kinds of interactions occurring between man and man as well as between man and machine. In addition, the selected functions will influence techniques used for the measurement of man's performance and the assessment of the total performance of the system.

This view of man's functions in relation to those of machines poses a number of interesting questions to be answered by scientific research on human behavior, some of which are described here. In a more general sense, the chapter may be considered as suggesting the possibility that the classification of human functions provides a structure within which research questions on human behavior can be framed with considerable usefulness.

HUMAN FUNCTIONS IN SYSTEMS

Robert M. Gagné

A basic assumption of the system development point of view is that man can be considered as one of the major components of a total system. This view is opposed to the notion that man simply plans, buys, develops, and uses a system once it is built. Any reasonably complex system requires a true interaction between man and the other parts of the system, which may be machines, other men, or combinations of these. Some way must therefore be found for thinking about the functions of machines and the functions of men within a framework which makes possible the relation of these two kinds of functions to common goals—that is, to system goals. Even in a system as familiar and as relatively simple as the automobile, it is easy to see that the goal of transporting passengers over roads requires not only the functions of the machine itself but also a considerable variety of human functions performed by the operator, as well as auxiliary functions performed by such people as traffic policemen and filling-station attendants. The design of a system which is to be successful in achieving some socially defined purpose requires thorough and continued consideration of the interacting functions of both men and machines.

What we propose to do in this chapter is to describe some of the functions of man and to show how these can be related to the functions of the machine environment in which man is placed as part of a system. We shall attempt to do this by developing and using a language that relates *input* for the human being to his *output,* which in turn becomes an input to some other portion of the system. In other words, in dealing with man's *functions,* we shall be identifying the *kinds of transformation* which an input undergoes in order to be reflected as a human output. The nature of such a language is fundamentally not very different from the kind used by equipment designers who speak of machine functions as "coding," "searching," and "storing."

However, we shall aim to be as precise as possible about definitions, using "operational" language.

Why should one be concerned with the description of human functions in systems? The reason is not far to seek and will be abundantly illustrated in this and later chapters. Knowing what human beings must accomplish in systems, to express these accomplishments as functions makes possible the accurate description of man's required capabilities. These accounts in turn permit inferences to be made concerning the various techniques needed to develop these human capabilities, whether they be matters of selecting men, training them, or providing them with adequate environments for their work. These techniques constitute the subjects of later chapters. In a fundamental sense, they all rest upon decisions that concern the nature of human functioning and its relation to that of machines.

We shall attempt to develop this description of the varieties of human functioning in the context of a fictitious system of increasing complexity, whose goals can be related to those of other existing systems. We shall also find it informative to relate the human functions we are able to identify to those with which the science of psychology has traditionally dealt. As will be seen, placing man in a system context makes possible a novel and instructive view of some of the categories of human functioning with which psychology is concerned.

Man in the Man-Machine System

In order to develop definitions of man's functioning in systems, we need first to set the stage. In a very general way, we need to describe what a system is and how man fits into it.

A system is developed to fulfill some human purpose or intended use. Its purpose may be to protect against enemy military attack or to harass or destroy an enemy in wartime. But systems, of course, are not confined to military enterprises. They may have distinctly civilian social purposes, such as those of an airport-to-city transportation system, a mail-sorting system, a check-cashing system. Any system is defined in terms of its purpose.

In order to fulfill a purpose, a system must meet certain *standards*, often expressed (particularly in military systems) as criteria of *operational effectiveness*. The idea of operational effectiveness deserves emphasis. System developers have been known to take the point of view that if only the hardware subsystem can be made to run (perhaps in a specially prepared test location), somehow human beings with the proper characteristics will be found and "fitted into" the system. Such a view places too much dependence on the range of human talents and on the availability of suitable manpower, as well as on the extent of human adaptability. On many occasions this restricted view of systems and system development has led to failures, breakdowns, costly programs of retrofitting, and even to virtual system abandonment. No system is complete until it can be shown to operate within a total setting that includes human beings; no system can truly be said to be successful until its operational effectiveness is demonstrated. The best system development is that which includes consideration of system operation (rather than merely hardware operability) from the very beginning of system design.

There have been several attempts to describe the place of the man-machine subsystem in a total system, as well as the place of the human component within a subsystem. One of these is by Taylor (1957), whose conception of man's role in a system is shown in Figure 2.1. Here, the human operator is pictured as a *data transmission and processing* link inserted between the displays and controls of a machine. An input is transformed by certain mechanisms into a signal, which is displayed as a pointer reading, a pattern of lights, an oscilloscope wave form, or the like. This information is read by the human operator and transformed into responses—the pushing of switches, the moving of control handles, and so on. These in turn generate control signals which are transformed by mechanisms into system outputs.

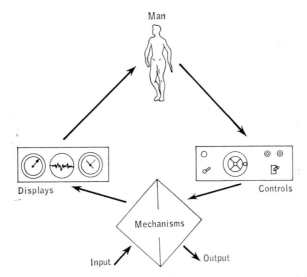

Figure 2.1.   The place of man in the man-machine system (after Taylor, 1957).

In some systems (the *closed-loop* type) this output works back upon the displays, so that they reflect the human operator's response; in others (*open-loop* type) it does not. As Taylor points out, if the designing of the mechanical components of a system is to be done successfully, it must proceed in such a way as to take into full account the characteristics of man and his role in the system.

Man's functioning enters into complex systems at many points and in many particular ways. Furthermore, the display of information, the controls to which the individual responds, and the mechanisms which provide the transformations for these components of the system are of considerable variety. Accordingly, we need to recognize at once that Taylor's generalized picture, while it indicates man's position as a system component, does not provide the means for a detailed analysis of the variety of human functions. It would be a mistake to think that because man typically "occupies a space" between machine displays and controls, his functioning can be related in a constant set of ways to such inputs and outputs. The fact is, neither the input nor the output by themselves will tell us the nature of man's functioning. For there are different kinds of transformations which may be performed (by the human nervous system) in turning inputs into outputs.

To understand the variety of these transformations, we must first recognize that there are *internal functional units* in man, some of which may be active or inactive (that is, shunted out or shunted in) for any particular kind of functioning which the system may require. The science of psychology may be considered as having the purpose of discovering and defining the functions of these internal units, as well as their interrelationships. The extent to which this process has been successful to date will determine the adequacy with which the functions of these internal units can currently be described.

Although we shall be concerned with describing the functioning of these units throughout the chapter, perhaps it will be desirable at the outset to illustrate the point that human functioning can be understood in terms of what kinds of internal mechanisms are activated by an input and what kinds are shunted out in any particular instance.

Suppose that a system has available an oscilloscope as a basic unit for display. On the face of this scope appears a 60-cycle wave form which can be adjusted in amplitude to a particular size, the required size being given by two fine horizontal lines on a transparent overlay placed against the tube face. Let us assume that the system requires the amplitude of the wave to be determined within very close tolerances before further operation of the system can take place. Following this, what happens is that an external signal distorts the form of the wave, and it is the human operator's task to "report" the nature of these distortions by pushing one of five buttons. If there is an amplitude distortion (vertical displacement from the overlay markers), he pushes button 1; if there is a frequency distortion (horizontal displacement from other markers), he pushes button 2; if there are additional frequencies present (irregular wave pattern), he pushes button 3; and so on.

Now, saving certain details for later consideration, let us consider the difference between what the operator does in "getting the equipment ready to operate" and what he does in "operating." Actually, he is utilizing two different functions in the two cases, even though the display may be the same in both.

In placing the equipment into proper operating condition, the human operator is making use of the function of *sensing*. That is to say, he is using his visual receptors, nervous system, and effectors simply to "report" (to a machine, typically) the presence or absence of a difference in physical energy. In this case, the physical difference being reported is the coincidence of two points (or small areas), each of which lies along a narrow band of light (a "line") which makes an abrupt gradient of intensity with its surround. The operator is exercising a function called *visual acuity,* a particular name for one of his sensing functions.

It may be noted, however, that the operator *is able* to do much more than this, even within the equipment-readying stage of operation we are considering. He is perfectly capable, for example, of making an output which reports the amplitude of the wave along some scale such as millimeters or volts. He is able to tell us the color of the wave form, to estimate whether it is bright enough, or whether it has a regular appearance, and many other things. Why does he not do all these things in this situation? There is no mystery to this question at all: he does not simply because we have not told him to (or perhaps told him not to). But this means we must recognize that there is more to the matter of input than simply the presence of a display. In order to get the output required by the system, the operator must be provided with a set of *instructions.*

One basic purpose of these instructions, we are now able to see, is to determine which functions "higher up" than sensing are to be *shunted out.* The combination of the oscilloscope display and the instructions is what determines the output that will be made. The instructions say to the operator, in effect: "Report coincidence between a set of lines. Do not report their shape, or size, or brightness, or regularity, or meaning, or anything else." Thus it is apparent that the effect of presentation of the oscilloscope display plus a particular set of instructions is to put into operation a particular kind of human function, *sensing,* and to shunt out other kinds of functions of which the human operator is capable. The situation is depicted in Figure 2.2.

Now let us contrast this elementary kind of behavior with what occurs when the equipment is being operated rather than merely turned on. In this

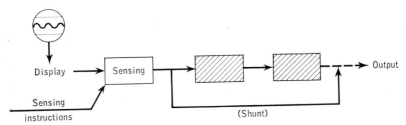

Figure 2.2. The combination of a display and "sensing instructions" as input to a human operator produces an output which reports the presence or absence of a difference in physical energy, the function of sensing, and shunts out other functions of which the operator is capable. Compare with Figure 2.3.

case the human operator must function in quite a different way. He must provide five different output responses (press one of five buttons) whenever a particular kind of deformation of the sine wave appears, whether it is a change in the horizontal dimension produced by variation in frequency, in the vertical dimension (amplitude), or in one of several other types. In other words he must identify five different classes of patterns appearing on the scope.

When the operator is engaged in this function of identifying, has the internal mechanism for sensing been shunted out? Of course it has not, because the physical differences which determine the existence of classes of stimuli to which the operator responds must be sensed in order for identification to take place. Thus we see that, on the input end, human functions have a hierarchical arrangement. The use of a function like *identifying* requires that a function lower in the hierarchy, *sensing,* be put in operation as well.

Again, however, we can see that certain even higher functions have indeed been shunted out when we ask for identification. For example, the operator may be capable of telling us that a deformation of the sine wave in the vertical dimension "means" a change in amplitude. But we have not asked him that; we merely asked him to press a button indicating the presence of a particular class of change in wave shape. Or again, he may be capable of interpreting this kind of change as indicating the presence of a type of remote signal received at the other end of the system. This too would be a function at a higher level than identification, and we shall consider this later on. At the moment, our point is simply to contrast the situation of Figure 2.2, depicting the *sensing* function, with Figure 2.3, showing *identification.* Again in this figure we see that one of the primary effects of instructions is to keep the human being functioning at the proper level and to shunt out other, higher-level functions.

Another internal mechanism must be added at this level, too, and that is *memory.* For we know that without some kind of long-term storage of representations of the five different changes in wave shapes, the achievement

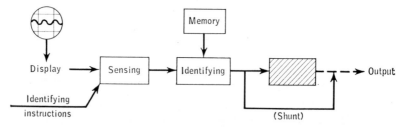

Figure 2.3.   The function of identifying in response to the same display as shown in Figure 2.2. This function requires "identification instructions" and a memory which provides an internal set of standards for the wave shapes to be identified by different outputs. Again, the instructions operate to shunt out higher-level functions of which the human operator is capable.

of five different outputs would be impossible. Instructions alone will not do the job. To be sure, we can describe to the individual what he is expected to do, by means of instructions, but he will nevertheless not be able to do it by this means alone. He must have an *internal* means of matching the external display to one of five classes in order that he can make five different responses, as required in our example. This means he must have previously acquired the "representative shapes" in his memory, by means of learning preceding the occasion when he tackles the job of operating his equipment. And this provides the basic reason for *training,* as well as for the crucial part it plays in the system development process.

Now, this description of two examples of human functioning has not involved very high-powered psychology; we are well aware of that. We have, in fact, been describing the functions of *sensing* and *perceiving,* which have been studied by psychologists for many years. But the purpose of our account has not been to review basic principles. Rather, it has been to show that the fundamental operations of psychologists in describing the functions of man's behavior are, in fact, very much like the operations of a design engineer in describing a machine. Psychologists make the same kinds of inferences about human behavior as designers do of machines, and they are based upon the same kinds of objectively defined operations. It should therefore be quite easy for the psychologist to communicate to others the nature of human functions, provided he remembers to state clearly *what input conditions must be met* and *what the output achieves* (as an input to the next unit of the system). In our further delineation of human functions, we shall find it useful to refer back to the conceptions developed in these relatively simple examples.

▣ HUMAN FUNCTIONS

Now let us undertake to view the nature and variety of human functions which are employed in systems. We shall do this by using illustrations of typical human tasks that occur in actual systems, such as telephone systems, aircraft, and missile systems, traffic-control systems, and air-defense systems. But the major technique we shall use will be one of describing a variety of tasks which could be performed by a *single subsystem* of a fictitious system. We can imagine the system as a whole as having any of a number of purposes, but we shall concentrate on the basic unit of a man-machine combination (similar to the one depicted in Figure 2.1). In this way we shall be able to set several different kinds of tasks for the subsystem, progressing from the simple to the complex, with the expectation that these will permit the illustration of the varieties of human functions and the conditions under which they operate. Of course, a total system may consist of many such man-machine subsystems connected by either human or machine "communication links." But if we chose a particular system, we might miss some of the kinds of human functioning we want to describe. Accordingly, the subsystem becomes the initial focus of interest for our discussion.

Imagine, then, that we have a subsystem which presents to the human operator certain information in the form of a display panel containing one or more "pictures" of various sorts. Such pictures may include a dial with a graduated scale and a pointer, an oscilloscope with various forms of visual information, and an aerial photograph of selected portions of the earth's surface. The operator, seated at a console containing these displays, has at his fingertips several switches, a small joystick mounted in a universal joint, and a means of verbal communication (telephone) with another human being who constitutes a link with another portion of the total system. The ultimate purpose and mission of this is not important for our present purposes; it might be a manned space satellite intended to land on Venus.

What are the possible kinds of functions this human being can perform? And what are the conditions which have to be established for the proper functioning to take place; in other words, for the desired kind of input-output transformation to occur? It is necessary to ask this last question because, as we shall see, the particular kind of human functioning which is going to occur at any particular time has to depend upon the provision of conditions to sensitize, to trigger, and to control the function, and not simply on the nature of the display itself. We have already seen that this is so in contrasting the functions of sensing and identifying. A human being is not fixed in his operation, but flexible. Accordingly, one must consider several different sources of input which determine the kind of input-output transformation that is made on any given occasion. Besides the display itself, we have mentioned verbal instructions as one of these additional conditions. There are others, such as visual and auditory signals; check-lists; pictures; and general aspects of the physical environment. And in addition, it is necessary to take account of those inputs to the function which come not directly from the external environment, but rather from short- and long-term memories within the individual. A complete description of any given human function requires that we take account of these memorial sources of input as well as of the external sources.

Output Characteristics

Our relatively uncomplicated examples have given a great deal of emphasis to the possible differences in input which may characterize human functions. What about output? Are there not differences here too? Of course there are, and the fact that we have supplied the human operator in our fictitious system with at least two kinds of controls bears witness to this fact. Pressing a single switch appears somehow to be a qualitatively different type of act from tracking a continuously moving target with a joystick. Such differences are, however, hard to define satisfactorily, and it may even be that separate classes of output do not exist. In other words, it is possible that human responses may simply vary in a continuous fashion along several dimensions (such as duration, speed, and force), without actually requiring different categories of neural organization.

For practical purposes, three different categories of human responding are often recognized. There is, first of all, the kind of output which performs a required action (like pushing a switch) in a relatively brief time, without change in direction during its occurrence. These may be termed *unitary responses* and occur fairly commonly as output modes. Secondly, there are responses which require a continuous, uninterrupted movement, like turning a crank, but which appear to be relatively self-contained and internally controlled. These outputs may be called *autonomous sequences.* They are characterized by the capability of "reeling themselves off" with very little guidance from external stimulation during their occurrence. The operation of cranks, handles, and wheels, as well as the use of familiar tools, are common examples of this kind of output. Finally, there is responding in a *flexible sequence,* as one does in tracking an irregularly moving target. Such sequences are guided and modified in critical ways by input signals from displays and the other parts of the human operator's environment. Tracking tasks are of quite frequent occurrence in systems, although the limitations of speed and accuracy of humans responding in such tasks sets some restrictions on their use. Both fixed and flexible gunnery in aircraft, for example, have to a large extent given way to tracking performed by computers, because of the rapidity of tracking movements required in modern aerial combat.

It is apparent that these or other categorizations of human output do not provide a means of distinguishing human functions, any more than do the kinds of displays used to provide input. We are forced again to a realization of the necessity for consideration of input-output relationships, or transformations, in order to find meaningful categories of human functioning. It is easy to realize, too, that a particular human function may be expressed in any or all types of output. The function of identifying, for example, may be expressed as a set of unitary responses; the human operator may identify five wave forms by pushing five switches. Or again, the same function could be expressed as a set of autonomous sequences; one wave form may set off a cranking motion in the clockwise direction, another a cranking motion in the counterclockwise direction, and so forth. Or continuous variations in amplitude of the wave form may be made to require a continuous following by means of a flexible sequence output, while similar continuous variations in frequency require another kind of "tracking" output. (The hovering of a small helicopter, for example, may require as many as four different sets of tracking responses at the same time.)

For the purpose of describing human functions, the *mode* of response is unimportant. What is important, however, is the nature of the information which the output provides concerning the input. In other words, if we consider that the output *tells us, or tells the next member of the system,* we get a valuable set of clues about the nature of the function with which we are dealing. For example, if the pressing of a switch is employed to convey the information that a change in physical energy has occurred, we can say that the human function of *sensing* is being utilized. If the pressing of a switch (one out of five) is done to provide the information that a particular class of wave form is present in input, then we may suspect that the function of *identifying* is being used by the human operator. The fact that the output is unitary or sequential, made to a switch or joystick or handwheel, is not of consequence. But the way this mode of response is related to the input is what provides us with an essential criterion of human functioning.

The Varieties of Human Functioning

Now let us return to our fictitious system and see if we can first illustrate and then describe the nature of various human functions, beginning with the simplest. We shall imagine that a single human operator is seated at a panel having several different kinds of display and several different controls. What we shall try to do is to state the following conditions for each function we come upon, noting in each case that these differences are what determine the kind of human function with which we are dealing:

1. Minimum display requirements
2. Filtering conditions
3. Shunting conditions
4. Memorial inputs (long-term)
5. Memorial inputs (short-term)

These five conditions differ for each of the functions we shall describe. A succeeding section will give an account of a typical human task for each of the functions and an idea of the differentiating features of each.

Every function may be described, as we have said, as a kind of input-output transformation. It is important to note that a full delineation of such a transformation requires the statement of all five of these varieties of input; it would be quite insufficient to specify only the nature of the physical instruments or other energy sources that constitute the "display." Before considering the other input conditions, however, we may note that this type of input must be specified in terms of *minimum display requirements*. One cannot expect to transform some information which is not there; thus if sensing is the function of interest, there must be a physical difference to be sensed, rather than a blank screen. A second requirement is the establishment of *filtering conditions*. The individual does not respond to the entire range of potential inputs in his environment; in fact, he responds at any given moment to only a few of them. If he is required to identify certain shapes on an oscilloscope, the chances are that he is at the same time required to ignore other shapes which are considered as "noise." Third, as we have already mentioned, there must be a persisting condition of *shunting,* so that the individual will make the desired kind of transformation. If he is expected to identify patterns (an intermediate-level transformation) it may be required that he avoid reporting the meaning of these patterns (a higher-level transformation). Both filtering and shunting conditions are frequently provided by instructions, but these instructions establish a continuing state in the human being, often called a *set,* which is what accounts for the persistence of these conditions throughout the performance of any given task. It may be readily seen, therefore, that such sets are carried by a mechanism of short-term memory, or "buffer storage."

The mechanisms of short-term and long-term memory are presumably very different in the human being, just as they are in the computer. Short-term memory has a distinctly limited capacity, as many studies have demonstrated (see, for example, McGeoch and Irion, 1952). But in the human being it also possesses an enormous flexibility; and as a consequence, the *programming* of shunting and filtering conditions may be changed readily and frequently, simply by providing suitable instructions. Relatively short sequences of action may also be held in the short-term memory. Long-term memory, on the other hand, has a very considerable capacity, the limits of which have not yet been very well described. Programs of filtering and shunting may be retained in the long-term memory for extensive periods of time, if one desires, but changing them within the long-term store is not an easy matter. However, the major use of the long-term memory can be seen in the retention of internally organized routines which are variously referred to as "models," "rules," or "action sequences." For example, in order for a change in wave form to be identified by the human operator as a "frequency change," there must be an internal model of such a change, stored in long-term memory, with which the input from the display can be compared. Furthermore, as we shall see, such a model is a highly complex routine, relative to those of a typical machine.

Sensing

We need spend very little time on this simplest of human functions, not only because it has served us so well already as an example, but also because it is not of tremendous importance in modern complex systems. In our fictitious system, a task which required the individual to report a difference or lack of difference in alignment of two small line segments provides us with a typical example. In general terms, the function is one which *indicates the presence or absence of a difference in physical energies.* As is well known, such a difference may take the form of light intensity or wave length or wave composition, so far as visual displays are concerned, and comparable differences may be sensed when input is fed through other senses, such as hearing or touch. Considerable quantitative information has been collected concerning these varieties of sensing, particularly for vision and hearing (see Chapter 4).

As we have said, the function of human sensing is not used with particular frequency in modern systems, largely because machines can be designed to do a superior job. However, the specific variety we have used as an example, visual acuity, is sometimes utilized to good advantage in such tasks as alignment of vernier scales and in aligning instruments such as transits and gun sights. It is difficult, though, to think of an example of the use of brightness or color sensing as a function of a human operator in a system. Similarly, although auditory inputs are often employed in systems both as warning signals and as conveyors of voice communication, the sensing of slight physical differences in sound energy does not often occur as a task for a human operator. Although the mechanisms for sensing are activated in the use of higher functions, sensing itself has extremely restricted employment in systems.

A number of studies of sensing thresholds have shown that filtering conditions have important effects on the exercise of this function; in fact, the various constant errors which occur in psychophysical experiments may be considered to reflect the limitations of the filtering mechanism (compare Woodworth, 1938). The differences in results obtained in psychophysical experiments with trained *versus* untrained observers are also relevant to the establishment of filtering conditions. Evidently a trained observer does not "sense better" because of his previous training, but he does "attend better" and thus is able to report extremely small physical differences with a high degree of probability. The implication is that certain observational routines may be acquired and stored in long-term memory and that these may facilitate filtering. Although filtering conditions for the sensory function may readily be established by instructions ("As soon as you see a difference in brightness in these two patches of light, press this switch"), these will not be optimally effective in untrained observers.

What about the other conditions for the sensing function? Shunting conditions are readily established by instructions ("Report *only a difference* in brightness, but not how bright the patch is, or what color it is, or anything else"). As our previous discussion has implied, there are presumably no effects of training on the sensing function; inputs from memory affect the function only indirectly, through their influence on the filtering conditions. From the point of view of systems design, perhaps the most important aspects of conditions for sensing are the minimum display requirements expressed in terms of physical measures. Because the sensing mechanism is the initial avenue for all higher functions (see Figure 2.2), the physical limitations of this function sometimes have an important bearing on equipment design (see Chapter 5). These limits of sensory functioning are described at greater length in Chapter 4.

Identifying

A much more important and widely used function than sensing is the function of identifying. Recall our example in which the human operator is asked to "report," by pressing one of five buttons, which of five wave-form patterns is being displayed. This kind of function is perhaps the most ubiquitous in which human beings engage, whether in their daily lives or in the context of systems operation. A stock clerk identifies merchandise; a pilot identifies panel instruments; an office manager identifies his staff; an equipment repairman identifies the parts of equipment with which he deals; a file clerk identifies file cards. Learning the names for and locations of the various controls of a machine, or the words to be used in verbal communication within a system, are examples of this function. In identifying, the human operator *makes a number of different responses to a number of different classes of stimulation.* The transformation which takes place from input to output performs the specific function of identifying (distinguishing among) different input qualities. In more traditional psychological language, this is the function of *perception.*

A particular case of the identifying function must be recognized, in the situation which requires the identification of only two input classes, as opposed to three or more. For example, we may want to require an operator to report the presence of a "blip" on the oscilloscope face. But this means that we expect him to distinguish a blip (a small bright patch having certain size limits) from that large class of other small bright patches, the "noise" in the machine. In such a form, this function is often called *detection.* Although it may be said to have a certain simplicity in this form, since the inputs to be distinguished are only two, the function is still basically one of identifying, that is to say, of making different responses to different classes of input. In all probability, the conditions for generation of this function are basically the same, whether we are dealing with twenty input classes or only two.

Filtering Conditions. In getting the operator to report certain classes of input qualities, one must utilize a set of instructions which prevent the reporting of *other* input qualities (since such reporting would contribute "noise" to the next input). If we require the identifying of changes in wave amplitude and frequency, for example, this may mean that we do *not* want the reporting of changes in wave brightness, or its position on the scope face, or its "thickness" as a line, or any of a number of other qualities it may possess. If the input is Morse code, we want the human operator to identify the particular combinations of sound that are used to make letters and words, but not such other stimulus qualities as signal speed or loudness. Instructions, as well as memorial inputs from previous instructions, define the identifications required.

Shunting Conditions. Another purpose of instructions is, of course, to shunt out the employment of higher-level functions on the part of the human operator. The task may be one which requires him to perceive but *not* to interpret. For example, if he is asked to identify five different wave forms, this may imply that he is asked *not* to report any of several *meanings* of these wave forms, such as their possible means of generation or their implications as inputs for the next stage of the system. Reporting such meanings may be easy or hard for the individual. But if the designed task calls for identification only, then the shunting conditions must also be designed to keep the individual functioning at this level, or else his output will be likely to contain errors as well as noise.

Memorial Inputs. Obviously the filtering and shunting conditions of such a task are carried as programs (or *sets*) in the short-term memory, after having been established by instructions. The long-term memory, on the other hand, provides the "models" of wave forms with which the external inputs are compared and which thus make possible the differentiation of output that is required in five different responses (for example, pushing five different buttons).

The nature of these stored models is an interesting and remarkable matter. As is well known, the physical nature of the input may vary over a relatively wide range without disturbing the identifications which are made. This is what is meant, in its broadest sense, by *perceptual constancy,* and it is a property which has not yet been built into a machine, except in the most limited sense. As a simple example, it is evident that a human being can readily identify the digits 0 1 2 3 4 5 6 7 8 9, whether they are printed, stamped, or written, and even when they are subject to wide variations in size, stroke width, or other changes in form. Up to the present, at least, there must be a close physical resemblance between two digits for a machine to be able to "recognize" them as the same; for a man, the physical resemblance required varies over a wide range. Because of such models in long-term memory, a photograph of an object is an input equivalent to the direct sight of the object itself; a chord in the key of F is equivalent to the same chord in the key of G; a round knob among a group of square knobs is identified regardless of changes in its size. In a more complex setting, a ground radar return may make possible the identification of objects such as railroads, bridges, and bodies of water as equivalent to those depicted on a printed map.

Identification routines, or *models,* are chiefly acquired by a process of learning. It is true that there appear to be some kinds of models which are innately determined, such as those which underlie figure-ground identifications, or the identification of certain figures and patterns, emphasized by Gestalt psychologists (see for example Woodworth, 1938). But models like those used in looking at photographs, reading maps, recognizing printed and spoken words, examining tissues under a microscope, or filing cards in a catalogue must be learned previous to the performing of the task requiring the identifications. The optimal conditions for such learning appear not to be too well understood even today, although experiments on human learning have a history extending back several decades (McGeoch and Irion, 1952). Perhaps the clearest set of conditions which emerges from work on paired-associate learning is that of contrasting right and wrong examples of the model to be acquired in successive practice trials, and providing immediate "knowledge of results" after each trial. In this way the models to be acquired become progressively "differentiated" (see Gibson, 1942), as shown by the progressive reduction in errors as learning proceeds.

Identifications are sometimes put together to form sequences of action, rather than being acquired one at a time in any order. Such sequences are usually referred to as *motor skills,* or *perceptual-motor skills.* In a common example, reading out loud from a printed page, the individual must identify each word in the sequence by making a response appropriate to it (that is, by pronouncing the word) and then going on to the next. Of course, an entire sequence of this sort may also be committed to memory, in which case the input for each identification becomes, not the printed word itself, but the sound of the previous word uttered by the speaker. Similarly, in a skill such as bicycle riding the input for each successive identification (such as pushing downward on the left pedal) is a complex which includes both the currently present external stimulus situation and the proprioceptive feedback from the movement just previously made (extending the right leg). When the human individual is required in a systems context to track a continuously moving display element, such as a spot on an oscilloscope, he is similarly required to use the identifying function in response to an input that includes both the current position of the spot and the feedback from his previous movement, in a continuous action sequence.

Interpreting

In many system instances, the most important function performed by the human being is *interpreting.* Here the individual makes outputs which, in effect, place inputs into categories whose basis is their *effects* rather than their *appearances.* In other words, interpreting is a matter of identifying the meaning of inputs. Suppose that our human operator, seated at his console containing oscilloscope and response buttons, is given the task of reporting whether a blip on his scope represents a friendly or a hostile aircraft. He cannot, of course, decide on the basis of its appearance, since this is not distinguishable from that of other blips. Instead, he may have to decide primarily on the basis of certain rules which form a part of the memorial input in this case—the blip is approaching from the northeast, flying at a certain altitude and with a certain speed, following no previously reported "track," and so on.

The contrast between identifying and interpreting is well exemplified in the task of aerial photo-interpretation. The initial part of this task is one in which the human being identifies objects such as piles, bridges, buildings, or lakes. But in interpreting the photograph, he takes another step as well. He *interprets* an airplane as a "combat aircraft," or a building as a "power plant," or a tank as a "water tank." It should be noted that he is not able to do this on the basis of the appearance of these objects (a water tank may be indistinguishable in appearance from a fuel tank) but only by making inferences about the *expected effects* of the actions they lead him (or others) to take. In other words, he begins to work with "if-then" relationships, which can be approximately illustrated by the statement "If it is a power plant, then I should see transmission lines." Psychologists have given this kind of behavior many names, including "expectancy," "hypothesis-using," and "thinking." In *interpreting, the human being identifies inputs in terms of their expected effects.* Interpreting thus involves a choice among "courses of action" available through memorial inputs.

The minimal display conditions required for interpreting are determined by the fact that the function of identifying must precede the interpretation itself. In the case of the task of interpreting a blip on an oscilloscope, for example, the human operator must have been able to identify the northeast approach, the altitude, the speed, and the type of track followed in order to be able to make the interpretation required. In the photo-interpretation task, he must be able to identify transmission lines, transformers, and a number of other objects in order to perform the interpreting adequately. Unless the required objects are displayed, and unless they can be identified by the human observer, correct interpreting cannot be accomplished.

Shunting and Filtering Conditions.   At this level of human functioning, shunting conditions are not required. The channels are open, and the human operator is being asked to function in a manner which he seems to prefer and at which he often excels.

Filtering conditions, however, are quite as essential with this mode of functioning as with others. Instructions are used to "set the problem," or, in other words, to tell the human operator what to look for. If he has the task of reporting enemy aircraft, he must be instructed, in effect, not to report such things as the volume of traffic on local airways, or the fact that a scheduled commercial airliner is ten minutes late, or a whole host of other interpretations which he is perfectly capable of making. Sometimes he may have time to make such interpretations, to attend to such inputs; but on those crucial occasions when the load is heavy, filtering will be essential to the prevention of errors.

Ordinarily, as we have said, filtering conditions are established by means of instructions which activate sets carried in short-term memory. There are occasions, however, on which system functioning may depend upon the discovery of suitable filtering conditions by the human operator himself. For example, suppose the task to be performed were that of interpreting an aerial photograph of enemy territory for "military significance." In such a case, it is perhaps not possible, or at least not desirable, to specify by instructions "what to look for." The individual will likely proceed by developing a number of filtering conditions of his own—he will adopt his own sets by *giving himself instructions.* He may try several of these self-instructions in a row before finding some which make it possible for him to perform the task successfully to his satisfaction. Such self-instructions appear to be equivalent to what a number of psychological investigators call "strategies" (see for example Bruner, Goodnow, and Austin, 1956). System development procedures are sometimes designed to take advantage of the highly adaptive characteristics of human beings in discovering their own best filtering conditions. We shall have occasion to return to this point in a later discussion of "systems learning."

Memorial Inputs. Short-term memory provides, as we have said, the sets which determine filtering. There may also be brief sequential routines, actually a part of the filtering mechanism, which determine certain sequences of behavior. For example, such a routine might read: "First, check the altitude, next the range, and finally the speed." Such routines must of course contain a limited number of steps if they are to remain within the limitations of the short-term memory. In any case, it can be seen that their function is to provide for the filtering of inputs in a certain order.

One kind of input from long-term memory is a familiar one: the models which make identification possible. The individual, it is often said, must *perceive* the situation before he can *interpret* it. We have already emphasized this point. If the human operator is being asked to report "enemy attack," he must be able to identify such things as altitude, range, speed, and nature of track. This means he must possess a mechanism which compares the actual inputs with models available in his long-term memory. Similarly, the photo-interpreter must be able to identify, on the basis of stored models, power transmission lines, transformers, and many other objects, in order to make the interpretation, "power plant."

The second type of stored input is new. It consists of the *rules* by means of which objects, regardless of appearance, are classified into categories of "expected effects." They are the action categories which are so essential to interpreting. In landing a large aircraft, the pilot perceives instrument indications of a number of aspects of the plane's performance, or even more immediately, in terms of the courses of action available to the pilot himself. Thus an overly high altitude may "mean" the alternative courses of action of nosing down or making another landing approach. The rules that define these courses of action are available to the trained pilot from his long-term memory. These rules can be expressed as verbal statements; whether they are stored in this form or some other is a matter psychologists argue about, but which need not concern us here. Similarly, the photo-interpreter who has identified a "pile" has in his memory a whole set of rules which determine a number of courses of action, such as "Look for vehicle tracks" or "Look for nearby chimneys," which enter into the process by means of which he arrives at the interpretation "coal pile" that is the output response. It may be noted, too, that these stored rules are not necessarily of an all-or-none sort; rather, they frequently represent probabilities and have been studied as such by a number of investigators (see Gagné, 1959).

Interpreting in Sequence: Dynamic Decision Making. It is not at all uncommon for interpreting tasks to occur in sequential form. The step-by-step nature of *problem solving* has frequently been emphasized (see for example Johnson, 1955), as well as the fact that the information available for each later step is likely to be contingent on the consequences of earlier ones. In a task of equipment troubleshooting, for example, the initial interpretation may lead the individual to check an input voltage; his next step is an interpretation of symptoms which include the initial information plus this voltage reading. At each step of the way, the input to the human problem solver is changing, because of his own actions, and continues to do so until he is able to make the final interpretation that locates the malfunctioning part. Aerial photo-interpretation also frequently proceeds in this sequential fashion (Gagné, 1954).

Obviously, this kind of dynamic decision making requires successive reprogramming, at each step of the way, of the filtering conditions in short-term memory. Thus at each new stage the individual must provide his own instructions to establish the filtering set which tells him "what to look for." This kind of flexible reprogramming constitutes one of the most striking characteristics of human functioning, and one which distinguishes it markedly from that of most machines. In performing in this manner, the individual must have available in his long-term memory the variety of "filtering rules" necessary and relevant to the problem to be solved. Choosing among them is the major task accomplished by interpretation. The rules themselves then come into play in determining the particular filtering set employed in the next stage of the problem; they are self-instructions, or *programs*.

A more complex form of dynamic decision making occurs when the feedback loop from the preceding action step involves interacting with another person. In such circumstances the input situation for each step in the sequence becomes highly variable and unpredictable, since it depends not solely on the effects of the individual's own output, but also on that of the second individual. Suppose that two air-traffic controllers must share the task of guiding traffic into an airfield, having as a primary display two PPI (Plan Position Indicator) radarscopes displaying the same information. This is a "load-sharing" task, and it is obvious that each decision made by individual A will result in an action that changes the input for individual B. In periods of heavy traffic, such a system could presumably not be operated without some externally imposed filtering instructions concerning the sector, range circle, or destination to be covered by each controller (Kidd and Hooper, 1959). However, even when this has been done, the task is one in which frequent interaction is required between the individuals, in the sense that each new situation for decision making is determined in part by the preceding action of the other person. The possibility of flexible programming is obviously a necessary condition for successful operation of this type of system.

Inventing. We have seen that the high adaptability of human beings is exhibited in their capability for frequent reprogramming of the filtering (as well as shunting) conditions applicable to the transformation of inputs into outputs. There is also another, and even more striking, way in which the flexibility of human behavior is demonstrated. This is in the *invention of new rules*. It is reasonable to suppose that "having a new idea" is fundamentally a matter of using old rules (ideas) in utterly new situations. The history of science contains many examples in which a principle from one sphere of knowledge is transferred by analogy to another sphere, with the result that the entire outlook on the second problem is changed, the problem is "redefined," and a great upsurge of novel theory results. Invention also occurs with some frequency in other areas of human activity as well, and its occurrence as a requirement in certain systems cannot be overlooked. A successful leader is often an inventive leader, in the sense that he achieves new solutions to problems of social interaction and group productiveness. Military tactics and strategy also require new solutions for new situations if they are to remain successful.

Inventing occurs when the individual makes an interpretation of inputs in accordance with a set of rules which he has not previously applied to the situation or to similar situations. Thus, for the individual, every "original" solution of a problem is, in a sense, an invention. Whether or not it is an invention in a broader social sense of course depends upon whether other people have previously made the same interpretation. Much of the evidence about inventing is anecdotal (see for example Platt and Baker, 1931). It is interesting and suggestive, but of limited scientific usefulness. "Brainstorming" (Taylor, Berry, and Block, 1958) is a technique which was designed to stimulate invention in group situations, and its encouragement of "wild ideas" is a feature which suggests a possibly new experimental approach to the topic.

Review of Human Functions

It will be useful now to summarize what we have said about the three basic types of human functioning, which we can do by reference to Figure 2.4. In addition we need to discuss some of the implications of this description of functions, and particularly to see where they lead us in relation to the development of systems.

Human functions are varieties of transformations which the human being, considered as a system component, performs upon inputs to produce outputs. They have been identified and described by considering a typical unitary *subsystem,* composed of a human being who is presented with an equipment *display* and a set of *controls* that include manipulable buttons and knobs as well as a microphone for verbal communication. In such a setting, it can be seen that the input from the display (which itself is a machine output) is transformed by the human being with the use of controls into an output (which in turn becomes an input to the next element of the system). Thus the transmission of information is, in general terms, the use which human beings fulfill in systems.

When we analyze the nature of inputs to the human being in their totality, we find they are composed of several parts, as Figure 2.4 shows. Besides the display itself (shown here as an oscilloscope wave form), there are *instructions* which establish sets in short-term memory (similar to "buffer storage"). These

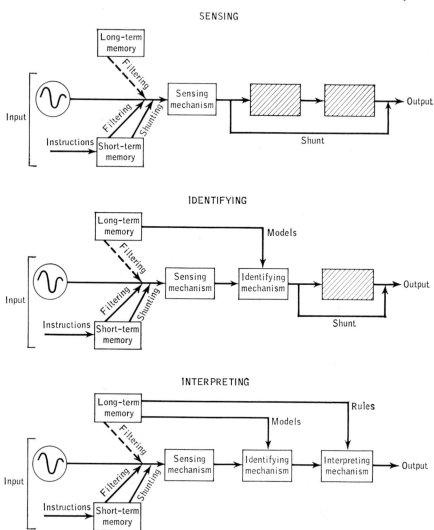

Figure 2.4.   The basic varieties of human functioning.

sets determine the *shunting conditions,* and thus the level of functioning at which the individual operates in the situation. In addition, they establish *filtering conditions,* which have the very important role of selecting inputs— that is, of determining what the human operator attends to. Brief sequential routines of observation may also be held in the short-term memory. Finally, there are inputs from long-term memory, the most important of which are the *models,* which make possible comparisons with display inputs to produce identification, and the *rules,* which represent courses of action to be compared in the function of interpreting. *Sequences of action* are also stored in long-term memory, forming the basis of perceptual-motor skills.

Sensing is a function that requires a difference (or change) in physical energy as a minimal display condition. Filtering conditions establish attention to a particular difference, while shunting conditions act to prevent the reporting of "things" and "meanings." Filtering conditions are often partly a matter of observational routines stored in long-term memory, as is shown by the superior performances of "trained observers." While many sensing functions of human beings are very acute (see Geldard, 1953) they are nevertheless readily excelled by those of machines; as a consequence, this kind of human function is not widely employed in systems. However, sensing obviously must be accomplished in every human activity, and in this manner it sets the limits to all functioning.

Identifying represents the next level of functioning, as shown in Figure 2.4. When suitably defined, this function is equivalent to "perceiving." Minimal display requirements are the presentation of two or more aspects of stimulation to be reported differentially by an equal number of responses. In the simplest case the presence or absence of an input feature (such as a "blip") is to be identified against a background of "noise"; and this variety of identifying is usually called detection. In identifying, instructions play their usual role as inputs for the establishment of shunting and filtering conditions. The most important memorial inputs (from long-term memory) are the models, which provide standards against which display inputs are compared and thus identified.

Interpreting is the highest level of human functioning and takes place when shunting conditions for lower functions are removed. The individual makes output responses which classify inputs in terms of their effects, rather than in terms of their appearance (as in identifying). To do this he must use rules that are stored in long-term memory and that represent alternative courses of action. A particular variety of interpreting, called inventing, occurs when the individual uses rules which are novel (for him) with respect to the inputs he is responding to. Actually, there are many specific varieties of interpreting (like numerical computing, aerial photo-interpretation, equipment troubleshooting) in systems, and we shall be returning to these later.

One characteristic of interpreting deserves a special mention, which will also be considered more fully in a later section. As Figure 2.4 shows, a total act of interpreting requires the exercise of the preceding functions of sensing and identifying. However, it is well known that the interpreting mechanism is able to use inputs which simply *represent* the actual inputs of the task. These are *symbolic* inputs which, in a sense, simulate the outputs of the identifying mechanism as they would normally occur. For example, if the actual task involves as inputs the digits 1, 2, and 5, it is possible to represent these with the words *one, two,* and *five.* Interpreting can then proceed without error, provided that the rules used have been learned in such a way that the digits and the words are equivalent, as is often the case. This provision, however, must be satisfied: one would have to make sure, for example, that words such as *un, deux,* and *cinq* were identified in an equivalent manner to 1, 2, and 5 before the former could be successfully used as "substitute" inputs for an interpreting task. This feature of interpreting has important implications for training as well as for the use of simulation in systems.

The occurrence of interpretations in sequence, in response to input events which are contingent upon the individual's output in the previous step, constitutes a variety of interpretation called dynamic decision making. It involves frequent changes in the filtering sets, a mechanism which appears analogous to reprogramming in the sense that new self-instructions must be provided by the individual for each stage of action, consistent with the new input situation occasioned by his just-previous response. When another link is added to this feedback chain in the form of another individual, the input for each decision becomes accordingly more complex and more difficult to predict.

Some Implications

What have we accomplished by viewing the individual as a system component having the purpose of transforming inputs to outputs? Have we added anything that would not be available by a study of psychology in more traditional terms?

The answer appears to be yes and no. It is clear, for example, that the psychologist is fundamentally dealing with the same set of phenomena. Inputs are called stimuli, outputs are called responses by the psychologist. In using one as the independent variable, the other as the dependent, his purpose is in fact to make inferences about the mechanisms in between. In so doing, he long ago established the categories of *sensing, perceiving,* and *thinking* (all of which are sometimes given various other names) as forms of behavior related to qualitatively distinct sets of experimental operations. Furthermore, he has for an equally long time investigated the properties of *memory* as well as *immediate memory*. The selective or filtering function of *attention*, acting through the mediation of *sets,* has often been a focus of interest for the psychologist. In this sense it cannot be said that we have made new distinctions, nor identified new phenomena.

Actually, we believe that the mechanisms we have described, as well as the functions they define, represent a basic set of inferences that one is forced to make when he observes the variety of behavior possible in a human being. They are not what is meant by "hypothetical constructs," and they do not go very far to explain behavior in the sense that theory is supposed to. (In the language proposed by Northrop [1947], they are "concepts by intuition" rather than "concepts by postulation"). Accordingly, they are not intended to account for the why and how of sensing, perceiving, and thinking, but only to distinguish these as human activities requiring different sets of manipulations of the system environment.

These functions are considered to represent the initial, organized way which must be used to deal with human behavior in the framework of systems. They appear to be quite compatible with the functions used to describe machines, so long as the latter are expressed in terms of "data transformation." In addition, the conditions needed for their use are quite analogous to such machine mechanisms as filtering, programming, and shunting. They should therefore provide a language which can be related directly to the other events and operations that occur in systems.

In thinking about man in a systems framework, it is essential that one deal with functions rather than with the unitary events that compose them. *Stimuli* and *responses* are perhaps necessary to psychological analyses, but they contribute little, if anything, to precision of thinking about human functions, over and above the concepts of input and output. As for S-R "relationships," our analysis leads us to believe that these can be no simpler than the mechanisms we have described, and therefore offer no advantage in this respect. A number of implications flow from the consideration of human functions as we have described them, important to system development and perhaps also for psychological science. Let us take a brief look at some of these.

Selection and Training. The men who take part in the operation of a system have to be selected and trained (see Chapters 7 and 9). They may be selected because they already possess the capabilities for performing in a system; or more typically, because they are capable of rapidly acquiring, by means of training, the specific capabilities needed. The human functions as described here have immediate implications for selection and training, and these may be seen to be generally applicable to all kinds of jobs that occur in systems.

If the task to be performed involves sensing, selection must screen out those who fall below a given standard applicable to the particular sense mode concerned, whether it be a matter of visual acuity, brightness discrimination, auditory-frequency discrimination, or whatever. Training can be designed to establish stable sets for filtering (that is, it can produce the "trained observer"), but beyond this nothing can be achieved. If identifying is involved, the main function of training is to establish the models required for this function, whether these be wave forms, objects in aerial photographs, foreign words, or symbols used to provide computer inputs. A somewhat different and additional purpose may be the establishment of sequential routines such as are used in perceptual-motor skills. Selection may be employed to pick out those individuals who can acquire and store these models and routines most rapidly. If the task involves interpreting, one must first insure that the prior function of identifying can be performed and that the required models have been established by training. Beyond this, the function of training is to insure the acquisition of the rules needed to make the desired transformations, as well as the programming rules used in the establishment of filtering sets. Again, selection may be used to find those individuals who can most readily accomplish the storing of these rules.

Job Aids and Manuals.   There are also some obvious implications of our analysis of human functions for the development of printed aids and manuals used by the human operator in the course of system operation (see Chapter 8). First of all, we have found it necessary to recognize at the outset that inputs to the human components are not limited solely to the display of equipment. A highly important input source is the instructions provided to the operator. While these may on occasion be oral, they are most frequently printed, occurring as a portion of job manuals, as standard operating procedures, as check lists, and in other forms. One of the main purposes of such instructions is to bring about reprogramming—in other words, to accomplish the necessary changes in sets for filtering and shunting which are needed as the individual proceeds from one mode of operation to another. There is a second major purpose of printed materials, in addition to this instructional one. Such materials are needed as a means of maintaining retention of the models and sequential routines in the long-term memory, particularly when these are complex. For example, a lengthy procedure for putting a piece of equipment into operation may be expected to involve a stored routine which profits from frequent "relearning" trials undertaken with a check list. Similar reasoning applies to a complex model such as that needed in equipment trouble shooting; retention of the model may require frequent reference to a "functional diagram" provided in a job manual.

The Composition of System Tasks.   A later chapter (Chapter 6) will consider in some detail how the structure and purpose of a system defines the tasks to be performed by human operators and how these tasks are combined to form jobs. As we shall see, the tasks generated by a system are simply small parts of larger operations and are describable in common-sense terms without resort to technical language. Thus a *task* may be a suboperation such as "plotting tracks of aircraft," "locating targets on a map," "aligning set X prior to operation." It is clear, however, that the description of a task does not in itself provide an indication of the human function involved in it (see Miller, 1953). Locating targets on a map could be a task requiring fairly simple identifications, or relatively complex interpreting, depending on the kind of input-output transformation required. Thus the set of tasks which make up a given job may vary widely in terms of the human functions they involve; and a given task may partake of more than one function.

For these reasons it will be apparent that descriptions of system tasks, whether organized into jobs or not, provide only the starting point for the problem of utilizing human capabilities in systems. Proceeding from this point, one must make an analysis of each task to obtain an indication of the *human functions* that are required, together with the input conditions needed for each of them. This is the kind of information required for the specification of selection and training requirements, as well as for the design of job aids, as we have already mentioned. Thus it may be realized that the identification of human functions in system operations provides the key to many of the steps that have to be taken in developing the system as a whole, and particularly the human components of the system. It is these human functions which will basically determine how the human beings are to be selected, what is required for their training and retraining, how they are to be instructed during system operations, and what standards can be set for their performance.

Limitations in Human Functioning

Our discussion of human functioning has revealed a number of limitations of human functioning, some of which we have mentioned rather casually as we proceeded. It is worthwhile, however, to take a direct look at this problem. What are the limitations of the human functions we have described, and how do these compare with those of present-day machines? This is a question of particular importance in the design stage of system development, when the designer may be faced with the necessity of comparing the consequences of substituting a machine for a man or vice versa.

What are the limitations of human functions, relative to those of machines? Several authors (see for example Chapanis, 1960) have contributed lists of advantages and disadvantages of men and machines, expressed in such terms as "flexibility of programming," "size of channel capacity," "perceiving organized patterns," and so on. Is it possible to express these ideas, perhaps in more highly organized fashion, using the functions and conditions we have described? Table 2.1 makes this attempt.

Table 2.1
Some Comparisons of the Limitations of Machine and Human Functions, in Relative Terms

Conditions for function	Limitations	
	Human	*Machine*
SENSING		
Display	Limited to certain ranges of energy change affecting human senses	Range extends far beyond human senses (X-rays, infrared, etc.)
	Sensitivity: very good	Sensitivity: excellent
Filtering	Easy to reprogram	Difficult to reprogram
IDENTIFYING		
Display	Can be varied over relatively wide range of physical dimensions	Can be varied only in very narrow range of physical dimensions
	Channel capacity: small	Channel capacity: large

Table 2.1 (continued)
Some Comparisons of the Limitations of Machine and Human Functions, in Relative Terms

Conditions for function	Limitations	
	Human	*Machine*
IDENTIFYING (cont.)		
Filtering	Easy to reprogram	Difficult to reprogram
Memory	Limits to complexity of models probably fairly high, but not precisely known	Potential limits of complexity very high
	Limits to length of sequential routines fairly high, but time-consuming to train	Potential limits of length of routines very high
INTERPRETING		
Display	Same as Identifying	Same as Identifying
Filtering	Easy to reprogram	Difficult to reprogram
	Highly flexible, i.e., adaptable	Relatively inflexible
	May be reprogrammed by self-instruction following input changes contingent on previous response (dynamic decision making)	
Shunting	Can be readily reprogrammed to lower levels of functioning	Difficult to reprogram
Memory	Limitation to rule storage not known	Limits of rule storage ("logic") quite high
	Speed of reinstatement of rule sequences relatively low (as in computing)	Speed of using rule sequences high (e.g., computing)
	Use of novel rules possible (inventing)	Limited in use of novel rules

As the table indicates, limitations may be described and understood in accordance with the input conditions to which they relate, whether these be characteristics of the display, of the filtering and shunting conditions of short-term memory, or of the long-term memorial inputs. When each of these is spelled out, the nature of man versus machine limitations becomes rather clear, and it is possible also to see what future possibilities are likely to develop in machines yet to be designed.

For the *sensing* function, the limitations of man are quite apparent. The physical-energy changes he can sense are limited to those which affect his receptors of vision, hearing, touch, smell, taste, and so on (see Chapter 4). In contrast, machines are able to sense changes beyond these limits, in the ultra-violet and infrared regions of the electromagnetic spectrum, above 200,000 cycles in the mechanical spectrum, and so on. Within the limitations of his senses, a man's sensitivity is quite good, since it is known that he can sense very small differences (compare Geldard, 1953). But the number of changes he can respond to at one time is relatively small—that is, his channel capacity is limited. Beyond this, it will be realized that reprogramming man's filtering conditions is a matter readily accomplished by instructions; in a machine, this would be expensive or time-consuming or both.

Identifying is a function at which man currently excels the machine. Primarily, this is because the stimuli to be identified can vary over a wide range in their physical dimensions, as well as in the context in which they are imbedded, without producing errors in identification. In other words, the models man can learn and store are extremely "flexible." Machines have not yet been designed which can perceive inputs of such variability in a reliable fashion. Instead, the routines that function as models for the machine must have relatively fixed patterns. When these routines can be unvarying, but are composed of long sequences (as, for example, in certain types of tracking), a machine can readily outperform a man. Long sequential routines require fairly lengthy periods of practice on the part of a human being.

A number of varieties of *interpreting* can be performed better by machines than by human beings. Complex and lengthy sequences of rules can readily be designed into a machine, and tasks such as computing can be performed in a fraction of the time required by a man. Computers can be designed also to include probabilistic rules, and such interpretation can often better be done by a machine than by human beings. The filtering of inputs, however, can be easily reprogrammed in man, whereas this is difficult in a machine. In addition, it has been found desirable in a number of instances to permit human beings to develop their own filtering rules, and this sort of "adaptation" may be shown to improve man's performance. Can machines invent new ways of using rules? Perhaps they will be able to someday, although as yet their performance in this function is distinctly limited. The kind of task at which man clearly excels, compared with present-day machines, is one which requires interpreting of inputs which require complex identifications in the first place. Aerial photo-interpretation, for example, is such a task. Perhaps a machine could be designed to follow the rules required in deciding that a picture contains an "aluminum plant"; but a human being would first have to identify the objects in the photograph which enter into these rules. When these functions are used together in a man, we have a task which appears to be peculiarly a human one, and which can on occasion use man's capabilities to the limit. Another kind of human function which reveals man's remarkable capabilities is that of dynamic decision making, in which input changes at each step of an interpretation sequence produce reprogramming of the individual's filtering sets. The facility and rapidity with which such changes can be brought about stand in marked contrast to the capacities of a machine.

▣ **HUMAN FUNCTIONING IN SYSTEM TASKS**

We have already had occasion to note that tasks, forming as they do the parts of system operations, do not hold a one-to-one correspondence with human functions. There are tasks which utilize a single human function in their performance, and there are tasks which utilize several functions. Man is a relatively versatile "package." It is not surprising, therefore, that he is used to carrying out a great variety of tasks, which are typically designed to "fit in" with the functions of machines, rather than being designed specifically to conform to the conditions of the separate human functions.

There appear to be certain typical kinds of task situations in which man is used as a part of a subsystem, and these have come to be called by special names. It is doubtful that these tasks have any more general significance than that they occur frequently in many different systems. But each of them reflects the employment of human capabilities in a manner which exploits one or more of the advantageous features of human functioning. Let us examine a few of these here, in order to show clearly the involvement of human functions as we have described them. In doing this, we return to our example of the human operator seated at a console, the two components forming a link in a larger set of system operations.

Coding

There are many varieties of coding tasks in systems. Characteristically, the input comprises stimulus patterns which must be identified in terms of outputs designed to be employed as inputs to the next link in the system. Suppose, for example, that the operator must receive messages through head-phones in Morse code and transform these messages into typed English sentences for transmittal to the next system component (which in this case is another human being). Clearly these activities utilize the function of identification. Filtering sets must be established by instructions which insure that the individual will attend only to certain kinds of auditory sounds received through the headphones and ignore the noise. The individual must utilize some stored models which represent the pattern of dots and dashes he hears in order to identify them as letters and words. There is also a second stage to this task, which also has the characteristics of identifying: the words must be transformed into an output which involves the use of a typewriter. There is thus a motor skill required, and the sequential routines involved in typing must also be available to the individual through his long-term memory.

If we look a little more closely at this total task, we can see that the first stage of identifying (transforming Morse code into English prose) can be more efficiently accomplished by interpreting. In fact, this is what usually happens if we give an individual enough practice at receiving code (as Bryan and Harter [1899] suggested many years ago). As practice continues, the experienced code receiver begins to be able to *anticipate* whole sequences of dots and dashes, because he is interpreting the message in accordance with well-practiced "rules" of English prose. This method turns out to be more efficient for several reasons. The human message receiver can perform accurately even when subjected to rather extreme distractions; he can receive even when the noise level is very high; and he can receive when there are gaps in the message. These facts have some particular significance for the system design decision as to how the human operator can best be employed in this coding task. If the Morse code can be depended upon to provide a relatively constant physical input, a machine can readily be used to translate these fixed patterns into English letters and words. However, if reception is going to be characterized by frequent noise and lapses, a human being may be needed to perform both the identifying and the interpreting required for producing reliable (and meaningful) English prose.

The second stage of this task, the typing, presents a somewhat different picture. The input in this case will be meaningful English sentences supplied by the individual to himself. He must now identify the letters and spaces which make up these sentences in terms of responses made to the keyboard of the typewriter. In order to do this, he must have acquired the sequential routines that constitute the basis for this motor skill. This, of course, is well within his capabilities; after sufficient practice a high degree of typing proficiency can be attained. Thus, if a human individual has been chosen to do the interpreting task of the first stage, he can readily be used to perform the identifying (motor skill) function required at the second stage. The crucial decision has therefore already been made, and can be seen to characterize a wide variety of coding tasks. When inputs can have a fixed relationship to outputs, a machine can perform the entire coding operation very well indeed. In contrast, when inputs must be *identified* which are variable in their physical dimensions; or when they must be *interpreted,* because inferences about meaning have to be made to fill gaps; then the task is one at which a human being excels.

Another Example of Coding. Let us change the situation a little, so that we can look at another coding task. Suppose we set our operator-console subsystem the task of reporting "deviant courses" of aircraft which are being tracked by radar and displayed as a track of points on a scope face. What we want the subsystem to do is to identify as "deviating" or "nondeviating" from preplanned courses the tracks of a number of aircraft shown on the scope. Obviously there are several ways of going about this. One may think of doing it, for example, by requiring the human being to report the specific variables of speed, heading, and altitude to a computer, by punching them in a set of buttons. The computer then compares these variables with a set representing the preplanned course stored in its memory. When the task is designed in this manner, we are requiring the use of the identifying function of the human being, in a relatively simple and straightforward way. He identifies the speed of a given track, making his output by punching buttons. Similarly, he identifies heading and altitude, by comparisons of the display dimensions in each case with models stored in his long-term memory. But depending on the situation, the computer may have been given a difficult, or even impossible, task. What ranges of variation in speed, heading, and altitude is it going to report as "deviating"? What combinations of these variables is it going to choose to distinguish "deviating" from "nondeviating"? Can it take account of, and ignore, certain gaps in the information it receives, certain errors made by the human operator, or the presence of occasional "noise"? Of course, this depends on the nature of the operating situation, as we have said.

Suppose the task were performed by a man-machine display combination in a different way. This time the machine will take note of and measure the speed, heading, and altitude of the tracked aircraft. This it can do quite well because these variables are relatively "fixed" in character; they are definite physical variables which can be fed to the machine as inputs that do not change significantly in their other dimensions. The machine will then display a track for the aircraft in question, plotted out on a visible screen. At the same time, it will also display the preplanned track of the aircraft, taken from its memory. The display as a whole, then, will be one which shows the human operator the two tracks simultaneously, each in its dimensions of speed, altitude, and heading. Now the human being is confronted with the necessity of using his identifying function in a way that will exploit it effectively. He can ignore small changes, gaps, noise, and other variations in input in perceiving the patterns which he reports as "deviating" or "nondeviating." Once he has acquired the proper models, he will be able to perform such a task with a high degree of efficiency. Furthermore, his performance can be easily reprogrammed: if the task demands that he ignore speed on a particular occasion or for a particular aircraft, a filtering set established by instructions enables him to do this easily without loss of effectiveness. On the whole, then, this can be seen to be a much more efficient arrangement than that previously described. The machine is being asked to do what it can do best: sensing, measuring, and perhaps computing, such things as speed, altitude, and direction. And the human being is being required to perform the kind of function at which he excels: identifying patterns of stimulation that are subject to variation in a number of dimensions, but which must be reported as equivalent despite these variations.

The implications of a coding task for selection and training of human operators are clear enough, but we can also recognize that they depend on the kinds of functions involved. If, as in our first example, a transformation of Morse code is to be made into English prose, training will need to establish, not only the models required for identification of the dot-dash sequences in terms of letters and words, but also the rules for anticipating the meanings of messages. Some of these latter, of course, may be already available because of long acquaintance with the language; others may have to be learned as special technical language peculiar to the system. Our second example, coding aircraft tracks, involves the function of identifying, and the models to be acquired are either those pertaining to speeds, altitudes, and headings (first instance), or to track deviations (second instance). In all these instances, selection has the purpose of choosing individuals who can most rapidly acquire and store the necessary memorial inputs.

Scanning and Detection

Scanning and detection together provide another and different sort of example of a subsystem task in which the human observer plays a prominent part. Suppose we ask our observer to report the presence of buildings in a relatively unpopulated area which is being scanned by radar mounted in an aircraft and displayed on a scope. The aircraft approaches the area and flies over it at a height of 30,000 feet, and the human observer is required to report as soon as possible the position of each building he can identify. The radar picture on the scope changes with each sweep, so that terrain features become increasingly clear as the aircraft gets closer to the area. The scanning and detection task begins at a distance of 20 miles.

Anyone who has observed a terrain picture on a radar scope will realize at once that the basic identification function being utilized in this task is one which requires a model by means of which "buildings" and "things that are not buildings" can be distinguished. It is the kind of model which bears little resemblance to that used in viewing an aerial photograph, for example. Buildings are distinguished in radar returns on the basis of brightness and shape differences, but they are recognized as buildings only after the human observer has had considerable experience in viewing such returns. Furthermore, the variations in these dimensions as well as in the background against which they occur are quite extensive, particularly since each successive antenna sweep brings an altered picture. Fundamentally, then, this task uses the identification function, requiring output responses which indicate the presence or absence of buildings. (As we previously pointed out, the identification of a single category of input from all others is usually called *detection*.)

But obviously something else has been added to this task which makes it different from simply "looking at a radar picture." It is performed under pressure of time. And in order that it be performed efficiently under these conditions, a sequential routine called "scanning and search" has been added. This routine is an essential part of the filtering conditions—by means of it, the individual continues to "tell himself" where to look and what to look for throughout the whole operation. Scanning and search routines may be carried in short-term memory, as is usual unless they are extraordinarily lengthy. They may be reprogrammed; for example, one might need to give the instruction, "Look in the northwest quadrant." If there is a requirement that filtering routines be particularly systematic (as is true, for example, in airplane "spotting"), they may be practiced and stored in long-term memory. In any case, scanning and search frequently are preliminary to, and coupled with, detection.

Scanning and search routines as a prelude to detection have often been taught successfully to military personnel who must carry out missions in the dark (compare Sharp, Gordon, and Reuder, 1952). In this case an initial act of sensing some change in visual stimulation (a movement in the dark) puts into operation a systematic routine of observing "out of the corner of the eye" in order to bring to bear on the situation the more sensitive extrafoveal receptors. Such routines must be deliberately trained, because they are directly opposite to those used in daytime vision, when the "natural" thing to do is to look at the object foveally. The function ultimately employed is again one of detection, in which the individual attempts to identify "a moving thing" or perhaps "a moving enemy soldier" against a background of nonmoving shapes.

Monitoring

Another relatively common kind of task that involves the function of detection is called *monitoring*. A monitoring task is one that requires detection of events which occur at relatively rare, randomly distributed intervals over a lengthy period of time. The events may be the appearance on the display of an object which must be reported, or they may be out-of-tolerance conditions of the equipment. The human individual may be required to detect one or a number of different events, when and if they occur, during the same time period.

The basic function utilized in monitoring tasks is detection, and this means that the individual must have available the models required. If he is to report the appearance of a blip on an oscilloscope, he must have the model which distinguishes the blip from noise. Or, if he must detect out-of-tolerance readings on twelve gauges, he must have the model for each of these. However, since the events he is looking for are infrequent and sporadic, a monitoring task is not easy for a human being to perform with high efficiency over periods of time greater than half an hour or so. Scanning and search routines become excessively tiresome and subject to inhibition. Attention is said to wander; that is, the sets for filtering which are held in short term memory tend to fade away, and the inputs to be detected are missed (compare Deese, 1957).

There are two general ways of effectively designing a monitoring task assigned to a human operator. One is to establish the necessary models in long-term memory and to depend upon a strong alerting stimulus (like a loud noise or bright light) to take the place of filtering conditions. This method is often used with danger signals. The maintenance of filtering conditions within the individual becomes unnecessary with this method, since the warning signal is strong enough to capture the attention and to block the reception of all other inputs for a time. The second way is to provide for the occurrence of events at frequent enough intervals so that the filtering sets are in a sense "reinforced" and thus maintained (compare Garvey, Taylor, and Newlin, 1959). A human operator who must watch for the appearance of a blip representing an aircraft in an isolated portion of the earth may be looking for something which seldom happens. A satisfactory way to maintain the filtering conditions necessary for such detection is to increase the frequency of the events—that is, the blips. This can be done by deliberately designing the machine to "help out" the man, by including a program which simulates the occurrence of blips (representing aircraft) at relatively frequent intervals. By thus insuring the maintenance of filtering sets, the efficiency of the human operator can be substantially raised.

Actually, as the work of Mackworth (1958) and others has shown, monitoring is not the kind of task which human beings perform well, except under the conditions described in the previous paragraph. The equipment designer needs to consider the instances in which the machine can be built to perform this function, which is the case when the events to be detected can be reflected as changes in single physical variables. In contrast, when these events partake of the perceiving of forms and patterns varying widely in their physical dimensions, the detection may have to be done by a man. In such cases some provision must be made for insuring the maintenance of sets for filtering.

Tracking

The tracking of a continuously moving target is a kind of task which has occurred with some frequency in military systems. This is the task which characterizes antiaircraft gunnery, for example, and, in a somewhat more complex form, aerial gunnery. The function utilized in tracking is obviously identification, and the models involved pertain to the "sighting picture" provided by the reticle, or gunsight, which displays the target in reference to the positioning of the gun, usually represented as the intersection of cross hairs. The directions of movement of the control (the output) reflect the identification of a variety of different positions of the target in the field of the gunsight. The task is one in which successive pictures are reacted to (identified) one after another by movements which blend into each other and form a more-or-less continuous movement.

In this kind of tracking task, the sequence of movement required is not only variable but unpredictable from one moment to the next. This is in contrast with a motor skill like that involved in rendering a particular composition on a piano, in which the sequence of movements is entirely determined by the sequence of notes. Consequently, the models of primary importance to the tracking task are those which represent relationships between target position at any given moment and direction and speed of movement of the control handle (or wheel). However, since the input to tracking performance also includes kinesthetic feedback from the just-previous movement, it is impossible to provide for the learning of wholly adequate models except by giving practice with the use of the specific control used in the actual task. This is the reason for the insistence upon "realistic" representation of control pressures and movements in training devices and simulators for tracking tasks such as gunnery and aircraft maneuvering. It is noteworthy, however, despite the correctness of this position, that models acquired for identification of the sighting picture alone (without accompanying kinesthetic feedback) may nevertheless have the most marked effects on tracking performance. Studies of flexible gunnery, for example, have shown the critical importance for good tracking of training in recognition of correct sighting pictures (compare Goldstein and Ellis, 1956).

When the identifications involved in tracking can be reduced to simple inputs varying in a single dimension, it is obvious that machine performance can easily be made to exceed that of a human operator. Extensive training in sighting-picture models can thereby be avoided. But the primary reason for machine excellence in tracking is one of speed (compare Table 2.1). The human individual's time of reaction (not less than ¼ second for each identification) presents a definite limitation to his tracking performance, as a number of studies have shown (compare Fitts, 1951). This speed is slow indeed, compared to what can be accomplished with the use of such mechanisms as servomotors and analogue computers. Since the demand for speed in gunnery has greatly increased in recent years, it is not surprising to find that this kind of task is to an increasing degree performed by machines, without the participation of the human operator.

The task of flying an airplane constitutes an interesting and instructive example of tracking. The tracking required for control and maneuver of the plane in flight have long ago been taken over by machine (except, of course, for small private aircraft). Even before the automatic pilot was extensively used, it became apparent that the identifications required in the course of flight were being made with reference to instrument readings, which represent extremely simple models for the human being and, in fact, could readily be reduced to single-dimension inputs to a machine. The "seat of the pants" soon became unnecessary as a source of input for the identifications made in controlling the aircraft. The situation in landing the aircraft, however, is quite a different one. Here the identifications required are based upon models with a variety of "built-in" variations, of the sort that are used by human beings in perceiving distance. Automatic landing of airplanes can presumably be accomplished, but only when the input variables which establish the requirements for the plane's performance can be specified with great precision. Again we can realize that this particular tracking task is performed better by a human operator because of his ability to acquire and store complex models (of distance) which are applicable to a great variety of specific situations.

Troubleshooting

Our account of some typical system tasks has up to now emphasized those that involve the function of identifying. It is time to turn our attention now to some examples of more distinctly "intellectual" tasks which utilize the function of interpreting. One of these is troubleshooting, or the diagnosing of malfunctions. While this kind of task occurs most frequently as a part of system maintenance, as opposed to system operations, it is important to recognize that troubleshooting in a more general sense is not confined to maintenance. In many instances, the operation of modern systems requires this kind of task as an integral part of "running" the system, or of "putting it into operation." Strategic missile systems provide an example. While the popular image of the "operation" of such a system may conceive of this as beginning at the time the missile leaves the launching pad, military users of such missiles are well aware that the major portion of system operations takes place on the ground minutes, hours, and even weeks before the time of launching. The missile and its components are "checked out" in many different ways during these periods of time, and even the final countdown before launching may be considered to be a standardized checkout procedure. Checking out equipment is a task of *troubleshooting*.

A typical troubleshooting problem is depicted in diagrammatic form in Figure 2.5, which shows the situation faced by the radar mechanic in diagnosing a malfunction whose initial symptom is that no north-south displacement in range is being displayed on the scope, regardless of the value of inputs to the north (-south) chain. The difficulty could lie in any of components concerned with north-south information, including *A, C, G, J, K,* and *N.* The circles indicate check points, and the dotted crosses show where the mechanic would find faulty indications if he were to make these checks. (This information, of course, is not available to the mechanic unless he seeks it.)

Finding the malfunctioning unit in this case may be done by sequences of checking which vary considerably in their efficiency. One could, for example, simply check at every available point. An efficient procedure, however, is as follows: Point *4* is checked to determine whether both the "angle chain" and the "range chain" are involved. Since *4* is faulty, this means that the trouble must lie at or behind the linked units *G* and *J.* This reduces the area of uncertainty to that portion of the equipment which includes units *A, C, G,* and *J.* Checking in the center of this complex, check point *7* yields a faulty reading, which narrows the search to units *A* and *C.* When a check is made at *6,* unit *C* is found to be receiving the correct input. Consequently, the trouble is definitely located in *C.*

A task such as this evidently utilizes both identifying and interpreting functions. The mechanic must first of all have been trained so that he has available in his memory the models which represent the components of the equipment and their check points, as well as the instrument readings that

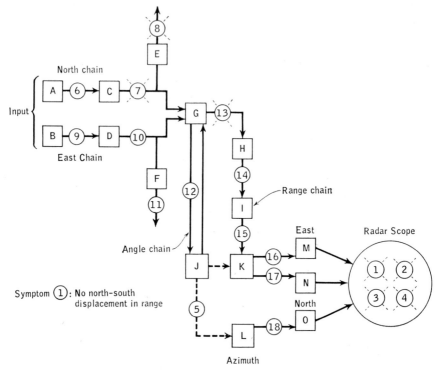

Figure 2.5.   Diagram illustrating an equipment malfunction in a set of radar equipment (from Gagné, 1954, by courtesy of Mr. Norman Crowder)

indicate "good" or "faulty" when he makes the checks concerned. It is noteworthy that training in equipment nomenclature and locations and in reading test instruments are prominently emphasized features of courses of training for radar maintenance. One cannot troubleshoot successfully without being able to make these identifications.

The interpreting function is used at every step of the way in the troubleshooting sequence. The choice of the first check, for example, involves a decision among courses of action which are the rules for equipment functioning previously acquired by the mechanic. He responds to check number 4, not simply on the basis of its appearance, but in the sense that it is connected by rule with the functioning of the combined "angle" and "range" chains. It may be noted that these chains themselves do not correspond with the packaging of the equipment and are not at all apparent from looking at it. Instead, they represent the kinds of conceptual rules which the mechanic must acquire and store if he is to perform troubleshooting effectively. Accordingly, training for the troubleshooting of specific equipment must concern itself prominently with the establishment of such rules in the individual.

We have no wish here to oversimplify the nature of the dynamic decision-making activity involved in such a task as troubleshooting. Human thinking is indeed complex behavior, and the mechanisms that make it possible are by no means well understood. We want only to make it clear that troubleshooting, as a typical systems task, requires the use of the human functions of identifying and interpreting. The individual must exercise filtering and shunting routines that take him through the problem in a systematic sequence of steps. At one moment he is identifying a check reading (for example, an instrument value which indicates "good" or "faulty"), while at the next he is interpreting the effects of this reading (for example, "Information is distorted in the range chain"). Thus he must have in his memory the models which make identifying possible, the rules which are utilized in interpreting, and the potential programs needed for the establishment of a variety of filtering sets. Selection and training procedures will need to be instituted taking each of these functions into account.

Flexible Programming with Interaction between Persons

The operation of total systems usually requires the interaction of people, as well as the interaction of an individual man with a machine. As later chapters will show (see Chapters 11 and 13), the consequences of such interaction are to greatly expand the range and variety of inputs to which a given individual must respond, as well as to introduce the necessity for frequent reprogramming of behavior. Even at the subsystem level with which we are dealing, some notion of the consequences of human interaction may be gained by a consideration of *load-sharing* situations, in which two individuals are required to operate in parallel from the same display (or from a duplication of the same display). An example may be found in the task of air-traffic control.

An investigation has been made (Kidd and Hooper, 1959) of the task of radar-approach control under high traffic-load conditions, in which the question of load sharing between two operators was explored. The two operators received inputs from identical PPI scopes displaying representations of incoming aircraft. Their task was to direct aircraft entering the system into one or the other of two GCA (ground control approach) gates, using minimum flight times and minimum fuel consumption, while maintaining prescribed aircraft separations. The laboratory problem was designed to provide a complete and realistic representation of an operation involving several aircraft types. As a part of the experiment, instructional inputs were systematically varied, to the effect that the operators initially adopted filtering sets of three different sorts: (1) rotation control (one controller responsible for every other aircraft); (2) sector control (control assigned on the basis of entry); and (3) destination control (control assigned on the basis of landing field). When operators were permitted to transfer control of an aircraft to each other, it was found that no exchanges were made in the destination-control condition, whereas a high proportion of exchanges were made under both the other conditions, in each case to bring about a destination-control configuration. Thus load sharing was effectively accomplished by the reprogramming of filtering sets by the two operators.

Basically, the task of recognizing and controlling aircraft can readily be seen to involve the functions of identification and interpretation. The PPI display must first be perceived as a pattern of aircraft having certain positions and directions of movement in space, and in relation to runways on the ground. The controller must also interpret the situation in accordance with a number of previously learned rules, having to do with acceptable conditions of heading, altitude, and speed. He is carrying out sequential interpretations, and stating vector and descent instructions, so as to insure that the aircraft under his control will land in the shortest time possible, using as little fuel as possible, and with maximum safety.

Under reasonable traffic conditions, a single controller would probably be able to accomplish this task successfully by adopting a filtering set comparable to "rotation control"—that is, by simply taking responsibility for each aircraft in the order in which it appears. But when traffic is heavy, and another controller is added to the subsystem, the load must be shared. In such circumstances, it is possible to prescribe the kind of filtering set to be adopted; but, as the study we have described suggests, it is not possible to predict which of these is going to work best. Alternatively, this aspect of the task may be deliberately allowed to remain *flexible,* and when it is, reprogramming of filtering sets will be done by the individuals concerned so as to adopt the sets which optimize performance of the task. At a relatively simple level, a kind of "system learning" has taken place with these two operators. Their basic skills have not been altered; but they have achieved a higher level of subsystem performance by discovering what self-instructions will work best in the execution of this load-sharing task.

With a total system, the number and varieties of interactions between people are, of course, greatly increased. The possibilities of flexible programming are similarly increased, not only by the sharing of tasks, but also by the performance of tasks in which communication among individuals is required. In such instances, flexible programming takes on a new dimension in which "self-instructions" become "instructions to other people." There are, accordingly, greatly augmented possibilities for achieving effective filtering sets within each individual operator by means of system training exercises, which will be further discussed in a later chapter (Chapter 11).

REFERENCES

Bruner, J. S., Goodnow, J. J., and Austin, G. A. 1956. *A study of thinking.* New York: Wiley.
Bryan, W. L., and Harter, N. 1899. *Studies on the telegraphic language.* The acquisition of a hierarchy of habits. *Psych. Rev., 6,* 345–375.

Chapanis, A. Human engineering. 1960. In C. D. Flagle, W. H. Huggins, and R. H. Roy (ed.), *Operations research and systems engineering*, Chapter 19. Baltimore: Johns Hopkins Press.

Deese, J. 1957. *Changes in visual performance after visual work.* Wright-Patterson Air Force Base, Ohio: Wright Air Development Center. Technical Report 57–285.

Fitts, P. M. 1951. Engineering psychology and equipment design. In S. S. Stevens (ed.), *Handbook of experimental psychology.* New York: Wiley, 1287–1340.

Gagné, R. M. 1954. *An analysis of two problem-solving activities.* Lackland Air Force Base, Texas: Air Force Personnel and Training Research Center. Research Bulletin TR–54–77.

Gagné, R. M. 1959. Problem solving and thinking. *Ann. Rev. Psychol., 10,* 147–172.

Garvey, W. D., Taylor, F. V., and Newlin, E. P. 1959. *The use of "artificial signals" to enhance monitoring performance.* Washington, D.C.: U. S. Naval Research Laboratory. Report 5269.

Geldard, F. A. 1953. *The human senses.* New York: Wiley.

Gibson, E. J. 1942. Intra-list generalization as a factor in verbal learning. *J. exp. Psychol., 30,* 185–200.

Goldstein, M., and Ellis, D. S. 1956. *Pedestal sight gunnery skills: A review of research.* Lackland Air Force Base, Texas: Air Force Personnel and Training Research Center. Research Report TN–56–31.

Johnson, D. M. 1955. *The psychology of thought and judgment.* New York: Harper.

Kidd, J. S., and Hooper, J. J. 1959. *Division of responsibility between two controllers and load balancing flexibility in a radar approach control team. A study in human engineering aspects of radar air traffic control.* Wright-Patterson Air Force Base, Ohio: Wright Air Development Center. Technical Report 58–473. ASTIA No. AD214616.

Mackworth, N. H., and Mackworth, J. F. 1958. Visual search for successive decisions. *Brit. J. Psychol.,* 49, 210–221.

McGeoch, J. A., and Irion, A. L. 1952. *The psychology of human learning.* (2nd ed.). New York: Longmans.

Miller, R. B. 1953. *A method for man-machine task analysis.* Wright-Patterson Air Force Base, Ohio: Wright Air Development Center. Technical Report 53–137.

Northrop, F. S. C. 1947. *The logic of the sciences and the humanities.* New York: Macmillan.

Platt, W., and Baker, B. A. 1931. The relation of the scientific "hunch" to research. *J. chem. Educ., 8,* 1969–2002.

Rossman, J. 1931. *The psychology of the inventor.* Washington, D. C.: Inventors Publications.

Sharp, L. H., Gordon, D., and Reuder, M. 1952. *Review of studies on the effects of training on night vision ability.* Washington, D.C.: Personnel Research Section, The Adjutant General's Office, Department of the Army. PRS Report 974.

Taylor, D. W., Berry, P. C., and Block, C. H. 1958. Does group participation when using brainstorming facilitate or inhibit creative thinking? *Admn. Sci. Quart., 3,* 23–47.

Taylor, F. V. 1957. Psychology and the design of machines. *Amer. Psychologist, 12,* 249–258.

Woodworth, R. S. 1938. *Experimental psychology.* New York: Holt.

CONSIDERATION OF THE FUNCTIONS OF MEN and machines would indeed be incomplete without a discussion of that most modern and versatile machine, the computer. The development of these system components and their technology has broadened and sharpened the issues pertaining to assignment of functions to man and machine within the system framework. With a machine as intellectual as a computer, the decisions about what capabilities for specific kinds of tasks can be built or programmed into the equipment, as opposed to those which can be assigned to system operators, obviously become highly critical decisions, which can markedly affect the success of a system's operation.

The basic functioning of computers is described in this chapter, together with the nature of programming, its techniques and tribulations. This is followed by an examination of the problem of allocating tasks to computers and men, based upon a comparison of their functions. This in turn leads to a consideration of the kinds of system tasks which human beings perform in interaction with computers. Finally, the chapter provides a brief account of an area of research of considerable current interest to behavioral scientists—the problem of simulating intellectual processes by means of computers.

Perhaps no combination of man and machine could be imagined which would pose livelier or more intricate problems of behavioral description and analysis than the man-computer combination. The development of computers has forced equipment designers to think and talk about machines as though they "behaved." As this chapter demonstrates, the behavior of men and computers can reasonably be considered within a single frame of reference which facilitates valid decisions for system design.

MEN AND COMPUTERS*

Ward Edwards

Man-machine systems exist to do work. They are worth developing only if the work they do cannot be done easily or correctly by men alone. Consequently, the machines in such systems are usually designed to perform tasks which men cannot easily perform. Examples are obvious: bicycles triple speed of locomotion, binoculars may increase by a factor of five or more the effective range of vision, books increase information storage by unmeasurable amounts. Machines which enhance the speed or power of man's muscles, the accuracy or acuteness of his senses, or the durability and precision of his memory are as old as man himself.

All machines obey orders. But most machines either obey only an extremely limited set of orders, like a toaster, or gain versatility only by using constant human control, like a pencil or an automobile. Perhaps the most extraordinary technological achievement of the last century is the development of machines which do better something men do very well: take and give orders. Machines which can sense and execute many diverse orders very rapidly and accurately are called *computers*. We usually think of computers as order takers, but the advent of automated factories illustrates the fact that computers are fully as adept at giving orders to other machines (it might be better to say, other parts of the same machine) as they are at taking them from other computers, such as men.

* The work reported herein was sponsored by the Astrosurveillance Sciences Laboratory, Electronics Research Directorate, Air Force Cambridge Research Laboratories, Air Force Research Division (ARDC), under Contract No. AF 19(604)–7393, monitored by the Operational Applications Office, Directorate of Technology, Air Force Command and Control Development Division. This chapter is identified as ESD-TR61—18.

Computation, interpreted broadly, is required in any man-machine system complicated enough to be worth talking about. And consequently, all such systems have computers in them. Two kinds of computers are available to system designers: wet or dry. The wet computer, known as the human brain, is an extraordinarily rapid, accurate, flexible, and inexpensive device. For this reason, system designers until this century have never felt much need for any other kind of computer. But in the last 100 years, and especially since World War II, engineers and mathematicians have become able to design dry computers which for some specific purposes are so much superior to the wet computer inside the human head that system designers have had to learn how to use dry computers effectively. Their efforts have been so successful that it is safe to predict that any man-machine system costing more than $1,000,000 and designed after 1965 will include at least one dry computer.

How should computers be used? How should functions be allocated between computers and men? What kinds of intercommunication devices and techniques are most effective? This chapter examines these questions. It begins with an expository discussion of computers and computation. It then compares men and computers with an eye to function allocation within large systems. It next discusses the nature of human jobs in systems which include dry computers. It concludes with a discussion of computers as models for men and of the artificial intelligence problem.

Much of what follows may sound like science fiction. But computer technology is developing so rapidly that the statements contained in the chapter are likely to be woefully unimaginative compared with what will actually happen. The task of predicting today the future of man-computer systems resembles the task of predicting in the days of James Watt, who invented the steam engine, the future of mechanical replacements for human muscle power.

▣ WHAT ARE COMPUTERS?

There are two kinds of computers, analogue and digital. An analogue computer is one which performs operations such as addition, division, or integration on continuously variable quantities, usually voltages or shaft positions. Such machines are relatively cheap, can be made fairly accurate, and can execute surprisingly complicated orders. Unfortunately, they are very difficult, relatively speaking, to give orders to, since the orders must be set up as externally wired connections, and they are subject to a number of kinds of inaccuracy which limit their usefulness. Nevertheless, they are widely used. A computer which is wired into a larger machine for the purpose of executing the same computation over and over again for its entire working life is almost always an analogue computer. The controls of an automatic washer are a very simple kind of analogue computer; an alarm clock is another. Note that such machines intermingle digital with analogue elements, a common characteristic of analogue, but not of digital, computers. But when we speak of computers we are usually interested in digital computers, and this chapter will be confined to them, although some of the things said apply to analogue computers as well.

Digital computers deal with discrete quantities, digits. The technology of manipulating digits by machine is so well developed that almost anything which can be done on an analogue computer can also be done on a large digital computer, just as fast, much more precisely—and, at present, rather more expensively. More important is the fact that logical operations of the kind discussed in classes of formal logic can easily be expressed in digital form. Most of the important and interesting properties of digital computers result from their ability to perform logical operations, or to mingle logical operations with arithmetical ones. In fact, some computer-plus-program combinations are incapable of adding two and two; they are concerned only with logical operations.

Computers are often talked about as though they were chunks of hardware, like desk calculators. There is an important sense in which the machine called IBM 709, for example, is not a computer at all. A computer must be told what to do before it will do anything other than take up space and generate heat or cold. Each computer comes equipped with a language, so that someone who wants to have it execute an order can communicate his desires. But that language is so inconvenient for human beings to use that it is often used only long enough to provide the computer with some other more convenient language. A computer plus a language—machine language or some other easier one—can obey orders; the hardware itself cannot. The reason why this point is important is that the computer changes its characteristics radically whenever its language is changed. For example, it is often possible to program a larger computer like the IBM 704 to behave as though it were a smaller computer like the IBM 650; such a program permits other programs originally written for the smaller machine to control the larger one without additional programming effort. The language in which a program is to be written plays a far more central role in programming than does the identity of the machine which is to be used, except, of course, for the fact that most programming languages are intended for specific kinds of machines. Hereafter, whenever the word "computer" is used without further qualification, reference to a machine-plus-language system is intended. Ordinarily, all properties other than speed, size, and cost are properties of the language rather than of the hardware. Of course, the hardware puts restrictions on what languages are possible or useful, but these are less important than the restrictions on languages which reflect the needs and ingenuity of their inventors.

Parts or Functions of Any Computer

The ordinary desk calculator, a simple digital computer, has an input mechanism; an output mechanism; an arithmetic or logical unit; a storage mechanism or memory; and a means for controlling its operation, or control unit. The input is a keyboard. The output is a set of digital dials. The arithmetic or logical unit and the storage mechanism or memory are the gears and cams inside the machine, and in some cases auxiliary digital dials. The control mechanism is partly the function keys and partly the operator, who determines the sequence in which keys will be pressed. Distinct parts which perform each of these five functions are found in most contemporary computers. The input devices on most large computers are magnetic tape, punched cards, and buttons on a console. The commonly used outputs are magnetic tapes, high-speed printers, and card punches. Most slow-access long-term storage uses magnetic tape, although stacks of magnetic disks are also coming into use. Rapid-access short-term memory now usually uses magnetic cores which store bits of information by means of a hysteresis effect; smaller, slower machines may use magnetic drums. Until recently, control and arithmetic units were electronic, but contemporary machines use transistors in preference to vacuum tubes, and so are sometimes called solid-state devices.

Computer technology is changing. Computer designers know more about how computation can be done than they used to, and new kinds of devices with fantastic properties will soon be available. So new ideas about the design and organization of computers are likely to make the statements in the previous paragraph about the parts of a computer obsolete within a few years. Input and output devices will continue to be easily identifiable, but the functions of short-term memory, control, and arithmetic or logic will probably not be distinct and recognizable. A very highly abstract analysis of any kind of computation is embodied in the notion of a Turing machine, which consists of a tape, a "read" operation and a "write" operation, which respectively take information from and put it onto the tape, and a designation operation which specifies where on the tape each read or write operation is to be performed. Any set of functions reducible to these three operations could in principle be used as the functions of a computer.

History of Computers

Of the devices listed above as standard for today's computers, only push buttons, punched cards, and vacuum tubes were available in 1940. The history of computing is, however, primarily the history of memory devices. The most important single development in that history was the invention in 1899 of the Hollerith card, the punched card named for its inventor. The punched card stores quite a lot of information permanently without error, gives the information back easily, and can be manipulated remarkably fast, at least by the standards of the 1930s. Techniques and hardware designed to exploit these useful characteristics of punched cards were developed; devices which sort punched cards are still extensively used in business operations.

In August, 1944, the first automatic calculator was put into operation. "Automatic" here means that the sequence of operations which was to be performed was set up in advance, using plug-in wires. Such machines are still in use. They are a great advance over desk calculators or sorters for Hollerith cards, in that no intervention by an operator is required in the course of the machine's work on a problem. But they lack flexibility and convenience and can handle only programs of very modest size.

The idea which makes modern computers possible is the idea of the stored program. It emerged shortly after the end of World War II; John von Neumann played a central role in developing it. The gist of the idea is this: since a calculator must have some kind of memory anyhow, it is desirable to store the instructions which the machine is to obey in the same way that data are stored within the machine. The instructions are numbers, in fact, and are interpreted as instructions because they are called out of memory in the right manner and at the right time. A stored program has two advantages over other kinds of programs: first, the instructions can be called out and used much more rapidly than would be possible otherwise; and secondly, the instructions can be modified within the program, during the course of the problem, as they are used.

Stored-program machines were a gigantic advance; computer hardware development since then has been mostly concerned with making fundamentally the same sort of machine bigger, faster, more reliable, and more convenient. In 1950, the earliest successful stored-program machines could perform one million additions in about eight minutes. In 1956, it took about 30 seconds to perform a million additions. In 1960 the fastest machines available could perform a million additions per second—and faster machines are on the way. Similar improvements in size of memory and cost per operation occurred. The upper limit on the number of operations per second in serial computers is imposed by the speed of light; information must move around the machine, and it cannot move faster than that speed. Computers now in development operate at about five eighths of that upper limit.

Advantages of Computers

What is gained by using large, fast computers? The most important gain is *speed*. It is not just a matter of performing computations in an hour which might otherwise take a week or a month; the improvement is much more dramatic than that. Computers routinely do in an hour or two computations which would take an unlimited staff of mathematical clerks with paper and pencil centuries to perform. So computers routinely perform calculations which otherwise would not be performed at all. Furthermore, this immense gain in speed makes possible the use of what mathematicians call numerical methods to find answers to problems which do not easily yield to intellectual effort. Numerical methods are brute-force methods; for example, one method for solving equations which do not yield to analysis is to try out possible answers one by one until a satisfactory one is found. (Most numerical methods are rather more sophisticated than that!)

The second gain is in *reliability*. No machine is perfectly reliable. But a present-day digital computer, properly used and maintained, may make errors less than once in a billion operations—and if it makes an error, it may be able to detect the fact and make appropriate corrections. One of the advantages men have over computers is a kind of reliability—but that kind of reliability has more to do with overcoming the consequences of errors than with not committing them. At not committing errors, computers are clearly superior to men.

The third gain obtained from using computers is *precision*. Within limits, the computer can carry as many significant figures as are needed through a calculation at no extra cost. The main consequence of this is that many calculations can be designed for precise though difficult, rather than imprecise though easy, procedures.

A final gain obtained by using computers is *reduced cost*. It is often and incorrectly argued that, since a computer greatly decreases the cost of computation, all computations should be performed by a computer. The premise is correct only for some computations. Specifically, a computing job must be of at least a certain size to be appropriate for a computer; the larger the computer, the larger is the smallest appropriate problem. Any computation must be programmed, and programmers are well paid. Moreover, almost all newly written programs contain bugs (errors); debugging time on the computer usually costs as much per hour as production run time. A large computer like the IBM 709 rents for somewhere between $250,000 and $1,000,000 per year, depending on what is being rented and who is paying the rent. Building, air conditioning, and auxiliary machines cost about $500,000 to purchase outright. A staff of 25 to 35 men to program and operate the machine and take care of the building is not uncommon; these men plus the others who are needed to support them might cost as much as another million a year. If the machine is rented, men to maintain it are provided by the owner. Typical time charges for computers such as the IBM 709 run in the region from $300 to $800 per hour, depending in part on whether programming services are included in the time charge or paid for separately. So if a computation can be done by hand with reasonable economy, it is a good bet that little if any money will be saved by transferring it to a computer. The savings obtainable from large computers result from the fact that the computer can easily and quickly perform repeated calculations which would otherwise be impossible. In business applications, such computations may save amounts of money literally thousands of times as great as their cost.

▣ PROGRAMMING

The most important fact about computers is that they do what they are told, no more and no less. The generic name for the art of telling a computer what to do is *programming*. More precisely, four steps intervene between problem and solution. The first step, usually called *analysis*, is that of figuring out just what the problem is. It often requires collaboration between the customer, who may not know exactly what he wants, and the programmer. The second step, usually called *programming*, is that of deciding in some detail how the computer should go about solving the problem. The third step, *coding*, is writing down the list of instructions which the computer will obey. The fourth step, *execution*, is the production runs on the computer. *Debugging*, or correction of errors, occurs at each step, though the word is often used with special reference to correcting errors in coding.

A program, sometimes also called a code, is simply a list of instructions written in some language the machine can understand; if that language is different from the machine's native language, then the program is put into the machine along with a previously prepared program which tells the machine how to perform the translation into machine language. Certain basic operations appear as instructions in almost all programming languages. The meanings of *add, subtract, multiply,* and *divide* are obvious. *Transfer* tells the machine to look for its next instruction in a place different from the place where it would ordinarily look. *Conditional transfer* tells the machine to take its next instruction from either location A or location B depending on some fact it can investigate, such as whether the number stored at location C is positive or negative. The meanings of *read* (from the input mechanism), *print*, and *store* (in memory) are obvious, as are *start* and *stop*. Some of the most modern machines have neither *start* nor *stop* available as programming instructions. In addition, programming languages always include some kind of location or address code, so that the instruction can specify not only what operation is to be performed but also where the raw material is to be obtained and what is to be done with the finished product. Characteristically, such addresses are simply numbers, which are thought of as serial locations, sometimes called *buckets*, in the machine, in which something of value may or may not be stored. A program is a series of numbers stored in a sequence of buckets; the machine ordinarily reads and executes the instructions in serial order, unless told otherwise by a transfer instruction.

Instructions vary in the number of different addresses which must be supplied in one way or another so that they can be executed. An unconditional transfer instruction requires only the address of the next instruction to be obeyed. An instruction to change sign requires only the address of the number the sign of which is to be changed and the next instruction address. A conditional transfer requires two next instruction addresses, plus the address of a quantity to be tested in order to determine which next instruction address will be used. An add instruction requires four addresses; the addresses of the two quantities to be added together, the address of the place where the sum should be stored, and a next instruction address.

Seldom if ever is explicit listing of all these addresses necessary, or even permissible. The next instruction address is usually simply the next instruction in the list of instructions beyond the one now being executed; most computers require that it be named explicitly only in the case of transfer instructions. There is usually one special location, often called the *accumulator,* in which all arithmetical operations take place. Thus in a single-address machine, if an addition is to be performed, one of the two numbers to be added together is already in the accumulator; if not, it must be brought there by an extra instruction. The address of the other number to be added to the one in the accumulator must be provided. The sum is left in the accumulator; if it is not to be used in the next instruction, an additional instruction must be used to store it elsewhere. Most modern machines are single-address machines.

Loops

The most important intellectual tools of computer programming are loops, subroutines, and address modification. A loop is simply a set of instructions which uses transfer or conditional transfer in such a way as to execute the same sequence of operations a number of times, usually modifying the addresses each time. For example, consider the following problem. There are 100 numbers, P_i, in cells 100 through 199, and 100 numbers, Q_i, in cells 200 through 299. The program is to form the 100 products P_iQ_i and store them in cells 300 through 399. The following loop will do it:

1. Store the number 100 in bucket S1, 200 in S2, and 300 in S3.
2. Take the number whose address is in bucket S1, multiply it by the number whose address is in bucket S2, and store the product in the bucket whose address is in bucket S3.
3. Add one to the numbers in S1, S2, and S3.
4. Conditionally transfer to instruction 2 if the number in S3 is less than 400 and to instruction 5 if the number in S3 is equal to or greater than 400.
5. Go on to the next part of the program.

Instruction 1 illustrates the most important feature which all programming languages other than machine languages have: symbolic addressing. The machine will substitute some currently unused buckets for S1, S2, and S3, and will remember which they are. Instruction 3 operates on a number which is part of an instruction, and thus uses the basic advantage of stored-program machines. Instruction 4 is, of course, the crucial instruction which sets up the loop. Instruction 5 might sometimes be included within instruction 4 but more often would be a separate instruction, into which a next instruction address would have been inserted by the instruction which led into this subroutine; that permits the subroutine to be used a number of different times within the program without being rewritten each time. Note that the buckets S1, S2, and S3 are left with numbers in them. Such unwanted numbers are often called *garbage;* it is standard programming practice to assume that buckets contain garbage and so to use initializing instructions like instruction 1 before using them for any purpose.

Almost all brute-force, or numerical, methods for solving problems which are intractable to analysis can be placed in one or the other of two categories. *Iterative* methods use series or other similar approximations. *Monte Carlo* methods, appropriate for use with functions or problems which involve probabilities, solve the same equation over and over again, using random values generated from random numbers, according to probabilities specified in the equation. The mean and variance of a large number of such solutions might be an appropriate output for some Monte Carlo computations. Loops are well adapted to both of these methods, of course; that is why these methods are so frequently used in practical computation.

Subroutines

The undiscussed major intellectual tool is the subroutine. Suppose a statistical computation requires extracting square roots. The programmer will have to select some technique for extracting square roots, break it down into component operations which appear in the programming language, and then code the program. But he need do it only once. Thereafter, whenever he wants to extract a square root within that problem, he need only transfer control to the first instruction of the part of the program which he has already used for extracting square roots, let that sequence of instructions operate, and then, when the square root has been extracted, return control to the next instruction of the unexecuted portion of the program. Such a portion of a program is called a *subroutine*. Subroutines can be generated within a program and used again and again, as in this example. But they can also be generated independently of any particular program, and either included as a single instruction in a programming language or made available as a previously prepared set of instructions which can be copied into a program or added as an extra card or set of cards in a program deck. Subroutines can, of course, be used in hierarchies; a process as complicated as a factor analysis can be used as a single subroutine, containing many subsubroutines. Some programming languages even permit a subroutine to contain itself as a subsubroutine; a brain-twisting arrangement.

Simplification of Programming

Progress in computer programming has consisted in large part of development of programming languages different from, and hopefully easier to use than, machine language. Symbolic addressing, loops, and subroutines have already been discussed. Their systematic use leads to the development of such languages. Many instructions in certain programming languages represent long and complicated subroutines in machine language. Almost all programming languages other than machine language use symbolic addressing; the machine, rather than the programmer, keeps track of where things are stored. Most programming languages use *mnemonic operation codes*. Instructions in machine language may include numbers or letters or both. But in a programming language the part of each instruction which specifies the operation to be performed is usually part of a word; examples are REA (read), MUL (multiply), and TRA (transfer). Many programming languages permit the use of *floating point* notation. This is the familiar scientific notation in which twelve million is written 1.2×10^7, or, in the form more appropriate for computers, 0.12×10^8. The advantage of floating point for computation is that it makes it easy for the computer, rather than the programmer, to keep track of the decimal point during calculations and to round off properly when necessary. And although most computers use binary numbers, most programming languages use decimal numbers; the machine does the translating.

Mnemonic operation codes, symbolic addressing, instructions not present in machine language, and provisions for conveniences such as floating point notation are the characteristics of most programming languages. Each such language is defined by a "package" of instructions which permit the computer to translate from the programming language to machine language; that package is usually simply a deck of punched cards or a reel of tape. The translation may work in either of two ways. Some language packages simply instruct the machine to translate the program into machine language. The machine reads the language package and the program and produces an output which is simply the program rewritten in machine language. Thereafter, in a second operation, the rewritten program plus the data enter the machine, which then performs the computation desired. Such languages are called *assemblers* if each instruction in the language in general corresponds to a single instruction in machine language. If, instead, each instruction in the language is likely to correspond to some large set of instructions in machine language, the language is called a *compiler*. The second way in which a programming language may work is that each instruction in the language is interpreted by the language package back into machine language and then immediately executed; such languages are called *interpreters*. Again, interpreters may ordinarily generate one or many machine-language instructions for each interpretive language instruction, though one-to-many interpreters (such as IPL-V) are relatively rare.

Compilers and one-to-many interpreters have in common the characteristic that any one instruction in the language replaces many (perhaps as many as 100) instructions in machine language; the use of such languages is often called *automatic programming*. The name is a bit misleading; writing programs in these languages is far from automatic.

To illustrate the amount of effort a programming language can save, Table 3.1 contains five different subroutines all designed for the same purpose and for the same computer, but each written in a different programming language. The advantage of powerful compilers like FORTRAN or MAD is obvious.

Table 3.1
One Subroutine in Several Programming Languages

The following subroutines look up a particular number in a table A of N numbers. If the particular number in fact appears in Table A, the subroutine reports its index (for example, serial position) in the table; if not, the subroutine reports zero. A subroutine for this purpose is written in each of five different programming languages.

IBM 704 Octal Numeric with no indexing (machine language)

```
   77   +050000 0 10000
  100   +060100 0 10002
  101   +040200 0 10003
  102   +060200 0 00104
  103   +050000 0 10001
  104   +040200 0 00000 address part to be filled in
  105   +010000 0 00112
  106   +050000 0 10002
  107   +040200 0 10004
  110   +010000 0 00112
  111   +002000 0 00077
10003   +040200 0 20000
10004   +000000 0 00001
```

IBM 704 Symbolic Assembly Language with no indexing (SAP)

```
          CAL   N
  LOOP    STO   COUNT
          ADD   CONST
          SLW   HERE
          CLA   TEST
  HERE    SUB   **
          TZE   OUT
          CLA   COUNT
          SUB   ONE
          TZE   OUT
          TRA   LOOP
  OUT
  ONE     DEC   1
  CONST   SUB   A
```

IBM 704 Symbolic Assembly Language with indexing (SAP)

```
          LXA   N, 1
  LOOP    CLA   TEST
          SUB   A, 1
          TZE   OUT
          TIX   LOOP, 1, 1
          LXA   ZERO, 1
  OUT
  ZERO    DEC   0
```

Table 3.1 (continued)
One Subroutine in Several Programming Languages

IBM 704 Formula Translation Compiler (FORTRAN)

```
        DO   6, I = 1, N
        IF   (TEST — (A(I)) 6, 7, 6
   6    CONTINUE
        I = 0
   7
```

Michigan Algorithmic Decoder (a compiler) for IBM 704 (MAD)

```
   X        THROUGH X, FOR I = N, −1, I. E. O. OR.
                    A(I). E. TEST
```

Every programming language has a name; examples are SOAP, SAP, PACT, FORTRAN, FLOWMATIC, MAD, IPL-V. Until relatively recently, each language was completely specific to a particular kind of computer. Now, however, IBM has FORTRAN packages for its 704, 709, and 7090, and packages for languages like IPL-V, which was developed by computer experts at RAND Corporation and Carnegie Institute of Technology rather than by computer producers, are or shortly will be available for different computers not even in the same family. It seems likely that the number of languages will decrease as the practice of designing both languages and computers for maximum compatibility becomes more widespread.

Automatic programming is a great time and error saver for the programmer, but it costs heavily in computer operation time. It may take a program five or ten times as long to run if it is written in an automatic programming language as it would take if it has been written in machine language. For this reason, many professional programmers proclaim proudly that they write in machine language, rather than any automatic programming language. Of course the speed advantage of writing in machine language may sometimes be an illusion. Programmer time is at present cheap compared with machine time, but debugging on the machine often costs just as much per minute as production runs would, so a machine-language program with many bugs may be more expensive than a much shorter, easier program which produces the same result but has been written in a highly automatic language. Some programs now in use—for example, some of the chess-playing programs—run to 10,000 instructions or so in a very highly automatic language. Each instruction in a highly automatic language may correspond to twenty or more instructions in machine language. Some of these extra instructions are housekeeping instructions required by the language, and so would be unnecessary if the program were written in machine language, but even so the program might become ten times as long if written in machine language as it is in the automatic language. It seems unreasonable to set out to write a 100,000-instruction program simply to save machine time. On the other hand, some large programs must be written in machine language to reduce their demands on the machine's storage capacity, or to save computation time if the program is to be used over and over again. Many of the programs used in military systems have this character.

One relatively recent development in automatic programming is the invention of *list languages* like IPL-V. Such languages use a storage structure which resembles a stack of plates in a cafeteria; only the top plate (bucket) is immediately accessible, and as soon as it is removed, the next plate pops up into its place. Such a stacked memory structure, of course, is ideal for storing serial lists. The essence of a list language is that its memory can contain arbitrarily many lists, a list being a variable sequence of items, each of which may be itself the name of another list (or of the same list). Each list can easily be changed by free application of operations such as *insert* and *delete*. It is particularly easy to define recursive processes in terms of list structures. The Information Processing Languages developed by Newell, Shaw, and Simon, of which IPL-V is one, are not really designed for mathematical applications; instead, their primary purpose is to perform logical manipulations.

Writing the Program

The working tools of a programmer are a language and a flow chart. Languages have already been discussed. The flow chart is, as its name suggests, a diagram of the logical design of a program. It looks very much like a block diagram of an electronic device. Once a good block diagram of the logic of a program has been prepared, the actual coding of the program is a fairly routine matter, provided that the problem is neither unusually large nor unusually complicated and that the block diagram is not too abstract. This description of programming is somewhat idealized, perhaps. Few, if any, programmers customarily prepare flow charts before coding; more often the flow chart is reconstructed from the code, if it is ever prepared at all.

Debugging is at first a hand operation; for example, flow charts are debugged before coding commences simply by tracing information through them. Later, hand simulation, which means working through the instructions of a program by hand for some simple sample problem, is used to debug the actual program. Eventually, the program must be put on the machine; if it still has bugs, they usually show up at this point. Bugs which stop the program completely are much more common and much easier to find than bugs which permit the program to continue running but cause it to produce incorrect results. And even those bugs which lead to incorrect results rather than halts usually produce such ridiculous-looking errors that they can be spotted at once; the bug which produces a subtle error is fortunately rare. This is a nice instance of complementarity between men and computers; the computer is accurate in detail but has little capability for detecting ridiculousness, while the man can often tell whether an answer is "in the right ball park" but usually cannot tell whether or not it is right in detail.

One fundamental fact about computer programming outweighs all others: the computer does what it is told. Unfortunately, present-day computers never do what any fool could tell the programmer wanted; they do what they are told to do instead, often with disastrous results. This *idiot savant* characteristic of even the most highly developed automatic languages is what makes them hard to use and computer programming hard to perform. The problem is that computers do not learn anything from experience, except in the rather peculiar sense that they develop libraries of available languages and subroutines. Human beings do not approach each new problem afresh; their most heavily used intellectual tool is their ability to apply wisdom gained from past experience to the present problem. It is the application of this wisdom which permits a man to do what another person obviously meant instead of what he said. This restrictive characteristic of computers is evidence that they are still in infancy; fortunately, it is not a permanent flaw. Programs capable of learning from experience exist, and the computers and languages of the future will certainly embody this ability in their interactions with human beings.

▣ THE FUTURE OF COMPUTERS AND COMPUTATION

Micro Computers

At present, the high-speed memory of all large computers consists of what is called magnetic cores; there are about 1,180,000 of them in an IBM 709. These magnetic cores are connected to other cores and to other elements of the machine by means of wires. They are far superior to other kinds of storage, such as magnetic tape, magnetic drum, electrostatic tube, delay line, or relay, in speed of access, accuracy, or both. But at $1 apiece they are expensive; they are of substantial size, in the sense that they can be seen by the naked eye; and they are strung on wires. Major steps in the further development of computation await the overcoming of these difficulties.

The next step, almost here now, is the transition to cryogenic computers. These computers operate at temperatures very near zero degrees Kelvin, in order to take advantage of a phenomenon called superconductivity. When metals are cooled to within a degree or so of absolute zero, they lose all electrical resistance; a pulse of current induced in a loop of superconductive wire will continue to circle within the wire more or less indefinitely. Tiny etched loops, kept very cold, will be used as high-speed memory elements. They are exceptionally cheap to produce, can be read somewhat more rapidly than magnetic cores, and permit a kind of multiple access not easily achieved with cores. They are also smaller and more reliable than cores.

Beyond the cryogenic computers, experts in the new field of microelectronics promise that soon it will be possible to etch a sort of laminar structure which has on a very minute scale the regular design required for basic units of a computer. So powerful is this technique that an expert speculates that in ten years or less it will be possible to obtain cubes one inch on a side, each of which will contain 100,000,000,000 (or 10^{11}) distinct units, each roughly comparable to a single magnetic core and capable of being separately used as a core is separately used (Shoulders, 1960). The speed of light will still provide a kind of limit on the rate at which such a unit can be used; but its small size severely reduces the significance of that restriction, and highly parallel computer organization (Holland, 1959, 1960) will reduce it still further. A much more serious problem is that of getting information into and out of the elements in that one-inch cube. It is already true that the processes of putting information into and out of any large computer are so hopelessly slow that they are seldom done directly. Instead, the punched cards are passed through a machine which transfers their information to magnetic tape, the tape is then read into the machine, the output of the machine goes into tape, and then a separate off-line machine translates that tape into a print-out. Even now this procedure is clumsy and only just acceptable; it will be entirely too slow for full exploitation of a micro computer based on units like the one-inch cube discussed above. This area looks like the next serious bottleneck in computer technology.

Fortunately, a computer with 10^{11} or more memory units, other internal equipment in proportion, and an operation rate near the speed of light need not be used at all efficiently. This means that the computer can be used to generate as much as possible of its own input, and to reduce the output to a quantity small enough to be printed. Since the information-handling capabilities of men are more or less fixed, it will be up to the computer—or, more precisely, to those who plan its use—to adjust its input and output requirements downward until it can be in communication with those who wish to use it. Obviously, this will leave room for very highly interpretive languages, approaching English in their convenience and flexibility (see Newell, 1960). Furthermore, these micro computers will be able to devote large parts of their storage to becoming generally sophisticated about computation, so that they will be able to report back with such statements as "That is not the most efficient way to attack your problem" and to respond appropriately to such instructions as "Oh, hell, you know what I mean."

Monsters and Aides

How will this fantastic capacity and speed be used? It is already clear that computer design is moving in two quite different directions: large central computers and small technical aides. A current specimen of each type is shown in Figure 3.1. The distinction between these two directions may become more important as computers get bigger and faster. The growth of computers in size and complexity will not be retarded particularly by the development of micro machines. If the central data-processing unit is a one-inch cube, it will

Figure 3.1.   A large and a small digital computer. The large computer
is an IBM 709; the small one is an LGP–30. (By permission of the International Business Machines Corporation; and the Royal McBee Corporation.)

nevertheless be true that the auxiliary equipment, particularly for input,
output, and long-term storage, will be very extensive and expensive. As has
already been mentioned, the larger the machine the larger is the minimal
problem appropriate for it. Furthermore, the larger the machine, the more

work it must have in order to keep busy, and the less time it takes on any single problem. Consequently, really large computers will never be common; there will be a few of them, in central locations, with lines tying them to a ring of peripheral points for problem origination and solution delivery. The computer will have elaborate monitoring and interrupt procedures, so that all customers get equal treatment and the machine never waits, doing nothing, for some one to make up his mind. Such arrangements, of course, are most appropriate for very large continuing data-processing operations; inventory control is one obvious example, the census another.

But large central computers have one serious flaw: it is difficult, though not impossible, to use them in real time. ("In real time" is computer slang which means that the computer is made a part of a larger machine, performing some tasks whenever they are called for in the course of the larger machine's operation.) Less important but perhaps more annoying, the really large machines cost so much per hour that one cannot afford to interact with them in a groping, tentative way, and so cannot have a dialogue with the computer or ask it to help in formulating a problem. This sort of need is better met by a much smaller machine, which sits in the office or laboratory of the man who uses it, available whenever needed. At present such smaller machines have smaller, slower memories and less auxiliary equipment than larger machines. Whether this will or will not be the case in future depends on the cost of micro computing units; it is conceivable that smaller machines may be developed which differ from large ones only in having less auxiliary equipment.

An exciting concept which combines the best of both kinds of computers is the concept of the large central computer connected to many satellite computers. The satellite computers can perform the functions which small computers now perform but can also use the services of the large computer when necessary. The realization of such a system requires the development of housekeeping or executive programs for the large computer orders of magnitude more sophisticated than anything now in use and opens new vistas of difficulty in programming and programming languages. Invention of a programming language which is easy and natural for human use, well within the limited capabilities of a satellite computer, and nevertheless efficient or capable of being translated efficiently when the large computer is being used is a staggering task.

One way in which the capabilities of future computers may be exploited is by using them as technical assistants. Newell (1960, pp. 267–268) says:

> It is difficult to differentiate [a machine that is an intelligent processor of information] from an extremely compliant, fairly bright human technical assistant, backed up by an impressive computing establishment. The user will converse with such a machine about his problem with the freedom of ordinary technical discourse. . . . The machine will return answers with a rather breath-taking rapidity. . . . All our lives are spent learning to live with other intelligences, and relating to an intelligent machine will seem more familiar than strange. Since we want machines to help us solve

problems, the more intelligent we are able to make it, the more unobtrusive it should be in providing this help. . . . I do not consider the vision radical. Indeed, the programming and computing world is already on its way to achieving it.[1]

It is reasonable to assume that languages and input-output equipment appropriate to this sort of application will be developed. It has been suggested, for example, that the human could write his question in longhand on the surface of a desk, and the computer could write its answer below the question. Such an arrangement substitutes the very difficult handwriting-recognition problem for the perhaps still more difficult speech-recognition problem.

Whatever the specific configurations adopted, the following predictions concerning the world ten years from now seem as safe as any:

1. Computers will be far, far cheaper for a given capacity, but their manufacturers will increase capacity rather than cutting prices.

2. Computers will exploit micro techniques by using parallel rather than series processes; this means that only capacity and nature of the problem put upper limits on the speed with which any particular problem can be solved.

3. The trend, already highly visible, toward using computers for symbolic and logical rather than numerical operations will increase, and the development of programming languages will reflect the fact.

4. Very flexible, very easy-to-use programming languages will develop. Such languages will have a high degree of ability to resolve ambiguities and to exploit vague and uncertain information and instructions.

5. The meaning of the word "think" will become more and more restricted, because our society will continue to define it to mean that which computers cannot do but men can, and the list of such capabilities will steadily shrink.

▣ MEN VERSUS COMPUTERS

The system designer faces a choice between men and computers at many places in his system. To help him make that choice, many different kinds of information are relevant. This chapter will ignore information concerning the economic and social problem of technological unemployment and the relative production costs of men and machines, all of which are of major importance in any real decision of this sort. Instead, it will simply consider the strengths and weaknesses of men and computers in the face of tasks which either might be asked to perform.

Tasks in which Computers Excel Men

It has already been pointed out that the fundamental virtues of computers are speed and accuracy. The performance of many individually easy

[1] Quoted by permission of the National Joint Computer Committee.

information-handling tasks, time after time and without error, is not at all easy for men; it is what computers do best. Consequently, any high-volume information-processing task in which the rules for processing are simple and easy is just right for machine performance. And tasks which are not of this nature can often be made so by appropriate redefinition.

One very important kind of task which is not naturally of this high-volume easy-rule nature but which can easily be made so is the task of *search*. Suppose a man has forgotten the combination to his safe. He will scurry to his files to see if it is written down, and then rack his memory to see if he can recall or reconstruct it. But not so a computer. The computer will simply try all possible combinations (which might take a couple of seconds to compute) until the right one is found, and then stop. This sort of try-them-one-by-one-until-one-fits strategy is the computer's solution to many intellectual problems. For example, in order to generate a move, a chess-playing program goes through a series of searches. First, it generates a permissible move. Then it examines many plausible sequences of moves which might follow the move under consideration, for a sequence length determined by the capacity of the machine. It evaluates the position reached at the end of the sequence, according to some criterion. It thus finds the best, or perhaps only a good, continuation of the original move being evaluated. Having done all this for one move, it goes on to other possibilities, and eventually selects the best move, or perhaps only a good one. If only computers had enough capacity, they could carry the consequences of each possible move on to checkmate and thus could produce the perfect chess strategy; the amount of capacity required for this is far beyond the ambitions of even the micro computer designers.

The search process, important though it is for any logical operations the computer might wish to perform, contains a serious flaw: most search problems lead to unreasonably large sets of things to search. Even a safe can be made computer-proof by adding a few additional numbers to the combination. The key to getting around this is what has come to be called *heuristic programming*. A heuristic is a rule of thumb which greatly reduces the set of things to be searched, and so reduces search time. The cost of heuristic searches is that if a stopping place is specified, the search may not be exhaustive, and so may be unsuccessful. A way around this is to make the search exhaustive but use the heuristic principles to determine the order in which the possibilities are to be searched. (For more on heuristic programming, see Minsky, 1956; Newell, Shaw, and Simon, 1957, 1958b.)

Another task in which computers excel men is *long-term storage*. They remember immense amounts of information, and can reproduce it extremely accurately. It is seldom desirable for a man to commit something to memory if he can conveniently use a machine—perhaps as simple a one as paper and pencil—to remember for him. However, machine storage has a serious disadvantage, which will be later described.

The other ways in which computers excel men as technical assistants mostly reflect human imperfections from which computers are free. Among them are: emotional attack on problems, slow speed of learning and necessity for repetition, egotism and unwillingness to be treated as a slave, laziness, and dishonesty. Note that illness is not listed; computers are often exasperatingly "sick"—which means that they do not give the right answer, for no easily discernible reason.

Finally, man-machine systems exist for human purposes, not the other way around. No matter how skillfully a machine can achieve an end, that end is a human end, not a machine end. This characteristic of computers is in principle unnecessary, but in practice it seems unlikely that men will make any serious attempt to liberate this powerful race of willing slaves.

Tasks in which Men Excel Computers

Many computer experts agree that the most important respect in which men excel computers is in the accessibility of the items in storage. Men can get at a single memory in many different ways; in particular, they can recover memories on the basis of similarity alone. Computers, by contrast, have no such efficient cross-indexing. If they did, it would be possible to write programs which rely on the computer to locate and produce any item in memory without specific instruction concerning where that item is. At present, no such procedure is possible. Cryogenic computers will have capabilities of this sort which excel those of current computers, but they will still be much inferior to the capabilities of men.

Psychologists and computer experts would also list pattern recognition, particularly visual pattern recognition, as an important capability in which men far excel computers. A great deal of research on how to make machines recognize patterns is in progress. The fundamental difficulties result from the fact that men recognize patterns in spite of transpositions, rotations, translations, and many other varieties of systematic and random distortion. Machines cannot do nearly so well: it is a great achievement that Selfridge (1955, 1956, 1959) has been able to train machines to recognize Morse code sent by human operators. Note the use of the word "train." The assumption underlying almost all attacks on the pattern recognition problem is that the complex structure of equivalence classes of stimuli necessary for pattern recognition must be learned, rather than built into the machine. There are even some comparatively unsuccessful attempts to train machines by means of reward and punishment, in the absence of any specified structuring of the machine (Friedberg, 1958). At any rate, the problem of pattern recognition is very far indeed from being solved, in spite of the strident newspaper stories concerning various pattern recognition programs which appear from time to time. Until it is solved, computers will be unable to interpret complex visual displays such as aerial photographs, will be unable to recognize spoken words, will have difficulty recognizing longhand, and in general will be markedly inferior to men in a crucially important technological skill. But this deficiency may well not exist 15 years from now, in view of the rapid rate of progress now being made in research on mechanical pattern recognition.

A major virtue of men is that they have a high tolerance for ambiguity, vagueness, and uncertainty. Men are able to detect what other men mean through the smog of what they say, and they customarily do so and behave accordingly. Such tolerance for ambiguity is based on a life-long history of experience with ambiguity and on the ability to argue by analogy from one's own purposes to those of other people. Neither of these characteristics seem likely to be available for computers in any near future. So long as computers cannot tolerate and exploit ambiguity, they cannot be given major executive responsibilities unsupervised; social control is usually based on vague mandates which permit wide but not unlimited latitude in interpretation (for example, platforms of political parties). This means that man-machine systems will necessarily continue to have men with veto power over computer-generated decisions, rather than vice versa.

One reason why men are good at tolerating and exploiting ambiguity is that they can effectively translate uncertainty into probability—another task in which men far excel computers. Consider the statement, "Before you go to bed tonight, you will consume a bottle of beer." Presumably that statement is neither impossible nor certain. A computer could probably go no farther; a man can attach a number to the statement which represents his evaluation of its probability of being correct. Such numbers are, it turns out, excellent guides to action; men can accurately translate uncertainty into probability. Computers, on the other hand, are far superior to men in taking probabilities and payoffs and computing from them the best course of action. These considerations suggest that a military-information processing system which must cope with relatively unreliable data (such as a sonar system) might profitably use human operators as transducers for probabilities. These probabilities could be entered into a computer, which would then compute the optimal course of action in the light of them. No such system now exists, but it seems entirely possible that there might be one ten years from now.

The preceding virtues of men in competition with computers, though important, are rather remote from current system applications. The next three to be mentioned are crucial for most current man-versus-computer problems in man-machine systems.

The first of these is that in a very important sense men are far more reliable than computers. It has already been pointed out that computers make far fewer mistakes than men. But in general the mistakes computers make either remain unchecked or stop the computer completely. Man, on the other hand, can detect his own mistakes and spontaneously work out a plan to correct them or remedy their effects. Furthermore, once he has learned how to perform a task correctly, man does not repeat and repeat the same error, as will a computer with a broken part. In short, if a little allowance is made for the approximate nature of human reliability, man is far more reliable than any computer yet invented, or any likely to be invented in the near future. Of course, some computers are to a degree self-correcting even now, and most large future computers will embody various kinds of self-correction features. But the versatility of human beings in dealing with error is an extremely remote goal indeed for computer technology. This human reliability characteristic is so important that major systems are likely to continue to include human components for a long time to come for this reason alone.

Perhaps the most practical advantages of men over computers, of course, are in cost and availability. Consider a system which has an expected life of ten years. Over that period, it might cost $120,000 in salary to employ one man to tend the system. The system for personnel support and other indirect personnel costs might over that time cost another $120,000. That puts the cost of one human brain, for many purposes the most effective computer now available, at something like $240,000 over a ten-year period. By contrast, an IBM 709, for many purposes much inferior to the man, costs something like $1,000,000 *per year,* or more than 40 times as much as the man over the ten-year period. Even if the system were to operate 168 hours per week, which requires at least five men for each operator position, the computer would be much more than 10 times as expensive (since the cost of supporting it would go up with round-the-clock usage). Of course, the 709 can do many things that men cannot do, and vice versa; which is preferable depends on the specific nature of the job to be performed. But the man has a powerful built-in economic advantage, which is not likely to change very much with time.

Availability is important also. There are many men, and at least a third of them can be trained to perform difficult intellectual tasks. There are few computers, and the number of really large ones is unlikely to become as large as, say, one millionth of the number of men. So men not only are cheaper, they are also easier to obtain.

▣ OPERATOR JOBS IN A MAN-COMPUTER SYSTEM

How can a system be designed to exploit the special abilities of men and of computers? The art of designing man-machine systems which include computers is too new to have very many well-understood and generally accepted principles. Nevertheless, most military information processing systems which include computers have a family resemblance to one another. Some unsystematized wisdom has evidently accumulated about how to design such systems.

Communication of that unsystematized wisdom is difficult, because parts of the detailed designs of every military information processing system are classified. Release for publication even of descriptions of such systems which contain no classified information is difficult or impossible to get. In an attempt to get around these difficulties, the following paragraphs contain a somewhat detailed description of an imaginary military system. The system setting, naval hunter-killer operations, is real, and the ideas presented are, in fact, drawn from experience with a number of real military (but not naval) information processing systems. All the technical ideas presented have previously been included in nonclassified technical publications; only their integration into a system context is original here. This means, of course, that no classified information is presented. Of course naval hunter-killer groups do exist and must be controlled somehow. But the system for controlling them described below deliberately violates some Navy policies concerning allocation of command functions, and so would be unacceptable to the Navy.

The HUK-Master System

The following paragraphs describe the HUK-Master System, an imaginary Navy system assumed to have been designed in 1952–1954, to have passed tests of a prototype in 1958, and to be becoming operationally available in 1960–1961. (HUK is Navy slang for hunter-killer. A hunter-killer operation is one in which a number of ships, planes, and possibly submarines collaborate to detect and destroy enemy submarines patrolling coasts or shipping lanes which are to be protected.)

Since the system is carried on board a ship, it must be relatively small. For this reason it uses a number of relatively small analogue computers rather than one large digital computer, and many operations which in larger systems might be automated are in this one performed by men on line. The following description is confined to operator positions; of course large numbers of maintenance and support personnel are required in connection with any large system.

The HUK-Master System receives information from long-range sonar devices located on land, on its ships, and on sonar buoys—as well as information about courses and speeds of friendly ships and submarines and intelligence information about enemy activities and plans. This sonar information in general reports the location, course, and speed of objects which might be enemy submarines—or might be friendly ships or submarines, or whales, or schools of fish, or layers of shrimp. It attempts to identify these returns, and tracks those which are not identified as friendly. It sends planes or ships to investigate possible enemy submarines, providing information which is designed to enable the investigating ship or plane to find the proper area and then to acquire the unknown object on its own sonar or other sensors. It keeps track of attacks by its controlled ships and planes, their success or failure, and initiates further action with respect to enemy submarines if necessary.

The heart of HUK-Master is its central station, located in a few compartments on the largest ship (a small aircraft carrier) in the HUK Group. The main room is a large one, designed somewhat like an amphitheater, with a large manually operated display where the stage would be, a set of auxiliary status boards, and a number of operator positions, each one having a computer-controlled cathode ray tube display and a complex console. The illumination of this room is blue, because the dim orange dots on the operators' cathode ray tube displays are best seen if the over-all illumination is dim and blue. The large stage display is made of edge-lighted transparent plastic; marks made on it with grease pencil show up in vivid color in the edge lighting.

The first important operator position within this room is that of the entry operator. He first instructs the computer to initiate a track on an unidentified moving object which appears in a long-range sonar return. Next he tries to identify the object. The first question is: is it on the surface or submerged? Comparison of the sonar return with a radar return or the results of a visual search covering the same area usually makes the answer to this question easy; submerged objects do not generate radar returns and cannot be seen by the naked eye. The next task is to examine the scheduled movements of ships and of friendly submarines in an effort to identify the object specifically. If the object can with fair confidence be identified as a man-made moving object but cannot be identified as friendly, the entry operator next transfers the track to one of several tracking operators. He may monitor the performance of any tracker, and sometimes moves tracks from one operator to another in order not to overload one operator. He also obtains information about the pattern of temperature layers in the water at the location of the tracked object from an operator who has custody of this information; this information permits some inferences to be made (by the computer) about the depth of the object being tracked. Finally, the entry operator keeps track of what happens as a result of any attack initiated by the system against the object, and he can, if necessary, propose further action to the tactical officer. All these operations go through the computer; the system has phones which permit one operator to talk with another, but they are not the intended primary channels of communication. The entry operator can look at either live sonar returns or computer-generated symbols or both, at his choice.

The next operator in the sequence is the tracker, who simply monitors and corrects the computer's track of several moving objects. The computer has a linear extrapolation routine, which assumes that a moving object will continue to move in the same direction and at the same speed as before. If the next sonar return does not indicate an object in the expected location, the computer has a search routine which searches a circle around the predicted position, finds the object if one is there, and modifies the extrapolation routine accordingly. Unfortunately, this procedure fails all too often; frequent causes of failure are losses of contact caused by temperature layers in the water and intersecting tracks which may confuse the computer about which object is which. The tracker intervenes whenever the computer is having trouble maintaining the track, and uses his much more flexible extrapolation abilities to help the computer out. He has the same display options as the entry operator.

The next operator job, perhaps the most difficult in the system, is that of the tactical officer. He must decide which ship or plane should investigate or attack which object (a decision often suggested by the computer in larger land-based systems) and inform the computer of the decision. Of course he must first present his decision as a proposal to the task force commander, and that commander must approve it, but such approval will in general be routinely given. (Only the fact that ships and submarines move relatively slowly permits this time-consuming on-line monitoring operation. In systems designed to control aircraft or missiles which are attacking other aircraft or missiles such an arrangement would not be possible.) Once the decision has been made, the tactical officer informs the computer about it. The computer informs the ship, if a ship is to investigate or attack, or informs the aircraft control center, if a plane is to investigate or attack. The ship or aircraft control center is provided with a display of estimated location of the object, based on its HUK-Master track. The ship's captain or the aircraft controller can use this information to vector the ship or plane to the right place and to enable the ship or plane to pick up the object on its own sonar, or magnetic detection gear, or other sensor. When the attacking unit sees the object on its own sensors, this information is passed on to the HUK-Master computer, which in turn informs the tactical officer. If the ship or plane has difficulty in locating the unidentified object, its officers can talk directly by radio-telephone with the HUK-Master tactical officer. The tactical officer has no access to live sonar displays; he sees only computer-generated symbols. The same is true of the commander of HUK-Master.

Finally, there is of course a commander of the HUK-Master System; he has a small command post of his own, which overlooks the main room in the central station. He has no specific responsibilities during operations other than that of general supervision of the system. In this system as in many others, the commander has elaborate displays to look at, but his command post is separate from the place where the work is being done and his only means of generating an output is a telephone. As military-information processing systems become more complex, commanders have fewer and fewer occasions to intervene in the actual operation of the system. After all, the reason why any such system exists in the first place is because the information relevant to decisions is too complex and too abundant to be satisfactorily processed in the heads of a few men. For the commander to intervene effectively, he must perform with little help the task for which the system was designed, and must perform it more satisfactorily than the system is capable of performing it at the moment. Only if the system is very seriously malfunctioning is he likely to be able to do so. In effect, in the more complex modern weapons systems much of the command function has been delegated to complex man-machine systems, and in particular to the computers within those systems, because the tasks inherent in the command function in these systems are beyond unaided human capability. Of course this process has gone much farther in systems which must deal with fast-moving objects such as aircraft or missiles than it has in slower systems dealing with ships and submarines, or with columns of trucks or tanks. It is very unlikely that antimissile missile systems, for example, will make any substantial use of men on line; such systems must act so rapidly that human delays will not be tolerable. So the major functions of commanders in most future systems will come increasingly to consist of bearing ultimate responsibility for system performance, managing the people who operate the system, and managing the personnel support system behind them.

Design Principles for Systems which Include Computers

Computers and men perform little-understood functions in competition with each other, and the system designer must, for each function included in his system, resolve the competition in favor of one or the other. Unfortunately, the necessary scoring system is hard to find; these functions in human beings are not well understood, and in computers the score is constantly changing as technology advances. Still, some principles appear to be relatively valid and stable guides to good design practice.

The first question the designers of a new system must face is whether or not the system should include a computer. The sheer economic considerations already discussed are important but not conclusive; social costs, such as technological unemployment and the cost of training system operators and technicians, must also be considered. Once the decision to put a computer into the system has been made, several general principles concerning the design of computerized systems can be used to guide design. Some of these principles are illustrated by HUK-Master; some are not.

1. Allocation of functions among men and computer should consider the best skills of each. It is seldom wise to allocate to the computer everything the designer knows how to mechanize, and to parcel out among the system operators whatever is left over.

2. If possible, the computer should be about 80 per cent used; if it has too much unused time or capacity, either a smaller computer should be used instead or tasks for which it is less than ideally suited (such as long-term memory) should be given to it. Computers do not profit from rest periods, other than the necessary halts for maintenance and repair; men do. On the other hand, tasks change, and a little flexibility is therefore desirable.

3. Provision of one sort or another must be made for system function during computer malfunction. This often implies either a second computer or a manual back-up system. In some cases, of course, no meaningful provision is possible or worthwhile.

4. Operator jobs should not be homogeneous in difficulty. Some jobs should require a relatively high level of ability and training; others should not. This reduces the requirement for high-IQ operators and provides for a career structure within the system.

5. Man-to-man communications should be relatively rare. In general, human outputs should go into the computer. The process of man-to-man communication is so often clumsy and imprecise that the system is usually better off if any two functions performed by different men are separated by a function performed by the computer. This principle is controversial; some experts insist that a great deal of informal man-to-man communication is both necessary and desirable.

6. Men should function as aids to the computer in sensing, extrapolating, and decision making. The entry operator in HUK-Master senses which spots of light on a sonar return are really ships, decides which of the ships should be tracked, and so informs the computer. The tracker helps the computer when its mechanism for extrapolating is inadequate for the job. In each of these functions, the computer can be given the primary responsibility so long as a man is ready to back it up when it fails (though this is not done in HUK-Master for the sensing and decision-making functions). The idea of using men as back-up systems for computer functions is very widely applied; most manned space vehicle designs are designed that way. There is some question whether in many applications it might not be cheaper and just as effective to have the man perform the function in the first place.

7. If at all possible, the computer rather than a man should have primary responsibility for maintaining vigilance and detecting when, after a period of inactivity, some system action is required.

8. A number of specific tasks which must be performed in most information processing systems are usually allotted to men because they use man's best skills. The functions of detection, identification, and tracking have already been discussed; they exploit human pattern-recognition ability and ability to cope with uncertainty. Another common function is goal-setting for searches. Computers very often solve problems by means of directed search through a very large set of possible solutions. Searches should usually be guided by hypotheses concerning the most fruitful places to search first—that is, by using heuristic principles; it is arbitrary whether searching continues until a solution is found or whether it stops after the most likely possibilities have been searched. A computer program can induce these heuristic principles from experience with the problems, but more often in practical applications men will supply computers with heuristic principles to guide search. Little use of this sort of technique has so far been made in military-information processing systems, but they will obviously be very important, for example, in the design of systems for processing the immense volumes of information which will be generated by reconnaissance satellites.

9. Yet another important human function in computerized systems is censorship. Men monitor the output of computers, with responsibility to veto computer actions when it seems appropriate to do so. Unfortunately, as systems get more complicated and their tasks become more demanding, it will be more and more difficult for men to censor system output effectively.

They cannot assimilate enough information to be sure whether the system is right or wrong, except in the case of gross malfunction. More important, systems can seldom tolerate the response of doing nothing, and men often cannot accumulate the information or the time to supply alternatives to the computer's recommended course of action. So the veto function will become more and more symbolic, and the commander's telephone line will play a less and less important role in the system's functioning.

10. It will continue to be true that systems which include computers exist to serve human purposes, so system goal-setting will continue to be a human function, the most important human function in the system. However, that function will be performed mostly by the designers of the system and those who write the computer program; the nature of system design pretty completely determines the goals which it can effectively further.

The most serious problem which can arise as a result of using men as on-line components in a system which also includes a computer is caused by the severe mismatch in rate of performance between men and computers. Computers ordinarily perform their operations very fast indeed, while human beings are ridiculously slow by comparison. To make a computer wait while a man performs some function on line is extremely wasteful of computer time. It is worth doing only if the function cannot be satisfactorily performed in any other way. The assumption which underlies the preceding discussion is that cases in which that penalty is worth incurring are fairly frequent. Some psychologists and computer experts disagree, arguing instead that men should perform only off-line functions such as goal-setting, monitoring, and censorship. Some systems must function so quickly that human bottlenecks cannot be tolerated; it seems probable that antimissile missile systems would fall into this category. But for most slower systems, and in particular for most civilian systems, the advantages of exploiting human skills far outweigh the disadvantages of putting up with slow human reactions.

The Man-Computer Interface

Any man-machine system must provide displays and controls for its operators. In a system which includes a computer, such interfaces between man and hardware must be very carefully designed. Unfortunately, there is a serious mismatch between what is best for man and what is easiest for the computer to use or generate; much design effort must be devoted to minimizing the consequences of this mismatch.

Computer-controlled displays are usually presented on the face of a cathode ray tube (CRT). Special equipment permits combination of blips or spots, outline maps, and alphanumeric information on the same tube face. Such displays nicely fit some characteristics of computers. They are electronically generated and therefore easy for the computer to control directly. They can change as rapidly as the computer changes the information to be displayed. And they are well adapted to what psychologists call *contingent programming*. "Contingent programming" is a phrase denoting the simple idea that the operator can control what information his display presents to him. It is well established that operators can use such capability to reduce the amount of irrelevant information presented to them. Unfortunately, experience indicates that operators often prefer to look at more information than they need, and that the excess information actually hinders them. Thus many systems, including HUK-Master, restrict the classes of information at which any one operator can look.

CRTs with many different kinds of phosphors are available. This means that many different colors, brightnesses, and persistences are available to the designer. The question of persistence is important. A short-persistence phosphor rapidly fades when the beam of electrons which excites it is turned elsewhere; this means that the same information must be put onto the tube many times. On the other hand, a long-persistence phosphor, though it preserves information longer after each application, cannot change nearly so fast when the operator wishes to look at something different. Systems which include an auxiliary storage device, often a magnetic drum which receives from the computer the information which is to be displayed on the tube, can alleviate but not cure these difficulties.

No military system now available uses multicolor CRT displays. Color coding is less important than one might suppose; only somewhere between four and eight absolutely identifiable distinct colors are possible, and the same sort of coding can often be achieved by contingent programming. Nevertheless, it seems likely that the development of color TV technology may have as a by-product the development of color CRT displays for military systems.

No tube-generated display can include as much detail as, for example, a photograph. Thus photographs, as well as drawings such as maps, are likely candidates for inclusion in systems where rapidly changing information which does not demand high resolution is blended with relatively static high-resolution information. One way of doing this is to project a color slide onto the front of a CRT, simultaneously producing blips or other similar displays from the rear. Such displays, having the potentiality of combining the best aspects of two systems, are now coming into use. Elaborate systems for handling slides mechanically under computer control are now under development for just such applications.

One interesting possibility available in some computer-controlled displays is *time compression*. If information changes only every five or ten minutes, it may be helpful to the operator to be able to review the history of a situation rapidly, perhaps looking at each display generated during the past four hours for a second or two. If even faster time compression is used, apparent movement like that obtained in movies or TV may occur; this may help to distinguish signals from clutter. Recent research suggests that for many purposes a multiple-exposure photograph may be a better time compression device than a serial presentation of successive times; equipment such as the Polaroid Land Camera permits multiple-exposure photography without significant processing delay.

Computers can, of course, control other kinds of displays. The only important other one, however, is the print-out. This can effectively be used for system purposes. One interesting possibility is the direct printing of map-like information.

The fundamental nature of the display mismatch between man and computer is simply that man cannot deal with displays which change in time nearly as fast as computers can generate them. He can use detailed information at a given time more effectively than computers can usually display it. This is especially true in CRT displays, with their inherently poor resolution. Thus, much of the art of designing computer-controlled displays consists of reducing the time-variability of the display and, if possible, of trading space for time.

Continuous control systems, like those which might be used to control a high-speed submarine or a hovering helicopter, present problems which can be attacked by using computer-controlled displays. A submarine, for example, has great inertia in moving up or down; it is often hard to get this movement started and often even harder to stop it once the desired depth is reached. Such characteristics, which produce complex relationships between what is done to the operator's controls and what the system being controlled does in response, are called *control dynamics*. When the control dynamics of a system produce severe control problems, computer-controlled displays can often alleviate them. One class of displays useful for this sort of purpose is called the *quickened* display (see, for example, Taylor, 1957). Quickened displays are concerned with error signals for rapidly changing continuous-control tasks, such as controlling the hovering of a helicopter. They display a combination of error and the first derivative, and possibly higher derivatives, of the error signal. Thus they permit the operator to change his control setting when the rate at which error is accumulating starts to rise, before the total amount of error has changed seriously. A quickened display looks very jittery and changes very fast; one might suppose that it would be exceedingly hard to use, and it is true that operators do not particularly enjoy using it; but when used appropriately, it produces error scores orders of magnitude lower than those obtained with unquickened displays.

Another kind of processed display is called a *predictor display*. This display is concerned with systems which have very large control dynamics, so that any action of the control will continue to affect the behavior of the system for a long time after the action is terminated; maneuvering a ship or a submarine is an obvious example. In predictor displays, the computer uses a mathematical model of the system. It continuously calculates ahead and displays to the operator what the system will be doing at a series of future times (for example, 1, 2, 3, . . . 60 seconds ahead) if the control is immediately returned to a null state. Thus the operator can rapidly change his control setting to one which produces the desired state of the system a minute or so from now if the control is returned to a null state, and then do so. The advantages of predictor displays, in suitable situations, are even greater than those of quickened displays—and operators love them. Figure 3.2 is an example of such a display.

There is a much smaller degree of mismatch between man and computer when information is going from man to computer than when it is going from computer to man. The push button is an entirely satisfactory technique for communicating human decisions and instructions, provided that only a few items of information need be transmitted, and the stick is a very satisfactory device for inserting continuously varying information. One practical problem of some importance arises when an operator wishes to designate a particular object on a display when giving instructions to a computer. The old-fashioned way to do this was to use cross-hairs or some other movable marker attached to the computer. A more modern way of doing it is to use what is called a light gun—an object shaped very much like a pistol, which contains a photoelectric cell. When placed over a blip on a tube face, the photoelectric cell is excited by the pulse which renews the blip. The exact time when that blip was renewed is detected by the circuitry controlled by the light gun. Since only one blip is renewed at a single instant, the computer can thus figure out which object the operator had in mind. This is a clumsy device, only slightly less so than cross-hairs or an electronic cursor. New systems use smaller, less bulky, light pencils, but the task of putting the light pencil exactly on the blip is still a nuisance; it is to be hoped that a better solution will be found.

Of course, in controls, as in displays, there is great room for ingenuity in designing computer programs and auxiliary equipment to maximize human effectiveness by using computer capabilities to make human tasks easier. But the only important idea of this sort that is apparent at present is the idea of making one push-button initiate a sequence of events. Surely greater ingenuity ought to be possible in the future.

The Future of Man-Computer Competition

It should be clear by now that even the fantastic progress anticipated in computer technology will not permit a clear-cut victory in the man-computer competition. It will continue to be true that men and computers differ sufficiently from one another in skills so that large systems will use both. Men are not about to become obsolete. Therefore the future of the man-computer competition lies in symbiosis rather than in extermination. Systems must and will be designed to exploit harmoniously the best virtues of both. The technological basis which the system designer will have to use to promote this happy marriage is a clear understanding of the capabilities of both men and computers, and detailed knowledge of the mechanisms available for use at the interface between them.

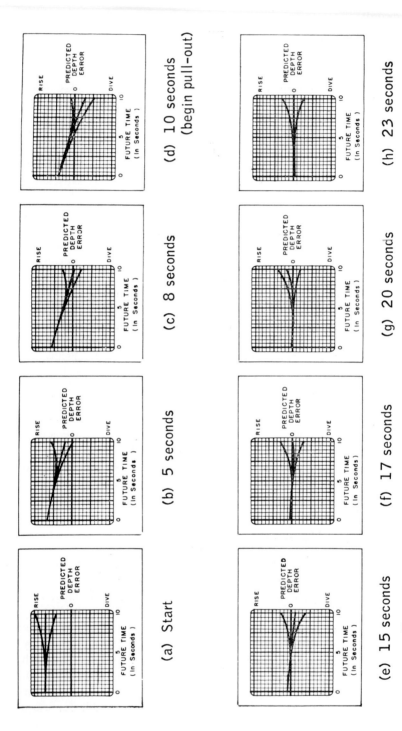

Figure 3.2. A sample three-trace predictor display for depth control in a submarine. The maneuver represented is a rapid dive. The inner trace represents the prediction if the stick is returned to center; the outer two traces represent the predictions if it is moved to either extreme. (From Kelley, 1960.)

▣ COMPUTERS AS MODELS OF MEN

Although it is not really crucial for system design, a chapter about men and computers would be incomplete without a discussion of the old, emotion-laden, unresolvable question: can machines think?

In an important sense, the question is meaningless. Contemporary lay definition of "thought," or, for more sophisticated laymen, "creative thought," usually is: what man can do but a machine cannot. By that definition, machines cannot think and never will be able to, no matter how able they become. Unfortunately, that definition is difficult to replace with a more meaningful one; psychologists have never been able to decide what thought is or how it can be recognized when a man or a machine does it. The whole question of what thought is and whether machines can do it has become so emotion-laden and so meaningless that computer experts who are engaged in enabling their machines to think have now widely chosen to circle around it by calling their field the creation of *artificial intelligence*. From this point of view, the problem that these workers are attempting to solve is the problem of designing machines which have particular valuable intellectual skills which intelligent animals (including men) also have, such as pattern recognition and problem-solving ability. It seems safe to say that any intellectual process recognizable in man or animal can now be simulated, though often very crudely, by a computer program. It is out of research on simulation of human intellectual processes that much of the progress in computer technology, particularly in programming, is coming; it is reasonable to hope that this research will be even more fruitful in the future.

Simulation of Neural Structures

Three main streams in research on artificial intelligence can be distinguished: simulation of neural structures, simulation of intellectual and behavioral processes, and applications for artificial intelligence. Of these, simulation of neural structure may possibly be the least promising, although it is the farthest advanced. Such programs usually take Hebb's (1949) conception of how the nervous system works or one very much like it, simulate that conception by creating within the computer a network of "elements" (subroutines) which behave like neurons, and then attempt to show that this network can exhibit at a very low level some intellectual functions, most often pattern recognition. Rosenblatt's Perceptron (1958a and b) is a program which does this with a substantial amount of structure initially applied by the program. Holland (1959) is attempting much the same with an initially quite unstructured nerve net; his main interest is the emergence of functional organization among the "neurons." No real attempt is made to simulate any very complicated process; no simulated nerve net has so far contained more than 10,000 neurons. It is unlikely that computer technology will in any reasonably near future be able to supply elements remotely as versatile and abundant as human neurons, so it is unlikely that we will even be able to evaluate this approach soon. Of course, the neurophysiologists find it very valuable thus to be able to simulate their more general ideas about how the nervous system works; this technique is therefore a very valuable research tool in neurophysiology, even if not in the study of artificial intelligence. (See McCulloch *et al.,* 1956; Milner, 1957; and Rochester *et al.,* 1956.)

Simulation of Intellectual and Behavioral Processes

Research which attempts to simulate intellectual and behavioral processes seems to be divided into two kinds, each based on a particular viewpoint about psychology. One kind starts from the radical behaviorist's view that the only kind of process which matters in behavior is the fixation of responses as a result of reinforcement. In artificial intelligence, this has taken the form of evolving programs by random processes. In effect, the computer is provided with an initial random set of instructions, combined with a feedback mechanism which evaluates the product of this random set and administers a reinforcement making successful instructions more likely to occur and unsuccessful ones less likely to occur (compare Friedberg, 1958). It has been demonstrated that such a machine can, in fact, develop a program which will achieve a desired effect, starting from a random initial set of instructions. Unfortunately, it took about 300,000 reinforcements to be successful. That remarkably large number can be reduced somewhat (perhaps to 100,000) by more efficient management of the basic idea, but there is no reason at the moment to suppose that it will manage either to simulate human learning or to be an effective means for developing programs. Unfortunately, reinforcement of a program contingent on its consequences cannot be very effective if the number of steps in the program is at all large, since the number of possible combinations of randomly selected instructions soon becomes astronomical.

A more reasonable line of research simulates specific intellectual functions without limiting itself in the matter of tools used in the simulation. One outstanding example is Selfridge's Pandemonium program; another is Newell, Shaw, and Simon's General Problem Solver. Pandemonium (Selfridge, 1955, 1956, 1959; see also Dineen, 1955) is a pattern-recognition program based on a kind of parallel processing. A large set of tests is applied to the pattern to be examined. Each of these tests reports its outcome to a "demon." Each demon represents a different weighting of the various basic tests. Each demon shouts to a decision maker, "Choose me," with a loudness proportional to the weighting of the tests for that demon and also proportional to the outcomes of the tests, and the decision maker chooses the demon who shouts loudest. If that decision was correct, that demon weights still more highly the tests which came out favorably and still less highly the tests which came out unfavorably on that occasion; if the decision was incorrect, it weights less highly the tests which came out favorably and more highly those which came out unfavorably. Thus in due course a demon whose tests are optimally weighted for the particular diagnostic category which he represents is evolved. A more elaborate version of this general idea would presumably use higher-order demons to weight differentially the outputs of the first-order demons, and so on. The program can also be designed to invent and evaluate new tests.

Newell, Shaw, and Simon's (1958b) General Problem Solver is simply a search program which uses some very general heuristic principles and which is capable of modifying its heuristic principles or developing new ones. It evolved out of an attempt to develop a program which would invent proofs for the theorems about logic found in Chapter 2 of Whitehead and Russell's *Principia Mathematica* (1925). It recognizes three fundamental entities: expressions, differences between expressions, and operators. The program attempts to apply permissible operators to expressions in such a way as to reduce to zero the difference between two expressions which might be called the original problem and the solution. Thus the program can be used to solve problems of the form "Given expression *a* and a set of admissible operators, derive expression *b*." It does this by means of goals, subgoals, and methods. There are three types of goals:

Transform Goal: Find a way to transform expression *a* into expression *b*.
Reduce Goal: Reduce the difference *d* between expressions *a* and *b*.
Apply Goal: Apply operator *q* to expression *a*.

One method is associated with each of these goals. The method associated with the transform goal consists in (1) matching the two expressions to find a difference *d* between them; (2) setting up the reduce subgoal of reducing *d*— if that goal is attained, a new transformed expression *a'* is obtained; and (3) setting up a transform goal of getting from *a'* to *b*. The method associated with the reduce goal consists in (1) finding an operator *q* relevant to the difference *d*; (2) determining if the conditions are met for applying *q* to *a*; and (3) if so, applying the operator; if not, setting up the transform subgoal of reducing the difference between *a* and the conditions necessary for applying *q*. These goals and methods are applied initially to developing a plan for solving the problem; the plan is obtained by substituting for the original problem a simplified problem from which some of the detail has been omitted. If the simplified problem can be solved, the steps in its solution can serve as clues to the solution of the original problem.

It is already clear that this sort of general problem-solving program can prove theorems in logic; other uses for it are likely to develop as refinement of it continues.

Game-Playing Programs. A particularly lively field in which computer problem-solving is being studied is the development of game-playing programs. It is, of course, elementary to write a computer program which will play a perfect game of tic-tac-toe. More complicated programs have been written for large computers which play excellent games of checkers (Samuel, 1959). But the interesting games are the more complicated ones, such as chess and go, for which optimal strategies are not known. A number of chess-playing programs have been developed (Bernstein, 1958; Kister *et al.,* 1957; Newell, 1955; Newell, Shaw, and Simon, 1958; Shannon, 1950); no chess program has, in fact, yet been able to beat even a rank human amateur. It seems likely that the general principles included in such programs could be used to write a really expert program if only large enough machines were available. But it is doubtful if a world's-champion program could be written, no matter how large the computer, with present-day understanding of the game; the heuristic principles necessary for championship play are too imperfectly understood. There appears to be no current attempt to write a go-playing program. This is unfortunate, since go is a more elegant game than chess, in the sense that its rules are far simpler and more general; the difficulty of this extraordinarily difficult game arises solely out of strategic and tactical issues that arise in the play, rather than out of idiosyncrasies of particular pieces. Thus a go program might be a better simulation of human problem solving than a chess program.

Applications for Artificial Intelligence

Three varieties of research on applications of computer technology make extensive contributions to knowledge about artificial intelligence. One is the development of convenient programming languages; enough has been said already about that (but see U. S. Dept. of Commerce, 1954). The second is research on information retrieval. The practical problem, of course, is that as the amount of information relevant to any particular scientific, governmental, or business topic increases as a result of research or any other information-gathering process, the problem of locating any particular item of information becomes ever more difficult. Obviously a computer could serve very effectively as the agent for such retrieval, if only a satisfactory cross-indexing and question-interpreting system could be found for it. The development of such a cross-indexing system requires solution of the problem of providing the computer with multiple-access long-term memory; the multiple-access feature is crucial. Much progress has been made, but the problem is at present far from solved (see McCarthy, 1958; Perry, Kent, and Berry, 1956). The third kind of application-oriented research on artificial intelligence is research on machine translation of foreign languages. The practical importance of this problem is obvious. The deficiencies in computed performance which must be remedied in order to make machine translation possible are pattern recognition, for the purpose of identifying phrases, as distinct from single words; multiple-access long-term memory, to perform vocabulary look-up operations for phrases rather than for single words; and problem solving, to make it possible to put together meaningful sentences. It is now possible to perform a very crude kind of machine translation; the translation can be cleaned up into a rather accurate translation by a man who need not know the language of the original. Steady progress in this area is to be expected. (See Brown, 1958; Locke and Boothe, 1955; Yngve, 1958.)

The March, 1961, issue of the IRE Transactions on Human Factors in Electronics (IRE-HFE-2, No. 1) is devoted to automation of human functions. It contains fascinating review articles about list languages, man-computer decision processes, speech recognition, and problem solving, among others. And it contains a complete bibliography of the literature on artificial intelligence, with a detailed topical index. It is therefore the indispensable tool for anyone who wishes to pursue further many of the topics in this chapter, especially those of the final section.

▣ CONCLUSION

> I think that I shall never see
> A calculator made like me.
> A me that likes Martinis dry
> And on the rocks, a little rye.
> A me that looks at girls and such,
> But mostly girls, and very much.
> A me that wears an overcoat
> And likes a risky anecdote.
> A me that taps a foot and grins
> Whenever Dixieland begins.
> They make computers for a fee,
> But only moms can make a me.[2]
>
>   Hilbert Schenck, Jr. (1960)

REFERENCES

Bernstein, A. 1958.   A chessplaying program for the IBM 704. *Proc. 1958 West. Joint Computer Conf.*, May.

Brown, A. F. R. 1958.   Language translation. *J. Assoc. for Computing Machinery, 5,* 1–8.

Clarke, W. A., and Farley, B. G. 1955.   Generalization of pattern recognition in a self-organizing system. *Proc. 1955 West. Joint Computer Conf.*, IRE, March.

Dineen, G. P. 1955.   Programming pattern recognition. *Proc. 1955 West. Joint Computer Conf.*, IRE, March.

Friedberg, R. M. 1958.   A learning machine, part I. *IBM J. Res. Develpm. 2,* 2–13. (*Cf.* also 1959, *3, 282–287.*)

Gelernter, H. 1959.   Realization of a geometry theorem proving machine. *Proc. International Conf. on Information Processing.*

Gelernter, H., and Rochester, N. 1958.   Intelligent behavior in problem solving machines. *IBM J. Res. Develpm., 2,* 336–345.

Gilmore, P. 1959.   A program for the production of proofs for theorems derivable within the first order predicate calculus from axioms. *Proc. International Conf. on Information Processing.*

Hebb, D. O. 1949.   *The organization of behavior.* New York: Wiley.

Holland, J. H. 1959.   A universal computer capable of executing an arbitrary number of sub-programs simultaneously. *Proc. East. Joint Computer Conf.,* 108–112.

Holland, J. H. 1960.   Iterative circuit computers. *Proc. West. Joint Computer Conf.,* 259–265.

Kelley, C. R. 1960.   *Developing and testing the effectiveness of the "predictor instrument."* Stamford, Conn.: Dunlap and Associates. Office of Naval Research, Technical Report 252–60–1.

Kister, J., Stein, P., Ulam, S., Walden, W., and Wells, M. 1957.   Experiments in chess. *J. Assoc. for Computing Machinery, 4,* 174–177.

Locke, W. N., and Boothe, A. D. (ed.). 1955.   *Machine translation of languages.* New York: Wiley.

McCarthy, J. 1958.   The advice taker. *Proc. Sympos. on the Mechanization of Thought Processes.* Teddington, England: National Physical Laboratory.

McCulloch, W. S., *et al.* 1956.   Symposium on the design of machines to simulate the behavior of the human brain. *IRE Trans., Elec. Computers,* EC–5, No. 4.

Milner, P. M. 1957.   The cell assembly: Mark II. *Psychol. Rev., 64,* 242–252.

Minsky, M. L. 1956.   *Heuristic aspects of the artificial intelligence problem.* Lexington, Mass.: MIT Lincoln Laboratories, December. Group Report 34–35.

Newell, A. 1955.   The chess machine; an example of dealing with a complex task by adaptation. *Proc. 1955 West. Joint Computer Conf.,* IRE, March.

Newell, A. 1960.   On programming a highly parallel machine to be an intelligent technician. *Proc. West. Joint Computer Conf.,* 267–282.

Newell, A., and Shaw, J. C. 1957.   Programming the logic theory machine. *Proc. West. Joint Computer Conf.,* 230–240.

Newell, A., Shaw, J. C., and Simon, H. A. 1957.   Empirical explorations of the logic theory machine: A case study in heuristic. *Proc. West. Joint Computer Conf.,* 219–230.

Newell, A., Shaw, J. C., and Simon, H. A. 1958a.   Chess playing programs and the problem of complexity. *IBM J. Res. and Develpm., 2,* 320–325.

Newell, A., Shaw, J. C., and Simon, H. A. 1958b.   Elements of a theory of human problem solving. *Psychol. Rev., 65,* 151–166.

Newell, A., and Simon, H. A. 1956.   The logic theory machine: A complex information processing system. *IRE Trans. Information Theory,* IT–2, 61–79.

Perry, J. W., Kent, A., and Berry, M. N. 1956.   *Machine literature searching.* Cleveland, Ohio: Western Reserve Univ. Press.

Rochester, N., Holland, J. H., Haibt, L. H., and Duda, W. L. 1956.   Tests on a cell assembly theory of the action of the brain, using a large digital computer. *IRE Trans. Information Theory,* IT–2 (3), 80–93.

Rosenblatt, F. 1958a.   *The perceptron: A theory of statistical separability in cognitive systems.* Buffalo, N. Y.: Cornell Aeronautical Laboratory, Inc. Report No. VG–1196–G–1.

Rosenblatt, F. 1958b. The perceptron: A probabilistic model for information storage and organization in the brain. *Psychol. Rev., 66,* 386–408.

Samuel, A. L. 1959. Some studies in machine learning, using the game of checkers. *IBM J. Res. Develpm., 3,* 210–229.

Schenck, H., Jr. 1960. Me. In *The best from fantasy and science fiction: Ninth series.* New York: Doubleday.

Selfridge, O. G. 1955. Pattern recognition and modern computers. *Proc. 1955 West. Joint Computer Conf.,* IRE.

Selfridge, O. G. 1956. Pattern recognition and learning. In C. W. Cherry (ed.). *Third London Sympos. on Information Theory.* London: Academic Press.

Selfridge, O. G. 1959. Pandemonium. *Proc. Sympos. on the Mechanization of Thought Processes.* Teddington, England: National Physical Laboratory.

Shannon, C. E. 1950. Programming a computer for playing chess. *Phil. Mag., 41,* 256–275.

Shannon, C. E., and McCarthy, J. (ed.). 1956. *Automata studies.* Princeton: Princeton Univ. Press.

Shaw, J. C., Newell, A., Simon, H. A., and Ellis, T. O. 1958. A command structure for complex information processing. *Proc. 1958 West. Joint Computer Conf.,* IRE.

Shoulder, K. R. 1960. On microelectronic components, interconnections, and system fabrication. *Proc. West. Joint Computer Conf.,* 251–258.

Sluckin, W. 1954. *Minds and machines.* Harmondsworth: Penguin.

Taylor, F. V. 1957. Simplifying the controller's task through display quickening. *Occup. Psychol., 21,* 120–125.

Turing, A. M. 1950. Computing machines and intelligence. *Mind, 59,* 433–460.

U. S. Dept. of Commerce. 1954. *Proceedings of a symposium on automatic programming for digital computers.* Washington, D. C.: Office of Technical Services.

Whitehead, A. N., and Russell, Bertrand. 1925. *Principia mathematica.* Vol. 1, 2nd Ed. Cambridge: Cambridge Univ. Press.

Yngve, V. 1958. A programming language for mechanical translation. *Mechanical Translation, 5,* 25–41.

HAVING SEEN IN PREVIOUS CHAPTERS SOME-
thing about the kinds of things man can do, so long as
his inputs and outputs are adequately provided for, we
need now to look more closely at these two latter
aspects of man's functioning. What are his sensory
capabilities, that is, the characteristics of his input
mechanisms? Similarly, what do we know about the
nature of his output, his motor response capabilities? And for both these
aspects of his behavioral make-up, what are the limits within which they
operate, under normal conditions as well as in certain environmental extremes? These are the questions with which this chapter deals.

Considerations of man's sensory and motor capabilities and limitations
enter importantly into decisions made in a very early stage of system development—in particular, those concerning the allocation of functions to man and
machine. In participating in or contributing to such decisions, the psychologist
has as a part of his repertoire a systematized body of knowledge called psychophysics. There are precise methods by means of which psychophysical data
are collected, and there is much detailed information, particularly about the
functioning of the senses. Regardless of the amounts of these existing data,
there is much that is not yet known, and the psychologist often finds he is
required to conduct experimental measurements in order to answer some
specific questions about system design.

The authors of this chapter offer an account of some of the ways in
which data on human capabilities are applied to the solution of system problems. Realistic examples are also provided to make possible an understanding
of the many alternatives and the successive decisions that enter into this
process. A description of the relations of data on sensory limitations to system
planning and design is followed by a discussion of human motor capabilities
and their relevance to man-machine functioning, and finally by a treatment of
the effects of environmental stresses on performance.

The problem of using information on man's sensory and motor limitations in the allocation of functions to men and machines is conceived as one
of determining trade-off equations that predict system effectiveness. In the
pursuit of this effort, the needs are seen to be for more psychophysical data,
expressed in the probabilistic terms which will fit predictive formulas, as well
as for rules of interpreting such data over broad ranges of variables.

HUMAN CAPABILITIES
AND LIMITATIONS

Joseph W. Wulfeck
and Lawrence R. Zeitlin

If man is proposed as a system component, an understanding of his unique sensory and motor capabilities and limitations is required. An appreciation of the methods by which man's performance as a system component may be predicted during system design, assessed during system development, or evaluated during system test is also necessary. Clearly, there are certain steps in system development which can only be taken effectively by applying principles that are uniquely psychological. At these points the engineer, mathematician, or statistician is at a handicap without the content of psychology; the medically or physiologically oriented worker is at a handicap without the methodology of psychology.

It is not the purpose of this chapter to presume to present a concise review of the literature on human capabilities and limitations. A bibliography of the literature documenting human capabilities and limitations and of the methodology for determining them would fill this book. It is the rather more humble purpose of this chapter to attempt to illustrate the significance of basic data on human sensory and motor capability, and the appropriate manipulation of those data, in system design and development. Therefore, we are concerned primarily with defining the contribution to system development of data normally obtained by psychophysical and psychophysiological methods, and secondarily with documenting the manner in which those data are typically applied to system development.

Psychology in System Development

In an ideal world, the psychologist would participate in system development through any and all of the following system development activities:

1. Establishing system goals
2. Determining system requirements
3. Allocating system functions between men and machines by:
    a. Determining information requirements
    b. Determining transfer requirements
    c. Determining control requirements
    d. Establishing a maintenance and logistics philosophy
4. Equipment design and workplace layout
5. Establishing manning requirements
6. Determining training requirements
7. Training
8. System test and evaluation

The point in the sequence at which information on human capabilities and limitations is first required depends upon the preliminary definition of goals to which the system aspires. If, for example, the goals of the system are stated initially as being to put a human observer on the surface of the moon to sort and gather significant geological specimens, data on human capabilities and limitations in an inferred lunar environment are of immediate importance in assessing the realism of the systems' goals. If system goals are stated initially as the obtaining of significant geological specimens from the moon, information on human capabilities in an inferred lunar environment may not be required until decisions on man-machine function allocation are necessary. If goals for the system are stated initially as the obtaining of significant geological specimens from the moon by means of a fully automated, unmanned system, information on human capabilities and limitations may not be necessary until the point at which a maintenance and logistics philosophy must be developed.

The point in system development at which information on human capabilities is first required bears little relation to the ultimate significance of that information to final system effectiveness. A so-called "fully automatic" system can fail just as abjectly due to lack of information on human capabilities required late in system development when maintenance equipment is designed, as a manned system may fail due to lack of such information required early in system development when operational equipment design decisions are made. However, the earlier in system development that information on human capabilities is required, the more significant the information becomes for structuring subsequent decisions.

More frequently than not, system goals are stated initially in general terms of the sort used in the second example cited, so that information on human capabilities and limitations is required early in system development, during feasibility studies and the process of allocating functions to man and machine. Decisions made at that time will provide the substrate and will have profound, if not constraining, implications for the nature of later decisions involving human performances. For that reason, we can conclude that information on human capabilities and limitations is most significant to the psychologist in system development when it is applied during feasibility studies and man-machine function allocation. In the process of allocating man-machine functions, it is assumed that the role of man in the operation of the system will derive mainly from the intrinsic properties of man. If that assumption is accepted, it can further be assumed that man's role in the system should be relatively independent of the nature of the system under consideration, but will be contingent upon his capabilities and limitations. The more exact information that can be provided on the capability of the human component, the better can system effectiveness be predicted in consideration of various man-machine function allocations.

At this point in system development, the psychologist is assuming the role of an engineer and is concerned with the question: "What can I expect of the human operator, and what will the effectiveness of my system be if I design the system this way?" When we undertake to discuss this question, we are looking at the fairly well fixed capabilities and limitations of the human operator through a matrix of possible equipment functions. In the next stage of system development (and in the next chapter of this book), we must dash around to the other side of the fence and look at the matrix of equipment functions allocated through the human operator in order to answer the question: "If my operator is to use his capabilities this way, how must I design my equipment so as to optimize system effectiveness?" The difference between the two points of view is subtle, but it is of considerable significance in applying psychological principles to system development. It defines not only the kind of psychophysical and psychophysiological data which will be required in subsequent stages of system development, but also the nature of the psychophysical methods or modification of them which should be applied in obtaining the data. Since the difference between the points of view has as yet lacked clear definition or demonstration in system development, it will not always be easy to distinguish between them. In fact, it may not be possible, or even desirable, to attempt to differentiate them unequivocally in every practical situation in system development. More likely than not, the same individual must comprehend both points of view and be able to work within the constraints of each, shifting from one to the other and back again in rapid succession. We may consider the vigilance problem an illustration of the first point of view, and the ambient-lighting problem an example of the second.

Vigilance. Suppose that some of the requirements of a particular system are continuous search, target detection, target identification, and threat evaluation. Because target identification is difficult for machines to perform well, and threat evaluation is expensive for them to perform well, the possibility is considered of using a radar system which presents a visual display of raw radar data to a human monitor who will perform the detection, identification, and threat-evaluation functions. Given the characteristics of the radar and of the targets in question, how will the vigilance behavior of the human operator affect system performance if the system requires that 90 percent of the targets which appear be detected within five seconds of their appearance? An entirely hypothetical conclusion might be that, if 90 percent of targets *exceed* the *detection threshold* within five seconds, 4 percent will fail to be detected for an additional three seconds after their appearance, simply because of the operator's vigilance behavior in that situation. Therefore, 90 percent target detection will be achieved only after eight seconds of target appearance on the display, and such a level of detection will not quite meet the requirements of the system. This result has been reached by looking through the equipment at the operator's capabilities and by drawing a conclusion which relates to system effectiveness. Since the conclusion was negative, one may choose to look at the operator's capabilities through another piece of equipment—say, a longer-range radar—in order to find one which, when combined with the operator's vigilance characteristics, will meet or exceed system requirements. If a longer-range radar would cost more than automatic target detection equipment, one might choose to reallocate the functions to man and machine.

Ambient Lighting.   As an alternative to finding a different piece of equipment (the longest-range radar available may have been employed), one might instead look at the equipment through the broad matrix of the operator's capabilities. If there are requirements arising from cost, weight, size, or power restrictions to use that particular radar and display; and if, combined with the operator's vigilance characteristics, it fails to meet system requirements; can the equipment be modified or the situation be designed so as to meet system requirements by utilizing some other aspect of the operator's capability? An entirely hypothetical answer to that question might be that a special chromatic filter over the display and a restricted spectrum of ambient lighting would increase the apparent contrast of the targets as well as the sensitivity of the eye, so that 90 percent of targets reach the detection threshold in two rather than five seconds. Even allowing for the vigilance characteristics of the observer, 90 percent will then be detected within five seconds of appearance on the display—a positive conclusion that the system will meet its requirements.

Data on human capabilities are the stuff from which both sorts of design decisions are made. In the first case, the data are needed to assign operator functions and predict performance of them in meeting system requirements. In the second case, the data are needed to design the man-machine interface and the operating environment for maximum performance of the assigned operator functions.

It is both significant and comforting to realize that the same kinds of data are required to make both sorts of decisions. However, it is also significant and distressing to realize that the time pressures under which the two sets of decisions must be made are very different, and that the magnitude of those pressures is usually inversely related to the importance of the decisions which must be made. It was pointed out earlier that decisions regarding the allocation of man-machine functions influence subsequent decisions throughout the remainder of the system's development. They are important indeed. However, it is precisely these decisions which must be made and revised under the greatest time pressures.

Experimentation

Occasionally, during the stage of man-machine function allocation, frequently during equipment design, and always in a basic research program, it should be possible to do the experimental work necessary to nail down a particular human capability in relation to the physical or physiological variables which would be expected to affect that capability. The experimental work which is part of a basic research program may be directed ultimately at an understanding of the psychophysical or psychophysiological implications of a particular stimulus-response process. But many other variables must be simultaneously considered in any given system-design decision. For example, in a response indicating a visual detection or acuity threshold, parameters of the stimulus, such as size, intensity, wave length, contrast with background, as well as psychophysiological factors, such as state of adaptation and retinal area, may be directly relevant to a considerable variety of specific man-machine function allocation decisions.

Experimental work done during the man-machine function allocation stage of system development will usually be designed to determine human capability within ranges of physical variables in which gaps have been left in existing basic research data or in ranges of variables beyond those covered by existing data. Experimental work done in support of the equipment design stage of system development will normally take the form of studies designed to discover optimum levels of particular physical variables in relation to the human function allocated.

Use of Existing Data

Time is usually not available to generate experimental data specific to the initial decisions allocating functions to man and machine, nor is formal experimentation ordinarily possible as allocation revisions are required. Such initial decisions must, therefore, frequently be based on interpretations and extrapolations from existing data. Since those data will rarely be specific to the situation, the process requires explicit generation of hypotheses but allows only for implicit test of these hypotheses *a priori* and revision of them *a posteriori* based upon observational or, at best, cursory experimental data. Generally, the hypotheses can only be stated in terms which in an experimental situation would lend them to rejection by a one-tailed *t*-test.

As an example, let us consider another hypothetical system. Goals for the system are stated as usual in general terms: to develop a vehicle-borne antitank weapon system which will provide first-round kill probability of 98 percent. Some specific system requirements are that:

1. it be adaptable to all armored vehicles now operational or which will become operational during the next 15 years;
2. it be a daylight system, with potential for adaptation to night-time use;
3. it defend against tanks up to a range of 5000 yards and as close as 500 yards;
4. it destroy a target at maximum range within 23 seconds of sighting the target.

Pure engineering considerations determine that the weapon will be a missile. Could the system be fully manual? Could it be fully automatic? If neither, what would be optimum allocation of functions between man and machine? Innocuous, straightforward questions! A partial and very fragmentary list of the information related to human capabilities required to answer them follows:

1. How is daylight defined? What is the lowest "daylight" brightness under which the system must operate?
2. Can the *target* be seen by the operator under all conditions?
   a. What visual angle does an enemy tank subtend today? What angle 15 years from now?
   b. What is the reflectance of the tank?
   c. Against what sorts of backgrounds will it appear? What range of contrasts?
3. Can it be tracked at maximum speed and minimum range?
   a. How fast can it travel today? How fast 15 years from now?
   b. How fast can it change direction and speed?
4. Could the *missile* be seen under all conditions?
   a. What visual angle would it subtend at 5000 yards?
   b. Would it have a visible plume?
   c. What is its reflectance?
   d. What is its range of contrasts against expected tank background?
5. Can it be tracked under all conditions?
   a. How fast does the missile accelerate?
   b. What is its maximum velocity?
6. What is the relation between optical sight magnification and
   a. target detection and tracking;
   b. missile acquisition and tracking?
7. What is the relation between optical sight reticle design and
   a. target detection and tracking;
   b. missile acquisition and tracking?
8. If the missile firing vehicle is standing still with its engine idling, what are the effects of its vibration on
   a. target detection and tracking;
   b. missile acquisition and tracking?

9. What are the effects of heat shimmer along the line-of-sight on
    a. target detection and tracking;
    b. missile acquisition and tracking?
10. What are the effects of recoil-producing firing transients on
    a. target detection and tracking;
    b. missile acquisition and tracking?
11. What are the effects of missile propellant ignition; glare and smoke on
    a. target detection and tracking;
    b. missile acquisition and tracking, especially at very low daylight brightness?
12. What are the effects of maximum rates of own weapon mount slewing on
    a. target tracking;
    b. missile tracking;
    c. gunner's nystagmus?

Answers to these questions require a considerable amount of the data available on human visual performance and manual tracking functions. They also require data on the complex interactions of a variety of physical variables on these functions. Most significantly, if time is not available for experimentation, they require extrapolations from available data to allow tentative hypotheses to be drawn regarding the effects of unexplored ranges of the physical variables on the human functions. For example, the effects of various degrees of heat shimmer on target detection and tracking are not yet known, especially throughout broad ranges of target size, rates of target movements, ambient and target brightness, and target range. For the present, crude approximation of these effects must be inferred from scanty and marginally related data on the effects of vibration, blurring of the contour gradient, and the like upon visual functions. We can conclude, then, that to answer questions such as (1) can a human operator detect and track a target under the conditions required for system performance, and (2) can a human operator detect and track a missile under the conditions required for system performance, man-machine function allocation must be based on:

1. basic data on human capabilities;
2. data on the interactions of many physical and physiological variables on human capabilities; and
3. extrapolation from the data to ranges of variables or higher-order interactions not yet included in available data.

The classical psychophysical methods and modern adaptations of them are the primary means by which it is possible to relate man to his environment in any truly quantitative fashion. If one disregards the polemics which have surrounded development of psychophysics as a set of techniques for relating mind and body and refuses to be involved in the question of reality or universality of the psychophysical law, one can accept the psychophysical methods as fundamental tools of psychological measurement. Without them there would be precious few psychological principles to apply to system development.

Since the psychophysical methods were designed specifically to identify and define the stimulus and to relate change in stimulus magnitude to changes in response magnitude, they make it possible to identify those aspects of the system environment which can be manipulated effectively to mate with man's capabilities and to attempt to quantify the effects of manipulating them on human performance as a system component. In certain cases, the psychophysical methods also enable one to establish the limits of system effectiveness when those limits are dependent directly upon man's own limitations.

All the psychophysical methods in use today (including, for example, attitude scales) are modifications or refinements of three so-called classical methods: the method of adjustment, the method of limits, and the method of constant stimuli. A clear understanding of the means by which they are applied, of the controls necessary to produce reliable data with them, and of the pitfalls inherent in their use is assumed, for in the remainder of the chapter we shall present considerable illustrative data obtained by them.

▣ MAN AS A SYSTEM COMPONENT

The primary role of a human in a complex system is that of an information-receiving, processing, or transmitting element. Depending on the specific allocation of functions to man and machine, the human may be asked to sense a variety of stimuli, evaluate the implications of the stimuli in accordance with instructions, and produce a control output. If we draw a block diagram of a system, we often indicate the position of man by a little rectangle labeled "operator," through which information vital to the functioning of the system passes. The characteristics of this little box are of great interest to both psychologists and systems engineers. For psychologists, much of the interest lies in the fact that prediction of the characteristics of the box serves as an excellent validation tool against which to test the findings of laboratory experiments. This is the "real world" which is spoken of so mysteriously in the classroom. For the systems engineer, a detailed knowledge of the characteristics of the box are important for specification of the input and output devices necessary to incorporate it into the system.

At this point, a fundamental problem in system design arises. Since the description of the information integral to a system which must be processed by man or machine usually comes in engineering language, a conversion must be made to the terminology of psychology in order to enter the body of accumulated experimental data on human sensory and motor performance. It is at this point that one must compare the information-handling characteristics of the various sensory modalities with the characteristics of the information to be displayed to the operator; considering, of course, the unique demands of the situation and other sensory demands on the operator. It is at this point also that one must specify the nature of the decisions to be made and the control outputs to be taken from the operator.

For the moment, let us restrict ourselves to the information-input side of our operator box. We shall assume here that we have made *a priori* assignment of specific information-handling functions to the man. The information comes to the operator as a stimulus, specified as to content, spectral characteristics, dynamic range, and the like. How is this information to be presented? What sense modality is to be exploited?

Engineering design has progressed to the point where one type of signal energy can be converted to another type of energy with little loss in efficiency. In a radar, for example, radio waves carrying information coded in a time domain are translated, for the operator, into pulses of light coded in a spatial pattern. If one chooses, he can convert the same information into a series of tones to be presented as an auditory display. It has been suggested that such information be presented to the operator by means of vibratory or tactical displays; and we suspect that in the not too distant future someone may seriously propose an olfactory display. Generally, however, vision or audition is the sense modality of choice. In Table 4.1 we have presented summary data for several senses. The rows of the table represent various parameters of sense modality response; the columns list the senses themselves. By scanning across a row, we can compare various human input channels along a single parameter. By scanning down a column, we can assess over-all capabilities of a given sense modality. As a consequence of the nonlinearity between stimulus and response, the interactions between the various cells in Table 4.1 may become more important in some situations than the data in the cells themselves. The psychologist experienced in system development work keeps such a table, or a reasonable facsimile, in his head. He unconsciously matches cell entries with developments in the art of information display, in terms of engineering feasibility, cost, or general desirability. Of course there is no *best* method of presenting information to an operator, although there are preferred methods, which cover a variety of generalized situations. Often a change in sensory modality is effective because it permits the man to recover information which was previously ignored or discarded from a stimulus. We will illustrate an example of this later in this chapter, in describing the case of a radar in which the best display proved to be a pair of earphones rather than a cathode ray tube.

Going beyond the information in Table 4.1, it is possible to extract a limited number of sets of data characteristic of the sense modality chosen, which schematize much of the information about functions within the modality as well as the variables that affect these functions. By recognizing certain sets of data within each sensory and response modality as "basic curves," it is possible to attack and possibly evolve first-cut solutions to a great number of function-allocation and equipment-design problems which one encounters in system development. We shall present such data in the following sections. Each set of data chosen illustrates a different aspect of the modality under

Table 4.1

Characteristics of the Senses

Parameter	Vision	Audition	Touch	Taste and Smell	Vestibular
Sufficient stimulus	Light-radiated electromagnetic energy in the visible spectrum	Sound-vibratory energy, usually airborne	Tissue displacement by physical means	Particles of matter in solution (liquid or aerosol).	Accelerative forces
Spectral range	Wavelengths from 400 to 700 mu. (violet to red)	20 cps. to 20,000 cps.	>0 to <400 pulses per second	Taste—salt, sweet, sour, bitter. Smell—fragrant, acid, burnt, and caprylic	Linear and rotational accelerations.
Spectral resolution	120 to 160 steps in wavelength (hue) varying from 1 to 20 mu.	$\sim$3 cps. (20 to 1000 cps.) 0.3 percent (above 1000 cps.)	$\dfrac{\Delta \text{pps}}{\text{pps}} \cong 0.10$	—	—
Dynamic range	$\sim$90 db. (useful range) for rods = 0.00001 mL to 0.004 mL; cones = 0.004 mL to 10,000 mL	$\sim$140 db. 0 db = 0.0002 dyne/cm²	$\sim$30 db. .01 mm to 10 mm	Taste $\cong$ 50 db 3×10^{-5} to 3% concentration quinine sulphate. Smell = 100 db.	Absolute threshold $\cong 0.2°$/sec/sec
Amplitude resolution $\dfrac{\Delta I}{I}$	contrast = $\dfrac{\Delta I}{I}$ = .015	.5 db (1000 cps. at 20 db or above.)	$\sim$.15	Taste $\cong$ .20 Smell: .10 to 50	$\sim$.10 change in acceleration
Acuity	1° of visual angle	Temporal acuity (clicks) $\cong$ 0.001 sec.	Two point acuity = 0.1 mm (tongue) to 50 mm (back)	—	—

Response rate for successive stimuli	~0.1 sec.	~0.01 sec. (tone bursts)	Touches sensed as discreet to 20/sec.	Taste ~30 sec. Smell ~20 sec. to 60 sec.	~1 to 2 sec. nystagmus may perist to 2 min. after rapid changes in rotation.
Reaction time for simple muscular movement	~0.22 sec.	~0.19 sec.	~0.15 sec. (for finger motion, if finger is the one stimulated).	—	—
Best operating range	500 to 600μ (green-yellow) 10 to 200 foot-candles	300 to 6000 cps. 40 to 80 db	—	Taste: 0.1 to 10% concentration.	~1G acceleration directed head to foot.
Indications for use	1. Spatial orientation required. 2. Spatial scanning or search required. 3. Simultaneous comparisons required. 4. Multidimensional material presented. 5. High ambient noise levels. (Javitz, 1961)	1. Warning or emergency signals. 2. Interruption of attention required. 3. Small temporal relations important. 4. Poor ambient lighting 5. High vibration or G forces present. (Javitz, 1961)	1. Conditions unfavorable for both vision and audition. 2. Visual and auditory senses. (Javitz, 1961)	1. Parameter to be sensed has characteristic smell or taste. (i.e. burning insulation).	1. Gross sensing of acceleration information.
References	Baker and Grether, 1954 Chapanis, 1949 Woodson, 1954 Wulfeck, et al., 1958	Licklider, 1951 Licklider and Miller, 1951 Rosenblith and Stevens, 1953 Stevens and Davis, 1938	Bekésy, 1961 Jenkins, 1951	Pfaffman, 1951	Wendt, 1951

consideration. Considered together, they demonstrate the complex interactions among visual or auditory capacities. It should be mentioned that for exemplary purposes single variable functions are often presented for visual capacity, while multivariable functions are frequently chosen to describe fundamental auditory capacities.

Vision

In providing illustrative data for the visual sense, we shall deal with: (1) brightness sensitivity, (2) brightness discrimination, (3) color discrimination, (4) visual acuity, (5) dark adaptation. The basic curves to be presented deal primarily with stimulus characteristics. However, the first basic curve, Figure 4.1, is simply an anatomical plot of the *number of rods and*

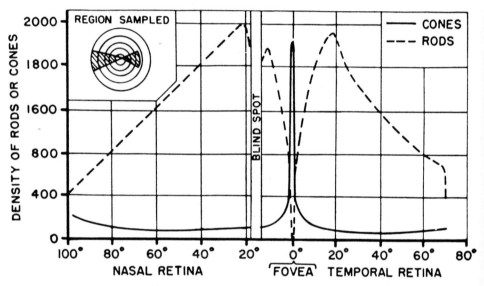

Figure 4.1. *Basic Visual Curve 1:* Rod-cone population curve. Density of rods and cones from nasal to temporal edge of the retina. (After Chapanis, 1949. Data from Osterberg, 1935.)

cones per unit area along a line drawn from the nasal to the temporal retina. It provides the anatomical basis for understanding many aspects of visual performance. If we remember that the cone system is largely responsible for detail and color vision, while the rod system provides for detection of minimal amounts of light, much can be inferred about visual performance by knowing the stimulated area of the retina. Brightness sensitivity is a function of the amount of the radiant energy and the wave length of that energy. Basic curve number two, in Figure 4.2, illustrates the spectral *sensitivity of*

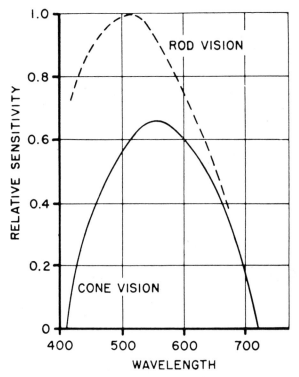

Figure 4.2 *Basic Visual Curve 2:* Spectral sensitivity curve. Relative sensitivity to light as a function of wavelength. (After Wulfeck *et al.,* 1958. Data from Hecht and Williams, 1922.)

the rods and cones. From cone vision to rod vision, the region of maximum sensitivity shifts towards the blue end of the spectrum. The change from cone to rod vision occurs as luminance is decreased. As the eye becomes adapted to dark, sensitivity increases gradually and the peak wave length becomes shorter. Generally speaking, therefore, the rods require much less radiant energy for vision than do the cones. However, rod response is achromatic.

The third basic curve, Figure 4.3, is the *dark adaptation* curve. It has been selected because it illustrates how sensitivity behaves as a function of time in the dark. The first segment begins with a very rapid decrease in threshold and levels off after about ten minutes in the dark at a value approximating the cone threshold. The second segment of the curve begins in about ten minutes and, for practical purposes, levels off from 35 to 45 minutes after adaptation has begun. The final value approximates the rod threshold. Colors are not recognizable as an aspect of sensing represented in the second portion of the curve.

Basic curve number four, Figure 4.4, presents the *brightness contrast*

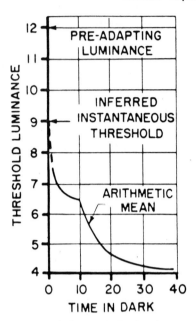

Figure 4.3.   *Basic Visual Curve 3:* Dark adaptation curve. Luminance
that can just be seen as a function of time in darkness. (After Chapanis,
1949. Data from Sloan, 1947.)

threshold as a function of background luminance. Threshold contrast decreases
as luminance increases until it reaches a limit at high illumination. This means
that the capacity of the human eye to detect differences in the brightness of
objects increases as illumination increases. Contrast discrimination also increases with the size of the test object. The sharp discontinuity in the curves
occurs at luminance values at which rod vision shifts to cone vision.

In most systems, it is rare that the operator is called upon to make simple
judgments of brightness or contrast of a stimulus. He is generally asked to
separate two stimuli, describe the form of a stimulus, or discriminate relative movements of stimuli. In those instances it is the relation between stimuli
on various parts of the retina which is important, not the absolute magnitude
of a particular stimulus. In responding to various visual patterns on the retina,
visual acuity is generally considered the parameter of primary interest. Basic
curve number five, Figure 4.5, illustrates one type of visual acuity, *minimum
resolvable,* as a function of background luminance. At zero degrees displacement on the retina, no acuity can be measured at background luminances
less than minus 4.6 log units. However, foveal acuity increases very rapidly
with background luminance up to one millilambert where the curve levels off.
At both four and 30 degrees from the fovea, large objects can be discriminated at very low luminance values. Beyond 30 degrees, there is no further

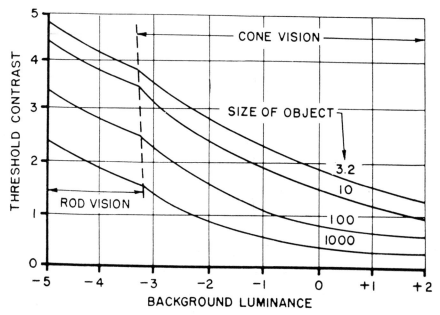

Figure 4.4   *Basic Visual Curve 4:* Contrast discrimination curve. The smallest brightness contrast that can be seen as a function of luminance. (After Baker and Grether, 1954. Data from Blackwell.)

improvement in acuity at luminance values above those where foveal vision begins, and minimum resolvable acuity never falls below 30 minutes. At four degrees, on the other hand, acuity improves with increasing luminance up to about one millilambert. The interaction among background luminance, contrast, and visual acuity is summarized in Figure 4.6.

Other visual capabilities of importance in system development are *distance judgment* or *depth perception, form discrimination,* and *temporal discrimination* including *flicker discrimination,* but the functions which we have presented are sufficient for present purposes. The primary functions are deceptively simple; it must be emphasized that each simple function is presented as a pedagogical device to illustrate the *general* form of the family of functions of which it is representative. Table 4.2 illustrates the interactions between variables and several visual functions.

Throughout our five basic curves and all families of functions deriving from them, the principle is clear: *in no case is human response linearly related to the stimulus.* In no case is the nonlinear response function a *simple* one: it is dependent upon a variety of stimulus parameters. Note, however, that the *general form* of a function is retained through the effects of a wide range of different stimulus parameters. It is for that reason that we have chosen and emphasized the five basic curves. If their general forms of nonlinearity are

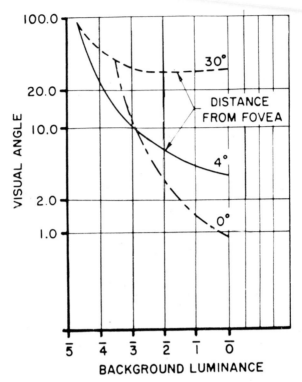

Figure 4.5.   *Basic Visual Curve 5*: Visual acuity curve. Visual angle of the smallest detail that can be discriminated as a function of background luminance. (After Wulfeck *et al.*, 1958. Data from Mandelbaum and Rowland, 1944.)

understood, and if the nature of the families which they represent remain familiar, a giant step can usually be taken in relating human capabilities and limitations to system requirements.

No one would pretend that applying the five basic sets of data will solve all system problems which require information on human visual capability. It is entirely possible that applying the data will not completely solve any single problem. But applying these data will give better problem solutions than would be possible without them. Even more important, *attempting* to apply the data when appropriate to a particular system problem may identify those aspects of it for which data are inadequate or lacking and may thereby efficiently pinpoint critical areas for basic or applied research. Let us apply the "basic curves" to another system example.

System goals: effective continental air defense.

Among system requirements: a high-speed, high-altitude, daylight manned interceptor system.

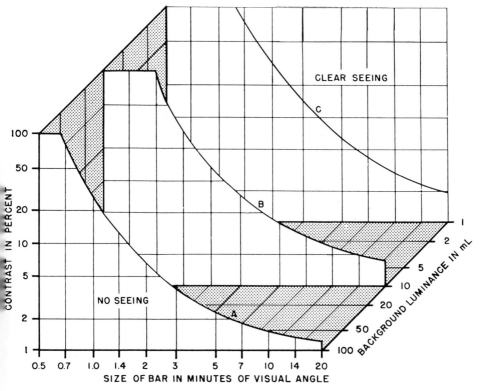

Figure 4.6. Background luminance and contrast required for bars subtending various visual angles to be seen under daylight conditions. (After Cobb and Moss, 1928.)

Question in man-machine function allocation: can the pilot be allocated the functions of monitoring and using a search and fire control radar and also the function of visual search of the daylight sky?

Answer: a qualified yes—if we can be sure that the difference in brightness between the daylight sky and the radar display will not demand a period of dark adaptation to detect radar signals which would compromise system performance.

Our scope must be small, so that it can be centrally located. The scope proposed uses a phosphor which presents green blips against a yellow-green background. A very likely first question becomes: what happens if we push the luminance of the scope face up toward sky brightness? We find the following:

From the curve of Figure 4.1, it is apparent that since the pilot will be using central (foveal) vision, he will be using only cone receptors to fixate the blips on the scope face.

Table 4.2

Variables that Must Be Kept Constant or Carefully Controlled when Measuring Some of the Principal Kinds of Visual Performance

Type of Visual Performance	Variables to Be Controlled												
	Level of Illumination	Region of Retina Stimulated	Stimulus Size	Stimulus Color	Contrast between Test Object and Background	Adaptive State of Eye	Duration of Exposure	Distance at which Measured	Number of Cues Available	Movement	Other Objects in Field	Monocular vs. Binocular	Stimulus Shape
Visual acuity	X	X	(MV)ª	X	X	X	X	X		X			X
Depth discrimination	X		X	X	X	X	X	X	X	X	X	X	
Movement discrimination	X	X	X	X	X	X	X	X	X	(MV)ª	X		X
Flicker discrimination	X	X	X	X	X	X	X						
Brightness discrimination	X	X	X	X	(MV)ª	X	X			X		X	X
Brightness sensitivity		X	X	X	(MV)ª	X	X			X			X
Color discrimination	X	X	X	(MV)ª	X	X	X	X	X		X		

ª Variable being measured
(From Wulfeck *et al.*, 1958)

From the curve of Figure 4.2, it appears that raising intensity is a better approach to the problem than changing color, since the cones are already most sensitive in the yellow-green portion of the spectrum.

From the curve of Figure 4.3, it can be seen that less time will be required for adapting to the raised level of illumination.

However, *from Figure 4.4* one can determine that the blip will be detected more quickly with a low contrast at high luminance values than it would with the same contrast at low luminance values. By calculating visual angle subtended by the smallest target blip and using the actual luminance values of blip and background, we could use Figure 4.4 to find whether the blip would be detected at the contrasts involved. However, a "safety factor" should be incorporated to make certain that contrast will be sufficient, even if the pilot is not fully adapted to scope illumination.

From Figure 4.5, it is seen that acuity will probably be reduced as a function of the decrease in contrast that will occur when scope-face brightness is increased toward blip brightness.

Actually, Figure 4.5 shows that acuity decreases as a function of *decreased* background luminance. However, this curve is based on data for a *dark* object against a *light* background; as background luminance is decreased, contrast between object and background is also decreased, and it is obvious that the decrease in acuity is due to the change in contrast rather than to the absolute change in background luminance. In the case of *bright* radar blips against a *dim* background, *increasing* the luminance of the background reduces contrast, and therefore acuity. (If one requires exact information on visual acuity for the radarscope, data should be consulted that give acuity as a function of contrast for the actual luminance values involved and for the yellow-green portion of the spectrum.)

From the foregoing, it can be seen that if the luminance of the scope face is increased, other variables will probably have to be manipulated so that the pilot can detect target blips and locate them accurately on the scope face. If the position of the scope cannot be changed, so that its size can be increased without pushing other instruments out farther, one might alter, for example, spectral composition, luminance of blip, or shape of blip.

Spectral Composition. We have already seen that the eye is most sensitive to the yellow-green illumination of the scope face. However, contrast may be improved by changing the wave length of the phosphor or the scope illumination or by changing the filter (if there is one) for optimum contrast. In other words, to make up for the decrease in brightness (achromatic) contrast, one can increase color (chromatic) contrast. Perhaps a change to yellow phosphor would be best, since visual acuity is best for yellow.

Luminance. In view of the foregoing, one might better increase brightness contrast by brightening the blip, so that it again stands out from the brightened scope face. However, limits are imposed by (1) the nature of the phosphor, and (2) the diffusion of the image that occurs as brightness of a small luminous object is increased. At this point it is also desirable to reconsider what the best background luminance would be for the *radarscope.*

Let us consider the following data: In the first place, if the pilot must shift his eyes back and forth from the daylit sky to the radarscope, must the scope be as bright as the sky for the pilot to see it clearly? The answer is, no; a surface up to 100 times less bright than a previously viewed surface can still be seen with little adaptation time. Since the brightness of a daylit sky is about 2000 millilamberts, scope brightness should therefore be set up to 20 m-L or higher to ensure visibility of the scope face (without target blips).

Now, how bright must the target signal be to be detected against a background of 20 m-L? Figure 4.4 shows that as over-all luminance values increase, lower contrast ratios can be discriminated. Therefore, a signal of 50 m-L should be more than bright enough to detect against a background of 20 m-L.

Shape of Signal. In addition to changing color and brightness, one might make the blip easier to detect by designing the input to change its shape. One might also make it bigger, but the position of a large blip cannot be determined accurately. If it were desired to explore this approach, however, the data in Figure 4.6 indicate that the visibility of the blip at a given contrast could be increased by making it larger.

Auditory Capabilities

The auditory capacities we shall deal with are (1) absolute thresholds, (2) differential thresholds, (3) subjective measures of audition, (4) masking, and (5) perception of speech.

The auditory stimulus consists of only one element, the rapid fluctuation of air pressure at the eardrum. No matter how complex a sound, it can be represented as a variation in air pressure over time. This comparative simplicity of the auditory stimulus is a mixed blessing. On the one hand, it makes it possible to generate, transmit, and reproduce a wide variety of sounds with relative ease; on the other hand, it interferes with investigation of human response to single attributes of the auditory stimulus. It is difficult, for example, to separate the influence of frequency from intensity in a practical experiment. Suppose the attempt is made to measure the intensity difference limen by presenting a sound to a subject at a given frequency and changing the intensity of the sound over a short period. What gets introduced is not only a change in intensity, but additional frequency components which may be detectable independent of the change in intensity. Licklider (1951) states this quandary quite aptly in pointing out that it is impossible to change any of the parameters of a pure tone and still leave the tone pure. Hence we find that most auditory basic curves show the effect of more than one variable.

The auditory threshold has been defined as the least amount of acoustic energy in the presence of which the subject will report a sound (Rosenblith and Stevens, 1953). Those of us who are high-fidelity fans are well aware that the frequency range over which vibratory energy can be perceived as sound extends from roughly 20 to 20,000 cycles per second (cps). The difference in the amount of energy necessary to perceive sound over this frequency range is enormous. If one uses as a base point the amount of energy necessary to just detect a sound at the 1000 cps as zero decibels (db) (a sound pressure of .0002 dyne per square centimeter), then the amount of energy necessary to detect a sound at 20 cycles is approximately 10,000,000 times greater, or 80 db above the base point. The human ear is actually somewhat more sensitive at frequencies higher than 1000 cps, the threshold of audibility being 5 to 10 db lower at about 3000 cps. Figure 4.7, our first basic curve in audition, shows the threshold of audibility plotted as a function of frequency. The upper threshold, the threshold of feeling, appears to be relatively independent of frequency and occurs at approximately 140 db across the audible range.

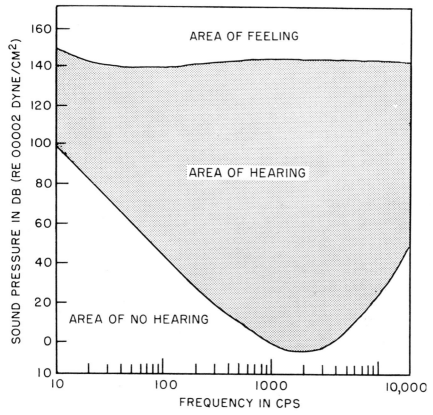

Figure 4.7. *Basic Auditory Curve 1:* The threshold of audibility as a function of frequency.

Our second basic curve, Figure 4.8, shows the differential intensity threshold as a function of the frequency and intensity of the stimulus tone. This figure is a three-dimensional surface, since, as mentioned earlier, it is difficult to manipulate single attributes of an auditory stimulus. Representation of auditory space by a three-dimensional surface makes it possible to consider simultaneously the implications of change of either frequency or intensity upon perception of the test stimulus. We can see from this figure

that the size of the difference limen (DL) for pure tones depends rather criti-
cally upon the sensation level of the stimulus. In general, the DL is constant
for sensation levels above 20 db, and is close to .5 db.

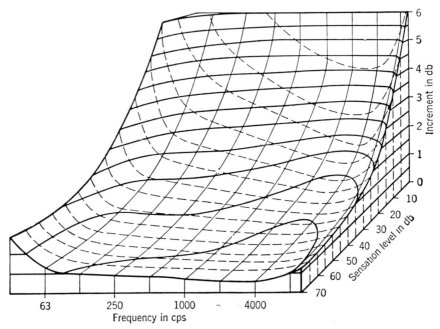

Figure 4.8.   *Basic Auditory Curve 2:* Intensity discrimination curve. The
differential intensity threshold (DL) as a function of the frequency and intensity of the stimulus tone. (After Licklider, 1951. Data from Riesz, 1928.)

Basic curve number three, Figure 4.9, illustrates the other side of the
coin. It represents frequency differential threshold as a function of the frequency and intensity of the stimulus. From this curve one can see that frequency discrimination is poor near the absolute threshold and at high frequencies. At the middle intensity and frequency ranges, however, a change of
about 3 cps can be detected. The magnitude of the frequency DL is subject
to wide individual differences. We have personally tested subjects who can
reliably report changes in the frequency of a tone of .5 cps at 1000 cps. This
is a variation of .05 percent and generally pushes the limits of test instrumentation (Zeitlin, 1956).

In specifying man's auditory capacities, it is important to remember the
difference between the objective and subjective dimensions of auditory experience. Intensity and frequency of a tone are physical characteristics and can
be measured by test instruments. Loudness and pitch are subjective attributes
and can be determined only by subjective scaling techniques. While it is true

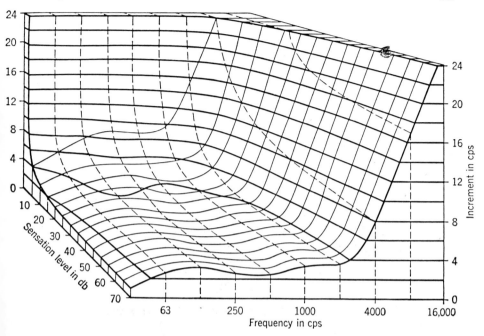

Figure 4.9. *Basic Auditory Curve 3:* Frequency discrimination curve. The differential frequency threshold as a function of frequency and intensity of the stimulus. (After Licklider, 1951. Data from Shower and Biddulph 1931.)

that there is a correlation between intensity and loudness and between frequency and pitch, this correlation is by no means invariate. The loudness versus intensity function is different for different frequencies. The pitch versus frequency function is highly dependent upon loudness. Basic curve number four, Figure 4.10, is another three-dimensional surface, this time showing loudness as a function of intensity and frequency. Loudness in this figure is represented in units of measurement called sones. (A sone is defined as a loudness of a reference tone of 1000 cps at 40 db sound pressure level. A sound whose loudness is 2 sones is twice as loud as one whose loudness is 1 sone, and so on [Rosenblith and Stevens, 1953]. It may be seen from the figure that the loudness of a tone increases rather slowly as the intensity of the stimulus is increased from the threshold of audibility to 60 or 70 db. The loudness then begins to increase quite rapidly as the intensity of the stimulus is increased. At 1000 cps, an increase in the intensity of the stimulus from zero db to 40 db produces an increase in loudness of five sones. The same 40 db increase in energy from 60 to 100 db, however, produces an increase in loudness of 65 sones.

Masking. Acoustic stimuli are rarely presented in isolation. The

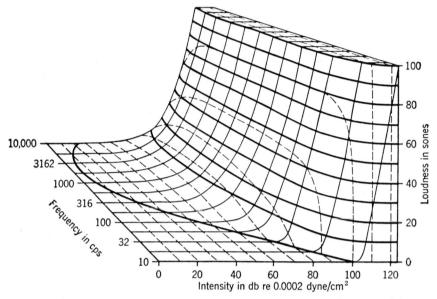

Figure 4.10.   *Basic Auditory Curve 4:* Loudness as a function of intensity and frequency. (After Stevens and Davis, 1938.)

desired stimulus must usually compete with other auditory stimuli, ambient noise, and transmission noise, all of which may interfere with perception of the desired tone or message. This phenomenon is known as *masking.* The percentage of masking is usually defined by determining the amount that the desired stimulus must be increased before it is perceived. It is obvious that the amount of interference between two stimuli will depend very much on what the stimuli are. Two pure tones will behave differently from a combination of a pure tone with a noise. A number of experiments have been performed in which one pure tone masks another. The conclusions which can be drawn from these experiments are briefly as follows: (1) There is more masking between tones that lie close to each other in frequency than for tones which are farther apart. (2) A low frequency tone is more effective in masking a high frequency tone than vice versa. (Licklider, 1951.)

Of greater concern to the system designer is the effect of noise on masking of a desired stimulus. Figure 4.11 shows the effect of random noise (white noise) on the perception threshold of pure tones. The masking effect of such noise appears to be relatively constant across the frequency range.

Speech. Most communication to and from operators in systems functions is in the form of speech. We are often apt to overlook the fact that the operator's earphones may be the most important display in the entire system. Some of the physical properties of speech are quite unlike those of the stimuli we have been considering. Perception of speech differs sufficiently from perception of other stimuli to justify separate treatment.

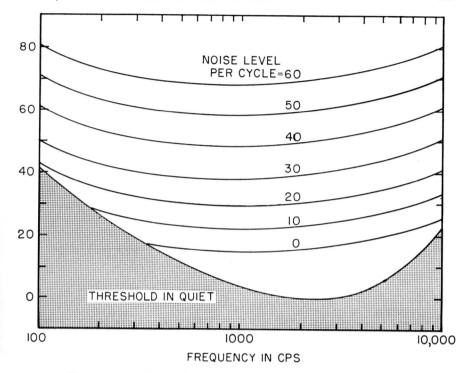

Figure 4.11.   The masking effect of random (white) noise on the perception threshold of pure tones. The ordinate indicates the intensity required for the pure tone to be just audible against random noise masking
of the level shown as the parameter of each curve. (After Hawkins and
Stevens, 1950.)

The average speech power emitted by a speaker on a conversational level
is quite small and corresponds roughly to a sound from 80 to 85 db. The
distribution of speech power with frequency is reasonably constant for both
male and female speakers. Figure 4.12 illustrates average speech spectra.

In many applications, the presence of unwanted masking noise impairs
the listener's ability to interpret all speech sounds correctly. The articulation
score, a quantitative measure of the efficiency of speech communications,
represents the percentage of test words which can be transmitted correctly
over a communication channel. If the channel is nearly perfect, the articulation score is close to 100 percent. Figure 4.13 shows the articulation scores
for three different types of test material. The test items were masked by white
noise, and the percent items correct are plotted as a function of the signal-to-
noise ratio in decibels. We can see from this figure that the amount of masking
is not only a function of the signal-to-noise ratio but also of the content of
the material. The more familiar the material, the less it is masked. It appears
that the contribution of human interpreting functions to speech reception is

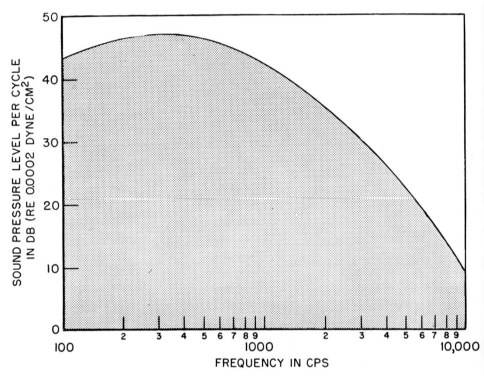

Figure 4.12. Average speech spectra. (From Licklider and Miller, 1951. After Dunn and White, 1940, and Rudmore *et al.,* 1944.)

quite marked. If we distort speech by passing it through a system that is selective in respect to frequency, as in the case of a high- or low-pass filter or a frequency-restricted earphone or microphone, the articulation score also changes. Figure 4.14 illustrates the effect on the articulation score for speech passed through high- or low-pass filters. From these curves we see that there is only a small increase in articulation score if we pass all frequencies above 5000 cps. If we pass only those frequencies below 300 cps, the articulation score drops to zero. Likewise, a filter passing all frequencies above 300 cps gives an articulation score close to 100 percent. The crossover point occurs at 2000 cps, hence a speech communication system passing either all frequencies below or above 2000 cps will yield equal results, providing about 70 percent syllable intelligibility (French and Steinberg, 1947). Speech over such a system will not sound natural, but it will be intelligible. In general, however, a frequency range of from 600 to 3000 cps is considered as the minimum desirable for speech transmission.

Speech can also be distorted considerably in amplitude before the articulation score drops to an unusable amount. In fact, deliberate amplitude dis-

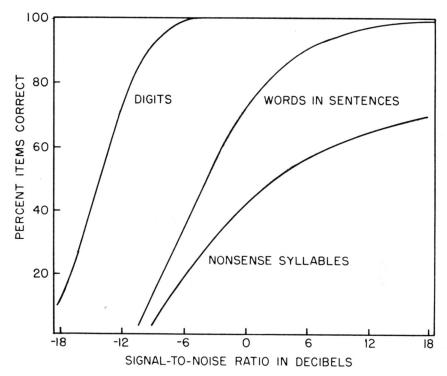

Figure 4.13.   Articulation scores for three different types of test materials. (After Hudgins *et al.*, 1947.)

tortion or peak clipping is commonly encountered in speech communication devices as a means of using available transmitter power more efficiently. The number of decibels by which the amplitudes of the peaks are reduced by limiting defines the amount of peak clipping. Infinite peak clipping will reduce the speech to a succession of rectangular waves. Surprisingly enough, speech can be distorted to this extent and still retain an articulation score above 70 per cent (Licklider, 1946).

In general, we may say that speech reception is a human capability that has almost defied automatic or mechanical duplication. Humans can interpret speech distorted in frequency, amplitude, phase, and under conditions of high masking noise. Some of this capability lies in the analytic ability of the ear, but by far the larger part lies in the nature of speech itself—a highly redundant communication process—and in the higher nervous centers of the listener. If the number of speech commands or messages is limited, only a small fraction of the message must be perceived to enable the listener to reconstruct the message in its totality.

Example.   As with data on vision, we have attempted to identify basic

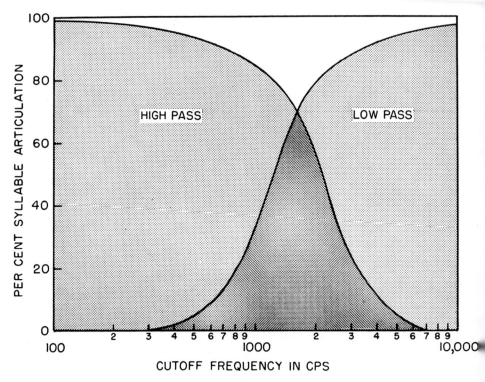

Figure 4.14. The effect on syllable articulation score of passing speech through high-pass or low-pass filters. (After French and Steinberg, 1947.)

auditory facts which may be committed to memory for retrieval in system development during man-machine function allocation and equipment design. The complex interactions among those functions and the fact that they are representative of families of functions have also been illustrated. An example of the manner in which such data for audition may be applied in system development follows.

Radar engineers have been aware for some time that a radar return carries considerably more information than azimuth, range, and general reflective size of the target. The return carries information about rapid changes in the reflective area of the target due to moving parts (propellers and wings), changes in the refractive index of the air, and Doppler shifts due to the relative motion of parts of the target or the target and its surrounding objects (clouds, chaff, ground). For the most part, such information is ignored because (1) it is irrelevant to the task at hand, and (2) the traditional means of presentation, the cathode ray tube, uses phosphors which have a persistence long enough to integrate rapid fluctuations in intensity of the radar return. For many purposes the integration of return energy is valuable, however. Systems designers have recently become aware that the fine information on the radar return can aid in identification and evaluation of the gross aspects of the return. This is particularly true in the case of weather radar.

A weather radar detects clouds by bouncing radiation off the rain drops within the cloud. The radar return gives position and general size, but it does not provide significant information about conditions within the cloud. By recovering fine-grain information from the radar return, it is possible to assess turbulence within the cloud by observing the relative motion of areas of rain-laden air. How is this material to be presented to the operator? The video display is already being used to give size, distance, and azimuth; the response rate of the eye is also limited. It has been suggested that the material be extracted from the video signal and presented to the operator through ear-phones. Turbulence modulation of the radar signal is relatively rapid, although somewhat below the audio range. Thus, it cannot be presented to the operator directly. It can, however, be used to modulate another tone well within the operator's range of hearing. The problem we are now concerned with is the location of this tone in the auditory spectrum and the type of modulation to be impressed upon it. One must ask the following questions:

1. What frequency should the carrier tone have?
2. Should it be frequency or amplitude modulated; that is, should it change in frequency with a change in turbulence, or change in intensity?
3. How loud must the carrier tone be against a noise background of at least 60 db?
4. Will it interfere with speech perception?

From Figure 4.7, it may be seen that the desirable range of frequencies for the carrier tone is between 400 and 4000 cps. If a tone outside these limits is chosen, the amount of power necessary to present the display may be excessive.

From Figure 4.8, it is evident that it takes a change in intensity of at least 1 db for a tone 30 db above the threshold before an observer can detect the change. This increment drops to about .5 db at 60 db above threshold. This gives an amplitude sensitivity of from 10 to 30 percent of the stimulus power, depending upon the sensation level chosen.

From Figure 4.9 one can see that the DL for frequency modulation is somewhat smaller in terms of percentage of variation of the test signal at reasonable sensation levels. Above 30 db and at 1000 cps a .3 percent change can be detected.

On the basis of the information presented so far, it is difficult to make a decision between frequency and amplitude modulation. It is known, how-ever, that pitch stability tends to be greater than loudness stability over a period of time. Consequently, a frequency-modulated tone would be preferred. More important, if the carrier tone is to be presented at various levels of amplitude, a given percentage change in intensity will not be perceived as a constant percentage change in loudness (Figure 4.10).

From Figure 4.11, it is apparent that a pure tone to be detected against a random noise background of 60 db must have an intensity of at least 80 db. If amplitude modulation is used, extreme changes in the carrier intensity level may force the signal, on the one hand, into a near painful area, and on the other hand into an inaudible region. If frequency modulation is chosen, the tone can be made comfortably discernible against the random noise background and held at approximately the same amplitude.

What should the carrier frequency be? Will it interfere with speech perception? These questions are intimately related. From Figure 4.14, one sees that a low-pass communication system which cuts off at 3000 cps permits at least 80 percent syllable articulation. A communications system with syllable articulation score of 80 percent will transmit words in sentences virtually unimpaired. If the carrier frequency is positioned at 4000 cps, permitting deviations of $\pm$ 1000 cps, it may be possible to present both speech and the auditory display on the same communication channel without too much mutual interference. At the same time, it can be seen from Figure 4.7 that this is still a rather sensitive area in the auditory spectrum.

Conclusion: a frequency modulated carrier tone of 4000 cps, at least 80 db above threshold, meets the stated requirements. In an actual system it would probably be undesirable to stop the design effort here. Of necessity, other factors would be considered, including the pulse repetition rate of the radar, the characteristics of the audio system, the characteristics of the earphone, and the nature of the ambient noise.

Other Senses

The contribution of information about system operation obtained from other sense modalities may be extremely important to system performance. Noxious olfactory stimulants are often incorporated in liquid and gaseous materials to serve as warning indicators of leaky hydraulic or pneumatic systems. Gustatory sensitivity identifies a spoiled steamed clam long before it becomes a dangerous agent in the human digestive system. Body heating may indicate a faulty air conditioning system. Indirect sensory effects may identify a malfunctioning oxygen-breathing system.

Excessive vibration, stimulating tactile and kinesthetic receptors, ordinarily indicates a malfunction in any mode of transportation. Vestibular sensitivity may provide the only sensory inputs useful for orientation in certain kinds of system operations conducted at night. Overheating commonly indicates malfunction in electronic and some mechanical equipment.

However, with the exception of shape-coded controls and skin "buzzers" displaying information to tactile and kinesthetic receptors, the senses other than vision and audition have not been called upon in system development as candidates in the man-machine function allocation process. Their significance in system development to date has fallen mainly in the area of equipment design for *comfortable* human operation, in optimizing performance through controlling the operating environment, and in determining the requirements for radical system environments, such as those necessarily encountered in submarine, high-altitude, underground, or completely closed ecological systems. In most cases basic sensory data, such as absolute or discrimination thresholds, have little significance, for the emphasis is on meeting environmental requirements for maximum work efficiency and minimum fatigue. For those reasons we will omit presentation of basic data for senses other than vision and audition, with the realization that the data do exist and can be organized efficiently for application to system development if necessary.

◙ MAN AS AN ELEMENT IN CONTROL SYSTEMS

For every manned position in a man-machine control system provision must be made to permit the operator to return processed information to the system. The output device may be as simple as a pencil and pad of paper, or as complex as the fully instrumented cockpit of a high-performance aircraft. In many cases, the operator's function is to control some system parameter to agree closely with a command function derived from the external environment. The general control operation comes under the rather broad general category of "tracking"; however, the task may vary from a simple trapping of a blip with a light gun on a radar screen to driving an automobile at 60 miles an hour on an ice-covered expressway during rush hour. In effect, the operator is performing as a servo link whose objective is to reduce system error in following the desired forcing function to a tolerable quantity. What differentiates the human operator from an electrical or mechanical servo link is the ability of man to modify his own characteristics to match the requirements of the controlled situation.

Transfer Functions

The analogy between human performance as an element in a control system and servomechanism theory has prompted much research into the specification of *transfer functions* which would describe the nature of human response for specified inputs and outputs in the same manner as the response of a servo system. Unfortunately, from the point of view of theory, the range of variables which importantly affect human performance in control systems is far greater than the range handled by servomechanism theory. Among these variables are the mode of control, the kind of tracking, display, and control relationships, and the nature of the forcing function itself. The interaction between motor performance and sensory performance is extremely great. Transfer functions developed from a simple application of servomechanism theory in human performance could only apply if the human operator's responses were completely or very nearly linear. However, we have seen in earlier portions of this chapter that human responses to stimuli occur in a generally nonlinear fashion.

If one chooses to restrict the scope of investigation to information presented along a single continuum of a sensory modality and measures a control response in the absence of complex system dynamics, human transfer functions can be developed which are reasonably accurate for certain types of control tasks. According to Goode and Machol (1957), three sets of performance criteria are applicable to servomechanism design. These are transient response, steady-state conditions, and stability. Transient response refers to the manner in which a device settles down to steady performance after an abrupt change in the input stimulus. Steady-state conditions refer to the error between input and response which remains when all transients have died out. Stability, of course, refers to the consistency of performance of the system to a variety of inputs. In this section, we shall use these three criteria to describe human capabilities in a control system.

Human Responses in a Control System

In most studies investigating human transient response, a stimulus moves sharply in one direction and the operator is required to track the position of the stimulus with the controlled element. Human response in this type of input occurs in three phases. During the first phase there is no appreciable motion at all. This is the reaction-time delay. At the end of this dead period, the subject moves the controlled element rapidly toward the position of the stimulus, ending with a small error. During the final portion of the response, the operator moves the controlled element slowly toward the final position of the stimulus, eliminating the remaining error as much as possible. The average duration of the reaction-time delay is about .25 second and generally agrees with other reaction times recorded to simple visual stimuli (McRuer and Krendel, 1957). The dynamic portion of the response, at least the first controlled movement, is generally ballistic, that is, the operator forcefully moves the control element by a single muscle impulse. It makes relatively little difference how far he must move the control element. The time taken for simple ballistic responses is generally the same regardless of the extent of motion. This time is about .1 second. The operator determines the amount of error between the position of the controlled element and the stimulus, then gradually reduces this error. Depending on the dynamics of the situation, he may overshoot the stimulus position once or twice before the final position. The total time taken to track a step function is usually .4 to .5 second.

If the stimulus is not moved in steps but is moved continuously, one can measure the operator's steady-state response characteristics. If the results are to be generalized to a wide variety of input conditions, it is best to use an input stimulus which appears random or nonpredictable in nature. Low-frequency white noise has often been used to control stimuli in tracking experiments. The results of studies using this type of input show that the highest input frequency which a man can track successfully is somewhat less than one cycle per second. Tracking accuracy drops off severely when the input frequency exceeds 2 cycles a second (Elkind, 1956). This figure compares well with the transient response of the human operator indicated within the previous paragraphs. Since a random input stimulus is nonpredictable, the operator may be considered to be tracking a series of step functions of arbitrary amplitude and duration. Table 4.3 shows what happens to the correlation between input and output of a human operator as the frequency of the input becomes higher.

Table 4.3

Tracking Capability of Human Operator

Forcing function bandwith [a] (cps) [b]	Average linear correlation
0.16	0.995
0.24	0.99
0.40	0.995
0.64	0.98
0.96	0.92
1.6	0.75
2.4	0.58

[a] Random-appearing function made up of 40–120 sinusoids giving any desirable rectangular spectra.
[b] Passband from 0 cps to upper limit.

(After Elkind, 1956)

Elkind (1956) summarizes the basic characteristics of human visual-manual responses somewhat as follows: (1) The human operator is fundamentally a low-pass device. Considered as an amplifier, his gain approaches zero at high frequencies. (2) For low bandwidth inputs, his low-frequency gain can be very high but is finite, because of limitations of visual, motor, and memory systems. (3) All performance in tracking unpredictable complex stimuli must contain a delay analogous to the reaction-time delay or stimulus-response latency of the human operator in a discrete tracking task.

If the stimulus moves in a completely predictable manner, the operator will learn the control motions which must be made to minimize his error. A low-frequency sine wave is a stimulus of this sort. Three types of response occur to this form of stimulus. The first is "nonsynchronous," in which the operator lags behind the motion of the stimulus. As the operator learns to anticipate the stimulus movements, his response changes to a "synchronous" mode, in which there is no lag. At this point he may be said to have learned the response. The mode of operation can be maintained for long periods of time provided the stimulus frequency is less than 3 cps. If the frequency of motion of the stimulus is much faster, the operator tends to drift out of synchronism and, for a time, his actions may serve to increase error rather than decrease it (McRuer and Krendel, 1957). The control system then becomes unstable. If this occurs when piloting an airplane through buffeting, or driving a car down a winding road, the effect, of course, can be disastrous.

In summarizing human performance as a control element in a servo system, we can state that man has a transient response of .5 second, can track forcing functions with high accuracy provided the input does not contain frequencies above 2 cps, and can track predictable, repetitive phenomena if the frequency is not much higher than 3 cps. At frequencies higher than 3 cps, instability of response occurs, the operator sporadically getting out of phase with the input, and error may be increased.

▣ ENVIRONMENT

In the design of complex systems, man must be considered as an element which operates best in a fairly narrow range of environmental conditions. As mentioned in previous sections, environmental factors have a direct bearing on operator performance. Their effect on performance can be exerted in two ways. First, the environment may be such as to degrade a sensory modality directly. For example, visual performance suffers if the environment does not provide adequate illumination; auditory performance suffers in an environment containing high ambient noise levels. Second, the environment may introduce physiological stresses which indirectly affect sensory or motor performance. Temperature, atmospheric contamination, inadequate oxygen, and radiation fall in this category. To some extent, a single environmental condition may operate both directly and indirectly upon human performance. Noise and vibration fall in this category. Of course, in addition to their influence on operative performance, severe deviations from an environmental norm can cause physical injury or endanger life. The magnitude of the absolute limit of environmental stress is, roughly, inversely proportionate to the amount of time the stress must be endured. The absolute limits of human tolerance greatly exceed normal expectations, provided the time of exposure is extremely short. For example, a properly clothed man can exist for one hour without sign of injury at temperatures ranging from $-60°$ F to over $140°$ F. For shorter periods of time, this range can be extended from $-100°$ F to over $200°$ F. A man in a supine position can survive transverse accelerations of over 20 G for periods of 30 seconds and over 50 G for periods of 1 second (Eckenrode and Abbot, 1959).

For the most part, however, interest centers on a much smaller environmental range. One must assume, in systems design work, that equipment designers will not provide modes of system operation which subject an operator to environmental stresses greater than his tolerance limits. For the purpose of illustration, we will consider environmental stresses in three areas: temperature, acceleration, and noise.

Temperature. Temperature is a stress which does not interfere directly with a sensory or motor mechanism, but influences the general comfort and psychological functioning of an individual. The temperature of the human body depends upon the balance of heat produced and lost by the body. Under normal conditions, the body adapts to changes in temperature, humidity, and air movement, regulating the sweat glands and the rate of flow of blood in the skin to maintain the body temperature at about $98.6°$ F. As long as the individual can readily adapt to external changes, heat equilibrium is maintained and the body feels comfortable. There is a slight physiological penalty which must be paid for this maintenance of equilibrium, however. If the ambient air temperature rises to much greater than $80°$ F, there is some slight impairment in performance. By the time the ambient rises to $90°$ F, there is a demonstrable impairment in man's mental and physical processes. If one does not consider extreme temperature ranges, the effect of temperature on performance is slight for simple motor and sensory tasks, but increases as the complexity of the task increases. Table 4.4 indicates the critical effective temperatures at which performance impairment may be demonstrated.

Acceleration. One important use of a human in systems operation is as a vehicle controller. In this kind of task, the operator may be subject to accelerative forces with every change in vehicle velocity or orientation. These forces must be controlled so as not to become too great an influence on perception of pertinent systems information and the performance of necessary tasks. It goes without saying that men function best at an acceleration of 1 G directed in a head-to-foot direction. If the acceleration in this direction increases, sensory degradation occurs, due to drainage of blood from the brain. Vision is lost first, followed by loss of hearing, and then loss of consciousness. The "blackout" phenomenon generally starts at 3 G's acceleration but can be postponed by the use of appropriate clothing. If the acceleration is directed in the opposite direction, from foot to head, sensory performance is also impaired.

The human is much less sensitive to acceleration in a transverse direction. Sensory performance is generally not affected unless the acceleration reaches 10 G or greater. In this case, there may be some blurring of vision because of the distortion of the eye.

The most important effect of acceleration on human performance, after sensory degradation, is the restriction of gross body movements. Regardless of direction of acceleration, a man cannot move about freely at greater than 2 G. The arms and the hands become difficult to move freely at greater than 3 G. These limits of perception and motor performance determine the limits of operator participation in the control of high-performance vehicular systems.

Noise.   Noise is one of those environmental parameters which interferes directly with a sensory function and indirectly with over-all human performance. As mentioned previously, noise directly affects speech perception, and consequently can influence system functioning to a great extent. However, in addition to masking speech, it is possible for noise to have an effect on other kinds of human behavior, particularly performance of tasks requiring con-

Table 4.4

The Critical Effective Temperatures at Which Impairment May Be Demonstrated, According to Various Sources

Name and type of test	Investigator	Temperature (°F)	
		Max. at which performance remains normal	Demonstrable impairment
Typewriter code (scrambled letters)	Viteles	80	87
Morse code reception	Mackworth	87.5	92 [a]
Locations (spatial relations code)	Viteles	80	87
Block coding (problem solving)	Mackworth	83	87.5 [a]
Mental multiplication (problems)	Viteles	80	87
Number checking (error detection)	Viteles	80	87 [a]
Visual attention (clock test)	Mackworth	79	87.5 [a]
Pursuit (visual maze)	Viteles	80	87
Reaction time (simple response)	Forlano	93 [b, c]	—
Discrimeter (complex response)	Viteles	80	87
Lathe (hand coordination)	Viteles	80	87 [a]
Pursuitmeter	Mackworth	87.5	92 [a]
Motor coordination	Weiner	64.5 [c]	91 [a]
Ergograph (weight pulling)	Mackworth	81 [d]	85.3 [a, d]
Bicycle ergometer (heavy work)	Liberson	64.5 [c]	91.5 [c]
Weight lifting (heavy work)	N. Y. Ventil. Comm.	64.5 [c]	70 [c]

[a] Deterioration statistically significant.
[b] Provided wet bulb does not exceed 86°F.
[c] Effective temperature estimated from data in report.
[d] Midpoint of a range of conditions.

(After Eckenrode and Abbot, 1959)

centrated attention. For the purpose of discussion, it is convenient to divide behavior into mental and manual tasks and to divide noise levels into intense (above 100 db) and low-level noise. Over short periods, less than two hours, there is no clearly demonstrated effect of low-level noise on human performance. If the time of exposure is extended, it may be possible to discern a slight degradation of performance for manual tasks.

Intense noise generally has an effect on performance. The effect on manual tasks is usually small, the effect on mental tasks is somewhat greater. If the noise is very intense, ear damage can result, which can influence system functioning long after cessation of the noise. Table 4.5 lists the effects of exposure to noise on human performance (Eckenrode and Abbot, 1959).

Table 4.5

Some Effects of Exposure to Noise as Compared to Quiet on Human Performance and Other Processes

Type of performance	Noise level (db)	Noise duration	Quiet level (db)	Effect of noise
Addition problems	50	Continuous	Not given	No difference in number of correct solutions. Considerable increase in energy expenditure under noise as compared to quiet, especially during first few days.
Continuous tracking	120	Intermittent and random	" "	No effect
	120	12 × 2 min. in 4 hours	" "	Performance improved
	130	3 min. at middle and end of 4 hours	" "	Performance improved
Stereoscopic ranging	120	3 minutes	" "	No effect
Inserting pegs in pegboard	high	Intermittent clicks and complex noise	" "	Initial performance slowed but over-all performance showed no difference
Tracking requiring hand, foot, and eye coordination	115	continuous	90	Reactions in noise 5.4% slower
Card sorting	115	continuous	90	No effect
Marksmankship	115	continuous	90	No effect
Joystick pursuit tracking	115	continuous	90	No effect

Table 4.5 (continued)

Some Effects of Exposure to Noise as Compared to Quiet on Human Performance and Other Processes

Type of performance	Noise level (db)	Noise duration	Quiet level (db)	Effect of noise
Hand or foot key-pressing	115	continuous	90	No effect
Key pressing to translate letters to numbers	120	10 minutes	not given	Time required initially longer; greater tension in noise
Monitoring clock for erratic hand movements	114	last 1½ hours of 2-hour trial	83	Significantly poorer in last ½ hour
Conversation	0–60	continuous	—	Normal
	60–80	"	—	Raised voice
	80–100	"	—	Very difficult
	100–115	"	—	Shouting
	< 115	"	—	Impossible
Comfort level in aircraft	0–60	Continuous	—	Quiet and very comfortable
	60–80	"	—	Comfortable
	80–90	"	—	Acceptable
	90–100	"	—	Noisy
	100–115	"	—	Very noisy and disagreeable
	115–125	"	—	Uncomfortable
	< 125	"	—	Painful

(After Eckenrode and Abbot, 1959)

▣ SOME GENERAL IMPLICATIONS

This chapter has emphasized the position that psychophysical and psychophysiological information on human capabilities and limitations is most significant to system development when applied during the process of allocating functions to man and machine. It has attempted to show why the information becomes significant, what kind of information is available, and how the information that is available must normally be applied. It is time now to take a close, hard look at the implications of the position taken and of the material presented for past and especially for future system development.

As indicated in Chapter 2 and reiterated here, the decisions made during man-machine function allocation establish the requirements for equipment design, work–place layout and environmental control. They determine manning, selection, training, and organizational requirements. Finally, they define to a large extent the nature of system test and evaluation. On the face of it, the position has such validity that we may well accept it as a psychological principle of system development. But how can such a clear-cut principle have been so difficult to establish and so marginal in application? The answer is a painful one; Jordan (1961) makes the point nicely. He begins with a statement from Swain and Wohl (1961), to the effect that there is no adequate systematic methodology in existence for allocating functions between man and machine. This lack, Swain and Wohl suggest, is probably the central problem in human factors engineering today. They point out that ten years of research and experience have failed to bring us any closer to the goal than did the landmark article by Fitts (1951). Jordan then questions the utility of the "Fitts lists," which instruct us to compare man to the machine and choose the one who fits a function best. He concludes that if men and machines are not comparable, it is not surprising that the attempt to compare them proves fruitless.

Jordan summarizes Craik's (1948) arguments, which recommend that human functions be described in terms *comparable* to the terms used in describing mechanical functions, and concludes that whenever human function can be reduced to a mathematical formula, it is generally possible to build a machine that can do it more efficiently than a man; therefore, to the extent that man is comparable to a machine, he can be replaced by a machine. Birmingham and Taylor's conclusion (1954) that, speaking mathematically, man is best when doing least, is extended to a *non sequitur*—if man is best when he does least, the best he can do is nothing. Clearly the rules for making man-machine function allocations have not been agreed upon.

An attempt to seek an answer to this problem can be made with the assumption that man-machine function allocation decisions may be made as a series of trade-offs which *predict* desired operational effectiveness for the system. Those trade-offs must include data on human capabilities and limitations, but they also require data on machine and human size, weight, reliability, availability, maintainability and cost (in the human case, the cost of training, of environmental support, and the like). The trade-offs can be made properly in terms of *cost* or *value:* what will be the *cost* to desired system operational effectiveness of using the limited-reliability but easily reprogrammed human being, rather than the reliable, inflexible machine? Applying the techniques for making such trade-offs *a priori,* and predicting their cost, is therefore a growing necessity which demands that psychophysical and psychophysiological data as well as standard design data be evaluated by system analysts and operations researchers. Some psychologists have participated in application of these techniques to man-machine function allocation and system-design feasibility studies, and they have sometimes been criticized for being *macro*analytic when *micro*analytic techniques are required to deal with the human.

To date psychologists have been and continue to be somewhat limited in the initial stages of system design in the extent of participation and the significance of contribution because of the *form* in which psychophysical, psychophysiological, and more general behavioral data are ordinarily available.

This is not an epistomological problem. It is not solved when one calls stimuli "inputs" and responses "outputs," or when one relates stimulus and response in psychophysical terms and concludes that the human may be considered an amplifier or some other electrical or electronic component. The problem is uniquely psychological, and it appears to be fundamentally a problem in psychophysics.

The most stringent demands on the form of psychophysical and psychophysiological data occur in the development of mathematical models for system simulation, cost analyses, or value studies. Probablistic data in the form of error functions are required for single-stage analytic probability models and for numerical probability or Monte Carlo models used in complex simulations. The only general psychophysical method which produces sensory data in that form is the method of constant stimuli. However, the method of adjustment and the method of limits have been used so extensively that a tremendous amount of the data available on human capabilities and limitations have been obtained by them. Unfortunately, variability indices obtained with those methods have not been, and are not normally, reported in sufficient detail to allow the statistical manipulations necessary for deriving probabilistic conclusions from them. Furthermore, the method of constant stimuli is the most laborious and time-consuming to apply when gathering new data; the method of adjustment is much simpler to instrument, and the method of limits is much faster to use. These differences are of considerable significance within the operational framework, for when the opportunity for experimentation presents itself, the techniques used must be quick, easy, and efficient. Tanner and his associates (1956) have been active in adapting the constant stimuli method to operational problems, but much progress remains to be made. New psychophysical methods or efficient modifications of the old ones appear to be required. More needs to be known also about the rules for inferring the relations among sets of psychophysical data and for relating psychophysical data across different modalities. These rules depend ultimately upon principles of psychological scaling. In addition, psychophysical scaling problems are relatively simple compared to the problems which must be solved if one is to scale, and therefore be able to trade off, in areas of complex decision making, such as threat evaluation or troubleshooting.

Finally, knowledge is needed of the rules for interpreting psychophysical data obtained over broad ranges of variables, and of methods of designing psychophysical experiments which will give maximum interpolation accuracy through the widest ranges of variables with minimum administrative and computational difficulty.

These requirements are severe and will not be met easily. However, they are requirements which must be realized as rapidly as possible if the mass of psychophysical and psychophysiological data describing human capability and limitations is to be uniformly useful in establishing the psychological principles of system development.

REFERENCES

Baker, C. A., and Grether, W. F. 1954. *Visual presentation of information.* Wright-Patterson Air Force Base, Ohio: Wright Air Development Center. Technical Report 54–160.

Bekesy, G. V. 1961. Pitch sensation and stimulus periodicity. *J. Acoust. Soc. Amer., 33*, 341–348.

Birmingham, H. P., and Taylor, F. V. 1954. *A human engineering approach to the design of man-operated continuous control systems.* Washington, D. C.: U. S. Naval Research Laboratory. NRL Report No. 4333.

Chapanis, A. 1949. How we see: A summary of basic principles. In *Human factors in undersea warfare.* Washington, D. C.: National Research Council, pp. 3–60.

Cobb, P. W., and Moss, F. K. 1928. Four fundamental factors in vision. *Trans. Illum. Engng. Soc., 23*, 496–506.

Craik, K. J. W. 1948. Theory of the human operator in control systems, Part I. *Brit. J. Psychol., 38*, 56–61.

Dunn, H. K., and White, S. D. 1940. Statistical measurements on conversational speech. *J. acoust. Soc. Amer., 11*, 278–288.

Eckenrode, R. T., and Abbot, W. C. 1959. *The response of man to his environment.* Stamford, Conn.: Dunlap and Associates, Inc.

Elkind, J. I. 1956. *Characteristics of simple manual control systems.* Lexington, Mass.: MIT Lincoln Laboratories. Report No. 111.

Elkind, J. I., and Forgie, C. D. 1960. Characteristics of the human operator in simple manual control systems. *IRE Trans. on Automatic Control*, May, 44–55.

Fitts, P. M. 1951. Engineering psychology and equipment design. In S. S. Stevens (ed.), *Handbook of experimental psychology.* New York: Wiley.

Fletcher, H., and Munson, W. A. 1930. Loudness: Its definition, measurement and calculation. *J. acoust. Soc. Amer., 5*, 82–108.

Fletcher, H., and Steinberg, J. C. 1929. Articulation testing methods. *Bell Syst. tech. J., 8*, 806–854.

French, N. R., and Steinberg, J. C. 1947. Factors governing the intelligibility of speech sounds. *J. acoust. Soc. Am., 19*, 90–119.

Goode, H. H., and Machol, R. E. 1957. *System engineering.* New York: McGraw-Hill.

Hawkins, J. E., Jr., and Stevens, S. S. 1950. The masking of pure tones and of speech by white noise. *J. acoust. Soc. Amer., 22*, 6–13.

Hecht, S., and Williams, R. E. 1922. The visibility of monochromatic radiation and the absorption spectrum of visual purple. *J. Gen. Physiol., 5*, 1–34.

Hudgins, C. V., Hawkins, J. E., Karlin, J. E., and Stevens, S. S. 1947. The development of recorded auditory tests for measuring hearing loss for speech. *Laryngoscope, 57*, pp. 57–89.

Javitz, A. E., and staff of Dunlap and Associates, Inc. 1961. Engineering psychology and human factors in design. *Electro-Technology, 5*, 107–130.

Jenkins, W. L. 1951. Somesthesis. In S. S. Stevens (ed.), *Handbook of experimental psychology.* New York: Wiley.

Jordan, N. 1961. *The allocations of functions between man and machines in automated systems.* Santa Monica, Calif.: Rand Corporation. Paper P–2310.

Licklider, J. C. R. 1951. Basic correlates of the auditory stimulus. In S. S. Stevens ed.), *Handbook of experimental psychology.* New York: Wiley.

Licklider, J. C. R. 1946. Effects of amplitude distortion upon the intelligibility of speech. *J. acoust. Soc. Amer., 18,* 429–434.

Licklider, J. C. R., and Miller, G. A. 1951. The perception of speech. In S. S. Stevens (ed.), *Handbook of experimental psychology.* New York: Wiley.

Mandelbaum, J., and Rowland, L. S. 1944. *Central and paracentral visual acuity at different levels of illumination.* Randolph Field, Texas: U. S. Air Force School of Aviation Medicine. Project No. 220, Report No. 1.

McRuer, D. T., and Krendel, E. S. 1957. *Dynamic response of human operators.* Wright-Patterson Air Force Base, Ohio: Wright Air Development Center. Technical Report 56–524.

Miller, G. A., Heise, G., and Lichten, W. 1951. The intelligibility of speech as a function of the context of the test materials. *J. exp. Psychol., 41,* 329–335.

Osterberg, G. 1935. Topography of the layer of rods and cones in the human retina. *Acta Opthalmol.* Suppl. Vol. 61, pp. 1–102.

Pfaffman, C. 1951. Taste and smell. In S. S. Stevens (ed.), *Handbook of experimental psychology.* New York: Wiley.

Riesz, R. R. 1928. Differential intensity sensitivity of the ear for pure tones. *Phys. Rev., 31,* 867–875.

Rosenblith, W. A., and Stevens, K. A. 1953. *Handbook of acoustic noise control. Volume II, Noise and man.* Wright-Patterson Air Force Base, Ohio: Wright Air Development Center. Technical Report 52–204.

Rudmore, H. W., et al. 1944 *Effects of high altitude on the human voice.* Cambridge, Mass.: OSRD Report 3106, Harvard University (PB19820).

Shower, E. G., and Biddulph, R. 1931. Differential pitch sensitivity of the ear. *J. acoust. Soc. Amer., 3,* 275–287.

Sloan, L. S. 1947. Rate of dark adaptation and regional threshold gradient of the dark-adapted eye: Physiological and clinical studies. *Amer. J. Opthal., 30,* 705–719.

Stevens, S. S., and Davis, H. 1938. *Hearing.* New York: Wiley.

Swain, A. D., and Wohl, J. G. 1961. *Factors affecting degree of automation in test and checkout equipment.* Stamford, Conn.: Dunlap and Associates, Inc.

Tanner, W. P., Swets, J. A., and Green, D. M. 1956. *Some general properties of the hearing mechanism.* Ann Arbor, Mich.: Electronic Defense Group, Univ. of Michigan Research Institute. Technical Report No. 30.

Wendt, G. R. 1951. Vestibular functions. In S. S. Stevens (ed.), *Handbook of experimental psychology.* New York: Wiley.

Woodson, W. E. 1954. *Human engineering guide for equipment designers.* Berkeley, Calif.: Univ. of California Press.

Wulfeck, J. W. et al. 1958. *Vision in military aviation.* Wright-Patterson Air Force Base, Ohio: Wright Air Development Center. Technical Report 58–399.

Zeitlin, L. R. 1956. *Frequency discrimination of pure and pulse tones: Part II.* Fort Knox, Ky.: U. S. Army Medical Research Laboratory. Technical Report No. 237.

BEGINNING AT THE DESIGN PHASE OF SYS-tem development, a series of critical decisions is made which have profound effects upon the parts to be played in the system by human operators, as well as upon the effectiveness of their performance. These decisions are based upon a determination of the nature of human tasks required by the system and have an effect upon

the design and configuration of equipment. Psychologists customarily partici-pate in such design decisions, functioning as members of a design team, as consultants to designers, or as independent investigators of a design-relevant problem in human performance. The body of technology which is drawn upon for this effort belongs to the discipline called "human engineering" or "engi-neering psychology."

The principles of design available to the engineering psychologist have their fundamental basis in the psychologist's conceptions of behavior func-tions, as well as in a considerable amount of data on human capacities and limitations. Beyond this, as shown in this chapter, a most productive approach to the design of human tasks has been the identification of *human errors* and the search for means to eliminate them.

The elimination of human error requires first of all that the designer attain a clear conception of the nature of human tasks and the varieties of human functions embodied in them. Armed with this knowledge of what the human operator is "really doing" in interaction with a machine, it is then possible to draw the necessary conclusions concerning what his inputs and outputs should be. These in turn lead to a consideration of those particular features of equipment that link the man and the machine: displays and con-trols. For the engineering psychologist, then, this aspect of design is not simply a matter of "knobs and dials." Instead, it is a question of designing links between the man and the machine which will permit optimal human func-tioning in the kinds of tasks to be performed by the human operator and, at the same time, efficient attainment of system goals by the man-machine combination.

Some examples of what is meant by designing equipment for human use are described and discussed in this chapter, together with some empirically derived principles which pertain to information-processing and decision-mak-ing tasks. These are related to the problem of reducing human error in sys-tems, to some of the probable causes of such error, and to the need for a theory of human performance.

HUMAN TASKS AND
EQUIPMENT DESIGN*
J. S. Kidd

Systems exist to facilitate man's control over his environment, or, expressed in another way, to aid him in achieving an adjustive relationship with his environment. A system is best understood in terms of its intended use: the goals or purposes for which it was contrived. The instrumental aspect of the system in combination with its goal or purpose constitute a process whose primary characteristic is the elimination of a discrepancy between a predetermined, intended state of affairs and an existing state of affairs. When such a discrepancy exists, the system is active; when it has been eliminated, the system is quiescent but retains the potential for action. A system is one of the major means by which man interacts with his environment in accomplishing his purposes.

Psychologists have good reason to be concerned with system development. In the broadest sense, anything that influences man's behavior—his interaction with his environment—is psychologically significant. For the purpose of this chapter, however, the subject-matter coverage may be substantially narrowed. The intent of our discussion is simply how to achieve effectiveness: how can one design and develop complex systems in such a manner that their intended purpose can be achieved most effectively? Since systems are used by and for people, how can our knowledge of human characteristics be introduced into the system design and development effort so as to derive the maximum human benefits?

* The preparation of this chapter was in part supported by Air Force funds under contracts Nos. AF 33(616)–6166 and AF 33(616)–7122. Permission is hereby granted for reproduction in part or whole, by or for agencies of the United States Government.

On grounds of both logic and experience, psychologists have come to believe that they have a distinct contribution to make to what appears to be, fundamentally, an engineering activity. A semi-autonomous discipline, having both scientific and professional components, has been in the process of development during the past 15 to 20 years. It is too young a specialty to have even a reliable nomenclature for itself. It has been called variously engineering psychology, human engineering, human factors, human-factors engineering, ergonomics, and applied experimental psychology—to indicate some of the more popular labels. Whatever the title, however, the goal is coherent and consistent: it is to enhance man's capability by providing him with tools and tasks which are appropriate to system goals and which are commensurate with man's nature—his human capacities and limitations.

Generally speaking, psychologists participate in the equipment design process in two major ways. First, they may function as "experts," perhaps as members of a team of designers, who propose the criteria on the basis of which practical decisions are to be made. When they are operating in this manner, it is apparent that they are engaged in the extrapolation of principles and rules about human performance which have been verified in other contexts under the usual procedures of scientific inference. Their contributions are limited by the range and variety of knowledge obtained in such previous studies which can be brought to bear upon a current problem in design. The fact that such knowledge is limited often sets the stage for a second important function, which is the design and conduct of empirical studies for the purpose of discovering and defining new principles about man-machine relationships. As the problems of system design become better understood in their total sense, the kinds of experimental studies that the psychologist designs likewise become increasingly useful in their yield of generalizable information. The use of concepts like "information," "load," "channel capacity" in modern research on human performance have made possible a significant increase in the application of measurements taken in one task situation to those of another. Many design questions, however, still require the execution of carefully controlled empirical investigations to provide answers that can become the basis of practical system decisions. Finally, looking forward to the time when the application of psychological principles can be made with maximal confidence, the psychologist is concerned with a theory of human action. Presumably, the degree of generalizability of findings regarding man-machine activities would be greatly enhanced by a comprehensive theory of human performance, only the barest outline of which can be said to exist today.

The purpose of the present chapter is fourfold: (1) to define and elaborate some of the relevant psychological principles that enter directly into the system development activity; (2) to provide an operating framework or schema that indicates how these principles can be used; (3) to give some appreciation of how such principles are obtained and how they are validated; and (4) to confirm the application of such principles with some concrete examples of contributions to the system development effort.

▣ THE CHARACTERISTICS OF THE OPERATOR

Systems are operated by people. One must know what people are like if he is to design the system so that it can be used effectively. Much of the relevant detail of human capacities and limitations has been made explicit in a previous chapter (Chapter 4). However, since the point of view of the present chapter differs somewhat, it may be helpful to review some of the most critical points in this section.

Error Analysis and Elimination. A convenient point of reference for discussing human operator characteristics is *error analysis*. In somewhat over-simplified terms, the psychologist's contribution in system engineering is often one of interposing decisions which minimize the opportunity for human error, while maintaining the contributory resources of the human operator. Frequently, the method chosen is merely *simplification:* the elimination of ambiguities. Since simplification is often commensurate with good engineering practice and economy (Chapanis, 1960), there is considerable temptation to limit concern to that aspect. However, as the task itself (as contrasted to the system intended to accomplish the task) becomes intrinsically more complex, it is often not possible to determine in advance what operator action will be "correct" or what will be "incorrect" in any given circumstance. Often the circumstances of activity themselves cannot be anticipated. Thus, it may be possible to do a very adequate job of "human engineering" on an electric range or a telephone handset, because the purpose, circumstances of use, and characteristics of the user population can be relatively well established in advance. In contrast, a motor vehicle perhaps exemplifies a good intermediate case: its operation is inherently more complex, the circumstances of its operation are extremely varied (involving, for example, weather, traffic, roads) and the driver population, if not more varied, at least possesses a far greater range of goals for the use of an automobile than is the case for the use of an electric range.

The most complex systems of all are those used in competitive situations. The environment that includes a competitor or opponent (as in military operations) is likely to contain vicissitudes which are purposefully unpredictable. That is, the intelligent enemy will make the circumstances of system operation as variable and unsettling as possible. In view of this circumstance, it is not surprising that the man-machine systems which seem to attract most attention from behavioral scientists are predominantly of the military type. More to the point, however, is the implication that simplification, as such, is not an adequate answer to the systems engineering problem. One must think beyond mere "idiot-proofing" in order to do a reasonable job in developing man-machine systems which can cope with involved and indeterminate situations. Such a requirement takes us back to the matter of operator characteristics and their effects in the production of error.

Operator Functioning in Systems. In examining the operator for the purpose of identifying those of his characteristics which are germane to system performance effectiveness, the most productive framework appears to be one which involves the specification of the operator's *role* or *function* in the system. While this function varies in detail from system to system, there appear to be some general, normative aspects. By and large, the human being has two interrelated functions in almost any system: he may perform an *information-processing* or "input-interpretive" role, and he may perform a *decision-making* role, in which input integration, synthesis, prediction, comparison, and response selection may comprise the major subelements of action. The emphasis, then, in classical psychological terms, should quite obviously be on perceptual and cognitive mechanisms. Moreover, these mechanisms should be conceived as operating in an interactive context; that is, the operator manipulates the system equipment, and in just as genuine a sense, the equipment manipulates the operator.

As Chapter 2 pointed out, traditional categories of human functioning for the psychologist are sensing, identifying (frequently called perception), and interpreting (cognition), and we continue these same distinctions here. What we need to consider here specifically, however, is some of the particular emphases that system task and job design gives to these human functions in their various modes. What are the questions concerning human functions which the psychologist meets when he faces the problem of designing equipment and tasks to optimize human capabilities? We shall describe these here as related to input mechanisms in identifying and interpreting, to the mechanism of memory, and to response (or output) mechanisms.

Identification Functions

Some of the basic issues involved in a consideration of human capacities in identification functions have been described in the preceding chapter, and we need not review them here. However, one or two matters seem worthy of additional emphasis. First, there is the question of *channel capacity* for identifications associated with various kinds of sensory input. As posed in terms of information theory, the bit-per-second rate is known to be limited (Miller, 1956). Some idea has also been gained of the relative capacity of the various sensory modes, such as vision and audition (Henneman and Long, 1954) and the tactile sense (Geldard, 1960). Not yet known, however, is the extent to which capacity limitation is a function of the sensory apparatus itself or is dependent on central nervous system processes. As we shall see later, the issue of peripheral versus central sensory capacity limitation is the key to certain system design problems. However, it is of interest to note that one can go far in task and system design on the basis of the simple principle that perceptual capacity has distinct and stable upper bounds.

A second area of increasing relevance to system design concerns the phenomenon of attention. Since it is not possible here to review the literature on this topic, it will suffice to point out that interest in attention is currently going through a revival under the heading of *vigilance* research. The problem, stated briefly, is how to insure the attention of an operator to the highly infrequent signals of a monitoring task. At first, this seems to be the opposite of the sensory-capacity problem: the distinction between too much and too little sensory input. However, there is reason to believe that altogether different psychological processes are involved in the two types of task. For vigilance, one of the most promising explanations appears to be a hypothetical inhibition-arousal mechanism, based on the notion that any reiterative repetition of either a stimulus or response raises the detection and elicitation thresholds respectively for all stimuli and all responses (that is, induces a state of somnolence or fatigue). The organism (operator) is either aroused "all over" or, in a sense, encapsulated "all over." This effect appears to depend on the heterogeneity of the stimulus-response pattern; the more heterogeneity, the greater the arousal.

The third question relevant to the identifying function concerns perceptual interference: the detection of signals in noise. Noise is here used in its broadest sense, as a background stimulus which can mask a critical signal, whether the signal be visual, auditory, tactual or some other. The problem of masking of signals by noise has often been studied as a problem in sensing, in which the basic determining factor is the similarity (psychophysical) between the signal and the noise stimuli. However, when the task is one of detection (in the sense of identifying a particular signal), humans have a remarkable capacity for selectivity. Somehow, they are able to do a remarkable job of preventing extraneous material from becoming an interference to the detection task. Often very minute and fractionated cues presented against a heavy background of noise are all that is necessary to enable a person to reconstruct a complex picture. For equipment design, however, the question exists as to how to enhance a man's ability to abstract the signal from the noise components of his stimulus environment; or, secondarily, how to minimize the noise itself.

Interpreting

Given the fact that signals are available to the operator through his sensory channels, what do we know with respect to their meaning to him? Most of the signals in man-machine system operation are symbolic; that is, they have assigned rather than intrinsic meaning. The problem is whether the intended meaning and the understood meaning are the same. A discussion of this question by Campbell (1958) emphasizes the point that the human operator has certain tendencies to distort the meaning of stimuli, or to assign meaning that was not intended. A part of this distortion originates in the process of identification; that is, the tendencies for redintegration, closure, and the like in response to fragmentary or noisy inputs constitute sources of perceptual errors, as suggested by the Gestalt psychologists.

Closely related, yet generally conceived as a cognitive process, is the mechanism of *expectation* or *cognitive set*. People recognize what they expect to recognize. Such expectations can be very general and sustained; they can be established over brief experimental exposure (for example, the Einstellung effect, Luchins, 1942); or they can be imparted symbolically by instructions. Despite man's remarkable capabilities for adaptation or adjustment, there are contrary mechanisms which give both the advantages of continuity and automaticity to certain complex responses (Bahrick and Shelly, 1958) and the disadvantages of rigidity.

There are emotional components involved in the interpretation process also. While "perceptual defense" may be a slightly disreputable concept nowadays (Freeman, 1955), it still appears that our cognitive experiences are influenced by our motives to some extent (Eriksen and Brown, 1956). Thus the individual recognizes, in a meaningful sense, not only what he expects to recognize, but also what he *wants* or *needs* to recognize.

Memory

Probably the most significant aspect of memory for system design considerations, as opposed to system training (compare Chapter 2), is the short-term, or buffer, memory. One can consider this aspect of behavior as possessing a capacity similar to the channel capacity of perception, although we know somewhat more about the buffer storage mechanism. Perhaps the most important factor affecting its operation is *interference*. It seems certain that a simple decay hypothesis is inadequate to account for storage loss in short-term memory; that is, nonretention of intelligible and significant inputs appears due to their displacement in storage by later arriving inputs (Bahrick et al., 1961). The process transpires very rapidly, and small amounts of information are involved. A simple demonstration is provided by an attempt to retain a list of random digits. By the time one has heard the seventh or eighth digit in the series, the second one cannot be remembered. (The first may be remembered, but providing an account of that phenomenon would take us too far afield.) Suffice it to say that a distinct limitation in operator capability exists with respect to short-term memory, but it is one for which realisic compensations can be made in task and equipment design.

Response Factors

When we look at it analytically, it is always somewhat surprising that man can do so many varied things with such a limited effector apparatus. Man is neither particularly strong nor particularly precise in his muscular actions. This, after all, is the *raison d'être* for man-machine systems in the first place—to augment the muscles, as well as the brain, of man.

Two aspects of man's response attributes are worthy of mention. First,

man's most significant response domain is language. It is in this response area
that man's adaptability, flexibility and problem-solution synthesis capabilities
are most apparent. In language, human beings have the widest possible range
of response alternatives. However, the human operator can introduce his
action choices back into the mechanical portion of the system only by overt
manipulation of some control device. This fact differentiates the man-machine
system from many other classes of environments. As things stand at present,
the verbal response mode, while the most ubiquitous and elaborate output of
the human organism, must be translated into other forms of response, such as
turning a dial or flicking a switch, before it is accessible to the machine. This
is not to say that the actions of the human operator cannot be expressed in
verbal form, or that in multiman systems indirect control by verbal means is
not possible. The point to be emphasized is that ultimately the verbal response
must be transformed into physical motion, in order to affect machine elements
in the system.

As stated previously in connection with input capacity, the human operator is conceived as a mechanism with a wide but bounded range of responses.
As a system element, the human operator may be required to utilize only a
small fraction of this response repertory. The speed and accuracy of a prescribed set of such actions may be the critical parameters for human responding. In many systems, the human operator is called upon to choose from a
finite set of possible actions; and in some systems, the operator may be called
upon to develop his own novel responses.

Even in the highly prescribed situation where a minimum number of
response alternatives is relevant, however, the *sequence* of response alterna-
tion is likely to be critical to successful performance. Thus one can usefully
regard human performance as a series of discrete actions. Skilled performance,
particularly as exhibited in such manual skills as steering an automobile, tends
to mask the discrete nature of the responses and their trial-and-error characteristics. The apparent smoothness and rapidity of the behavior suggests both
continuity and stereotopy of response. The performance of even a highly
skilled driver under stressful circumstances, as when he is driving on slippery
pavement, however, re-exposes the basic elements of the process. Under such
conditions the driver's movements become dislocated in sequence as they are
interrupted by needed revisions of the normal series. Thus even seemingly
highly coordinated, continuous behaviors may be seen as a tightly linked set
of discrete response events.

▣ HUMAN FUNCTIONING IN SYSTEM TASKS

The broad categories of human participation in the system have already
been specified: they are predominantly the information-processing and decision-making functions. In a word, in spite of the advances in computer tech-

nology, man is the "brains" of any system. His role may well become progressively more remote from the moment-to-moment operations as computers are developed to take over more of the subordinate functions. But the executive role, especially with respect to the specification of goals, will presumably always be man's prerogative. Computers which can learn, in the sense of being able to adopt new means (a potential but as yet unrealized characteristic), are not expected to be capable of setting their own goals (compare Chapter 3).

For the present, we may safely concern ourselves with attempting a generalized description of some of the most important varieties of information-processing and decision-making functions that are typically allocated as tasks to human operators within systems. The categorization used here is an arbitrary one, and it is not intended to describe complete tasks assigned to human operators.

Information-Processing

Signal Detection and Classification.   Except in the carefully contrived environment of sensory deprivation studies (see Solomon *et al.,* 1957), an individual is under continuous bombardment of stimuli in all the sensory modes. He must separate from this "blooming, buzzing confusion" that which is relevant. He must isolate the "signal" from the "noise." Once the *presence* of a signal is established, the signal must be classified or given meaning. Signal classification is a typical identification task, in which differential responding to different signals is the performance expected. Thus detection is a matter of distinguishing signal versus noise, while classification is a matter of distinguishing among signals.

The sonar operator's task in an antisubmarine warfare system is a good example. The sonar operator looks at a moving oscillograph (paper tape) record. If passive sonar is being used, there is a continuous output from this display. Most of this output is a quasi-random effect from a myriad of non-target sources. Occasionally there are very minute discrepancies in the display output: these are targets, which the operator must distinguish from the background clutter. Then there are subtle differences among such target signals. He can make appropriate responses to indicate that a given target is a surface vessel, a conventional submarine, or an atomic submarine, and sometimes he can make even finer distinctions. System design can either help or hinder his capabilities for handling both the detection and classification functions, particularly by enhancing the distinguishability of the wave forms displayed on the tape.

Recoding.   One of the conceptually rather simple requirements in information processing is that of translation, or *recoding.* The telegrapher who receives in Morse code provides one instance of this kind of task, which requires him simply to recast the dots and dashes into English words. He need not be concerned with the message content, and indeed may not remember what he has translated. Nevertheless, it is apparent that this task is aided by the use of the interpretation function, which provides word meanings and probable word sequences. Codes vary in the degree to which they can be conveniently interpreted: some are quite meaningless in the sense that they are completely arbitrary. Some codes, on the contrary, are constructed on the basis of learned associations already available to the operator. An example of this latter situation is provided by the recent development of a graphic code for use in cathode ray tube displays; symbol forms were selected on the basis of their compatability with existing response tendencies (Howell and Fuchs, 1961). The format of the codes and the degree of the correlation between a signal in one code and a signal in the other are design factors that have obvious implications for performance effectiveness. Many of the findings from the extensive literature on associative learning are relevant to such design considerations.

Accumulating and Summarizing. In some traditions, such as computer technology, transformations of information by accumulation and mathematical manipulations are the essence of information processing. Indeed, such arithmetic and statistical tasks are increasingly allocated to machine rather than to human components. However, it is well to understand the processes involved, since some traces of tasks of this type may remain man's prerogative in even highly automated systems. Moreover, in some systems, such as large-scale business and military organizations, the raw inputs are nonquantitative or only partly quantitative, and therefore may not be susceptible to machine manipulation.

An example of the latter occurrence derives from an analysis of military intelligence systems. Part of the total intelligence picture of a foreign nation would be the attitudes of a populace toward their current regime. Barring elaborate attitude scales, such incoming intelligence data would be highly qualitative. Nevertheless, some summarization would be necessary to make the information ultimately usable. Human operators would need to go through a quasi-statistical operation, from which summary information such as "average" attitudes would emerge.

The general process is further exemplified by the tradition of "briefing." Higher-management levels in an organization or system are kept abreast of the status of subordinate units by presentations of selected items or summaries of activities. The format may have a distinctly statistical flavor by including such things as average productivity rate and accident frequencies.

The system design problems associated with this type of task are predominantly those of allocation. To what extent can and should such operations be automatized? Secondary issues involve the design of sensing and measuring equipment and displays and the establishment of optimal reporting procedures.

Output-Processing. While the examples and terminology employed up to now have emphasized the input side of information-processing in the man-machine system, it should also be remarked that the system itself generates information as well as accepting information from its environment. Some of the signals generated within the system may be conceived of as system-regulatory in character. Such signals are for "internal consumption only" and contribute to the maintenance chores that are a part of every system operation. Other such system-initiated messages make up the output of a particular subsystem, and such material may require processing before emerging from the system as a whole. Classifying, encoding, and accumulating are frequently required. In a ballistic missile launching system, for example, the "output" portion of system operation often appears to contain most of the stress and drama. Actually, since the weapon is not manned and is aimed at a preselected target, the "count-down" is the most dynamic man-machine system contribution. The count-down is essentially an output activity based on inputs gathered over an extended time period. Thus, information processing can in reality be one of the most highly essential components of what appears to be an output operation.

Value Weighting and Destination Routing. The information processor and the decision maker may be, in some man-machine systems, one and the same individual. When they are not, there is usually a transitional process whereby the decision maker, in effect, continues the information-processing function for his own particular ends. Underscoring the continuity between information processing and decision making, there is at least one kind of system task that clearly partakes of both. Once the information is "in the system," it must be acted upon. Although decisions are involved, they pertain to the message, rather than to the environment the message purports to describe.

While closely related to the signal classification task, the activities of weighting and routing deserve particular attention. The two activities of weighting and routing may be called "scheduling" tasks. The operator determines the importance and destination of a message, and by so doing rearranges the sequence of messages in the channel flow. There are many system characteristics that can influence the efficacy of such a function—not the least of which are the clarity of system objectives and the feedback from the user of the messages. For example, a military-equipment maintenance organization might generate a routine flow of reports describing events on the line and in the shops. Parts-supply reports would be routed to a logistics-support agency, while some kinds of malfunction reports would be routed to safety agencies or engineering agencies. Under such circumstances, value weighting would enter into the operation as the discovery of faulty or mislabeled parts. Reporting these to decision makers might be designed to get priority over routine messages because of the potential consequences.

Decision Making

Selection and synthesis.   In performing decision-making tasks, the individual may not treat equally the total output of whatever source of information he has. He may select and reject various of his incoming messages, and he will certainly add his own evaluation to that which has already been done. His criteria may be different and superior to those of the subordinate information processor, since he is likely to have overlapping information from a greater variety of sources. He can thus interpret the content, and include his experience with respect to the consistency and veracity of alternative sources in his assessment. For example, the battlefield commander may well have several subordinate agencies feeding in information with overlapping content. The perspective of these agencies will vary; air reconnaissance will reveal some aspects of the battlefield situation, and ground patrols will give other aspects. Neither perspective alone could yield a "correct" picture. Both may contain incongruities or fragments that fail to make sense in a historical perspective. The commander or his staff must select out the useful from the non-useful and put the useful pieces from various sources together.

Pattern Construction.   Closely related to selection and synthesis is the decision-making task of creating a coherent whole out of discrete fragments. In any very complex system, a picture of the state or condition of the system environment is built up like a complex jigsaw puzzle in which competing pieces fit the same gap, all the pieces are not available, and the picture itself is changing from moment to moment. In the battlefield example just cited, the data received from even a very comprehensive intelligence and reconnaissance effort would be incomplete. The completed image of "what is going on out there" is, then, partly logical, rather than empirical; the gaps are filled by what "makes sense," rather than solely by what is known. In classical psychological terms, this action partakes of *redintegration* on a grand scale.

Cause-and-Effect Attribution.   Once a coherent picture of conditions exist, the human decision maker is forced to assume or determine, as best he can, *why* conditions are as he perceives them; that is to say, he must undertake to classify inputs in terms of their effects, as opposed to their appearances. Let us consider an example. A military command-control system is responsible for the tactical air support of an infantry operation. Some of the environmental factors of concern would be disposition of enemy troops, hit frequency on assigned targets, proportion of secondary targets attacked, proportion hit, and cost of operations. As each bit of data is presented to the commanding officer, he must, as a matter of course, ask and derive a hypothetical answer to the question of why. Only through dealing with or acting upon the cause-and-effect dynamics of its environment can a system function effectively.

Time-Line Analysis and Prediction.   Coordinate with the attribution of cause to observed events is the evaluation of time-contingent processes in the environment of the system. Many phenomena for which either the immediate or ultimate causes cannot be easily determined are time-contingent. Organismic growth or the fluctuations of the stock market are examples. The reason why the changes take place are not known, but it is often possible to predict what they will be, since they have some orderliness against a time base. The decision maker in a man-machine system has both the ability and the necessity to consider time-linked phenomena, and to extrapolate from observable trends in completing his picture of the system's operation.

Critical-Cause Selection.   As the complex picture of conditions approaches completion, there is usually a necessity to compare that picture with that which is desired or required by the avowed goals of the system. In performing in this way, the human being must assess the discrepancy, if any, and focus his attention on the dimensions of that discrepancy, whatever they may be. It is, obviously, the *cause* of the particular discrepancy with which he must contend. Moreover, he must at this stage begin to consider his resources with respect to what needs to be done. More often than not, his resources are not sufficient to do all that is immediately necessary. He must then determine a priority system and decide what is critical for immediate action. In essence, he must determine what factor or limited combination of factors in his task environment *can* be manipulated, given his limited resources; he must next decide which of these potential manipulations will lead most directly to his goal. For example, a military unit commander may decide that an enemy installation atop a given hill is *the* factor retarding his advance. Such factors as his own troops' fatigue, bad weather conditions, and the like may be highly contributory, but they are beyond the decision maker's control or not compatible with goal achievement. He must thus select a critical cause for the allocation of effort.

Action Selection.   It would be a poor system indeed that had but one response for all occasions. Most systems are typified by a multitude of means for each end; the particular means and the extent of its use to be determined by the decision maker's assessment of conditions. Indeed, the most interesting systems are those having what might be called modular or "building-block" means, such that novel combinations or patterns of response can be put together to meet virtually any exigency. The performance of the human decision maker faces its crucial test when he makes his choice of action from among the alternatives, few or many, that he has at hand. A nonmilitary example is provided by an airline manager who must assign various types of aircraft to different routes. With a single aircraft type at its disposal, an airline could not be operated very efficiently. However, in most instances, the decision maker would have some variety of resources for meeting such problems as high-traffic short hauls versus low-traffic short hauls. He might even synthesize a solution by converting some of his aircraft to cargo or mixed cargo-and-passenger carriers.

Effect Evaluation. The loop is closed by the consequential feedback subsequent to action initiation. The decision maker can assess, through the effects wrought by his action upon the system environment, whether his perception of the environment was valid and whether his choice of action was correct. Did the impact of his selected action have the desired effect on the environment? If not, was the direction of effect appropriate but the extent too great or small? Such questions ordinarily cannot be answered in a single cycle of action-reaction, of course. But the process of system operation is a continuous action, providing the opportunity for the decision maker to assess his hypotheses and response predilections and to revise them. Thus, the man-machine system has the potential for continuing development through action.

▣ THE DESIGN OF HUMAN TASKS

Having described some categories of human tasks in systems, we can turn now to their interpretation for system design purposes. We shall attempt to fit the task categories discussed in the previous section into the mold of system design requirements in the realm of task and job definition. Although general rules usually suffer from oversimplification, some degree of simplification nevertheless appears appropriate in this discussion. To this end, we shall consider only the major functional categories of information processing and decision making. From what is known concerning the activities required of human participants in man-machine system operations, as well as of human capabilities and limitations (see Chapter 4), we are now ready to describe the principles that enter into the process of *designing human tasks*.

Design Factors in Information-Processing Tasks

A most important principle relevant to designing tasks involving information processing can be reduced to the short phrase *load constancy and input variability*. By *load* is meant the momentary demands placed upon the operator's limited identification and associated memory capacities. Load needs to be constant, in the statistical sense of not being susceptible to violent fluctuations; it is also intended to imply that the level of load should be "intermediate." When the signal input rate exceeds the perceptual/mnemonic capacity of the operator, not only are the excess signals "lost," in the sense that they are not detected and identified, but they also come to function as additional noise. When this happens, these excess signals act as distractions, and they have the effect of masking residual signals that otherwise would be within capacity limits.

In the opposite case, when the input signal rate is low, loss of vigilance (breakdown of filtering sets) takes place. The behavioral mechanisms which account for these events are subjects of theoretical controversy, but the phenomenon itself is demonstrably valid, and the effect occurs across sensory modalities. Thus, for optimal task design, the rate of signal presentation should be at a steady, intermediate level.

Methods of display of signals—such as their coding and the presence of noise—will be discussed in a subsequent section. However, a general rule concerning the nature of signals is germane to the problem of task design. It would appear that a good case can be made for the desirability of *content variability* of signals. Without content variability, the system is exposed to the possibility of "getting in a rut." There are many anecdotal instances which corroborate this notion. One need only visualize the automobile driver who uses his car only to drive from home to work and back—never anywhere else. Were such an individual to move his residence or place of work after many months of such a practice, his response-error frequency, and the delay occasioned by his equivocation, would seem likely to be higher than they would be had he driven a wider variety of routes under a wider variety of circumstances.

The concept of *habituation* also seems to be relevant to the problem of task design. In fact, it can scarcely be overemphasized that the system, insofar as its human components are concerned, is always in the process of learning. The conditions which are experienced by the human operator on any occasion serve to determine his subsequent reactions, whether this is intended to be so or not. If a single or highly limited range of conditions is displayed and a restricted set of responses is emitted, there will probably be resistance to change, or to the accommodation of new conditions as they arise. In order to insure that a system will be capable of utilizing its full capacity and response repertory when it must, some variety in signal display is essential. This does not necessarily mean that the precise conditions of infrequent events must be artificially introduced into the system inputs. Rather, it means that sufficient variability needs to be included in order that a tendency is maintained by the human operator to "expect the unexpected."

Design Factors in Decision-Making Tasks

For tasks involving decision-making functions, there is a second principle, cast in the same form as the first. It is *goal specificity and means flexibility*. Goal specificity does not mean that the system must have but a single goal, nor does it necessarily imply that multiple goals be altogether compatible. It simply means that the ultimate objectives of the system, the various subgoals, as well as the interrelationships among these, need to be explicitly communicated to the decision maker.

The relationship of means to ends, however, should be left as unspecified and flexible as possible. Of course, the responses available to a decision maker are always limited. They are limited by his own repertory and imagination, by the facilities at his disposal, and often by administrative fiat or organizational directive. The last-named reasons, however, are often the least justifiable.

Our reasoning with regard to decision-making tasks parallels that used to explore the information-processing function in task design. The "what" of a task should be clear (and having a correlative "why" helps); but the "how" should be left as open as possible. The decision maker must have a standard or criterion if he is to function as an adaptive unit, as is implied by the cybernetics or servomechanism model. If the *means* are designed to make optional behavior possible, the consequent flexibility makes provision for such factors as individual differences among operators and unpredictable combinations or patterns of operating conditions.

It will be useful here to describe one example. Experimental studies of human activities in radar air-traffic control have used the general variable of "procedural flexibility" repeatedly. One of the earlier ones in a series devoted to this operation explored the effect of giving operators a set of fixed flight paths to use in guiding aircraft in a blind landing situation, as opposed to a condition in which no fixed paths were available. The hypothesized trade-off centered on the possibility that fixed paths would reduce confusion and help the controller keep track of a heavy traffic load. He was expected to use paths and check points to *organize* the traffic flow. It was discovered, however, that the operator's performance—as reflected by flight delays and by frequency of near misses (midair conflicts)—was relatively poor under these rigidly set conditions (Kinkade and Kidd, 1959a). In the terminology of the operator, he "had no elbow room" to take advantage of exploitable situations. Even in the absence of continuous target identification, the highly structured configuration of an approach path did not help. The means provided were too inflexibly specified.

The main import of these findings was corroborated in a later experiment (Howell, Christy, and Kinkade, 1959). Under normal conditions of operation, maximum freedom of action was facilitative to performance. Under emergency conditions (radar failure), increased specificity of the means of action was useful in providing a substitute for adequate informational inputs. It was in the area of communications, rather than in the decision-making domain, that procedural rigidity resulted in greater effectiveness, even under conditions which were intended to capitalize on the structured aspects of the situation. Other studies in the series provide further substantiation of the main point (Kinkade and Kidd, 1959b; Kidd, 1961).

▣ DESIGNING EQUIPMENT FOR HUMAN USE

Having stated some general principles applicable to the design of human tasks, we can turn our attention to the ways in which design is actually made concrete within the system development process. It is apparent that the human operator, whether functioning as an information processor, a decision maker, or both, occupies a position as a link between two other portions of the system. This means that he (1) responds to the preceding unit's output as his input and (2) by his action provides an input to the next unit. When provided by a machine, the configuration of output events that constitute input to the human operator is generally called a *display*. The physical objects which he operates (particularly with his hands and feet) in order to provide an input to the next unit in the chain are called *controls*. Obviously, the way the human operator must function within the system will be determined by the nature of these displays and controls. Accordingly, considerations of effective design for the man-machine configuration usually result in decisions concerning the physical characteristics of these aspects of equipment.

Display Design

The goal of display design is to provide the operator with usable information germane to his task within the system. One can usually begin with the assumption that the system has at the outset the basic means of acquiring all the information that might conceivably be useful. But once the information is attained, how and in what manner should it be distributed among, and presented to, the human elements of the system? The problems can be defined somewhat more specifically. The variables of interest in the design of displays have been classified in the following ways (Williams, Adelson, and Ritchie, 1956):

1. *Readability, legibility*. Obviously the operator must be able to hear or see or in some other way sense the signals being provided for his use. He must also be able to sense differences among different signals; variables concerning both the display proper and the viewing or sensing environment (for example, illumination) come within this class.

2. *Sensory modality*. The question raised by this category concerns which sensory mode should be employed to convey various kinds of information.

3. *Multiparametric or combined displays*. Here are included questions of what and how many different kinds of information can be incorporated within a single display and how this is to be accomplished most effectively.

4. *Display coding*. This category implies questions as to the language form or the kind of symbols to be employed in presenting information.

5. *Filtering*. Questions of this class concern ways of preselecting information inputs so as to simplify the interpretation task.

6. *Clutter and noise*. Included in this category are problems pertaining to the elimination of false or masking signals in the display.

Let us look now at a specific case or two, in order to gain an idea of the steps involved in dealing with such problems. The caution should be given, however, that the separation of display design, control design, and procedures specification, while useful for purposes of analysis, is actually somewhat artificial. System design, as opposed to component design, stresses the total system and the total compatibility between all system elements. Though these elements may at times be studied in isolation, one should not lose sight of the reintegration that must eventually be accomplished.

Instruments. For several reasons, the most intensively investigated topic within the class of display-design problems has been that of airplane cockpit instruments. During the latter stages of World War II and subsequently, as aircraft continued to become faster, heavier, and more complex, instrument reading errors became less and less tolerable. Since pilots were being trained in large numbers and often being placed in stressful situations with minimal experience, dramatic instances of instrument-reading errors became almost commonplace. The responsible military agencies turned to psychologists to help with solutions to these problems, with the effect that many of the pioneers in engineering psychology were introduced to their eventual specialty through this particular kind of work. A classic example of cockpit instrument evaluation is Grether's (1947) study of altimeters. In that experiment, nine alternative altimeter configurations were compared with respect to both speed and accuracy of reading. Both experienced pilots and inexperienced students were used as subjects. The standard three-pointer circular dial altimeter (which is still widely used) was found to be among the poorest of the display alternatives. A counter, moving tape, or a combination of counter and single-pointer dial were among the best alternatives. The difficulty with the multiple-pointed instrument can probably be accounted for, at least in part, in terms of its demands on the short-term retentive capacity of the operator. With such an instrument, the operator must read one pointer, store that information, read the next pointer, store that information, and finally read the last pointer. Having done this much, he has then assembled the necessary digits of the altitude figure. In addition to this basic difficulty, the operator must not confuse the order of the pointers (the shortest pointer reads in 10,000′ increments, the medium sized pointer in 1000′ increments, and so on) and must be able to interpolate when a pointer rests between two scale graduations. Pointer obfuscation of dial numerals can also contribute to the difficulty of reading this instrument.

Obfuscation of scale marks and the need for interpolation are related by an interesting example of a "trade-off" relationship. If scale units are too close together, obfuscation results; if they are too far apart, readings based on interpolation decline in accuracy. Thus, a graphic plot of reading errors against the size of the space between graduations yields a U-shaped function with a minimum between .05 and .07 inch (Grether and Williams, 1947). Related research on dial reading has also been carried out by Kappauf and Smith (1951) and by Kappauf, Smith, and Bray (1947).

Another interesting aircraft instrument problem centers on the attitude bank and roll indicator. Loucks (1947) reported a carefully executed series of comparative evaluations of various attitude indicators. He used a group of

137 air cadets with an average of 6.5 hours of flight training. A Link Trainer was used to provide the task situation. Loucks found that an arrangement in which the horizon line is fixed and the aircraft symbol moves in the same direction as the roll of the aircraft was reliably superior to the standard instrument, in which the aircraft symbol is fixed and the horizon line is the dynamic element. Measures of the maintenance of level flight by the operator in standard trainer missions were the criteria of performance employed.

Despite this carefully tested finding, the design implications of this study remain somewhat equivocal for two reasons. First, the subject population was composed entirely of novice aviators. Transfer of training on the part of experienced, senior pilot personnel, who were accustomed to the standard instrument, was not measured, but might be expected to be of the negative variety. Second, the task situations as presented by the Link Trainer was greatly simplified relative to actual instrument flying. Although such abstraction often characterizes a sound research approach, the method did not provide a way to assess possible interactions between the varied and complex circumstances of instrument flight and the particular design in question. The study nevertheless remains a classic in its demonstration of a method for approaching such display problems and finding meaningful answers by the use of measures of human performance.

A recent proposal (Fogel, 1959) has been made to combine the features of both instruments. The so-called Kinalog display system shows the aircraft symbol as moving during the first few seconds of a coordinated turn. As the maneuver progresses, the horizon line begins to tip from the horizontal until, at the completion of the maneuver, the aircraft symbol has returned to horizontal and the horizon line is tilted to represent the roll or bank angle. This technique is designed to resolve the transient perceptual conflict experienced by pilots flying blind, when the visual inputs from their instruments and the proprioceptive inputs from the equilibrium sense are incompatible. The dynamics of the Kinalog instrument incorporate a mathematical representation of the typical human operator's adaptation to acceleration sensitivity. At the present time, no empirical validation of the ideas suggested has been made.

The design principles implied by the preceding discussion are fairly obvious: a "systems" approach to display design is essential. Modification of standard configuration is unlikely to be effective if it results in a patchwork array. The needs and values of the ultimate user must be paramount; this means that the boundaries set on what constitutes the "system" of concern should be as wide as possible. An example of the latter approach is provided by efforts on the part of the Air Force and the Navy to design a fully integrated cockpit in which all the advances in display technology can be implemented at one time (Svimonoff, 1958).

Radar Displays.   Let us turn to a second major topic in the display design area: the design of radar and other ground-based system displays. Coming as it did in the early years of World War II, radar provided a novel, fresh, and therefore desirable testing ground for many advancing technologies, including that of applied psychology. In several series of experimental investigations, both the display itself and the viewing environment have been examined, in an attempt to make such devices compatible with human characteristics and task requirements. One relatively recent example of such studies will be described here as an illustration of method employed.

The problem centered on the presentation of altitude information to radar air-traffic control operators. Ordinarily such operators are given the lateral position of the aircraft under radar surveillance through a cathode ray tube display. Since the display face is a flat surface, it provides no direct altitude data. In order to get altitude confirmation, the operator (controller) must query the pilots of each aircraft by voice radio. Voice query and reply are rather time-consuming and generally require five to six seconds at a minimum. Accordingly, it seemed reasonable to propose that a visual display which provided continuous altitude information would enhance the effectiveness of the system.

Such a display was designed and constructed, and then tested in the laboratory in a detailed simulation of the radar approach control operation (Schipper et al., 1957). It was found empirically that little, if any, performance enhancement occurred when the visual display containing altitude information was employed. Since the PPI display and the altitude display were contiguous but separate instruments, it seemed likely that the visual time-sharing load imposed by this arrangement offset the time gained by direct access to the altitude data. Consequently, a series of laboratory experiments was conducted to determine how the display layout could be modified to combine lateral position and altitude information in a single display. Several such formats were evaluated under a number of explicit task requirements. It was observed that a very substantial interaction obtained between the display design characteristics and the various task modes, insofar as speed and accuracy of operator performance were concerned (Kraft, Boyes, and Alluisi, 1959).

It may be noted that these experiments did not yield a single, unequivocal answer to the general question of the absolute utility of the visual display of altitude information. One of their main contributions, aside from the specifics of the test setting, is in suggesting a research approach. But beyond this, their findings reaffirm the caution against arbitrary isolation of system components and task elements in designing displays for human use. In all cases, the results showed optimal design to be dependent on an interaction between equipment, task requirements, and operator characteristics.

Computer Displays. A third example of display design derives from the context of the increasing tendency to employ computer display combinations in complex decision-making tasks. In order to understand the problem faced by the system designer of such a combination, one may consider the job of a corporation vice-president in charge of sales, with his data inputs automatized and the pace of his job accordingly multiplied a hundredfold. A man in this position is faced with the problem of making a number of decisions on the basis of a large amount of information. Some of this information is continuous, some is discrete; some of it is determinate, some is indeterminate or probabalistic at best. For some of the data presented, the evidence is complete, for some the evidence is spotty or sporadic; for some the validity of the data and the veracity of the source is known, and for some the validity is unknown and the sources are of dubious veracity. Imposing automatic data-processing and mechanized display facilities on such an operation is obviously fraught with difficulty—yet similar operations are being automatized in military operations.

The processing and display elements of this kind of system are obviously intended to *simplify* the human's decision-making task. The simplification takes place in the form of both logical and mathematical operations performed by a computer. For example, if our vice-president were faced with assigning a set of new salesmen to various territories, factors such as the differences between the salesmen in ability and personality, the past relations of the firm in the market areas, and the sales potential of each area would have to contribute to his decision. A computer might act on these factors and generate a set of "acceptable" alternatives much fewer in number than the original set of combinations of salesman and territory. The vice-president could then employ yet a different set of criteria (for example, how the salesmen's respective wives feel about their husbands' being out of town for long periods) in making the final choice.

Somehow, the computer display combination has eliminated much of the ambiguity of the original situation. The computer has already made a large number of "formal decisions" in its rejection of the largest portion of the possible alternatives. A question remains, however: is such predigestion of the information-processing and decision-making task compatible with the nature of the problem and the characteristics of the final arbiter, the human decision maker?

Since our problem was hypothetical to begin with, we can dispense with it in summary fashion. Insofar as the data inputs to the system meet certain criteria of scalability and quantifiability, and insofar as there is a *known* pattern of cause and effect relationships, computerization of the problem is possible and, in many instances, advisable. The advantage of using computers, at the present stage of their development, resides in their capacity to do reiterative work rapidly, without error and without complaint. Otherwise, computers are governed by the logic of the *program* and will do only what the program can do (see Chapter 3). When the vital question is asked, "Can the operation be programmed?" what is meant is: "Can the process be accurately reproduced, using a fixed set of rules, logic, and computational operations?" An increasingly frequent possibility of error in system design appears to stem from the fact that human functions which cannot conveniently be programmed may either be simply ignored or grossly distorted by the designer, in order to *make* them fit the criteria for computerization.

Human characteristics relevant to the task provided by a computer display raise other issues. For example, under normal operating conditions, how well does the executive conceptualize and interpret the cause-and-effect relationships of his task that *are* susceptible to formal logic and computational treatment? Can he distinguish between the logical and "intuitional" aspects of his task? What kind of subroutines does he use when faced with such situations? Assuming that he has experienced similar problems in the past and has developed a consistent approach, is it possible that computerization will distort the decision-making context to the extent that the existing approach is invalidated? If so, can the executive be trained, using his past experience as a basis, to make effective use of the predigested materials he gets from the computer display facility? At present, it can only be said that none of these questions has been directly subjected to psychological experimentation, although they appear to be eminently susceptible to that form of evaluation. Equipment design must currently proceed by extrapolation from research findings obtained with different ends in view.

Design of Controls

We now turn to the effector end of systems operations and consider the *controls* by which the decisions for action are actually carried out. Again, we avoid detailed descriptions of human control movements, such as are contained in handbooks (for example, Woodson, 1954), in order to achieve general orientation and widest applicability.

The ruling concepts in control design should be *order, coherence,* and *organization.* Rather than flexibility or changeability, one wants control devices to have the properties of being orderly and consistent in their operation and action consequences. From the standpoint of the human operator, perhaps predictability may be thought of as the most desirable characteristic.

The layout of control panels and consoles is a good place to begin consideration of control design problems. The basic technique for the designer consists in analyzing the task. The task analysis provides a map of what the operator is supposed to do in carrying out his job. Traditionally, the analysis is a description of isolated actions in sequence. For relatively simple tasks (for example, mechanical assembly) the classic *therblig* of industrial engineering is appropriate (Gilbreth, 1911). With increasing operational complexity, as well as the necessity to develop equipment for tasks which are almost entirely novel, newer techniques are needed (see Chapter 6). By whatever means obtained, however, an analytic map of the task is essential.

Just as the system as a whole may be functionally organized according to operations, the control layout can be so organized. Functional grouping, ease of access, differentiability of suboperations, and the like then come into play as criteria for console design. Unfortunately, the criteria are not always (in fact, are rarely) independent of each other. Functional grouping and frequency of use may dictate contrary arrangements.

Missile Guidance. In a hypothetical case of a guided-missile system, an operator might have three main suboperations in the control guidance of a single weapon. These could be prelaunch checkout, flight control, and arming control. Let us say that the operator spends six tenths of his time in prelaunch checkout, three tenths of his time in flight control, and one tenth of his time on adjusting the warhead. Each of these main operations might be equally complex in terms of the total number of discrete suboperations involved. It is conceivable, however, that one of the arming control suboperations (for example, proximity-fuse adjustment) might take up almost all the total fraction of time devoted to that main operation. Proximity-fuse adjustment might even be the one single most frequent action in the entire task. How, then, should the control panel be arranged? Should the main suboperation of prelaunch checkout be given a priority position because all its suboperations add up to the biggest block of time? Or should arming control be given precedence because one of its suboperations is the most frequent of all? Then again, the flight control operation might require the most delicate and exacting control settings and thus be a suitable candidate for maximum accessibility. Obviously, with so many factors to consider, any given system may require some very insightful analysis or, in many instances, specific empirical comparisons of alternative configurations. When the rules of functional arrangement are freely applicable without internal contradiction, they have every appearance of consisting entirely of simple common sense. Indeed, such is the case. The specialist in human design factors makes his contribution, whether it be by means of an analytic or an empirical study, when the straightforward application of rules *cannot* be accomplished.

Principles of Control Design. Certain principles of control design have by now attained the status of familiar and frequently employed rules of thumb. Although some of these rules have been implicit in the preceding discussion, they need to be stated here in more complete form:

1. *Accessibility.* All control should be accessible to the operator without requiring that he contort himself or otherwise take an awkward stance or position.

2. *Functional arrangement.* This principle contains several parts, as follows:

    a. Controls should be grouped according to logical and easily comprehensible categories.

    b. The categories should be based on the system or subsystem goal structure (that is, on the operations such as fueling, guidance, arming); not on the action called for (such as switch setting, vernier adjustment, rate control).

    c. Priority in location should be given to controls which require the most frequent use.

    d. Priority in location should be given to those controls which require the greatest deftness of action or which are the most difficult to handle.

    e. Critical controls—those having a "life-death" effect on the success of the operation—should be prominently placed.

3. *Differentiability.* Controls should be arranged so that their differentiability is enhanced by their location. The purpose of the control should be apparent by its location, physical characteristics, color, mode of use, and the like. The coding and cue-enhancement logic should be consistent for a given station. (Ideally, coding would be made consistent across systems to facilitate operator training and transfer of skills.)

4. *Safety.* Provision should be made to prevent the accidental (nonintentional) activation of any control. Critical controls should be covered or protected under lids, and provision should be made for locking some types of controls.

5. *Reliability.* Controls should, when possible, signal their state. As an example, the "on-off" positions for a switch should be clearly marked. The mode of action correlated with direction of turn should be clearly indicated on all knob controls. Mnemonic cues should be included when feasible, in such a way that desired-setting or last-setting data are available in proximity to the control device.

6. *Display compatibility.* In the total configuration of displays and controls making up the operator station, display control arrangement should be correlative; that is, controls governing the process being displayed should be in proximity to their related display. Display format and content should be dimensionally similar to control location and direction of action.

As our previous discussion has suggested, it is often not possible to follow all these rules with equal vigor. The design of controls and control layouts is, of course, a matter of practical compromise, as is true of other aspects of equipment design. Nevertheless, this set of principles represents the factors that are based on empirical findings of studies of human functioning, which can successfully be brought to bear on design decision having the aim of optimal system effectiveness.

▣ REDUCING HUMAN ERROR

On the whole, our discussion of design problems has been carried out in the context of human functioning, and particularly in consideration of the ways of eliminating the kinds of functioning that result in error. The analysis of possibilities of operator error leads to the conclusion that its causes may often be identified as deficiencies in equipment design, whether of displays, controls, or the expected interactions between these two types of elements. The information obtained from such analyses is exhibited in summary form in Table 5.1. It will be noted that many of these difficulties provide the possibility of correction by means of equipment design (for example, unclear code form), whereas others would appear to be avoidable by the provision of external instructions, possibly by means of job aids (for example, inappropriate filtering set). In still other instances, it appears that corrective action would take the form of training to be undertaken after the equipment configuration has been determined (for example, action-control relationships not understood by the operator).

Table 5.1

Typical Human Errors in Equipment Operation and Their Possible Causal Factors

Type of Error	Possible Causal Factors

Failure to detect signal	Input overload
	  a. Too many significant signals
	  b. Too many separate input channels
	Input underload
	  a. Too little variety of signals
	  b. Too few signals
	Adverse noise conditions
	  a. Poor contrast
	  b. High intensity of distraction stimuli

Incorrect identification of signal	Code form or typology unclear Lack of differential cues Inappropriate filtering set (expectation) Conflicting cues Conflicting identification requirements
Incorrect value-weighting or priority assignment	Nonlinear predictions required Multiple or complex value-scaling required Values poorly defined or understood Contingencies vaguely defined

Error in action selection	Matching of actual and required patterns faulty
	Consequence of courses of action not understood
	Appropriate action not available
	Correct action inhibited
	  a. Cost considerations
	  b. Procedural prohibitions

Error of commission	Correct tool or control not available Action-control relationship not understood by operator Action feedback unavailable or delayed

It seems evident from the table that there are a number of ways of preventing, minimizing, or reducing the deleterious effects of operator mistakes, when one recognizes that such errors may be understood as matters of inadequate functioning of human information-processing and decision-making activities. In many cases, the avoidance of faulty human functioning can be specifically related to the design of equipment displays and controls, and particularly to the extent to which they define sensible human tasks. If one looks beyond these "rules of thumb," he can foresee the possibility of a systematic theory of human performance, for which currently acceptable categories of human functioning provide only the bare framework.

REFERENCES

Bahrick, H., Kidd, J. S., MacDonald, B., and Schumacher, A. W. 1962   Short term retention and interference effects. *J. exp. Psychol.*

Bahrick, H. P., and Shelly, C. 1958.   Time sharing as an index of automatization. *J. exp. Psychol., 56,* 288–293.

Campbell, D. T. 1958.   Systematic error on the part of human links in communication systems. *Information and Control, 1,* 334–369.

Chapanis, A. 1960.   *On some relations between human engineering, operations research and systems engineering.* Baltimore: Johns Hopkins University, May. Report No. 8.

Eriksen, C. W., and Brown, C. T. 1956.   An experimental and theoretical analysis of perceptual defense. *J. abnorm. & soc. Psychol., 52,* 224–230.

Fogel, L. J. 1959.   A new concept: The Kinalog display system. *Hum. Factors, 2,* 30–37.

Freeman, J. T. 1955.   Set versus perceptual defense: A confirmation. *J. abnorm. & soc. Psychol., 51,* 710–712.

Geldard, F. A. 1960.   Some neglected possibilities of communication. *Science, 131,* 1583–1588.

Gilbreth, F. B. 1911.   *Motion study.* New York: Van Nostrand.

Grether, W. F. 1947.   *The effect of variations in indicator design upon speed and accuracy of altitude readings.* Wright-Patterson Air Force Base, Ohio: Air Materiel Command. Report TSEAA 694–14.

Grether, W. F., and Williams, A. C. 1947.   Speed and accuracy of dial readings as a function of dial diameter and angular separation of scale divisions. In P. M. Fitts (ed.), *Psychological research on equipment design.* Washington, D. C.: Army Air Forces Aviation Psychology Program Research Reports, 101–109. Report No. 19.

Henneman, R. H., and Long, E. R. 1954.   *A comparison of the visual and auditory senses as channels for data presentation.* Wright-Patterson Air Force Base, Ohio: Wright Air Development Center. Technical Report 54–363.

Howell, W. C., Christy, R. T., and Kinkade, R. G. 1959.   *System performance following radar failure in a simulated air traffic control situation.* Wright-Patterson Air Force Base, Ohio: Wright Air Development Center. Technical Report 59–573.

Howell, W. C., and Fuchs, A. 1961.   *The study of graphic language.* Griffis Air Force Base, N. Y.: Rome Air Development Center. Technical Report 61–76.

Kappauf, W. E., and Smith, W. M. 1951. A preliminary experiment on the effect of dial graduation and size on the speed and accuracy of dial reading. *Annals of the New York Academy of Sciences, 51.*

Kappauf, W. E., Smith, W. M., and Bray, C. W. 1947. *A methodological study of dial reading.* Princeton, N. J.: Princeton University, Department of Psychology. Report No. 3.

Kidd, J. S. 1962. *Some sources of load and constraints on operator performance in a simulated radar air traffic control task.* Wright-Patterson Air Force Base, Ohio: Wright Air Development Center.

Kinkade, R. G., and Kidd, J. S. 1959. *The effect of different proportions of monitored elements on operator performance in a simulated air traffic control system.* Wright-Patterson Air Force Base, Ohio: Wright Air Development Center. Technical Report 59–169.

Kinkade, R. G., and Kidd, J. S. 1959. *The effect of procedural variations in the use of target identification and airborne position information equipment on the performance of a simulated radar approach control system.* Wright-Patterson Air Force Base, Ohio: Wright Air Development Center. Technical Report 58–629.

Kraft, C. L., Boyes, F., and Alluisi, E. 1959. A comparison of six grossly different methods of presenting altitude information in ATC systems. In J. S. Kidd (ed.), *Research on human engineering aspects of air traffic control.* Columbus, Ohio: Ohio State Research Foundation. Final Report, AF Project 7184.

Loucks, R. B. 1947. An experimental evaluation of the interpretability of various types of aircraft altitude indicators. In P. M. Fitts (ed.), *Psychological research on equipment design.* Washington, D. C.: Army Air Forces Aviation Psychology Program Research Reports, 111–135. Report No. 19.

Luchins, A. S. 1942. Mechanization in problem solving: The effect of Einstellung. *Psychol. Monogr., 54,* No. 248.

Miller, G. A. 1956. The magical number seven, plus or minus two: Some limits on our capacity to process information. *Psychol. Rev., 63,* 81–97.

Schipper, L. M., Kidd, J. S., Shelly, M., and Smode, A. F. 1957. *Terminal system effectiveness as a function of the method used by controllers to obtain altitude information.* Wright-Patterson Air Force Base, Ohio: Wright Air Development Center. Technical Report No. 57.

Solomon, P., Liederman, P. H., Mendelson, J., and Wexler, D. 1957. Sensory deprivation: A review. *Am. J. Psychol., 114,* 357-363.

Sviminoff, C. 1958. *Air Force integrated flight instrument panel.* Wright-Patterson Air Force Base, Ohio: Wright Air Development Center. Technical Report 58–431.

Williams, A. C., Jr., Adelson, M., and Ritchie, N. 1956. *A program of human engineering research on the design of aircraft instrument displays and controls.* Wright-Patterson Air Force Base, Ohio: Wright Air Development Center. Technical Report 56–526.

Woodson, W. E. 1954. *Human engineering guide for equipment designers.* Berkeley, Calif.: University of California Press.

THE PROCESS OF SYSTEM DESIGN IS RE-
flected in two sets of specifications: one for equipment,
and another equally important set which describes
human tasks. Just as the former descriptions guide the
development of equipment components, the latter constitute the basic reference for all of the actions that
determine the capabilities of the human components of

the system. *Task descriptions* are the statements of those events which constitute the interactions of men with machines and with their system environments, including other men. They are, of course, continually revised and
refined as system development proceeds. They are necessary in order that
system developers can provide themselves with answers to continually recur-
ring questions about what functions men are performing in any part of projected system operations. In addition, they form the point of origin of most,
if not all, the procedures used in developing the "man" part of the system,
the personnel subsystem.

Once it is known what men will do in the system, it is evident that the
system psychologist will then be required to determine what human capabilities are necessary. He therefore undertakes a *task analysis*. By this is meant
that he makes inferences, based upon knowledge of the nature of human
functioning, concerning what kinds of abilities, skills, and knowledges are
required in order for a human being to carry out the specified tasks. The
results of task analysis provide the means for decisions about those individual
qualities which can be selected, the kinds of performances which can be
supported by job aids, and a firm basis for the design of individual and team
training programs. In addition, they provide immediate definitions of the
various human performances required, and suggest the measures which will
have to be applied to these performances in the assessment of human capabilities.

It is apparent that the technologies of task description and analysis have
been markedly advanced in technique and objectivity since these have
occurred within the framework of system development. In fact, the contrast
between these techniques and traditional "job analysis," with its unsystematic
procedures and poorly defined terminology, is quite striking. The techniques
described in this chapter have been remarkably successful, on the whole, in
forecasting human performances required by newly developed systems,
together with the human capabilities that need to be selected, trained, and
supported on the job. At the same time, the gaps in scientific knowledge about
human behavior are all the more pointedly apparent when these techniques
are applied to systems development. Chief among these, as the chapter makes
clear, are first, knowledge about dimensions of human functions, and second,
how these dimensions are affected by the process of human learning as it
operates in training programs and on the job.

TASK DESCRIPTION
AND ANALYSIS

Robert B. Miller

The process of system development generates many kinds of descriptions—of system purposes and limitations, of hardware characteristics, of schedules and costs, of techniques and operating procedures. None of these descriptions is so intimately connected with the development of the "man" portion of a man-machine system as is the set of documents which contain *task descriptions:* these are the specific statements of all the interactions of man with machine and of man with the system environment. Task descriptions are developed on the basis of the decisions which determine the assignment of functions to man and to machine, and which therefore influence both hardware operations and human tasks within the system. Once developed, task descriptions serve as a basic reference for all later designs and plans for the personnel subsystem. One of their initial uses is for the purpose of *task analysis*, a process whose results provide data about human functions, which in turn are used to determine the characteristics of job aids, training programs, and the assessment of performance of the system and its components.

In this chapter, we shall first describe these purposes of task description and analysis and indicate their relation to the process of system development. Following this, we shall discuss the general rationale for task description within the framework of system development. Then we turn our attention to the nature of task description, the categories of operation with which it deals, and the language it employs. Finally, we shall deal with the topic of task analysis and the behavioral structure of tasks. Here we shall be particularly concerned with the kinds of questions which this technological enterprise raises for psychological science.

187

▣ PURPOSES OF TASK DESCRIPTION

It is important to differentiate heuristic description from scientific description of a set of events. A scientific description generally seeks to describe a set of events with variables which are mutually exclusive and have fixed, usually quantitative, relationships to each other. The volts, ohms, and amperes of electricity are examples, as are the variables of distance, time, and mass in mechanics. In contrast, although heuristic descriptions may aspire to the rigorous characteristics of scientific description, they may be satisfied with much less. A sufficient criterion for a heuristic description is that it aids a job or class of jobs to get done.

Task analysis at present is a heuristic description of activities at the functional interface of the human operator and the objects and environments with which he interacts. As such, its value is proportional to its utility and economy in the design, evaluation, and operation of systems. We must hope that fundamental research may eventually provide us with a descriptive system for behavior which can provide the factors and measurement operations for an equation of all input-output relationships of potential interest in man-machine systems. This hope may, however, contain a paradox. One of the major uses for the human in systems is as an improviser, to meet contingencies the nature of which can be anticipated only in part, and these imperfect anticipations of system activities make for imperfect specifications of human input-output requirements. Nevertheless, it is a properly pious hope, not only that science will be reduced to practice, but that on occasion that practice will be reduced to science.

Having now dispensed with illusions that task descriptions may have to meet the canons of scientific rigor, let us examine the purposes which in fact do provide canons of utility for behavior description.

Support for the System Design Enterprise

The act of design consists of identifying functions and activities to be accomplished and of inventing or selecting mechanisms for accomplishing these functions and activities (Flagle, Huggins, and Roy, 1960). The progress of functions and mechanisms is a two-way affair. A function such as "signal amplification" calls for a mechanism. The introduction of this mechanism calls, in turn, for the function of maintenance, perhaps of a special kind. Fulfilling the maintenance function may in turn call for mechanisms to be selected from those available or invented or adapted for special purposes.

It is particularly desirable during the formative stages of system design for the descriptions of functions, activities, and mechanisms to be fluid on the one hand, so as not to curtail the free flow of ideas, but on the other hand to be capable of being reduced to denotative detail when necessary. Design constructions and decisions are made in the following contexts (Miller, 1954).

Human Engineering. Conventionally, human engineering has been associated with the design of the displays and controls with which the human and the machine plus their environment interact. The description of at least a tentative arrangement of displays and controls being used by the human for the purposes intended may suggest modifications and improvements of a general or specific nature. Since the construction of tryout hardware is often expensive and inevitably time-consuming, descriptions on paper may be prepared and used as rough "simulations" of actual configurations and events. In some kinds of tracking tasks (steering, guiding, aiming, and others) the nature of the human control function can be quantified and equations prepared. What is known about human "transfer functions" (see Chapter 4) can then be applied to the design of displays, controls, and their dynamic interactions, for the tracking tasks. Only rarely, however, does a human's job consist only of a straightforward and predictable tracking activity. In fact, machines are doing this kind of task more effectively every year as there are improvements in the engineering art.

The identification of human activities permits many questions to be asked about the proposed design. "What will happen if . . . ?" is the kind of question. Attempts to answer this question in terms of a particular design configuration may lead to additions, changes, refinements. Some of these changes may be made in the procedure whereby a task is performed, rather than in displays or controls. The description of the procedure for performing a task is itself a task description if the display and control objects, and their indications and actions, are included.

Task description, of course, must be only tentative until the human engineering of the task environment has been frozen. At that time, the human requirements are relatively fixed if the environmental conditions with which the man-machine entity must cope have been thoroughly designated.

Job Design. In a large system the question inevitably arises as to what tasks will be done by whom. This is the question of job design: the best organization of human tasks into the job requirements of individuals. This patterning will be dictated in part by exigencies of time and space: the same man cannot be in two places at the same time. But within these exigencies, there may be options that will tend to optimize selection, training, turnover, stand-by, vulnerability, and other factors of operational and economic significance in the system enterprise. Task descriptions provide input information for patterning tasks into job design.

Selection. The proper source of information leading to selection procedures for personnel is description of the behavioral requirements. Selection may then be based on already-established abilities, or on estimates of amount of transfer from previously learned tasks to the subject task; or the selection methods may have to be based on inferences and tests of aptitudes for learning the tasks. An adequate task description may not only provide precision in selection methods, but also avoid downright irrelevance due to semantic vagueness. For example, a superficial description of a job might lead to the requirement of "numerical ability," which in selection testing could be interpreted as ability to perform mathematical operations in which background in calculus and algebra seems suited, although in actuality the task might call for no more than the ability to quickly memorize six to ten digits and recall them while performing other operations—an ability required, for example, in a long-distance telephone operator. Task descriptions provide reference information for reducing such ambiguity.

Training. Task descriptions certainly provide the substance for the content of training; in addition, they may suggest the form and sequencing of training. They reference the operations to be used in evaluating both the training and the trainee.

Objectification of Performance Criteria

Since the task description is virtually a statement of human performance requirements, the description serves as a statement of the task criterion. As such it is a fundamental reference for personnel and system actions and decisions, and for evaluation and prediction of personnel in the system context. By being explicit, it may have the advantages of a contract in stating: if Human X does all the things listed according to the conditions spelled out, *and nothing more,* he is doing his job (or task) acceptably. This should put the proper burden of responsibility on the system designer and his representatives: the human-factors engineers and the writer of specifications for the humans. These specifications are the task descriptions; they are also performance criteria.

Actually, this account describes only an ideal state of affairs, and in fact, responsibility for design and operation of a system is generally as changeable as the shape of Proteus. From a realistic point of view, it is impossible to anticipate all contingencies to which a system and its components (including humans) may be exposed in operations. Nevertheless, the task description should provide at least the variables in the population of operational events which should be sampled (representatively, it is to be hoped) for presentation to the human component in testing him, as well as a thorough set of output characteristics to measure and relate to test inputs.

The advantage of a good task description is that it is analytic and may thus permit subsamples and subtests to be prepared for testing purposes, with a consequent gain in exhaustiveness of sampling and efficiency in testing. Some of these features will be explained more fully later.

Common Reference for the Personnel Subsystem

The personnel subsystem may be considered to consist of all the design and operating decisions and activities that are associated with the human component in the system. These have already been individually identified in this chapter. They consist of the design of the man-machine-environment inter-face (human engineering), procedure design, design of job aids, task and job design, selection, training, exercising, and evaluating. (Other factors—such as incentive structures, supervisory and monitoring features, job promotion, personnel rotation, supply of new personnel—are tentatively excluded from this discussion. See Chapter 7.) Definitive statements of task and position requirements in the form of task descriptions provide a common, explicit reference from which design and operational decisions can be made with some hope of consistency. That is, selection, training, and evaluation may be made consistent with each other if they are based on a single set of performance objectives anchored in system operation.

System development and operation is frequently a vast and often a sprawling enterprise. There are many offices, agencies, departments, and services that add their bits and pieces to the construction and ongoing activity of a system. Coordination is practically impossible without common references which are made public to all participants. Coordination is made possible by documents which specify system requirements and, by explicit implication, the requirements of its components—including, of course, the human com-ponents—in terms of specific performances.

▣ THE RELATION OF SYSTEM DESIGN TO TASK DESCRIPTION

Design is not a rigorous process except at certain stages. It is true that each design decision puts constraints on what further decisions can and must be made for a workable and economically feasible system or system com-ponent. But a new concept for a mechanism or process may be invented or a new discovery made in a natural phenomenon—or old principles may be used in a new mechanism.

It is important to have some idea about what the design process con-sists of, in order to recognize that the design of the personnel subsystem is also an inventive process. Inventions, of course, may be effective or ineffective, efficient or inefficient, in performing their intended functions. There is ample reason to believe that practices in the design of personnel subsystems is cur-rently limited in effectiveness and certainly in efficiency as a means for per-sonnel subsystem design. This is partly true because the nature of it *as a subsystem* is generally not recognized.

In subsequent sections, we shall consider why task descriptions are important to the design of the personnel subsystem. We shall also see, perhaps idealistically, a picture of its formal requirements. The reader is reminded that at present task description is not a rigorous procedure with a rigorous set of terms and definitions. Actually, it now consists of not much more than a general, conceptual format: the substance of this concept is that the "re-quirements" for any mechanism can be specified by a description of what its work responses should be to the stimuli presented to it. The challenge of a classification structure for behavior in what we now loosely call "tasks" remains before psychologists. The reader is invited to consider this challenge and the many-faceted utility of even partial solutions.

Implicit in the concept of design is innovation. Innovation may extend to the perception and organization of patterns of functional "requirements" for a system or component, to devices and to operational procedures. The fundamental value consideration in choosing a design option is some ratio of performance to cost of the mechanism chosen. But "performance" of the mechanism may have to be measured by a variety of criteria, many of them incompatible with each other (such as speed and accuracy), and costs may have to be measured in a variety of ways not entirely compatible with each other (such as long-term versus short-term costs).

Design therefore rarely proceeds by formula, although features of it may seem to become "programmable." Changes in engineering technology, while opening new possibilities, also create new problems. Changes in the technology of behavior (such as may result from improved training techniques) also change the pattern of decision options.

Heuristics is a way of coping inventively or improvisationally with unique events, requirements and combinations of ignorance and knowledge. The "heuristic man" says: "I will do the best I can under the circumstances with what I have, and try to improve as I go along." In this sense—and applied to the context of system design—task description and analysis is heuristic rather than rigorous. This is likely to be true, although perhaps to a lesser degree, even if we had a task taxonomy constructed along the ideal lines proposed in later paragraphs. Each man-machine-environment interface in new systems is likely to pose unique problems. Providing a good answer (the "best" answer is best only among known and tested design alternatives) will require new thinking, originality, imagination, inventiveness. To the extent that old methods of description of behavior raise barriers to inventive thinking, any standard rubrics should be used tentatively.

The concept of "inventing" behavior and behavior settings may seem strange to the laboratory and classroom-trained psychologist. Nevertheless, this is precisely what the systems designer has responsibility for doing, unless he is running some comparative studies on design alternatives which someone else has already thought up.

Decision Structure in the Personnel Subsystem

The development of a design entity may be thought of as a network of interrelated decisions (Miller, 1954). Each decision may be characterized by a number of response options. For example, there are decisions as to the extent to which a particular man-machine system function should be automated, or the extent to which to train a complex human behavior requirement by extensive rote training for each combination of operational circumstances or to train by problem-solving technique and general concepts and principles. This decision is also related to a decision in selection, since training to operate by principle, as opposed to rote recall, may require a difference in kind or degree of some abilities as opposed to others.

At present there is no systematic pattern of subsystem design decisions laid out in explicit form. Personnel design decisions are generally intuitive, segmented, and local. This procedure permits organizational and administrative flexibility but also evasion of direct responsibility for feedback: if failures and difficulties arise, each administrator may point to the person next in line as the culprit. The resulting inadequacies tend to prohibit growth in capability of the entire design operation.

Still considering an idealized state of affairs, a proper behavioral taxonomy could help to make explicit the structure of alternatives in personnel subsystem design. This could increase and make articulate communications and choices in design operations and later in system monitoring. Design decisions and terms used in classifying behavior requirements would have direct interplay. The facts are that this ideal state of affairs is very far from being realized, and no formal route that will lead to it has been publicly charted. The student of system design may perceive the challenge to conceptualization in breadth and depth in this problem area. The nature of this problem is an example of the difference between conventional problems consisting of a dependent variable with a few independent variables and the "systems type" problem.

Description through Terms in a Task Taxonomy

Let us now briefly examine the nature of an ideal method for identifying and describing tasks or behaviors that comprise tasks. It is ideal in that it is standardized, efficient, directly teachable, reliable with respect to different observers, and requiring minimum interpretation in coordinating and directing action in each facet of the personnel subsystem.

A taxonomy differs from a mere glossary of terms. Terms used in a taxonomy are formally related to each other by explicit principles of inclusion and exclusion. The terms are systematically related to each other. They are also related to each other by concepts about the operations denoted by the terms. In biology, the taxonomic terms "photosynthesis" and "carbon synthesis" provide descriptive and analytic means of differentiating life forms. Note how much more significant these terms are than "animal life" and "plant life": they point to a major basis for relating and applying knowledge as well as making an observation and test of differences between "plants" and "animals." Note also that these terms need not be mutually exclusive with respect to an organism in order to be highly useful. There is some evidence, for example, that some viruses may live by some combination of photosynthesis and carbon reduction.

For purposes of behavior description, we would ideally have a set of categories that would permit any kind of stimulus-response relationships which could be found in tasks of any kind to be readily identified and labeled. Certainly the total set of these terms should be exhaustive to the extent that any kind of behavior requirement can be specified by one or a combination of terms in the taxonomy. Mutual exclusiveness of terms may be, from an operational standpoint, a vainly sought objective for a taxonomy.

In addition to simplicity in attaching categorical labels to features of behavioral events (or behavioral requirements), each term in an ideal taxonomy would point to design operations for efficiently controlling the behavioral phenomena denoted by the term. Let us for example, assume that the term "visual scanning" appeared as a term in the taxonomy. Having this term in the ideal taxonomy would imply that there would be a body of knowledge about selection factors relating to this behavior; and also that there would be a body of knowledge on efficient and effective training and evaluative devices, operations, and sequences of operations particularly appropriate to "visual scanning." In a taxonomic sense, the term "visual scanning" might have further value in that it should point to relevant subcategorizations such as "scanning through visual noise" where a subbranch of knowledge could be brought to bear on human engineering, training, and so forth.

It can now be seen that an ideal behavior taxonomy would, on the one hand, permit the use of terms to identify and label behavioral events and, on the other hand, point to a body of design knowledge about the effective development, control, measurement and prediction of the behavior in systems contexts. Since there are some developments along the line of a selection taxonomy, the need might be greater for the development of a taxonomic structure for particular use in training and transfer of training. The classification rubrics would permit determining similarities and differences among tasks used for research in the learning literature. On these grounds one could ascertain the task conditions under which the given research findings were applicable and not applicable. The glossary of terms of the behavior taxonomy would thus become the relevant index for determining applicable research findings and principles for training.

Presumably, a taxonomy would also provide guidance to researchers for setting up and describing their experimental studies. The scientific advantage of a taxonomy of this kind for the development and interpretation of research data should be obvious.

A few researchers are currently becoming interested in this problem. It is likely to defy conventional approaches which subject small range samplings of data to intricate statistical meshes and which disregard the criterion of utility of the taxonomy for training and human-engineering decisions. It is, in fact, likely that a breakthrough of some kind in research technology may be required in order to move effectively toward a task taxonomy, just as a new research technology is perceived as a necessity for the development of a systems theory and systems taxonomy.

The reader has now been exposed to the challenge for the future in task description and task analysis. Let us forthwith return to the limping practices of the present.

▣ SYSTEM OPERATIONS AND TASK DESCRIPTION

The description of human tasks in a system has a fundamental relation to the purposes for which the system is designed in the first place. Just as these system goals lead to the statement of hardware characteristics, to an equivalent degree they determine the characteristics of the personnel who interact in various ways with this hardware. The description of human tasks must therefore be carried out within the context of the major categories of functions associated with the expected operation of the system.

There are obviously various levels at which the description of the total operations of a system may be stated. As one progresses from the general to the more specific identification of system functions, he comes progressively closer to the level at which individual man-machine interactions can profitably be described. Generally speaking, this point is reached at what we shall call the *subsystem level,* in which one or more human individuals are engaged in the performance of some distinguishable portion of the system's purposes, a portion which could conceivably be observed as a separate entity.

Let us consider, for example, the levels of operational description which might be applied to a strategic missile system.

Level 1. At this level one can distinguish the broad categories of functions which are necessary to insure that the system will fulfill the purposes for which it has been designed. These categories, a sample of which is shown in Figure 6.1, are traditional even to the formation of organizational charts and assignment of responsibilities. *Administration* is the name given to the activities which govern the flow of information and decisions from one part of a system to another, and between a given system and other systems. *Operations* is the branch of system activities specialized for carrying out the primary missions for which the system was designed. It is a mistake to think, however, that operations in this specific sense is synonymous with total system functioning; instead, such operations are merely part of the story when viewed at this level. *Maintenance* refers to the prevention and repair of any form of hardware malfunction. Although treated as a distinct function, it should be integrated during the design conceptualization with system operations, since the time lost on account of maintenance often penalizes the mission effectiveness of a system, or may jeopardize it altogether. *Logistics* deals with the problem of supply and demand of materials within the system. The problems of inventory, procurement, and transportation may be more significant to system success, at least in the long run, than many refinements in design for operations and maintenance.

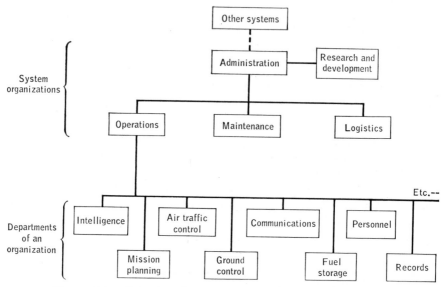

Figure 6.1.   Example of organization and department structure in systems.

Level 2.   So far, the kinds of system functions described may be applied to almost any system, regardless of its purpose. The next level of specificity of description, however, brings us again to the purposes of a strategic missile system. Each of the general categories of Level 1 can now be seen to have a number of subordinate goals in fulfilling the mission. For example, *Operations* might include such functions as *range safety, fuel storage, missile preparation,* and *missile launch.* Such categories might be called *departments,* and it will be recognized that they can be distinguished for each of the categories of Level 1 (see Figure 6.1). However, the description of human tasks can seldom if ever begin at this level, since the variety and number of people and equipment involved are too great.

Level 3.   If one now considers a particular department of operation, such as missile preparation, it will be apparent that this can be divided into a number of subcategories such as engine checkout, guidance system preparation, and so on. In other words, one has now arrived at the *subsystem level,* in which human individuals or teams interact with equipment in a manner which makes possible the identification of a unified, subordinate function which contributes to the total operation of the system. It is at this level that one can begin to describe the specific interactions among men and machines that constitute *task descriptions.* It is essential to note, however, that such task descriptions are made with full cognizance of the ways in which they contribute to the system's goals, as these are conceived at the progressively more general levels of description which we have just identified.

The Difference Between Task Description and Task Analysis

A task description may best be understood as a statement of *requirements*. Although the operations of producing a good task description may be substantially aided by a task analysis, we can differentiate between the objectives of a requirements statement and an analysis statement.

Task description specifies along a time scale the cues which the human should perceive in the task environment and the related responses which the human should make in his task environment. For example: *"Must* run one mile in ten minutes on straight, level, and smooth concrete roadway, with no wind blowing on a sunny day at 70° F., carrying 30-pound load in addition to wearing 2 pounds of summer clothing and 2½ pounds of normal GI boots." The word "must" establishes this statement as a job or task "requirement." The statement seems extraordinarily complete.

A *task analysis* of load-carrying tasks would quickly reveal that the above statement is indeed lacking a most critical factor: a description of the load. Will it be strapped to and supported on the back or carried in the arms? What is its bulk? Its contour and center of gravity? Must it be carried only in one position? Clearly it is a different requirement to run with a bucket filled to the brim with 30 pounds of corrosive liquid acid than with the same 30 pounds composed of nuts and bolts in a padded knapsack on a shoulder harness.

It is possible for a task description to be complete simply by denoting and enumerating all the circumstances in the stimuli and responses that can occur in the operational settings in which tasks may have to be performed. Where this is realistic, it is indeed the direct way to establish completeness. But in many cases, this would result in huge volumes of documents of description. Some analysis of the behavioral aspects of the task will tend to direct the task description to more detail about the behaviorally important variables, and less detail about variables less critical to successful performance of the task. A behavioral understanding (that is, an *analysis*) of the task requirements when viewed in both their physical and psychological settings will therefore aid the preparation of task-requirements description in several ways. It will point out what should be described in detail and what does not need detailed identification and description for use in the personnel subsystem. Thus there will be completeness of description without undue length. These are the values that a psychological understanding of the task to be described can bring to the physical description of the task requirements.

This issue is more than academic. It has been widely proposed that the preparation of task-requirements descriptions can be performed by laymen, more or less as a clerical activity. This is a dangerous part-truth. It is as if a layman in engineering were to undertake the performance specifications of an electronic component to fit between two electronic interfaces.

With these warnings in mind, we can now proceed to the superficially simple mechanics of task description as such. We will go into task analysis in

further depth a little later. For the time being, the description of task requirements is a description of what has to be accomplished in physical terms.

The Mechanics of Task Description

Task descriptions can be made at any stage of the development of the
man-machine interface. They can begin as early as the conceptualization of
this interface, and they can be done from blueprints on drawing boards, and
later from nonfunctional and functional mock-ups. In each of these cases the
definition of system requirements (input conditions and output responses)
must also be available. And, of course, the fewer the details available about
the physical cues shown and the physical responses required to them, the less
the detail in the description. The most detailed and obviously the most valid
description of requirements can be obtained from the task actually being
performed by sample humans in operational settings. On the other hand, the
earlier in system development task information can be generated, the more
valuable it is likely to be for system design and timely design of the personnel
subsystem.

Like the progressive development of architectural drawings for a new
building, task description most sensibly proceeds from general "blocking out"
statements to specifics and details. The following is a summary of steps that
can be followed in task description procedures. (Compare Miller, 1953b.)

General Statement of Job and Task Functions.   The general functions
(input-output relationships) assigned to the human component(s) will probably have been specified at least loosely by the system designers during their
layout of what the general functions of the system are to be. They will also
have determined what classes of components (including humans) will perform
them. Thus, electronics maintenance consists of the general duties (another
term for "function") of inspection and checking for in- versus out-of-tolerance
indications; troubleshooting; replacing; and repairing down to the replaceable
entity in the machine.

Another way of getting a bird's-eye view of position requirements is to
get a dozen or more terms that describe the sequence of major events in a
"typical" mission or job cycle. Thus, in the operation of vehicles we generally have:

Briefing: the statement of purpose, destination and routings for the mission.
Inspection of the vehicle.
Start and warm-up.
Guiding the vehicle on route to destination.
   Guiding vehicle through traffic.
   Navigation: the proper identification and choice of route indicators.
Entering into "homing pattern."

Debarking.

Unloading.

Debriefing, completion of records.

Each of these activities may be called a *segment* in the mission or job cycle. A simple version of mission segments is shown in Figure 6.2.

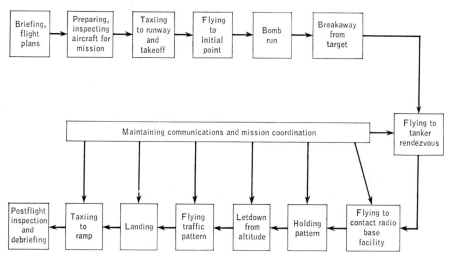

Figure 6.2.   Position segments in a "typical" mission. (Note that a variety of contingencies should qualify each box.)

The major *environmental conditions* affecting a mission cycle, or segments of it, should then be identified. Will the vehicle be operated at night as well as by daylight, in rain or snow as well as in dry conditions, in fog as well as in clear weather? If it is a surface vehicle, will it be driven over rough terrain as well as smooth? What varieties of cargo will require special treatment, and of what kind? This may also be a good time to determine the tightest tolerances which will beset successful task performance: the narrowest and lowest apertures through which the vehicle will have to be guided forward or backward, the tightest curves to be negotiated (also forward and backward). Will operation be required through mud, over ice, through shallow water?

Other *contingencies* should be identified. Besides those arising from the environment, such as a few suggested above, the malfunctions which may occur must be identified, and it must be determined whether the operator is to cope with them or not. (The methods for coping with them should be deferred until the details are put into the picture.) Contingencies which may be critical to mission success should, of course, come high on the list. Tire blowouts on the road, brake failure, steering failure are examples of contingencies in the operation of surface vehicles.

Besides environmental contingencies and those arising from machine malfunction, there are those brought about by *human error*. Any mechanism which can operate can also malfunction—whether it is a machine or a man. At a later stage in task analysis, more careful thought may be given to situations likely to lead to error; and information obtained about what provisions the human has for detecting his errors and what means will be available to him for correcting errors or their consequences.

The analogues of the factors which guide the preparation of a general statement of position requirements as outlined above may be applied to any job ranging from cobbler to president of a corporation. The sum of these statements should provide a fairly good bird's-eye view of the job. In many cases a flow chart of "mission" segments may be drawn, major contingencies labeled where appropriate, and time-shared activities indicated by placement of boxes along the time baseline. (Time-shared activities are those performed at about the same time, and which have overlap in cues that must be searched for, remembered, put with other information, and acted upon when proper.) With such a general picture of the total pattern of tasks prepared, details may be added to any part without loss of perspective because of preoccupation with those details. It is particularly important to identify contingencies (environmental, machine malfunction, human error) because these often do demand the highest level of skill and, at the same time, may put the success of the system in greatest jeopardy.

Some Task Varieties. A task is a group of activities that often occur in temporal proximity (but not necessarily so) with the same displays and controls, and that have a common purpose. A task is a fairly arbitrarily bounded set of activities—a rigorous operational definition cannot (and therefore should not) be sought. It is a heuristic term. The general job-cycle statement guides the selecting and relating of tasks for more detailed description.

Tasks may be broadly classified into *discrete* and *continuous*. A discrete (or discontinuous) task is one in which stimulus-response behaviors can be marked off into readily differentiated separate steps. On the other hand, the general example of a continuous task is that of tracking a moving object such as gun aiming, steering a vehicle, and keeping a continuously changing target position on a scope centered or matched with a controllable cursor.

Discrete tasks are of several varieties. One is called standard routine: the same series of steps is always followed in the same order. A nonstandard routine may consist of a group of steps *not* always followed in the same order. In either kind of routine, the procedure is fixed and specified by step. Nonroutinized tasks are generally problem-solving in nature. General procedures and strategies (principles) may be provided, but the human must also perform some logical operations or calculations with the data available to him before he is able to make an appropriate response.

There are two general varieties of tracking task. One is that of aiming or getting coincidence of a cursor and target. In general the objective is to aim at the center of the target, or at least some point which may be thought of as target center. The device may be either what is called "pursuit" (aiming a gun at a flying duck) or "compensatory" (keeping a target airplane in a center ring on a radar scope). A second general type of tracking task is that of steering vehicles through apertures—for example, guiding a car on a roadway and through traffic. In either case, both target and cursor may be moving or one of them may be stationary. Somewhat different behavioral principles may operate in each of these classes and subclasses of continuous tasks.

Obviously there will be examples in which the above distinctions between continuous and discontinuous tasks will be blurred. After altitude and course has been reached in flying an aircraft, many adjustments are procedural, even though events are changing continuously.

Detailed Task Description. Let us assume that a general job cycle statement is available to guide the identification of tasks, task clusters, and their relationships. The next step is to describe the specific behaviors within the tasks. In time-critical tasks (and are there any that are not?), reaction and performance times for stimulus and response should be marked along a time baseline.

The first step is to specify the cue or cues, and their context, that tells the human that the task is to be performed. Then each *task activity* consists of the following:

An indicator on which the activity-relevant indication appears.
The indication or cue which calls for a response.
The control object to be activated.
The activation or manipulation to be made.
The indication of response adequacy, or feedback.

An *indicator* may be any object that provides the activity cue. It may be an aircraft instrument or it may be a piece of paper on which a message is written; it may be the windshield through which one sees to drive. The indication, in its broadest sense, is some out-of-tolerance signal which calls for a work response—the difference between a present condition and a goal condition or information that establishes that difference. The *indication* may appear all at once, or it may have to be assembled by the human by recall through periods of time.

The *control object* may be a telephone, steering wheel, or another human. *Activation* is any motor response necessary and sufficient which satisfies the demand of the indication and the response requirement to it.

Indication of response adequacy may be *proximal,* as by the feel of a switch when it is moved into a detent, or *distal,* as when one hears the motor starting up. In many routinized tasks, the feedback from one step or activity is the indication for the next step.

The simplest concept of a behavioral step assimilates several of these categories and consists of

Indication (stimulus) → Activation (response) → Feedback

In order to get a proper picture of task complexity, two additional kinds of information should be provided. One is the kind of disturbance and irrelevance (perceptual noise) which can make the indication difficult to detect and identify. The other is the number of activities—overt or covert—which the human must be performing at about the same time in one or more tasks. Describing the task of a big-game hunter would be incomplete if one did not specify that the detection and identification of the tracks of the prey will be confused by other tracks, grasses, and stones; and that if the hunter is not continuously scanning his environment to assure himself that *he* is not the hunted, there is severe risk of "mission failure." Generally speaking, the level of detail for specifying task activities is about that used in a good manual of instructions to a novice. In fact, one of the uses of a good task description is precisely that of a procedural manual for the job. Figure 6.3 shows an example of task description of routinized activities.

The preparation of good task descriptions calls for imagination, an insatiable ability to ask questions, and an unflagging determination to get (or figure out) the answers. It is easy to be content with identifying "normal operating conditions" and not think—or take the trouble to find out—about the contingencies. It is easy to be overwhelmed by details and ignore the possibility that a delicate manipulation may have to be performed under time stress in bombardment or in severe aerial turbulence or while wearing protective gloves. It is very easy to accept precedent in the new performance of various tasks (such as troubleshooting, for example, which is generally done in a haphazard, bungling fashion), rather than get to the roots of the information-handling operation and expose these for the guidance of training method.

▣ TASK ANALYSIS AND THE BEHAVIORAL STRUCTURE OF TASKS

The task requirements description, as has been pointed out, provides the basic reference for the design and development of the personnel subsystem. It is the basis, one step removed, for decisions leading to the design of selection and classification procedures, training, and evaluation. The step from task analysis to specifications for selection and training cannot be made directly. Instead, the psychologist must first engage in a process of systematic analysis of the behavioral implications posed by the statement of physical task requirements. In some cases, these behavioral implications may point to deficiencies that must be remedied in the task requirements description by

JOB ELEMENT FORM					
Position	Line mechanic -- Radar system				
Duty	1. Adjust system			Date 5 May 19	

TASK	TIME minutes		ELEMENTS			REMARKS Alternatives and/or precautions
	In seq.	Out seq.	CONTROL	ACTIVITY	INDICATION (Include when to do task and frequency of task)	
1.1 Adjust radar receiver	40	40		→	Adjust every 25 hours of a/c time. See a/c log.	
			1.1.1 POWER ON Button	Press	Inverter starts and makes audible hum, pilot light comes on, range indicator lights come on, tiltmeter pointer comes on scale.	Avoid starting system with covers removed from high voltage units: personal hazard
			1.1.2 AC voltage adjustment (screwdriver)	Turn	AC voltmeter aligns to 117±4 volts.	
			1.1.3 POS regulated voltage adjustment (screwdriver)	Turn	POS regulated voltage meter indicates 300±5 volts.	
			1.1.4 BRIGHT control knob	Turn clockwise	Sweep trace becomes visible on CRT.	
			1.1.5 FOCUS control knob	Turn as required	Sweep trace becomes sharper (focused).	

Figure 6.3. Sample of detailed task description.

obtaining more information. This systematic study of the behavioral require-ments of tasks is called *task analysis*.

A task description of a typist-keypunch operator may include the state-ment: "Must be able to read messages in a variety of handwritings." The task analysis statement attached to this description might read: "The operator must be able to distinguish between those parts of a message in which she can fill in unrecognizable characters from context and those parts of the message in which she cannot depend on context but must go back to the source of the message for interpretation. Both the ability to interpret from message context and deciding when context is not to be trusted require judgment—that is, intelligence of at least average or above. Errors introduced into the system at this point will be difficult to correct in system operation, and can have catas-trophic consequences if not detected and corrected."

Let us use another example. The task description reads in part: "Operator must back vehicle into areas with no more than 18 feet clearance on top and sides." The analysis might read: "This requires absolute identifications of size required for the vehicle, and the vehicle may be loaded in different ways at different times, so that the operator must be able to memorize these different dimensions. Operator will not have complete visibility of aperture into which he is backing, since rear of vehicle cuts off view. Operator must therefore properly gauge size of aperture before backing into it, and then use cues available only on the driver's side of the vehicle for properly steering while backing. *Differences in illumination* will modify nature of cues available, hence of *aperture judgment* and of *steering*. Task when performed under time pressure and fear of discovery by the enemy may generate constant errors in judgment and steering, which need to be investigated empirically under different conditions of illumination." The major points of psychological interest are in italics. The particular significance to selection and training of the phrase "identification of absolute size," as opposed to, say, "sensing of size differences" will be evident.

A task analysis document will tend to provide information parallel to that on the task requirements description. Both could form parts of the same document, which might be divided into right- and left-hand sides. Both kinds of information, the physically descriptive and the behaviorally analytic, may be generated by the same effort—and in fact, this is likely to be an ideal arrangement, for reasons to be cited later.

The source information to the task analyst is task requirements information plus all that is known and much that is conjectured in the full area of experimental psychology. This is a tall order and invites much randomness. The behavior structure of tasks is offered as a guide for organizing a way of looking at tasks and task information that is compatible with a way of organizing knowledge in experimental psychology according to task settings. This task structure may also be regarded as an intuitive first pass at a task taxonomy at a very general level.

If the term "task" is made to apply to a group of activities sufficiently extended and complex, that are all surely related to a system goal, we can generally find a common structure. If we disregard the specific stimulus-response content of a large, randomly selected group of tasks, we will find that tasks differ from each other mainly in the relative weighting of the factors in this common structure. Except for some additions, the reader will notice substantial similarity to the classification scheme proposed in Chapter 2; these parallels are intentional.

Goal Orientation and Set

A task is never initiated in a psychological vacuum. There are a number of features about the psychological task setting which have rather obvious importance. The first of these is the clarity with which the human operator has in mind a set of goal conditions: how thoroughly he knows what is expected of him in operational terms. There are some tasks in which a major (but often concealed) requirement is to discover a proper set of goal conditions. In some respects, this requirement characterizes the inventive situation.

Where there may be more than one human interacting in a coordinative fashion, there may be some occasional uncertainty as to what functions should be performed by each. This ambiguity may under some circumstances lead to inefficiency; in others, it may provide that flexibility which permits teamwork through improvised work arrangements.

Another factor in the task setting is the motivational context in which it occurs. Is the atmosphere "do or die," or is it "business as usual"? Is the emphasis in performance on speed or on accuracy? Where there are multiple criteria of goodness in task performance, which have priority and under what conditions? What is the operator's concept (or what should it be) as to the relationship of what he does to subsystem and system performance? Where are his attitudinal identifications as to competition and cooperation?

Finally, what context of stimulus events indicates to him that the task must be done, and that it is time to initiate its performance?

These various conditions may be allowed to develop spontaneously in the operator, or some control over them may be undertaken through indoctrination and training. It should be obvious that unless the operator has a clear picture of proper goal conditions, he is in a poor position to profit from feedback information—either during training or in operations—about his performance in a way that will aid him toward improvement. The task analyst should have reference to criteria of system performance in order to ascertain, directly or through inference, conditions that should initiate a task and the task goals relevant to those conditions. These goals should ideally, of course, be specified in quantitative terms, and include acceptable tolerance ranges, for the variables that enter the task picture. Where possible, relative priorities in task output should be determined in the form of policy and criticality to success of the system's mission.

Reception of Task Information

It is of critical importance to identify various requirements associated with the reception and interpretation of task-relevant stimuli. Naiveté about "the task stimulus" is both common and disastrous among run-of-the-mill task analysts, except in the relatively narrow problem area of target tracking on a scope. Because of this common deficiency, considerable attention will be given here to problems of identifying task inputs.

Search and Scan.   Both early and late in learning to perform tasks, it is frequently a practical necessity to search out relevant task cues. This is true in vigilance tasks, such as that of lookout. It is also true in many types of combat condition, where the operator must not only attend to some ongoing set of activities, but must also scan his general environment for surprise attack from unexpected quarters. The maintenance technician learns to look at an engine and note secondary cues such as frayed or loose wires, burnt terminals, fuzz or dust on relay terminals, or bolt heads that have been worn from frequent removals. The reconnaissance man—whether looking at natural terrain, a radarscope, or various kinds of map—develops practices of selective searching out of cues. The competent driver occasionally looks at his dashboard instruments to be assured that all is well. Where these scanning responses require the operator to deviate from a strong primary attention to ongoing tasks, this requirement needs special recognition, so that proper attention can be given to it at various stages of training. Human-engineering modifications of the work station may be suggested. The issue may also influence selection of operators. The description of the search-and-scan requirements is obviously incomplete unless the context of concomitant task activities is also identified.

The search activity in reference here differs psychologically—or at least operationally—from the kind of search which accompanies serial decision making, such as in troubleshooting. In this latter case, the *interpretation* of one cue leads to a locus of search for the next task-relevant cue. But in the case at hand, search and scan are literally a sensory enquiry of a work environment that, to the scanner, may be neutral or not, depending on the presence or absence of a task-relevant cue.

Identification.   This consists in perceiving a pattern of cues in such a way as to permit it to be named by the perceiver or reacted to by some other particular response. The name may be a class name (enemy soldier) or it may be a specific name (Joe Jones). The cues perceived may consist of objects, symbols, attributes or values of attributes, activities, or conditions. The value of an attribute would consist of, say, a speedometer reading of 50 miles per hour. Identification of an activity might consist of the recognition that the driver ahead is decelerating.

The cues that make up an identification may be together or they may be separated in time and space. Other conditions being equal, the more they are separated, the more difficult the identification may be. This is especially true if parts of a pattern must be perceived through periods of time, and especially when this time is interspersed with irrelevant cues and other activities. When the identification acquires this kind of complexity, it may be difficult to distinguish identification from *interpretation,* which may enter to guide search in filling out a cue pattern.

Verbal listing may be the first of the various kinds of identification required by an operator in a task. But since words are often inadequate surrogates for physical cues, diagrams and other visual (or sensory) representations should be prepared in order to guide selection and training. One should remember to include the conditions that should lead to the identification of contingencies by the operator, and these in turn should include identification of the operator's errors. It is also important to identify the class characteristics of noise and disturbances which will interfere with identifications during operating conditions.

Noise Filtering.   A signal is information which leads to the selection of a response. In a sense, it "throws a selector switch" (but let us not go too far with this analogy to human processes). Noise consists of information which either incorrectly throws the response switch or obscures the "true and proper" signal when it occurs and prevents the throwing of the selector switch. Or it may result in the wrong response being selected.

Much training of the human consists of his learning how to filter these disturbances in his task environment. Noise may be environmentally produced, as in the case of rain on the windshield, glare of lights at night, static in radio, radar, or television. Noise may arise from the sensing equipment itself, as through electronic artifacts or malfunctions. And noise may arise from within the human himself, as when he is distracted, is motivated by other activities, or "projects" incorrect hypotheses about the cues presented to him.

Stimuli irrelevant to the task at hand, therefore, are potential noise. There are some qualifications, however. Studies in perception of radar returns have shown that *small* amounts of relatively homogeneous background noise actually improve detection and identification of target information. We recall that studies have shown that sensory deprivation (people kept in the dark under constant water pressure for hours and days) leads to complete disorientation, confusion, and hallucination. Studies in the area of attention and rapid recognition also support the idea that some kind of sustained stimulus (change of energies in the stimulus field) facilitates perception, apparently by maintaining alertness. Speaking physiologically, this is like keeping a neuron's threshold low by a low level energy input not quite adequate for firing it. In any event, the problem here is not so much the elimination of noise as the identifying of it and preparing to train for task performance under various conditions of disturbance and irrelevance.

The complexity of noise signals tends to baffle the descriptive powers of the communications engineer in electronics. Because of the much greater complexity of the response mechanism in the human, the description of perceptual noise is virtually impossible. Noise that affects human tasks must therefore be coded by class names and denoted by specific examples of the noise phenomena in task contexts. There seems some reason to hope that the human ability to read through environmental noise has some degree of generalization within a class of responses. Telegraphic code is an example of what is meant here by "class of response." Another response class would be radar returns on PPI (Plan Position Indicator) scopes. Still another would be the human voice speaking a language well-known to the listener.

Retention of Task Information

There are two classes of retained information in human tasks. *Short-term retention* is like buffer storage in a communications or data processing system. It is information peculiar to a single (task) cycle of operation which must be retained for seconds, minutes, or even hours, so that it can be combined with other information and used at the proper time to effect appropriate response. *Long-term retention,* on the other hand, is like a set of instructions that is "programmed" into the computer and is valid over any and all cycles of the task in operations. There is reason to believe that there is at least some psychological discontinuity between short-term retention as here defined and long-term retention.

Short-term Retention. This factor has sometimes been confused with "memory span," but this is far too restricted a context for our purposes in task description. The waiter's feat in memorizing the order of several patrons while they are speaking and later serving each with the dish he ordered, is an example of short-term retention. So is the motorist's effort in trying to negotiate a route just described to him by a passerby. The player's recollection of the designation and position of each card played in a hand of bridge is another example.

Skill in virtually all human activities includes some special classes of short-term retention. The typist learns to read a phrase or a line ahead of her fingers; the motorist memorizes the configuration of traffic around him while maneuvering through a busy street; the administrator retains information about half a dozen variables each about several people being considered for a promotion. By whatever means this ability comes about in a given task context, there seems clear evidence of improvement by the learner, from "novice" to "old pro."

Far less seems known about the acquisition, retention, and transfer of abilities in short-term retention than its importance to behavioral economy suggests. It seems clear that a significant factor in skill at decision making is the range and precision of short-term memory.

It is difficult to classify kinds of short-term memory with any hope of utility. The task analyst must therefore depend on being fairly specific in tabulating the kinds and amount of short-term information which must be retained in task cycles and job cycles. He should also try to spot "confusion-likely" situations that may arise in task contexts.

Long-term Retention. Long-term retention includes the identification, nomenclature, and background knowledge for interpretations of perceptual information. The present context of this chapter, however, focuses on the retention of procedures. A procedure may be retained in one or a combination of several forms. It may be retained as a set of verbalizations, more or less in the form of sentences. The first few lessons in starting an airplane would consist of memorizing verbal rules. In order to put the verbal rule or statement into practice, the operator must be able to identify the task stimulus from its verbal surrogate and must be able to generalize and perform the task response from the verbal surrogate of that response.

Tasks may also be performed by recall of general knowledge and concepts and by making deductive inferences from them. This is generally the case in "problem-solving" activities, of which troubleshooting with limited job aids is an example. Activity is guided by strategy (general rules) rather than by specific rules applicable to individual stimulus-and-response identities.

With sufficient repetitive practice, the symbolic mediators between environmental stimulus and overt response will tend to drop out from performance. Such non-mediated performance can conveniently be called "automatized response." Automatization is likely always to be a matter of degree. Larger and larger clumps of stimulus-response members may be performed without mediators, although the clump may be initiated by a symbolic activity. In highly skilled performance, this symbolic initiator may be little more than the concept of a particular goal state. When we decide to get a drink of water in our own home, the concept of getting it may initiate a train of "automatic" responses in rising, walking, selecting a glass, turning on the faucet, and running water into the glass.

These distinctions among the ways in which stimulus-response associations are encoded in long-term retention have more than academic significance. If activities are to be time-shared, then it is clear that some of them must be to some degree automatized. One cannot think of the words in two sentences at the same time; nevertheless, one can drive a car and converse at the same time. If the range of contingencies which can beset a mechanism or a task environment is very large, it may be more efficient to teach by general concept rather than by specific procedures for each contingency. By acquiring a concept of the sequence of events in the mechanisms of an aircraft engine, it becomes somewhat possible to *deduce* what to do in a variety of situations. The operator recalls cause and effect in the action linkages.

But where high reliability of behavior is required, and it is feasible to do so, a straight listing of procedures which can be performed with or without the aid of a check list may be the most effective method of instruction with the goal of learning a verbally mediated set of operations. This may also produce a flexibility somewhere midway between the stimulus-bound behavior in automated response and the uncertainty of deduced response.

Where high reliability of infrequently practiced tasks may be required—such as is the case in a large range of potential emergency conditions—some of all three classes of S-R encoding may be attempted. This would provide "associative redundancy," a variety of recall routes and mnemonics which, taken together, would tend to increase probability of recall of the correct mode of response to the unusual circumstances.

Here is a situation in which the task analyst, by specifying modes of response, clearly points to the need for getting more information about "the system" than is necessarily given by the bald task requirements. He is suggesting not only what must be done but, behaviorally, how it is to be done. His knowledge about the task should put him in a better position to exercise these insights than personnel people down the line who might receive only "task requirements" information. He must remember that the task analyst must frequently anticipate many of the circumstances of task behavior, rather than observe them. He is working during relatively early stages in the design of the total system, perhaps even before hardware is completed, and generally before it is fully operational.

A method of describing a procedure has been previously outlined (see page 201), applicable to routinized procedures. Where a procedure has a large variety of conditions and alternatives ("subroutines," in computer language) it may be desirable to consider treating the task as a problem-solving task.

It should be clear from the discussion on long-term retention that the description of task requirements should take into account not only what must be retained by the operator, but the conditions which may prevail at the time that recall is required. Reports and observations have shown in a large variety of jobs and tasks in the operational world that the incumbents were seriously deficient in verbalizing and performing the procedures both central and peripheral to their responsibilities.

Memory for Codes. A special but important form of long-term memory applies to human coding and decoding operations. These operations consist of a direct translation of symbols into other symbols in a one-to-one relationship, where speed and accuracy are indicators of skill. Typing is an example of translating written or typed messages into typescript through manual outputs. In this case, the output symbols may be individually identical to the input symbols, but the arrangement of the symbols on the source document may differ from the arrangement on the output document. This is likely to be true in tabular layout of numerical data. Keypunchers on tabulating and data-processing equipment perform similar tasks. The telegraph operator literally translates from one code (alphabetic and numeric characters) into another (Morse) when he is sending, and again, in reverse, when he is receiving telegraphic code.

The description of task requirements should include some specifications on the range and characteristics of the set-up procedures and formats for the translation of symbols on source documents to output documents or messages. Many errors in keypunching data onto punched cards are attributable to inadequate skills of the operator in shifting from one "field" (or category) of data to another. When practical, a large number of representative *patterns* of symbols should be provided for training purposes. Words and phrases are patterns of alphabetic symbols, for example, and the highly skilled operator tends to apprehend symbols in such patterns and "emits" them as patterns. Apprehending information in patterns has the value of redundancy ("meaningfulness"), hence greater reliability, in perceiving the message (as well as the symbols) and in translating the message. Even numeric data that ordinarily are more nearly like "nonsense" symbols and symbol patterns may acquire some degree of context, and both human engineering and training should capitalize on such contexts. Needless to say, severe requirements of speed and skill in shifting rapidly from one format to another require several levels of "automatization" between the stimulus code terms presented to the operator and the emitting of the responses of translation. This automatization will certainly be necessary where the operator must exercise a higher order of attention on the data he is transmitting, as when he has to deal with the *meaning* of the symbols as well as with their translation. Tasks required of some air-traffic control jobs require this dual type of performance. Human engineers are aware of some of the dangers that arise in task combinations that require continuous automatic responses by the operator as well as his vigilance and "thinking." It seems quite possible that training can have its content and organization directed at least toward "face validity" in such dual skills. The vast increase and proliferation of data processing will call for increasing numbers of individuals with these skills.

Interpretation and Problem Solving

Interpretation requires bringing some context of information to bear in addition to what is directly presented at the moment to the senses. In this context, the information immediately presented to the senses consists of "symbols" from which the interpretation (meaning) is established. Thus the visual shapes of the word C A T and an open switch before an onrushing train are both symbols. The problem of the task analyst is to specify that "context of information" which the operator should have which will be necessary and at least sufficient for the operator in establishing the meaning or interpretation.

But the "meanings" of any sign are practically infinite. Which one will be chosen? This is indeed a critical question. The answer is direct. The information context that the operator should have in his head (or otherwise directly available) is that which will enable him to select or contrive *the course of action* essential to his assigned task responsibility when he is presented with the sign (or symbol) and sign context. If we bear in mind that task performance implies goal-directed activity, then, in its rawest terms, the *relevant* meaning of a stimulus consists of the responses or response classes permitted and required of task performance (compare Chapter 2).

For example, a railroad yardman should probably perceive an open switch in front of an oncoming train with the following "meaning": "Close the switch immediately," or "Stop the train immediately," or "Reroute the train immediately," whichever is most practicable at the time. If none of these primary task responses is practicable, another "meaning" may come into play: "There will be a train wreck, hence injuries." This raises another response option: "Call out the ambulances."

Notice that if the open switch were interpreted only as "train wreck," the response *directly linked* to this interpretation would be the calling out of the ambulances. True, the possibility of the train wreck would establish motivation to take some avertive action rapidly and correctly, and in human affairs this kind of information may not be irrelevant. But, in engineering language, let us not confuse the need for a power supply to our control mechanism with the design of the control paths and control activations. Precision here permits economy of design (in this case of training) and efficiency of operation (lack of confusion in performance).

At least in some limited respects, this analysis of the train-and-open-switch situation shows us the intimate relationship between interpretation and problem solving. We have defined problem solving as the selection of a task response through mediating (thinking) processes. Let us examine the variables of our example, schematized in Figure 6.4, in greater detail (Miller and Van Cott, 1955).

Stimulus and Stimulus Variables Directly Presented. The open switch is perceived on a given track at a given time.

Variables of Stimulus Not Directly Presented. Let us assume that the yardman has not yet actually perceived the train on the horizon, so that the stimulus is not directly presented. He has "knowledge" that the train is due at this point in five minutes. The factors which establish the response options that may be effective are: distance of train from the open switch, rate at which train is approaching, and perhaps the location of other switch points on its track. Still another variable may be the location and effectiveness of an automatic warning or control signal to the train.

Classes of Response Options. Response options make up the alternative kinds of control options that are available to the operator. In our example, they include throwing the open switch, throwing some other switch, signaling the train. Within each option class, specific responses, such as which switch alternative to select, are available for effecting a favorable outcome in a task responsibility.

Response Implications. In many decision-making situations, the selection of an appropriate response alternative may depend in part on knowledge which permits conceptualizing the outcome of the response *in the context of the particular situation.* (One might think of this as "response meaningful-

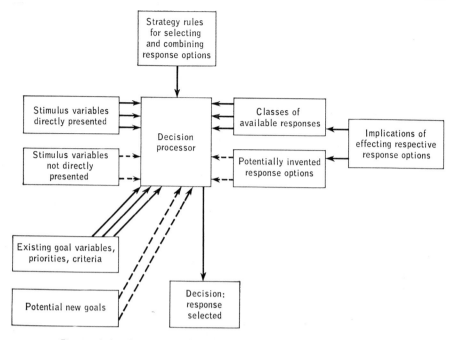

Figure 6.4.   Decision making: classes of information required.

ness.") In some cases, the response has implications for the operator's own future task responsibilities; we have, as an example, a response of "searching for more information." In other cases, the responses have implications for effects in the system which may occur beyond the purview of the operator's job. Thus, the oncoming train might be shunted onto a siding, but with the probability that a train immediately following would miss the block signal and plow into the first train. Another facet of response implication is the subjective probability estimates of the relative success of one response in achieving a task (or system) goal versus some other response in the situation.

Goal Priorities.   Decision making frequently requires making some compromises among several desired outcomes. It is important that trains meet schedules, but at least up to a point passenger safety is more important. It is more important that the express trains rather than local trains be on time. (As another example, in defense systems, one might ask whether it is more important to avoid shooting down a friendly aircraft because it was not recognized than to risk letting an armed enemy get through the defense barrier!)

Rules for Selecting Responses to Problem Situations.   Decision-making rules will tend to be generalizations about strategy rather than rigorous specifics. If they are the latter, however, a quantitative model of the operations, and computers or reference to a table, will be more effective than subjective human mental activities. Strategy rules will apply to classes of situations and classes of responses rather than to specific cases.

One broad class of problem solving consists in localizing a cause from one or a group of symptoms. This is diagnosis, or troubleshooting. The efficient solving of this type of problem depends on a strategy of sequential tests for information: choosing at each step of inquiry that check or test or inspection that yields the greatest relative amount of information about the physical or functional location of the object sought. The game of Twenty Questions, for example, is generally played most effectively with what is called a "binary search" strategy. (This has also been called the "half-split" method of troubleshooting.)

Another broad class of problem solving calls for surveying a situation, establishing a goal, making a response, watching for the opponent's response in reply, and letting the opponent's reply be in part the stimulus for selecting the next response. This is an example of battle tactics; it also applies to business. In general, strategy rules are intended to optimize gains per unit expenditure of resource.

Strategy rules, indeed, comprise an important class of information for the training of decision-making types of task. They have been elaborately formulated for card games such as bridge and chess and at some ultrahigh levels of the military and government. Rarely do they seem to accompany task requirements information, although the reader may have glimpsed how important they are to job behavior. It is easy to imagine and verify the difficulties that arise if the operator must, with his often limited resources in logic or specialized operations research know-how, develop his own strategies. The task analyst may have to accept the responsibility for trying to get answers to the question: "What general principles can be used to guide behavior sequences in relatively ambiguous task situations?"

We have seen that decision making depends on various classes of stimulus information and of response information, and means by which the operator can make appropriate links between stimulus and response. Decision making is generally difficult because it requires "holding so much information in the head at the same time." The task analyst may be a key factor in organizing the information structure of decision-making requirements so as to make it more amenable to training and ultimately to performance in task operations. Decision making is almost inevitably required in meeting complex contingencies in task operations, where any one configuration of circumstances happens rarely. Problem solving which produces improvisation and invention calls for a treatment outside the context of "task requirements."

Motor Response Mechanisms

Although it is often rather meaningless to think about motor responses apart from perceptual stimuli, there are some tasks in which such examination can pay off. The pianist's performance is a notable example: he is subjected to a variety of exercises and procedures for acquiring sheer skill in dexterity. In degree, this is true of all tasks calling for physical manipulation of objects. The task analyst may, through suitable examination of the controls of a device, anticipate some of the "likely human errors" that will occur. This anticipation, ideally accompanied by data, should pinpoint training content that may offset these error likelihoods. The human automatization of individual and sequenced responses may create both necessary capabilities and some liabilities. Physical and psychological stresses may have various effects on motor performance, some of which may be partly predictable.

Implication of Task Structure for Task Analysis

The foregoing factors in task structure are, in some degree, inevitable parts of every task and certainly of every job. Some tasks may have a high degree of some one of these factors present; vigilance tasks have a high degree of search, scan, and identification, for example. The task analyst can look at a set of task requirements and translate their usually molecular statements into the molar features of behavior by perceiving them in task structure terms. These terms should be more directly translatable into selection procedures, training procedures, and human engineering, because the terms are behavioral rather than expressing relations between signals and activations of controls. The human component is not a passive wire link, but an active mechanism with some built-in properties. By the same token, the collection and organization of task requirements information should be made more useful when guided by task structure concepts, as is indicated, for example, by our previous discussion of interpretation and problem solving.

Furthermore, there are some bodies of literature about scanning tasks, signal interpretation, noise filtering by the human, decision making, and motor performance. This literature can be used for further inquiry into definition of task "requirements," and also in linking requirements information to personnel decisions in selection and training. The nature of the behavioral "problem" becomes more apparent. Liabilities in the human component tend to become exposed when examined in behavioral terms, especially when we recognize that the operator does not perceive and retrieve information like a network of wires and switches summoning data pulses from fixed memory cells, but that he perceives and recalls through associative networks that are imprecise, "noisy," full of "cross-talk" between recall channels. These features, while liabilities in one context, are the basis of his flexibility and trainability.

As we shall see in the next section, task structure as described here lends itself to the outlining of the training program. Some dimensions of task performance omitted from discussion because of considerations of space and the primary objectives of this chapter but which are also of great importance are: physiological and psychological stress; the dynamics of social and team interactions; job and task motivation.

▣ TASK INFORMATION AND TRAINING DESIGN

Let us recall that task information is not an end in itself. Its purpose is to aid in the design and operation of the total system. We may think of the human component, once he has been selected, as being "designed" for system operation through training. Here we shall consider the implications of task analysis for the design of training.

First, however, we should recapitulate the kinds of information we have available. By following the route thus far outlined in this chapter, we have obtained a total picture of system requirements. We have a fairly clear but continuously unfolding picture of the functional requirements of the system as a whole, and of the functional requirements generated within the system by the kinds of components we have selected. Within this context of information, we have sought out the functional requirements of the human components in the system. These are stated in greater or lesser detail by pairings of task stimuli—actually or potentially available to the operator—with the responses and response supports appropriate to those stimuli. We have used system information to provide quantifications in the time dimension for stimuli, delays required and permissible between stimulus and response, and response rates. We have charted the temporal overlaps that may occur for one task with another. We have called the sum total of these data *task requirements information*.

Next, we have examined the behavioral implications of these task requirements. In each task and group of time-related tasks we have looked for the behavioral implications of search and scan of stimulus fields, identification and interpretation of stimulus patterns, short-term recall, long-term memory, decision-making and problem-solving operations, and effector responses. This examination was made in the light of what we, as psychologists, know about the economics of behavior and the peculiar characteristics of the human component before, during, and after training. We have tried to organize and analyze task information around knowledge (or at least hypotheses) about how the human mechanism organizes the information-processing that goes on within itself. The result of this examination of task requirements for their behavioral structure and implications is called *task analysis*.

The next question is: how do we use information about system requirements, task requirements, and task analyses as guides to training? We will want training that is (1) valid—transferable to system operations; (2) complete—to minimize trial-and-error learning on the job; and (3) efficient—in that the training objective is accomplished with minimal cost in resources and time.

System and Task Requirements Data as Performance Criteria

To the extent that task requirements are specified completely according to the operational universe of task inputs and outputs and their time relationships, we have at hand complete performance criteria. Generally speaking, the operator has fulfilled training objectives if he can pass these criteria. As training specialists, we have therefore a clear target toward which to aim every feature of our training enterprise. This in itself constitutes a significant achievement in training design. (How these data are sampled and put together for representativeness and economy in building evaluation tests is not within the scope of our present discussion.) And however we may break up the total training regimen into pieces of training, we will still have stimulus-response references in corresponding portions of the task requirements data.

Selection and Organization of Parts of Training

Now, where does one begin? Let us bear in mind that the design of training, like the design of any other object or process, is a creative and inventive enterprise. The total job can probably be partitioned into training segments in a variety of ways, all of them equally effective in supporting each other. Take for examples the operator of a vehicle, a member of an assembling crew of a missile, an electronic maintenance technician, a guidance operator, and an air traffic controller. These are complex jobs made up of a number of interlocking tasks.

One approach consists of examining what we have called a "mission cycle" or "job cycle" in order to find natural "break points" in the cycle. These would break the job into job segments, set off from each other on a time baseline. The trainee would be taught all he had to learn within one job segment before he proceeded to training on the next job segment. By another approach, an attempt is made to find those knowledges which seem to be common to a number of tasks in the job and to organize training around these clumps of knowledge. The same kind of organization would be made of clumps of mental and physical skills that exercised these knowledges. The latter procedure seems to have better promise of efficiency in learning, at least in the earlier phases of total job learning (compare Miller, 1956).

Let us examine the successive stages and phases of a typical learning situation—say, of an electronics maintenance technician. He has been selected for training on the basis of various aptitude tests, but he has no background in electronics.

Orientation Training

First, we will want to provide a motivational background for the technician in training. He is given a general survey of the functional and physical features of the system in which his tasks are embedded. He learns the purpose of the system at large and, more specifically, the functions of the equipment he is to service, and how each of the outputs of this equipment contribute to the operation of the system complex. He learns the operational consequences of various kinds of equipment failure or malfunction. He also learns the sources of signal and power input to the equipment, so that he can better appreciate, and later anticipate, disturbances of input to the mechanism in his charge. He will also get, as part of his orientation training, some general concepts on how the equipment does its job and a preliminary picture of its physical layout.

The content of this orientational training obviously comes from information about system requirements and the functional organization of the system.

The orientation serves not only to get the trainee motivationally "identified" with the system as an operating, organic entity. It also gives him a general map of the physical and functional context in which his various tasks fit. This mental map will, of course, become more specific and concrete as he continues training. Nevertheless, it can provide an associative reference for relating what might otherwise be random bits and pieces of task learning. If, however, the orientation material is too detailed and too extensive, the general map he should be learning will be obscured by trivia.

Nomenclature and Identification of Work Objects and Work Actions

Words and sentences tend to be meaningful to the extent that they conjure some mental image of the object and operation denoted by the word. Before the technician can read books, interpret diagrams, or profit from other instructional material, he should learn to recognize and name dials, test points, adjustment knobs, power supplies, input signal lines, and so on. He must also learn to identify in-tolerance conditions and out-of-tolerance conditions. (We might adopt the general definition of an out-of-tolerance condition as any stimulus which incites some active task response or change in a task response.)

In order to profit best from instructional materials about a task, it is desirable that identifications pertinent to a task be learned to a fairly high degree of reliability. These reference images provide a high degree of "meaningfulness" to the verbal materials, making them easier to learn and retain, and with higher guarantee of generalization from classroom and study hall to actual task context. Thus when the student reads: "Turn gain control to moderate intensity," he will have a mental picture of the gain control knob and an image of a signal of "moderate intensity" on the screen of the scope.

Similarily, we would teach the meanings of nonverbal symbols that occur in the task. Numerical names, graphic symbols, and special codes, such as binary numbers, are examples. It is inadequate to provide practice merely to bare mastery in learning these identifications. It is difficult for the student to learn and link ideas and concepts if he is fumbling with the meanings of terms that appear in those concepts.

As a matter of training technique, we should recognize that the student has two sets of differentiations to learn in making identifications. One is the differentiation among *objects* and other task stimuli. The other is differentiation within the lists of *symbols* that apply to objects. Furthermore, a two-way association must be developed: the task stimulus should suggest the symbol applied to it; and the task symbol should suggest the task stimulus. ("Task stimulus" here refers to an object or a signal emitted by an object.)

The need to learn nomenclatures suggests that in our task requirements description we should not omit communications which the operator should send or interpret: these may include informal communications to his team-mates on task-related operations.

Search for Job-Relevant Cues

A dimension of training that can and should be directly related to the learning of nomenclature and identifications is that of search for job-relevant cues. In its simplest terms, this information answers the question of the naive operator: "What tells me that I am supposed to do something?" In the routinized portions of tasks, of course, job-relevant cues appear from predictable places at predictable times. But as any person who is familiar with real-life operations knows, a large number of system difficulties arise because the operator keeps his nose too close to the grindstone: he is not alert to contingencies such as the bare wire, the broken junction, the too-hot chassis, the wisp of smoke from a coil, the pattern of hash marks that precede the full image when a radar screen is turned on.

Every job is filled with nonroutinized contingencies, hence it demands alertness. This dimension of training should probably begin as early as during the learning of nomenclatures and identifications and should continue through-out the rest of training. In tasks that call primarily for monitoring activities, of course, search skills may be formalized through concentrated training.

Training for Short-term Recall

Psychologists have reported relatively little about this important class of behavior. We do know from personal experiences that the naive bridge player may not be able to recall half a dozen cards in his hand after the hand has been played, whereas after a few years of motivated practice at the game, he may recall not only all the cards in his own hand, but most of those in the hands of the others in the game. The acquisition of skill in short-term recall seems to be somewhat related to the phenomena generally subsumed under "meaningfulness," but the associative nature of meaningfulness is not itself very clear.

Short-term recall of task-relevant information seems to improve with general familiarity about the material to be remembered, and with a fairly high degree of practice at observing and recalling such information. The information should be presented in task-simulated situations. This requires that it be apprehended from the manner in which it is typically presented, and recalled under situations which the performance of the task demands.

In corrective maintenance, the technician is frequently given one or more symptoms of malfunctioning. These symptoms must be noted and written down or remembered. They must be borne in mind (recalled) both in searching for additional symptoms (which also must be recalled) and in making inferences about the probable locus of the trouble. Unless he marks them down in some way, the technician must also recall the checks he has made and, through inferential processes, the portions of the equipment which have been cleared from suspicion in narrowing down the cause of the trouble. These are only a very few of many more examples of short-term recall required in this type of job. Although short-term recall is by no means limited to problem-solving activities, it does weigh heavily in them.

There is good reason to believe that under stress, either emotional or from environmental overload, the function of short-term recall deteriorates more rapidly than that of long-term recall. Whether this comes about through failure to notice the cues or to remember them—or both—is beside the point. However, problem-solving abilities may frequently be most highly taxed under the stress of coping with contingencies. This observation suggests the importance, not only of highly learned and "overlearned" procedures applicable to such situations, but also of extensive practice in short-term recall as required by the concurrent task requirements of such situations.

Unexplored, except in popular books on memory aids, are procedures for providing through controlled training the assistance of special mnemonics and techniques whereby the operator will rehearse and organize short-term information.

Training of Procedures

It is characteristic that on-the-job studies of proficiency almost inevitably show that the majority of job incumbents are deficient in knowledge of both standard operating procedures and special or "emergency" procedures. Examination of training curricula frequently shows deficiencies in amount of training given to procedures and inadequacies in the procedures that are taught. Among other reasons for these deficiencies are lack of knowledge by the instructor as to what the operating procedures for a given job actually are, and criteria for establishing proficiency. As one might guess, all these deficiencies are especially marked in procedures that we have called "contingency operations" in this chapter. That is, the contingencies which may beset the performance of "routine procedures" are frequently unknown, hence neglected during training.

The significance of information about system requirements and task requirements is clearly evident in specification of training in procedural performance. A procedure may be loosely defined as a series of steps, where each step consists of a stimulus, a response, and a response feedback.

The teaching of a procedure may begin with "orientation" as to the purpose of the procedure in the context of system operation. It may be followed by teaching of the nomenclature and identification of work objects, symbols, activities. This enables the student to associate the task stimulus with a concept of the stimulus, and the task response with a concept of the task response. When these two sets of associations have been established, a considerable amount of pretraining can be done at the verbal level, with expectation of positive transfer to the task situation. This verbal training can cut down on the confusion and trial-and-error with which the student approaches learning in the actual task environment. It also permits rehearsal of procedures when away from the actual equipment and task environment, as well as some degree of anticipation (hence of getting "set") from one activity to another in the actual task setting.

These conceptualizations also permit, in some cases at least, more extended delays for corrective feedback about task performance. If the student can, through conceptualization, reinstate the stimulus and response of the task, he can associate with these concepts the feedback he receives (Miller, 1953a). Thus if, as a driver, I have taken a wrong turn and I am later given instructions as to where I turned incorrectly, I may on the next occasion take the proper turn *if* I was able to associate the corrective information with my concept of the turning place and my concept of the response I erroneously made. It might be sufficient merely to be able to conceptualize the stimulus as well as the response I should have made. This kind of conceptualization may frequently account for what seems to be "one-trial learning."

Procedures should, of course, be practiced both symbolically and actually in a variety of task settings. Frequently these settings in operations will include disturbances ("noise") or the need to effect time-sharing with other tasks. In time-sharing, one task may have to be performed more or less concurrently with another task. This requirement imposes, among other things, additional skill in short-term memory for each of the tasks involved. Such practice in various task environments will, of course, tend to guarantee the generalization from training to the operational scene. The operational scene itself almost inevitably varies somewhat from one task cycle to another.

In cases where it is highly important to system success that a procedure be performed correctly and within prescribed time limits, or where there may be infrequent opportunity for practice on the job, or where the performance may have to be under internal or environmental stress, additional steps must be taken in training. Additional reliability can be built into task performance by providing the operator with a variety of "recall routes."

Where flexibility of behavior in the performance of procedures is desired, one or more of the following conditions should be met. The operator should have "automatized" many of the stimulus-response relationships. He should also have had sufficient practice so that he is at least fairly adept at handling the short-term recall requirements during task performance. The task situation should permit him some degree of anticipation of the next stimulus in the action series, so that he is not stimulus-response-bound in time. He should have a conceptual reference for his ongoing and oncoming performance.

The meaning of "conceptual" reference deserves some amplification.

The novice musician generally depends on "finger memory" for playing a composition from memory. But if there are any changes in the pattern of muscle action, he may break down. He must play the composition the same way every time. The highly accomplished musician "hears" the music internally, and although he may be partly guided by muscle memory, he is also guided by this implicit "image" or conceptualization of the music. He is able to play, at least partly, the composition "by ear." This permits him flexibility in modifying his performance from one time to the next without breakdown, and with continuity.

The same is true, in a slightly different sense, for the accomplished driver of an automobile. He drives from a concept of what he wants to have happen. If he wants his automobile to move into another lane, he does not instruct his arm responses to turn the wheel: the motor responses are geared to the concept of the goal condition. Thus he can combine a goal concept of accelerating and turning so that a smoothly graded and continuous adjustment is made.

Training for Decision Making and Problem Solving

For purposes of the present discussion, let us define decision making as the cognitive processes that lead to the selection of one from among a "known" set of response alternatives—where these are known by the decision maker. The selection process may include computational and other logical operations for combining information. Thus, examples of the decision process as defined here would range from (a) the selection of a particular one of a group of enemy targets against which to aim a missile to (b) the aiming of the missile as a result of calculating azimuth, elevation, and rate for intercept with the target. The choice of heads or tails in the toss of a coin; the businessman's allocation of budget respectively to the following year's plant operations, product research, market research, and promotion and advertising; troubleshooting for the cause of a given gross effect—these are additional examples of decision making.

The information essential to training for decision making has been described in a previous section. In summary it consists of:

1. The stimulus variables in the problem.
2. The response alternatives.
3. The variables in the goal conditions and their relative priorities.
4. Implications of the exercise of response alternatives.
5. Strategy rules for selecting response alternatives in order to optimize goal conditions in given stimulus situations. Such rules may include procedures for efficiently getting additional information towards an ultimate decision.
6. Allowable time between the situation arising and control action (compare Miller and Van Cott, 1955).

It should be clear that only when these kinds of information are available can there be effective *practice* undertaken in decision making relevant to the job. In general, this information is almost totally lacking in training situations; in many cases the fact that decisions must be made by the operator is only fuzzily recognized. The consequence of lacking a picture of the structure of the decisions required and of information about stimulus, response, strategy, and goal variables is that training degenerates into an attempt to teach "all about the situation," with the hope that personal wisdom and logical improvisations by the operator will somehow cope with the job problems. Thus the maintenance technician is taught "all about" the operation of the equipment and then thrown, willy-nilly, into troubleshooting, where he may sink or swim—as may the system itself. Thanks in general to human adaptability, a semirandom midway kind of motion between sinking and swimming is usually the result. Large amounts of on-the-job "experiences" are required for even minimum competence, where even competence is undefined except by comparison with other individuals similarly benighted. Extensive backup in system time, material, and human resources must support the muddling and errors in such misty cognitive environments.

It would be misleading to conclude, however, that all the knowledges and rules sufficient to cover all job situations and contingencies can be precisely identified and neatly wrapped up in a training package. There is always the possibility that some mechanic's chance knowledge of the materials used in manufacturing a hairpin could put a machine back in shape and save the world. The question, however, is really which stimulus and response demands are probable and which are critical to mission success, as well as the degrees of probability and criticality in a population of missions. Training should center around this core of probable and critical events as they bear on the man's job, and decreasing values in probability-multiplied-by-criticality should be given training time *only* after the central training has been concluded and only if additional time and funds are available for "education" as an altruistic principle.

This last point of view brings us to the matter of problem solving. Whereas we defined (for this chapter) decision making as the selection from responses and resources already known to the operator, let us define problem solving (again for this chapter) as the activity of *inventing* or *improvising* resources and response alternatives beyond those already known to the operator. Obviously, we can find many examples which would make the distinction between decision making and problem solving a hazy one. Let us not be concerned with hairsplitting on definitions or metaphysical arguments about whether it is possible "to produce anything new under the sun." We can point to examples in which a problem was solved by a person with a "new idea."

It should be clear that the requirements for invention cannot be precisely specified in a task description. Task description specifies and denotes the response to be made to the stimulus. Where this is done only in general terms of stimulus and response, the reason should be for short-cutting the tedium of more detailed description. With this in mind, we must tend rather to educate as well as train for inventive acts. A few classical suggestions may be made:

1. Indoctrinate by concept and example that there are always many levels of "causation" for any event.
2. Indoctrinate by concept and practice to differentiate the function from the mechanism that performs the function.
3. Teach, with examples, the variety of classes of mechanisms and physical principles that may perform a function.
4. Teach synonyms (in the form of a thesaurus) for function names.
5. Teach, by any means available, contemplation of a problem situation.
6. Teach criteria and, by practice, balance between contemplation that provides analysis and hypotheses and the testing of hypotheses.
7. Indoctrinate the motivation to search for alternative modes of response to system situations.
8. Indoctrinate that a new method of control is not a sufficient reason for adopting the method. It must improve over an existing ratio of performance-to-cost.

But aside from formal inventions, the development and operation of a system containing humans inevitably is accompanied by considerable informal improvisation. This has been vigorously demonstrated by the RAND studies of group behavior in complex man-machine tasks (compare Chapter 11). The nature of the supervision of the system may tend to reduce such actions, or it may be permissive or actively inducive to improvisations. Informal means of reallocating task inputs and even task responsibilities will tend to arise under conditions of heavy load and contingencies on a group. Team training should be so set up as to encourage a particular group to explore for optimum interactions. Obviously, individuals and the group should be provided with feedback which will let them perceive what has been successful (and unsuccessful) and why.

Since continuous dynamic changes in a system make it resemble in many respects a maturing organism, recognition should be made in system and task description of these generally unpredictable changes. They do constitute unknown variance in projections of system and task requirements, but this uncertainty should not invalidate a best attempt at such projections. Task requirement projections tend to guarantee at least a minimally acceptable system performance with respect to mission success. Internal optimization of resources by system components then becomes a bonus in reliability over a somewhat wider range of potential catastrophes.

A significant, if not determining, variable in the successful maturation of a system is the nature of its leadership and human supervision. This topic is outside the scope of the present book. Nevertheless, insofar as this leadership may influence the extent of improvisation by individuals and groups within the system, the topic should at least be mentioned. Even where there is a high degree of automation in a system complex, the quality of human leadership must remain a critical factor in system reliability. Maintenance and logistic operations must be accomplished by people who think, plan, and make decisions, and do so quickly and alertly or sluggishly and ineptly. At least in the long run, these are functions of leadership. Unfortunately, we seem to be learning much more about job design, selection, and training of people for man-machine tasks than for patterns of specific supervisory responsibilities. We can hope that studies in man-machine system laboratories will provide us with guiding data and principles in this direction, too.

Training for Motor Response

We have discussed training for perceptual, procedural, decision-making and problem-solving behavior. We turn, finally, to motor response and some of its properties that should influence training (compare Miller, 1953a).

The task analysis, rather than the description of task requirements, should be of major help. The analysis should have identified likely human errors as a function of the response mechanisms. For example, study of the task may reveal operations that require the location and activation of controls by kinesthetic, rather than visual, cues. Special patterns of motor coordination may be shown to be necessary. Occasional reversals of customary actions may be required, such as starting a nut on a screw from an upside-down position. Sequences of motor response may reveal error tendencies in the task. Responses may have to be made immediately following a response which culminates a difficult task: for example, shutting off the ignition after maneuvering a particularly difficult crash landing.

The possibilities of negative transfer effects from previous learning of a reversed control or the failure to conform to a "population stereotype" may be recognized as a basis for special training. And a study of the motor demands and the task requirements in context may show what response groupings or patterns should be learned and "automated" as a performance unit. Where timing of the motor response is critical, special exercise material for anticipation, attack, and release of the body movement may be prepared.

These are examples of what inquiry of the motor requirements of tasks may reveal for training purposes. They are certainly not exhaustive even of the classes of motor problem that may be investigated.

Organization of Training Content

Obviously one cannot teach or learn everything at once. The question then becomes one of finding the sequence of the content of training. The organization of training into units, segments, and part-tasks, probably cannot be put into formal prescription. The topics identified above do suggest an approach to organization and sequence of content at least at the task level. In review these consist of:

1. *System and task requirements data as performance criteria.* This is orientation as to the goals of task performance and what the task is all about.
2. *Orientation.* A general functional flow-chart of the operations supported by task performance and the mechanisms on which it is performed.
3. *Nomenclature and identification of work objects and work actions.* Relating the terms, symbols and work objects to each other so that the student can read and execute verbal instructions, understand feedback, and communicate his actions to others.
4. *Search for job-relevant cues.* Techniques for paying attention to his job environment for cues that indicate he should take some kind of action.
5. *Short-term recall.* Learning to remember task-relevant items of information peculiar to each task or job cycle, or between the perception of stimulus units and motor response.
6. *Procedures.* Acquiring relatively invariant associations between stimulus events and response actions.
7. *Decision making and problem solving.* Patterns of stimulus variables, response alternatives, goal variables and priorities, and strategy rules for selecting responses in decision making and for inventing or improvising new responses in the form of concepts, mechanisms, or operations in the course of problem solving.
8. *Motor response.* Efficiency and reliability in the mechanisms of execution of stimulus-response patterns.

Except for *short-term recall* and *motor response,* we have in this list at least a reasonable order for teaching a task, including its contingencies. The two items named do not fit into any special place in the order of training, and their position in sequence is likely to be highly dependent on the nature of the task. But the remainder of this general order seems best to fit the requirement for efficient training that emphasizes building upon what is already known by the student. Nevertheless, pending considerably more programmatic research in task learning, the foregoing recommendations should be regarded as tentative, although psychologically reasonable.

▣ TASK DESCRIPTION AND PERFORMANCE EVALUATION

Evaluation may serve two related purposes. One is to establish the readiness of the component to be put into the operational entity we have called a system. The other is to predict the level of performance of the system itself with the component in it. Level of performance includes, of course, reliability of performance across the totality of events and contingencies that will act on the system throughout its career.

Evaluation is generally expensive, both in time and material resources; system evaluation is almost overwhelmingly expensive. Therefore it is usually possible to obtain only a relatively small number of samples with a limited number of variations among hundreds, and possibly hundreds of thousands, of variables potentially capable of interacting with each other. To many engineers, the uncertainty of performance as it affects error probability of the human component seems prodigious. In some respects this is true. In others, the human capacity for task adaptiveness (or should we say, the capacity of *some* humans for task adaptiveness?) is also prodigious. In any event, the evaluation of human performance poses special problems in sampling of stimulus events in order to predict system performance in some kind of probabilistic structure.

The combination of task requirements and task analysis should reveal how to sample situations so that performance measurements can be most precisely taken and generalized. A relatively large number of expected "trouble spots" in performance may be sampled in exercises with the human component in local (nonsystem) evaluations. Large numbers of samples are less expensive to get and easier to control if restricted to such local exercises. Performance in this range of sample problems can then be measured. Subsamples of problems can then be intelligently selected from these "local tests" and put into system exercises or observed in system exercises. Better extrapolations of systems results to a universe of problems for that system can then be made. This is the conventional problem of efficiency in getting representativeness and validity.

The reader should be warned that what may seem a significant local criterion in a portion of a system may turn out to have little importance to total system success or failure. And the converse may also be true. Hence the need for total system exercises, expensive though they may be. Paradoxically, the total system sometimes performs better than the sum of the performances of its components measured individually and calculated into system performance. (Perhaps this is because the enemy—or the system environment—is not as hostile, clever, or reliable an opponent as we thought he or it would be.)

In any event, the selection of exercises for system component evaluation is in itself fraught with difficulty and uncertainty. The programming of total system exercises is a monstrous task. So is the analysis of the mountains of data that ensue. Precision in the identification of system and task requirements may supply at least order and guidance to the task.

With the function of evaluation, we have come full circle in the use of system and task information. It has guided the development of the system and served as a measuring stick of the system's adequacy.

REFERENCES

Churchman, C. W., and Ratoosh, P., (ed.). 1959. *Measurement, definitions and theories.* New York: Wiley.

Flagle, C. D., Huggins, W. H., and Roy, R. H. (ed.). 1960. *Operations research and systems engineering.* Baltimore: Johns Hopkins Press.

Miller, G. A., Galanter, E., and Pribram, K. H. 1960. *Plans and the structure of behavior.* New York: Holt.

Miller, R. B. 1953a. *Handbook on training and training equipment design.* Wright-Patterson Air Force Base, Ohio: Wright Air Development Center. Technical Report 53–136.

Miller, R. B. 1953b. *A method for man-machine task analysis.* Wright-Patterson Air Force Base, Ohio: Wright Air Development Center. Technical Report 53–137.

Miller, R. B. 1954. *Some working concepts of systems analysis.* Pittsburgh: American Institute for Research.

Miller, R. B. 1960. *Task and part-task trainers.* Wright-Patterson Air Force Base, Ohio: Wright Air Development Center. Technical Report 60-469; ASTIA No. AD245652.

Miller, R. B., and Van Cott, H. P. 1955. *The determination of knowledge content for complex man-machine jobs.* Pittsburgh: American Institute for Research.

ONCE THE TASKS THAT MEN MUST PERFORM and the jobs they must fill within a system have been defined, the development process can proceed to identify the men to occupy these jobs. The process of choosing human beings and categorizing them for the channels of individual development which will lead to their effective performance of jobs is based upon procedures of *selection and classification*. Task analysis must have previously been carried out, to identify the human abilities required for various human performances. Selection and classification is begun by designing psychological tests to measure these abilities. Such tests have the purpose of predicting the facility of learning specific skills in later training programs, as well as ultimate effectiveness of human performance on the job. The following chapter describes the basic rationale which applies to the design, development, and use of these predictors of human performance in systems.

The predictions of performance undertaken by selection and classification procedures occur within a framework of certain important assumptions. First of all, there are some essential differences between men and machines which must be taken into account, including such things as man's versatility, his temperamental make-up, and his variability. In addition, one must consider the characteristics of that larger complex of techniques which are used to obtain and maintain the people for the system, which is sometimes called the *personnel subsystem*. The administrative features of this subsystem have an effect upon the kinds of selection techniques which are appropriate, as well as on its mission. In addition, the decisions which have been made regarding the variety of jobs, the training, and the measurement of proficiency, as parts of the personnel subsystem, will determine the requirements for selection and training.

The technology of selection and classification has been with us for a relatively long time and has achieved many successes in connection with both military and nonmilitary systems. Despite continual refinement, these techniques obviously suggest many as yet unanswered questions for psychological research. There are perhaps three major areas of research which remain to be invaded by new ideas. The first concerns the question of how to derive the abilities to be tested by aptitude measures from descriptions of the performances for which prediction is desired. Related to this is a second and equally challenging question of just what is being measured—what exactly an ability *is,* and how it functions in a causal sense to determine behavior. Finally, there is the matter of designing ever more complex and intricate models for prediction, in order to take into full account more of the variables which are now treated as assumptions. This chapter provides a systematic basis for consideration of these problems, as well as others, seen from the standpoint of a highly useful technology in system development.

THE LOGIC OF

PERSONNEL SELECTION

AND CLASSIFICATION

Paul Horst

Previous chapters have provided many illustrations of the occurrence within systems of interacting man-machine combinations having specified goals, which are called subsystems. In addition to these operational units of the system, there exists also another kind of subsystem, which is identified with the procedures employed to obtain the personnel who constitute the "man" part of various man-machine combinations and to keep them functioning. This is often called the *personnel subsystem,* and it may be considered to have a most important supporting role in the total operation of any system.

In this chapter we shall be concerned with the personnel subsystem of a man-machine system. This leads us to discuss the decisions that must be made as to which particular persons shall constitute the personnel subsystem and also how they shall be distributed or assigned throughout the total system. As a basis for discussing the personnel subsystem, we shall first consider some important respects in which men and machines are different and what impact these differences have on the logic of personnel selection and classification. Following this, we shall describe the essential properties of the personnel subsystem and how it operates. The consideration of these topics will then make it possible for us to describe the requirements of the *selection and classification model,* the variables which it takes into account, and the ways in which it operates to produce the required personnel for a system. Some important research questions which arise in connection with such a model will also be indicated.

Purpose of Selection and Classification

As indicated in earlier chapters, systems are developed to satisfy the needs or desires of people. They may be systems for opening cans or for mowing lawns. They may be systems for providing transportation, like automobiles, or systems for producing the automobiles. They may even be systems developed for an entire nation or alliance of nations for the purpose of destroying or subjugating another nation or group of nations. Within such systems, of course, will be found many component and contributing systems varying widely in degree of complexity. Typically, such systems involve the interaction of men and machines. In most systems the trend has been for machines to take over more and more of the functions of man, and this trend bids fair to continue at perhaps an accelerated rate. Thus far, however, the over-all and long-term result has not been a progressive reduction of men as components of systems. Rather, as machines take over functions currently performed by men, new systems emerge, providing new and different functions for men within them. Although automation creates temporary dislocations, the trend has not been to reduce progressively the man component of systems, but rather to change the systems and the specific functions of men within them. It can be argued, of course, that increased mechanization and automation has reduced the average yearly time spent by men on jobs—that is, within systems—as evidenced by shorter hours, shorter work weeks, and longer vacations. But while the average time spent by men within systems has declined, there has been no systematic decline in the proportion of total available persons utilized by man-machine systems within this and other industrial countries. Such a trend would be reflected in the proportion of unemployed, whether forced or otherwise, in the total employable population. Presumably, one of the objectives of modern societies is to utilize its total manpower resources within the productive systems which in a very real sense are these societies. The strength of a society is, in fact, largely a function of the effectiveness with which its manpower resources are utilized within the systems which constitute it. It is probably inherent in the nature of man that the systems he generates will continue to incorporate men as essential components of these systems. In any case, in the development of systems, jobs are created which are performed by men. Other chapters indicate in some detail the sorts of things men can do better than machines and vice versa. In the next section we discuss some of the essential differences between men and machines. But so long as men can do some things within a system better than machines, the system, if it is to be maximally efficient, will require a personnel subsystem.

This means that men must be selected for the system and classified or distributed throughout the system so as to yield maximum congruence between the abilities of men and the requirements of the jobs within the system. The problems and principles involved in the selection and classification of personnel for the system are discussed in the following sections of this chapter.

▣ SOME DIFFERENCES BETWEEN MAN AND MACHINE

The subject has been discussed in previous chapters, and we shall consider it here only as it bears on the logic of personnel selection and classification. It is instructive in this connection to delineate some of the important ways in which men and machines differ. In this way, we shall be able to see clearly the demands which must be made upon a personnel subsystem in order that suitable men shall be available to the system as essential parts of a variety of man-machine combinations.

Functional Characteristics

Versatility. Although it is possible to design machines which can perform many different kinds of tasks, most men can perform more different kinds of tasks than machines can. However, in the development of a system one is ordinarily not concerned with the construction of versatile machines; similarly, one does not typically require men to do many different kinds of jobs, even though they may be capable of them. In a different sense, though, *versatility* is a most significant kind of characteristic of the personnel components of a system. Most men can do some things better than they can do other things, even though they can do a number of things reasonably well and perhaps only a few things not at all well. What is important in developing the logic of personnel selection and classification is that one man can do task *a* better than tasks *b* or *c,* whereas another can do *b* better, and another can do *c* better. The personnel selection and classification problem arises in part from this lack of correspondence between the relative abilities of men for different kinds of activities. In the design of machines for a system, the procedure is to design the machine specifically for what it is supposed to do, and in general there is no concern about how many other tasks it can perform or how well it can perform them.

Individual Differences. Another important difference between men and machines is this: for any particular action to be accomplished, there are great individual differences with respect to how effectively a group of men can carry out a specified performance; whereas machines are usually designed to specifications for a particular purpose, so that there will be no great variation among them. For example, in the case of bomber planes such as B-52s, little variation in performance characteristics may be expected. However, one may expect considerable variation in a group of trainees with respect to their aptitudes for piloting B-52s.

Upper Limits of Performance. Another important difference between men and machines is that for any particular function there is a definite limit to how well or how much of something a person can do, whereas these limitations are often greatly exceeded by machines. As a matter of fact, one of the primary roles of machines is to do better in, or more of, a particular activity than men can do. For example, with rare exceptions, men cannot lift 500-lb. weights, whereas machines can be developed to lift many tons.

Temperamental Factors. Men differ from machines also with respect to personality or temperamental characteristics. One may facetiously refer to "temperamental" machines, but in general machines do not get angry and avoid performing their functions because they do not care to. Unless there is some mechanical or organic malfunction in the machine, it will not refuse to respond appropriately to its foreman or supervisor who gives it proper instructions. Neither will it try to make its operator think that it is doing a better job than it really is in order to get promoted to more important functions. Unless the machine is ill, it will not fail to cooperate with another machine simply because it does not like the other machine, or because it would prefer to receive from or give to some other kind of machine. These kinds of differences create many problems in the selection and classification of personnel for man-machine systems.

Modifiability. Another important difference between men and machines is that while both may be modified, the nature of this modifiability requires entirely different procedures. It is true that machines within systems are often modified so as to change or improve their functioning. It is also true that with training and experience the functioning of individuals or men can be modified. But it is much more difficult to predict how and to what extent men's functions can be modified than it is for those of machines. The difficulty in predicting the extent to which performance can be modified or improved for different individuals creates one of the most troublesome problems in personnel selection and classification. We can make machines to specification, given the raw materials. It is misleading, however, to press the analogy and say that given raw recruits, we can also train or modify them precisely to specifications. This, of course, is the purpose of training programs, the effectiveness of which is dealt with in more detail in another chapter (Chapter 9).

Checking Specifications. Another important difference between men and machines has to do with their specifications. Presumably, in a man-machine system, just what the machines are to do has been spelled out in considerable detail. Presumably, also, there are reasonably straightforward procedures for determining how accurately the machines meet these specifications. This is true whether one wishes to find out how closely a ballistic missile will find its target ten thousand miles away or to check the washability of an army private's work fatigues.

The problem is far from being as simple in the case of the man component of the man-machine system. Although a task description and analysis for the various elements of a man subsystem may be provided in great detail, and although there may be a pretty good knowledge of human capacities and limitations in general, the problem of determining whether a particular individual satisfies a specification based on these various analyses is nevertheless not simple. Instruments may exist which may be assumed to measure these functions and so give an indication of the potential performance of the individual in a man-machine complex. But the problem of selecting and classifying individuals from a potential pool into the personnel subsystem of a man-machine system is one which, in the current state of our knowledge, requires in addition adequate models for testing the validity of the hypotheses and instruments employed.

Checking whether individuals meet the specifications before being assigned to job activities is only one of two very important related problems. The second involves the determination of how well personnel assigned to job activities are actually meeting the specifications of those activities. Estimates of how well men are satisfying requirements of the job are called criterion measures. The logic of assessing human performance is considered in some detail in a later chapter (Chapter 12). As we develop the model of personnel selection and classification, however, we shall see that an essential part of this model consists of assessing human performance within the man-machine system. The problems of such assessment are comparable to those of checking specifications of individuals before they are placed in the man-machine system.

We may hypothesize that if individuals satisfy certain specifications, they will also satisfy corresponding job requirements. One of the great problems in verifying hypotheses is to get enough experience on the basis of which reliable conclusions can be drawn. We must have an adequate number of cases on the basis of which to validate our logical analyses, and this requirement must be incorporated in the personnel selection and classification model.

Administrative Factors

Other differences between men and machines result primarily from administrative considerations. But, as is so often true, practical and administrative considerations play a large role in the development of useful theoretical models.

Turnover or Attrition.   Within any man-machine system, machines wear out and must be replaced, or better machines are developed to replace older ones, so that we may have turnover in the machine components, resulting in a flow of machines through the system. For any specified system, however, the nature of turnover or the flow of these components through the system is essentially different with respect to men and machines. In the case of men, it is not typical that they leave the system primarily because they wear out. Neither is it typical that they leave the system because new and better types of men are required; although the latter occasion could occur in the development of an entirely new kind of system, such as man in space.

Since the personnel selection and classification model requires a flow of personnel into and out of the system, let us consider briefly the causes of this flow. The outflow from the system or from components of the system may be of two kinds, favorable and unfavorable. The unfavorable type of outflow may be due to faulty selection in the first place, resulting in persons who must be removed from the system. The second type of outflow is that resulting from persons who prefer to go to other systems or are more urgently needed in other systems.

The inflow of the system may be of two kinds, the first of these being the inflow required to replace the outflow from the system. The second kind is that resulting from expansion of the system. System development should proceed so that expanded systems may benefit from the experience of smaller initial systems. The flow of personnel through a system is an essential feature of the personnel selection and classification model. Without taking this into consideration, it would be impossible to develop a man-machine system unless great reliance were placed on crystal balls or supernatural guidance.

Supply and Demand.   Another practical consideration which bears on the theoretical model is that of supply and demand. Within rather wide limits, the problems of raw materials from which to produce the machines within a system are not crucial. Although raw materials may be limiting factors, if more are needed to produce more machines, they usually can be found. But a selection and classification model which is based on the assumption that the problem is primarily one of selection and that the resources from which to draw are theoretically infinite is doomed to failure in practical application.

The problem of classification is imposed because of the fact that the total available manpower is limited. We must consider how this restricted volume of available manpower may be made best to satisfy the needs of the man-machine system. Presumably, the requirements of the man-machine system will be spelled out; the different kinds of functions and the number of persons required for each job will be specified (compare Chapter 6). But for any man-machine system, no matter how defined—whether it be a weapon system, a manufacturing system, an educational system, or, for that matter, an entire nation—it is most unlikely that the various kinds and degrees of abilities required to perform the operations demanded of the system will happen to be just those represented within the personnel pool available for manning the system. This disparity is the basis for the classification model we shall discuss later.

▣ THE NATURE OF THE PERSONNEL SUBSYSTEM

In developing a logic of personnel selection and classification, several aspects of the personnel subsystem are crucial. One of these is its administrative character; one cannot divorce the model from the administrative framework in which it must operate and which imposes restrictions upon it. Second, the mission of the system, both with respect to objectives and scope, will have a bearing on the way in which a personnel subsystem may be defined. Since a central concept of a personnel subsystem is that of jobs to be done, we cannot discuss the characteristics of the system without a consideration of the jobs within it. But the jobs to be done presuppose some kind of requirement of the men who are supposed to do them; so that job requirements are an essential feature or characteristic of personnel subsystems. Presumably, also, an individual does not just work at a job, but he also works at it with some degree of proficiency; thus, as we have indicated previously, the logic of personnel selection and classification involves the concept of proficiency evaluation. A selection model which provides for verification or validation must define the personnel subsystem so that flow of personnel may be assumed to characterize it. Another characteristic of the personnel subsystem which the selection and classification model must take into account is the modification of human functioning, which implies a consideration of training programs, formal or otherwise.

This enumeration does not perhaps include all relevant characteristics of a personnel subsystem, but it should serve as a reasonably satisfactory basis for the development of the model.

The Administrative Organism

Perhaps one of the chief reasons why personnel selection and classification systems have not been more adequately developed is because of the failure to define systems in such a way that the conditions required by the model can be satisfied. We have said that for an adequate selection and classification model we presuppose a large number of people. We also presuppose a large number of different kinds of tasks. This is one of the reasons why a large number of men are required in the model.

Types of Personnel Systems. We may identify four different types of personnel systems. (For convenience, we use the phrase *personnel system* to refer to what may be the larger framework within which specific *personnel subsystems* are embedded.) The first of these we shall call a *completely autonomous system*. The second is an *autonomous subsystem within an autonomous system*. A third type of administrative organism, from the standpoint of a selection and classification model, consists of *homogeneous groups of autonomous systems*. A fourth type consists of *homogeneous groups of autonomous subsystems*.

The completely *autonomous system* may be defined as one which for all practical purposes operates without restriction except of the most general sort imposed from outside, such as may be provided by government controls. The typical example of such a system is an industrial organization, such as General Motors or Procter and Gamble, or a governmental organization, such as the Department of Defense or the Treasury Department. In the educational field, we have autonomous universities and colleges. Other examples are small business organizations or small independent government bureaus, or similar enterprises which are relatively small in scope and operation. These last are noted because when they are defined as unitary man-machine systems, they usually do not individually include a large enough man subsystem to make possible the application of an effective selection and classification model.

Autonomous subsystems may be regarded as departments or divisions of a large autonomous system which in themselves may operate with considerable autonomy. Examples of such subsystems are the Chevrolet and Buick divisions within General Motors, or the Army, Navy, and Air Force within the Department of Defense. Or we may consider as subsystems of a large national industry its distribution and manufacturing divisions.

Examples of *homogeneous groups of autonomous systems* are provided by cooperative associations of autonomous systems, such as trade or professional associations. For example, an association of independent grocers within a town would be a homogeneous group of autonomous systems. One may consider the high schools within a state cooperating in a state testing program as a group of autonomous systems. From the point of view of personnel volume, the concept of homogeneous groups of autonomous systems is extremely important. It also presents some problems and difficulties from a practical point of view. One notable example of a homogeneous group of autonomous systems cooperating in the development and application of a large-scale personnel selection model is the Life Insurance Agency Research Bureau, which represents most of the major life insurance companies in the country. Unfortunately for the development of adequate personnel selection and classification models, such patterns are very rare in this country.

The fourth kind of administrative organism, the *homogeneous groups of autonomous subsystems,* is exemplified in a voluntary association of similar types of subsystems drawn from larger, completely autonomous systems. Such an administrative organism might be represented by association of the ballistic missiles departments of the various Army, Navy, and Air Force groups. Another example might have been (but was not) the voluntary association of agencies in the Army Air Forces and the Bureau of Naval Aeronautics during World War II, for the purpose of developing personnel selection and classification models for air crew personnel. Such examples are hard to come by, since men, unlike machines, become ego-involved in their own activities and jealous of what they regard as outside threats to these. Such differences between men and machines may often militate against the structuring of administrative organisms to satisfy the requirements of the ideal theoretical personnel selection and classification model.

The Mission

Man-machine systems may evolve because of objectives previously established. Sometimes, too, a definition of objectives helps to structure more effectively an existing system. Often analyses of man-machine systems may reveal unrelated objectives which have developed by accident. For example, the general objectives of a small business system may be to manufacture grinding mills and household vinegar; accidents of history may combine apparently unrelated objectives. Usually, however, in the modern man-machine system the spelling out of general objectives, as in the development of specific weapon systems, occurs before the system is set up. But the development of personnel selection and classification models proceeds from the more specific objectives which contribute to the over-all mission.

In defining the administrative organism so that it will satisfy the requirements of an efficient selection and classification model, the scope of the mission is also relevant. The organism may be monopolistic, so that we have only one completely autonomous system, as in a single ballistic missile man-machine system. If this is the case, then the administrative organism is automatically defined to include the maximum amount of personnel available within a political or social system for the particular mission. If, however, the mission is competitive with other systems, such as competing weapon systems within the Defense Department or competitive missions among small business organizations, then it is difficult to establish either homogeneous groups of autonomous systems or autonomous subsystems to satisfy the requirements of an ideal personnel selection and classification model.

On the other hand, let us suppose the combined output of a group of autonomous systems or subsystems is no more than adequate to meet the total need, and that the cooperative effort of homogeneous groups of autonomous systems or subsystems is recognized as contributing mutually to the objectives of the members. Then we may have the basis for a more adequate and logical personnel selection and classification model. The Life Insurance Agency Research Bureau is one example previously referred to of cooperative groups of autonomous subsystems.

Another example which has been regarded by many observers as a most unhappy illustration of competitive scope is that of the many competing commercial organizations who are asked to bid on military contracts involving the development of costly systems. This makes for tremendous waste of highly technical personnel. It also results in a fragmentation of the man subsystem, so that an efficient selection model cannot be applied.

So much for the implications of the administrative organism for a logical selection and classification model. We shall now consider briefly how the jobs to be done within a man-machine system relate to the development of such a model.

The Jobs in the Man Subsystem

As indicated in Chapter 6, it is important to describe jobs in such language that inferences about selection can be made. These descriptions must enable us to distinguish between the activities and the objectives of the job. It is from the job descriptions that hypotheses for the development or procurement of appropriate selection instruments are formulated.

Perhaps one of the most interesting and also difficult aspects of the man subsystem has to do with grouping of jobs into homogeneous subgroups. How this grouping shall be defined or what shall be the basis of the grouping has not been well worked out. However, if those individuals who can function satisfactorily on one of two jobs can do so on the other with little or no training, and if in general those who cannot function satisfactorily on the one cannot do so on the other, then the two jobs may be said to belong to the same group. In general, jobs calling for the same functions are regarded as similar. Many jobs which have different names and objectives may be similar in their requirements, whereas other jobs which have similar names may have different requirements.

Supervision Factors in Jobs.   In discussing jobs in terms of supervision exercised, one may consider roughly three different levels. These are: no supervision, first-line supervision, and executive or administrative supervision. The selection and classification models as traditionally formulated are applicable almost entirely to jobs involving no supervision. Such models, of course, ignore the systems approach. It has been common for many years in large industrial organizations to select, not only men who will perform the actual productive operations of the system, but also those with potential supervisory and administrative abilities, who will be scheduled for special programs of executive or managerial development. These sorts of abilities and the kinds of functions involved in them do not appear to have been as thoroughly investigated as some of the simpler individual functions outlined in Chapter 2. However, some elaboration of interpretative and inventive functions are almost surely involved.

In any case, one cannot ignore the administrative functions in man-machine systems in discussing the logic of personnel selection and classification. Systematic efforts to distinguish between the types of supervision involved in first-line supervision and in the more remote executive and administrative types are at best limited and sporadic. Such efforts should be an essential part of the analysis of the task in a man-machine system. It is not unlikely that malfunctions or failures to achieve mission objectives could frequently be traced to a neglect of this aspect of a system. For example, a technical sergeant may have misread a gauge or failed to check a particular valve and thus caused a mission to fail. On the other hand, if a lieutenant, colonel, or a general is not functioning adequately within the system, even though the individual parts of the man-machine activity complex may be operating satisfactorily, the mission will very probably fall short of its objectives.

As one goes up the line of supervision, the problem of applying an adequate selection and classification model becomes more difficult within a narrowly defined man-machine system, because of the relatively small numbers of men involved at these levels.

Manpower Requirements. It has been pointed out that the number of men required for each particular kind of job is an important item of information for the selection and classification model. The more naive models which have been in use for many years have tended to neglect this factor, and have assumed in principle that the source from which persons could be recruited for any particular job was for practical purposes infinite, so that one did not need to be concerned with how many people were required. World War II taught clearly, as must any large-scale mobilization program, the existence of a close relationship between manpower requirements and sources.

An adequate model must distinguish between classifying men into different kinds of jobs and classifying into different levels within a given job. For example, one might classify a group of men into six different kinds of jobs and then, on the basis of their classification indices, subdivide each kind of job according to the level of abilities required for its successful performance. For example, let us suppose the jobs are those requiring interpretation of symbols, such as numbers. Appropriate evaluation indices for this function may be used to classify the higher group into accountants and the lower into bookkeepers. This is, of course, an oversimplification, since other abilities and other factors would also be involved.

Job Requirements. Chapter 2 proposes a set of basic human functions derived from an analysis of input-output transformations in human behavior. Descriptive systems which have traditionally been used to outline job requirements and worker characteristics have been essentially empirical and have not evolved from an analysis based on human functions. No attempt will be made here to elaborate this conceptual framework bridging the gap between such an approach and the commonly used empirical approach. As a matter of fact, even the vast volumes of psychological tests—achievement, aptitude, personality, motor skills, and the like—have not in general been developed from theoretical analyses of human functions. It is likely that more fundamental approaches, taking their cues from psychological laboratory investigations, would be extremely useful in structuring, organizing, and integrating the vast and confusing array of arbitrarily labeled measurement and evaluation devices which flood the market.

Frequently, job requirements are spelled out in terms of education and experience, as well as in terms of specific psychological or achievement tests. From the point of view of the selection and classification models, both education and experience, on the one hand, and aptitude, achievement, and personality measures, on the other, may be regarded as providing estimates of proficiency in the functions required by specified jobs. Actually, the selection and classification model including its validational mechanisms can test the adequacy with which these assumptions are satisfied. However, well-defined rationales for specifying and evaluating items of education and experience in terms of more fundamental human functions are not currently available.

One important aspect of the role of job requirement specifications has to do with the evaluation of personality characteristics. Presumably personality variables are important for the efficient functioning of a man-machine system. They are important because men differ essentially from machines in that they do cooperate, they do get angry, they do dislike one another, and so forth. But the entire area of personality analysis and evaluation has not yet reached the point where it can be articulated satisfactorily with the type of analysis set forth in Chapter 2.

Proficiency

One of the important activities within a personnel subsystem which must be considered in the evolution of the selection and classification model is that of proficiency evaluation, or assessment of human performance on the job. Without taking into account this aspect of a personnel system one cannot have a model which can be validated. Chapter 12 is devoted to the topic of assessing human performance. In this chapter we shall discuss the subject only briefly in order to relate it to the development of the selection and classification model.

Proficiency Evaluation. One of the characteristics of the selection and classification models is that it is concerned with prediction. On the basis of behavior previous to selection, predictions are made as to how well individuals will function in specified job situations. In spite of continuing violations of this principle, it is axiomatic (for anything except a crystal-ball model) that we have available, on the same group of individuals, measures of performance for a specified set of activities prior to introduction into the man-machine system, and also measures of performance in job activities after introduction to the system. One modification of this principle is that the evaluations on the variables normally taken prior to participation in the jobs may be taken while engaged in job activities. This variation in the model, however, assumes that performance on nonjob activities while on the job will provide an adequate index of performance on these activities had they been assessed before coming on the job. These two types of measurement of nonjob performances as a basis for predicting job success have been discussed in various textbooks on personnel selection. Not always, however, have the assumptions been clearly stated, and usually they have not been validated.

Three broad types of evaluation on the job may be employed. One of these is in terms of objective measures, such as length of time on the job, number of salary increases, current salary, units of production, spoilage, and the like. Another kind of measure which may be used is based on objective or achievement tests. A third type of evaluation is that of supervisors' ratings. Here many specific methods are available, and this is not the place to describe them. The important point is that each of these three types results in some sort of quantitative or numerical value.

Let us next consider an important aspect of supervisory ratings as it relates to the supervisory framework of a proficiency evaluation system, as well as to the types of administrative organisms which we considered earlier. A given supervisor can be responsible only for a limited number of persons. Ordinarily, such a supervisor cannot be responsible for a group large enough to be considered the N for a typical selection and classification model. Neither can it be expected in any typical man-machine system that all persons doing the same kind of work are subject to the same supervision and evaluation. Therefore, where evaluations are based largely on subjective appraisals by supervisory personnel, the problem of accounting for individual differences in the standards and discriminatory abilities of different supervisors is germane to the logic of personnel selection and classification. A general approach to the solution of this type of problem has been outlined elsewhere (Horst *et al.*, 1941). The problem of obtaining comparable ratings is intimately tied up with the administrative structure of a man-machine system. The ideal system requires a hierarchical order of supervision such that a next higher-order set of evaluations will overlap or in part bracket evaluations of lower orders of supervision.

One aspect of a proficiency evaluation program which is important for the implementation of an adequate model of personnel selection and classification is the frequency and regularity with which such evaluations are provided. For any selection program which makes provisions for improving the accuracy of the system on the basis of ongoing experience, it is important that a systematic and periodic evaluation procedure be set up. Although this is a requisite for a dynamic personnel system, it is also essential for other aspects of the efficient operation of the man-machine system, as indicated in

Chapter 12. At any rate, proficiency evaluation must provide feedback to the selection and classification subsystem. These evaluations must be readily and freely available to the selection subsystem if the model is to include self-correcting mechanisms.

Selection Procedures

Among the major considerations in typical selection procedures are the kinds of instruments used, the basis on which these instruments are used, the allocation of responsibility for selection within the organizational structure, and, perhaps most important, the relation of the selection procedures to the proficiency evaluation program within the system.

Types of Instruments. The kinds of instruments used may profitably be discussed under four major groups: psychological tests and measures of various kinds, biographical inventories, personal references, and interviews. By far the most important of these groups from our point of view is the first. We have already referred to worker characteristics and capacities, and have indicated that a great volume of instruments has been developed to assess these various capacities, abilities, and personality traits. We have pointed out that the approach has been largely pragmatic and has not followed a comprehensive, systematic analysis of human functions. We shall point out here that the underlying philosophy of psychological tests—whether these be tests of ability, proficiency, aptitude, personality, temperament, or interests—is that they constitute specific and presumably relevant kinds of stimulus situations which will elicit behaviors considered relevant to job requirements in a man-machine system. Measures of this kind are supposed to elicit samples of behavior characteristics of the reacting individuals. Implicit in this reasoning is the assumption that the sample behaviors are representative of the typical or usual ways of reacting to similar stimulus situations, and that therefore these behaviors may be used as a basis for predicting behavior in subsequent similar situations. That these assumptions are all too frequently not met in actual practice is beside the point. It is a function of the personnel selection and classification model to test and revise assumptions of this sort.

A particular example of this approach is provided by the biographical inventory. This is one sort of scatter-gun approach to the sampling of past behaviors, stimulus patterns, and environmental influences. The essential characteristic of the biographical inventory, as of other tests, is that the stimulus situations are set up in the form of items with controlled responses and methods for evaluating these responses objectively.

Another common type of selection instrument is the personal reference. Actually, personal references can be provided in the form of answers to objective questionnaires or they may be given in free-answer verbal form. Perhaps the type calling for objective responses to a structured questionnaire could be used with profit much more extensively than it has been. In general, the purpose in using references is the same as in using tests—namely, to elicit samples of behavior. Here, however, the behavior samples are not directly those of the individual, but only reactions of other persons to behaviors of the individual. In spite of the extensive use of references in personnel selection and classification, experimental evidence for the value of such instruments is still surprisingly lacking.

Perhaps the most commonly used selection instrument of all is the interview. Its use is almost universal in all systems of personnel selection. In the interview, the stimulus situation is usually provided in terms of auditory stimulus symbols by the interviewer, to which the interviewee responds. The assumption, of course, is that the stimulus symbols are directly related to specific job requirements and that the responses of the interviewee will be predictive of his functioning or responses in a particular situation. The interview may be highly structured and follow a specified pattern, or it may be completely unstructured. It is not unusual in interview situations for the interviewer to do most of the responding, giving the interviewee little opportunity to do so. Therefore at the end of the interview the interviewer may have only a small and irrelevant sample of behavior from the interviewee on the basis of which to make selection and classification decisions or recommendations.

Perhaps the greatest advantage of the interview as a prediction instrument stems from one of the essential differences between men and machines suggested earlier. This is that the effectiveness of the man component in the man-machine system is a function, in part, of his interactions with other people, whereas this is not the case, except in a superficial mechanical sense, with machines. The interview provides just such a stimulus environment—namely, one in which another individual interacts with the interviewee. This characteristic of the instrument also applies in part to personal references. Objective tests, on the other hand, aim to remove personal judgment of the individual from the behavior situation. It is true that with some types of testing situations, the interaction of the tester and the subject may be regarded as important. Experimental and objective evaluations of such approaches are, however, very limited, and in general such results as are available are not strikingly positive.

Reasons for Choosing Selection Instruments.   The bases for the use of selection instruments fall into at least three important categories. These are *a priori* or rational considerations, informal and unsystematic experience, and systematic experience or research.

In putting together a man-machine system, *a priori* or rational procedures must often be the basis for the initial selection and classification procedure. Much as this approach offends the validation purists, there may be no alternative in practical situations where we are faced with the necessity of producing an operating system as rapidly as possible. It is inevitable in such cases that rational bases must play a large role in initiating selection procedures for man-machine systems. But it can well be argued that all logical and rational approaches must consist of applications or extrapolations of past experience.

When a new man-machine system is initiated, a great deal of experience with personnel may be available from similar types of systems and with reference to similar types of analyses in previous situations. Interpretations and certain assumptions can be made in taking over in part or in modified form procedures which have been verified in similar systems. In this way, bodies of quasi-scientific results may be used in the preliminary establishment of selection instruments for a newly initiated system.

Finally, the basis for determining the instruments for selection and classification which concerns us most is that based on systematic and structured experience according to a prespecified model, in accordance with the procedures of scientific research.

Responsibility for Decisions about Selection.   One of the characteristics of selection procedures which can influence the development of the selection model has to do with the allocation of responsibility for critical decisions in the selection of personnel. This responsibility can be allocated in one or both of two different ways.

In the first approach, line personnel responsible for the work of a new employee may make the final or critical decision in the selection procedure. This sort of allocation is common in most industrial organizations. The philosophy underlying the procedure seems to be that, since a large part of the success of an employee will depend on his interaction with his supervisors, the supervisory personnel under whom he works must assume final responsibility for his induction into the man-machine system.

The other approach to selection and allocation of personnel assumes a staff organization or subsystem responsible for the induction and distribution of men to the system. The philosophy here appears to be that selection and classification procedures are not only sufficiently adequate and accurate but also sufficiently specialized and complex, so that a staff division can function more effectively in the optimal selection and assignment of personnel than a system depending largely on supervisory personnel. This latter type of philosophy is exemplified in civil-service and military organizations. Many systems employ combinations of these two extremes.

Relation to Proficiency Measurement.   An important characteristic of selection procedures is the nature of their relation to the proficiency evaluation program within the organization. A selection and classification program can in general be no better or more effective than the proficiency evaluation program within the system. An interesting exception to this statement occurs in the case of a system which measures performance of the man subsystem reliably but not validly. It is possible that a proficiency evaluation program may measure with great accuracy factors which are largely irrelevant to mission objectives. To the extent that selection and classification procedures are based on such programs, the system will fall short of achieving its mission objectives. On the other hand, even though a proficiency evaluation program measures only roughly or crudely the factors relevant to mission objectives, it may provide a more adequate basis for the development of selection and classification procedures than one which measures irrelevant factors with great accuracy. This phenomenon is generally not well recognized. A technical and detailed treatment of the issues involved is given by Thorndike (1949).

Personnel Flow through the Man-Machine System

A major characteristic of the personnel system which is essential for a dynamic personnel selection and classification model relates to the flow of personnel through the system. We have previously pointed out that although new units of both men and machines are introduced into the system and existing units leave the system, the nature of the inflow and outflow for each is essentially different. The phenomenon of personnel flow into and through a system is utilized in developing essential aspects of the personnel selection and classification model. Personnel flow may be discussed in terms of loss of personnel from the entire system or subsystems within the system, and also in terms of the induction of personnel into the system.

The loss of personnel from subsystems within the system which does not result from over-all loss is due chiefly to promotions and transfers. These two types of losses from subsystems are important because they imply different problems in the logic of personnel selection and classification.

Promotion may be of two kinds. The promotion may be along the supervisory scale, where a person goes from one supervisory level to a higher one or from a nonsupervisory level to a supervisory level. There may also be promotions *within* a given kind of activity, where the change in performance is from a less difficult to a more difficult level of the same kind of function. In general, promotions can take place only if more room is being made at the top, because of expansion of the man-machine system, or because of the escape of personnel from the higher echelons of the total organization. We have indicated that when a system is initiated it must rely in part on rational bases for its selection procedures. In general, the lower the validity of these rational considerations, the higher can we expect the ejection rate of personnel from the system to be. In the case of transfers, we have the implication that either the design of the man-machine system is changing or that the classification or assignment part of the selection procedure was not functioning adequately in the first place. The rate of transfer from one kind of job to another at the same level of job requirements may be used inversely as an index of the efficiency of the classification model.

Personnel may leave the total system for one of two reasons. Individuals may be ejected from it because they do not meet the requirements of available positions within the system or because the available positions do not satisfy them. Voluntary resignations occur because the individuals can presumably find more satisfactory jobs in other systems. But resignations may be due either to faulty classification or to inadequate functioning of persons in supervisory levels. In any case, promotion of any kind, whether from within a given type of activity or from one type to another (such as to a supervisory level), transfers, resignations, and discharges all imply vacancies to be filled by new personnel.

It is the phenomenon of vacancies existing within a system which makes possible the development of a selection and classification model incorporating within itself a self-correcting submechanism. If by some omniscient scheme or program it were possible to staff a newly established man-machine system so that each person were perfectly fitted for the job he is to do, then the personnel problem would already have been solved. Realistically, of course, this is not the situation, and the most conspicuous features of the personnel selection and classification model are derived from the assumption that the hypotheses from which the model is developed are assumed to be subject to error, so that the model must provide for feedback and self-correcting mechanisms operating dynamically throughout time.

Recruitment into the System.   Both practically and theoretically, the recruitment problem must be concerned with the sources of personnel to be inducted into the system and the total supply available. The ratio of supply and demand is one of the constraints of the selection and classification model. The sources of personnel are important characteristics of a model because of their implications for both competing and cooperating man-machine systems which must compete with one another for the total unutilized reserve pool of manpower. These are problems we cannot discuss at great length here; their analysis seems to be far from complete at the present time. It is interesting to point out that during World War II recruitment procedures and recruitment sources for the armed services involved important theoretical assumptions. Some of these assumptions were that the mission of the U. S. Army Air Forces required a higher order of abilities than did those of the other Army organizations, and that the job of pilot required a higher order of ability than did those of other types of aircrew personnel. The efficient operation of an ideal personnel selection and classification model is dependent to a certain extent on how sources of supply are defined and what restrictions are placed on these.

Training Programs

One important aspect of the functioning of a personnel system within the total system concerns those operations responsible for systematically modifying the performance characteristics of men within the system. The extent to which effective training programs, whether systematic or informal, exist within the system has considerable bearing on the development of the selection and classification model. Other chapters in this book are concerned with procedures, devices, and concepts involved in modifying or improving the functioning of men within the man-machine system (compare Chapters 9, 10, and 11). Here we shall be concerned only with those characteristics of the training problem which have theoretical implications for the development of the selection and classification model. This model must take into account how training relates to the mission objectives of the system, as well as how the training activities are distributed over the available jobs in the system.

The relation of training programs to mission objectives may be discussed from the point of view of those programs concerned directly with these objectives, and of those programs concerned with preparing men to participate in these objectives. These two kinds of training may readily be recognized as on-the-job training and formal, or classroom, training. In on-the-job training, systematic supervision and tuition is provided the individual performing the functions of a particular job. On the other hand, many organizations have vestibule schools or formal classroom sessions, where employees listen to lectures, observe demonstrations, read books, watch movies, operate simulators of actual hardware, and the like. The distinguishing characteristic of this kind of activity is that it is not in itself productive, as is on-the-job training. There are, of course, many systems whose primary mission is that of formal training or the modification of human functions for the purpose of satisfying mission objectives in other systems. Schools, colleges, and technical training schools in and out of the Department of Defense are such systems.

Before hypothesizing the types of stimulus situation which are presumed to evoke samples of relevant behavior, it is important to know for what kind of training situations, if any, personnel are being selected. It is likewise important to know to what extent the ability to profit from experience on the job under appropriate supervision and tutelage is required; or to what extent ability to profit from formalized classroom situations is necessary.

Within a given system, there may be a great deal of variation from one type of job to another with respect to the extent and kinds of training procedures employed. Before it is possible to develop an over-all selection and classification model for a particular man-machine system, specifications need to be provided as to the training available for each of the jobs within the system. These specifications must be set forth in sufficient detail so that the worker characteristics may be reasonably hypothesized, as outlined in Chapter 6.

We have considered various aspects and characteristics of the personnel system within the man-machine system which are particularly relevant to the development of the selection model. We shall now proceed to a more precise description of the selection model, using the concepts we have discussed in this section.

▣ THE SELECTION AND CLASSIFICATION MODEL

The terms "selection" and "classification" used in combination are somewhat misleading. The implication seems to be that if one has a man-machine system which requires, let us say, a thousand men, one segregates or isolates from an available pool one thousand men for the system. After one has selected or segregated this group, he then classifies its members according to the various jobs within the system. This procedure leaves us in the dark as to how the men were selected in the first place. As a matter of fact, one cannot logically segregate or select the total number of men required for a man-machine system without selecting each man for a specific assignment in the system.

But before the model can be developed, we must introduce certain basic concepts. We assume that certain hypotheses or sets of hypotheses are developed from whatever source, and that then experimental data are collected and analyzed to test the adequacy of the hypotheses. The most conspicuous, if not the most important, part of the model is that of testing the hypotheses, rather than that of constructing them. Perhaps this is because it is much easier to specify the "hypothesis-verifying" part of the model than to describe the "hypothesis-construction" part.

The basic concepts we require for the development of the model are three. They are *attributes, entities,* and *measures*. We assume that in the personnel system, as in any system subject to scientific investigation, there are attributes or variables of some sort with which we are concerned. We also assume that these attributes do not exist in and of themselves but that they are manifested in some kinds of entities. In the case of the personnel selection model, as in most psychological studies, the entities are human beings. We therefore have attributes or characteristics of human beings. The third basic concept with which we are concerned is that of measures or indices. We assume that, if entities are characterized by attributes, these attributes exist in some quantity, so that we have a measure for an attribute of an entity.

The Attributes

Attributes may be defined as broadly or narrowly as we wish for our purposes. The personnel selection model which we shall develop involves two distinct types of attributes. One of these we shall designate as *predictor attributes* and the other as *criterion attributes*. Sometimes, in more general settings, predictor attributes are called independent variables, and criterion attributes are called dependent variables. In general, predictor attributes are so called because they are used to make predictions. Criterion attributes are those which are predicted or estimated by the predictor attributes.

Predictor Attributes. First, let us consider some of the characteristics of predictor attributes. Because of the use to which predictor attributes are put, they have certain essential characteristics. In the first place, predictor attributes are available prior to criterion attributes. Usually they are also much easier to evaluate than criterion attributes. For example, a test score is usually considered as a predictor measure. It is relatively inexpensive and takes perhaps not over a matter of minutes or hours to get a test score for particular individuals. In the second place, predictor measures are usually not regarded as important in themselves. The product of a response obtained from a predictor measure cannot be utilized in any useful sense. One cannot do anything useful with a person's response to a two-hand coordination instrument or to items in a test of mechanical aptitude. It is only because these are thought to be correlated with useful responses that they are of interest.

Many kinds of predictor measures are available for the selection model. For example, one could consider the types of stimulus (input) situations described in Chapter 2 and the kinds of functions available for each of these situations. Once could then introduce any number of variations or special cases for each of the stimulus situations and various manifestations of each type of response. For various combinations of these, one could then invent test situations or instruments for prediction purposes. Actually, many of the available test instruments may obviously be regarded as special cases of sensing, detecting, identifying, interpreting, and inventing with respect to stimulus differences, stimulus objects, or symbols. Systematic efforts at such classification have not been made. It is possible that such efforts would be productive, not only in providing clues for better selection of predictor instruments, but also in providing clues for elaborating the system of human functions proposed in Chapter 2.

In general, then, we may think of predictor variables or attributes as those attributes of individuals evaluated by means of tests and other selection instruments prior to selection and classification for man-machine systems.

Criterion Attributes. The criterion attributes are attributes which are to be predicted. In the personnel selection and classification setting, the criterion attributes are those attributes of individuals exhibited in their performance on the job. By definition, therefore, the criterion attributes have certain important characteristics. First, unlike the predictor attributes, they are not available until after the individual begins to function within the man-machine system. Also unlike the predictor attributes, the assessment of criterion attributes is relatively expensive and time-consuming. For example, it is much more expensive and time-consuming to find out how well an individual can fly a B-52 bomber aircraft under all sorts of conditions than it is to find out how well he can function on a mechanical comprehension test or on a simple eye-hand coordination test. Also in contrast to the predictor variable, the criterion variable is important and significant of itself. It is of direct concern to mission objectives whether a pilot can fly a B-52 effectively; or whether a technical sergeant can properly carry out his specific functions in the launching of a ballistic missile.

We have previously discussed the problem of proficiency evaluation as it impinges on the selection model. Ideally, we should have a common language which will bridge the gap between criterion measures and predictor measures; that is, we should be able to evaluate criterion or job performances in terms of the basic types of response functions in relation to specified types of stimuli. Chapter 12 is primarily concerned with such problems, and no attempt will be made here to characterize the different types of criteria.

Dual Functions of Attributes.   There is a third kind of attribute, which may serve a dual function. At one period in time the attribute or variable may be a criterion attribute and at a later time it may be a predictor attribute. For example, performance on a particular job may be a criterion attribute at one time, but this performance may be also used to predict performance on a job at a later time. Performance on a lower-level job may be regarded as a criterion attribute which has been previously predicted by some predictor variable, but which may also be used as a predictor to predict success in a higher-level job.

One example of this is found in systems which have established training programs as part of the man-machine system. Before the individual is admitted to the training program, whether on-the-job or classroom, one may predict success in these training activities. Performance in the training activities would then constitute the criterion attribute. But the same performance may also be used to predict success in later phases of productive activity on the job; in this case they are regarded as predictor variables or attributes.

The Entities of the Selection Model

We have said that the attributes must inhere in some kind of entities, and have pointed out that in the personnel situation the entities are individual persons. In order further to develop the personnel selection model, let us examine the concept of entities more specifically. It is important in discussing the entities of the selection model to consider two major types. One of these we shall call the experimental entities, because it is on the basis of these that the selection model is developed. The other we shall call administrative entities, because these are the entities to which the procedures developed on the experimental entities are applied.

We begin to see now why the concept of flow of personnel in the man-machine system is important for the selection model. The model assumes that we have a group of experimental entities on the basis of which selection procedures can be established, and that these procedures may then be applied to entities known as the administrative entities. Specifically, we find out how to make predictions on the group of experimental entities and we make these predictions for the administrative entities.

We have said the model assumes that for an attribute we have a measure with respect to an entity. These measures must be numerical if the model is to have more than journalistic significance.

Let us now summarize these basic concepts in terms of Figure 7.1. In

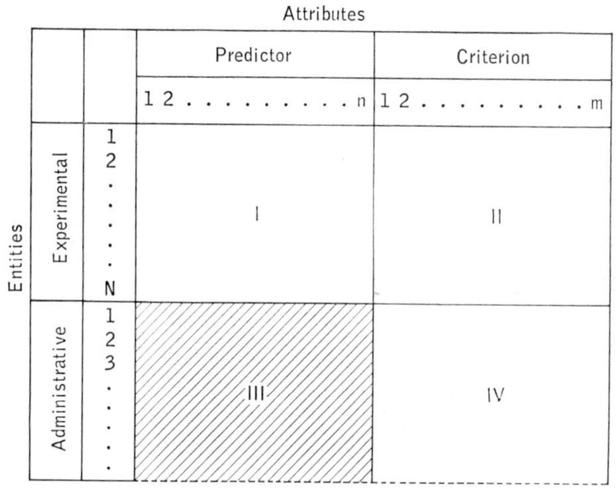

Figure 7.1. The complete multiple prediction data matrix. The first quadrant is the submatrix of n predictor measures on the N experimental entities. The second quadrant is the submatrix of m measures on the same N experimental entities. The third quadrant is the submatrix of n predictor measures on an unspecified number of administrative entities. The fourth quadrant is a submatrix with unknown criterion elements which are to be predicted from the predictor measures of the administrative entities.

the first place, the number of experimental entities is specified beforehand in setting up the experimental part of the model. This is indicated by the column on the left in the upper part of the diagram, which goes from 1 to N. We notice that the upper part of the diagram consists of two quadrants. Quadrant I represents the measures of the predictor attributes for the experimental entities. Quadrant II represents the measures of the criterion attributes for the experimental entities. It is important to note in this model that we assume measures of all the experimental entities for each of the predictor attributes. This characteristic of the model implies that the number of different types of functions required in a particular man-machine system are definitely limited. Similarity of functions may be defined in terms of the correlations between measures of these functions for a group of individuals. A particular type of analysis known as factor analysis has as its basic function the determination of the number of statistically or functionally independent attributes within a specified system. Although authorities disagree, there is good evidence to indicate that the total number of socially significant kinds of different behaviors which can be measured by objective procedures does not exceed thirty or forty. This applies to psychological functions rather than to specific achievement variables involving specialized knowledge or facts.

Furthermore, the model assumes measures of the experimental entities on the criterion attributes. Very rarely, however, is it possible in practical situations to have measures of experimental entities on all the criterion attributes. In a later part of this section we shall consider in more detail the submatrix of measures in Quadrant II of Figure 7.1 with respect to the pattern of missing data.

Next let us examine the essential characteristics of the administrative entities represented by the lower part of the diagram in Figure 7.1. An essential characteristic of the administrative entities is that their number or quantity may not be specifically defined. This is indicated by the fact that we start with the numbers 1, 2, 3, but then do not go on to some general symbol for the total number, and that we have a broken line at the bottom. The administrative entities, let us remember, are those to which the procedures derived from the experimental entities are applied. We may have a fairly unitary group of entities, such as an Army quota calling for a thousand inductees at a time and place. But more typically, in most man-machine systems the experimental entities come in a more or less even flow from day to day, as is the case with job applicants for positions vacated as a result of expansion of the system or exits from the system. The fact that Quadrant III is shaded means that we have measures on all of the experimental entities for the predictor attributes. The fact that the space in Quadrant IV is blank indicates that we do not have measures on any of the experimental entities for any of the criterion attributes. Figure 7.1 is the fundamental model from which we must work in developing the elaborated model of the selection and classification subsystems. The basic scheme of the selection model shown in this figure is a special case of what is known as the *generalized multivariate prediction model.*

We have said that the selection model implies some sort of index or measure of an attribute for an entity. In Figure 7.1, the entries in Quadrants I, II, and III are figures or indices of this kind. We shall now discuss in more detail the measures of the attributes.

The Measures of the Attributes

We need in our model two basic concepts in discussing measures of the attributes for the entities. First, as we have indicated already, these measures must be in the form of number symbols, or such that they can be translated to number symbols. Second, we need the concept of more than one estimate of the attribute for the entities. That is, we need the notion of replication or repeated samples of behavior with reference to a particular defined function or performance.

Numerical Score. Although in many cases it is not feasible to have a measure or an index of performance for each entity with respect to each attribute, it is essential that, if such an index is available, it be in the form of a number. These numbers often are scores on a test, such as the number of items correctly answered according to a predetermined scoring key. Or they can be the number of seconds or minutes it takes to assemble a particular group of objects, the number of errors made in typing a piece of copy, the rating assigned to a person by a supervisor, or the monthly salary of a person in a particular job.

As a special case, the number may be restricted to either zero or one. This is called a dichotomous measure, and the fact that we may have such a simple type of measure makes it possible to quantify practically any attribute in which we may be interested. For example, sex may be regarded as an attribute. Here we may assign a value of one for female and zero for male. Another variable of this type of attribute is college graduation. We may give a score of one for "graduated from college" and zero for "did not graduate." Many important models of scientific research and investigation in the social, biological, and even physical sciences utilize in their designs this notion of zero-one measures.

Replication. The second characteristic of measures which is important in the selection and classification model is that of replication. By replication is meant that there is more than one measure of an attribute for an entity. A simple example is a test score. Objective test scores are made up of scores on individual items in the test. A mathematics test includes a number of items, and the score is a function of the total number of items answered correctly. This is a very simple example of replication, or of taking a sample of a number of different responses from the individual with respect to the same kind of stimulus situation. We may also consider repeated responses to the same stimulus pattern or group of patterns in successive time intervals. For example, we may give the same test to a person today and again next week. Here we have two different measures for the same individual or two different measures of the same test. Or in the case of an observer's rating, the observer may give repeated evaluations for successive weeks or months. We may also have observations or evaluations with respect to the same function by different observers. The concept of replication is crucial in the multivariate prediction model as well as in its special applications to the personnel-selection and classification model.

Characteristics of Measuring Instruments

Selection and classification programs may fall short of being maximally effective because they do not take into account certain characteristics which the measures of attributes should satisfy. All of these characteristics of measures must be considered in relation to the particular group of individuals to whom the model is applied.

Measures of attributes must satisfy certain conditions with respect to a particular experimental group. The first of these we shall discuss is that of *average level of performance*. The test of a function should not be too easy or too difficult for the group of individuals who are supposed to perform the function on the job. For example, an arithmetic test used to predict success on a job should not be so difficult that people functioning satisfactorily on the job make poor scores on the test. Neither should it be so easy that all persons could finish the test with a perfect score in the time allowed.

Another characteristic of the measure is that when applied to the group which is to be considered for jobs there should be *variation in scores* among those tested or measured. Some people should make good test scores, others poor, and others in between. This means that the standard deviation of the distribution of scores should be adequate to make possible differentiation among group members. Even in the case of dichotomous measures, the experimental group must have some people who get *one* scores and some who get *zero* scores. Otherwise the attributes will not function in the selection and classification model. For example, sex cannot be used as a potential predictor variable in the experimental group unless some of the persons are males and some females. A measure of an attribute which does not discriminate among the members of the experimental group is of no value in the selection and classification model. Other things being equal, it may be said that those attributes which have the largest dispersion in the experimental group will serve the most useful function in the selection and classification procedures.

A third characteristic of the measures applies more specifically to continuous measures than to dichotomous measures. This characteristic is known as *homogeneity*. It applies to those measures which may be regarded as made up of replications. For measures of this kind, it is desirable that the stimulus elements be as nearly comparable as possible. That is, the items within a test should all be of the same type, in the sense that they require the same sort of response function. This point can be put in statistical terms. If we have separate measures on the individual parts of the sample of behavior for each of a group of individuals, the intercorrelations of these measures of unit responses should be as high as possible. In particular, the measure of a unit response to an objective test will ordinarily be zero or one. The responses to unit elements of psychomotor or eye-hand coordination tests may be arbitrarily defined units of time, such as the first five seconds of performance or the next five seconds.

A fourth important characteristic of the measures is that they should be *objective*. The method of arriving at the numerical index should be such that there is high agreement among observers as to a particular person's measure on a particular attribute. Psychological tests are good examples of objective measures. In general, it is not a matter of argument whether the individual has 20 or 30 items correct according to a specified answer key. On the other hand, if the task is to write an English essay on a given subject, then there may be considerable disagreement as to whether a person should get a score of 75 or 100.

Another characteristic of measures which applies both to criterion and predictor attributes is that of *stability*. This refers to the consistency of the measure for a particular individual over a period of time. If the criterion function to be measured is such that the measure of it fluctuates wildly up and down over a period of time, it may be impossible to predict. It is important to construct measures of performance which will exhibit stability for individuals over a period of time. Measures which exhibit this characteristic are said to be reliable, and those which do not, unreliable.

Reliability is of particular importance for measures of predictor attributes. If the measure of a particular function today gives little indication of what the measure of this function will be next week or within a month, we cannot expect such a measure to predict later performance on the job. It should be noted, however, that stability may be achieved simply by taking evaluations of performance over a sufficiently long period of time. It should be noted that stability, like homogeneity, involves the concept of replicated evaluations of the same attribute for a given entity. The essential difference between the notions of homogeneity and stability is that in homogeneity we are concerned with responses to a number of the same type of stimulus patterns, whereas in the case of stability we are concerned with repeated responses to the same stimulus pattern over a period of time. In both cases, we collect a number of behavior samples involving the same function.

The next characteristic of the attributes we shall discuss is called *specificity*. The first five characteristics we have mentioned—level, discrimination, homogeneity, objectivity, and stability—all refer to a measure of a specific attribute. Specificity concerns the relationship of one attribute to another. It is desirable in the personnel classification and selection model that the predictor attributes be as independent of one another as possible. In statistical terminology, the intercorrelations among the predictor attributes should be as low as possible. The reason for this is that, the higher the intercorrelations between two variables, the more nearly do they measure the same functions, even though we may use different methods for measuring them. A commonly observed phenomenon in attempts to measure a large number of rationally defined psychological functions is that intercorrelations among many of them tend to be high. This can have one of two causes. First, it may be that the rational analysis on which the measures are based, while appearing to yield logically different psychological variables, nevertheless fails to define essentially different functional unities. Another reason may be that, although functions have been described which are in themselves relatively independent and unitary, efforts to measure these functions do not result in instruments which actually do measure different functions. Some of the instruments may duplicate others even though they may seem to be different.

It should be obvious that merely by applying different labels to different instruments we do not ensure that we are measuring really different kinds of functions. Nevertheless, this assumption is made in many presumably responsible testing programs and frequently leads to disappointing and misleading results. The higher the intercorrelations among a set of predictor measures, the less useful will these measures be for predicting in which of a number of different kinds of criterion activities (job functions) a person will be most successful. Another way of stating this important principle is that the higher the intercorrelations among a set of predictor measures, the less useful these will be for personnel classification.

The final characteristic of measures which we shall discuss is what has traditionally been called *validity*. In recent years, a number of different kinds of validity have been defined, but only one of these will concern us in the personnel selection and classification model. By the validity of a measure we mean the accuracy with which it predicts performance on a criterion activity. More generally, statistical validity refers to the correlation between a predictor and a criterion measure. We refer to the coefficient of correlation between a predictor measure and a criterion measure as a validity coefficient. In this sense it is clear that a test may have, not a single validity, but as many validities as there are criterion measures with which it may be correlated.

It is also possible to speak of the validity of a criterion measure, although this is not as commonly done. For example, we may consider supervisors' ratings of performance on a particular job as a criterion measure. We may then raise the question, "Do these ratings give an indication of how well the person is performing in relation to the specific mission objectives of the particular job, or do they instead reflect personal interactions between the supervisor and the employee?" In other words, do these ratings also indicate how well the supervisor likes the employee? If this latter is the case, and he likes the employee whether or not he is adequately performing the specific mission objectives of the job, then we may say that the criterion measures are not valid measures of job performance. Another example may arise when objective achievement or information tests of some sort are used as criterion measures for individuals in a particular job. These measures are objective; they may also be stable and reliable. They may place emphasis on what the subject knows about a job, such as technical terminology, but they may not indicate how well he is actually performing the specific mission objectives of the job. In this case, while the test scores may be regarded as objective and reliable measures of the criterion performance, they may not be valid measures.

It is often difficult to separate these characteristics of a measure in the case of criterion activity. In many man-machine systems, it is particularly difficult in team situations to determine for any particular individual just how well he is performing the mission objectives of the job. In a straightforward assembly job, where each person works independently, valid proficiency measures may be more easily arrived at. In general, it is probable that insufficient effort has been devoted to the designing of man-machine systems so that the contribution of a single individual can be isolated or segregated from the output of the group to which he contributes. Certainly in an assembly line the productivity of individuals is largely paced by the tempo of the assembly line itself.

From the motivational point of view, it is possible that systems designed so as to permit each individual to contribute independently as much as he can may be generally more productive. This is a separate problem, however, and is more appropriately expanded in other parts of this book. The essential relevance of this point for personnel selection and classification is that the less the productivity of a man-machine system depends on the independent sums of the productivity of the individuals in the man subsystem of it, the less effective can be the development and validation of a selection and classification model.

In terms of Figure 7.1, then, we may summarize the characteristics of measures as follows. The characteristics of level, discrimination, homogeneity, objectivity, and stability are concerned primarily with the measure of each of the individual attributes in Quadrant I. With the exception of homogeneity, these also apply to the measures of each of the attributes in Quadrant II. The characteristic of specificity refers to the interrelationships of the attributes among themselves and involves only Quadrant I. (If the criterion activities are based directly on arbitrary job designations, there is nothing one can do about the interrelationships of these, so that ordinarily specificity does not involve Quadrant II.) Finally, the characteristic of validity refers to the interrelations or correlations of the attributes in Quadrant I with those in Quadrant II.

We have referred several times to the fact that the complete selection and classification model requires not only the development of hypotheses but also the verification of these hypotheses. This requirement of the model is reflected in Figure 7.1 by the fact that measures of both predictor and criterion attributes for a group of experimental entities are indicated in Quadrants I and II. We have also pointed out that the flow of personnel into or out of the man-machine system is an essential phenomenon in the specification of the personnel selection and classification model. It is evident that, in setting up a man-machine system "from scratch," there is not available a group of entities in the man-machine system on whom we have both predictor and criterion measures. The system has not existed previously, therefore the experimental group could not have performed the tasks for which criterion measures are required.

For any such newly constituted man-machine system, some assumptions must be made about the variables important for predicting success in the newly constituted system and how they should be measured. It is possible to develop hypotheses structured somewhat along the lines of Chapter 2 on the basis of information provided by the kinds of analyses outlined in Chapter 6. Hypotheses must be formulated about the extent to which each of these predictor attributes enters into predicting success in each of the jobs for which personnel are to be selected and classified. In other words, there must be some procedure for *weighting* test scores differentially for each of these particular jobs, so as to get predictions of success for each job. At this point, however, one must operate on the basis of hypotheses alone. Only later, as men are absorbed into the system and measures of criterion performance become available, can these hypotheses be tested and modified on the basis of experience.

Prevalidation Administration

Both from the theoretical and practical points of view, it is important that whatever measures we adopt shall satisfy as well as possible the characteristics we have just outlined. It is essential, then, that the complete model for the system include a preliminary *prevalidation procedure,* to assure that the measures of the postulated predictor variables satisfy the required characteristics of such measures. This principle is illustrated by the simple diagram in Figure 7.2. Here we have a matrix similar to that in Quadrant I of Figure 7.1. Operationally, this means that, having worked out a set of predictor measures, we administer these to a prevalidation group, so that our hypotheses with reference to the essential characteristics of the measures may be tested and so that the measuring instruments may be modified on the basis of these

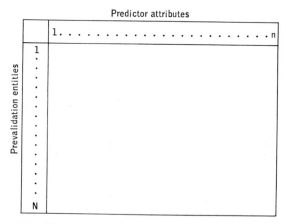

Figure 7.2. The matrix of *n* predictor measures on a group of *N* prevalidation entities.

results. Frequently, selection instruments turn out to be much less effective than they might be because this preliminary feature of the general model has been neglected. In general, the kinds of analyses to be performed on the pre-validation entities are those of difficulty, dispersion, homogeneity, stability, and specificity. These are discussed in detail in textbooks on measurement and evaluation, such as Cronbach (1960) and Anastasi (1954).

It is of some relevance to the development of the model to consider the source of the prevalidation entities. We have several possibilities. First, these entities may be the same as the original group of men taken into the new system. In general, however, this is an extravagant and impractical procedure because, in any case, the revised set of predictor measures must be applied to the group considered for induction to the system. If the prevalidation material is given to this group, the group will then have to be subjected to the second administration after the material has been revised to meet the required specifications.

It is usually desirable to administer the material to groups external to the system which may be available for such experimental purposes. In actual practice it may be difficult to find such groups. In military situations, new inductees are often used for such purposes. In industrial situations it is sometimes possible to get school systems to cooperate in such projects. If the system is an autonomous subsystem of a larger system, such as a missile division of a large aircraft company, then it may be possible to use the time of employees in other parts of the company for such experimental purposes.

It is not uncommon in the development of predictor measures for a selection and classification procedure of a new man-machine system to use batteries of material already available. This is common in the armed services, where extensive work has been done on the development of personnel selection and classification batteries. Unfortunately, however, many of these batteries do not exhibit adequately the essential prevalidation characteristics of a battery of predictor measures.

The Criterion Data

The selection and classification model cannot be completed until we have measures of criterion performance on the men operating within the new system. Let us now consider in more detail the nature of the criterion submatrix.

It may first be observed that, typically, in the selection and classification model the chief emphasis in the past has been on selection as such; that is, a particular job has first been thought of and has led to a concern with finding a battery of tests or measures to predict success in this job. If the battery is given to a group of individuals, a composite score may be derived by appropriate statistical techniques and the persons who score best on these predictions may be selected for the job. This has been the traditional approach to personnel-selection programs using objective measures. This model concerns itself only with a single column of the criterion attributes in Figure 7.1. It should be observed, however, that what we have indicated for convenience as a single column may actually involve a number of different kinds of functions. If the attribute is on the basis of job designation—such as typist, lathe operator, or pilot—the job itself may be complex and require a variety of different functions. This, then, suggests the possibility of a criterion of over-all effectiveness as a pilot or a typist or a lathe operator. But there is also the possibility of breaking the job down into a number of different functions, such that performance on each of these may be evaluated. The kind of analysis which may be undertaken has been described in Chapter 6.

For a single job, then, we may have just one measure or we may have a number of functions, in each of which an entity has an evaluation for a given criterion. The question of whether one wishes to predict performance in each of these attributes or to combine these evaluations into an over-all measure of proficiency is relevant for the model. The technicalities involved in carrying out these alternatives are discussed in detail by Thorndike (1949).

The model we have just discussed is not useful for *classification* purposes, since it takes into account only a single job or kind of activity. The appropriate model from the systems point of view involves all the jobs within the system. This means a consideration of the entire submatrix represented by Quadrant II of Figure 7.1. Here we have a number of different criterion attributes or job designations. But again it can be seen that the alternatives exist of an over-all evaluation for each job designation or of breaking each job down into a number of different kinds of functions and providing measures of proficiency on each of these.

Theoretically, one may have the same system of categories for segregating the functions required for each of the jobs. Ideally, from a psychological and perhaps even from a practical point of view, this is the best approach. The same categories would then occur in Figure 7.1 for the predictor and the criterion attributes. The criterion measures would then be set up on the basis of psychological or behavior functions rather than job designations. This procedure would have immense advantages relative to the problems involved in the fragmentary criterion-data matrix.

In general, there are enormous problems in getting the actual evaluations on the job on the basis of a common set of designations and of making the measures comparable from one job to another and one supervisor to another. The practical difficulties, however, should not blind us to theoretical and practical advantages or prevent us from seeking methods of achieving such a treatment of criterion attributes. Perhaps one of the most pressing needs is not only the development of a common terminology for functioning of men and machines, but also the extension and utilization of this terminology in the development of predictor and criterion measures. We would then predict performance in terms of these functions.

Criterion Measures. We are now ready to discuss characteristics of the pattern of measures in the typical criterion submatrix. We have pointed out that, typically, job designations are used for criterion attributes. If this is the case and if we are to have criterion measures on all entities for all attributes, this means that each person in the experimental group must have an opportunity to perform on each of the jobs within the system in order to determine his proficiency in each of these. This is precisely the model which has been suggested by some experimenters in the field.

Specifically, the proposal is made in connection with technical training schools where courses in a large number of technical specialties are provided. A battery of differential prediction tests is given to students before they enter the school. Each student is then required to take all the courses, and each course or technical specialty is then regarded as a criterion attribute. Here, then, we have measures for each of the students on each of the criterion attributes and also measures for each of the students on each of the predictor attributes. This is the ideal model from a theoretical point of view, but in general it is not feasible in operating man-machine systems. However, the evaluation of job performance on the basis of a standard or universal set of behavior categories would best exemplify this approach to a measure on each criterion attribute for each experimental entity.

A second type of criterion submatrix is one in which the criterion attribute is defined in such a way, and the administrative structure and procedures of the system are such, that for any given entity there may be measures of performance on several, but not all, of the criterion attributes. Practically, what this means is that within a system, persons may participate in several different jobs. Their time may be divided among two or more jobs or they may be transferred over a period of time from one job to another. The most common example of this overlapping type of criterion participation is in an educational system such as a college or university, where the student may be regarded as the man subsystem of the system and the output is performance on examination papers, lab work, and the like. The measures of these performances, then, would be grades assigned to the student in the various course areas. In such a case, a student would ordinarily have grades in a number of different course areas offered by the system, but in general he would not take all of the courses offered. If we think of the criterion submatrix coming from such a discretionary procedure, we have the situation depicted in Figure 7.3. Here elements are missing from the submatrix. This means that students for whom elements are missing did not take the particular course represented by the column in which the missing element occurs. In general for overlapping participation, there is no systematic pattern to the presence or absence of data.

A third type of criterion-data submatrix occurs when the person engages in only a single criterion activity. For each person there is an entry only in a

Criterion attributes

1 . . . . m	
1	X XX XXX XX X XXX X X XX
.	XXX X X XXX XXX X XXX XX X
.	XX X XXX X X XX XXX X X X
.	X XXX X XXX X XX XXX XXX XX
.	XX X XXX X X XXX X X XXX
.	X XXX XXX X XXX XX XXX XXX
.	XX X XX XXX X XXX X X XX
.	X XX X X XXX X XXX X X
.	XXX XXX X XX XXX X XXX X
N	XX X XXX X XXX X XXX XX

Experimental entities

Figure 7.3.   The typical case of *m* criterion measures and *N* experimental entities, where not all the measures are available for all the entities,
and where the missing data exhibit no systematic pattern.

single row of the submatrix. An example of this type is indicated schematically
in Figure 7.4. This type of criterion data submatrix is by far the most common
in man-machine systems where a criterion attribute is defined in terms of a
job designation. This we may call the mutually exclusive type of criterion
submatrix.

It may be seen, therefore, that methods of describing performance within
the man-machine system and the structure of the system itself determine very
materially the kind of criterion submatrix which becomes available for the
experimental group of entities.

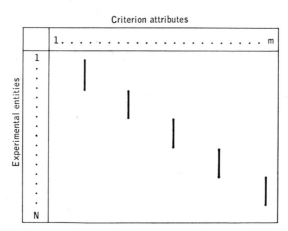

Criterion attributes

Figure 7.4   The case of *m* criterion measures on *N* experimental entities, where a measure on only a single criterion is available for each
experimental entity.

In the model represented by Figure 7.1 there are straightforward solutions for the statistical establishment of prediction procedures for personnel selection and classification. However, the situation in most man-machine systems is not of this type, and even though there is a possibility of defining criterion attributes to yield such a matrix, the problems involved are far from solved. In actual practice, we are almost entirely restricted to the types shown in Figures 7.3 and 7.4.

The mathematical procedures for using the data from the predictor and criterion attributes on the experimental entities as a basis for developing prediction procedures for the administrative entities are well known for the case in which the criterion submatrix has no missing elements. These are known as multiple regression techniques (Thorndike, 1949). Special problems, however, are encountered with the more typical cases represented by Figures 7.3 and 7.4, where we have missing data in the criterion submatrix. These we shall discuss briefly.

Criterion-Data Analysis. The methods for handling the more typical cases indicated in Figures 7.3 and 7.4 have not been nearly as well worked out mathematically as those for the more atypical case of a complete criterion-data submatrix. In general, use is made of subgroups of experimental entities, including in each analysis only those cases which have criterion estimates for a particular criterion attribute. Such a procedure is not optimal for the case of Figure 7.3, where there are indications about the interrelationships of performance on various criterion attributes only to the extent that there is overlapping among those who have performance estimates on two or more of the criterion entities. However, for the case of Figure 7.4, where mutually exclusive participation rather than discretionary participation occurs, standard procedures for estimating criterion performance on the various criteria from the predictor data utilize all the information available. Here, as in the overlapping case, the analysis proceeds by segregating subgroups according to those having criterion data for a single criterion category. Such subgroups are of course mutually exclusive.

Sample Selection

We have said earlier that the measures of both criterion and predictor attributes must show dispersion or variation for a particular group. But variation with reference to an attribute is a function, not only of the way the attribute is measured, but also of the particular sample on which the measures are taken. If these entities are selected so that they have no variation on the functions measured by the assessment procedures, the measuring devices themselves can show no differences. For example, one cannot show differences in height for a group of individuals who are all exactly five feet ten inches high. As an instance of a special case, one may have a set of valid predictor measures on the basis of which persons are selected for a particular system. Those who fall below a critical score are rejected. For those who enter the system, criterion measures subsequently obtained will not have as much variation as if the entire group had been accepted. Selection procedures which affect directly the dispersions of some of the predictor attributes may also affect the degree of relationships among the various predictor and criterion attributes. A body of theory and technique is available for handling such cases of sample selection (Meredith, 1958).

These techniques apply particularly where the selection is of a systematic sort. One example is when all persons exceeding certain critical scores are assigned to one kind of activity—say, pilot training—and others with other scores to bombardiering or navigation. Methods of analysis are concerned with the effect of such selections directly on the means, variances, and correlations of the attributes on which direct selection is made and on the means, variances, and covariances of other variables affected by direct selection.

Some of these techniques may be applied with limited assumptions to the cases of criterion subgroups such as indicated by the Figures 7.3 and 7.4. Here, however, we may have indirect, rather than direct, selection. For example, students decide which courses they are going to take, and we do not know in general on what basis these decisions are made. Also, persons decide to go into a particular job, instead of being assigned to it on the basis of certain predictor measures. The problems of adjusting data and incorporating the adjustments into the selection and classification model are important. The techniques currently available still leave a number of problems unsolved and require a number of assumptions which are known to be imperfectly satisfied.

▣ KINDS OF PREDICTION

We have discussed various aspects of the prediction of criterion performance from predictor variables. Now we shall consider more systematically the kinds of predictions which are relevant to the personnel selection and classification model. We shall discuss five different models in more or less common use. These are the *single-criterion* model, the *multiple absolute-prediction* model, the *multiple differential-prediction* model, the *optimal-classification* model, and the *multiple discriminant-function* model.

In the *single-criterion* model we have indicated that the system is so defined that there is only a single criterion attribute. This model makes no distinctions among various kinds of activities carried on in the man-machine system. It assumes a single-criterion attribute, so that in Quadrant II of Figure 7.1 there would be only one column. This assumes that the interest is in predicting success only in a very general way within the man-machine system, irrespective of what functions within the system a man may perform. The screening procedure used in the aviation cadet program during World

War II is an example of this. An Aviation Cadet Qualifying Examination was given to persons in the ground forces who wished to go into air-crew training. A single score was provided by this test, although the test consisted of a number of different parts which measured several different kinds of psychological functions. The assumption involved in this procedure was that if a person achieved a score above a specified cutting point, he would be successful in some kind of air-crew activity. Another example of the single criterion is found in attempts to predict success in college irrespective of what courses a student takes. The Army General Classification Test is another example of the single-criterion model. The prediction is made that a person will or will not be successful in the Army, regardless of what kind of assignment he is given.

In general, the single-criterion model is concerned primarily with rejection of unqualified individuals. Cutting scores are established, so that it is a reasonable assumption that all people below this cutting score will most likely be unsuccesful in almost any kind of activity within the system. People above this score may be successful in some kinds of activities and not in others. The basic function of a screening test is to eliminate those persons who will almost surely not succeed satisfactorily in any of the major activities of the man-machine system. Thus the single-criterion model may be considered a rejection, rather than a selection, model.

The next model we shall consider is that of *multiple absolute-prediction* (Horst, 1955). Here one assumes a set of criterion attributes such as are indicated in Figure 7.1. The number of attributes depends on the system and the manner of definition of the criterion attributes. It is assumed that with an adequate set of multiple predictors and the use of appropriate statistical procedures for a group of experimental entities, estimates of success in *each* of a number of criterion categories can be provided. The model assumes that interest is centered on predicting absolute performance in each of these criterion categories.

Another kind of prediction has been called *multiple differential-prediction* (Horst, 1954). Here again success is predicted with reference to a number of different criterion activities such as those indicated in Figure 7.1. However, in this case the emphasis is not in predicting absolute performance so much as in predicting relative performance for each of the criterion activities. This model assumes that each person can make some sort of worthwhile contribution in any particular job activity, even though it may be very small, and that one is interested in knowing in which of the various activities he can make the best contribution. The aim is to provide not absolute prediction but the prediction of relative success in various job possibilities. Differential prediction can be important in the case of predicting success in college, where within wide limits the concern is not with how well a person will do absolutely in a particular course area, but rather with which course areas or majors he is apt to do best in.

In most practical cases the differential-prediction model must be supplemented with the multiple absolute-prediction model, for the assumption is nearly always valid that in any kind of activity a person must have a minimal amount of ability in order to continue in the activity. For example, it is usually not enough to know that a person could do better in English than in mathematics if we know that his absolute performance in either of those would be failing in any case.

One important distinction between the multiple differential-prediction model and the multiple absolute-prediction model is that for any given set of predictor measures the techniques and the formulas for making the predictions are exactly the same. However, the predictor variables most useful for multiple absolute prediction are generally not the same as those which are most useful for multiple differential prediction. For example, if there is a set of criterion measures defined, say, according to job designation, such that there are high correlations among the various criterion measures, this means that these measures have one or more factors in common which cause the high correlations. If in the group of tests there occurs a subgroup which predicts the factors common to all the criterion measures, this group will be useful in predicting *absolute* performance in each of the criterion measures. But if one is interested only in predicting *differences* in criterion measures, the tests will not be needed which measure whatever the criterion measures have in common. It is in this sense that multiple absolute prediction and multiple differential prediction are essentially different. It should be noted, however, that if that group of tests has been selected which gives the best multiple differential prediction and if certain tests are added to it which measure also the factors common to the criterion variables, the result will be a total battery maximally efficient for both differential and absolute prediction.

It can be seen from the description of the multiple absolute and the multiple differential models that both of these offer possibilities of classification or assignment of men to the various jobs within the system. Suppose, however, that we have a group of predictors, as suggested in the preceding paragraph, which are capable of both optimal absolute and differential prediction. These predictions should then provide a basis for determining in which of the various job categories each of a group of persons should be assigned. Suppose that each person is assigned to the job for which his prediction of success is highest. (The assumption is made that comparable scales for the various predictions are available.) Suppose there are 50 different kinds of jobs to be filled and that 20 persons are required for each job. Suppose further that 1000 persons are available to fill these jobs. If each person were to be assigned the job for which his prediction is highest, there is little reason to expect that precisely 20 would be assigned to each type of job. The ideal personnel selection and classification model is one which will yield from the available sources the number of persons required for each job.

For these reasons, the need is evident for a system for making estimates of success which will take into account not only the abilities of the persons but also the number of persons required for each job. This model, called the *optimal classification model*, is much more complex mathematically than either of the other multiple-criterion models which we have considered. Various methods are, however, available for approximating a solution (Horst, 1960). The general principle is to assign each person so that the over-all effectiveness of the organization will be maximal. This means that people should be assigned so that the sums of the estimated performances for all persons with respect to the jobs to which they have been assigned are maximal.

One elaboration of the optimal classification model provides not only for the classification of individuals within the system, but also for the rejection of part of the applicant group from the system. This model assumes that the group of individuals available is larger than the total number required for the system. In addition to optimally classifying or assigning each of the individuals within the system to meet quota demands, it also rejects the remainder of the group not required, in such a way that those rejected would have contributed least to the over-all efficiency or productivity of the system.

A fourth kind of prediction model is based on what is called *multiple discriminant-function analysis*. This model also assumes a multiple-criterion system, as in the case of the other three multiple-criterion models. It assumes further that each criterion category corresponds to a special class of individuals and that a person belongs only to one of these classes. The technique calls for utilization of the predictor variables in such a way that individuals can be assigned to the classes to which they "really" belong. The general notion is to construct predictor measures in such a way that the number of misclassifications resulting from the use of these measures is minimal.

The philosophy underlying the multiple discriminant-function technique may be subject to some question. From what we know about human beings, they do not belong to only one of a specified number of classes. It is unlikely that psychological functions are of this all-or-none character; rather, an individual tends to have more or less of some kind of proficiency. Various techniques have been worked out to combine multiple discriminant-function techniques with other multiple prediction procedures (Horst, 1956).

Predictor Selection

Perhaps the most important problem of all, and one which we have barely touched on, has to do with the verification of the personnel selection model. It is concerned with empirical methods for selecting predictor variables which will be most efficient in the predictor system. Considerable work has been done on predictor selection techniques. Actually, however, all of these leave much to be desired, because of the fact that theoretically one may include an extremely large number of potential predictor variables in a multiple predictor system in lieu of a demonstrably satisfactory rational approach. All of these methods encounter problems involving degrees of freedom. Methods have been worked out which attempt to tell when an adequate number of predictors have been selected for a particular system. These, however, appear to be far too conservative. But both the technical and philosophical problems involved in this subject are beyond the scope of this chapter.

Predictor Formulas

So far we have implied that there are specific procedures for utilizing the predictor measures in making predictions of the criterion measures. It is not possible in this chapter to go into the technical details and statistical procedures involved. However, a brief general discussion may be useful.

In general, there are two ways that predictions of success can be made from the predictor variables. In either case, these are established on the experimental entities indicated in Figure 7.1. The first of these may be called the method of *optimal cutting scores* and the second the method of *linear combination*.

The method of *optimal cutting scores* proceeds on the basis that for each criterion attribute there can be established a set of cutting scores on the predictor variables so that persons in the experimental group who meet these cutting score requirements also have sufficiently high criterion measures.

The method of *linear combination* assumes that for any particular criterion measure a linear combination of the predictor measures can be found so that for the experimental cases on whom criterion measures are available the weighted scores are as close as possible to their actual criterion measures. The method commonly used is called the multiple-regression technique. In this procedure a set of *weights* corresponding to criterion categories are applied to the predictor variables. There are as many weights for a given criterion variable as there are predictor variables, and as many sets of these weights as there are criterion variables.

It should be remembered that these cutting scores or weights, as the case may be, are of no value for the experimental group, since their criterion measures are already known. These procedures are used on the administrative entities as a basis for predicting their success prior to participation in job activities.

Of the two methods just considered, it is probable that the latter is by far the best, both theoretically and practically, in spite of the fact that the cutting-score method has been extensively used, often by the employment of multiple cutoffs successively applied. One of the assumptions in the multiple cutoff procedure is that a certain minimum amount of ability is required to function in a particular criterion category so that no matter how good the person in other functions, these cannot compensate for inadequacies in a particular function. The method of linear combination, on the other hand, assumes that for a specified criterion activity, superior functioning in one of the predictor attributes may compensate for inferior functioning in another. It is true that the former assumptions may apply in some cases. However, it is possible to introduce certain interaction variables into a predictor system which have much the same advantages as multiple cutoffs and are more easily handled from a mathematical and computational point of view. For this procedure the weight assigned to a given variable is not based solely on that variable but is a function of other variables as well (Horst *et al.*, 1941).

It must be remembered that the variables chosen for use in prediction represent hypotheses which constitute the basic framework of the selection and classification models. The experimental group of entities, together with the predictor and criterion measures available on them and the determination of optimal procedure for using the predictor variables, constitute the verification part of the model. For the experimental group, methods are available for determining how accurate the estimates of the criterion measures based on the predictor measures actually are in terms of the observed criterion measures. These statistical tests of significance indicate the accuracy or validity of the hypotheses set forth. If the hypotheses are regarded as accurate enough for practical purposes, the procedures may be applied to administrative entities. These will be persons who are accepted into the system to replace those who leave, or to fill jobs created by an expanding system.

REFERENCES

Anastasi, Anne. 1954. *Psychological testing.* New York: Macmillan.

Cronbach, L. J. 1960. *Essentials of psychological testing.* New York: Harper.

Horst, P. 1954. A technique for the development of a differential prediction battery. *Psychol. Monogr.*, No. 380.

Horst, P. 1955. A technique for the development of a multiple absolute prediction battery. *Psychol. Monogr.*, No. 390.

Horst, P. 1956. Least square multiple classification for unequal subgroups. *J. clin. Psychol., 12,* 309–315.

Horst, P. 1960. Optimal estimates of multiple criteria with restrictions on the covariance matrix of estimated criteria. *Psychol. Reports, Monog. Suppl.,* 6–V6.

Horst, P., *et al.* 1941. *The prediction of personal adjustment.* New York: Social Science Research Council. Bulletin 48.

Meredith, W. 1958. *The estimation of criterion parameters from a biased sample.* Unpublished Ph.D. dissertation. University of Washington.

Thorndike, R. L. 1949. *Personnel selection.* New York: Wiley.

Votaw, D. F., Jr. 1952. Methods of solving some personnel classification problems. *Psychometrika, 17,* 255–266.

THIS CHAPTER DEALS WITH THE DESIGN AND development of a class of materials that can be used to support various performances required of human beings in system jobs. They are given the general name of *job aids,* and they include such things as printed instructions, check lists, diagrams, and the contents of technical manuals. Without such aids, the human performer

would be required to retain in his memory a much larger store of models and to learn many more procedures and identifications. Thus, if job aids were not used to support such job performances, system technicians would have to be selected according to more stringent standards, and trained over longer periods of time, because job aids, training, and selection are complementary methods for obtaining job performance.

Obviously, then, the design of job aids must take place after human tasks and jobs of the system have been decided upon and in conjunction with decisions about how to select men and how to train them. Job aids to be used for supporting human performances during system operations may range in complexity from simple printed check lists through technical manuals to actual pieces of equipment affording visual or auditory displays. In a strictly engineering sense, they are simple to develop and produce. Yet they can and do have profound effects in reducing the complexity of selection and training procedures necessary to achieve the required performances from human system components.

The psychological problem posed by the design of job aids is here conceived as one of stimulus control of human performance. How can stimulus situations be arranged so as to produce optimal performances by controlling human behavior? It is recognized that this question cannot be sensibly answered by attempting to categorize the bewildering variety of human performances in systems. But it may be possible to classify the varieties of *change* in performance that can be brought about by the introduction of job aids. The problem of defining such classes of change, and of relating them to characteristics of the performance aid, defines in a general sense the area of scientific questioning discussed in this chapter as a challenge to future psychological research.

AIDS TO

JOB PERFORMANCE

J. Jepson Wulff
and Paul C. Berry

Within the process of man-machine system development, the term *job aid* has a special meaning. Since that special meaning cannot be given without some preliminary discussion, however, we begin by providing a preliminary definition in common-sense terms: *A job aid is something which guides an individual's performance on the job so as to enable him to do something which he was not previously able to do, without requiring him to undergo complete training for the task.*

An example of a job aid with which many people are familiar is the piece of paper which accompanies a new bicycle or an unfinished furniture kit, telling the purchaser how to assemble the parts. The task of assembling a child's bicycle may be one which the purchaser has never before encountered. Yet with the aid of a piece of paper together with his previously acquired general skills (reading directions, using a screwdriver, and the like), a new performance can be produced without any lengthy period of special training. Almost everyone has had experience with the deficiencies exhibited by such printed instructions and will recognize at once that there is room for improvement in the construction of such job aids.

Two kinds of psychologists are commonly concerned with job aids. The first is the psychologist engaged in man-machine system development. He is interested in job aids because they provide him one means for obtaining the human performances that are necessary for system performance. The second is the research psychologist. An effective job aid is an article which serves to elicit and control human behavior, and this of course is central to the research psychologist's domain of interest.

Objectives of the Chapter.   This chapter is directed primarily toward the research interest of the psychologist. Its aim is to show the relation between the practical job-aid problem facing the system developer and some of the questions about human behavior faced by the research psychologist. If this chapter achieves its objective, after finishing it the reader should be able to identify some major research problems that require solution to enable the psychologist in industry to construct better job aids, and to relate these research problems to the subject matter and to the common concern of research psychologists.

Contents of the Chapter.   The body of this chapter is divided into two main parts. The first is designed to provide useful background information about the development and use of job aids in man-machine systems. In reading this part, the reader should recall that our aim is not to teach him how to go about building a job aid of his own, but rather to foster a research capability. The information that is presented about the development and use of job aids is provided for the purpose of defining the practical requirements which basic research must sooner or later satisfy so that the psychologist in industry can improve his capability to develop effective job-aid materials.

The second part of this chapter is concerned with the psychological aspect of research and development on job aids. This part is focused directly upon the main objective of the chapter. It is designed to relate the job-aids problem to psychological principles and findings with which the research psychologist is familiar, and thus to relate the practical problem of producing job aids to the research psychologist's major interests. It is intended to provide the reader with an orientation that will permit him to carry out his own research and development work. It is not a review of what has been done in the field; in fact, it needs to be borne in mind that very little research has been done that has been focused specifically on the problem of developing job aids.

▣ JOB AIDS IN SYSTEMS

The users of complex systems naturally think of job aids as essential adjuncts to system hardware, necessary for its operation and maintenance. To think of job aids merely as adjuncts, however, can be misleading. It is more useful to conceive of job aids as integral parts of the total system, produced during system development to provide for the reliable operation of the total man-machine system in the field.

The Role of Job Aids in System Operation

A job aid is an item which is delivered as part of an operational man-machine system along with the hardware and personnel. A job aid may be printed on paper, it may be a simple device, or it may be a motion picture. But whatever form it takes, its purpose is to foster some performance that is required in the operation or maintenance of a system. Once a job aid is delivered for use by system personnel, it is normally not expected to be modified in the field. Therefore, although the research psychologist will be interested in the job aid in system operation, his major interest is likely to center upon the research and development that can be brought to bear upon its effectiveness before the item is manufactured and the manner of its use can be determined.

The principal thing that the research psychologist needs to know about job aids in the field is the manner in which they are properly evaluated. A job aid is delivered as part of an operating system for only one reason—to support some performance on the part of an operator or technician that is needed to keep the system "on the air." This means that job aids are given their final evaluation by determining whether or not they actually support the job performance that is required. Further, any such performance evaluation must be accomplished under the actual operating conditions that will obtain when the job aid is used with serious purpose. Under proper conditions, job aids will not be evaluated in terms of their appearance nor by expert opinion, but rather by measuring observable human performance under representative field conditions. To know how job aids are evaluated is to know the objective of job aid development, and thus to know what practical purpose research on job aids must serve. Research must be focused upon the development of techniques for obtaining job *performance* by means of job aids and upon the development of techniques for producing the performance under the specific kinds of conditions that will obtain in the operating system.

Job-Aid Development in System Development

It is primarily during the development stage that research findings can be brought to bear upon the job-aid problem. Therefore, in order to define the development task which requires supporting psychological research, let us turn to a description of the way in which job-aid development is integrated into a man-machine system development cycle.

Man-machine systems are, of course, developed in many different ways if one considers the detail of individual development cycles. However, there is a pattern to what is done in system development which can be abstracted in general form, and which can be said to be typical of development cycles. A general description of such a development cycle is presented here to provide the context for talking about job-aid development, and it is presented schematically in Figure 8.1. The figure shows that the development cycle is partitioned into two major parallel functions, a hardware development cycle and a personnel development cycle. The personnel development channel is separated from the hardware, not because it provides logically distinct contributions to the system, but rather because the problems associated with the actual provision of one or the other are so different. Thus the hardware channel accounts for the development of all the hardware means needed to implement system performance, while the personnel channel includes all the activities needed to produce those functions allocated to personnel.

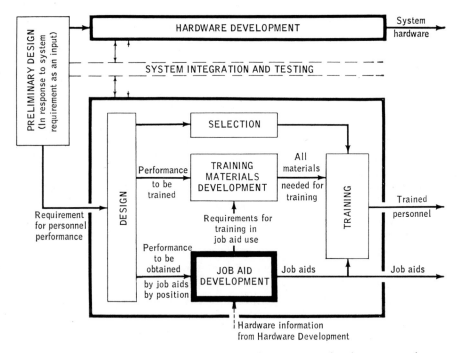

Figure 8.1 Schematic description of a system development cycle emphasizing job aid development.

The job-aid development task is embedded within the personnel development cycle. In this figure, the job-aid development task is defined in terms of the inputs it receives during the development process and the outputs which are required of it. As shown in the figure, job-aid development is preceded by job definition (design), which results in a description of all the objective performance requirements for all the operator and technician positions within the operational system. Job definition further breaks down each job into a list of those performances which will be obtained by selection, those which will be obtained by means of training, and those which will be obtained by means of job aids.

The last of these is the major input to the job-aid development unit. It is therefore worthwhile to examine the nature of this input in detail. Specifically, this input will be made up of a series of "orders" for job aids, each order implying a need for a job aid. An order will be identified with respect to the position that it is associated with, and it will define in objective terms the on-the-job performance that must be fostered by the job aid. An order is thus, in in a sense, a description, not of the details of the needed job aid, but of the way in which the job aid will be evaluated in the operational situation. To be complete, the order must also specify the relevant capabilities which can be assumed on the part of the man who will use the job aid, and it must specify the conditions under which the job aid will be employed that will influence the physical characteristics of the job aid.

The Nature of Job-Aid Development.   Since the job-aid development unit operates upon each order in much the same manner, we shall undertake to describe the operation of the unit for a single typical order. Ignoring for the moment the other inputs which must be made to the job-aid unit, let us turn to a description of the major output of the unit, because this defines the principal objective of unit operation. That output is a job aid which will actually foster the job performance specified when it is employed by a technician who has the relevant capabilities (also described in the order). This output is, as shown in the diagram, a major final output of a system development cycle, just as hardware and trained personnel are final outputs. The output of the job-aid unit is something which appears in the operational situation as an integral part of the operating system, necessary to provide accomplishment of the system mission with a given reliability.

Some of the secondary inputs and outputs of the job-aid unit also need to be considered here. In order to respond to an order for a job aid to be developed, it is necessary to collect detailed information about the hardware upon which the technician is required to perform; and this calls for an input of information from the hardware development cycle. Further, in the actual development process, interaction is required with the selection unit, and the system training and test functions, although these are not shown in the figure (compare Chapter 13). An important secondary output which must be obtained is one which goes to the training-materials development function, carrying the requirements for training in the use of the job aid. This output is an important one to note because, by providing it, we take particular notice of one characteristic of job aids: it is not necessary for a job aid to be constructed so that it can be used with no prior training at all. It is only required that a job aid reduce the amount of training below that which would be required if no job aid were provided.

In the context of man-machine system development, the job-aid development problem is simply this: the job performance to be supported by job aids must be identified, and then a means must be found to proceed from the initial statement of the performance that must be produced (together with the description of the hardware and the prior capabilities of personnel), to the production of the actual materials that will guide the performance appropriately.

What Does the Job-Aids Development Specialist Do?

By describing briefly the work of the job-aids specialist within the development cycle that has just been depicted, it will be possible to call attention to the kinds of development actions that require supporting research. The developer of job aids contributes to two of the functions shown in Figure 8.1: The design unit and the job-aids unit. The major development actions that he will take are described below. This account should not be taken as a prescription for job-aid development, however. The order of the actions, and even the need for some of them, will differ from one system development problem to another. The list is simply intended to be a representative one.

1. The job-aids specialist is first involved in system development within the unit called "design." As shown in the figure, the function of this unit is to prepare job definitions in terms of the performances required and to break down each job into requirements for selection, training, and job aids. In order to accomplish this three-way breakdown, it is necessary to draw upon the talents of selection specialists, training specialists, and job-aid specialists. This kind of cooperative endeavor is necessary because the determination of how to obtain performance must be based upon consideration of the state of existing technology. Thus, it is inefficient to mark a particular performance for training if it is within the state of existing technology to accomplish it by means of a job aid, and it is also inappropriate to mark a performance for development by means of job aids if there is no known job-aid technique that can be employed to accomplish it. Therefore, in deciding upon the means that will be employed to obtain all of the performance for a given position, it will be necessary to foresee where current technology will allow the use of job aids, where it will allow the use of a training method, and where selection can be employed. One end result of this effort should be "orders" for the development of job aids which will be passed on to the job-aids unit for processing.

2. Once an order has been given to the job-aids unit, the first major step to be taken within this unit will be to prepare a very specific description of the performance that must be fostered by means of the job aid. There are two different cases to consider in undertaking this step. The first is the case in which the detail of the actions which must be supported by the job aid is completely determined by the equipment in the system or by other factors external to job-aid development. In this case, the action to be taken within this step is simply that of finding out what the detailed performance is and of describing it. The second case to be considered is that in which there are alternative ways that could be employed to achieve the performance that is specified in the order. Typically, alternative performances are possible when

the human activity to be fostered involves problem solving or dynamic decision making. Therefore, this step in job-aid development may be a rather difficult one; it may be necessary to describe and then to choose among a number of different ways of leading the technician to carry out the required performance. In either case, at the end of this step in job-aid development, there must be a detailed description of the actions to be taken by the technician, and these actions will be the ones to be supported by the job aid to be developed.

3. A job-aid medium must be selected. Given a detailed description of the actions which must be supported by the job aid, and given a statement of the on-the-job conditions which must obtain, the best medium for presenting job-aid information must be chosen. The medium chosen may be a printed page, an auditory guide, a motion-picture film clip, an automatic information-selecting device, or some other medium. Whatever one is chosen, it must be compatible with the operational requirements of the job aid and of the job.

4. The detailed content and format of information to be presented by the job aid must be developed and prepared in a form suitable for use in the medium selected for presentation. The specific stimulus materials that will be the job aid must be designed, and whatever they may be, they must be calculated to support the specific detailed job performance required.

5. The prototype job-aid materials must be subjected to evaluation and must then be refined and specified for production.

6. The job aids must be produced and delivered as part of the operational system. They must also be supplied to the training program, where technicians under training will learn to use them.

7. The training requirements generated by the development of the job aids must be specified and forwarded to the training materials development unit, where materials will be prepared for training technicians to use the job aids.

▣ THE NATURE OF JOB AIDS

Now that we have described the system development context within which job aids are designed, we can return to the question of definition. As we have pointed out, a job aid may be defined in terms of its use in an operating system, but such a definition is not of greatest utility to the research psychologist. Instead, the characteristics of a job aid are here conceived in terms of the problem of job-aid *development*.

A job aid is an item whose purpose is the support of performances by system personnel, which are necessary for over-all system performance. It is developed as an alternative to training as a means of obtaining the necessary performances, and is therefore designed deliberately to complement training. The job aid is developed in response to a requirement which specifies the performances that must be supported and the conditions under which these performances must be obtained. It is an end product of a system development cycle which is delivered as part of an operational system.

This kind of definition can be useful to the research psychologist because it identifies the situation in which research findings must be brought to bear. That is, the definition states that the research findings must be useful for a situation in which development starts with a performance requirement, is integrated with training development, and ends with the delivery of an item that will be assessed in terms of the performance which it is supposed to support. The definition also implies that job aids are articles which are developed as job aids; it is not useful to classify all items which "look like" job aids as job aids, if they have been developed for other purposes.

Referring back to the stages in job-aid development outlined in the previous section, we can identify two particular points at which support from basic research is to be sought. The first (step 2) is in connection with the detailed description of performances that must be supported by the job aid (compare Chapter 6). When the job-aid developer must prepare such a performance description for a problem-solving or decision-making activity, he is likely to find that the research literature on these topics has many relevant findings. The second major step which creates a need for research is that concerned with the development of stimulus conditions to be presented by means of a job aid in order to bring about the required performance (step 4). Research on the relationships between stimulus input and performance output is of central interest to the human learning theorist. The psychological research requirements generated by these two job-aid development steps are described in a later section of this chapter.

Some Examples of Job Aids

Before going on to a discussion of the psychological problems associated with job-aid development, it will be useful to examine some examples of actual job aids. There are two major classes of job aids which we need to consider particularly. The first class is composed of job aids which foster the same performance steps that would be taken by the technician if he were to be trained to do the task without the use of job aids. A common example of a job aid of this kind is a lubricating chart. Such a chart calls for essentially the same activities on the part of the technician as would be exhibited if he were to learn the task "by heart." The advantage of the job aid in this case is that it obviates the requirement for training without sacrificing performance capability, and perhaps with a gain in performance reliability. In other words, a somewhat lengthy sequential routine, rather than having to be memorized as a "model," has simply been provided to the technician so that he can refer to it on the job.

A second class of job aid is composed of aids which make it possible to obtain the desired performance without requiring the user to go through all the steps that he would normally take if he were to perform the task after having learned it. An example of a job aid of this kind is a transformation table. Job aids in this class are usually prepared by experts who carry out all of the detailed performance steps required and then encode the results of their labor in such a way that the user need only perform the first and last steps in the sequence.

Thus, in using a transformation table, one must perform only the steps of identifying the initial given information and of identifying the answers by decoding the table; it is not necessary to go through all the intermediate steps of calculating, which one would normally perform if the job aid were not available.

The diagram shown in Figure 8.2 is part of a troubleshooting job aid for a complex electronic equipment. It is an example of the first kind of job aid, the kind which supports the same job performance as the performance which would be carried out if training were used instead of the job-aid method. In the case of this example, the circles in the diagram identify all of the indicators which the technician must read out as his first step in the troubleshooting procedure. The circles thus support the read-out performance in the place of a memorized list. The boxes in the diagram identify the functions in the system to which a malfunction can be isolated by means of the given read-outs. Therefore, like circles, boxes make it unnecessary for the technician to commit information to memory—in this case, the list of functions. The fact that the boxes and circles are arranged in a certain order, which is shown by the arrows connecting them, is also useful to the technician. The arrows connecting the boxes and circles show the information flow in an operating system, and this is information which the technician must use to determine where to find a malfunction. These relationships are much more difficult to remember than the list of functions or the list of read-outs, and it is primarily to make it unnecessary for the learner to remember these relationships that this job aid is provided. In general, the job aid materially reduces the amount of training that is required to teach a technician to troubleshoot the system. (It should be realized that only a portion of the total troubleshooting diagram is shown in the figure. The total diagram is a great deal more complex, but it is based on the same principles as the portion shown.) In using this job aid, the technician goes through the same procedures as those he would perform if he had to memorize all of the information contained in the job aid in order to carry out his troubleshooting.

Now let us consider an example of the second kind of job aid, one which *changes* the job performance of the technician, as compared with the case in which he must perform the same duty without a job aid, on the basis of training. The diagram shown in Figure 8.3 is a simple example of this kind of job aid. It is a type of transformation table used in troubleshooting. To use the diagram shown in Figure 8.3, the technician must have gathered some information which will allow him to enter the table. Specifically, he must have

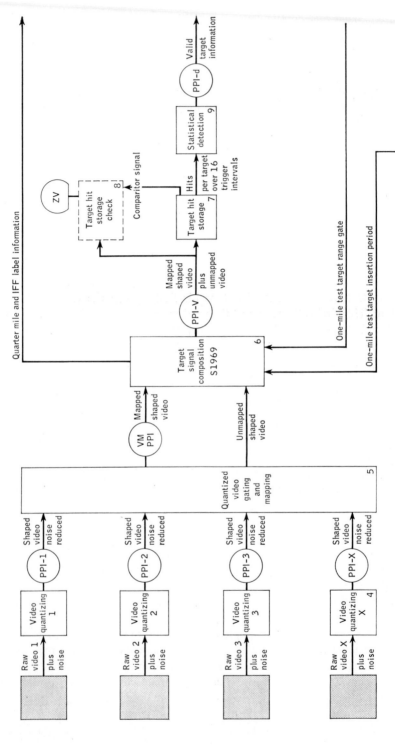

Figure 8.2. Examples of a job aid which fosters the same performance steps as those which would be taken by a technician trained to perform without a job aid. (From Psychological Research Associates, 1961.)

USE THIS TABLE IF THE SYSTEM DOES NOT HAVE SIF:

	BOX 12	BOX 13	BOX 14			BOX 15
			BOX 14a or BOX 14b	BOX 14b ONLY	BOX 14c ONLY	
With NORMAL TARGET DATA you had these alarms:	NO ZL	ZL	ZL	ZL	ZL	ZL
PPI-S with Wedge	BAD	BAD	GOOD	GOOD	GOOD	GOOD
RAPPI with Wedge	BAD	BAD	Display like R or S below	Display like T or V below	BAD	GOOD

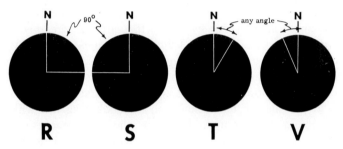

Figure 8.3 Example of a job aid which reduces the performance steps, as compared with the steps which must be taken by a technician trained to perform without a job aid. (From Psychological Research Associates, 1961.)

guessed which function, or box, in the system contains the malfunction. He then enters the table from the top and reads the column below the suspected malfunctioning function-box. In this column he will find a pattern of three read-outs which he must obtain in order to confirm his guess about the location of the malfunction. The technician who uses this table to check out his troubleshooting guess must perform significantly less work than the technician who carries out the same task without the table. That is, if the table were not available, after the technician had made a guess about the bad box, he would then have to work out for himself a plan by which he could check his guess. Working out such a plan involves a considerable amount of time and effort. The preworked plans which are shown in the table were developed by an engineer who spent several days working with the equipment for that purpose. His work has been encoded in the table and need not be repeated by the technician each time he wishes to carry out one of the troubleshooting checks described in the table.

The two examples of job aids which have been described exemplify the two classes of job aids we have defined. However, job aids appear in many different forms and are used for many different purposes. The reader should not assume that these examples constitute a representative sample of all of the varieties of job aids in use. Related discussions of job aids and their development can be found in treatments by Hoehn and Lumsdaine (1958) and by Miller (1956).

Varieties of Tasks Supported by Job Aids

We have said that job aids are used to support the performance of many different kinds of tasks. It is therefore natural to want to categorize job aids in some way that will identify the tasks for which they are useful. Any attempt to classify the tasks for which job aids are used should, however, serve some useful purpose; such an endeavor should do more than satisfy a natural human requirement for order. One reason for classifying tasks might be to assist in identifying the situations for which job aids should be developed for new systems. We might attempt this by noting that job aids are used with good effect to support the performance of lengthy procedures—especially when the lengthy procedures are used only infrequently and would otherwise be subject to forgetting. Job aids are also used to foster stimulus-identification tasks, as when pictorial presentations of oscilloscope read-outs are used in maintenance handbooks to provide the technician with a standard against which he can compare his obtained read-outs to determine whether a signal is good or bad. Job aids are also used to support problem-solving tasks. These, as described above, are sometimes used to reduce a problem-solving task to a fixed procedure by the use of a transformation table. Job aids are also used quite frequently to replace memorial inputs, as we have also exemplified above. If we continue attempting to identify the situations for which job aids are useful, however, we will sooner or later come to tasks for which job aids are sometimes useful, but for which it is at other times impossible to construct useful job aids. We will also come to tasks for which job aids are not used. An outstanding example of a class of tasks for which job aids are not used includes those tasks which involve complex motor performance.

A little reflection about those tasks for which job aids are not used will shortly suggest the conclusion that they are not used simply because no one has yet developed job-aid techniques which are suitable. In fact, just a few years ago, some of the tasks for which job aids are now used would necessarily have fallen into the category of tasks for which job aids are not used, simply because the development of appropriate job-aid techniques had not yet taken place. The truth of the matter is, job aids are used whenever a way can be thought of to develop a job aid that will effectively support some performance demanded of a technician; job aids are not used when a way of constructing them cannot be conceived. Perhaps the time will come when job aids will be developed to support the performance of complex motor tasks. Right now, however, it is not known how such material could be presented. But the realization that one might at some time be able to do so points up the fact that the categorizing of tasks for which job aids can be used is a dangerous practice. Such a list can never be comprehensive and must continuously be revised as the technology of job-aid development improves. Later on, we will discuss a way to categorize tasks for a quite different purpose—namely, for the purpose of deciding how to build a particular job aid rather than for the purpose of deciding whether or not a job aid might be useful. For the latter purpose, it is much more reasonable to use criteria such as the following when deciding whether or not to use a job aid:

1. The use of a job aid to support the performance of a task should be considered if a job aid can be projected that will actually support the performance. If no job aid that will provide the required performance support can be described, there is no need to consider the matter further.

2. If a job aid which might be used can be described, the next consideration should be whether or not its use will actually reduce the amount of training time that is required. Sometimes it will take so long to train a technician to use a particular job aid that it would be more economical, in terms of training time, to teach him to perform the task without the use of the job aid. There may be no gain in using a job aid if the training time required is not lessened by using it.

3. If the use of a job aid will save training time, one should next consider the cost of developing and using the job aid. If the cost in terms of dollars is much greater when the job aid is used than the cost of the training approach, consideration should be given to abandoning the proposed use of the job aid.

4. Finally, if there is an available job-aid technique that will support the required job performance at a saving in training time, and if it costs less than training, one must ask what effect the use of the job aid will have on the reliability of performance. Most often, job aids will improve the reliability of human performance over the reliability that is obtained when training is employed. However, deliberate attention should be paid to this fact, because a job aid should not be used if it will degrade the percentage of times that the human performs correctly below that which can be tolerated within the system.

When criteria like the above are used to determine whether or not to use a job aid, there is no need to categorize the uses of job aids. Rather than categories of uses for job aids, the job-aid expert needs a large repertory of job-aid techniques, so that he will be able to think of a job aid to match almost any task required. In the last section of this chapter we will discuss what is required to build a large repertory of job-aid techniques.

We have considered how requirements for job aids are developed, how job aids themselves are developed in response to these requirements, what job aids look like, and how to decide when to use a job aid. With this background established, it is appropriate now to turn to consideration of those aspects of the job-aid problem which relate directly to the content and approach of psychology.

Two major aspects of job-aid development are of interest to psychologists. The accomplishment of both of these requires the development expert to utilize presently available psychological information, and both steps also call for further research by psychologists to develop new information which is needed to improve our present capability to develop job aids. The first is the problem of describing in detail a selected set of performance steps which must be supported by a job aid when there are alternative ways of accomplishing a task. The second is the determination of the stimulus characteristic of a job aid, such that the job aid will provide appropriate stimulus control to insure that the technician will carry out the performances which must be supported. We will now consider the research problems associated with these two development problems.

▣ RESEARCH PROBLEMS

The first problem to be discussed—that of selecting and describing a detailed sequence of performance steps to be fostered when there are alternative ways to accomplish a task—is one common to both the development of training materials and the development of job-aid materials. However, in the development of job-aid materials this problem is of even greater significance than when training has been selected as the method for obtaining job performance. This is true because job aids must necessarily be constructed to promote the performance of very specific actions. Training, on the other hand, can be carried out in such a way that considerable latitude is left on the part of the operator or technician when it comes to doing the job. Thus, when a training approach is applied, it may be possible to give considerable basic or background training with respect to a decision-making performance or problem-solving performance, such that the technician can employ ingenuity in selecting his own methods of solution when he meets with a real problem on the job. In general, this kind of latitude is not possible when the job-aid method is used. The specific performance to be fostered must, therefore, be decided upon in advance and must be described in great detail before the job aid is constructed.

Identifying Performances for Job-Aid Support

We have already encountered one example of job performance which poses a problem when it comes to defining the specific actions which must be fostered by means of a job aid. Thus, in order to construct the job aid shown in Figure 8.2, it was necessary to describe the desired actions in detail. The job aid in Figure 8.2 is designed to support troubleshooting performance for a complex electronic system. Troubleshooting is a problem-solving performance, and for many systems there are alternative ways of troubleshooting. For example, one kind of performance routine might call for the technician to start by taking a reading of system performance at an indicator on the output side of the system and then to work backward through the system, step by step, taking additional readings which would gradually partition the system. Eventually, by this process, he would narrow down the location of the malfunction to a replaceable component. An alternative routine might be to gather information from many read-outs of system performance as the very first step, for the purpose of isolating the malfunction to a rather large functional area by using the pattern of read-outs as a syndrome. If this approach is taken, the indicators to be used for this first step must be carefully selected, so that isolation to a functional area will be possible. As a second step, the process might be repeated within the functional area identified in the first step, and so on until the malfunctioning replaceable component is identified. Other performance routines could be described, but these two will suffice to demonstrate that alternatives are possible and to make the point that a particular one must be selected before a job aid can be constructed.

Figure 8.2 is based on the second of the two performance routines described above, and it therefore contains only that information necessary for carrying out that kind of troubleshooting. Had a different troubleshooting routine been selected, the job aid in Figure 8.2 would be structured quite differently. The conclusion here is that when decision-making or problem-solving behavior is called for, there may be alternative ways to carry out the process, and a particular one must be selected and described in detail before an appropriate job aid can be constructed. This creates a research problem. Specifically, we need to know something about problem-solving and decision-making behavior as it is carried out by human beings and as it might be carried out by human beings. Thus, not only is it necessary to be able to describe in detail some kind of problem-solving or decision-making behavior which will work, but it is also necessary to be sure that the routine which is prescribed is one which human beings are capable of carrying out. Only then can a job aid for a decision-making performance be constructed.

Thus far, the terms "decision making" and "problem solving" have been used rather loosely. The phrases commonly refer to processes internalized in the human brain by which information is processed and to which the more general term "thinking" is also applied. In this discussion, the reader should not seize upon what may seem to be inappropriate usage of these terms, but should remember, rather, that these terms are used here to refer to a class of internalized processes which meet the following criteria: they must be specifiable on the input side by an objective description of the stimulus situation which initiates the process; they must be described on the output side by an objective description of a correct answer or state of affairs which must be achieved when the process is complete; and the process which mediates between input and output must be one which is not fixed, but which can be carried out in two or more ways with at least occasional success.

For thinking tasks whose structure is fairly simple and quite explicit, logical analysis of some of the available procedures is possible, and it is a comparatively straightforward task to select an efficient rational procedure. For example, alternative procedures may be evaluated in terms of the number of steps required to carry them out or the expected cost or time implied by the steps. For many complex problems, however, there does not yet exist any rational procedure by which the information can be processed. In some cases a perfectly rational procedure may be conceivable, but it is also obviously impractical. It is therefore necessary to fall back on temporizing procedures that will work some of the time or may be preferable to no action, but which lack the elegant assurance of success that characterizes rational approaches to simpler problems.

Let us take, for example, the problem of specifying moves in a game of chess. In principle, one could examine every possible move, every possible reply of one's opponent, every possible move after that, and so on. But even if computerized assistance were used, this task would take far longer than a chess player's lifetime. This means that a strategy must be adopted which will inevitably leave many possible moves unconsidered. The devising of such strategies and the evaluation of alternative ones becomes an extremely difficult task. And this is a difficulty which exists quite apart from our consideration of the limitations of the human being who must provide this performance. The difficulties we have mentioned are logical difficulties in the nature of the problem and in the information processing required to solve it.

Now let us suppose that a rational strategy of some sort can be concocted for approaching a particular information-processing problem; it still remains to specify this strategy in terms of the repertory of information-processing abilities of the human operator. This is undoubtedly our area of greatest ignorance. While the processes of human thought were once considered the central subject matter of psychology, remarkably little progress has been made in analyzing them. Certainly we are utterly ignorant of the physical and chemical bases of thinking, and we can say little more about the thought process than that it is probably located in the brain. It seems more optimistic to attempt to describe human capabilities in terms of the information processes of which human beings are capable. But this too is an area about which we have so far only the most rudimentary knowledge. Early attempts to study thinking by introspection rapidly revealed that men are largely unaware of the processes by which they think. Research since then has had to be content with examining only some of those peripheral conditions which may facilitate or inhibit the final output of a thinking process.

It can be seen, then, that one research problem which is particularly important for the development of job aids for decision making and problem solving is the development of ways to determine good strategies for carrying out these activities. A second research problem, and one which is more relevant to the interest of the psychologist, is the determination of what functions (either primitive or learned ones) human operators may have in their repertories. This determination is essential to the job aiding of the specific steps the human is to utilize in carrying out his strategy. At the same time, this determination will have considerable bearing on the selection of strategies that are feasible of accomplishment by human performance.

The Programming of Thinking Activities

Let us now turn to consideration of ways in which these research problems might be attacked. This discussion will center on the use of computer techniques which have only recently been developed and which promise to provide new methods both for the rational solution of information-processing problems and for examining the processes involved in thought. In considering this research approach, it should be kept in mind that the program for the computer serves a function comparable to that of a job aid for human being. In each case, once the desired performance has been specified, a strategy must be developed that is capable of solving the problem and which can be built up from the more primitive actions of which the man or machine is capable. As the programmed instructions call out machine operations, so must the elements of the job aid call out human operations. Thus, in a sense, a job aid is to a human as a program is to a computer.

Use of the Computer in the Study of Thinking. The invention of the computer has given a new boost to the study of thinking. It is interesting that it should have done so, because no new discoveries about the nature of thought have followed from the use of computers, and computers are not capable of activities that could not have been undertaken long before the first computer was built. Rather, the existence of the computer and of advanced computer programs has made undeniable the fact that activities that we would ordinarily describe as "thinking" can be undertaken by machines. This has served to remove some of the mystical flavor which surrounds this topic.

It was not long after the use of high-speed computers for problems of arithmetic that programmers turned to the exploration of some of the other logical possibilities of the machines, and in particular the use of heuristic strategies for approaching problems of extreme complexity. The results of some of the early pioneering efforts in this field are provocative for several reasons. First, they indicate that by employing heuristic methods as opposed to algorithms, computers may be set to work on problems in areas heretofore considered solely the province of man's imagination. By processes which remain completely explicit (for computers can deal with no others), computers have been set to work making economic choices, playing chess, and solving theorems. (See also the discussion of the capabilities of computers in Chapter 3.)

The second provocative result of heuristic programming of computers is that computers thus controlled sometimes make mistakes. This, of course, is the inevitable consequence of the rejection of the algorithms. Now it is interesting to note the kinds of mistakes that are made and the relation of these limitations to the type of information processing employed. Computer programmers have begun to compare the strengths and weaknesses of their artificial thinkers with those exhibited by human beings. This effort was undertaken at first simply to see if any machine method might be devised which would reproduce some of the characteristics of human thought. Gradually the programmer psychologists have become emboldened to make more direct comparisons between the processes that they know exist in the computer with those that it appears might exist within the human head. Thus the development of heuristic information-processing programs for computers offers not only an approach to the solution of complex problems in a rational manner (or at least an explicit manner), but also a language and a way of thinking that may then be applied to the study of human thought processes.

Obviously, the mechanisms within the head do not even faintly resemble the hardware employed by computers. Just as obviously, some sort of information processes are used within the brain. Because of the extreme flexibility of digital computers, it may be possible to make the computer imitate the information flow (although not the physical mechanism) that occurs within the brain. Certainly, human thought exhibits many characteristics of radically heuristic programming: it is extremely rapid for many tasks, is capable of handling problems of great complexity, and yet is not always highly reliable. With the development of computers more specifically designed to imitate some of the characteristics of human thought, it may prove possible to pursue these comparisons much further. Already there is available a whole new approach that may be applied to the study of thinking, and that is to ask (with or without computer assistance) the question: what sort of information-processing heuristic would result in the operating characteristics actually observed in human thinking?

The techniques of the study of information processing remain so rudimentary that we can at present only hope that it will prove possible genuinely to obtain some new understanding of human thinking by this route. At present, the development of computer techniques in thinking is following two lines of development: *simulation* and *artificial intelligence*. Simulation refers to the construction of programs whose operating characteristics duplicate those of human subjects, with a view to making some inference about the nature of the information process used by the human being. Artificial-intelligence projects are concerned simply with using computers to think as best they can and, if possible, better than humans do. In this latter venture the interest is not in duplicating human errors but in providing thinking functions in the most efficient way possible.

Possibly much of the useful contribution of computer technique to the study of thinking will be the contribution of a language by which psychologists can describe their impressions of human thinking. These need not involve any electronic equipment at all. Those who debug (that is, troubleshoot) computer programs become fairly skillful at guessing in what processes faults may lie from inferences about the errors produced in machine output. This is just the position the psychologist is in: human output is readily visible, and process is not. By asking what sort of program might produce such outputs, psychologists may be able to arrive at useful hypotheses about human thinking.

Before significant gains can be made in the development of job aids that will effectively foster problem-solving and decision-making performance, psychologists must begin to identify through research those human functions which are involved in problem solving and decision making. Probably the way to identify these functions is not through the use of computers as research tools, but rather through the use of computers as an example which will help to keep the research psychologist focused upon the proper question. If one wishes to know what functional capabilities the human is endowed with, the proper object of study is the human. The suggestion made here is merely that the human be studied as though his output were the composite result of functioning components. The goal of research must be to identify those functions which the human can or should employ in problem solving and decision making.

Let us summarize by considering a hypothetical operator performance requirement for which we might wish to develop a job aid. Our hypothetical example is a decision-making performance which must be carried out by a submarine officer. His performance is initiated by a signal that one or more targets have been detected. The output of his performance consists of four orders: (1) identification of the target or targets that will be attacked; (2) identification of the weapon that will be used against each target; (3) a statement of the time at which each target will be attacked; (4) a plan for own ship retirement. In order to "job aid" the performance which must mediate between the initiating signal and the final outputs, we must be able to identify a set of specific performance steps which can be carried out by the officer and which will always bring problem solution to a successful conclusion. Only after we have done this can we construct a job aid which will successfully give the steps the submarine officer must take through the required performance. We have suggested above one type of research approach which might be used to obtain the required information about methods of problem solution, as well as about human functions in problem solution, to enable us eventually to develop a practical job aid for supporting such job performances.

There is yet another step which must be carried out in job-aid development before the entire problem is solved. If one pursues the parallel between the job aid and the computer program, it is evident that the computer must be provided with a highly explicit set of instructions to carry out problem solution; and so must the human being. After some idea has been gained of what functions are available in the human repertory, and of which ones human beings need to employ in order to carry out a specific task, a list of instructions must still be constructed which will, in fact, elicit the required performance components in the right order and at the right time. Let us turn next, then, to consideration of the research that is necessary to develop basic information about ways in which we can obtain some desired behavior by means of stimulus control.

The Stimulus Characteristics of Job Aids

The role of a job aid as a stimulus complex can be pictured as shown in Figure 8.4. In this figure, S_x stands for the signal which indicates that some specific performance is required and R_y stands for the state of affairs which must be achieved when the performance (response) has been completed

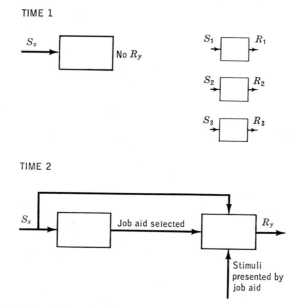

Figure 8.4   Schematic description of performance before and after the introduction of a job aid.

successfully. The figure shows that at Time 1, prior to the introduction of the job aid, the technician will not respond with R_y when S_x is presented. The figure also shows that at Time 1 the technician will be capable of certain elementary performances (S_1-R_1, S_2-R_2, and so on). Further, the figure states that at Time 2, when the job aid is introduced, the S_x-R_y capability will be exhibited. Specifically, at Time 2, S_x will lead to the selection of the appropriate job aids; and when the job aid has been selected, it will present stimulus conditions which, in conjunction with S_x, will elicit R_y by way of the elements of performance capability that existed at Time 1.

The symbolic representation in the figure calls attention to the principal research problem to be discussed here. Research is required to answer the question, "What kind of stimulus conditions must be afforded by the job aid to obtain the required job performance?" Here, then, concern will be with the form and content of a job aid; the objective is to develop pictures, words, devices, or sounds that will induce a technician to perform some specific behavior. When we reach this stage of consideration in job-aid development, it does not matter what technique has been used to generate a description of the behavior that the job aid must foster. Whatever the behavior is, the objective becomes one of developing a set of stimulus materials of some kind that will obtain the required performance both reliably and quickly.

The Need for Various Types of Job Aids.   The problem of developing a set of stimulus conditions which will constitute an effective job aid would be a relatively simple one if it were possible to formulate a single set of rules for doing so. However, it seems rather clear that rules for developing a job aid which might work well in one case are not at all appropriate for another. For example, although job aids have been constructed for guiding fixed procedural performance, the same type of job aid will not be useful for other kinds of performance.

As soon as it is recognized that there must be several sets of principles for developing job aids as stimulus materials, then it can be seen that the objective of research must be to create several kinds of information. The job-aid specialist must eventually be able to take any job performance and decide what class of performance it represents. Then he must be able to determine, for each of these types of performance, what rules to employ for generating a job aid that will be appropriate for the class of problem he has at hand. In order to generate a table of such information through research, it will be necessary to discover how to classify job-aid problems. And for each class, it will be necessary to discover rules which can be employed to generate stimulus materials that can be used as effective job aids.

What is the proper goal for research that is designed to obtain information about classifying job-aid problems? At first thought, one might offer the answer that research should be directed toward describing the kinds of job tasks for which job-aid materials are required. Thus, one might attempt to discover useful ways of classifying job tasks so that the job-aid expert could learn to classify any given task and then to enter a table by the type of task to find the rules for generating appropriate job-aid materials. Upon closer examination, however, it can be seen that there is not a constant relationship between job tasks and the characteristics which job-aid materials must exhibit. In fact, it is rather simple to demonstrate that this relationship must be a function of other factors. Consider almost any job task for which a job aid might be constructed. Even though the performance is held constant, the nature of the job aid must change as the initial repertory of capability of the technician changes. Thus, for a group of technicians who can do A, B, and C, a job aid of one kind is required; whereas for a group of technicians who can do only A and B, a somewhat different job aid will be needed to foster the same end performance.

If one cannot hope to discover what kind of job aid to build simply by considering the final performance that must be fostered by the job aid, where then should he look for a clue? Certainly not to the component performances which are exhibited by the technician before the job aid is introduced. The performance capabilities which the job aid must build upon are necessarily already parts of the technician's repertory, and the stimulus conditions which will elicit each one will have been determined by his past learning experience.

Classes of Performance Change.   If the classification problem is not that of classifying either the initial performance capabilities of the technician or the final job performance that must be exhibited, how indeed can the question of what to classify be answered? One answer is to say that it is the change between what the technician can do without the job aid and what he must be able to do with it that is important. If this point of view is taken, the research question becomes, "Of what classes of *change* in performance are humans capable, and what kinds of stimulus conditions are appropriate for fostering each kind of change?"

The nature of the "change" concept can perhaps better be seen if the similarity between the job-aid situation and the training situation is considered. Figure 8.5 is a schematic description of a training situation in the same terms as those used in Figure 8.4 to describe the stimulus role of job aids.

In this figure, S_x and R_y have the same meaning as in the previous figure. The figure shows that at Time 1 the learner will not respond with R_y when S_x is presented, but that at Time 1 there are certain capabilities in his repertory. Further, the diagram shows that, if S_x is presented at Time 2 along with certain training conditions such that R_y is elicited, and if this continues either with varying or fixed training conditions until Time 3, then it will be possible to present S_x and obtain R_y without any supporting conditions. It should be noted that the initial conditions in these two paradigms (Time 2 and Time 3) are the same, and so are the effective final conditions. The final conditions do, of course, differ in that when the job-aid method is used, the job aid remains as part of the final picture, whereas when the training method is used, all supporting conditions are withdrawn. The most important similarity between these two paradigms, however, is the similarity between Time 2 of the job-aid paradigm and Time 2 for the training paradigm. In both cases, at Time 2 the final response is elicited by means of supporting stimulus conditions.

This similarity at Time 2 is worth a good deal of discussion, because it provides a clue as to what must be done in research to develop information about how to construct job aids as stimulus materials, and because it suggests a way in which job-aid research can complement training research. Let us consider Time 2 in a training situation.

TIME 1

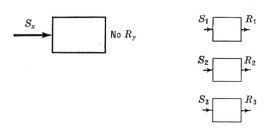

TIME 2

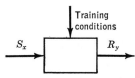

TIME 3

Figure 8.5   Schematic description of performance before, during, and after training.

In setting up the training conditions for Time 2, the training expert should accept responsibility for accomplishing the objective as quickly as possible. This means that he must, if he can, set up training conditions which will make it highly likely that the learner will make a correct response on the first training trial. It must also be observed, however, that although this might be desirable, it is not necessary in a training situation. If the training expert cannot think of training conditions which will work reliably on the first trial, he can fall back on a less effective procedure; that is, he can attempt to shape the desired behavior by means of rewards and punishments over a number of training trials. This throws the burden of figuring out the learning problem upon the learner rather than upon the training expert, and it is therefore apt to be much less efficient than a training situation which has been designed in such a way that the training conditions promote the acquisition of the desired stimulus-response relationships. However, it is a permissible way of solving the problem in the training situation, and it is one which one frequently falls back upon when he does not know how to set up optimal training conditions.

Perhaps it is because it is possible to fall back upon a technique of shaping behavior by means of rewards and punishments that little training research has been concerned with the question of performance functions of the type described in Chapter 2; that is, since we can fall back on rewards and punishments to effect training, we have not been motivated to explore another approach. It is important to note, however, that some of the functions described in Chapter 2 are functions which are subject to change. Thus, while sensing is probably not subject to change, the functions of identifying and interpreting almost certainly are subject to change through learning. For example, if we present a Morse code signal at a high rate of speed to a naive subject, the sensing function operates in the same manner as in a sophisticated subject. On the other hand, the naive subject will have difficulty in reporting whether or not confusable Morse code signals are the same or different; whereas the sophisticated subject has learned to make these identifications. That is, some change has taken place in the identifying function as it is used by the sophisticated subject from its use by the naive subject. If we consider those human functions which are subject to modification or learning, we can see that the training conditions which must be employed to effect a change in one kind of function are frequently different from the training conditions which would be employed for another. When it is desired to set up conditions to attempt to foster correct responding on the first trial of a training experience which involves a modification of identifying, those conditions will be quite different from the conditions that will be set up to foster memorizing of a sequential routine. When we attempt to control the learning experience by means of training conditions, it is apparent that the conditions selected must be tailored for the kind of function we are attempting to modify. It follows that a profitable line of inquiry in training research is to attempt to identify the different kinds of performance functions which are subject to change, and then to identify for each kind of function a type of training condition which can be used to promote effective learning.

Achieving Stimulus Control

In developing a job aid, the designer *must* develop completely reliable stimulus control. While this might be considered a potentially profitable line of research in training, it is almost a necessary approach in job-aids research. One cannot fall back on the alternative of shaping behavior by means of rewards, punishments, and corrective procedures over many trials. He must set up stimulus conditions which will with certainty elicit desired responses on the very first trial. The job-aids designer is in a position similar to that of the training designer who must be successful on the first trial. For similar reasons, then, the job-aids designer must be able to identify the kind of performance change which he is attempting to effect, and he must be able to specify the type of stimulus control that will work for that kind of performance change. Job-aids research must therefore be directed toward the identification of the different kinds of performance change which can be effected by stimulus control and toward the identification of the type of stimulus conditions which will be effective for each type of change. Because of the similarity between the job-aid situation and the training situation at Time 2, job-aids research of this type will almost certainly turn out to be useful to the training designer. It seems that the important feature of the job-aid situation is that it forces research to be concerned with the development of stimulus control, whereas this is not a necessary approach to training research—although it is certainly a desirable one.

There has been virtually no job-aid research specifically focused on the development of methods of stimulus control for specific types of performance change. Such research could well start with consideration of what has been accomplished in training research to control response during training. In turn, it can be expected that job-aids research focused on this problem will turn relevant findings back to the area of training research.

For the most part, the job aids now in use are employed to effect a change in performance which is comparable to memorization of a sequence. (See Rees, 1959; Rees and Copeland, 1959.) Most job aids substitute for the memory function by eliciting comparable performance by means of stimulus control. In order to round out discussion of job aids as instruments of stimulus control which must be tailored to the kind of function being controlled, let us consider another example of a requirement for a job aid which is concerned with identifying. Figure 8 6 presents two PPI oscilloscope patterns which must be employed in troubleshooting a certain electronic equipment. If the technician sees Pattern A, he knows that the malfunction is in Unit A of the

PATTERN A   PATTERN B   PATTERN C

Figure 8.6   Three patterns used in a job aid which require special job aid conditions to promote reliable "identification."

equipment; if he sees Pattern B, he knows that the malfunction is in Unit B of the equipment. The problem to be solved is how to present this information in such a way that the technician will always respond correctly by identifying Pattern A when he sees it on the PPI, and so that he will always correctly identify Pattern B when he sees it on the PPI. The problem is complicated by the fact that patterns like C also occur from time to time on the PPI. It is known that if Pattern A and Pattern B are shown on the job aid in the same way that they are shown in the figure, the technician will frequently confuse them. Certainly, if one were to approach this as a training problem, he would expect A and B to be confused during training, and that during early trials the learner would call Pattern A by the name B and the Pattern B by the name A a fairly high proportion of the time. The same condition occurs in the job-aid situation when the information is presented as shown in Figure 8.6. This looks like a rather simple sensing problem when Patterns A and B are seen side by side, and one might therefore wonder how a technician could ever confuse them. The fact that they are confused may be explained by noting that each is a triple-criterion stimulus. Thus, Pattern A must be a spiral, it must be segmented, and its segments must alternate; whereas, Pattern B must be a spiral, must also be segmented, but the segments must be parallel to each other. Hopefully, the problem of presenting this information on a job aid can be solved in such a way that the technician can rapidly and reliably identify Pattern A when he sees it on his PPI and also identify Pattern B. Such a solution will perhaps also make possible the specification of a stimulus-control technique which can be extremely useful in a training situation requiring the same kind of change in performance capability.

REFERENCES

Hoehn, A. J., and Lumsdaine, A. A. 1958. *Design and use of job aids for communicating technical information.* Lackland AF Base, Texas: Air Force Personnel and Training Research Center. Technical Report 58–7.

Miller, R. B. 1956. *A suggested guide to the preparation of handbooks of job instructions.* Lowry AF Base, Colo.: Maintenance Laboratory, Air Force Personnel and Training Research Center. Technical Memorandum ML–TM–56–15.

Psychological Research Associates. 1961. *A self-tutoring course for on-site training in SAGE AN/FST–2 troubleshooting.* Arlington, Va.: Psychological Research Associates. AFCCDD–TN–61–26, Vol. I–IV.

Rees, D. W. 1959. *Guide to design of air force check-list publications.* Wright-Patterson Air Force Base, Ohio: Wright Air Development Division. Technical Report 59–758.

Rees, D. W., and Copeland, N. K. 1959. *The effects of serial position in check-list design.* Wright-Patterson Air Force Base, Ohio: Wright Air Development Division. Technical Report 59–552.

THE PARTICULAR CAPABILITIES NEEDED BY men to perform the variety of tasks required in system operation are established by a process of *training*. The selection of men possessing certain fundamental abilities, and the classification of people into ability categories, primarily serve the purpose of establishing a desirable starting point for training, as a previous chapter has indicated. Following this classifying procedure, measures must be taken to alter the "raw" human capabilities, to mold them into the particular state of competence which will insure the smooth and efficient meshing of the man-machine combination when in operation. The procedures used to bring about this increased degree of capability in man, resulting in heightened and increasingly skilled performance, are what are referred to as training. Several different subordinate purposes of training may be distinguished, each having its greatest relevance at different stages of system development. The following chapter is primarily concerned with *individual training,* which is ideally designed to establish in the individual man the skills he requires to make effective use of a machine he will operate, or of tools he will use, within a particular subsystem. The varieties of team training and system training, carried out to establish and refine interactive procedures within the system, are discussed more fully in later chapters.

The procedures of training are based upon a number of principles and findings of the science of psychology, as well as on a growing body of technology. They are cast into practical form in several kinds of situations designed to foster human learning, including the individual practice session, the training device, the classroom, and on-the-job training. The effectiveness of these procedures is assessed, both during the training and afterward, by the use of tests of human achievement and measures of human performance within the system context.

The conduct of training for systems often gives new emphases to fundamental questions about human behavior which are of potentially great importance to the scientific understanding of the process of human learning. Among these are the meaning of "knowledge" and "skill" and their relation to human performance; the nature of inferences which may legitimately be made regarding the factors which determine the learning of these entities. The ways in which motivation operates in learning is another matter that is highlighted by training programs. Finally, there is the problem of arranging the content and sequence of training sessions, which is the kind of problem the learning psychologist thinks of as the "programming" of learning.

CONCEPTS OF TRAINING

Meredith P. Crawford

The concepts presented in this chapter concern both the process of training and the application of techniques of research and development to that process. The discussion is limited to the training of individuals, since the training of groups is discussed in Chapter 11. Also excluded from consideration are training devices, which constitute the subject of Chapter 10.

For purposes of this discussion, training is defined as that process by which individuals learn the knowledges, skills and attitudes, not previously in their repertories, which will fit them to function as human components in a system. This training may take place in a school, before the individual is a member of the system, or on the job, after he has become a human component within it. Major attention will be devoted to formal training given before the man enters the job, although some consideration will be given to on-the-job training. It is recognized, although not discussed in this chapter, that the individual will continue to modify his behavior even after he has reached a minimum level of competence on the job. This improvement in performance is, in part at least, a function of the individual's learning to interact with other members, and so is properly treated in Chapter 11.

The notion of a *system* will be employed in various ways. It may refer to a large organization, such as an industrial concern or one of the military services; to a subsystem within the larger organization, which performs some particular function within the larger system; or it may be limited to a particular man-machine or man-weapons combination. The idea will even be extended to the single individual in the treatment of his training for and function as a human component in a system. Since systems exist within systems, a particular system of interest may be regarded both as a sub- and a supersystem, depending on the level of analysis. Such catholic use of the term, which suffers from a lack of precision, is justified in order to gain the analytic advantage of attempting to specify, for each entity so labeled, its purpose and the nature of its input and its output.

To illustrate the usefulness of thinking in terms of systems, as well as to suggest the point of view from which this chapter has been written, a distinction will be suggested between the meanings of the terms *training* and *education*. While it is obvious that both are concerned with human learning, and the technical problems of content and method are shared by both, they differ in terms of purpose. Training is undertaken to serve the needs of a particular system, while education aims to fit persons to take their places in the many systems of society. In training, a program of instruction is designed to fit the trainee for a particular job within the system, while a specific job is usually not foreseen for the student in an educational program. Furthermore, the worth of the training program is to be estimated in terms of its contribution to the output of a particular system. Education, on the other hand, is evaluated largely in terms of the growth of an individual. Thus, in general, training establishments are owned and operated by business corporations and military services, and students are paid to attend as employees of the parent organization. In contrast, educational institutions are owned privately or by the state, and tuition and other costs are borne largely by the individual or by society in general. Therefore, the objectives, policies, and values of a *parent system* are incorporated in the training program. Such a program has its primary meaning and utility within the sphere of the parent system. It follows that the parent-system managers would tend to expend no more on training programs than, in their judgment, is required to develop the knowledges, skills, and attitudes in new employees believed necessary for their functions as various kinds of human components in their system.

In actual practice, many courses of instruction in training and educational institutions are very similar. This is particularly true at "higher-level" schools, such as the War Colleges of the military services, which are usually considered educational establishments. The reason is that they train (or educate) generalists, men who can function at the apex of various systems, understanding the relations between several systems, and who can bring innovations into the operation of their particular systems. Similarly, business and governmental organizations sometimes send employees to universities for courses of a general nature, the exposure to which is believed to be in the best interest of the parent system.

It is apparent that the training process about which this chapter is concerned is a creature of the system it serves. Much of what will be said about the nature of training and the methods of research and development appropriate for it can be deduced from this fundamental proposition.

The remainder of the chapter is divided into three principal parts. Beginning with an identification of types of systems toward which the training of individuals may be directed, the first section includes an account of the subsystems of a large organization which are concerned with personnel and training. In the second section, attention will be turned to research and development as applied to specific training programs, illustrated by an example from Army training research. The final section considers the central problem of training research, the management of the learning process, and the bearing of psychological science on this problem.

It will become apparent that this chapter is derived from experience in military training. Most of the illustrations will be taken from studies performed for the United States Army. While it is believed that many of the observations which will be made apply also to industrial training, particularly for defense industries, a relatively small amount of direct attention will be given to training in commercial establishments.

▣ SYSTEMS IN RELATION TO TRAINING

The Parent System

For a large organization, such as one of the military services or an extensive civilian enterprise, the term *parent system* is a convenient designation. Such an organization may be regarded as a system in terms of its single general purpose or its collection of interrelated purposes and in terms of its identifiable inputs and outputs. Some large organizations may be systemic in nature only with respect to a certain general purpose or as a function of some common interaction, such as the movement of money for the purpose of earning profit for the entire, but otherwise loosely federated, organization. The term *parent* suggests the creation of several entities within the over-all system, which contribute in various ways to the major purpose of the total system and are responsible to it for direction. The management group or headquarters organization of the parent system may also be regarded as a subsystem, whose purpose is to control the entire enterprise. This management group may even be regarded, for analytic purposes, as an extension of that single biological system represented in the person of the organization's chief executive.

Certain subsystems perform operations contributing directly to the major goals of the parent, yielding outputs which provide components of, or constitute without modification, the outputs of the parent system. These will be called *operational subsystems;* the various major units of a military service, the separate production plants of a large manufacturing concern, and the regional offices of a sales and service firm are illustrations of operational subsystems. Other subsystems provide support for some or all of the operational subsystems, among which are those that furnish and maintain the human components: the *personnel subsystem* and the *training subsystem.* The latter may be a part of the former subsystem or may be differentiated from it.

Types of Operating Subsystems

The kinds of functions required of the human components of operating systems are the primary determinants of training. As indicated in Chapter 2, information-processing is taken to be one of the principal functions of the human component, while functions involving the application of power, performance of heavy work, or transportation are largely relegated to machine components. However, for consideration of training, it may be worthwhile to suggest a range of man-machine systems which require human functions extending from heavy manual labor to the most sedentary forms of data processing or decision making. A useful continuum in terms of the relative amount of hardware critical to system function has been defined between extremes that have been labeled "man-ascendant" and "machine-ascendant" systems.[1]

An extreme example of the man-ascendant system is a football team. The only absolutely necessary piece of "hardware" is the football itself— many sandlot games are played without the appurtenances of goal posts, chalk-lined playing field, or ten-yard chain. The players themselves supply the power, the movement, the striking force, as well as the information processing, the memory and the tactical decision making. Hence, training for football involves increasing physical stamina, strength, and speed, along with the development of psychomotor skills such as blocking, tackling, and ball handling, as well as the more symbolic or intellectual signal memory, perceptual judgment, and planning.

The machine-ascendant system, on the other hand, is well illustrated by a guided-missile battery, where the power output of the system is infinitely greater than the combined muscular output of all the men in the battery, and in which even the erection of the missile for launching is powered by the nonhuman devices. The major function of the personnel is in interpreting, coding, troubleshooting, information processing, and decision making.

A third example, the typical infantry unit, seems to occupy a position somewhere between these two extremes. Weapons supply a destructive power output much greater than the human muscles can provide, yet physical strength and stamina are essential for walking, running, and climbing, and for providing support for hand weapons. Symbolic behavior in coordination and decision making is, of course, also required.

A distinction which often parallels the contrast between the man-ascendant and machine-ascendant systems is particularly interesting from the training point of view. The man-ascendant system characteristically takes its physical form, its spatial configuration, from the men themselves—the infantry squad moving in diamond formation is, as a whole, a physical weapon, flexible, yet dependent for fire and maneuver on its several "Gestalts." In the machine-ascendant system, as the bombardment aircraft, the naval combat ship, or the complex newspaper printing press, the machine itself defines the

[1] Follettie, J. F., personal communication, 1959.

physical position and lays obvious constraints upon the performance of the men. Differences in the extent to which the machine defines the function of the crew result in different requirements for individual skills and modes of communication, as well as for different techniques of control and leadership.

The Personnel Subsystem

The functions of recruiting, selecting, classifying, training, upgrading, promoting, and counseling members of the parent system may be accomplished for the parent system as a whole or for some large operating subsystem by a personnel subsystem, whose operation reflects the policies of the parent system on the management of people. Insofar as there is a differentiated personnel organization, it may be regarded as a subsystem whose purpose is to furnish competent human components for operating units at the right place at the right time. This competence is in part determined by the nature and effectiveness of the training subsystem which, if not a component of the personnel subsystem, is obviously critical to its function of personnel supply.

Personnel policy and the functions of the personnel subsystem are of prime consequence to training. The average and range of general and special aptitudes, prior knowledges and skills, and attitudes of students furnished for training are among the determinants of the content and mode of instruction. The efficiency of the distribution of graduates of training to jobs in operating subsystems for which they are trained contributes to the effectiveness of the operational support rendered by the training subsystem. Finally, policies on rotation of personnel for upgrading and career management affect the extent to which training programs will be specific to particular jobs or will offer general training for a hierarchy of positions of increasing breadth and responsibility.

The Training Subsystem

Certain general features of typical training subsystems are of consequence to the psychologists who intend to make a contribution in this field of research and development. These concern the training subsystem as a whole and its relation to the parent system. Many characteristics will have to be taken as constraints in the planning for new training; others are subject to some alteration on the basis of research information.

The training subsystem consists of the entire group of courses, facilities, and personnel devoted to training by the parent system. One of the largest training subsystems ever invented served the Army Ground Forces during World War II. An instructive account of the interlocking operation of several different training schools and facilities for the formation of an Army division is presented in a volume by the Historical Division of the Department of the

Army (Palmer, Wiley, and Keast, 1948). This account of the determination of appropriate schedules, quotas, and attrition rates for the system as a whole, as well as the content of individual courses, indicates the extent and complexities of a large training subsystem. While research and development have been performed mainly on particular training programs within the subsystems, as will be discussed in subsequent sections, it will be profitable at the outset to view the training subsystem as a whole. This will be accomplished under the common systemic rubrics of purpose, input, and output, together with a listing of other important characteristics.

Purposes of the Training Subsystem. Within the general purpose of providing individuals with requisite knowledges, skills, and attitudes which enable them to take their places in the operational systems of the parent organization, more specific objectives are incorporated. To highlight some of these, one may begin by asking why a formal training system should exist at all. Why not apprentice new people directly to older workers already on the job?

Apprentice training works well enough if certain conditions prevail in the operating subsystem. It must be stable, operating in its normal mode, and experiencing little time pressure for bringing new employees up to minimum proficiency. In addition, the jobs must be relatively simple and safe. Neither modern industry nor a military establishment operates under these conditions. Jobs have become increasingly complex, especially in their demands for information processing and symbolic manipulation. In addition, the possibilities for damage to the person or equipment from incompetent handling have become greater. Furthermore, there is constant change in military and industrial job requirements, which call for quick regrouping of skills and knowledges among operators and maintenance personnel. Finally, and perhaps most important of all, separate training subsystems are required to train people for jobs in new operational subsystems which are still under development, so that they may function as soon as the equipment is ready. Therefore, a subsystem for training exists which keeps employees away from the operational scene until they have acquired a certain minimum of knowledges and skills. Training may then be completed on the job in an operating subsystem.

The training operation must provide for a uniform performance in a particular kind of job as it may exist in several operating subsystems of the parent system. A man trained to the specifications of a particular occupational specialty must be able to fill exactly the requirements of that human component position. For better or for worse, military personnel systems have adopted the hardware production philosophy of "the interchangeability of parts, mass produced." When, in a large training subsystem, individual training programs for the same job are offered at different locations by different instructors, controls must be exercised to insure uniformity of the trained product. The development and exercise of these controls in terms of proficiency assessment constitutes an important administrative and research problem.

The provision for innovation in operations is a purpose also served by the training subsystem. For example, men must be prepared for jobs which do not yet exist. To provide the means for accomplishing this training, planners need to team up with hardware planners and equipment developers to share advance information required for building new training programs. It is not always easy to specify the types and sources of this kind of information. To facilitate this exchange, there is embedded within the United States Army's over-all training subsystem the Combat Developments System, whose function is to look ahead toward new doctrine, weapons, and tactics, and to anticipate training requirements. Innovation may also be provided by the training subsystem even when no new major concepts or weapons are involved. Often new operational concepts and new procedures are devised within a training subsystem when training developers carefully examine the jobs for which they are constructing training. In this way, the industrial or military school system may furnish something of the same novel approach to operational system practices that is provided by the universities for our culture as a whole.

In response to requirements of the personnel subsystem, training fulfills another purpose in providing for the upgrading of personnel and the storage of knowledges and skills within them. This practice has important benefits to the individual, in adding to his knowledge, broadening his systemic outlook, and increasing his self-esteem. Training is equally important to the parent system in that it can provide a supply of potential managers and leaders who may be called upon for additional duty and responsibility in the future. This is especially true in the military services, where advanced work in higher-level schools prepares field-grade student officers for assumption of responsibilities commensurate with higher rank in the event of rapid expansion in time of emergency. Incidentally, it may be observed that training research on such programs suffers from one serious handicap: since the graduates of such schools often do not immediately perform the duties for which they are trained, it is difficult to measure the effectiveness of the training programs.

It is apparent that these several purposes of the training subsystem may all be subsumed under the major purposes of the operational subsystems and of the parent organization to which they belong. It is therefore clear that the ultimate test, for example, of military-training effectiveness is in the contribution it makes to performance of units on the battlefield. However, to ferret out this contribution from the many other sources of variance within the total system is extremely difficult. Similarly, the quarterly earnings report of a large corporation should reflect, in some measure, the effectiveness of the company training programs. While several articles on the costs of industrial training have appeared in *The Wall Street Journal,* the writer has not yet seen a financial statement which attributes a change in company profits to a change in the proficiency of personnel brought about through training.

Input to the Training Subsystem.   Members of the parent system, or candidates for membership, with various sets of knowledges, skills, and attitudes within their repertories constitute the input to training. The content of their repertories must be assessed very carefully and completely if training is to be maximally effective, which is the purpose of selection and classification procedures (see Chapter 7). Because of limitations in available manpower, the possession by possible candidates of incorrect or inadequate information about available job opportunities, and imperfect selection procedures, the personnel system may work in less than ideal fashion. Heterogeneity of input places particular burdens on a training system which has a rigid output quota to meet on a fixed schedule. Adaptation of training to varieties of aptitude and background characteristics of trainees constitutes a major research problem.

Output of the Training Subsystem.   Individuals who can perform the functions of a human component in an operating subsystem constitute the output of school or on-the-job training. The minimum level of performance required of particular human components to produce an acceptable output from an operational subsystem is usually quite difficult to specify. While inadequate proficiency of graduates is the more common shortcoming of training subsystems, there are probably several instances of unnecessary overlearning of certain knowledges and skills for a particular job. Such additional capabilities of individuals may be of some use for career advancement to other positions, but their acquisition during a particular job-oriented training program should be evaluated in terms of training costs weighed against advantages gained by the parent system in subsequent employment of the individual. Smith (1960) has offered a system model for determining that level of proficiency of training graduates which should strike an economic balance among the costs of the training subsystem, the immediate requirements of an operational subsystem, and the long-term needs of the parent system. A judicious combination of school and on-the-job training may help in solving the equation. It should be added that learning continues to take place after the man becomes a component in the operational system. As will be shown in Chapter 11, teams continue to improve their total performance as their members learn to work together. Through group discussion and interaction, new and more effective ways of performing are invented in the operational situation.

Other Characteristics of the Training Subsystem.   In addition to these formal subsystem specifications, other kinds of characteristics are worth noting by the training researcher. He needs to find out about the general *policy* of the parent system with respect to the training subsystem. Does management consider training important, or does it put up with it as a necessary but unproductive expense? Does it grant status to training personnel? Most important, perhaps, does it look to the training subsystem to provide an important ingredient in the total system operation? During the past few decades, there has been a marked increase in the positive attitude of management toward training, which has ranged from shop-level training for beginning employees to management courses for potential executives. This interest perhaps reflects a general increase in public interest in education.

Another general point of concern is the *working relations between training and operational personnel*. In some situations, operational personnel have a tour of duty in the training establishment, while in other cases, training personnel have a career of teaching and school administration. Presumably, the former practice brings constant operational emphasis to the training program, while the latter provides for conservation of teaching and training-management skills. The crucial question concerns the extent of communication between members of the operational subsystems and the training subsystems. The importance of feedback of information about operations to the training subsystem can hardly be overemphasized. Whether this communication is best done by having training personnel make frequent contact with operators or by rotating operators as instructors is open to debate, but neither practice relieves training researchers from the responsibility for gaining a thorough knowledge of operations.

Finally, the training researcher must assess the *boundaries of the training subsystem*. He must form some idea of the likely funds, space, locations, and terrain which are currently devoted to, or may be potentially used for, training purposes. This kind of information provides a background for the necessary assessment of costs and gains which will have to be made before a decision can be reached by parent-system managers on the adoption of a new training program. Research personnel should be able to contribute to this kind of assessment.

▣ RESEARCH AND DEVELOPMENT FOR SPECIFIC TRAINING PROGRAMS

The methods for research and development discussed in the remainder of this chapter are directed at the construction or modification of specific courses of instruction, rather than at the management of entire school programs or the training subsystem as a whole. In this section, a discussion of the different contributions made by research and by development to the improvement of training will be followed by the presentation and illustration of a particular sequential method for developing training.

Research and Development in the Field of Training[2]

Methods for the planning and conduct of educational and training courses have a long history (see, for example, Brubacher, 1947). These methods have come to constitute something of an art. The kinds of information and skills which support it come from many sources, of which experimental psychology is only one. While the psychologist has the potential for contributing to this art through research on learning and behavior measurement, he has to add a demonstrable increment to its effectiveness to make his contribution felt. This contribution comes about through participation in development, psychotechnology, and basic and applied research.

Development.   The process of working with an idea or model or design until it is modified into an operable, maintainable, and salable item, usually capable of being mass-produced, is known as *development*. Often this is a long and difficult undertaking. Potable, fresh water can be realized from sea water by various processes of distillation or freezing; however, the determination of which process can do it cheaply and reliably enough for practical use remains a developmental enterprise. Often it is not theory but a vast amount of specific technical information and practical know-how that is utilized in the developmental process. Research may result in the basic idea for a new machine or product, but as a research result, it cannot be put to a practical use. Only after developmental steps are taken can the idea be of any practical significance to the general public.

A specific training program with its associated lesson plans, textbooks, manuals, training aids, and supplementary materials has to be selected and assembled, tried out, and put together to build a workable course. In a university course at the graduate level, this is often done on an *ad hoc,* nonstandardized basis by an experienced professor whose subject is unique in the university's curriculum and whose students are highly motivated toward self-help. However, a training program intended for large numbers of people, taught in several places by many different instructors, must be put together in advance into a carefully engineered, well-documented, and completely supported "training package," which can be effectively administered, if necessary, by persons relatively unskilled in the teaching arts. This package comes about through a process of development.

Psychotechnology.   The ideas which the developer of training programs uses may come from sources as diverse as papers on learning theory and the accumulated wisdom of an old drill sergeant. Insofar as the ideas are tested and predictable consequences are shown to follow the same antecedent conditions, a body of information is accumulated. Such a body of information

---

[2] The ideas presented in this section have been developed during discussion with Dr. John L. Finan, to whom the writer is greatly indebted. They are elaborated in greater generality in Chapter 14.

becomes highly useful in the limited field from which it is derived, and it may be called a technology. It is composed of a set of low-order laws which apply to the limited universe from which they were induced. The laws are not explanatory; they do not utilize constructed concepts to mediate between antecedent and consequent conditions. Instead, they are simply descriptive and useful in the context of the "if-then" relationship.

A technology of training is thereby in the process of gradual formation and is taking its place among other psychotechnologies relevant to the management of human behavior. The chief areas of this branch of psychotechnology will be specified in the exposition of steps in training development in a subsequent section. It may be noted, by way of comparison, that the psychotechnology of aptitude testing and performance measurement is much further advanced than that of training, reflecting the concerted effort of psychologists in these fields, particularly during and since World War II.

Basic and Applied Research. In the strictest sense of the word, basic research is undertaken from a theoretical point of view with the aim of testing hypotheses. The biological organism chosen for study and the methods employed are selected in terms of their appropriateness to the conceptualization under examination. The results of such research have wide generality along specified conceptual dimensions. The results from theoretical-learning research are a source of ideas for use in the psychotechnology of training. When an idea appears to be relevant to a particular problem, it is tested under the conditions of application; this is an activity within the province of applied psychology. It may be noted that research in the psychotechnology of training only rarely affords an opportunity to test for conceptual generality in the manner appropriate to basic research. The psychologist working in the practical field of training needs to keep well in mind the distinctions between basic and applied research, on the one hand, and psychotechnology and development, on the other. Otherwise, he may be frustrated in a misguided effort to accomplish both within the same investigation.

The Goals of Training Development

It is apparent from the above discussion that the goals of training development differ from those of psychotechnology or basic or applied research. In development, certain kinds of ends may be sought, depending on the needs of the parent system. Among the important objectives of training, three kinds of goals may be cited, not necessarily mutually exclusive. They are: increased proficiency, decreased training time and costs, and decreased aptitude requirements.

Increased Proficiency. Probably low proficiency of training graduates is the most common operational problem in both military and industrial training. It is often not easy to state precisely how deficient such graduates are, because it is difficult to specify in quantitative terms the proficiency requirements for each job within the operational subsystem. A performance test can often be used to assess the proficiency levels of persons holding various jobs within the operational subsystem, since it isolates the individual from the system and supplies, in a simulated fashion, the systemic inputs to the job. For example, in order to establish reasonable goals for a training program for Army radar technicians, a proficiency test was administered to men who had been on the job at air-defense sites around the country for varying periods of time (Baldwin *et al.*, 1957). Figure 9.1 illustrates the average performance of these technicians plotted against average months of experience. The base line of 100 is the average performance of training-school graduates, and the

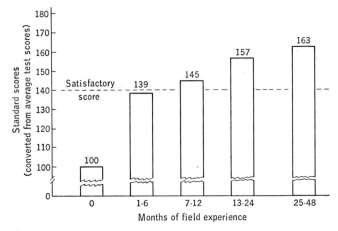

Figure 9.1   Average proficiency-test performance by months of field experience. (Adapted from Baldwin *et al.*, 1957, by permission of the Human Resources Research Office, The George Washington University.)

standard deviation was 20. The dotted horizontal line represents an estimate made by system managers of the minimum necessary level of proficiency. This estimate, while useful, was only a general judgment, rather than a precise, quantitative derivation from measured interactions within the operational subsystem. Since this level was not achieved until after men had been on the job for some time, the goals for a training program could be meaningfully set in terms of that level of performance achieved by experienced technicians after several months of on-the-job experience.

In the development of training for new jobs in new systems, it is necessary to specify in advance some level or range of performance which will be adequate for the needs of the system. The evaluation of the training program developed is then absolute, rather than relative, and training programs will be continuously engineered or developed until performance of trainees falls within tolerable limits. The specification of human performance, or the ranges through which job output may vary to meet the requirements of the system, serves a purpose analogous to the specification of component performance standards and reliability of hardware components in the operational subsystem. (For a fuller discussion, see Chapter 12.)

Decreased Time and Costs.   Since time spent within the training subsystem is essentially nonproductive with respect to the operational subsystem, it is usually important to reduce it. In industrial establishments, training time can be judged in terms of dollar costs—the longer, the more costly. In military systems, time is of the essence during a period of national emergency, when every day counts in readying a trained military unit for operational missions. Insofar as it is possible to divide the total training required between school and job, and accomplish a substantial part of it on the job, the new man may have a least limited utility in the parent system fairly early in his employment.

In addition to the personnel costs of training, involving the pay of students, faculty, and support people, which increases with the length of training, much expense may be involved in the buildings, outdoor training areas, and the operational or simulated equipment involved in training. An analysis of the specific knowledges and skills to be learned, and an inquiry into the simplest way of presenting training stimuli and providing for practice may reduce the expense of training. For example, an experiment (Denenberg, 1954) on the amount of learning achieved on a $27 wooden mock-up and a $10,000 realistic simulator revealed an equal amount of learning. Training devices and simulators, even though expensive, may be cheaper and more feasible than practice on certain operational equipment, as for example, certain modern missile systems.

Decreased Aptitude Requirements.   When the manpower supply is limited and trainees with high aptitudes for certain kinds of training are in short supply, an important objective of the training research and development effort may be to develop the content and method of instruction, or both, so that men of relatively low aptitude can learn to do the job, thus increasing the number of potential candidates. In some cases, this may be achieved if the training content is limited strictly to that which is relevant to a specific job, and no attempt is made to supply any underlying theory or more general instruction which might be useful to trainees of higher aptitude in fitting them for rapid advancement to positions of greater responsibility in accordance with some career pattern. Here, personnel policy and the operation of the personnel subsystem may have a very important influence on actions within the training subsystem. An illustration will be given later in this chapter of an instructional method designed to obtain this kind of result.

Major Steps in a Training Development Project

During the past several years of work in military-training research and development, the principal activities required in an orderly development of a training program have become apparent. A sequence of these activities is presented in diagrammatic form as Figure 9.2. While the seven steps indicated in the seven boxes represent somewhat arbitrary divisions of the work,

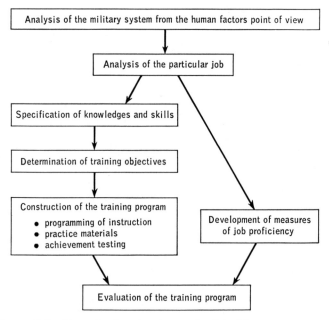

Figure 9.2   Steps in the development of training.

effort of the kinds indicated at each step must be expended in order to accomplish a complete job of building appropriate training and of testing the result. In the main, the work is dependent on an underlying psychotechnology, various aspects of which are treated in this and other chapters. When the psychologist is working at the development of a specific training program, he is functioning as an engineer, bringing his technological information and skill to bear on each step. In such work, he is able to see the utility and the limitations of the current technology, and so becomes well oriented toward further research designed to strengthen the technology. In succeeding paragraphs, each of the seven steps will be identified and reference will be made to chapters in this book where the underlying technology of each is discussed. In the next section, the developmental sequence will be illustrated by an account of the development of a military training program.

Analysis of the Operational Subsystem.   An analysis of the operating subsystem is the necessary starting point to determine the characteristics required of both the hardware and human components of the system. The human-factors aspect of the analysis is the basis for job allocation and specification, and from this aspect it is possible to determine the relative contributions to human component performance which may be made by selection and classification of individuals in accordance with the knowledges, skills, aptitudes, and attitudes they already possess; by human engineering in adapting displays and controls for optimum linkages between human and hardware components; and by training. The balance of effort among these three kinds of psychological work can be determined during the system analysis. In the case of a particular system and a certain available supply of manpower, the solution may involve much more effort along one of the three lines than along the other two. In addition to analyzing the operational subsystem to find the functional characteristics required of each human component, it is also in this step that personnel policies of the parent system are examined to determine whether people may be expected to move about within this subsystem from job to job or may be expected to leave it for other jobs in other subsystems. Such information has an important bearing on both selection and training procedures, as indicated in Chapter 7.

Analysis of the Particular Job. Next, out of the analysis of the whole system, the particular job is studied to determine the inputs to the job from the rest of the system and the required outputs. The type of job analysis which may also occur here—one that is useful to the personnel subsystem, involving classification for purposes of pay and promotion—is of secondary concern to the training developer.

At this point in the developmental sequence, a division of labor is introduced. On the left-hand side of Figure 9.2 are shown the steps involved in developing the curriculum of the training program itself, while the right-hand side pertains to the measurement of job proficiency. These efforts come together in the evaluation step at the bottom.

Specification of Knowledges and Skills. Within the parameters of required inputs to and outputs from the job, the processes by which the individual makes these transformations are identified. These are psychological in nature—sensing, discriminating, remembering, deciding and choosing, which are implied in the specification of the knowledges and skills required for the job. Chapter 6 discusses procedures of job analysis and knowledge and skill specification, while a suggested set of categories for the processes involved in transformation is given in Chapter 2.

Determination of Training Objectives. From the knowledge and skill specification, and from an assessment of the probable content of the repertories of persons to be trained, it is now possible to state in fairly precise terms the objectives of the training program as a whole. The goals may be limited to the specific job or may contain elements furnishing preparation for other jobs later in a man's career. In terms of the specific job, it is at this point that decisions may be made about the optimum combination of school and on-the-job training, and on the kinds of aids, such as manuals and check lists, which will be made available for use on the job (see Chapter 6).

Construction of the Training Program.   This step involves the selection of specific subject matter to be used in the instruction, the programming of the material, and special techniques which may be designed to motivate the trainee. Opportunities for practice may be provided in the form of training devices and simulators, whose general characteristics are specified at this point. Included in this "package of training" are achievement tests for each part of the training program, to provide a measure of the student's progress and to maintain his motivation. They measure only parts of the total required job performance. The technology for building this kind of test is quite well known, perhaps because the older technology of education has necessarily been limited to achievement tests, rather than to the ultimate job-performance tests. The technology available for the support of this step, as well as the preceding one, will be discussed in a subsequent section of this chapter as well as in Chapters 10 and 12.

Development of Measures of Job Proficiency.   As shown on the right-hand side of the figure, a proficiency test of the job as a whole is developed from the information about inputs to and outputs from the job determined in the job analysis. The test simulates these inputs yet isolates the man from the operational subsystem, in order to measure his output without interference with the subsystem. Acceptable standards of performance on this test are to be derived from the analysis of the subsystem, which, ideally, should quantify minimum necessary outputs from all the jobs. The technology of the measurement of human performance is considered in Chapter 12.

Evaluation of the Training Program.   The proficiency test is used as an instrument in evaluating the training developed. The measurement may involve the comparison of equivalent groups of persons trained by one or more methods, as in the case of a new training program's being proposed as a substitute for an old one. If the operational requirement is to increase proficiency, substantial gain in proficiency by the new training must be shown, while if shortened training time or decreased costs is the goal, it may only be necessary to demonstrate that the new program yields the same degree of proficiency as the old. This evaluation step serves two purposes: it supplies parent-system managers with information on which to base a decision for or against adoption of the training so constructed, and it contributes quantitative data to the store of technological information. Some of the technical problems in this kind of measurement, especially as they bear on the choice of proper research design for psychotechnology, as contrasted with basic research, are covered in Chapter 14.

An Account of a Military-Training Development Project

To illustrate the research and development process outlined above, an account will be given of a project of The George Washington University Human Resources Research Office (HumRRO) carried out at one of its field units, the United States Army Armor Human Research Unit at Fort Knox, Kentucky. The purpose of the project, known as Task SHOCKACTION, was to build a revised course of instruction for the armor crewman. The project was undertaken during a period of years from 1955 to 1959. Six subtasks were completed, covering each aspect of the developmental sequence outlined above, although the subtasks were not organized to correspond exactly with those six steps. While the final subtask of constructing and measuring the effectiveness of a new training program was foreseen at the outset of the work, the various stages were undertaken and reported as individual projects. Certain results of each step, although of primary value in furthering the developmental project, were of immediate interest and use to the Army.

The training program toward which the task was directed was the Army Training Program for Tank Companies, prescribed by the Department in an appropriate Army document (Department of the Army, 1957). This course, taken by graduates of basic combat training (the initial common training program for all new male enlisted personnel), leads to the position of armor crewman, a job in which the man is presumed to be capable of acting as a tank commander, gunner, driver, or loader of the main battle tank. The course is eight weeks long and is given at several Army installations. It is an important course because it serves as an introduction to all enlisted training in armor and serves many students, and was therefore judged to be worth a considerable investment of research and development funds. A previous survey of training problems in armor (Green *et al.,* 1954) recorded the opinion of many armor officers that the training of armor crewmen was not at a satisfactory level of proficiency.

Collection of Field Data. In order to define completely the objectives of the new training program, a number of determinations had to be made about the performance of tank crewmen in the operational subsystems represented by various kinds of armored units then on duty in the Army, both in the continental United States and overseas. The research team planned a series of studies which would result in job analyses of the four crew positions, together with a listing of the knowledges and skills required for each. In addition, a program was conceived in which various assessments would be made of the average existing state of knowledge and proficiency in samples of a wide range of armored units.

The first series of studies concentrated on groups of experienced armor personnel in order to determine the actual job duties, knowledges, skills, and levels of proficiency in those units which would be expected to be in the highest state of combat readiness. It was considered that such units would display most accurately the nature of the jobs as they existed in the best operational systems and as performed by the most proficient personnel. Toward these ends, members of the task team began their preparation by enrolling in appropriate courses in the Armor School, by reviewing Army manuals and training programs relevant to the tank crewman's duties, and of interviewing experienced officers. As a result of these preliminary efforts, several tentative data-gathering instruments were prepared, including an Individual Interview Form, Observational Check List, performance tests for each crew position, and an Activities Log on which crewmen were to specify how they spent a typical day in their unit.

For tryout purposes these instruments were used with 100 members of an armored cavalry regiment. The instruments were revised on the basis of this experience, and a second armored unit was identified, the members of which had at least three years of experience in armor and three months' experience on the job. The revised instruments were used with the 25 crews (100 crewmen) of this unit, to further test the suitability of the data-gathering materials for the main study.

While these preparations were being made for intensive study of experienced crewmen, another measure was developed to be used with crewmen of a wider range of experience for study of interchangeability of jobs among crewmen, since the ability of one crewman to replace another who might become a battle casualty is regarded by the Army as an important characteristic of armor crews. This instrument was a paper-and-pencil test of armor knowledge, the 157 items of which were grouped into four parts for the four crew positions (MacCaslin, 1956).

The task team visited Europe during September and October, 1955, where 256 experienced crewmen of three medium tank battalions and two armored cavalry regiments were studied with the pretested research instruments. With the tank commanders, for example, the researchers interviewed each commander, using the Activities Interview Form as a guide for asking questions about various tasks, his ability to perform them, the frequency with which he does so, and the degree of difficulty involved. From the 69 commanders studied, a count was made of the proportion who said they had engaged in, had responsibility for, or knew how to perform 61 elements of their job duties. Because of the large number of job elements, a sample of 20 elements was selected for proficiency measurement by means of performance checks, in which the percentage of men correctly responding on each task element was noted. The daily Activities Log was kept by each tank commander, and during the week spent with each unit, a ten-item descriptive rating scale was completed on each tank commander by his platoon leader. Similar procedures appropriate for each crew position were used for 57 gunners, 60 drivers, and 70 loaders.

Job Analyses and Knowledge and Skill Specification. From these observations, information on knowledges and skills and on proficiency were derived (Baker, 1958). A trial list of job duties for each crew position was compiled by listing each job element which was reported by 60 percent or more of the experienced men studied. These were submitted to experienced staff officers for evaluation and comment, and after conferences with them to resolve differences in opinion, a final criterion list of duties was prepared for each position. Eight "job duties" were specified for the tank commander, four for the gunner, nine for the driver, and five for the loader, of which the following are typical:

> The Tank Commander applies basic methods for collecting and reporting combat information and applies and supervises troop counter-intelligence measures.

> The Tank Gunner fires the main gun and the coaxial machine gun, utilizing direct fire procedures.

Under each job duty were listed "operations," "knowledges," and "responsibilities," ranging in number from 1 to 34. These lists of job requirements constituted the chief product of this first subtask of the program, supplemented by detailed job descriptions for each crewman which specified the behavioral steps in performing the tasks. They provided not only information for further training developmental work, but, as a by-product, also made available information on the basis of which the Army revised its published description of the Occupational Specialty Code pertaining to armor crewmen. This represents an incidental contribution from training research to the personnel management subsystem of the Army.

Assessment of Current Proficiency. The results of the field proficiency tests were reported in detail (Baker *et al.,* 1958) and formed the basis for a number of conclusions and recommendations, the principal one of which was that the beginning course for armor crewmen concentrate on the position of gunner, loader, and driver, leaving the special training for the tank commander to a more advanced course. In addition to the use of these proficiency measures in pinpointing particular job elements in need of improved training, the results—along with those from an administration of the 157-item paper and pencil test to a representative sample of active, National Guard and reserve units throughout the United States—furnished the Army with current information on the state of training and readiness of armored forces.

A Preliminary Study of Variations in Training Time. These studies furnished both the basis for reaffirmation of the requirement to construct a new training program and the information on which to formulate precisely the objectives of the new course. In addition, another study had been initiated, to determine the effect of halving, repeating twice, or repeating three times the training in selected armor subjects (Baker, Mathers, and Roach, 1959). This research in the psychotechnology of training was undertaken in advance of training-course instruction to obtain data on relevant learning phenomena to be used in the terminal phase of engineering design.

The increase or decrease in each subject was done by keeping the lesson content constant, and varying only the amount of instruction or practice. Through the use of comparable groups of armor trainees for each presentation condition for each of 20 selected subjects, the scores on achievement tests in each subject for some 2500 soldiers were obtained, analyzed in terms of low, medium, and high aptitude trainees (as determined by Army General Classification test scores) and plotted in the form of "learning curves" for each subject. Two such figures are displayed in Figure 9.3. The results as a whole indicated an increase in the percentage of test items answered correctly

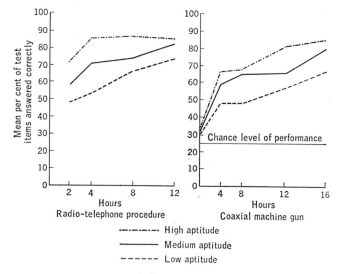

Figure 9.3. Achievement in armor subjects by amount of instruction. Each point represents the average score made by a group of trainees of specified aptitude level. (Adapted from Figures 21 and 22, Baker, Mathers, and Roach, 1959, by permission of the Human Resources Research Office, The George Washington University.)

with increased training, but considerably less than expected by Army instructors. Even with three times the standard instruction and practice, proficiency increased but little, while it decreased in only eight of the 18 skill areas when normal training was cut in half. Marked differences of achievement at all points along the abscissa were observed for the two extreme aptitude groups in most subjects, particularly the critical areas of communications, gunnery, driving, maintenance, and tactics. It was concluded that a mere increase in repetitive instruction would not produce the desired proficiency, and therefore special instructional techniques would have to be developed, particularly for the more difficult subjects. The almost negligible effect of halving instruction for some subject matters indicated those areas in which training time might be saved for use with new kinds of training on more difficult subjects.

Construction of the Final "Training Package." With the information gathered over the three previous years, the research team was prepared to begin a study of the existing program of instruction (Department of the Army, 1957) in terms of curriculum content, and instructional and administrative techniques, toward its modification to produce the product desired— "a tank crewman qualified to perform the job of gunner, driver and loader" (MacCaslin, Woodruff, and Baker, 1959, p. 3). On the basis of information gathered during the field studies, which showed that tank commanders do not achieve their position until after considerable on-the-job experience, the Army concurred in a recommendation that the objective of training tank commanders be omitted from the new course under development. However, as a by-product of this task, members of the task staff prepared the *Tank Commander's Guide* (Cook and Baker, 1959) which brought together revelant information from 90-odd Army publications and which was made available, through a civilian publishing company, for general Army use and as a text in a subsequent study on tank-commander training.

In planning the details of instructional procedures for the new course, seven psychotechnological principles served as guidelines:

1. Adherence to training objectives. This was accomplished by preparing lessons in advance for presentation by instructors, production of training films for some teaching points, recording certain presentations of complex lessons, and the use of picture guides, described below.

2. Emphasis on relationship of tasks to each other and to the program. The new course was designed to begin with a specially prepared orientation film on armor and on the training program. Each section of the program was introduced and summarized in an integrative manner.

3. Emphasis on learning by doing. Since the job descriptions broke down each task into steps, it was possible to direct each trainee through these steps under supervision and to correct his mistakes, a procedure facilitated by instruction in small groups.

4. Promoting understanding. All lesson materials were prepared in wording and illustration with the aim of maximum communication to the trainee. In particular, the job descriptions were used to develop a picture guidebook for each of the three crew positions. These books provided pictures and simple verbal statements of many job procedures and were put together after empirical testing of much of the material on trainees available at the Center. These were used as texts throughout the course (U.S. Army Armor Human Research Unit, 1957; 1958a; 1958b).

5. Knowledge of results. Performance achievement tests on each block of instruction were provided, and trainees were told their scores. When firing on the range, information on where his round went was transmitted to the trainee as quickly as possible.

6. Motivation as an integral part of training. On the first day of training, students were shown a specially prepared film, *Introduction to Armor,*

were given a chance to examine tanks and witnessed a firing demonstration, all designed to answer questions such as, "Why am I here?" and "What will I be doing?" The attempt was made to present the role of armor in modern warfare. Scheduling of training for individual participation, for remedial Saturday afternoon make-up sessions for poor performance, and for organized athletics and recreation was accomplished to enhance conditions of positive motivation. Additional general orientation to armor and the course was given during the first day of the third week.

7. Realism in training. Insofar as possible, training situations were designed to reflect conditions of combat. Activities not related to combat had been removed from the curriculum. The kinds of targets used in firing, the position and sequence of firing, and the courses over which student drivers operated their tanks were chosen to reflect combat situatons. A night firing problem was added.

To implement these general principles, administrative changes in the management of training were accomplished. The training company was divided into four platoons who lived, went to school, and performed other duties together, which resulted in only a few absences from class. The instructors for the experimental program were relieved of other duties and were trained for a two-week period prior to the experimental run. Those men normally held over from previous training classes to act as tank commanders for a new group of trainees were designated, for the new course, as "Assistant Instructors," rather than "Held-Over Tank Commanders," were promoted earlier than usual and had their duties arranged to permit them to stay with their crews throughout all training. To make this possible, it was necessary that ten additional men be retained for the duration of this study to remain with the tanks during periods of shop maintenance. The normal number of tanks were used but were driven by students more hours than in the standard course; because of scheduled economies in unnecessary driving by administrative personnel, less gasoline was used than in the standard course. The experimental company used fewer rounds of expensive ammunition for the main tank gun than in standard training, with some small addition of the less expensive machine-gun ammunition.

The over-all experimental program turned out to require 274 hours of regular scheduled training with four hours of additional concurrent training, while the standard program called for 352 hours of regular and 28 hours of concurrent instruction. This reduction of time from eight to six weeks was not a principal objective at the outset of course planning, but appeared to be possible during the detailed allocation of training time and facilities.

It is apparent that a great many variables believed to affect training were altered in some way for this experimental purpose. The results, therefore, represent the combined effect of particular curriculum and administrative and instructional conditions, all engineered into a single package. In the development of psychotechnology, it is desirable to determine the effects of each, varied while others are held constant, as well as their interactions, but such research requires time and resources not easily provided. Therefore, the evaluation is of the single combination of factors, weighted in terms of the best judgment of the research staff and combined in ways designed to be replicable by the Army in possible repeated uses of the new program.

Construction of the Final Proficiency Test. The Armor Mastery Test was built by a separate research group not associated with other members of the task team who developed the training program. The test battery comprised 21 subtests, made up of 405 items, constructed as mastery items— that is, they were designed to ascertain only whether the trainee had learned the essential skill well enough to perform a given job satisfactorily, and not to measure relative degrees of skill. Nine subtests were devoted to gunnery, six to driving, and four to loading, and two were general tests on the pistol and submachine gun, weapons to be used by all crewmen. Each subtest was of the performance type. In developing the tests, only key skills for each crew position were used, and practical considerations of time, equipment, and feasibility were guidelines. During the preparation of the tests, Army instructors criticized them, and they were tried out on trainees undergoing regular instruction. They were revised and standardized for administration by noncommissioned officers not associated with the research. In the experiment, conventional firing schedules were used because the criteria for new firing procedures, later developed by HumRRO, had not yet been fully developed (Woodruff, Stark, and Willard, 1962). A new driving course was prepared for the test.

Evaluation. The final measurement was performed with two training companies of about 160 men each, made up by the assignments to each in terms of scores on the Army General, Mechanical Aptitude, and Verbal Tests and in terms of educational level, race, and geographical origin. The control company took the current standard eight-week training program and the experimental company, the new six-week course. The former was started two weeks ahead of the latter, so that both companies were given the Armor Mastery Test during the same final week, alternating mornings and afternoons of each day for each company. Other precautions taken to eliminate bias on the test procedure included: selection of comparable officer or noncommissioned-officer cadres for each company; instructors for the experimental company chosen from those rated by supervisors in the Armor School as average or below average; assistant instructors (and hold-over tank commanders for the control group) chosen from those rated in the upper third of their training companies; and a briefing given to each company on the final day, explaining that they were part of an experiment, but without mention of competition with another company.

The results, in terms of the Armor Mastery Test as a whole, showed a slight superiority of the experimental group in terms of total score (experimental, 295; control, 285). Because the subtests differed in length and difficulty, a more meaningful analysis was made in terms of these. The experimental company was superior in 11 of the 21. The control company excelled in three. In seven the results were the same. In general, the 11 tests on which the experimental company showed superiority involved the more complex skills involved in gunnery, driving, and communication. Differences reflected, in large part, certain differences in emphases between the two courses. In addition to these results, the scores on the paper-and-pencil Armor Proficiency Test, used earlier in the field studies, showed no differences between the two companies.

The major conclusion was that the experimental six-week program produced trainees essentially equivalent in proficiency to graduates of the standard eight-week program. In considering this new training program for adoption, the Army considered the 25 percent gain in training time in comparison with the costs. This is, of course, a decision to be made by the proper military authority (as equivalent to the manager of the parent system). But it was important that the research report tabulate and discuss the differences in management costs in terms of the several enumerated factors. At this time of writing, it can be reported that the experimentally produced guides for the gunner, driver, and loader have been published as Army Training Circulars, new firing tables resulting from this study have been adopted, and a new training program, lengthened to the original eight weeks to comply with existing federal statutes and to provide for additional training, has been adopted by the Army on the basis of this developmental program.

▣ THE MANAGEMENT OF THE LEARNING PROCESS

This section is concerned with those decisions that are called for in the steps in the training development sequence designated above (and in Figure 9.2) as "Determination of Training Objectives" and "Construction of the Training Program." This account will be confined to the kinds of choices that have to be made; a few suggestions about the technological information available in support of these decisions will be added. To go further would require the study of a number of particular developmental efforts of diverse and unique interest. Generality in this field inheres more nearly in the specification of the orderly array of decisions that must be made than in rules as to how to make them in specific instances. At the outset, it should be emphasized that decisions in these three areas must be made simultaneously, since they are mutually interactive and supporting. Certain kinds of curricula indicate a preference for certain programming techniques, and motivation may be enhanced or reduced in terms of various choices of curriculum material and programming techniques. Since the learner is an active system, his management during the training process is to be done with a series of strategic and tactical decisions, simultaneously comprehending what he is to learn (curriculum), why he should learn it (motivation), and how he should learn it (programming).

Since the training subsystem is designed for the primary purpose of supplying the operational subsystem with capable human components, it follows that the chief concern in designing training, in psychological terms, is with *transfer of training* from the training to the operational situation. Much of what has been said before about feedback of information to the training subsystem from the operational subsystem, realism in training, and the pattern of gradual differentiation over the years of the typical training subsystem from the parent system, all point to the essential requirement that the learning must transfer to the place where it will be used. As Gagné and Bolles (1959) have pointed out, a good deal more is known about the conditions for efficient acquisition of learning than for transfer.

Major Decisions to be Made in Choice of Curriculum

The term curriculum is used here to denote the subject content of a course of instruction designed to qualify a man to perform a job in the operational subsystem. The instruction may be given in a school, on the job, or in a combination of the two. Choices about this content involve major decisions of where the training may best be done, and they involve determinations, if not already made, of the job aids which will be available in the operational subsystem.

The Derivation of Training Objectives. The clarity and adequacy of the specification of course objectives is primarily dependent upon the completeness and accuracy of the determination of knowledge and skills. If this is well done, the maximum curriculum coverage is readily apparent. Choice of curriculum material is then governed largely by particular considerations of time, cost, and equipment availability. For example, if the knowledge and skill specification shows a number of closely related items, a single unit of instruction may suffice. Again, all possible inputs of stimulus situations which occur on the job can probably never be economically reproduced in the training situation, and therefore representative inputs will have to be selected. These may be chosen if the knowledge and skill specification is based on the frequency of occurrence of various input conditions on the job. Such a frequency count, for example, is quite possible in the study of a repairman's job, where the number of different malfunctions encountered may be tallied. The objectives of the curriculum are thus set in terms of the acquisition of the most important, the most frequent, and the most representative of the knowledges and skills, and perhaps those most likely to be required when the man first goes on the job.

Certain general rules can be stated for the specification of course objectives which may encompass a number of specific choices. The training course objectives should be:

1. derived from the job, in terms of what is actually required for job performance;
2. arranged in hierarchical order, for the program as a whole and for each unit of instruction within the program;
3. cognizant of the knowledges and skills already within the repertory of students before the training begins;
4. reasonably within the achievement level of the students;
5. communicated to the students.

In following the third rule, for certain programs it may be necessary to prepare refresher training for some students whose prior repertories are inadequate, as, for example, training in mathematical operations before admission to technical courses requiring computation. The fifth rule is based on the fundamental characteristic of the human component in a system—his ability to modify his own behavior. Unless the objective toward which the modification is to be made is clear to him, one of the most important resources available to the training manager is overlooked.

Specific rules for the translation of knowledge and skill specifications into technical training course content have been described in Chapter 6, and also by Hoehn (1960a), who has illustrated them in the development of an electronics maintenance course. As previously stated, perhaps the most important single contribution to the development of training through research has been the determination of methods for the formulation of objectives of instruction.

Manuals versus Memory.   In planning the curriculum, a very important distinction must be made between what the man must be able to do from memory and what help he can expect from job aids, manuals, check lists, and other devices to provide cues for his action. The precise nature of such job supports needs to be foreseen at the time subject matter for school training is being selected, so that school training can be built around the supports which will be available on the job. It is often true, for example, that an electronics technician has the information he needs for troubleshooting within his manuals and schematics but has not learned how to use them in an efficient manner. If the design of these manuals can be anticipated at the same time training is being developed, training time will be used effectively, and the employment of job aids will be precise and rapid. In connection with the preparation of guidance for choosing training course content, Hoehn has suggested procedures for the parallel development of handbooks to be used on the job, especially for the presentation of hard-to-memorize performance sequences, infrequently used procedures, and specific equipment characteristics (Hoehn, 1960b). The design of job aids was discussed in Chapter 8.

School versus On-the-Job Training.   Another important decision which must be made early in the training development cycle is between the acquisition of knowledges and skills in the school or on the job. As has been previously indicated, training in the operational context has the advantage of realism, thus minimizing the transfer problem, and also allows for some gainful employment of the new worker in the operational subsystem. In some cases, the decision may be between the school and the job situation; in others, a judicious integrated combination may be made of the two. Some consideration of the advantages and disadvantages of on-the-job training was given in the earlier discussion of the apprentice system.

One of the most common difficulties with on-the-job training is that little systematic attention is paid to it. New employees may be put into the job situation and given sporadic explanations, instructions, or help by older employees, but without a planned program for learning. Usually, the older employee does not have the time to devote to instruction or special skills in planning learning experience. To meet the need for such programmed on-the-job training, Woolman (1960) developed a program for training of guided-missile operators on site. The instruction was prepared for men who report to Nike sites for duty directly from basic combat training, without any relevant experience. The development of this program generally followed the procedure outlined in the previous section. The Operational Context Training, as it was called, ". . . was to provide on-site training, flexible enough to produce operator skills without interfering with battery operations." Instruction was conducted in "training units" made up of an experienced operator and two trainees. It was scheduled around the regular duties of the crewmen, and was flexible enough to utilize parts of the equipment which were free from operational use. A "training guide" was prepared which not only presented in nontechnical language the standard operating procedures for all positions, emphasizing safety factors, but also provided for records of student progress on each block of instruction. For each operating procedure, the instructor was furnished a six-step training method which began with his own presentation of the over-all picture of the procedure and followed through steps of instructor demonstration, instructor talk-through, trainee-instructor talk-through, and finally, trainee practice. A set of proficiency standards was provided for each procedure. In a carefully controlled study, the field training in this operational context proved superior to previous unstructured training and produced, at far less cost, men with proficiency equal to graduates of school training.

It is probable that great advances, both in the efficiency of training and the performance of certain kinds of jobs, will be made through a judicious division between school and on-the-job training. The latter seems very effective when it is associated with a careful division of knowledge and skill support between training, on the one hand, and precisely designed manuals and other job aids, on the other. Following a comprehensive task-and-skill analysis, such a delineation of a program for preparing and supporting the human component in the system will yield important results.

Motivation of Trainees

The point of view has been adopted that the training subsystem is part of the parent system and that interest in learning is but a special case of an interest in performance. Therefore, it follows that the first examination of the conditions for motivation of training would be in terms of the general conditions for motivation of work in the parent system. In other words, the trainee is an employee of the organization or member of the parent system whose current work assignment is to master a training course. Consideration of trainee motivation will here be divided into two parts: factors which affect general employee motivation, and particular motivational conditions which promote learning.

Employee Attitudes and Motivation.   The new employee entering a company training program or the recruit entering basic training is making an important change in his life. The enthusiasm with which he begins may range from a keen anticipation, following a deliberate choice among several attractive employment opportunities, to a reluctant response to the notification from his draft board. His initial attitudes toward his first training program are therefore already determined. The early days of the training program may give promise of the realization of his highest expectations or of his worst misgivings. As the training progresses, he forms attitudes, not only about the training program and the knowledges and skills he is expected to acquire, but also about the parent organization which he has joined, as has been quantitatively demonstrated in a study of motivation for Army technical training (Heilman, Osburn, and Hausknecht, 1955). The way training is conducted, the apparent attitudes of instructors, and the facilities provided will offer cues by which the trainee formulates attitudes toward the parent system.

Since the trainee is already "at work," it is reasonable to assume that many of the conditions for good motivation which have been found in industry (Viteles, 1953; Maier, 1955, Chs. 4, 5, 13, 14; Industrial Relations News, 1960) and in the military services (Stouffer, 1949–1950) are generally applicable to the training situation. Perhaps one of the most important findings of recent research on motivation for work is the importance of factors other than financial reward. Many studies point to the fact that a feeling of achievement, interesting work, and recognition of accomplishment are more highly desired than pay, provided the latter exceeds a certain minimum level. The recent study by Herzberg and his associates (1959) on employees in engineering and accounting work found that motivational factors could be classified as "satisfiers" and "dissatisfiers." Among the former were such factors as achievement, recognition, the work itself, responsibility, and advancement, which could take positive values well above the zero, or indifference, point. The latter included such things as supervision, salary, and working conditions, which could be perceived as varying negatively below the zero point. The chief implication of the research was that, even if dissatisfiers were reduced to a minimum, satisfiers would have to be present in a finite amount to keep the employees from seeking other positions. Such results point to the importance of the work itself and its place in the parent system as a determiner of motivation.

It would seem important to capitalize during training on the same kinds of positive factors which will be important for good work throughout the parent system. Insofar as it can be assumed that the individual wants to get ahead in the parent system, doing work in which he has some interest, training can be conducted in a manner to allow some realization of this desire. Further, it seems reasonable that those incentives and motivational techniques which can be used in a particular operational subsystem to promote good work should also be used in training, because they would not represent artificial supports, to be removed when the man goes on the job. Attitudes toward the "work" of learning would transfer to the "work" of production. Looking at it another way, it is clear that an employee is expected to continue his learning on the job, with or without formal on-the-job training, so that, from the point of view of attitudes and motivation, learning in training is much the same as working at the job. Positive attitudes, reflected in a desire to learn, should be cultivated and reinforced during training in the hope that they will be taken into the job situation.

Motivation for Training. Within this perspective, both the motivating conditions for the training situation as a whole and those particular factors which affect the detailed acquisition of knowledges and skills are of interest. When the learner himself is regarded as a system, two characteristics that are important for his motivation as a learner become apparent. The first is his ability to acquire goals or purposes by which he governs the application of effort. The second is the fact that new outputs from this system come about through a sequence of inputs and outputs, a situation summarized by the accepted principle that the learner must be active. Further, the selection and acquisition of these new responses or modes of behavior is a function of the purposes or goals internalized by the learner. While it is recognized that people are often misled as to the nature of their own motives and the goal objects relevant to them, for this discussion the common-sense notion is adopted that a man will tend to learn what he wants to and will learn little if he does not want to.

Most writers on learning (for example, Hilgard, 1956) accept some form of the "empirical law of effect" concerning the use of rewards and punishments. They do not agree on the mechanisms involved. Rewards may be manipulated in the form of incentives. Insofar as the trainee wants to learn, the correct accomplishment of a learning task is itself rewarding and the probability increases that the behavior involved will become a part of the learner's repertory. For each learner, the hierarchy of interests and desires is probably unique, yet for any relatively homogeneous group of trainees, these hierarchies may follow rather predictable patterns. The relevance of the knowledge and skill to be acquired must be clear to the learner in terms of this hierarchy if the act of responding correctly is to be reinforced. In some cases, the learner can determine these relationships for himself; often it may be necessary to have these connections made explicit in the training situation. In any event, it is desirable that the material to be learned is perceived by the learner as a subgoal along the way toward a major goal desired by the learner. This process is facilitated by providing immediate knowlege of results.

To insure that goal orientation is maintained, various techniques of preliminary orientation, explanation of the interrelations between blocks of instruction, and techniques of programming have been employed. If goal-relatedness can be made explicit and reliance placed on the intrinsic motivation achieved thereby, it would seem to follow that training will proceed economically and should transfer to the job. The importance of selection of trainees in terms of interest, as by means of a biographical inventory, interview, or similar technique, is apparent in this connection. Also, the desirability of dividing new trainees into groups in terms of background and interest for their orientation and beginning training stems from this same technique for motivation.

When intrinsic motivation or goal orientation is insufficient, it is often possible to employ various sorts of positive but extrinsic types of incentives for training. Competition among individuals and among groups for small rewards can be effective. For example, a study of Army basic training (Findlay, Matyas, and Rogge, 1955) employed squad competition for week-end passes, relief from extra work details, and precedence in the mess-hall line. The squad making the highest score on the weekly proficiency test received these rewards, while the lowest squad usually received no passes, ate last, and formed most of the extra-duty work details during the following week. Two companies trained under these conditions made an average score on the final proficiency test 28 percent higher than four companies of the same composition trained under noncompetitive conditions. The assumption is that behavior acquired under conditions of extrinsic reward will develop the kind of functional autonomy which will carry through to the job.

In the military establishment and many other training situations, initial attitudes of trainees toward the parent system and interest in the knowledges and skills to be initially acquired do not offer the training manager much on which he can build a positive program of incentives. For specific learning situations in the classroom and laboratory, the evidence seems clear that reward is more effective than punishment, particularly since punishment alone does not offer the learner any cue to the correct response. In military training, and probably also in training for various positions in large organizations, there is a type of conformity required in many kinds of behavior, more or less related to the immediate job, which is brought about through the exercise of various kinds of social controls of a positive or negative sort. Punishment, as meted out by authorities or as developed by group attitudes and sanctions, is clearly operative and influences behavior. Information is not readily available on the extent to which the learning of specific knowledges and skills is so programmed in the military and industrial training that a form of punishment regularly follows an incorrect response. Nor, for that matter, is the writer aware of any systematic survey of the use of rewards. It is true that rewards and punishments are meted out in the practical training situations, often without precise relation to specific correct or incorrect acts. As noted in *The American Soldier* (Stouffer, 1949, Volume I, pp. 410–449), incorrect, nonconforming acts are easier to recognize, in the absence of reliable performance criteria, than are outstandingly good performances. This fact, together with the understandable impatience of training personnel burdened with heavy schedules and reluctant students, leads to a frequent use of some form of punishment. Stouffer reports that, in a sample drawn at the end of World War II, 46 percent of officers and 67 percent of enlisted men agreed with the statement: "The main reason most soldiers obey rules and regulations is because they are afraid of being punished." The real effectiveness of punishment—or better, the conditions under which it is an effective and wise technique for the management of learning—is yet to be determined. A discussion of its role in promoting discipline is beyond the scope of this chapter.

One other point in connection with motivation for learning should be noted. This concerns the problem posed for training by the possible presence of real danger during employment in the parent system. High-voltage electrical equipment, high-speed moving parts, and hazardous missions of one sort and another are characteristic of many jobs, both military and industrial. Although reliance can often be placed on volunteers for many such occupations, there are still problems involved in the control of fear. At present, we do not know, for example, at what point in the learning sequence it is best to introduce conditions promoting fear and stress, in order to insure that the behavior will be properly elicited under such conditions in the real-life job situation. Dependence on overlearning is perhaps the most common current solution to this problem.

The Programming of Instruction

The adaptation from the language of computer operation of the term "programming" offers the connotation of providing for an orderly, sequential set of operations by which the learner is to achieve a new behavioral output. The use of the term affirms the assumption that the learning process is an orderly one and expresses the conviction that it will eventually be understood. As yet, however, learning theory has not made explicit just how the process works on either the human or the infrahuman level.

For the reader interested in learning theory, it may be well to point out the level of discourse which is appropriate for training technology. Management of the learning of certain specified samples of persons, usually handled in groups, is the practical problem. The principal concern, therefore, is with those arrangements of antecedent conditions which can be accomplished within the constraints of the system in which we are working and with the kinds of behaviors which follow as consequents. The concern of technologists is not with the intervening or mediating events, whose construction through hypothesis formulation and testing is the province of the learning theorist.

Contemporary theory offers a number of insights into the learning process; the points of view of individual writers give differential emphases to the various phenomena of learning. Spence (1959) has indicated that at the present time much help cannot be expected from learning theorists in building practical training programs. This is undoubtedly true if simple, clearcut laws are sought, which can be applied directly to the engineering of a particular curriculum. However, it would be a great mistake for the developer of training programs to isolate himself from current discussions of learning theory (see, for example, Hilgard, 1956; Koch, 1959). Should he fail to keep up with the developments of theory, he would miss many valuable new hypotheses which might give him just the ideas he needs for tryout in a particular developmental assignment, and he might remain unaware of the exciting formulation of an important conceptual generalization which would move the technology far ahead in a single step.

General Considerations. To return to the more practical, if less exciting, problem of programming for learning, it may be observed that an ideal solution might provide a program adapted to the interest, aptitudes, and motivations of each single learner. The experienced instructor, thoroughly familiar with the material and with the general and specific characteristics of the learner, has been recognized as the most efficient programmer, ever since the enunciation of the well-known statement about Mark Hopkins and the log. While automated learning techniques may offer a practical approach to this ideal, as will be discussed below, first attention must be given to the programming for groups of learners in the conventional classroom, laboratory, simulator, and on-the-job situation. The need for uniformity in the training product, the frequent inexperience of instructors, and limitations of training facilities may require a fairly rigid prescription of the training program, so that it may often be best to present as much of the instruction as possible by previously prepared and fixed media, insuring at least a minimum comprehensive and orderly coverage of subject matter.

The vehicles for programming are the course outline and the lesson plan. The kinds of decisions which have to be made in the development of these were summarized from experimental studies of military training during World War II by Covner (1946). His list of choice points in building a course outline serves as well today as it did 15 years ago. The outline builder must answer questions about the time required for learning each knowledge and skill by the average trainee; the relative difficulty of topics; the optimum order of subject matter; the presentation of theory in relation to practical information; the allocation of time for practice, drill, testing and review; and the extent to which the outline may be altered to meet the characteristics of the individual learner. In preparing the detailed lesson plan, Covner indicates that the trainer must make explicit the purpose of each session, the necessary preparation of the instructor, the plan of presentation, the provision for student practice, and the method of conducting the review and summary in which the lesson is integrated with those coming before and after it. For the presentation, he indicates that the introduction of technical terminology, use of training aids, and the questioning of students should be specifically anticipated.

The making of these and similar decisions constitutes the work of program planning. What psychological principles are available for guiding the developer in making his choices? Summaries of such principles may be found in textbooks on learning (McGeoch and Irion, 1952; Kingsley and Garry, 1957) and in articles on training (Wolfle, in Stevens, 1951; Gagné and Bolles, 1959) as well as in chapters on learning in textbooks of general and experimental psychology. These principles constitute a kind of policy guidance for the programmer, rather than specific rules; like other types of policy guidance, they do not all apply to a single situation, and in some cases they may call for incompatible choices in a particular application. The reader is familiar with many of these, of which the following are typical:

1. Meaningfulness of material promotes learning.
2. The learner should be kept active in making responses.
3. Distributed practice tends to be more efficient than massed practice.
4. Immediate knowledge of results should be provided.
5. Stimulus material should be varied.
6. Accurate records of the learner's progress should be maintained.
7. Early guidance is useful.

While principles of this sort have been stated on the basis of the phenomena of verbal learning, they probably apply to the acquisition of a variety of behaviors which have some symbolic component.

Broad and general as are the above kinds of principles, they still offer useful guidance. Many existing training programs could be improved by their careful application, even though they are not very precise. A great many specific studies have been made on the acquisition of various knowledges and skills, as well as on the learning of different kinds of tasks. To examine this literature would require too much detail for the purposes of this chapter. It may be observed, however, that existing information is difficult to organize because categories for classification of both tasks and the relevant variables are still uncertain and because many of the existing training studies, done from the practical engineering point of view, necessarily confound variables whose interactions are unknown. As a first stage in the evolution of this technology, it seems likely that a number of provisional generalizations and specific guidance statements will be offered, to be revised and elaborated with further work, as has been begun by Hoehn (1960c) for maintenance training. Also, Jones (1961) has examined the specifications of several hundred Army enlisted jobs, classified the requisite knowledges and skills into several empirically useful categories, and suggested some important underlying dimensions for generality in training research.

Varieties of Training Media. Another series of decisions which need to be made in the building of a training program concerns the media through which the instruction is presented. This section will be confined to an identification of the major kinds of media and a few comments on their function. A thorough discussion of this topic will be found in the report of a symposium held under the joint auspices of the National Research Council and the Air Force Research and Development Command in August, 1959 (Finch, 1960).

The instructor himself is certainly the most universal, and in some respects the most important, of all of the media. The concept of his role should not be limited to that of classroom lecturer, quiz master or examination grader; rather, his function is that of a manager of student learning. In this role, he directs the work of the student in practical laboratory or shop activity, in the operation of trainers and simulators, or in the use of automated teaching devices. He may assign reading and the preparation of reports from printed material or field observation. In addition, he lectures, asks questions, grades examinations, and rates student achievement. His success will depend more on his skillful tactical employment of all the training resources (the various media) which are available to him than on his eloquence from the platform. In part at least, he also plays the role of supervisor or boss in the training subsystem, and in that capacity he holds a relationship with someone above and someone below him in the parent-system hierarchy. An important part of his job is as a motivator; his knowledge of the subject matter in its relation to the work in the operational subsystem and his skill in presenting that relation in clear terms is often crucial in providing the intrinsic, job-oriented type of motivation referred to above. His leadership of the student is often the key to successful training.

Melton (see Finch, 1960) has suggested another animate type of medium—the trainee's fellow students. Surely the attitude of the student group toward the training program, its purpose, and its conduct is of great influence on the effort and enthusiasm with which the individual learner attacks his work. The group atmosphere as well as the predispositions of new students may well be a function of the instructor's attitude and behavior. The frequency and intensity of student discussions, as well as study and work outside the classroom, may depend in large part on the climate of opinion among students as a group; they can learn much from one another. As Melton points out, little research has been done on how to promote an atmosphere conducive to learning among the students as a group.

The inanimate media are many, and their characteristics are discussed in Chapter 10. Some are offered by publishers and manufacturers, with little or no evidence of their usefulness for promoting learning. Claims often rest on nothing more than "face validity." The criterion for the evaluation of a training device as a medium for improving performance is, as Gagné has pointed out (1954), the degree of transfer of training to the operational situation. Such a criterion must be applied to all media, in systematic comparative studies for the improvement of technology, and when used in a training program, for the evaluation of a particular, developed training package.

Aptitude of Trainees. While most of our discussion thus far has assumed that the task of training management is to provide instruction for a group of students of somewhat heterogeneous background and aptitude, it is possible to divide trainees into relatively homogeneous groups when there are large numbers of students and valid classification tests are available. When this is not possible, it is important to choose methods and media which will be effective with a wide range of aptitude, particularly with men with intelligence-test or other test scores lower than may be ideal for certain kinds of training. As indicated in Chapter 7, there is a great deal of information on the relation between aptitude variables and achievement in different training programs, so that selection and placement in terms of background variables is done with practical economy. A good deal less is known about the relative appropriateness of various methods of programming training for different aptitude patterns and levels. A promising basic research study has been made by Allison (1960) on the relation between scores on a number of tests of human ability and rate of learning on 13 different short learning sequences. He finds significant relations between factors within the learning variables and factors representing the fundamental human abilities. This kind of research may lead to differential programming for learning in terms of various aptitude patterns.

A few studies have attempted to relate different teaching methods to aptitude differences. Edgerton (1958) showed that certain predictor variables correlated differentially with achievement in naval technical training taught under a "rote" method and under a "why" method. The results were clearer with aircraft familiarization than with material involving mechanics, mathematics, and physics. In a previous investigation, the same author (1956) found some advantages for a method of teaching "how to do" before the "why" parts of a naval aerographer's course, for men with higher numerical ability than rote memory, while the reverse tended to be true for those with higher aptitude scores in word fluency and reasoning. A somewhat different approach to the programming of training in terms of different abilities has been taken by Fleishman and his associates (Parker and Fleishman, 1959) in designing a motor-skill training program. From an analysis of the relation between different abilities to achievement scores at successive stages of practice, various types of instruction and verbal guidance were given at different times throughout the course of learning a pursuit rotor task. Students so trained showed an increase in performance of 39 per cent over those trained by the "common sense" method.

A rather extensive study was undertaken to evaluate several methods for programming learning to benefit men whose aptitudes fell slightly below the normal requirements for admission to Army technical training courses (Goffard et al., 1960). In the early part of the study, simple techniques—such as increasing the number of repetitions of important points in the lesson, improving training aids, or giving students mimeographed course notes—were applied to short segments of the course. These had small favorable effects which showed up in immediate mastery tests, but tended to disappear by the end of the course. Also, these changes seemed to be no more effective with the lower-aptitude group than with the average students. A more comprehensive kind of reprogramming, involving the first three weeks of an electronic-repairman course which were devoted to basic electronics, was developed in terms of the "functional context" principle, elaborated and tried out earlier by Shoemaker (Shoemaker, Brown, and Whittemore, 1958; Brown et al., 1959). The functional context principle contrasts rather sharply with conventional training, in that the emphasis is on a "whole to part" rather than a "part to whole" method of instruction. The conventional training begins with laws and principles and moves through individual circuits to a final combination in operational equipment. The functional context method, on the other hand, begins by immediately presenting the student with specific equipment. Principles of basic electronics are taught as they become relevant in the study of a succession of electronic components, so that the student learns the operation of the principles in the context in which they operate. In this study, the performance of students trained by the functional-context method was contrasted with that of a comparable group of men given the standard instruction by means of a basic electronic test battery. As a whole, the group trained with the functional-context method did better when tested on proficiency tests than did those trained under the standard method. However, when the analysis is made by levels of scores in the Electronic Aptitude Area of the Army General

Classification Battery, the functional-context technique had a different effect. For those groups at the lower and intermediate levels, the experimental group made about 10 per cent higher scores, while for the upper groups (above an aptitude score of 130) the standard instruction resulted in some 6 per cent higher scores. Apparently the lower-aptitude groups had trouble with conceptualizing general rules and facts before they were embedded in a relevant operational context, while the upper-aptitude men seemed to do slightly better when the principles and formulas came first.

This last finding suggests that there may be certain techniques which are particularly effective for trainees of high aptitude. For example, in a study of Army basic combat training (Cline, Beals, and Seidman, 1956) it was shown that high-aptitude men learned as much military information in a four-week accelerated program as comparable men did in the standard eight-week program. Special techniques of programming were employed, including an evening study period by squad members, using mimeographed material which reviewed the day's work and previewed the next. These may have facilitated the learning by high-aptitude men, although the experiment was not designed to isolate this factor. While there is considerable promise of gains in training time by adaptation of programs in terms of aptitude, often practical difficulties arise in segregating trainees into homogeneous groups, so that these potential benefits have not often been realized, at least in military training. The "multitracked system" of public school education seems to produce improved learning, associating, as it does, appropriate types of programming with each track.

Automated Instruction. The most dramatic and promising effects of careful programming are appearing in the field of automated learning. The current status of research on this topic has been conveniently brought together in the volume of readings by Lumsdaine and Glaser (1960), which includes most of the important original papers by Pressey and by Skinner, together with a representative sample of the current work. Because of the comprehensive and timely coverage offered by this volume, no attempt will be made to discuss the subject in detail in this chapter. Rather, we will add only a few comments about the promise, as well as the problems, the technique holds for the broad field of training.

If the total program of instruction for a particular job were entirely automated, it would represent the most precise kind of end product from the complete cycle of training development as outlined earlier in this chapter. The total kit of program materials, together with the device by which they are to be presented, would constitute the final training package resulting from all the research, engineering, trials, and tests of the developmental cycle. Such a program might be expected to achieve many of the objectives of the training development stated earlier. It would present a uniform coverage of subject matter whenever and wherever employed, would be independent of instructor skill, would allow for individual differences in rate of learning, and, from the results obtained with automated instruction to date, might prove to be a rapid and intrinsically motivating technique.

The complete automation of an entire training program has not, to the writer's knowledge, been achieved so far, nor is it implied that complete automation of a course is necessarily desirable. In fact, the allocation of teaching tasks to the instructor and the automated device may be regarded as a problem in assignment of function in a man-machine instructional system. Available, however, are large blocks of instruction materials, especially in the cognitive aspects of training, in the fields of mathematics, language, and even the arts, as well as the simpler skills of arithmetic, spelling, and technical nomenclature. In addition to cognitive materials, it is possible, with proper apparatus, to extend the range of stimuli for training well beyond words and diagrams to still and moving pictures, even with accompanying sound recording. Some studies are being done to apply the principles of automated feedback to the learning of motor coordination tasks as well as to the learning of perceptual judgments. In the vanguard of new developments, computers capable of varying the learning program in terms of student responses are being used, for example, in research at the System Development Corporation (1960, pp. 85–89).

As has been pointed out by many commentators on this new field, the programming, rather than the device, is the heart of the matter. The preparation of machines or books of various sorts does not pose very serious problems; choices can be made in terms of the material to be presented, costs, and requirements for portability or fixed installation. As for programming, a good deal still remains to be learned. Much of the discussion above concerning the programming of instruction for nonautomated use is suggestive of the kinds of problems which still need to be solved for machine use. It was noted that the facts about programming are little better than general rules or isolated segments of information. With the use of automated instruction for research purposes it is likely that the technology of programming will improve rapidly because the variables of content and presentation can be precisely controlled over several repetitions, so that it should prove more feasible to determine lawful relationships than is the case with animated instruction.

In terms of the main theme of this chapter, it seems reasonable to predict a renewed emphasis on careful job analysis and knowledge and skill specification because the programmer is forced to be precise in a much more challenging manner than is the lecturer. Objectives of instruction, as well as specific information and practice exercises, will have to be thought through with somewhat unprecedented precision. To build the large number of training programs required in the military establishment and in industry, a great body of programmers will be required. Training of men with content knowledge in principles of learning may be more economical than waiting for a few programming experts to master a variety of subject matter. Finally, the instructor, with automated facilities at his disposal, may become a full-fledged training manager.

REFERENCES

Allison, R. B. 1960. *Learning parameters and human abilities.* Princeton, N. J.: Educational Testing Service.

Baker, R. A. 1958. *The determination of job requirements for tank crew members.* Washington, D. C.: Human Resources Research Office. Technical Report No. 47.

Baker, R. A., MacCaslin, E. F., Kurtz, K. H., and Baerman, D. J. 1958. *An evaluation of the on-the-job proficiency of trained tank crewmen.* Washington, D. C.: Human Resources Research Office. Special Report No. 14.

Baker, R. A., Mathers, B. L., and Roach, E. G. 1959. *The effects of increasing and decreasing training time on proficiency in the critical armor skills.* Washington, D. C.: Human Resources Research Office. Technial Report No. 55.

Baldwin, R. D., Mager, R. F., Vineberg, R., and Whipple, J. E. 1957. *The AAFCS M–33 mechanic proficiency test.* Washington, D. C.: Human Resources Research Office. Technical Report No. 38.

Brown, G. H., Zaynor, W. C., Bernstein, A. J., and Shoemaker, H. A. 1959. *Development and evaluation of an improved field radio repair course.* Washington, D. C.: Human Resources Research Office. Technical Report No. 58.

Brubacher, J. S. 1947. *A history of the problems of education.* New York: McGraw-Hill.

Cline, V. B., Beals, A., and Seidman, D. 1956. *Evaluation of four-week and eight-week basic training for men of various intelligence levels.* Washington, D. C.: Human Resources Research Office. Technical Report No. 32.

Cook, J. G., and Baker, R. A. 1959. *The tank commander's guide* (Rev. ed). Harrisburg, Pa.: The Military Service Publishing Company.

Covner, B. J. 1946. Course outlines and lesson plans. In National Defense Research Committee, Applied Psychology Panel, *Human factors in military efficiency training and equipment.* Summary Technical Report, Vol. 2. Washington, D. C.

Denenberg, V. H. 1954. *The training effectiveness of a tank hull trainer.* Washington, D. C.: Human Resources Research Office. Technical Report No. 3.

Department of the Army. 1957. *Army training program for tank companies (except tank companies organic to infantry regiments), ATP 17–201.* Washington, D. C.: U. S. Govt. Printing Office, February.

Edgerton, H. A. 1956. *Should theory precede or follow a "how to do it" phase of training?* Contract Nonr 1722 (00). New York: Richardson, Bellows and Henry Co.

Edgerton, H. A. 1958. *The relationship of method of instruction to trainee aptitude pattern.* Contract Nonr 2313 (00). New York: Richardson, Bellows and Henry Co.

Findlay, D. C., Matyas, S. M., and Rogge, H. 1955. *Training achievement in basic combat squads with controlled aptitude.* Washington, D. C.: Human Resources Research Office. Technical Report No. 16.

Finch, G. (ed.). 1960. *Educational and training media: A symposium.* Washington, D. C.: National Academy of Sciences.

Gagné, R. M. 1954. Training devices and simulators: Some research issues. *Amer. Psychologist, 9,* 95-107.

Gagné, R. M., and Bolles, R. C. 1959. *A review of factors in learning efficiency.* In E. Galanter (ed.), *Automated teaching.* New York: Wiley.

Goffard, S. J., Heimstra, N. W., Beecroft, R. S., and Openshaw, J. W. 1960. *Basic electronics for minimally qualified men: an experimental evaluation of a method of presentation.* Washington, D. C.: Human Resources Research Office. Technical Report No. 61.

Green, E. J., Mathers, B. L., Olson, H. C., Willard, N., Jr., and Willmorth, N. E. 1954. *A survey of training problems in armor.* Fort Knox, Ky.: U. S. Army Armor Human Research Unit (HumRRO), (Revised 1956). Interim Report.

Heilmann, J. C., Osburn, H. G., and Hausknecht, R. O. 1955. *Changes in student motivation at an army technical training school.* Washington, D. C.: Human Resources Research Office. Technical Report No. 24.

Herzberg, F., Mausner, B., and Snydeman, B. B. 1959. *The motivation to work.* New York: Wiley.

Hilgard, E. R. 1956. *Theories of learning.* New York: Appleton-Century (2nd ed.).

Hoehn, A. J. 1960a. *The development of training programs for first enlistment personnel in electronics maintenance MOS's: II. How to analyze performance objectives to determine training content.* Washington, D. C.: Human Resources Research Office. Research Memorandum, Training Methods Division.

Hoehn, A. J. 1960b. *The development of training programs for first enlistment personnel in electronics maintenance MOS's: III. How to design the handbook materials.* Washington, D. C.: Human Resources Research Office. Research Memorandum, Training Methods Division.

Hoehn, A. J. 1960c. *The development of training programs for first enlistment personnel in electronics maintenance MOS's: IV. How to design training methods and materials.* Washington, D. C.: Human Resources Research Office. Research Memorandum, Training Methods Division.

Industrial Relations News. 1960. *The dollars and sense of human relations in industry.* New York: Industrial Relations Newsletter, Inc.

Jones, F. E. 1961. *A systematic analysis of army training requirements as the basis of more generalized training research.* Washington, D. C.: Human Resources Research Office. Research Report No. 7.

Kingsley, H. L., and Garry, R. 1957. *The nature and conditions of learning* (2nd ed.). Englewood Cliffs, N. J.: Prentice Hall.

Koch, S. (ed.). 1959. *Psychology: A study of a science. Study I. Conceptual and systematic. Volume 2. General systematic formulations, learning and special processes.* New York: McGraw-Hill.

Lumsdaine, E. E., and Glaser, R. (ed.). 1960. *Teaching machines and programmed learning: A source book.* Washington: National Education Association, Department of Audio-Visual Instruction.

MacCaslin, E. F. 1956. *The development of tests for two levels of armor proficiency.* Fort Knox, Ky.: U. S. Army Armor Human Research Unit (HumRRO). Staff Memorandum.

MacCaslin, E. F., Woodruff, A. B., and Baker, R. A. 1959. *An improved advanced individual training program for armor.* Washington, D. C.: Human Resources Research Office. Technical Report No. 59.

Maier, N. R. F. 1955. *Psychology in industry.* Boston: Houghton Mifflin (2nd ed.).

McGeoch, J. A., and Irion, A. L. 1952. *The psychology of human learning.* New York: Longmans (2nd ed.).

Palmer, R. R., Wiley, B. I., and Keast, W. R. 1948. *The procurement and training of ground combat troops.* Washington, D. C.: Historical Division, Department of the Army.

Parker, J. F., and Fleishman, E. A. 1959. *Use of analytical information concerning task requirements to increase the effectiveness of skill training.* Arlington, Va.: Psychological Research Associates. Contract Nonr 2489 (00).

Shoemaker, H. A., Brown, G. H., and Whittemore, J. M. 1958. *Activities of field radio repair personnel with implications for training.* Washington, D. C.: Human Resources Research Office. Technical Report No. 48.

Smith, R. G., Jr. 1960. *Scales and standards for military training research.* Fort Bliss, Tex.: U. S. Army Air Defense Human Research Unit (HumRRO). Research Memorandum.

Spence, K. W. 1959. The relation of learning theory to the technology of education. *Harvard Educ. Rev., 29,* 84–95.

Stevens, S. S. (ed.). 1951. *Handbook of experimental psychology.* New York: Wiley.

Stouffer, S. A. 1949–1950. The American soldier. In Vols. I and II of *Studies in social psychology in world war II.* Princeton: Princeton University Press.

System Development Corporation, Research Directorate. 1960. *Research directorate quarterly report No. 1,* TM 530. Santa Monica: System Development Corporation.

U. S. Army Armor Human Research Unit. 1957. *The tank gunner's guide (M48A1 Tank).* Fort Knox, Ky.: U. S. Army Armor Human Research Unit (HumRRO).

U. S. Army Armor Human Research Unit. 1958a. *The tank loader's guide (M48A1 Tank).* Fort Knox, Ky.: U. S. Army Armor Human Research Unit (HumRRO).

U. S. Army Armor Human Research Unit. 1958b. *The tank driver's guide (M48A1 Tank).* Fort Knox, Ky.: U. S. Army Armor Human Research Unit (HumRRO).

Viteles, M. S. 1953. *Motivation and morale in industry.* New York: Norton.

Woodruff, A. B., Stark, E. A., Willard, N., Jr. 1962. *An improved series of firing tables for the tank gunner.* Washington, D. C.: Human Resources Research Office. Technical Report.

Woolman, M. 1960. *On-site training of guided missile operators.* Washington, D. C.: Human Resources Research Office. Technical Report No. 64.

PLANNING A TRAINING PROGRAM TO INSURE
the presence of suitable skills and knowledges in system
personnel is an effort which requires a development
program of its own, but which must be closely integrated with the development of the system itself. Based
upon the concepts described in the previous chapter, the
procedures of training generate the need for specialized
types of equipment generically called training devices. The present chapter
provides an account of how requirements for training programs and devices
arise within the context of systems, and how the resulting designs are made
compatible with system functioning, on the one hand, and with the purposes
of training, on the other.

The goals of individual training and of team training (including "system
training") can both be seen to produce demands for training devices. The
varieties of these devices and the particular functions they can serve within
each of these portions of the total training program are briefly described in
the present chapter. The considerations that are necessary to insure proper
planning and design of training devices within the context of system design
and development are also described. Following this, the chapter undertakes a
detailed discussion of psychological principles relevant to the development of
training devices, giving separate consideration to the establishment of individual skills and to the attainment of optimal interactive working procedures
that represent the aim of system training. Particular emphasis is given in the
latter instance to the use of simulators and simulation techniques for the conduct of training exercises involving the operation of major subsystems or the
total system.

To a considerable extent, the psychological principles applicable to the
design, development, and use of training devices have a familiar ring to students of human learning. They include such matters as knowledge of results,
frequency of practice, and the relation of task similarity to transfer of training.
Yet when these principles are used as bases for technological decisions, certain
limitations in our knowledge of them, and even in their status as empirical
principles, become strikingly apparent. Thus the continuing need for subjecting
these principles to the careful scrutiny of experimentation and research, as well
as for attainment of the simplifying conceptualizations of theory, are once
more given emphasis by the contents of this chapter.

TRAINING PROGRAMS AND DEVICES

William C. Biel

The application of new developments in technology to meet the needs of commercial and of military and other governmental organizations for better performance has resulted in a variety of increasingly more complex man-machine systems. These systems create a major problem of training for the many persons who are to function within them. The many technical innovations, and the high costs associated with system development, production, installation, and operation have contributed to an increased emphasis on rapid and effective means of training large numbers of people. To realize the maximal value of these systems, human performance must be brought to a high level of proficiency and maintained at this level. Not only must individual proficiency be established and maintained, but in most systems people must be trained to work together as a team before the system can become operational. In some of them, of which military systems provide examples, much of the training must be directed toward the handling of emergency situations which do not often occur under normal conditions, but which are critical for effective operation when they do occur.

In situations where a more complex man-machine system is replacing one already in existence, the new one does not always have characteristics such that operational, maintenance, and support personnel can make an easy transition from the old to the new. In fact, new systems are frequently quite different from old ones, and many of the jobs require new and different skills. This situation creates the need for highly specialized transitional training for those who have had experience in older related systems. For example, needs of this sort have been created by the change from piston-engined to jet aircraft, as well as by the changes from aircraft to missiles, rockets, and space vehicles. In some modern systems, which require that much information be rapidly processed before decisions can be made, there is growing reliance on high-speed digital computers (compare Chapter 3). A computer makes it possible to process and use more information faster than would otherwise be the case. This information is summarized by the computer and displayed at critical points to the monitors and decision makers. Learning to make the rapid, accurate command or management decisions required by a complex computerized system is a new experience for most persons.

Training programs and their associated training devices are essential in preparing personnel for system tasks. These programs and devices provide the advantage in meeting the problem of training large numbers of persons to operate a system. To plan for training, to make critical and timely decisions affecting training, to design training programs with associated training aids and devices, should all be integral actions in total system development. The proper use of such programs and devices is a matter of major concern for the effective employment of a system.

The aim of this chapter is to describe the factors that need attention in the design and development of training programs and associated training devices for a system. To begin with, we shall provide an account of two major categories of training, *individual* training and *team* training, and shall describe briefly the kinds of training devices which may be designed for each of these purposes. We shall then consider the nature of planning for the development of training programs and devices. Finally, a section will be devoted to some of the psychological considerations which are relevant to the design of such programs and devices.

▣ TYPES OF TRAINING AND TRAINING DEVICES

The word "training" connotes the provision of the means and the environment necessary for individuals to learn skills and acquire information. Since there are many different views of training and of related types of training devices, many training areas have been studied and many techniques developed to meet diverse specific needs. These are reflected in the variety of terms used to describe types of training; among these terms are individual training, crew training, team training, unit training, system training, on-the-job training, and many others. The adjectives may imply techniques of training, content to be learned, numbers of persons to be trained, and many other considerations. Although only individuals learn, it is useful to separate the training techniques and devices necessary to train persons in their *individual* knowledges and skills from those used to train them as members of a team or as part of a system. This latter training is called *team training* or, under certain conditions, *system training*.

Individual Training

Individual training is directed toward the establishment of the capabilities of individuals so that they can perform on the job to an acceptable level or can progress to the next phase of their training. This process, when applied to individuals on a job which interrelates with other jobs in a system, is frequently described as training the individual as a component in the system. There are many system jobs which have as their major requirement that an individual must learn to operate and use equipment. In such instances the man and his equipment together constitute a component in the system, because there is an input (or inputs) of information to this component which must be processed, and there is a specific output from it. (Davis and Behan provide a further discussion of this topic in Chapter 13.) For this reason the training of an individual to operate his equipment can be called *component training*.

In the design of such training, it is necessary to identify those skills, concepts, and information which are needed by the trainee and to estimate the level of performance to which they must be learned for the trainee to perform his task in the system. Where appropriate, the training plan should include an assessment of the initial knowledge, aptitude, and skill level of the student. The purpose of the training program or device, then, is to change the level of the student from some initial status to the level required by the system task. Further, in planning the techniques to be used in establishing these capabilities, the planner must also estimate whether the materials to be learned can be acceptably absorbed in a single session or exposure or whether much practice will be required. It should be borne in mind that when only a few repetitions are needed and a large number of students must be taught, a communication method, like the lecture, may be quite efficient for presentation of the material. If more repetitions are needed to achieve the necessary level of performance, additional training techniques and devices become necessary. Some major varieties of these are described in the next section.

Training Devices in Individual Training

A *training device,* as the term is used in this chapter, is any piece or group of materials or equipment used to train individuals. This general term includes two-dimensional displays of verbal, symbolic, or pictorial materials (such as wall charts, photographs, slides, transparencies, and motion pictures), audio signals which may or may not be associated with displays (such as vocal directions associated with a video display of parts being assembled), as well as real or simulated displays and controls which trainees can operate in order to develop skills or to learn principles.

Training aids. Perhaps the most widely used kinds of training devices are *training aids,* so called because they are conceived as having the function of aiding the exposition of verbal information presented by a teacher. A great many different types of training aids have been used to supplement lecture materials in teaching concepts, information, and simple skills. Some of the major types of these classroom training aids are described briefly here. A more detailed discussion and evaluation of these devices will be found in Lumsdaine (1960a, 1960b).

Wall charts are for group display. Most commonly, they are photographs or schematic representations of system components, their connections, and their operation. Wall charts are easily produced, visible to all group members, and may be readily transported.

Transparencies and slides are drawings or photographs on transparent material through which light is passed for projection of the picture onto a screen. They can be easily projected with one of several standard projectors. The use of color, multiple overlays (additional transparencies placed over another transparency to add additional information to the basic drawing), and masks removed at appropriate times to reveal additional content of a drawing give these techniques a reasonable amount of flexibility. Transparencies are convenient to use and are often cheaper and faster to produce than many other training aids. Further, as components or major parts of the system change, only the transparencies need be changed. It is sometimes desirable to project materials from which slides or transparencies cannot conveniently be made— a student exercise, for example, or a page in a book. So-called opaque projectors are available for this purpose.

Motion pictures in their simplest form may be no more than recorded lectures. With this technique, a good lecture can be made available to many classes in which the original lecturer is not able to participate. Lecture demonstrations incorporating other visual aids can also be put on film. In addition, the possibilities of using certain features of the motion-picture medium for enhancing learning are considerable. As Gagné and Fleishman point out (1959, p. 408), motion pictures can (1) represent dynamic events where a sequence of events in time might not otherwise be visible; (2) represent the consequences of action where the learner can see and vicariously experience the results of an erroneous or a correct action; (3) show a situation from the point of view of the learner so that he feels himself a part of the action being shown on the screen.

Closed-circuit television is being used successfully as a classroom aid in teaching. It avoids the difficulty of all members of the classes being unable to see parts or locations of the device being described. The equipment to be demonstrated is arranged in a room, separate from the classroom, with the television camera and crew. Several variations of the teaching arrangement are used as appropriate. In one case, a demonstrator in the camera room, in communication with the instructor by telephone, carries out the directions of the classroom instructor, dismantling or assembling the equipment and pointing out the parts. In another, the instructor may be with the equipment, separate from the class, and instruct from there. In either of these cases, television receivers conveniently placed around the classroom allow all students to see the screens. Closed-circuit television is financially feasible only when large numbers of students are to be taught a particular subject or a series of subjects.

Open-circuit television as a training technique should be mentioned, since its use in education is growing rapidly. Its values are similar to those of closed-circuit television and of motion pictures, but its application to operator training for performance in systems has not as yet been undertaken.

Cutaway mock-ups are generally made of actual equipment, partially cut away to show internal appearance and relationships. A cutaway engine used for instruction is shown in Figure 10.1. The parts in this engine move by power from a supplementary electric motor. Such cutaway models are of value in giving a group of trainees an over-all view of a piece of equipment, showing how its parts fit together and how the parts work together. Unfortunately, it is often difficult for all members of a class to see at one time the parts being pointed out by the instructor. When the cost of a cutaway is considered, its value for detailed group instruction in comparison with other teaching techniques is low.

Operating mock-ups interconnect actual equipment components so that they function much as they do when they are installed. These devices (such as the hydraulic-brake system of an automobile) show the actual functioning of a system. When they can be used to give instruction in troubleshooting and maintenance in addition to their use for demonstration purposes, operating mock-ups have additional value. However, the difficulty of maintaining and storing them, the infrequency with which they are used, and their cost combine to reduce their attractiveness.

Nonoperational mock-ups interconnect actual equipment, or parts which closely simulate the actual components. These mock-ups are useful for lecture presentations when the objective is to give a general orientation to the device, its component parts, and their physical relationships. Such mock-ups can, if desired, be made lighter than operational ones if they are made of plastic or some similar material. These replicas can also be less expensive than operational mock-ups when enough copies are produced.

Animated-panel displays represent components of the system hardware pictorially or in the form of simple, semi-functioning models; sometimes both methods are combined. One form of an animated-panel display is shown in Figure 10.2. Essentially, this display is a large diagrammatic representation of a system, with simplified representations of the units within the system. Such

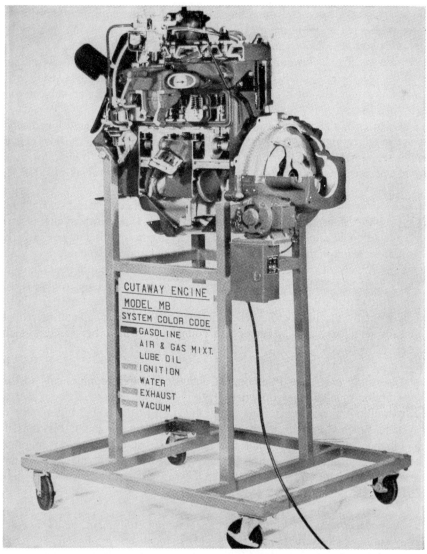

CUTAWAY ENGINE
MODEL MB
SYSTEM COLOR CODE
GASOLINE
AIR & GAS MIXT.
LUBE OIL
IGNITION
WATER
EXHAUST
VACUUM

Figure 10.1. A cutaway mock-up of an automobile engine used to show how parts fit and work together. (Courtesy of the Office of Naval Research, U. S. Naval Training Device Center.)

panels frequently have lines representing certain interconnections; they may also have tubes containing flowing liquids, indicator lights, instruments, transparent illuminated drawings, recorders, and the like.

The training aids described above vary considerably in their value as aids in the teaching process. Probably each of them has a place in this process depending on the intent and content of the course being taught. However,

—William C. Biel

- 349

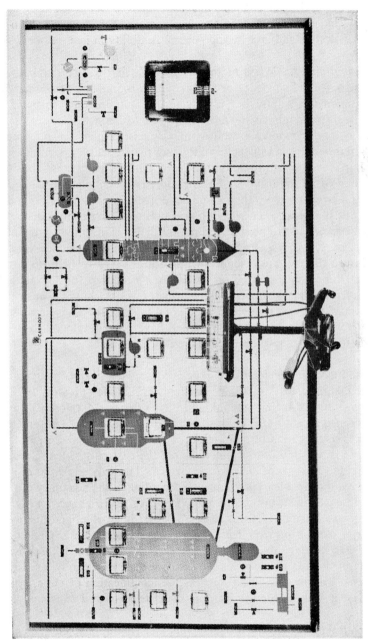

Figure 10.2. An animated panel display of Sohio's trainer for the reactor-regenerator section of a catalytic cracking unit panel board. The instructor's console is also shown. (Courtesy of Carmody Corporation and the Standard Oil Company of Ohio.)

before such an aid—particularly an elaborate one—is developed for classroom use, careful consideration should be given to the training objectives, the relevance of what can be taught by the aid, the effectiveness of the aid, its cost, the number of students to be taught, the time required for its construction or change, ease of storage and access, and general flexibility in its use.

Individual Trainers.   When more than several trials will be required for the trainee to learn the knowledge or skill required, training aids designed for group presentation are helpful but usually insufficient. In order to perform some system tasks, the human operator will need to learn to identify many parts, locations, and symbols, as well as many facts, principles, and procedures. The group lecture is satisfactory in giving the student an over-all view of the task; however, the lecture does not provide the necessary conditions for efficient learning of all these types of knowledge. For example, the tendency of the lecturer is to do no more than name and identify a part or location on a training aid; this is often not enough. Books and manuals help to reduce the material the instructor has to present and permit the student to review difficult material. But an active response in the form of repeated practice is still required to insure effective performance. Class drill is very expensive in terms of instructional time, since much practice is often necessary for satisfactory performance of many tasks which require a high level of skill. To meet the need for continued and varied practice, *individual trainers* are often employed.

Some of the devices or techniques which have been developed to meet training needs for skills requiring practice are described here.

Automated teaching devices were conceived a number of years ago, and some early development work was done on them at that time (Pressey, 1932). However, recognition of their potential, and their extensive development and testing have been a recent trend (Lumsdaine and Glaser, 1960). Automated teaching devices usually present material to be learned in a fixed sequence; a correct response is required of the subject before the next part of the material is presented to him. In some of the more sophisticated devices, the order of the material is varied during a learning sequence according to the adequacy of the learner's responses. Scores can be kept of the student's performance, for his or the instructor's use. Machines of this type are generally flexible, and different content material can be presented for different kinds of training. One such device which has considerable flexibility is shown in Figure 10.3. These devices can afford a wide range of learning experiences; they can be used for the more routine learning activities (such as the identification of parts, symbols, or words) as well as for the learning of more advanced concepts and principles.

A demonstration study using a digital computer (and related equipment) to simulate a teaching machine was successfully conducted by Rath, Anderson,

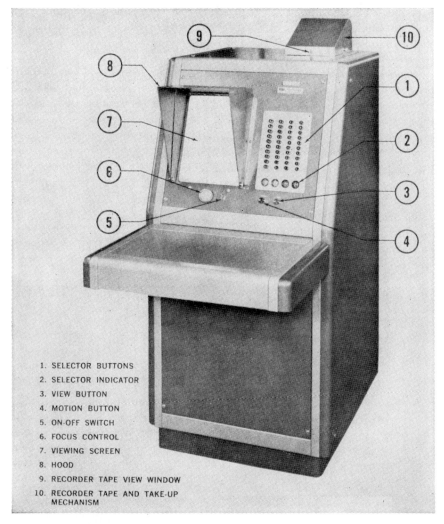

1. SELECTOR BUTTONS
2. SELECTOR INDICATOR
3. VIEW BUTTON
4. MOTION BUTTON
5. ON-OFF SWITCH
6. FOCUS CONTROL
7. VIEWING SCREEN
8. HOOD
9. RECORDER TAPE VIEW WINDOW
10. RECORDER TAPE AND TAKE-UP MECHANISM

Figure 10.3. An automated teaching device, the AutoTutor (a trade-marked name). (This device is described by Crowder, N. A., pp. 286-298, in Lumsdaine and Glaser, 1960. Courtesy of Western Design and Electronics, Division of U. S. Industries, Inc.)

and Brainerd (1959) with the computer program controlling the order and type of problems presented to the individual student, the scoring of the answers, the knowledge of results, and the modification of the presentation of the material if the student made an error. Coulson and Silberman (1961) report the use of a flexible computerized teaching machine, designed for research, to study the principles and procedures of value in this teaching technique. This research is also being extended to include the possibilities of using such a technique for multistudent classroom teaching, as well as for school administrative functions.

Concept trainers are used when the concepts to be learned are too complex to be absorbed in a few trials from verbal descriptions, and when the principles to be used in task performance can best be simulated by physical objects and real actions. A good example of this type of learning is the case of the maintenance technician who must find malfunctions in complex electronic equipment and repair or replace the parts. He must learn a set of rules and have understandings which are recalled and applied when he is faced with instrument readings, wave forms, or other physical stimuli from the equipment. He must be able to trace the flow of electricity from the instrument readings, isolate the malfunctioning circuit and replace the faulty unit.

Such a concept-training device is shown in Figure 10.4. The front panel is a miniature representation of the components, controls, and check points of a complex electronic system. After a typical malfunction is set up in the system

Figure 10.4. A concept trainer for training electronic technicians in the development and utilization of appropriate concepts for troubleshooting an airborne bombing-navigation system. (From Lumsdaine, 1960b; as described by French and Martin, 1957.)

with one of 200 individual switches on the side panel, the trainee isolates the source of this malfunction. An instructor may coach the trainee, also guiding him away from illogical or unnecessary checks. In this way the student technician can practice on a variety of equipment-malfunction problems of graded difficulty. With this type of trainer, the student learns the complex concepts of system functioning in direct relation to the stimuli which arise from the physical equipment. The device is convenient to use for practice and is relatively inexpensive compared to the cost of using operational equipment. This type of training device thus eliminates the need for spending time in disassembling complex parts in order to diagnose routine malfunctions. The concept trainer allows the student to devote most of his time to learning those things that are most difficult to learn (French and Martin, 1957).

Games embody a technique of training which is being applied in a variety of ways. Games have been used most widely for training in the areas of decision making and planning. For instance, the American Management Association's widely publicized top-management game is played as part of a course in decision making offered by the Association to business executives at the AMA facility at Saranac Lake, New York (Ricciardi *et al.,* 1958). The game allows the players to practice making and implementing business decisions in a simulated environment. Participants are divided into five teams or companies, each made up of three to five persons. These companies compete against each other in a hypothetical market with only a single product. The game is divided into periods each representing a quarter of a year; the five companies generally play for 20 to 40 periods. Following each period, the AMA staff takes the decisions made by the teams; with the help of a computer and mathematical formulas representing a simplified model of the business world, the complex interactions among companies are quickly worked out. The resulting information on its own business position at the end of each period is given to each company, as well as limited information on its competitors. This information and past history govern the decisions which must be made in the next period. The AMA game (and others which resemble it) contributes to the learning process by requiring each player to take part in decision making and in the discussion and analysis of play following each run.

Skill trainers are used for the many system tasks which demand highly developed perceptual-motor skills. It may be difficult to arrange for adequate or frequent enough practice on the actual task to develop and maintain the necessary level of performance on such skills. In other cases, it may be difficult for the operator to practice in the actual system without interfering seriously with the system's normal operations. Skill trainers typically provide conditions of practice which let the student know what results he has achieved. This characteristic is of particular importance since it is only by knowledge of results that the student can improve his performance.

An example of a skill trainer is a device which enables operators to attain skill in receiving code. Several types of these devices have been developed. A United States Navy device, called the Code Practice Keyer, can automatically transmit code from 10 to 30 words per minute. The operator can practice receiving code through head phones or a loud speaker or by means of a blinker light. Such a device has been very successful in training individuals (singly or in groups) to develop individual proficiency in receiving code.

Procedure trainers are mock-ups of part or all of an operator's work place on which the trainee can practice the sequences that he would go through in actually performing his task. For instance, in a cockpit procedure trainer for a jet single-place aircraft the trainee can be given training in normal and emergency operating procedures for the engine, the fuel system, and several other systems; likewise, training in procedures for take-off, landing, ditching, and several other operations. In the simulated cockpit those instruments, controls, switches, and other equipment which are simulated are accurately placed, although many controls and displays may be omitted altogether. Some of the controls can be moved, such as the flight controls which may move with a realistic feel, but such movement may not affect the displays. There is also a console or panel for an instructor. He can manipulate the cockpit instrument indications and can also introduce system malfunctions and failures from his console. Repeater instruments, telltale lights, and switches make it possible for the instructor to set up problems for the trainee and check his procedures. The trainee's information on his progress comes from the instructor.

Trainers of this sort have been used not only for establishing initial performances, but also in the transition training of skilled pilots from one type of single-place aircraft to another. In the latter usage, although it is assumed that the learning of suitable control skills for the new aircraft is relatively easy for an experienced pilot, responses to the quite different cockpit layout and many changes in procedural sequences, both normal and emergency, require much practice.

In some respects procedure trainers are like the skill trainers described above, particularly those skill trainers which may be called part-task trainers. In both, some part of the task requiring special training has been isolated for emphasis. The value, however, of practicing such procedures in isolation when they must be performed in context with other procedures has been questioned by Adams (1960). He argues that such training should be followed by whole-task practice, and that practice on a whole-task simulator (such as that described in the next paragraph) might better be used for total training right from the start.

Simulators integrate the various concepts and skills which an individual has learned into a complex or near-total job situation and permit him to develop and maintain proficiency. It is not always feasible for the trainee to practice such integration of skills in the actual job situation for reasons of safety, cost, or interference with system performance. A simulator is a special class of training device which attempts to reproduce or simulate the essential tasks of an operator or operators. In general it has a close physical resemblance to the operational equipment, particularly with respect to the display, the controls, and the way one affects the other when in operation (Gagné, 1954). In fact, some simulators use the operational gear; simulated inputs are fed into the displays so that trainees can carry out the normal operations and actions. Simulators range from those which present an individual operator's task to those which are used to train entire crews. In this section, only those which are used for individual training are described.

Some of the most highly developed simulators are used in the military services. Flight simulators, in particular, have been widely developed for the services and for major airlines. These accurately simulate such characteristics of the aircraft as the instrument panel, the indicator movements, the sound of the engines, the feel of the controls, and the effects of reactions made by the pilot. One use of such a simulator is in transition training—that is, the training required for a pilot who is proficient in flying one type of aircraft and must learn to fly another type with different characteristics. Figure 10.5 shows such a flight simulator for the F-106, a United States Air Force aircraft. In this

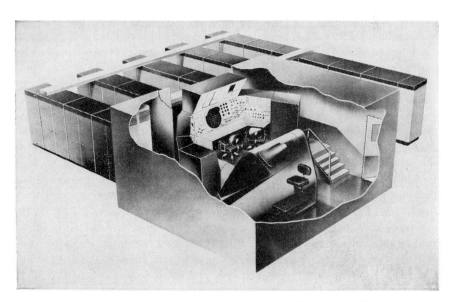

Figure 10.5. A flight simulator for the F-106 aircraft. The aerodynamic factors of actual flight are represented on the cockpit instruments, and as the pilot operates the controls, the controls and instruments provide realistic feedback to him. For integrated training of the pilot in flight, communications, and radar phases, a flight instructor and radar operator are necessary. (Courtesy of Link Division, General Precision, Inc.)

device, the pilot-trainee learns the skills required for the F-106 and practices them safely under the supervision of an instructor. The instructor can prescribe a simulated flight for the trainee and can record and observe his performance at the instructor's console. Special situations, including malfunctions, can also be inserted into the device. Such simulators also allow a trained pilot to maintain his proficiency. For example, pilots fortunately have only infrequent opportunities to practice certain emergency procedures in aircraft; yet they must maintain their proficiency in handling these situations should they arise. In every case, knowledge of results during and after each simulated flight allows the trainee to profit from his own actions.

On-the-job training is probably the most widely used type of training; for many types of jobs it is entirely adequate. However, the importance of the supervisor (as the responsible instructor) cannot be overstressed as a determining factor in the success of such a program. When the procedures to be learned are short and relatively easy, consideration should be given to having them learned on the job. In some cases, printed instructions will minimize help from the instructor.

When the procedures to be learned on the job are long, complex or diversified, the apprentice system is widely used. An experienced worker serves as the instructor, telling and showing the learner the procedures involved and gradually letting the learner carry on more and more of the procedures on his own under supervision. The experienced worker observes the trainee, judges when the procedures are adequately carried out, and provides the necessary feedback or knowledge of results. Training of this sort can be very useful in teaching principles of job performance. Even in the case of motor skills, the actual skill may be and often is learned on the job, although in some cases the skill might well be learned faster through the use of a training device. Once an adequate initial level of skill has been reached, however, the job provides a good setting in which to give satisfactory training in consolidating skills.

Another training procedure which should be mentioned briefly is one used in the flight training of pilots. At one stage of such training, an instructor flies in an aircraft with a student who carries out certain maneuvers under supervision. The instructor gives instructions, observes and corrects the trainee, and gives him specific knowledge of results. In one sense, this is on-the-job training; in another sense, the aircraft is being used as a training device.

Most of the types of individual training devices described above are tools that assist the instructor, but which only simulate or present a portion of the total task. The instructor must provide training continuity by what he tells the trainee and by how he uses the device. He must provide the necessary set or transitional instructions from earlier training to training with the device. Most devices are not perfect simulations of the physical equipment and environment; the instructor must point out what is accurately simulated and what is not. He must also have absolute control over the functioning and use of the device during the training situation. Most training devices have an instructor's console, which permits the instructor to control the training device and pace the material which he presents to the student. An instructor's console usually provides controls by which the instructor can present normal, non-routine and emergency procedures or events to the student. The instructor may also be expected to provide the student with feedback on how he is doing, and to motivate the student by appropriate praise and reproof. The design of the instructor's station and instructor's console requires considerable skill to make all of these responsibilities and duties possible of execution.

Team Training

As pointed out earlier in this chapter, many adjectives are used in connection with the word "training"; some of these describe the nature or size of the group being trained. Individual training and the kinds of programs and equipment relevant to it have already been discussed. In system terms, the typical form of individual training is *component training,* that is, the development of the skills necessary to permit the individual to "operate" his equipment so that the man-machine entity functions as a component of the system.

At a higher level of complexity is a group of men interacting with machines and with other men in such a way as to constitute a distinguishable portion of a total operating system. Such a group may man a bomber, the identification section within an air defense radar crew, a total radar unit, a ship (or a gun or some other equipment or function on that ship), a submarine, or any similar unit. This distinguishable portion of a larger system is called a subsystem. When training is directed at the functioning of such a subsystem, and particularly at the interactive procedures *within* the subsystem, one is dealing with what is often called *crew training* (or in system terms, *subsystem training*). This is one kind of *team training.*

Finally, an additional kind of *team training* is what is called *system training;* this, as its name implies, takes as its frame of reference the functioning of the total system, with particular emphasis on the interactive procedures that obtain between subsystems (or in some cases between components) and the effects of these procedures on achievement of the goal by the system. These subsystems perform related functions, they may be situated in separate geographical locations, and they may need to coordinate their work with that of a higher echelon which has to make decisions based upon information from these and other groups. This type of training is organized around the functions of the system, although only part of the total system may undergo training. It selects for training a large enough segment of the man-machine system so that this segment can carry out all of its normal functions. It undertakes to train the subsystems simultaneously on an integrated, realistic problem, and gives crews knowledge of results based on system performance. It requires well-planned and observable situations for training. Examples of such situations are Army battle maneuvers with combat situations simulated in the field, realistic mock-ups of the critical operating positions of a man-machine system for which personnel are to be trained, and operational set-ups in which the personnel to be trained can work at their normal positions. Realistic but simulated inputs to the training environment are needed in each case, as well as a way to record team action and feed it back to the crews for their evaluation.

Usually, system training is undertaken at a time during the training sequence which is relatively late, so far as the use of hardware in the system is concerned. Typically, it occurs at a time and under conditions in which both individual training and (occasionally) crew training are assumed to have been satisfactorily completed. It is designed primarily to train the many crews comprising the system to perform functions which it is difficult, if not impossible, to practice in any other integrated manner.

Training Programs and Equipment for Team Training

Several types of team training are useful in, and fitted to, particular training situations. Whatever the form of team training, it can be greatly facilitated by the use of training devices. Some of the programs and devices that are particularly useful for team training are described here.

Simulators.   Simulators allow a crew to train together when cost, safety, or general efficiency of training prohibit crew members from working with their actual equipment. For instance, pilot, copilot, and flight engineer transitioning to a new aircraft will have a certain number of hours of checkout and "flight time" on a simulator before they fly the actual aircraft. One such simulator is shown in Figure 10.6. In this simulator the members of the crew must learn thoroughly the standard operating procedures; in the process, they will probably also develop some crew operating procedures of their own. As in the case of an individual training on a simulator, a crew must also practice emergency procedures. A flight crew has special need for this training since each person is dependent on other members for specific information and actions, and they in turn are dependent upon him. Each member must learn his respective duties and responsibilities under operating conditions. Apart from considerations of low training cost and complete safety, the simulator affords great possibilities for flexibility and control in training. It makes possible a variety of special situations. In addition, crew actions can be monitored and recorded easily and accurately.

A simulator designed to provide integrated practice for personnel in certain key crew positions is the United States Navy's Submarine Attack Teacher (Figure 10.7). This is a training device which enables submarine conning officers and fire-control personnel to practice approach and attack. The device is also used to provide training of torpedo and diving-control crewmen integrated with the above personnel. The Teacher is set up in a

Figure 10.6. A simulator used for training the flight crew of a commercial jet aircraft. (Courtesy of United Air Lines.)

building of its own and has a conning tower and bridge with normal operative equipment. The periscope rises through a floor on which an operator maneuvers five target-ship models at apparent speeds up to 50 knots. Attack conditions are realistically simulated. The submarine, under the control of the students in the conning tower, is designed to respond normally to the helm. Periscope and radar presentations show depth changes; the periscope will not break surface when keel depth is more than 65′. A variety of submarine approach or attack problems may be run and evaluated with the Teacher. Possible problems include surface or submerged attacks on single fast or slow targets and on escorted or unescorted convoys; evasion of antisubmarine vessels; long-range radar tracking and approach; and submerged sonar attacks. Repeater instruments in a separate classroom allow additional students to follow the problem. One of the target ships can be made to seek out the submarine with sonar in an attempt to sink it, thus training the submarine crew in evasive tactics.

   Numerous other simulator devices and associated training programs for team training have been developed and used, and many others are under construction. Several such devices and programs in use, selected for brief

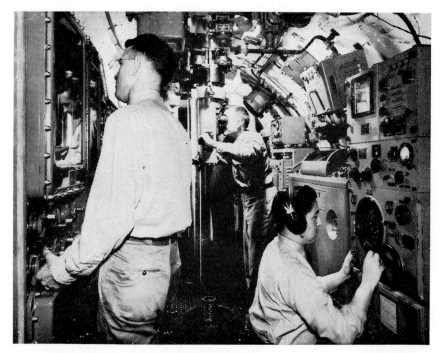

Figure 10.7. A device for the integrated training of submarine crew personnel in certain system functions. (Courtesy of Office of Naval Research, U. S. Naval Training Device Center.)

description to indicate their diversity in purpose and nature, are the Naval Electronic Warfare Simulator (NEWS) at the Naval War College (Davis & Tiedeman, 1960), and the Miniature Armor Battlefield (Baker, 1960) developed by the United States Army Armor Human Research Unit at Fort Knox, Kentucky.

The Naval Electronic Warfare Simulator is essentially an electronically controlled maneuver board for the simulation of naval warfare, used for the training of commanders and other participants. Commanders in combat information centers equipped with radarscopes, voice radios for communication with simulated forces under their command, and with other gear, move forces in large-scale exercises and have an opportunity to evaluate the effectiveness of their operating procedures. Over 100 persons are required to carry out a large-scale war game on this simulator.

The Miniature Armor Battlefield consists of an easily changeable terrain board over which can be maneuvered five miniature friendly tanks and five miniature aggressor tanks. Each of the ten tanks is controlled by a separate crew, the aggressor personnel sitting on an elevated platform at one end of the large room and the friendly tank-platoon personnel sitting on a movable steel platform at the other end. The movable platform is divided into five separate compartments, one for each three-man crew composed of a driver, gunner, and a tank commander. These crews communicate over a simulated radio network. The tanks are battery-powered, and their over-all movement, turret and gun movement (which are realistic), and simulated firing are radio controlled. The gun tube of each tank contains a small, bright light that projects a narrow beam, which when it strikes photoelectric cells on another tank, makes the "fired-upon" tank inoperable. Other devices for simulating mines, atomic weapons, and the like, are also employed. This Armor Battlefield device has the purpose of training crews to work together in many tactical aspects of operations. Use of this same simulator for proficiency measurement is discussed in Chapter 12.

Operational System Training. This kind of training is used in large, complex information-processing systems where information is collected, processed, summarized, and displayed, and where decisions are made and actions taken. In such systems, decisions may be made at several levels, with the decisions at higher levels being based on highly summarized and interpreted information. Individuals placed in such systems usually have enough training to be able to perform their particular specialty to at least a minimally acceptable level, but generally have not exercised their knowledges and skills in the context of this particular system. In fact, the skills may be new ones which they have never used in any system.

A specific system training program which illustrates the principles and operation of such a program is that in use by the Air Defense Command of the United States Air Force to train its Aircraft Control and Warning System (Biel, 1958). This program was first developed for the manual air-defense system. In this original system, all information-processing was done by human operators. The simulation techniques of this program have more recently been modified for the Semi-Automatic Ground Environment (SAGE) system of air defense, which has largely replaced the manual system in the continental United States. In SAGE, electronic computers process much of the air-defense data and display it in integrated form so that human operators can monitor many activities, make certain required decisions, and control many actions.

Although this system training program has been used for exercising the entire North American Air Defense Command (Carter, 1960; Miller, 1960), its equipment and design are such that it is very profitably used at more frequent intervals for training by smaller units of the system. In the present North American Air Defense Command, these units are called regions, divisions, and sectors. The earlier manual system organization was by forces and divisions. The program used is called the System Training Program even though the units, by our definition, are subsystems. The major units, however, are large geographically and include many crews.

For simplicity in describing the System Training Program, a hypothetical force of the earlier manual air-defense system will be assumed as the unit to be trained. This hypothetical force is shown in Figure 10.8. In preparing a training problem, an air situation is planned which covers all friendly and hostile aircraft that would be airborne in the force's area during a given three-hour period. The scan-by-scan location of each aircraft is computed for every radar in the force, then stored on 70-mm motion-picture film. A separate film for each radar site shows how the air situation looks to that site throughout the given three-hour period. At each radar site, a problem reproducer scans the film and translates the information into the video circuitry on the radar's operational consoles. A second device, also triggered by the film, generates electronic countermeasures which appear realistically on the site's radarscope and which are appropriately associated with the simulated transmitting aircraft. When a problem is to begin, all sites start the films in their problem reproducer equipment at the same time, and the crews process the simulated radar information from their radarscopes as though it were real.

Other materials in addition to the film, however, are necessary to complete the simulation and to carry out other parts of the training program. Some of these materials are in the form of scripts (lists, aircraft locations

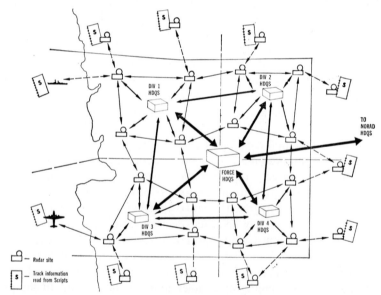

Figure 10.8.   Map of a hypothetical Air Defense Force showing locations of radar sites, Division Headquarters, Force Headquarters, and NORAD Headquarters, with the communication lines that exist between them. Among the many communication links not shown are those to the Federal Aviation Agency centers, the interceptor and missile bases, and the airborne interceptor aircraft.

shown on maps, and the like), which are used to simulate the informational inputs from those organizations or units with which the unit being trained has contacts or interactions. These surrounding organizations are referred to in this program as embedding organizations. For instance, flight plans associated with certain flights are called in normally from Federal Aviation Agency (FAA) installations in each division's area. In the System Training Program, these flight plans are computed in advance, tabulated, and sent as scripts with the film to each site. A trained individual, not a member of the crew being trained, simulates the FAA personnel's role; at the times indicated on the flight-plan script, he telephones the plans to the crew being trained.

Radar and other track information about aircraft penetrating the area of the force being trained is read from scripts and is called in over telephone or radio by selected crew personnel in other installations not participating in this training exercise. This information may be reported from radar sites in each of the adjacent forces, from airborne early-warning aircraft and from one or more picket ships, as shown in Figure 10.8.

Other personnel not participating in the exercise as crew-member trainees simulate interceptor-base personnel and interceptor pilots. They are located in another room. When required, the air-defense crew being trained sends simulated interceptor aircraft to intercept and identify unidentified aircraft. The responsible radar-crew members direct the simulated interceptor pilots, using simulated radio channels, and these pilots operate generators that produce simulated radar blips which indicate the location of the interceptors. The generators produce blips on all radar consoles in that site. These simulated interceptors which appear as blips on the consoles are maneuvered as directed by the crew according to a set of realistic flight rules for simulation. The simulated pilots have materials which provide them with detailed information on each aircraft which they might be directed to intercept and identify.

These integrated, simulated inputs are received and processed during the training exercise by crews in all the radar sites, at each division headquarters, and at force headquarters. Each crew trains in its normal environment using its operational consoles, its plotting boards, and its telephone network between air-defense radars and higher headquarters (but not to the FAA, interceptor bases, or airborne interceptor aircraft) and carries out its normal operating procedures. At division and force headquarters, of course, additional simulated inputs, such as intelligence reports, are put into the system.

Observing the crew at each headquarters and at each radar site is the Training Operations Report (TOR) Team. This team has printed materials which describe the details of the problem and on which records can be kept. While the problem is being run, the team observes and records crew actions, particularly those dealing with situations which have been identified in advance as important. The team verifies with adjacent radar site TOR Teams that critical messages were sent by and to the crew it was observing.

As soon as possible after the exercise, the TOR Team reports its observations to the crew or to the senior officer who, in turn, gives the results to his crew. Crews in subsystems in different locations, working together as part of the system, each get the over-all picture of system success and the results of their own performance. In addition, a debriefing or discussion session is held by the crew in each location to try to diagnose its problems as a part of the system, and to propose solutions which might be tried during the next training exercise.

The general intent in such a training program is for the participants to find out about the over-all system performance, their own subsystem performance, and to diagnose and solve their operational problems, particularly methods of crew interaction. Subsystem performance and even information from the crew personnel on individual actions must be used in the problem solving. This contributes to a feeling of group belongingness, group participation, group problem orientation, understanding of procedures, understanding of the group's problems, and a better understanding of what will be tried next. In fact, in this concept of system training it is difficult to find an appropriate use for the term "instructor." Although TOR Team members and simulator personnel record the actions taken and know in detail what the simulation situation was, the officers and the airmen in the crew do most of the problem solving.

The cost of a simulation training program to provide practice for such large-scale exercises is considerably less than the cost of flying real aircraft. The same exercise can be repeated many times; if desirable, it can be run with modifications. Such exercises are also less dangerous than flying real aircraft. And finally, since the location of each of the aircraft in the air situation is exactly known, and techniques are available for recording system performance, knowledge of results can be provided quickly and accurately. In this kind of training program, the additional training equipment required at each site is minimal but the production of integrated problems for large-scale exercises is a major task. As with all other training devices, the System Training Program must be used properly to be effective.

In System Training Program exercises, crews in the system practice as a team to improve their performance on peacetime situations, and on wartime situations on which they would otherwise have no chance to practice until an actual emergency arose. The operators in a system of this size must have an opportunity to develop and to shake down their procedures, finding out for themselves where improvements can be made (compare Chapter 11). With a system as large and as far-flung as the present SAGE air defense system, the operational system itself offers the only practical possibility for such training and the system itself is a part of the training device. An operational System Training Program such as this gives field commanders a means of carrying out on-the-job training against situations which they and their forces must learn to face and which they can learn in no other way.

▣ PLANNING FOR THE DEVELOPMENT OF
TRAINING PROGRAMS AND DEVICES

Planning for training programs includes planning for the development and use of training devices. It is closely related to, and should be an integral part of, system design and development of the system as a whole.

Training Design in the System Framework

Throughout all stages of system development, training requirements must be considered; as the details of the system are worked out, training plans must likewise become increasingly detailed. This is particularly essential in military systems, because training is one of the system functions which has to be carried out during peacetime. In consequence, system training must be recognized as an important, often independent, mode of operation of the system. A program is usually needed to develop and maintain human proficiency, and the capability for this type of training must be incorporated in the operational system and its equipment. Economy, quality, and timeliness of system training suggest the need to include facilities for training in the general operating requirements for the system, as well as in the operating system description. The operation of the training program can be worked out in more detail when the internal design of the system is prepared. In some military situations, only one integrated system is built and installed. To develop a high level of system performance, the system itself must be used for training.

The designers of a system training program should be intimately familiar with the requirements and design of the system. Whenever possible they should participate in the analysis and design process. This insures proper understanding of the goals of the system, its operational problems, information to be processed in the system, decisions to be made, actions to be taken, and so on. Informed judgments can be made as to *what* must be simulated in the system for adequate training, the *accuracy* with which it must be simulated, and *how* it can be simulated. These judgments may have to be modified as system development proceeds. Furthermore, the training program must be planned to be flexible, so that it can change as the system and its operating procedures change after installation (see Chapter 11). An operational system training program must also include plans for the production of integrated, simulated inputs. Since this is a major task, serious consideration needs to be given to how it will be achieved for an initial indoctrination training program, as well as for exercising and training after the system has attained operational status.

As soon as the component design is under way and operator tasks can be specified, a more detailed *task analysis* can be prepared for each operator position. This not only makes it possible to plan the *training objectives* and detailed *requirements* for the individual operator training, but also facilitates detailed planning for the system training program (see Chapter 6). In this analysis, it is necessary to consider the operator requirements for each man-machine task and man-man task to be performed. It is necessary to determine what cues or information inputs are important in the performance of the tasks, what information is necessary for making decisions, what information must be stored or memorized, what interactions are necessary between individuals performing closely related functions, what responses must be made and within what limits of accuracy, and what skills or procedures are necessary to perform the job. In other words, it is necessary to determine what must be learned and to what level. For a particular task, an analysis is made of the display problem and its variables, the decisions required, the control problem and the actions required, the feedback cues, and, where possible, the characteristic errors and malfunctions which occur. Consideration must also be given to the number of students to be trained and the level of knowledge and experience with which they begin the training.

The findings from these analyses must be integrated and decisions made as to what training methods or types of training will be used to teach the required knowledges, attitudes, and skills. These decisions include what content will need to be taught by classroom training, what operations by the use of skill, concept or other individual training devices, what operations by the use of team training techniques, and the duration of the training. The analyses will have shown equipment items, including displays and controls, which need to be considered along with the other task data in planning the training devices for those tasks selected for training. Following the plan for the training program, detailed specifications will need to be written for the training aids and devices to be developed. For devices, specifications must include the workplace layout, the display-control interactions and their ranges and tolerances, the simulation inputs to be used (their type, content, and in some cases, where and how they are to be introduced), computer programming requirements for training, techniques for observing and recording individual or system performance, feedback of performance data (consistent with any post-exercise debriefing plans), the design of the instructor's station, and the technology for the production of simulated inputs and other integrated materials (as in operational system training). Further, the importance of a detailed plan for the implementation, modification, and technical and management support of a training program cannot be overly stressed.

It is through study of a system and its training requirements early in its design and development, and through the taking of timely action for the design and development of the required training programs and devices, that these programs and devices will be available when required. Such action needs to insure that training requirements will influence the design of the operational system if this is necessary, in order that an effective training capacity may be achieved. In practice, of course, it has not always been possible to get potential training needs recognized by system designers early enough in the design and development of systems to follow in sequence all the steps described in this section, and to have appropriate training programs and devices ready when they are first needed. Such a situation is not satisfactory. When training plans are made late, it is clear that one must start from whatever point the system is in its development or operational phase to improve the training capability. However, this delay does not relieve training designers of the responsibility of thoroughly understanding the system and its operator tasks before designing the necessary training programs and devices.

Human Engineering and Training

Another very important activity must also be carried on during the design phase, particularly at the time of allocation of tasks to equipment and operators, as well as during the design of component hardware; it is that of designing the tasks and the equipment so that the human operator can perform his tasks efficiently. This, of course, must be done with consideration of what leads to optimal over-all system efficiency. This aspect of design activity is called human engineering and has been discussed in detail in Chapter 5. Good human engineering of equipment is of great importance to training, because it can simplify the training problem immensely. By making the displays easier to read and interpret, by simplifying the decisions required and the actions to be taken, and by contributing in many other areas where operator capabilities must be considered, the amount and type of training can be greatly influenced in the direction of increased efficiency. In addition, it may be noted here that appropriate human engineering of equipment has major implications for the selection of personnel to be trained and placed in system jobs, since good equipment design can bring about a reduction in the basic operator qualifications required for these jobs (Taylor, 1960).

Use of Simulation in the Design of Systems

In the design and development of many large systems, it is advantageous to set up a simulation of the system or its major parts, so that studies can be conducted and decisions reached about directions of development. Such simulation is useful in as early a phase as that of operational design. Hardware in such a simulation probably would include critical simulated consoles with essential displays and with operable controls. Ideally, for complex systems a computer is an integral part of the simulation. The computer can generate the simulated environmental situation displays for the consoles or other apparatus according to a plan, simulate certain characteristics of the system, and respond to and record the responses of the crew members.

Such a simulation, very general at first but more detailed as the design of the system progresses, can be very useful in providing a vehicle to assist the system designers and training developers in many ways. Some of its values are as follows:

1. It enables the designers of the system, as well as those designing the components, to determine what operational problems might arise in the system and to study these experimentally. As components are designed and built, they can be substituted for mock-ups. Results, even those which derive from trial and error, enable the designers to make better decisions.

2. Knowledge is gained concerning appropriate allocation of tasks to human operators versus machines, or between operators; more information is gained regarding display, information load, and control problems, workplace layout, operational procedures, potential capacity of the system, operator requirements for each job to be performed, and many other factors.

3. Experience gathered with simulation permits better determination of the need for and contributes to the subsequent planning for individual training devices; it also permits early decisions on the need for a system training program and associated equipment, and on the detailed nature of both.

4. In later stages of a more detailed simulation, the setup may itself be used as a training mechanism for the first crews prior to shakedown runs in the system.

5. From experience with the procedures used in the simulation laboratory and from known specifications for the equipment, it is possible to get an early start in the preparation of the operators' manuals.

6. The tasks incorporated in such simulation also provide good early work samples for developing techniques for the selection of operator personnel. Performance on these devices may be useful for providing the criteria for validating other tests to be tried as selection tools. Or the simulated tasks may themselves become the selection devices.

A different type of simulation frequently used in the design and analysis of systems is based upon mathematical modeling (Amer. Inst. of Indust. Engineers, 1957; Kibbee, 1960). The use of this type of simulation entails, first, a precise definition of the behavior of each component of the system— that is, a specification of the output of each component as a function of its input. Frequently, the inputs are a set of variables which are random in nature, and the operation of the component on the inputs is a random process which results in a spectrum of outputs with associated probabilities. Second, it requires an equally precise statement of the relationship between components. Using these specifications, it is then possible to devise computational sequences that result in pertinent measures of system performance as a function of the system input. Such a model, particularly with the use of a high-speed computer, makes it possible to make many runs and many different analyses through the use of compressed time. By this is meant the fact that one can, for instance, run through a year's real-time operation of a system in a matter of minutes to determine the nature of the interactions. Here, as in the case of other system simulation, before such a model is built and before such studies are conducted, a detailed operational analysis of the system to be simulated must be made if realistic or useful results are to be obtained.

▣ PSYCHOLOGICAL CONSIDERATIONS IN THE DESIGN OF TRAINING PROGRAMS AND DEVICES

There is a variety of factors, considerations, and principles which guide the training designer in the design and development of training programs and devices for complex man-machine systems. Some of these have been alluded to in previous sections of this chapter. In this section, they will be brought together and augmented by a few considerations which have not been made explicit earlier. For the most part, the emphasis in this section will be on the psychological principles influencing the training designer's decisions.

Human Problems in Complex Systems

Underlying the design of training programs and devices for today's complex man-machine systems must be an appreciation of the characteristics of such systems, including the psychological and social factors which make sophisticated training programs particularly necessary. Eckstein has discussed the characteristics of large-scale automated systems and their implications for training design (1959). As he points out, in today's computerized systems, the human operator perceives his significance relative to that of the machine as small and tends to feel loss of control over his working environment. His task may be narrowly constricted, as may be his knowledge of the total system and of the relationship between his task and the performance of the system. Operators may be isolated, sometimes in darkened rooms, with mechanized and formal communications, rather than enjoying natural face-to-face relationships. The operator receives little feedback on the effectiveness of his actions, and consequently his ability to improve his performance is limited. The effective training program must recognize these factors and provide specific measures within the training program for dealing with them. One antidote to these particular factors lies in system training, and especially in the provision of means for effective informational feedback in the context of group problem-solving sessions.

In addition to this appreciation of systems in general, the training designer must, of course, become intimately familiar with the particular system for which he is designing a training program or specifying a training device. He must understand in detail such things as the system mission, system performance specifications, system characteristics and procedures, operational problems, and the system environment. With this background and intimate knowledge of the task analyses of the operator positions, he is better able to make intelligent decisions about what skills must be trained, to what level, and by what techniques. In addition, he will be prepared to determine what system characteristics need to be simulated, with what degree of realism; where simulated inputs should and can be introduced into the system; where performance can be observed and recorded; and what the significant elements of system performance are which need to be reflected in post-exercise feedback.

Training Objectives and Training Requirements

The training designer must make explicit the objectives of the training program and devices to be developed. Generally, the ultimate goal of individual and team training is the same—maximum performance of the man-machine system. Practically, however, the goal of individual training is improvement in the performance of the individual to an adequate level in the shortest amount of time, whereas in team training the goal is more likely to be the achievement of maximum performance of the system. The determination of how best to attain these individual and system goals involves establishing the subordinate or intermediary training objectives. For example, in the case of a system training program, major intermediary objectives include, among others, the development of *system awareness* and the development of *system flexibility* (see Chapters 11 and 13). System awareness is the ability of the individual in a system to understand the relationship between his task and the functioning of the over-all system. As discussed above, today's complex systems promote an orientation on the part of the individual operator toward his own isolated position and tend to limit his knowledge of the total system. On the other hand, if the system is to perform effectively, the operator must develop an understanding of the interrelationships among components of the system and of the effects of his actions on other parts of the system. Thus, a comprehensive training program must emphasize, not only the development of skills and attitudes of individuals, but also a reasonable understanding of the functional interrelationships and interactions among components and among subsystems, seeking to clarify basic system problems. The program must then provide knowledge of results, enabling the individual to understand the relationship of his actions to those of others, to the solution of these problems and to the optimum functioning of the over-all system.

A second intermediary training objective, system flexibility, refers to the ability of the system to adapt to change, particularly to sudden and unanticipated circumstances. An effective training program promotes system flexibility through simulation of a wide range of conceivable conditions, through insuring that the personnel become accustomed to dealing with unexpected contingencies, and through providing experience in the development and use of alternate procedures.

Where a training program or device has multiple objectives, some of these may not be adequately served by the training instrument unless they are explicitly formulated. For example, a system training program must often serve as a vehicle for system diagnosis and revision as well as for system exercising, and therefore will require not only means by which existing procedures can be practiced but must also provide means for developing, testing, evaluating, and revising procedures. The training designer thus bases his statement of training requirements on explicit training objectives. He specifies the information, skills, and attitudes required by operators at each position in the system. These specifications also describe the level of proficiency needed to perform each job satisfactorily. Techniques for performing the analyses leading to such specifications have been described in Chapter 6.

From these requirements it is possible to make decisions concerning training content, methods, and devices, and it is also possible to develop the proficiency measures and standards used to evaluate individual and team performance. By using these measures during a training exercise, the training designer can establish how well the training objectives have been met; with these measures he can identify those parts of the program needing content or method improvement. Further, he can plan for the providing of guidance to individual operators concerning their proficiency.

Training Content

From the training objectives and requirements, the curriculum for the training program is developed. The three major parts of the curriculum are content, training methods, and training devices. Content includes the material to be presented, its organization, and its sequence. When planning the material to be presented, consideration is given to the previous experience, capabilities, and other characteristics of the trainees and to the training requirements of the tasks. These considerations determine what is to be taught, the level at which it is presented, the organization of the material, and the sequence in which the material is presented.

In addition to the content which is taught, early emphasis should be placed in the training on an overview of the system and its mission, with repeated clarification of the relationships of the tasks to the larger functions of the system. This contributes to the student's understanding of the purpose of his job in the system. Students need to be convinced that what they learn or do is important to them and to the system. Only with such motivation can it be expected that a high percentage of students will learn their tasks to the required level of proficiency.

Training Methods and Devices

The training program designer must decide whether the content to be taught and the required level of operator performance can best be achieved by individual training through classroom techniques and individual training devices, by subsystem or crew training, operational system training, or combinations of these. Some tasks will require skills and information which can be learned separately and therefore imply individual or component training; others require the integration of component skills through subsystem training; and still others require an appreciation of the operational relationship among components or subsystems, and therefore imply system training. In general, a minimum level of component performance is necessary, but not sufficient, for effective subsystem performance; similarly, minimum levels of subsystem performance are necessary, but not sufficient, for effective system performance.

Selection of training methods and devices is determined by a complex of considerations, such as type of task, stage of learning, required proficiency, initial skill level, and interactions among these variables. Thus, the optimal methods and choice of devices may vary, depending on whether the emphasis is on the learning of motor skills, conceptual skills, or system skills; whether training is being given at an early, intermediate, high, or transition stage; whether the objective is familiarization, understanding, or a working knowledge; and what skills, knowledge, and abilities are possessed by the individuals prior to the training.

Fidelity of Simulation and Transfer of Training

The use of simulation for training has many important applications and advantages. Use of the real system under live conditions for training may be too costly (in dollars or time), too dangerous, or too unwieldy. Further, using simulation techniques, it is possible to realize more precise control over the training process. For example, inputs can be manipulated readily to accomplish a particular training objective, and more accurate knowledge of results can be provided. Certain kinds of training under simulated conditions of emergency or system degradation can also be introduced, whereas these are virtually precluded under live conditions. However, simulation constitutes an abstraction or representation of reality, and therefore by definition implies some departure from reality. A key issue which the designer of a simulation-based training program must face is how much departure from reality is acceptable. Or, stated conversely: for the acquisition of particular skills, what degree of fidelity of simulation is required to insure maximal transfer of training to live operations? (Where there are practical constraints, as there normally are, "enough" usually substitutes for "maximal.") This issue translates into decisions about what elements of the actual situation must be represented in the training device or program, and how closely those elements represented must conform to reality to obtain maximum, or enough, transfer of training.

The question of what degree of fidelity of simulation is required must be considered with respect to two aspects of simulation. That is, the training designer must decide: (1) what *equipment* and *functions* must be simulated, and how precise the simulation must be, and (2) how accurately the *stimulus situations* on which training is given must simulate real life. In the first case, decisions need to be made concerning what critical tasks the operator must perform and what essential information is needed for the performance of these tasks. This leads to a concern with what instruments are required to display this information and with what precision they must display it. As a general principle, information of this type should be displayed in as realistic a fashion as possible,[1] although it may be appropriate for noncritical information to be displayed using simulation which is less accurate, or perhaps only to be represented by dummy instruments, or not to be displayed at all. In the second case—that is, fidelity of simulation of the *stimulus situation*—it is generally essential that the situations or "problems" which are used for training be realistic and show appropriate relationships between critical variables. These problems should be planned so that the operator can be exposed to a wide variety of situations of varying complexity which he might face in real life, ranging from normal through emergency. This is important in order to broaden the experience base of the operator and to cultivate flexibility and adaptability on the part of the individual or system. The proper sequencing of these training situations is likewise an important consideration in order to obtain maximum training value.

In most cases, the fundamental problem with respect to either of these two aspects of simulation (though it relates more clearly to the case of equipment and functions than to stimulus situations) is to optimize the relationship between fidelity, transfer, and cost. This relationship for the design of a training device has been shown schematically in Figure 10.9. Basically, the training designer hopes to be able to locate as accurately as possible the amount of fidelity of simulation required to obtain large amounts of transfer of training at a point where additional increments of transfer are not worth the added costs. This amount of fidelity is a point beyond which, if fidelity is increased, the transfer may increase, but not proportionately to the cost; in other words, it is a point of diminishing returns. For many reasons, this optimization is a complex problem.

The relationship between degree of fidelity and amount of transfer is not clear and unequivocal. For example, a number of studies have been reported in which transfer from several types of simulators to a single type of aircraft was investigated, where the simulators represented the aircraft characteristics with varying degrees of fidelity. Some of the studies report a significant relationship between degree of fidelity and transfer of training (for example, Dougherty, Houston and Nicklas, 1957; Ornstein, Nichols, and Flexman, 1954), while others do not (for example, Mahler and Bennett, 1950; Wilcoxon, Davy, and Webster, 1954). The inconsistent findings are difficult to

---

[1] It may be advisable, for purposes of emphasis, in the early phases of training to distort some aspects of reality purposely. This may take the form, for example, of exaggerating the amount of indicator movement resulting from a particular action, altering the relationships of information, or distorting true time relationships.

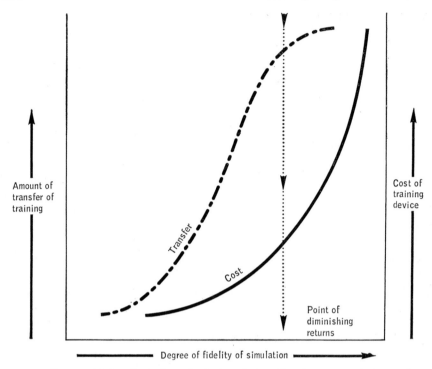

Amount of transfer of training

Cost of training device

Transfer

Cost

Point of diminishing returns

Degree of fidelity of simulation ⟶

Figure 10.9. One hypothetical relationship between degree of fidelity of simulation, amount of transfer of training, and cost of training device. (Adapted from Miller, 1954, p. 22.)

unravel because, as pointed out by Muckler and his associates (1959), the various studies were not always comparable with respect to such factors as levels of instructor ability, instructional techniques, types of simulators, student time on trainers, flight experience of subjects, and measuring techniques. We know very little about the parameters that contribute to the relationship between fidelity and transfer. As Miller points out (1954, p. 23), "Perhaps one of the principal difficulties has been that the various dimensions of the problem have not been made explicit." Fidelity and transfer relationships vary as a function of many variables external to a training device. For instance, the quality of instruction on the same device can influence the amount of transfer. Further, the objectives of the instruction can influence the relationships; if familiarization is the training objective, relatively low levels of fidelity are adequate, whereas if complete training on a high-level task is required, high-level fidelity of simulation probably is required.

Costs for simulation devices with a given amount of fidelity can be estimated at the present time with a reasonable degree of accuracy, although special requirements and technological advances may divergently influence the accuracy of these cost estimates.

In weighing the over-all relationship between cost and transfer in flight simulators, and perhaps in the case of some other simulators, one important point to consider is the goal or goals of the training. For example, there may be no opportunity for the live practice of certain operational flight tasks before the occasion arises when they must be performed. This is particularly true in the case of emergency procedures. When the occasion does arise, perfect execution may be required the first time. Thus, with respect to such tasks, it is imperative that simulator training be designed to meet the requirement that there be maximum transfer to the live situation on the first trial.

Knowledge of Results

Knowledge of results (KOR) provides learners with information on how well they are doing and whether or not their responses are correct. Laboratory studies consistently report either that KOR is essential for learning to take place, or at least that KOR produces more learning or more rapid learning than performance without feedback. Wolfle (1951) cites a number of studies indicating these consistent findings. Despite the extensive laboratory investigations of KOR, however, this factor deserves extremely careful attention when a training program or device is being planned and warrants a great deal more empirical study and field observation. There are many variables comprising KOR, including timing, type, amount of interpretation, relevance, accuracy, motivational value, individual versus team presentation, and other utilization variables. While many of these dimensions have been studied at length, investigation of their interactions is an area where the surface has hardly been scratched. Undoubtedly, for example, under one set of circumstances, one technique for presenting KOR is more effective than another, while under different circumstances (involving perhaps a different task or altered timing of KOR) the same relationship does not prevail.

Recognizing the complexity of the area, the multitude of studies, and the fact that much investigation has yet to be done, it is nevertheless possible to formulate some generalizations representing today's state of knowledge about KOR. This may serve as a useful frame of reference for the training designer. In this section such a set of generalizations will be listed, along with some brief comments. The generalizations relate principally to individual as opposed to team KOR, since most of the reported research has been done in connection with individual learning.

KOR increases the rate and level of learning. As discussed above, the experimental literature is consistent in the contention that KOR results in more learning or better performance, or at least faster learning, than performance without feedback. It is questionable, in fact, whether learning occurs without it. This contention is essentially universal, regardless of whether the observations deal with individual or group training, simple or complex material, motor or verbal tasks.

When KOR is removed, the level of learning and performance generally drops. Studies such as the one conducted by Morin and Gagné (reported in Gagné and Fleishman, 1959, p. 250) indicate that when KOR is removed, performance is degraded, though not to the level that would have prevailed had KOR not been provided in the first place. One explanation for the drop in performance, suggested by MacPherson, Dees, and Grindley (1948–1949) and others, is that KOR provides motivation. Not all learners show this drop. In the case of subjects whose performance does not drop when KOR is removed, some kind of substitute KOR or self-evaluation has apparently occurred. There are very few learning situations where some form of KOR is not available to the learner. Obviously, this does not mean that the providing of feedback can be left to chance. Performance can generally be substantially improved by formally providing KOR.

The more immediate the KOR, the greater the learning. This statement is something of an overgeneralization. Ammons (1954), for example, points out that there is probably an optimum delay for every task and every stage of learning. For the most part, however, prompt feedback is more effective than delayed.

The greater the amount of relevant feedback, the greater the learning. KOR can (and should) serve to help indicate or define the goal, and the learner's standing in relation to the goal; it can help to evaluate his hypotheses about how to attain the goal, and it can suggest new hypotheses. Within limits, the greater the quantity of feedback available to the learner, the more effectively these purposes are served, and, therefore, the more rapid will be the learning and the higher will be the level of performance. The exception to this rule is that when KOR is too complete and detailed, it can confuse the learner and impede his progress, particularly in the earlier stages of learning, when he is not prepared to integrate and utilize large amounts of information.

For a particular learning situation, some methods of providing KOR are better than others. Many different techniques for presenting KOR have been used. The most frequently used has been verbal report, but the techniques include lights and other visual displays, tones, and electric shock. The optimal method appears to depend on a number of variables such as type of task, stage of learning, and the nature of the information to be communicated.

KOR has motivational value. Many investigators point to a positive relationship between KOR and motivation. A number of them suggest that the positive relationship between KOR and learning is attributable primarily to the motivational value of KOR. Among others, MacPherson, Dees, and Grindley (1948–1949) come to this conclusion. These investigators further conclude that KOR affects motivation differentially in different stages of learning. They feel that in the early stages, KOR has a "directional" effect, serving to define the goal, while in the latter stages it has an "incentive" effect, reinforcing successful performance or indicating how it can be attained.

There are differences between individual and team KOR. For the most part, the generalizations discussed above, derived from investigations of KOR in the individual learning situation, do appear to apply to team KOR as well, although there has been very little empirical study of KOR on the team level. There are, however, important differences between individual and team KOR. Individual KOR refers to knowledge of individual performance which a person receives about his own behavior in performing a task individually or as a member of a group. Team KOR, in contrast, refers to the feedback which the group receives about team (or system) performance, goals, organization problems, and the like, and traditionally deals with individual performance only (if at all) as it relates to group goals. The variables discussed above require empirical investigation in the team context. In addition, those factors which are introduced, or greatly intensified, by virtue of the existence of a team, require appreciation and further study. Consider, for example, experience with respect to one aspect of KOR in the Air Defense Command system training program. In this program, the postexercise debriefings are viewed essentially as group problem-solving sessions. Detailed, objective KOR provides the stimulus for the group to identify system problems and formulate new solutions to be tried out in subsequent exercises or live operations. In this situation, it is important that a climate be created in the debriefings in which exercise observers, debriefing leaders, and crew members can communicate freely. In military settings, where the traditional hierarchy may tend to inhibit free communication, this issue calls for special attention and study.

Frequency of Training

When plans are made to employ training devices, the question of how often they should be used must be answered. No general principle can answer this question for all training devices, since optimal frequency varies with the training objectives, the tasks, the device, the trainee(s), the quality of the instructors, the length of each exercise, and many other factors. The best answers can be obtained empirically from experience with the device. From a practical point of view, training devices have generally been used too little rather than too much. However, frequency is important mainly because it provides opportunity for other factors in training, such as knowledge of results, to have their effects. Usually, frequent practice is essential for learning. Perhaps it may best be said that the optimum frequency is that which best achieves the training objectives in the shortest time at the least cost.

Evaluation and the Criterion Problem

When a training program or device has been developed, it is desirable to subject it to some sort of formal evaluation, in order to assess its effectiveness and in order to provide one means of determining requirements for its modification. The fundamental criterion for evaluating a simulation-based training program or device is the extent of transfer of training to the live situation. Thus, for example, a number of empirical studies—such as Ornstein, Nichols, and Flexman (1954), Mahler and Bennett (1950), and Wilcoxon, Davy, and Webster (1954)—have investigated transfer from flight-simulator training to flight performance in the actual aircraft. In these studies, experimental groups received a period of training on the flight simulators, where they practiced basic flight maneuvers such as climbs and turns. Their training was then continued in the actual aircraft. The control groups received equivalent total training time, but entirely in the aircraft. Flight proficiency of the experimental and control groups was compared by means of such measures as ratings on instrument maneuvers, accident rates, flight failures, and number of additional flights needed. The experimenters concluded that transfer of training took place; and in fact, that those trained initially on the simulators met the flight proficiency standards earlier than did those who had training only in the aircraft.

Many training devices and programs have not been validated to this degree. In many instances they cannot be, since rigorous evaluation would require that they be validated against the ultimate criterion—that is, performance of the individual or system in the live situation under the conditions for which the system was designed—and this ultimate criterion is often unavailable. This problem is particularly critical in the case of military systems. As an example, reasonably rigorous evaluation of the effectiveness of a system training program for training the air-defense system would require the fighting of at least two actual wars. One war would have to be waged while the system was manned by "experimental" crews who had received system training, and an equivalent war would have to be fought while the system was manned by "control" crews who had not received such training. Completely rigorous evaluation would require several more wars for crossvalidation of the results.

In cases such as this, where ultimate criteria are obviously unavailable, intermediate criteria must be employed. One example of an intermediate criterion is performance in a final examination. Thus, it is possible to obtain some measure of the effectiveness of a training device or program by comparing final performance scores, on some independent set of tasks, of groups which have been trained with the device or program and those which have not.

Sometimes improvement as measured by performance on the training device itself is the best measure available of the effectiveness of the device and its associated training program. One illustration is of interest here. Several field studies have been conducted that were designed to evaluate the effectiveness of the Air Defense Command system training program, or of aspects of the training program. In one such study (Alexander, Tregoe, and Kepner, 1961), conducted at an air-defense direction center, the effectiveness of the total training program (which included practice on simulated air defense problems, detailed knowledge of results, and postexercise debriefings or group discussions) was contrasted with training in which there was no formal feedback or debriefing. Two crews (experimental) received practice, knowledge of results, and debriefings, while two crews (control) received the same number of training exercises but no knowledge of results or debriefings. All crews were given the same test-retest and training problems. The experimental crews showed a consistent and large advantage on the various performance measures, which included such items as detecting flights, establishing tracks, maintaining continuity on critical or important flights, telling tracks to adjacent sites, and taking appropriate tactical action on critical flights.[2] This study suggests how effectiveness may be achieved with this particular type of training program, but more importantly, it illustrates one of the methods by which a training technique may be validated using intermediate criteria where the ultimate criterion is not available.

System Training Principles

Although the detailed characteristics of a training program are determined by the particular system which is to be trained, there are a number of general principles of operational system training which must be considered in designing such a program for any complex man-machine system. They have been established through experience in the analysis, development, and training of various systems, both in the laboratory and in the field. For the most part, they parallel principles which are used in individual training, but with some modifications and shifts in emphasis. The focus in the examples that follow is not on learning theory, but is on the conditions which must be established in a training program to optimize learning. The focus, further, is on the acquisition of complex rather than simple skills.

Promoting System Skills and Understanding. For complex systems to perform effectively, it is not sufficient for operators to be proficient at their individual tasks. Each operator must understand the relationship of his task to the functioning of the system, and must develop skills where necessary for interaction with other components in the system. Thus, an important feature of system training is the design of simulated system inputs planned in such a way as to require not only component skills but also a high degree of goal-oriented interaction among the operators in the system. Such, for example, would appear in situations calling for load balancing or load sharing, establishing priorities and procedures, or initiating the use of alternate facilities. The development of these skills implies a training vehicle which permits the operator to learn, not only what his task is and how to perform it, but also

---

[2] Also of interest in this study is the fact that the performance disparity between experimental and control crews was particularly great in the case of functions which were relatively "invisible." The visibility of a function meant the extent to which its performance could be observed or its consequences determined by the individual or another crew member.

what its purpose is, how the task relates to the goals of the system, and what the "environment" is in which the task is performed.

Understanding the environment means that he must understand the *organization* within which he operates, including its formal and informal structure, and the resources and communication channels which he can utilize in solving problems related to his tasks. He must understand the functions, capabilities, and limitations of the *hardware* components of the system; he most understand the *human* environment, including the functions and abilities of the people in the system with whom he interacts, and the relationship of their roles to his own. This understanding is gained partly by orientation and individual training, partly through participation in a variety of carefully designed system training exercises, and partly by means of postexercise group discussion and problem-solving sessions.

Encouraging Goal-Oriented Exploration.   In a team-learning situation, where alternate solutions or responses can be considered, learning will generally be enhanced if the working atmosphere permits the group (including the leaders) to explore alternatives, formulate hypotheses, and invent solutions. Where the penalties for failure are too great, defensiveness and resistance to change may be promoted and learning impeded. Further, the group must have a chance to validate its proposed solutions in the system context—that is, find how they affect system performance. The training situation is designed to provide sufficient understanding for generalization and transfer to take place. This happens when the opportunity for follow-up permits the group to test its hypotheses, receive information as to their adequacy, and explore new alternatives when the original solutions are not validated.

The *synthetic system exercise* is an ideal vehicle for providing the individual or group with the opportunity for such goal-oriented exploration. For example, in the manual air-defense system, the operating crew can improvise a technique for load sharing in the face of a simulated high-load attack, receive specific feedback as to its effectiveness, evaluate and modify the technique in group problem-solving sessions, and repeat the technique in subsequent exercises and, if successful, in live operations.

Training a Functionally Complete Unit.   In system training, a large and functionally complete unit (one which can carry out all of its normal functions) of the total system is trained in one integrated, synthetic exercise. The unit to be trained is not the individual operator; nor is it normally limited to the entire complement of operators at a particular site. In a given exercise, the unit may consist of an entire division, force, command, or whatever the major functionally complete elements of that military or nonmilitary system happen to be. Theoretically, it is desirable to train the entire system simultaneously on an integrated problem. In this way, those parts of the system which would be required to interact in live operations do so in the exercise, and it is not necessary to simulate all the various agencies "surrounding" each unit, as is done when separate, smaller-scale exercises are conducted. This results in a greater degree of realism, achieves more complete training, and affords a more valid indication of system effectiveness. However, it may be noted that other embedding organizations around the larger unit being trained still need to be simulated.

Completely simulated exercises of immense scope have been successfully conducted, such as those designed for the entire North American Air Defense Command (NORAD) (Carter, 1960; Miller, 1960). However, it is not practical to run exercises of this scope frequently. Special types of training must be provided for various sizes of subsystems to meet a variety of training needs. The training designer must plan carefully to insure a training vehicle which is adaptable to many different exercise configurations and system sizes, the selection of these being dictated by training considerations, such as current operator skill level, as well as by such practical considerations as scheduling problems, cost, and the maintenance of an acceptable level of live operations.

Simulating the Environment Adequately.   Although exact simulation is neither feasible nor necessary, an effective system training program must attain an adequate degree of realism. An attempt is made to simulate all inputs which significantly influence decisions and actions, doing so with enough realism that no important differences exist between simulated inputs and presumed live inputs. All significant interactions within the system, and outputs from the system, must also be able to take place realistically. And the system must be made to suffer the consequences of its own actions in a realistic fashion. Thus, in an air-defense exercise, if the system fails to defend an important target area which includes an air base, that base would be lost to the system. Adequate simulation is essential to insure that skills acquired during training will transfer to live operations. Realism also helps to stimulate the interest of the trainees, which in turn facilitates the acquisition of the necessary knowledge and skills. The degree of realism implied by this principle necessitates gathering large amounts of data about the live operations environment of the system to be trained, both with respect to normal day-to-day operations and potential emergency situations, and subsequently integrating these data into adequate simulation of the real environment.

Stressing the System.   A simulation-based system training program should be so designed that the designer of specific exercises should essentially have complete control over the nature and quantity of inputs to the system being trained. He then can design problems to stress the system in accordance with whatever the training needs dictate, as well as to "test the limits" for purposes of evaluating system capability. Thus, training problems can be designed to stress those system functions which are deficient or those parts of the system which must perform particularly critical functions. Most important, the system can be confronted with stressful problem situations it would not encounter in normal daily operations. Many systems have no opportunity to experience in live operations anything resembling the conditions that would prevail were they called upon to perform their ultimate mission. For example, in the case of a military system, the exercise designer can introduce heavier-than-normal input loads, enemy attacks, and various kinds of attrition to the system, such as communications failures, loss of weapons, loss of sensing devices or command facilities, as well as special problems posed by nuclear fall-out.

Providing the System with Knowledge of Results. This principle is based on the evidence that feedback is essential for effective learning. It holds that the personnel in the system must be provided with knowledge of results of system performance, and this must be prompt, relevant, accurate, unambiguous, and in appropriate detail to permit the association of antecedent actions with results. To permit this feedback, system actions during an exercise are recorded in considerable detail. In some systems the recording is done entirely by observers; in others, computers are used to provide a detailed record of the system actions that are taken in dealing with specific simulated inputs, while observers note critical incidents and significant behaviors that are not recorded automatically. A good deal of skill is required to make the detailed decisions about the amount and types of system performance information required, and how it is to be collected, processed, presented, and utilized in postexercise debriefings.

Debriefings are problem-solving sessions in which the group uses the system performance data as a basis for discussing the results of the exercise, diagnosing system difficulties, and working out new procedures for dealing with them. Again, the ingenuity and skill of those responsible for the use of this program are taxed in working with the system members to cultivate objective problem-solving attitudes toward operational problems, to provide a climate in which all system members can participate freely and contribute to system improvement, and to develop skilled debriefing leadership. Productive debriefings represent a key element in the effectiveness of system training. To a large degree their importance stems from the nature of complex man-machine systems, which tend in their operations to inhibit the kind of interaction and communication needed to solve operational system problems.

Integrating the Training Program into System Operations. Operational system training has a number of additional characteristics which differentiate it, in one or more respects, from each of the more traditional kinds of training. The common denominator of systems for which system training is appropriate is that each includes the training program as *an integral part of continuous system operations.* Thus, the training program is operated *on-site,* rather than in a central training facility; it is conducted in the *operational* setting, using the normal operational equipment and communications channels insofar as possible, rather than some form of simulators or mock-ups; it is an *ongoing* program rather than being limited to training for initial proficiency, with exercises conducted *frequently* throughout the life of the system, to insure that system potential is realized as system functions and characteristics evolve and change over time (and as personnel change through rotation or turnover); and it is *supported* by management or command level personnel as a regular and essential part of system operations.

REFERENCES

Adams, J. D. 1960. Part trainers. In G. Finch (ed.), *Educational and training media: A symposium*. Washington, D. C.: National Academy of Sciences, National Research Council.

Alexander, L. T., Tregoe, B. B., and Kepner, C. H. 1961. *The effectiveness of knowledge of results in a military system training program*. Santa Monica, Calif.: System Development Corporation, March. Report SP–271.

American Institute of Industrial Engineers, 8th National Convention, May 1957. *Report of system simulation symposium*. New York: Waverly Press.

Ammons, R. B. 1954. *Knowledge of performance. Survey of literature, some possible applications and suggested experimentation*. Wright-Patterson Air Force Base, Ohio: USAF Wright Air Development Center. WADC Technical Report 54–14.

Baker, R. A. 1960. The miniature armor battlefield. *Armor, 69*, 34–38.

Biel, W. C. 1958. Operations research based on simulation for training. Dayton, Ohio: *Aeronautical Electronics, National Conference Proceedings*, 319–322.

Carter, L. F. 1960. *Exercising the air defense system*. Santa Monica, Calif.: System Development Corporation. Report SP–47.

Coulson, J. E., and Silberman, H. F. 1961. Automated teaching and individual differences. *Audio-v. Commun. Rev., 9*, 5–15.

Davis, J. B., Jr., and Tiedeman, J. A. 1960. The navy war games program. *United States Naval Institute Proceedings, 86*, 61–67.

Dougherty, D. J., Houston, R. C., and Nicklas, D. R. 1957. *Transfer of training in flight procedures from selected ground training devices to the aircraft*. Port Washington, N. Y.: USN Training Device Center. Report 71–16–16.

Eckstein, M. R. 1959. *The theory, objectives, and methods of a system training and exercising program (STEP) for the 465L SACCS*. Santa Monica, Calif.: System Development Corporation. Report FN–LO–193.

French, R. S., and Martin, L. B. 1957. *A flight-line troubleshooting trainer for a complex electronic system: The MAC–2 trainer*. Lackland Air Force Base, Texas: Air Force Personnel and Training Research Center. Report TN–57–106,

Gagné, R. M. 1954. Training devices and simulators: Some research issues. *Amer. Psychologist, 9*, 95–107.

Gagné, R. M., and Fleishman, E. A. 1959. *Psychology and human performance*. New York: Holt.

Kibbee, J. M. 1960. Management control simulation. In D. G. Malcolm, A. J. Rowe, and L. F. McConnell (ed.), *Management control systems*. New York: Wiley.

Lumsdaine, A. A. 1960a. Design of training aids and devices. In J. D. Folley, Jr. (ed.), *Human factors methods for system design.* Pittsburgh: The American Institute for Research.

Lumsdaine, A. A. 1960b. Graphic aids, models, and mockups as tools for individual and classroom instruction. In G. Finch (ed.), *Educational and training media: A symposium.* Washington, D. C.: National Academy of Sciences, National Research Council.

Lumsdaine, A. A., and Glaser, R. 1960. *Teaching machines and programmed learning.* Washington, D. C.: Department of Audio-Visual Instruction, National Education Association.

MacPherson, S. J., Dees, V., and Grindley, G. C. 1948–1949. The effect of knowledge of results on learning and performance: II. Some characteristics of very simple skills. *Quart. J. exp. Psychol., 1,* 68–78.

Mahler, W. R., and Bennett, G. K. 1950. *Psychological studies of advanced naval training: Evaluation of operational flight trainers.* Port Washington, N. Y.: USN Special Devices Center. Technical Report SDC 999–1–1.

Miller, E. M. 1960. The day NORAD went to war! *Air Force,* August.

Miller, R. B. 1954. *Psychological considerations in the design of training equipment.* Wright-Patterson Air Force Base, Ohio: Wright Air Development Center. WADC Technical Report 54–563.

Muckler, F. A., Nygaard, J. E., O'Kelly, L. I., and Williams, A. C., Jr. 1959. *Psychological variables in the design of flight simulators for training.* Wright-Patterson Air Force Base, Ohio: Wright Air Development Center. WADC Technical Report 56–369.

Ornstein, G. N., Nichols, I. A., and Flexman, R. E. 1954. *Evaluation of a contact flight simulator when used in an Air Force primary pilot training program: Part II. Effectiveness of training on component skills.* Lackland Air Force Base, Texas: Air Force Personnel and Training Research Center. Technical Report 54–110.

Pressey, S. L. 1932. A third and fourth contribution toward the coming industrial revolution in education. *Sch. & Soc., 36,* 668–672.

Rath, G. J., Anderson, N. S., and Brainerd, R. C. 1959. The IBM research center teaching machine project. In E. Galanter (ed.), *Automatic teaching: The state of the art.* New York: Wiley, 117–130.

Ricciardi, F. M., *et al.* 1958. *Top management decision simulation: The AMA approach.* New York: American Management Association.

Taylor, F. V. 1960. Four basic ideas in engineering psychology. *Amer. Psychologist, 15,* 643–649.

Wilcoxon, H. C., Davy, E., and Webster, J. C. 1954. *Evaluation of the SNJ operational flight trainer.* Port Washington, N. Y.: USN Special Devices Center. Report 999–2–1.

Wolfle, D. 1951. Training. In S. S. Stevens (ed.), *Handbook of experimental psychology.* New York: Wiley, 1267–1286.

PREVIOUS CHAPTERS HAVE DESCRIBED THE techniques used in defining human tasks, in providing individual training to insure adequate levels of skill, and in measuring the performance of human beings in carrying out these essential portions of system operations. But there is an additional and highly important aspect of training that reaches beyond the capabilities possessed by the individual man-machine combination. This is the process of *team training,* the requirement for which arises out of the many and varied interactions that characterize modern, highly complex systems in an ever-changing environment. Many operating functions of such systems and their subsystems are performed by teams, made up of people and machines whose activities must mutually support and modify each other in a coordinated fashion in the attainment of common goals.

The successful operation of teams in the accomplishment of system purposes characteristically begins with the assumption that individual skills pertaining to the operation of machines by men have already been learned. Training which is undertaken by providing systematically planned team exercises has the quite different function of optimizing the conduct of one or more system operations. As described in the present chapter, team training is viewed as leading to the discovery and employment of effective working procedures which govern the interaction of men with machines, machine procedures, and other persons who are parts of the system. It is possible for some of these working procedures to be specified as established functions, which can be written down as standing operating procedures. But many of them cannot be so described. These may be called emergent functions, since they come into being as the system meets new, unpredicted, or unanalyzed situations for which operational procedures must be developed.

While other techniques are also employed to optimize team procedures in system operations, team training is the method of primary importance to this effort. Here are described a number of kinds of changes in work procedures which can result from team training. They include such factors as orientation to the team's goals, interdependencies of individual actions, analysis of error, sensing overload, and several forms of adjustment to load and work flow. For psychologists interested in training, it is a challenge of some proportion to consider the ways in which principles of human learning might be made to serve the purposes of bringing about such modification in human behavior. An account is given here of how such team training effects can be studied within the framework of system exercises, and some suggestions are made of the types of concepts required to describe the results.

TEAM FUNCTIONS AND TRAINING

Robert Boguslaw
and Elias H. Porter

Generally speaking, the term *team* is used to describe a collection of human individuals who work together to achieve a common goal. We are familiar with football teams, basketball teams, and even combat teams. A new type of team is emerging in the enormously complex, computer-based systems of today. This type of team requires new perspectives.

To understand the operation of large systems, it is necessary to consider something more than the attributes of the human beings working within it. Machines, computer programs, and, more generally, *programs of interaction* which can be adopted to achieve a system goal are all involved in the analysis of team behavior. Of particular concern in the examination of this behavior is its relation to the attainment of goals and some of the ways it may be altered to achieve greater effectiveness. As Forrester (1958) emphasizes in his account of industrial dynamics, the various parts of a total industry, although apparently independent, are markedly interdependent. The responses of retailers, distributors, and wholesalers can have the cumulative effect of overloading a manufacturer or causing layoffs, even though the rate of sales by the retailers remains fairly constant. Mail-order houses are plagued by problems incident to the apparently simple process of filling orders. The launching of missiles involves the development of highly complex procedures by members of a team whose members may be only dimly aware of each other's existence. A nurse finds that providing services in a hospital depends upon the effective cooperation of many people, upon equipment, and upon a variety of administrative arrangements as well.

While it is possible to have a team perform its goal-directed activities by following fixed procedures, the programming of which is under the control of external instructions or of previous training, this can be done only under special conditions, which we shall discuss subsequently. The effective operation of complex man-machine systems requires that provision be made not simply for the development of individual skills but for the adaptation of a team, in a manner which will insure the acquisition and progressive modification of flexible work procedures.

Contemporary culture has much to say about the most effective methods for training drill teams, basketball teams, football teams, and the like. It has much less to say about how a team like that in an automobile factory can be trained, or even about what the training needs of such a team might be.

We shall attempt in this chapter to provide a definition of a team which will be appropriate to work units of varying sizes, composition, and goals. The functions and training requirements of teams will be considered in the light of system development and system operation. Following this, a distinction will be made between those modes of performance which are "established" and those appropriate to "emergent" system situations. Some of the factors which differentiate these two kinds of team activity will be described. Finally, we shall turn our attention to the important matter of methods of training relevant to these emergent situations.

▣ TEAMS, TEAM FUNCTIONS, AND TRAINING

The Meaning of Team

To those investigators of system operations who have worked closely with teams such as the Air Defense Command and the Strategic Air Command— large teams, to be sure—the term "team" carries with it certain connotations that are frequently overlooked. First of all, it is necessary to differentiate the term "team" from terms such as "group," "small group," "organization," "social system," and "society." These latter terms are ordinarily used to connote aggregates of human beings with varying but identifiable relationships; among these are relationships which may be simple or complex, close or remote, direct or indirect. Ordinarily, it is the relationship among members which is implied. It seems desirable, however, to use the term "team" to connote more than the relationship among people. It is used here to describe a relationship in which *people* generate and use *work procedures* to make possible their interactions with *machines, machine procedures,* and *other people* in the pursuit of system objectives.

Teams are contrived by men to accomplish certain goals. The relationships among men, work procedures, machines, and machine procedures have meaning for the team only to the extent that they contribute to or detract from the effective and reliable attainment of the goals.

What does this imply for the system developer? In his conceptualizations of systems he must include work procedures, machines, and machine procedures (such as computer programs) as "members" of the teams with which he is concerned. The rigidities and flexibilities of procedures, equipment, programs, and their interaction with each other will do much to influence the effective and reliable attainment of goals. Further, the system designer must be prepared to take into account the impact on the entire team of a change in any one of these members.

To illustrate, let us consider a very simple, yet not necessarily obvious, equipment change which altered team functioning. The old-fashioned ball of American football used to be much thicker than the football of today. The ball was made slimmer to make it easier to pass with accuracy. Obviously, this new dimension markedly altered the tasks to be performed by most team members. Defense against passing required skills which were clearly different from defense against a running attack. Moreover, the increased complexity of the game demanded emphasis upon the higher-order skill of flexible "programming." Players today must be faster in shifting their defense (or their offense) in response to the particular way in which a preprogrammed play in fact is developing.

In the RAND Corporation studies of air-defense crews (Chapman *et al.,* 1959) it was found that the ability of the crews to alter their work procedures resulted in their eventual capacity to handle with the same degree of efficiency loads up to four times greater than the work loads they could barely handle at the outset. This increase in efficiency of the team operation was undoubtedly due in part to increased motor effectiveness of individual crew members; however, the most significant increases were due to the development of new work procedures. New procedures in their turn introduced new relationships of man to man and man to equipment, as well as new conceptions of the tasks to be performed by men and equipment.

As the age of computers comes upon us, it becomes increasingly clear that machine procedures (in this case, computer programs) constitute a vital aspect of team operations. When man first picked up a club to defend himself, it was an extension of his arm and a hardening of his fist. The modern high-speed computer is an infinitely more complex extension of the human organism (compare Chapter 3). Already it is an extension of human memory and computational ability; soon it may be an extension of man's ability to conceptualize or to recognize complex patterns. With much of memory, computational procedures, thought, and perception delegated to machines and their procedures, the role of human beings in team efforts is substantially altered. But the greater the degree of delegation of these activities to machines, the more obvious it becomes that machines and machine procedures must be thought of as team members.

These examples help convince us that the word "team" should be used to encompass human beings, work procedures, machines, and machine procedures as they interact in contributing to, or detracting from, the accomplishment of the defined goals of a system or subsystem.

The Meaning of Team Functions

For many years social scientists have looked at groups, cultures, and societies and have asked, "What function does this specific behavior pattern fulfill?" "What is accomplished by this behavior?" Systematic research has revealed that patterns of behavior are associated with keeping the family intact, with assuring an adequate food supply, with controlling sexual behavior, with providing for marriage, and so on. Presumably all behavior patterns have an underlying motivation, if one can but see the functions they serve.

An informative example of this type of functional analysis of teams occurs in the case of the Naskapi Indians as reported by O. K. Moore (1957). To determine the direction in which to hunt for caribou, members of this tribe hold a specially cleaned and dried caribou shoulder blade over hot coals. As the heat causes cracks and burnt spots begin to appear, the hunter divines the direction and the landmarks of the hunt he is to make. What possible function can this behavior serve?

A scientist would not be apt to take at face value the spiritistic explanations offered by tribal members for this behavior. On the other hand, the scientist might be very much impressed when he stopped to consider that (1) caribou learn to avoid game trails which are hunted regularly; (2) human beings are very poor at generating random responses (being originally designed to develop habitual responses); and (3) the divination from the burnt shoulder blade is about as effective a randomizing device as one could devise. Never to let the caribou know where one is going to strike next serves a very useful function indeed.

Bearing in mind that teams, as we have defined them here, are contrived to achieve certain objectives, one can think of team functions as special purposes which contribute to the attainment of the team's objectives. Conversely, team dysfunctions may be conceived as special purposes which either do not contribute to the attainment of the team's objectives or which detract from them.

The act of divining from the burnt shoulder blade serves the function or special purpose of randomizing hunting behavior. A radar transmitter-receiver, the scope reader, and the plotter serve the function or special purpose of air surveillance. The advertising department, the sales department and the shipping department of a business establishment serve the function of marketing manufactured goods.

In the analysis of systems, it is important that the system designer identify the functions which are being served by the actions and behavior of team members. This identification of purposes being served, as opposed to a description of the system in terms of actions or procedures *per se,* is important for several reasons. First and foremost among these reasons is that in almost all (if not all) systems the same purposes could be served by a great variety of different team organizations and work procedures. Because this is true, a failure to perceive a function or a malfunction may lead the system designer to miss an opportunity to improve team performance. To the extent to which the system designer foresees the functions which the team is to fulfill, he increases the choices of team organization which could accomplish them. Of vital importance, too, is the fact that system performance cannot be adequately evaluated if its functions are not understood. Last, but not least, is the fact that unless the important team functions are understood clearly, the training of team members is apt to be unduly unrestricted, as we shall point out subsequently.

So much then for the meaning and significance of the term team functions. Let us now consider a definition of *team training.*

The Meaning of Team Training

It is possible to define team training, in the broadest sense, as any experience in which a team engages which results in a change of team function, team organization, or team performance. This definition is made possible because of the following factors: (1) man-machine systems or teams are contrived to reach certain goals such as profit making, defense of the nation, or the education of students; (2) our modern, complex man-machine teams encompass men, work procedures, machines, and machine procedures; and (3) team functions can be fulfilled by a variety of combinations of men, machines, work procedures, and machine procedures. Effective training will result in more efficient attainment of team goals. Put in other words, the evidence that a team has learned is in the changes or adaptations it makes as a result of experience. The experience may be a planned one, as in a training program; or it may occur in the course of team operation—that is, the team can learn from experience. Furthermore, teams, like individuals, can have some bad experiences and can learn some bad habits. The learning which occurs is manifest in changes in work procedures, changes in equipment, changes in machine procedures, and changes in operator proficiency.

It is important to note here that this definition of team training goes substantially beyond the current, generally accepted, concepts of team training. It does not limit itself to saying, "These are the machines in this system; these are the machine procedures in this system; these are the work procedures in this system; and the job is to teach the personnel about the machines, the machine procedures, and the work procedures, so they can make the system work as it is supposed to work." Perhaps the most serious shortcoming in traditional team training efforts is the acceptance of work procedures, machine procedures and machines as given. When attention is focused on functions, changes in machines, machine procedures, and work procedures assume a significance which is directly comparable with changes in operator proficiency.

An alternative approach to team training which stipulates that the work procedures are fixed (as well as the machines and machine procedures) leads to a definition of the training problem solely in terms of increasing crew proficiency in the fixed procedures. Such an approach may be referred to as component training because it focuses on the component (human, in this case) and disregards the interaction between components.

Improvement by Simple Machine Alteration

Let us consider here some ways in which teams acquire new and more effective interactive routines by simple alterations in machines and machine procedures. Although many machines are fixed in character, such factors as communications lines can often be altered with some dispatch. Simple displays which have profound implications for team behavior can sometimes be developed with ease. We shall describe some instances in which the addition of simple machines (in this case, displays) were of substantial assistance to efficient team operation, and the kind of interaction adaptation which was brought about in each case.

In air-defense exercises, it is not unusual for one defense sector to sight an aircraft headed for a target area in an adjacent sector before the adjacent sector is able to "paint" the aircraft on its own radar scope. If the first sector passes information to the second sector early enough, it will provide that second sector with additional early warning time. Where air defense has been automated, this function of providing early warning is taken care of by the machine. In the manual (by hand, not by machine) parts of the air-defense system, however, this function must be accomplished by human operators situated before plotting boards and connected by telephone lines to adjacent stations.

It would appear that the task of lateral telling of a threatening, unknown aircraft should be simplicity itself. It would be, if a lateral teller had only to relay information on one track. However, he may have several tracks that must be laterally told to two or more adjacent sectors. He may also be responding to a request from an adjacent sector for information about a specific track. He must search the plotting board for tracks that will need to be laterally told. In addition, when there are several tracks about which information needs to be told, he must make decisions as to which track or tracks are more important to good defense and which therefore require more frequent information passing as opposed to very little or infrequent information passing.

It is this decision-making aspect of lateral telling which is crucial, especially during conditions of heavy work load. As the necessity for varying the amount of energy spent on different tracks increases, so does the difficulty of remembering just what has been done with any one track. Opportunity for error arises.

A simple machine introduced to aid the lateral teller's memory consisted of a simple 14″×16″ column-and-row display board. The operator recorded in the extreme left column the designators of the tracks to be told, and in time-labeled columns to the right he simply made check marks to show when he had told a track. This display, in effect, "remembered" for the operator the actions he had taken on every track. He needed only to glance at any row to tell how much or how little telling of the track he had done and when he had last taken action.

An unexpected benefit to the team operation arose from the fact that not only did the display let the operator know how he himself was distributing his energies but it also let the operator's supervisor know how the operator was distributing his energies. Before the development of the display board, the supervisor could sense what the operator was doing only by monitoring the telephone line for a period of time or by studying a log book kept by the lateral teller. The display board made the lateral teller's functioning highly visible and thus enabled the supervisor to give timely instruction.

Consider next the rather profound system changes that transpired when Whyte (1948) introduced to the short-order restaurant industry the device known as the spindle or wheel, on which waitresses could place their written order checks. As Porter (1961) points out, the wheel first of all acts as a memory for the cook; he does not have to remember orders, the wheel does it for him. The wheel also acts as a buffer drum. The input rate and output rate need no longer be one-to-one. Ten waitresses may come to the wheel almost simultaneously, but the cook takes the orders one by one. The wheel also acts as a double queuing device. Waitresses no longer need to stand in line to put in their orders; the wheel stands in line for them. Moreover, the wheel does not get the orders mixed up, but keeps them in proper queue sequence. Finally, the wheel also serves as a display of all the information in the system at a given time. The cooks, by having random access to the information, are enabled to organize their work around larger work units, such as the simultaneous preparation of three or four similar orders. The fact that the order is recorded on a check, equally available to waitress and cook to check back upon when an error has been made, permits feedback and the consequent elimination of habitual errors.

Improvement in Work Procedures

Work procedures governing the *interaction among team members* may also undergo distinct improvement in effectiveness as a result of training within a system context. Let us consider here two examples of this type of event.

In a manual radar station, the scope reader "reads" the blips on the scope to the plotter. The scope reader, by telephone, announces to the plotter the azimuth, range, and speed of a track. Traditional individual training might be directed at having the scope reader attain greater accuracy and speed—that is, to seek principally to reduce time and error scores. Zero time and error scores, under certain circumstances, are highly desirable. Under other circumstances they are not. As far as the *team's* efficiency is concerned, it may literally make no difference whether the scope reader is highly accurate and rapid or slow and inaccurate, as long as the other team members can compensate. This is a concept that individual training doctrine cannot readily take into account.

At an air-defense sector, one scope reader was extremely skillful, highly accurate, and very fast. During a simulated exercise, a number of unknown aircraft, flying in formation, were coming in from the northwest. There were many other aircraft in the air as well. The scope reader was kept quite busy, even allowing for his high skill level. The senior director, seeing three high, fast tracks on the plotting board, and being advised that there were no flight plans for these aircraft, sent up an appropriate number of interceptors. The attacking aircraft turned out to be "hostile"; two of them broke through and completed their "bomb runs." Later, in the postexercise discussion period, the crew was informed by the training personnel that there had been five, not three, aircraft in the simulated hostile formation. The senior director asked the scope reader whether he had seen all five, or whether two of them had not shown up on the scope. The scope reader affirmed that he had seen and called all of them to the plotter. The plotter's reply when queried was, "Well, sir, sometimes he just calls them in so fast that I can't always be sure I get them all." At this point the scope reader said, "Gee, I didn't realize that at all. Look, let's do this. When I get to calling them too fast, you cut in on the line and let me know. I'll check the board and repeat any that you didn't get. That way we can make sure we get 'em all." For the first time, the scope reader realized that his job on the team was not a matter of being the best scope reader, but a matter of working with the plotter to maintain a complete, accurate, and timely display. Thus, through team training in an actual system exercise came the development of new interactive work procedures and new programs of interaction within each of the individuals participating.

It may be thought that the need for working together is so obvious as to require no training. However, experience indicates that training methods which emphasize only the individual skills far too often develop such attitudes as, "I can't help it if he can't keep up with me. It's not my fault." The extensive implications of such a dysfunctional attitude are illustrated by the behavior of a senior director at one of the air-defense sectors during a simulated exercise. When a sector "goes off the air" by reason of some disablement, the adjacent sectors take over responsibility for predesignated parts of the disabled sector. In this particular case, the senior director found himself in a tight spot. He had but one interceptor left to scramble. Coming in over the ocean was an unknown aircraft, clearly in the "take-over" area of the adjacent sector which had gone off the air. Coming at him from inland was a second unknown, clearly in his own sector. Despite the fact that an inbound, unknown aircraft is substantially the more threatening, the senior director scrambled after the aircraft in his own sector.

As it developed, the aircraft coming from inland was a friendly aircraft, which had been erroneously reported as unknown. The aircraft coming in over water was a hostile aircraft that completed its bomb run. When the operations officer at division headquarters telephoned to the site to inquire why a friendly aircraft was scrambled on and a hostile aircraft left unmolested, the answer was, "I'm responsible for what happens in my sector. If we're able, we help out Dixie [code name for the disabled sector], but I had only one interceptor left and I had to look after my sector first." Such an attitude exhibits an admirable loyalty, but fails to accomplish the task of air defense. As a result of it, the senior director had a one-trial learning experience. He learned that his job was a matter of defending against threatening aircraft, and not simply of defending his sector.

So much then for the meaning of team training. A team consists of men, hardware, and procedures. All are subject to adaptation to the task as a result of experience.

▣ FUNCTIONS IN ESTABLISHED AND EMERGENT TEAM SITUATIONS

In considering the variety of system operations in which teams may engage, it appears desirable to distinguish a continuum of situations in which action can occur. One pole of this continuum consists of established situations; the other pole consists of emergent situations. An *established* situation is one in which (1) all action-relevant *environmental conditions* are specifiable and predictable, (2) all action-relevant *states of the system* are specifiable and predictable, and (3) available research technology or records are adequate to provide statements about the *probable consequences* of alternative actions. An *emergent* situation is one in which (1) all action-relevant environmental conditions have *not* been specified, (2) the state of the system does *not* correspond to relied-upon predictions, (3) analytic solutions are *not* available, given the current state of analytic technology (Boguslaw, 1961).

It is clear that a specific team may be called upon to deal with situations which vary along the entire length of this continuum. Team functions for established situations are tentatively planned for in the design of a system and are predictable at specific probability levels for varying states of system operation and environmental conditions. They include (1) the jobs assigned to the men and machines of the system, and (2) the agreed upon procedures for getting these jobs done. Team functions for emergent situations are frequently ignored on the formal level, although usually anticipated informally by experienced personnel. They include the actions which must be taken when communication channels unexpectedly fail, the procedures which must be followed to deal with an unanticipated input or threat or an operational crisis—for none of which are there "standard" or "book" answers, but which must be dealt with on the basis of adaptation to an immediate situation.

Predicting Functions for Teams

How does one formulate a comprehensive list of the established functions in a given system design? It seems essential that this is done prior to the initial operations date, and certainly it must be done if adequate training is to be accomplished. And yet it appears quite unlikely, in any given large-scale system, that a truly comprehensive list of system functions will be prepared; the reason is that not enough different perspectives will be used in solving the problem, or possibly that one perspective will be overemphasized. Let us consider some of these perspectives. Each perspective characteristically starts from a basic fact and exploits the body of knowledge which has grown up around the basic fact. Often the perspectives will overlap to some degree, yet each will have its individual, unique features.

The Human-Organism Perspective. It is a fact that men are limited in much of what they can do by reason of their physiological make-up. Human engineering, as a field, has grown up in answer to the need to fit the job to the man (compare McCormick, 1957). One would expect the human engineer to attend most closely to the interface between the machine and the man. The adequacy of displays and the ease of accurate response would be matters of central concern. Input rates, response times, and physiological demands all would receive special attention.

The Bureaucratic Perspective. Duties must be apportioned among the people who operate a system. There must be order, and there must be means provided for the resolution of conflicting demands between areas or functions. One would expect that this point of view would be most closely concerned with chains of authority, with the allocation of authority, and with the allocation of responsibilities (compare March and Simon, 1958, pp. 36–47).

The Interpersonal Perspective. People are known to exert influence upon one another. In some systems, a great deal of attention will be given to interpersonal relations. The vast literature on small-group research holds many implications for the relevance of interpersonal relations in system performance. The documentation of direct effects which interpersonal relations have upon productivity has a long history, which first achieved prominence with the Hawthorne Studies (Roethlisberger and Dickson, 1939). This prominence has been continued by the approach of the so-called human-relations school to problems of industrial productivity (Mayo, 1933, 1947a, 1947b). Related to these concerns are those regarding the flow of information in a system. To whom, at what rate, and in what order information should flow will loom as central issues in this viewpoint.

The System-Model or System-Engineering Perspective. The advent of operations research has formalized a somewhat different perspective. The fulfillment of any function has its cost in time, money, people, hardware, and the like. Operations researchers will want to examine the system to help achieve minimax solutions: minimum costs for maximum gains (Churchman, Ackoff, and Arnoff, 1957).

Several Perspectives. Other writers might well add to this list of perspectives, or even categorize them differently. The major point to be made, however, is that the experts in system design all too often bring to their work a singleness of perspective, while what is needed is to bring to bear many perspectives on the problems of system design from the very outset.

This involvement of many perspectives is probably most important in the design of today's large-scale systems. Consider, for illustrative purposes, the problems which face modern military systems. The advances in weaponry are so rapid and so bizarre that one cannot be certain of what a command and control system currently being designed will ultimately have to deal with. Adding to the difficulty, of course, is the fact that if our weaponry and control systems are "good enough," presumably they will never have to be used, since they will provide "deterrence." And if they are never used, no one will learn from experience whether or not the systems were effective. But in case they should have to be used, it seems wise to make certain that they are usable.

Consider again the short-order restaurant. The physiological perspective would contribute to better system design by looking at such factors as the perceptual distinctness of printing on the menu, the symbology used on the checks, the lighting, the air conditioning, the physical layout, and the flow of work. The bureaucratic perspective would consider problems of delegation of responsibility, working hours, wages, benefits, employment policies, and so on. The interpersonal-relations perspective would consider the impact of employment policies on employees and on supervisory relations, the handling of customers during rush hours, the distribution of work between old hands and new employees, and a thousand and one other status problems. The system-engineering perspective might well be concerned with the inventory problems involved, and seek a minimax solution which would involve the optimum amount of money tied up in supplies and equipment. It might also concern itself with the system design under conditions of overload. It would ask how the design would handle queuing, error, and omission problems. It would trace the "information" from its printed form on the menu through its verbal form as spoken by the customer, its written form as scribbled by the waitress, its display form on the spindle, its form as food, its form as money in the till, and so on through its total process. No doubt there are other perspectives in which team functions can be viewed. The more complicated the system, the more its design would seem to require a variety of perspectives.

Emergent Functions

In complex systems, characteristically, not all necessary situations will be foreseen or subject to *a priori* analysis. Every system will need methods for dealing with *emergent* situations. There are five major methods available to organizations for dealing with these situations: (1) the selection and use of managerial personnel, (2) the selection and use of equipment and facilities, (3) the formulation of policy guides, (4) the improvement of system analysis and computer technologies, and (5) team training.

Selection of a Manager. When an organization must deal with unpredictable events, and before the organization has had much experience with the events, the most common method adopted is to put a good man on the job; in other words, *to select and use a good manager.* He may not know what to expect and therefore have no ready answers, but his chief value is that he can see problems as they arise. To do this effectively, he must of necessity understand the organization's goals and the functions which must be served. Knowing only the organization's work procedures is not enough. This would tend to lead him to be restrictive in his answers; that is, there would be a marked tendency for him to see new events more or less as items to be fitted into established procedures. Understanding the organization's goals broadens his horizons and permits greater flexibility in his selection of custom-made work procedures.

Obvious examples of dealing with emergent functions through the selection and utilization of personnel include the State Department's use of ambassadors; industry's use of branch-office managers; and the use of local command responsibility in the armed forces. In successfully managed organizations, it is probable that top managements anticipate critical established functions and delegate to others responsibility for meeting them, while retaining responsibility for dealing with the emergent situations.

Selection of Equipment and Facilities. A second major method available to systems for dealing with emergent situations is the *selection of equipment and facilities.* For example, the selection of one computer rather than another for use in a system leads to the solution of future problems along distinctive lines which depend upon the specific characteristics of the computer that has been selected.

An example of planning the equipment in anticipation of emergent situations is found in the design of chemical manufacturing plants. Design engineers determine the theoretical capacity of the equipment and then deliberately add a 50 percent increase in input-output capacity, because experience has taught them that human operators will sooner or later devise ways to make the equipment exceed its theoretical capacity.

Formulation of Policy Guides. When a class of problems has been experienced over time by an organization, it becomes possible to formulate *policy guides.* A policy guide describes a type of problem, specifies the values and interest to be protected, and relates these values and interests to the organization's basic goals. The ostensible purpose of a policy guide is to aid people in dealing with all occurrences. In practice, it characteristically attempts to provide an action rule for each event. Thus, what is intended as a policy guide often becomes in fact a set of work procedures. Since, however, many events have not in fact been anticipated or predicted, many critical situations which actually do occur have no rule specified. It is for these emergent situations that a policy rather than a procedure is required.

Technology of System Analysis. A fourth method of dealing with emergent functions is through improvements in the *technology of system analysis* and in the technology of computer use. Christie (1956) points out that recent advances in these technologies are literally crying out to be used. To illustrate this, he notes that outmoded concepts of analyzing systems' needs lead to the building of more and more highways as practically the sole answer to the problem of traffic congestion, especially in urban areas. Updated system analysis techniques would uncover the dynamics of traffic flow. Computer technology could readily apprehend these dynamic changes and alter traffic-control signals to correspond wtih load and rate changes when and where they occur. It is the uncovering of relevant information and its timely handling that constitutes the fourth avenue for coping with emergent functions. Improvements in these technologies are being incorporated extensively in the design of modern military command and control systems.

Team Training. A fifth method of dealing with emergent functions is through *team training.* This we shall discuss in the following section.

▣ TEAM TRAINING TECHNOLOGIES

When one deals with established situations, many training techniques are available. There are all the conventional individual and group instructional procedures, such as classroom lectures and audio-visual methods. A rapid exploitation of teaching machines and simulators may be expected in the immediate future. On the other hand, severe problems are encountered when an attempt is made to adapt customary training procedures to the needs of team training as defined here. The tendency is strong in our culture to feel that if every man does his job, all will go well, and therefore all a man needs to know is how to do his job and to leave the next man's job to the next man. But training for effective team performance, even in established situations, should incorporate a number of additional considerations, which we shall attempt to describe here.

Orientation to Team Goals

While they may be expected to vary a great deal from one organization to the next, and from one level of job to another, the team's goals should be "spelled out" in every possible way. Illustration after illustration should be presented to show the consequences of errors to the team's output. (By consequences is not meant an evaluation of the team's performance as good or bad or right or wrong, but of the events which transpire subsequent to, and as a result of, an error.)

Let us consider for the moment a case in which cashiers were trained to disburse money to people on public relief. The standard work procedures consisted of receiving from the indigent person a form filled out and signed by a social worker, specifying that a payment of a certain amount was to be made. The money was disbursed, the form was stamped "Paid," initials were affixed, and the form was given over to the bookkeeper—simple and easy. But the work pressures were great: the indigents never felt they were getting enough money; they had just come from unsuccessful arguments with the social worker; they continued to press their case; the cashiers found themselves faced with situations over which they had no control; and occasionally an overpayment or an extra payment was made in error.

At intervals, the supervisor pointed out to the cashiers that they had made errors and admonished them to be more careful. They made the effort, and errors decreased for a time. This is a typical (although inadequate) training procedure, and had its typical results.

Finally, the supervisor called all the cashiers together and explained to them the consequences of an error. An overpayment or an extra payment starts a chain of events; as a public agency, the welfare agency has to account for every cent; when an overpayment is made, an effort must be made to recover it; someone must draw an interagency car and track down the indigent. Since the indigent does not feel he is getting enough money to meet his needs anyway, it is very rare that any money can be recovered; therefore, the matter goes to the legal department; the legal department must go to court with a suit against the indigent and obtain a judgment against him; the judgment can then be entered in the books, and the books can be balanced. The cost of an error of a few dollars runs into hundreds of dollars and results in very poor public relations. As an outcome of this explanation, some work procedures were changed. Errors decreased markedly, and the error rate stayed at a very low level. Understanding the consequences of error produced a significant change in the perspective of each of the cashiers. No longer were they simply disbursing funds; they were preventing expensive legal bills, preventing an indigent from public embarrassment, and preventing the agency from getting a bad name.

Training in Interdependencies

In organizations where the work flow is broken down into units of work (such as scope reading, plotting, movement identification, and so on) there will be interdependent relations between the team members. These interdependencies are seldom obvious from a chart of the work flow. As a consequence, they are seldom incorporated into training curricula; yet they are often the source of serious team errors. An example of such interdependence was described previously in the case of the scope reader who read plots to the plotter at too rapid a rate, resulting in a seriously inaccurate display of vital information.

In one air defense crew it was discovered that the senior director was placing great emphasis on the rapid identification of tracks. The movements-identification operator was not only very competent but highly motivated. The team, however, was making a high proportion of scrambles on friendly aircraft. It seemed that the movements-identification operator was not being very efficient; observation of his behavior, however, indicated a high degree of efficiency. He was exceptionally fast at his work—so fast, it was finally discovered, that whenever the plotter made one little misplot, an interceptor went up. This happened because the movements-identification man immediately reported a track to be uncorrelated with a flight plan, thereby virtually requiring the senior director to declare it unknown and scramble an interceptor in short order. The movements-identification operator learned that his effective performance was indeed a matter of working with the plotter to check for possible misplots, rather than simply accepting the information displayed.

Such examples emphasize the importance of the idea that in training personnel for operations, the facts of interdependency should be incorporated into the curriculum and given appropriate stress.

Training for Error Analysis

One of the most difficult skills to train, yet one of the most important skills in dealing with team functions, is skill in the analysis of one's own errors. For most of us, training in the notion that errors are bad and should be avoided began at home, was carried on in school, and continued in our workaday life. Most of us, in order to avoid the negative consequences of an error, have developed splendidly efficient methods of covering them up and denying really having made them. The most popular of these methods is to find someone or something to take the blame. This tendency to push errors aside may be a splendid device for protecting the ego, but it is employed at the cost of *not* learning how to avoid the error in the future.

The process of learning to deal with errors in a team situation appears to have some clearly identifiable stages. The first stage has already been mentioned: blaming errors on others. It is not at all uncommon to see the blaming behavior shift its focus from events or people quite distant geographically or in time ("It's the way those guys in the other department do things!" "That's the way my folks trained me!") to events or people in close proximity ("The machine didn't work right!" "He didn't tell me in time!").

It would appear that if others, especially supervisors, can seriously accept these statements, not as excuses to be ridiculed or brushed aside, but as honest efforts to explain what happened, many people will soon give up blaming errors on others and will enter the second stage, that of beginning to accept blame themselves.

Obviously, blaming oneself rather than others does not by itself lead to reduced team errors—but it is a step in the right direction, since it is clear evidence of a lessened defensiveness. When they accept the error maker as a person of integrity, as a person who is seriously trying to uncover reasons for errors, supervisors are rewarding objectivity and avoiding the reinforcement of covering-up behavior.

A third stage is apparent when a person achieves the insight that it is really not important that blame for an error be fixed on someone or something; rather, that it is important to find a way to avoid the error in the future. When a person achieves this stage of nondefensiveness, he is open to exploration of alternative work procedures. More often than not, he is now free to learn what *not* to do under certain circumstances as well as what *to* do.

The fourth stage of learning seems to be characterized largely by a shift in perception of the job. Rather than being seen as a set of established functions for which there are fixed work procedures, the job is perceived as a situation in which an emergent function can arise at any moment to demand a departure from the fixed work procedures. It is almost as though the learner accepted established work procedures as best working hypotheses, rather than as rigid rules. At this stage of learning, he is able to shift procedures at will in order to test a new way of proceeding. He can face the prospect of making errors because he can learn from them.

It does not appear possible at the present time to specify with precision the means of inducing this type of learning. Nevertheless, training personnel need to be as sensitive as they can to this area of skill or attitude development and to foster it when they can. It is conceivable that it would help to present trainees with numerous unusual situations which cannot be handled by simple adherence to standard operating procedures but which call for the application of a policy guide. Problem-solving discussions (rather than didactic presentations) might well help trainees to gain a problem-solving attitude.

Training for Sensing Overload

It is not infrequent in a team operation for one or more operators to be overloaded. When an operator is overloaded, errors of commission, errors of omission, and time delays are bound to occur. It becomes important that the operator learn to put aside the tendency to be a hero by trying to handle the entire job. He must learn *when* he is reaching the point of being overloaded and when to call for help. At the same time, other operators must learn to sense when a team member is nearing an overload condition and be prepared to watch closely for situations in which errors occur and for which they can take compensatory action.

During an air-defense system training exercise at one radar direction center, the team was given a very heavy load problem. After a period of time, the scope readers and plotters were "all fouled up." For the period of several minutes that were required for the surveillance officer to untangle the confusion, the senior director and the movements-identification operator took over the surveillance officer's normal duties in addition to their own. They were unable to do so for long, but they could manage it for just long enough. They had sensed the surveillance officer's state of overload and responded productively to it. A characteristic response in a conventionally trained team might have consisted of an attitude colloquially expressed in the statement, "Tough—but it wasn't *our* fault."

Training in Adjustment Mechanisms

When a team is overloaded, it may make adjustments of various types. The team may so operate as to permit *queuing;* that is, it lets things wait, or stack up, for a time. Restaurants have waiting lines; long-distance operators quote time delays; airplanes wait in line to take off.

The team may engage in *omissions;* that is, it may not accept all the usual inputs to the system. A factory accepts no new orders; a restaurant accepts no one who does not have a reservation; the telephone lines give a busy signal.

The team may so operate as to *commit errors;* that is, it permits certain errors to take place. The mail-order house finds it faster not to double-check all orders; the waitress brings relish, a tomato slice, and lettuce with your hamburger, whether it has been ordered or not; the telephone company permits people to dial wrong numbers rather than jam up the service by routing all calls through operators.

Another adjustment which may be adopted is *filtering;* that is, the team processes some inputs before it processes others. Special-delivery mail goes out of the post office first; customers are called from the restaurant waiting line in terms of the size of the party and the size of the most recently vacated table; the long-distance operator accepts only emergency messages.

The adjustment may be that of *approximating;* that is, a condensed message or a best guess may be sent. An observer reports a flight of "several" aircraft; the mail-order house sends the next-closest color of a dress; the restaurant hostess seats two unrelated customers at the same table.

The team may operate so as to increase the *number of channels* of work flow. The post office puts on extra men at Christmastime; decision making is delegated to lower levels of the organization; the telephone company switches in extra circuits.

The operation may involve the adjustment of *chunking;* that is, the team may reduce the number of categories of identification, using broad categories only. The postal clerk sorts only into local and out-of-city mail; the restaurant menu asks patrons to order by a number which designates the whole meal; the stock market report states that industrials are up while utilities are down.

And finally, the team may operate in such a way as to *escape;* that is, it may quit trying to handle the situation. The fire fighters abandon a hillside to the flames; the police cordon collapses; the student stops studying and goes to the movies.

Although at the date of this writing there is no published material available on the topic, Miller[1] has reported that his staff has conducted a number of experiments in which team members were trained in the theory of the adjustment mechanisms (except for escape) and subsequently performed significantly better on a laboratory task. Some imaginative applications of these concepts to operations training curricula may be expected to prepare operators to withstand greater periods of task overload and, in addition, to meet the demands of emergent situations with greater ease.

Training for Emergent Situations

So far in this discussion of team training technologies, the focus has been on the need for training in certain skills and attitudes necessary to effective team functioning which ordinarily are not provided by most of the broad range of training devices and technologies (compare Chapter 10). These skills and attitudes are those which must be brought into play primarily when the team is nearing or actually experiencing conditions of information overload.

It is probably not economical to try to train for these skills and attitudes in any more than a rudimentary manner in schools prior to assignment of personnel to particular jobs in particular locations of particular systems at

---

[1] Miller, James G., University of Michigan, Ann Arbor, Michigan; personal communication.

particular times. The reasons are twofold. On the one hand it would be next to impossible to anticipate and incorporate into a curriculum the multiple uniquenesses to be found at the many individual job settings, even though the importance of training for these uniquenesses is openly acknowledged. Traditionally, this particularized training is left for on-the-job training (OJT). Secondly, the time lags are great between changes in the environment of a system, the system's adjustment to the changes, and the incorporation of the changes into a school curriculum. To expect curriculum planners to foresee the changes in the system's environment and to foresee the changes which the system would make in adjustment to the changes would be to expect too much. For these reasons, then, the conversion of an individual operator into an effective team member is inherently the final responsibility of system operation.

Much can be done to heighten operator and team effectiveness by well-conducted OJT. It should be noted, however, that OJT is characteristically designed and conducted to train operators in functions which are clearly established. OJT in narrowly defined individual tasks is not calculated to train operators or teams to become effective agents for sensing the problems created by changes in a system's environment. It is normally not addressed to the problem of training operators or teams to become effective agents in changing work procedures, equipment, and equipment procedures, to meet the problems created by environmental changes. For an understanding of a training technology which does train for continuing adaptation to emerging functions, we must turn to the system training technology as described in Chapter 13, or as otherwise described by Biel (1958) and Goodwin (1957).

At the time this chapter is being written, system training is being conducted solely within military organizations. These organizations are complex, and they use equipment and procedures quite unfamiliar to most readers. Since it is often difficult to understand the training technology when it is described in terms of unfamiliar activities and procedures, the discussion of system training technology which follows is embedded in a system with which almost every reader has had experience.

▣ DESIGNING SYSTEM TRAINING

The system chosen as the vehicle for illustration of how system training technology is applied and how it operates is one that occurs in a public elementary school. The training need chosen for illustration is the need of the team members—pupils, teachers, administrators and maintenance personnel—to meet such emergencies as a fire or an explosion in the school building. As the reader proceeds, a helpful exercise would be to generalize from this discussion how the technology might be applied to other systems such as hospitals, airlines, telephone companies, railroads, or department stores, or to any other systems with which he has had enough experience to understand the structure, operations, and problems. With this enjoinder in mind, let us proceed to the illustration of system training technology.

Most readers are familiar with methods of emergency drill training in common use. A schedule for drills is established in the superintendent's office and is sent out to the schools. At the appointed time (unannounced to the children) the principal simultaneously sounds the alarm and starts a stop watch. The children drop what they are doing, form in colums of twos, march out the prescribed corridors to the prescribed doors, and march to a prescribed location.

One can envision how inadequate this training might be in the face of certain disrupting events, such as an exploding boiler, a fire, an aircraft plunging into the building, a runaway truck crashing into one of the rooms. Corridors might be aflame or filled with smoke. Stairwells might be blocked with debris. Some children might be injured and able to move only with assistance or not at all. Some classes might be able to use a stairwell at one moment, only to find it impassable a moment later. In other words, the team members—pupils, teachers, administrators, and maintenance personnel—are suddenly confronted with an unpredicted environmental condition, an unpredicted system state, and conditions for which tested solutions in the form of procedures are not available.

The major phases in the application of system training technology consist of identifying the kinds of environment and system states which could occur; developing techniques of simulating emergency situations; providing practice in dealing with such emergencies under simulated conditons; and providing knowledge of results in connection with this practice.

Identifying Training Environments

To determine what types of environment could be simulated in which practice is needed, detailed information must be assembled. Official reports of various school disasters could be collected and summarized. Fire-department recommendations to schools could likewise be collated. Reports of safety experts could be gathered and studied. A team of safety experts, experienced fire officials, police officials, insurance underwriters, architects, engineers, and teachers could be called in to study the reports, in an effort to isolate those emergency situations most likely to occur, and those emergency situations most likely to involve stress on each of the functions for which training is needed.

Experience with system training demonstrates that not all possible environmental conditions can or need to be simulated. There are restrictions in the cost of simulation, and it seems that there are limits in the need for extensity of simulation. For example, there seems to be no reason to think that one would need to simulate a fire breaking out in every possible location at a school, but there would be a need to simulate fires at a reasonable variety of the most probable locations.

Let us presume for the moment that a given school has been found to be vulnerable, among other things, to fire in a closet under a wooden stairwell. Consultations with fire experts reveal that the following sequence of events might be expected were a fire to start in the closet at ten o'clock in the morning:[2]

10:00   Spontaneous combustion takes place.
10:08   Smoke appears under closet door and at edges of the door.
10:15   Last possible moment that closet door could be opened by someone in erect posture without injury by flames.
10:16   Wisps of smoke begin to seep from under stair steps.
10:20   Flames appear at edge of closet door.
10:23   Flames have broken through closet ceiling and are beginning to burn stairway steps.
10:24   Wire to fire-alarm system destroyed; fire alarm impossible.
10:26   Heavy smoke fills stairwell and second-floor corridors.
10:30   Heavy smoke fills all second- and third-floor corridors.
10:32   Stairwell in open flames but still passable.
10:36   Stairwell no longer passable.
10:38   Flames race across second floor.
10:43   All stairwells to second and third floors cut off by impassable flames and lethal heat; escape possible only through exterior windows.

What would happen in a real-life situation, of course, would depend on such factors as the time when the fire was discovered, the time it was reported to the principal's office, the time the fire department was called, the time the fire alarm was sounded, and the appropriateness of any actions to the conditions at the moment. An exit might be available to first-floor classes but be blocked to second-floor and third-floor classes. Alternative routes might be necessary, but the people who would need to select them might have no way of knowing whether they were opened or closed.

Clearly, the training need is far beyond that of learning to march in orderly columns of twos to a designated space. In real disasters, some children will panic and, upon reaching the safety of the outdoors, will run for home. Parents and curiosity seekers will crowd around the school. Police will form in cordons. Hours and perhaps days may be needed to restore order.

Let us now consider how a suitable training problem might be designed, produced and run for such a public school disaster.

Functions in Which Training Is Needed.   First, one would ask: for what team functions is training needed and what priorities does each have? Let us suppose that this has been discussed, and that these functions have been settled upon with the priorities listed:

---

[2] The events listed are deliberately distorted here for purposes of illustration. For an accurate description of how fires develop, the reader is referred to *Operation School Burning,* National Fire Protection Association, 60 Batterymarch Street, Boston 10, Mass. 1959. This book reports on the results of test fires in a three-story school building.

1. saving human life;
2. averting property damage;
3. saving records and supplies;
4. maintaining order outside of the building.

It is important that these functions be identified and assigned priorities, since they will determine the correctness or suitability of actions taken by the trainees. Just how this is done will become apparent when postexercise discussions are considered.

Determining the Training Strategy.   Having determined the functions to be trained and the types of environmental conditions and systems states to be simulated, there then arises a need for designing a specific exercise and determining the training strategy.

Let us first consider the training strategy. If one has chosen the fire-in-the-closet problem, it seems probable that one would not want to present the problem with elaborate simulation to a group of children who are having their first system training experience, since panic might result. Because trainees have to learn how to learn from simulated experiences, one would want to work out a training strategy. Simulation might well be very simple and symbolic (as, for example, by using a sign that reads, "It is very smoky here") at the onset, and might advance toward complexity and realism over a period of time. The training expert designing the problem would of necessity work out the training strategy with the parents and the teachers—the people who know best what the children can accept.

Constraints on the Design of Problems.   It is obvious that the design of the problem, the complexity and extent of reality being simulated, will in part be determined by the training strategy. The age of the children, the frequency of training deemed necessary by the school officials, and the newness to the children of the type of problem, will all be involved.

Other constraints will be met as efforts are made to increase the reality of simulation. Just how smoke can be simulated without toxic effects might require some ingenious solution by a chemical engineer. A lighting expert might solve the problem of simulating flames. Some excellent solutions to simulation problems might be dropped because of their direct or indirect costs. To simulate smoke from an expanding fire, for example, might demand the installation of an elaborate system of pipes and valve controls, and the school board might find it necessary to settle for less verisimilitude. At the same time, the training expert might feel that such a decrease in realism would not materially affect the major lessons to be learned.

As a given group of children in a given school progresses, it will become clear that its training requirements will change. The children cannot learn everything at once. As proficiency in saving their lives increases, there will evolve requirements for training in what to do when they get outside. The needs which are foremost will be an additional factor to be considered in the design of a specific problem.

It is quite possible to imagine a problem in which a simulated disaster has already occurred and all the children are out in the street or yard. The training task might well be practice in getting out of the way of oncoming fire engines, of finding distraught parents, and of providing aid to the injured.

As the training needs of the school children change, the training needs of the community evolve. If fire is simulated, fire-department personnel may wish to participate in the exercise. If fire-department personnel start rolling fire trucks up to a school, crowds will gather. The police department may wish to use the opportunity for the purpose of permitting their own personnel to get experience with handling crowds or to pass out pamphlets telling onlookers how they hamper emergency efforts. Red Cross units may wish to simulate the setting up of emergency units. Hospitals may wish to participate for the purpose of testing their disaster plans.

The Problem of Cost. The costs involved in such exercises can vary over a wide range. The direct costs of some simulated events could be predicted with great accuracy. Less predictable would be costs arising indirectly from the degraded emergency posture of the fire department and the police department. There would be costs in the loss of educational time. In the final analysis, well-run training exercises would certainly exceed the cost of simply marching children out of a building.

The Training Team. When a problem has been designed and is ready to be run, the training team must be prepared. This is the unit which will contain observers and umpires. All results which are critical in terms of the functions being trained must be recorded. For example, in the fire-in-the-closet problem an observer-umpire stationed near the closet would observe and record the time and action of anyone who does or could take any action with regard to the smoke coming from the closet.

To record appropriate events, observer-umpires would need to know the problem design in advance and to have discussed thoroughly the consequences of the probable actions that might occur at their observation points. Additionally, they would need forms on which to record their observations quickly. The recording of observations should not be allowed to interfere with observing or umpiring.

Announcing the Exercise. The presence in the school building of the observer-umpires would very soon come to be a tip-off to the children that an exercise was imminent. This is a matter of no concern, since the children should be informed that an exercise will be held, but should not be told when or what type of emergency will be simulated.

There are two principal reasons for informing the children that an exercise will be held. First, it is desirable that the children be aware of the actions they are taking and that they think about their actions as they perform them. The training is aimed at developing a thoughtful and informed response rather than an uninformed, emotional response to emergencies. The second reason for announcing the exercise is to avoid panic. Panic could possibly ensue in the face of realistic simulation, were children not prepared for it either by knowledge of the exercise or by training.

Postexercise Discussion.   The conclusion of the exercise is the time to provide knowledge of results to the trainees, and in this operation a number of factors are of fundamental importance. At any one critical point in some problems, a number of different responses may be entirely adequate in terms of the purposes which must be served. If the situation develops somewhat differently, some of the responses may not be adequate while others, entirely new or previously inadequate, may now be adequate. In other words, there may be a number of correct responses at a critical point, but what is correct in one circumstance may be incorrect in another. Because of this circumstance, the discussion of these points should be focused on the consequences of actions as taken and on the probable consequences of alternative actions which might have been taken. Praising and faultfinding should be avoided, as should any effort to teach proper alternative action. Put another way, the discussion leaders should avoid using psychological techniques which tend to produce habitual responses. Rather, the discussion leaders should use those psychological techniques which tend to produce a correctly structured cognitive map, a knowledge of what actions result in what consequences under what conditions, in view of the necessary purposes which are to be served.

On the other hand, where a situation demonstrably has a single best response and this can be specified, the discussion leaders should capitalize on any psychological device which will help make a correct response automatic. An example of such a single best response is that of having children dive under their tables in the event of a sudden, brilliant flash of light as would occur in an atomic explosion. This presumably is the best response they can make under such circumstances.

Another problem for the trainers is to be found in the mechanics of setting up the discussion groups. Should children be handled separately from the teachers? Should all persons assemble in one location? Should the breakdown of groups be by home rooms?

The answers to these questions are not fixed at this point in the technology; perhaps they never will be. It seems most probable that they will vary by necessity. The best guide lines that can be suggested at this point are (1) to avoid attaching significance to any particular size of group as being an optimum size for a discussion group, and (2) to form the discussion groups around those individuals who, by the nature of the problem and how it unfolds, are more directly involved, have more to contribute, and can profit most from a detailed discussion. If the problem unfolds in such a way, for example, that the chief difficulty is in communication among the janitorial and teaching staffs, it seems pointless to involve the children in postexercise discussion. On the other hand, if the principal difficulty arose because the children were noisy and orders could not be heard, one might judge it best to deal with the children in small, intimate groups. Or, should the action taken by a single child turn out to be the most crucial event in the problem, possibly a short assembly presentation might be judged most effective and economical.

One final point relates to postexercise discussions. Chapman (1960) points out that in the RAND Corporation System Research Laboratory studies, marked improvements in crew performance at times followed postexercise discussions in which no apparent problem-solving behavior took place. These sessions seemed to follow problems which the crew believed they had handled poorly. The postexercise discussion periods were characterized by complaints and gloom. Porter (1950) notes a similar phenomenon in psychotherapeutic interviews. The implication is that the learning process possesses at time a strong emotional component. Porter (1961) attributes this type of behavior to the process of learning how to learn, and points out that the success of a postexercise discussion cannot be judged solely on the intellectual problem solving which takes place during the period. A second implication arises for the discussion leaders; they should be prepared to handle the emotional content of a discussion as well as the intellectual.

▣ A RESEARCH PERSPECTIVE

A recent commentary on small-group research, made by a distinguished researcher (Borgatta, 1960, p. 180), notes the enormous amount of "waste type" publication which seems to occur in this field. He points out that thousands of articles have been published on sociometric tests, projective tests, social perception and learning. The implication is clear that while much has been said, most publications on these topics have contributed little of practical usefulness to system designers.

Others have observed that the vast majority of studies directed toward increasing the efficiency of team performance and developing a greater understanding of the way small groups function have not been particularly relevant for improving the performance of typical working teams (Glanzer and Glaser, 1961; Klaus and Glaser, 1960).

Criticism of research as "not significant" seems to be most cogent when an emergent situation is studied as if it were an established situation. Conversely, criticism of theoretical investigations as "not true" is most cogent when an established situation is studied as if it were emergent (Boguslaw, 1961).

It is clear that research programs must avoid errors of both types if progress is to be made in improving our ability to increase the effectiveness of teams. Frequently this is done through research specialization in studies of established situations, on the one hand, or emergent situations, on the other. For example, a program of research at the Team Training Laboratory of the American Institute for Research seems to be concerned primarily with established situations. A report describing this program finds it convenient to differentiate between the terms *team* and *small group*.

According to the definition used in this program, teams (which represent the focal interest) generally:

1. are relatively rigid in structure, organization, and communication networks;
2. have well-defined positions or member assignments so that participation in a given task by each individual can be anticipated to a given extent;
3. depend on the cooperative or coordinated participation of several specialized individuals whose activities contain little overlap and who must each perform their task at least at some level of minimum proficiency;
4. are often involved with equipment or tasks requiring perceptual-motor activities;
5. can be given specific guidance on job performance based on a task analysis of the team's equipment, mission or situation.

Small groups, on the other hand, in terms of the definition used in this program, generally:

1. have an indefinite or loose structure, organization, and communication network;
2. have assumed rather than designated positions or assignments so that each individual's contribution to the task is largely dependent on his own personal characteristics;
3. depend mainly on the quality of independent individual contributions and can frequently function well even when one or several members are not contributing at all:
4. are often involved with complex decision making activities;
5. cannot be given much specific guidance beforehand since the quality and quantity of participation by individual members is not known.[3] (Klaus and Glaser, 1960, p. 2–3.)

Where it is assumed or judged that sudden changes or disruptions will not be a critical part of the task with which a team must cope, but rather that the team's own environment, operational state, and procedures will be essentially predictable, certain advantages accrue to the researchers. In the first place, they can abstract from real-life team tasks those central missions which characterize the operation and then represent them in simplified form within the laboratory. To abstract and simplify operations often saves a great deal of money, especially where complicated, expensive machines are involved in the real-life situation. Simplifying the operation means that "crews" can be experimented upon in finite time periods. Additionally, simplified operations can be kept track of more readily by the researcher. He does not, for example, have

---

[3] Reprinted by permission of the authors and the American Institute for Research.

to worry about nonprogrammed personnel changes due to terminations, transfers, sick leaves, and the like. He can more carefully control the events which would influence team performance beyond the experimental variables.

There are, on the other hand, some obvious disadvantages to an approach which deals solely with the established functions of teams. A central disadvantage arises from the loss of possibly significant variables which accompanies the simplified representation. As systems increase in complexity, it often seems that they become vulnerable to frequent breakdowns and self-generated problems, for which compensatory action must be taken. Excessive abstraction and simplification may result in a loss of opportunity to come to grips with problems which exist in the real world—that is, system problems which require solutions—if effective team training is to be achieved. Where total systems are subject to stress by overload or by sudden degradations, representations of established functions do little to help the researchers develop concepts for training teams to meet these overloads and stresses.

An example of a research program which seems specifically to have been concerned with improving team performance in situations of the kind we have described as emergent is that of the RAND Corporation System Research Laboratory's air defense experiments (Chapman *et al.,* 1959). These experiments postulated sudden changes, disruptions, unpredicted and unspecified interactions between subsystems, and rapid adjustment to these stresses, as a critical part of the team's ongoing operation. The experimenters began with the premise that "exploiting the ability of men in organizations to learn requires . . . understanding organizational adaptation" (Chapman *et al.,* 1959). They were dissatisfied with exploration of *ad hoc* hypotheses and addressed themselves to the problem of looking at the system as a whole to find significant variables rather than examining variables separately and postponing their integration. They described their experiments as a *search* for a framework for comprehending organizational behavior rather than as tests of particular hypotheses.

Engagement in studies of this kind involved extensive simulation of a system's continuously varying environment and internal structure. It is reported that the objective of getting organizational behavior into the laboratory was realized.

> Each of the four crews gradually came to behave as if it were in a real life situation. Crew members became deeply involved with the organization's goal and its successes and failures. During enemy attacks, the noise level in the station rose, men came to their feet, and the excitement was obvious. Crew members reported restless nights and bad dreams—attackers boring in without an interceptor available. On one occasion, an officer slipped while stepping off a dais and broke his leg. We were not aware of this event for some ten minutes because there was no perturbation in the crew's activity during the attack in progress. He was back the next day, cast and all, because as he said, they couldn't get along without him. The member of each crew became an integral unit in which many

interdependencies and coordinating skills developed. And each crew learned to perform more effectively. This learning showed itself in procedural shortcuts, reassignment of functions, and increased motor skill to do the job faster and more accurately.[4] (Chapman *et al.*, 1959, pp. 263–264).

This richness of realism permitted the problems of subsystem interaction to be studied in meticulous detail (see Figure 11.1). Additionally, it forced the researchers to formulate concepts at higher levels of generality such as Chapman's (1960) concepts of a processing coercion, a system inertia, an effectiveness coercion, and an adjustment cycle; concepts which view the team as a single organism which learns or adjusts to new and stressful situations. New levels of concepts such as these open entirely new vistas in team training, because they help one to see the problems of team training differently. In this case, the problem is shifted from one which asks "How can we get the crew to act in a specified way?" to one which asks "How can we stress a crew so it will mobilize its capacities to adjust?" Put in other words, the question changes from how one *teaches* a team, to the question of how one gets the team to learn.

High-fidelity simulation of a large system can be both costly and time consuming (compare Chapter 13). Space, equipment, and laboratory staffing constitute substantial investments in money and time. Because of the interactions of many variables involved, the problems of measurement are characteristically enormous. Exact replications of experiments become in effect impossible, since many of the specific tasks with which the team must cope are produced by the consequences of earlier actions. Once a large-scale simulation exercise has begun, the experimenters have little control over the events which follow. Often the nature of the research changes from what would generally be recognized as controlled experimental research into what might best be termed naturalistic observation. This, in itself, is not necessarily unsound or unscientific. It does, however, raise the problem of communication with other researchers who have not shared the same or comparable experiences.

It is clear that none of the methods currently available represent ideal solutions to the problem of team training. Historically, it has been assumed that rapid developments which are occurring in the technology of automation would provide early resolutions to the issues of system reliability and team effectiveness. Defining the team training problem simply in terms of man versus machine, or as more of one versus more of the other, no longer appears satisfactory as a conceptual framework. In some respects, many men are infinitely more rigid than the most rigid of computer programs. And at any given point in time, there exist definite limits on the storage capacites of available computational facilities, as well as marked limits on the range of adaptation available to automated systems. Methods which encompass not only modifications in operations of men but improvements in computer program-

---

[4] Reprinted by permission of *Management Science*.

ming, in machine implementation, and in the conceptual structure necessary for communication among all elements of modern teams, are all part of the new look which must be given to the problem of team training in contemporary large-scale systems.

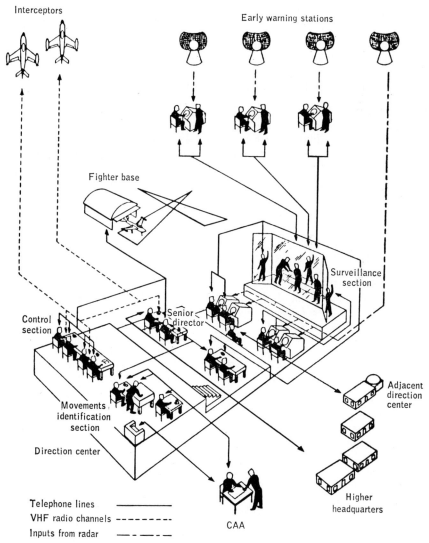

Figure 11.1. Diagramatic sketch of an air defense direction center and the simulated imbedding organizations as studied by The RAND Corporation System Research Laboratory. This sketch illustrates the richness of the realism which forced the researchers to formulate new concepts. (From Chapman *et al.*, 1959.)

REFERENCES

Biel, W. C. 1958. Operations research based on simulation for training. *Proc. Natl. Conf. Aeronaut. Electronics,* 319–322.

Boguslaw, R. 1961. Situation analysis and the problem of action. *Social Problems, 3,* 212–219.

Borgatta, E. F. 1960. A commentary on small group research. In D. Willner (ed.), *Decisions, values and groups.* New York: Pergamon Press.

Chapman, R. L. 1960. *Data for testing a model of organizational behavior.* Santa Monica, Calif.: The RAND Corporation. Research Memo RM–1916.

Chapman, R. L., Kennedy, J. L., Newell, A., and Biel, W. C. 1959. The system research laboratory's air defense experiments. *Management Science, 5,* 250–269.

Christie, L. S. 1956. The design and control of action groups. In *Proceedings of the seventh annual national conference, AIIE.* Washington, D. C.: American Institute of Industrial Engineers.

Churchman, C. W., Ackoff, R. L., and Arnoff, E. L. 1957. *Introduction to operations research.* New York: Wiley.

Forrester, J. W. 1958. Industrial dynamics. *Harvard Bus. Rev., 36,* 37–66.

Glanzer, M., and Glaser, R. 1961. Techniques for the study of group structure and behavior: II. Empirical studies of the effects of structure in small groups. *Psychol. Bull. 58,* 1–27.

Goodwin, W. R. 1957. The System Development Corporation and system training. *Amer. Psychol., 12,* 524–528.

Klaus, D. J., and Glaser, R. 1960. *Increasing team proficiency training: I. A program of research.* Pittsburgh, Pa.: American Institute for Research. Report AIR–264–60–TR–137.

March, J. G., and Simon, H. A. 1958. *Organizations.* New York: Wiley.

Mayo, E. 1933. *The human problems of an industrial civilization.* New York: Macmillan.

Mayo, E. 1947a. *The political problems of an industrial civilization.* Cambridge, Mass.: Graduate School of Bus. Admin., Harvard Univ.

Mayo, E. 1947b. *The social problems of an industrial civilization.* Cambridge, Mass.: Graduate School of Bus. Admin., Harvard Univ.

McCormick, E. J. 1957. *Human engineering.* New York: McGraw-Hill.

Moore, D. K. 1957. Divination: A new perspective. *Amer. Anthropol., 59,* 64–74.

Porter, E. H. 1950. *An introduction to therapeutic counseling.* Boston: Houghton-Mifflin.

Porter, E. H. 1961. *The system thinkers: Parable and paradigm.* Santa Monica, Calif.: System Development Corporation. SP–285.

Roethlesberger, F. J., and Dickson, W. J. 1939. *Management and the worker.* Cambridge, Mass.: Harvard Univ. Press.

Whyte, W. F. 1948. *Human relations in the restaurant industry.* New York: McGraw-Hill.

THE HUMAN COMPONENTS OF SYSTEMS MUST be given the skills they need by the techniques of individual and team training, in order to have the capabilities required to perform their tasks. But some determination must also be made to test whether these procedures have been truly and thoroughly effective in establishing these capabilities—to find out what individuals and teams can do in the system context. These questions are answered by techniques of assessing human performance called *proficiency measurement,* which are discussed in this chapter.

Measurement of the proficiency of human operators is an important aspect of system development, which has a number of different purposes within the entire development-utilization cycle. The results of such measurement are used to evaluate the processes of selection and training, as well as to estimate the contribution of human competence to total system performance. Measures of individual proficiency also establish a base line to which one can refer the gains in system effectiveness brought about by operating experience and by team training.

Some of the basic concepts of proficiency measurement have been familiar to psychologists for a long time, including reliability, validity, and weighting of component measures. These have been given increased precision of meaning in the assessment of performance within the context of system operation. Still other needs for assessment, like measures of on-the-job performance and those generated by the use of simulated operations, have imparted a new set of dimensions to performance measurement.

The chapter includes as a final section an examination of some of the varieties of measurement techniques that have been developed and employed within modern systems, and some of the problems these have suggested for future technological development in this area.

PROFICIENCY MEASUREMENT: ASSESSING HUMAN PERFORMANCE

Robert Glaser
and David J. Klaus

The output of the human component in a man-machine system requires measurement and assessment if its contribution to total system performance is to be effectively utilized. While primary interest in the development of a system is in perfecting the performance of the system as a whole and not with isolated man or machine components, the proportion of variability in system capability attributable to the human component requires the careful assessment of this component's contribution to system performance. Use of total system performance measures to evaluate contributions of the human component frequently confounds the information obtained, since information available from knowledge of the performance of the total system provides only indirect assessment of any individual component. Nevertheless, measurement of individual component performance is necessary in the assembly and analysis of the total system.

As an illustration of the methods used in the assessment of the human component in a total system, let us consider the performance of the driver in a man-machine system consisting of a driver and his automobile. Most of the measures that might be considered—such as speed, distance traveled, and ability to stop—are actually dependent upon interactions between the human and the mechanical components in the system. Total system performance is not only dependent on the skill of the operator, but on the capabilities of the machine in the system as well. To the extent that mechanical components can differ, the results of any comparison will be attenuated by factors independent of the human component. In this sense, it would not be realistic to contrast the performance of a driver using a jalopy with that of a driver operating a modern, high-powered automobile. It would be almost equally unrealistic to measure the performance of both drivers in the same automobile, since one driver or the other will then be required to operate an unfamiliar mechanical component. Even if the problem is solved by giving both drivers extensive experience with the same automobile, many additional factors must be considered before the skills of the two drivers can be accurately assessed. For instance, a decision must be made whether to use an actual performance test, to utilize information that might be obtained on past performance, or both. If an actual driving test is to be used, it is necessary to determine the importance and relevance of test conditions. Should the test include both icy and dry pavements? Should it measure skill in heavy traffic, or should it be conducted on a test course where the influence of nonparticipating drivers can be controlled? Should the drivers be examined on relevant job knowledge, such as skill in changing a tire, traffic regulations, and the design features of an internal combustion engine? How much weight should be given to these various kinds of performance? Should skill in turning be considered twice as important as skill in parking? If the driver's past record is used to assess his proficiency, is it possible to equate for the number of miles driven, the environmental conditions experienced, or the accuracy of the records themselves?

These questions illustrate the kinds of problems which arise in assessing human performance in even a simple man-machine system. As the number of system components, man or machine, increase and as the environment in which the system operates becomes less controllable, accurate assessment of human performance becomes increasingly difficult. This chapter considers some of the principles and techniques involved in proficiency measurement and illustrates the application of these procedures in several practical situations.

Proficiency measurement is the assessment of criterion behavior—the determination of the characteristics of present performance or output in terms of specified standards. As is true of other psychological measurements, proficiency measurement is carried out to obtain quantitative information on human performance, so that the behavior of individuals or groups can be ordered along some continuum. Proficiency measurement can be distinguished from aptitude measurement in that the measuring instruments used to assess proficiency are specifically concerned with the characteristics and properties of present performance, with emphasis on the meaningfulness of its content. In contrast, aptitude measures derive their meaning from a demonstrated relationship between present performance and the future attainment of specified skills.

Measures of proficiency, then, sample desired terminal or criterion performance, such as the proficiency of a radar operator, an auto mechanic, or a student of French. Aptitude tests, on the other hand, need not necessarily involve the measurement of terminal behaviors, and any aspect of behavior can be used for aptitude measures so long as it can be hypothesized that it is predictive of future performance. Proficiency measures are restricted to what can be called criterion behavior, but often such behavior can be used successfully for predictive purposes as well as for assessment. An individual's attainment in high-school geometry, for example, may indicate how well he can be expected to do as a navigator or architect. While this use of proficiency measures for predictive purposes represents an important contribution in the development of an effective man-machine system, the topic is more properly considered as an aspect of the selection and classification techniques described in Chapter 7 of this book; accordingly, the main emphasis of this chapter is on the measurement of proficiency for assessment purposes.

▣ THE CHARACTERISTICS OF PROFICIENCY MEASURES

The behavior of the human component in a system can be evaluated or assessed for several purposes. In order to understand these uses of proficiency measurement, the kinds of information conveyed by a proficiency test must be examined. The scores from proficiency tests are used both to indicate (1) the degree to which an individual has attained criterion performance—for example, whether man A can satisfactorily complete a maintenance check on a particular type of radar; and (2) the relative ordering of individuals with respect to a given task—for example, whether man B assembles fuses more quickly than man C. The principal difference between these two uses lies in the standard used as a reference. *Criterion-referenced* measures depend on an absolute standard of quality while *norm-referenced* measures depend on a relative standard.

Criterion-Referenced Measures

Underlying the concept of proficiency measurement is a continuum of skill ranging from no proficiency at all to perfect performance. In these terms, an individual's proficiency at a given task falls at some point on the continuum, as measured by the behaviors he displays during testing. The degree to which his proficiency resembles desired performance at any specified level is assessed by *criterion-referenced measures* of proficiency. The standard against which an individual's performance is compared, when measured in this manner, is the behaviors which define each point along the underlying skill continuum. When used in this way, the term "criterion" does not necessarily refer to final on-the-job behavior. Criterion levels can be established at any point in training where it is necessary to obtain information as to the adequacy of an individual's performance. Many jobs, for example, involve several grades or levels of skill. A machinist can be categorized as an apprentice, a journeyman, or a master at his trade. The specific behaviors implied by each of these levels of proficiency can be identified and used to describe the specific tasks an individual must be capable of performing before he achieves one of these skill levels. It is in this sense that measures of proficiency can be criterion-referenced.

Proficiency measures which reflect a continuum of attainment usually imply cumulative levels of achievement, in that a master machinist is also proficient at the tasks required at the apprentice and journeyman levels. Knowledge of an individual's score on a criterion-referenced measure provides explicit information as to what the individual can or cannot do. He can land an aircraft or he cannot; he can solve triangulation problems or he cannot. In this sense, criterion-referenced measures indicate the content of the behavioral repertory and the correspondence between what an individual does and the underlying continuum of proficiency. Measures which assess performance in terms of a criterion standard thus provide information as to the degree of competence attained which is independent of the performance of others.

Norm-Referenced Measures

Proficiency assessment can convey information about the capability of an individual compared with the performance of other individuals as well as with respect to a standard of achievement. In instances where an individual's *relative* standing along the underlying skill continuum is the primary purpose of measurement, reference need not be made to the criterion behavior. Educational achievement examinations, for example, are administered frequently for the purpose of ordering individuals in a class or school, rather than for assessing their attainment of specified course objectives. When such *norm-referenced measures* are used, a particular individual's proficiency is evaluated in terms of a comparison between his performance and the performance of other members of the group. Hence, information is obtained as to the performance of the individual with respect to the group average. These measures provide little or no information about the degree of proficiency exhibited by the tested behaviors in terms of what the individual can do. They tell us that one individual is more or less proficient than another, but do not tell us how proficient either of them is with respect to the job or task involved. The distinction between criterion-referenced and norm-referenced measures of attainment is similar to those previously made by Flanagan (1951) and Ebel (1960) with respect to educational achievement. They have suggested that most achievement measures currently employed in education are norm-referenced, and thus do not provide the degree of information made available by the use of criterion-referenced measures.

In education, norm-referenced measures of achievement are often referred to as "grading on the curve." Knowledge that a particular individual received an A grade in a course indicates that individual's relative standing or rank in the group, but does not indicate the degree to which he attained criterion performance. Perhaps the prevalence of this method of grading owes its existence to the difficulty encountered in attempting to specifically itemize the criterion behaviors being aimed for in the course of instruction. Both criterion-referenced measures and norm-referenced measures, however, indicate the desire to avoid assigning an arbitrary score to represent an individual's proficiency level. The utilization of course objectives as a standard against which to interpret a measure, as well as the use of group averages as the standard of performance, serve to objectify proficiency evaluation by providing a meaningful reference for an obtained achievement test score.

The expressions "percent" and "percentile" further illustrate the differences between criterion-referenced measures and norm-referenced measures. When criterion standards are used, it is reported that Johnny knows 80 percent of fifth-grade spelling words and Jimmy knows 70 percent; here, we have information both as to how they compared with one another as well as having information as to the content of their performance. When norm-referenced measures are used, it is reported that Jane was at the 90th percentile of her fifth grade class in spelling while Joan was at the 40th percentile. These scores convey information only as to the relative standing of the two students. It is apparent, then, that criterion-referenced measures are the more powerful of the two and must be used when information as to both behavioral content and rank in a group are to be obtained.

Standards of Reference

As is implied by the term "norm," norm-referenced standards of proficiency are based on data collected on the performance of a number of individuals having similar backgrounds and experience. Whether standard deviation scores, percentiles, or ranks are used to describe the position of a given individual depends largely on the kinds of data that are collected and the use to be made of the information. The size of sample used to establish the standard for norm-referenced scores is one of the factors which strongly influences the stability of the standard; too small a sample can yield measures of central tendency and variability that poorly approximate actual population values. In the same way, samples selected from among groups having widely differing backgrounds may fail to be representative of the population as a whole. Since the standard of performance is established by the group and the standing of an individual is determined by his relationship to the group when norm-referenced scores are used, the sample upon which the standard is based is of crucial concern. In this sense, the standard of proficiency for norm-referenced measures is set by the performance of the group.

When criterion-referenced measures are used, standards are established in terms of the behavioral content itself rather than in terms of comparisons with the group. Two kinds of criterion standards are available for evaluating individual proficiency. First, a standard can be established which reflects the minimum level of performance which permits operation of the system. A maintenance technician, for instance, must be capable of calibrating his test equipment before he can begin a checkout. In most cases, minimal standards are selected on the basis of relative cost by the system designer. In the case of the maintenance technician, test instruments could be produced which are calibrated automatically, but only when such devices were available would a man who was incapable of calibrating his equipment be acceptable as a component in the system. Minimal performance standards are those which represent the point below which the system will not operate. The proficiency of a given individual usually exceeds this lower limit, of course, but for the system to function as planned, the proficiency of an individual must be equal to or better than this criterion based on system requirements.

At the other extreme, proficiency can be defined in terms of maximum system output. The standard of measurement is then expressed as a function of the capabilities of other components in the system. The man loading a Navy gun, for example, never needs to load more rapidly than he receives shells from the magazine below decks. In this case, a fairly absolute standard of proficiency is available. When maximum system output is used as the standard, it is the limitations of the system rather than its requirements which determine the standard of proficiency for the human component.

In practice, proficiency standards can be established at any value between the point where the system will not perform at all and the point where any further contribution from the human component will not yield any increase in system performance. The proficiency of an individual can then be expressed as a percentage of either minimum or maximum performance standards. If a standard based upon minimum system requirements is used, an individual's performance can meaningfully exceed that specified by the criterion so that it is possible to perform at a proficiency level much higher than that minimally required. Once maximum proficiency has been reached relative to system capacity, however, the development of further proficiency serves no purpose. In summary, criterion-referenced measures of proficiency can be established using either of two standards; one, in terms of minimal requirements, assumes that the human is the weakest component in the system, while the other, in terms of maximum capacity, assumes he is one of the strongest.

As a concrete example of the use of the two references for proficiency measurement and their accompanying standards, let us consider the problem of evaluating the performance of an assembly-line worker whose output is measured by the number of items he turns out in a ten-minute period which fall within specified tolerance limits. Observing his output, one may determine that his production rate is 20 acceptable items per period. This raw measure obviously conveys little information as to his proficiency, except that he is turning out *some* product. In order to evaluate his performance, his score must be compared with some reference base. The rate of the worker across from him could be used, but such a restricted sample of a norm group may yield a comparison of limited value. An adequate sample of workers in similar jobs could provide a reasonably stable basis for measurement, however, and would permit the determination of any worker's relative standing. In many instances of proficiency assessment, norm-referenced measures are the only measures available. An individual's supervisory skills, for instance, are difficult to evaluate in terms of specific criterion behaviors and without reference to the performance of other supervisors.

Evaluating the proficiency of the assembly-line worker by means of criterion-referenced measures conveys information as to the individual's output when compared to specified performance standards as well as to his relative standing in a group of similar individuals. A criterion-referenced measure of the worker's proficiency can be based on a standard either of system requirements or of system capacity. Performance on the assembly line might be assessed in terms of the minimum human component output necessary for system function, assuming that a later component in the assembly-line system requires the processing of at least some minimum number of units per time period (as, for example, an annealing oven, which depends upon a minimum number of items passing through it to maintain proper temperature). In such a case, the assembly worker's output must equal the requirement for the system to produce as planned. At the other extreme, the individual's proficiency could be compared with a standard representing system capacity. If the system operated in such a way that the worker was supplied with a maximum of 40 items per time period, his output of 20 items for each period represents a proficiency level of 50 percent. Were the worker's rate to exceed the capacity of the system—that is, were he to have an output capability of 50 or 60 items per time period—the output of the system would not be increased and the additional proficiency would not represent any further contribution to total system performance. In certain systems, where the efficiency of mechanical components do not impose a limitation on system output, there is no upper limit to the potential contributions of the human component. There is probably no specifiable upper limit, for example, on such skills as inventiveness in systems where these behaviors contribute to over-all output.

In applications of proficiency measurement to educational situations, where it is generally the case that neither minimal requirements nor maximum effectiveness of the individual student are routinely specified, the selection of suitable standards is frequently difficult. Typically, school achievement is assessed by norm-referenced measures—that is, by "grading on a curve" of group performance. However, the lack of well-defined system standards does not preclude the use of criterion-referenced measures. Arbitrary proficiency levels can be established for minimum performance which are not based on comparisons with group performance. For instance, it is possible to select standards in academic training which reflect decisions as to the least amount of end-of-course competence the student is expected to attain, such as being able to perform long division or spell half the words in a given list. With respect to upper levels of proficiency in academic training, it is possible to use the maximum amount of course content presented to the student as a standard. A given individual's achievement can be assessed with reference to this kind of standard, for example, by stating the proportion of geometric theorems a student is able to prove from among those he has been exposed to, or the percentage of words he can spell correctly from among those taught by his teacher.

In summary, there are two principal types of proficiency measures. Criterion-referenced measures involve a comparison between system capabilities and individual performance. Norm-reference measures, on the other hand, compare the performance of an individual with a sample of other individuals. The standard for criterion-referenced measures may be either minimum system requirements or maximum system output. The standard used with respect to norm-referenced measures depends on the average and dispersion of the performance of a group of similar individuals.

THE USES OF PROFICIENCY MEASUREMENT

Basically, proficiency tests can be used for two principal purposes. First, performance can be assessed to provide information about the characteristics of an individual's present behavior. Second, performance can be assessed to provide information about the conditions which produced that behavior. The primary emphasis of the first of these uses is to discriminate among individuals. Used in the second way, proficiency tests are employed to discriminate among treatments—for example, equipment designs, training procedures, and working conditions—by an analysis of group differences.

Proficiency tests used primarily to provide information about individual differences are constructed so as to maximize the discriminations made among people having specified backgrounds and experiences. Such a test will include items which maximize the likelihood of observing individual differences in performance along various job dimensions, and hence maximize the variability of the distribution of scores that are obtained. In practice, the variability of test scores is increased by manipulating the difficulty levels and content of the test items.

Proficiency tests used primarily to provide information about differences in treatments are constructed so as to maximize the discriminations made between groups treated differently and to minimize the differences between individuals in any one group. Such a test will be sensitive to the differences produced by treatments. For example, a test designed to demonstrate the effects of training would be constructed so that it was uniformly difficult for those taking it before training and uniformly easy after training. The content of tests used to differentiate treatments should be maximally sensitive to the effects anticipated from the treatments in terms of performance changes.

In essence, the distinction between proficiency tests used to maximize individual differences and one used to maximize treatment or group differences is established during the selection of test items. In constructing a proficiency test to differentiate among *individuals* at the end of training, for example, it would be possible to begin by obtaining data on a large sample of items relating to training objectives. When the data were analyzed, it would be found that some items were responded to correctly by only some of the individuals in the group, while other items were answered correctly by all members of the group. These latter items, which failed to differentiate among individuals, would be eliminated, since their only effect was to add a numerical constant to every score. Those items remaining would serve to discriminate among individuals and thus yield a distribution of scores that was as large as possible considering the number and type of items used. If the test were constructed for the purpose of observing *group* instead of individual differences, the selection of items would follow a different course. In an instance where training was the treatment variable involved, for example, it would be desirable to retain items which were responded to correctly by all members of the post-training group but which were answered incorrectly by students who had not yet been trained. In a test constructed for the purpose of differentiating groups, items which indicated substantial variability within either the pre- or post-training group would be undesirable because of the likelihood that they would cloud the effects which might be attributable to the treatment variable. In brief, items most suitable for measuring individual differences in proficiency are those which will differentiate among individuals all exposed to the same training or other treatment variable, while items most suitable for distinguishing between groups are those which are most likely to indicate that a given amount of training or some particular treatment was effective. In either case, samples of test items are drawn from a population of items indicating the content of performance; the particular item samples that are drawn are those most useful for the purpose of the measurement (Hammock, 1960).

Assessing Individual Differences

The measurement of differences in individual performance is desirable at several stages in the development and utilization of the human component in a system. In a sense, the human component is "manufactured" by the process of training. As training progresses, the performance of individual trainees gradually approaches the desired minimum level of proficiency necessary for system operation. Assessing the behavior of the trainee at successive stages insures that the training process is achieving its goal of supplying properly qualified individuals to the system.

Selection.   Measurements of behavior are frequently made prior to the training process, when aptitude and achievement tests are used to select men and place them into courses of training appropriate to their background and initial skill levels. In general, tests used for this purpose are constructed not only to maximize test score differences between individuals but to maximize the relationship between these pre-training scores and later post-training scores which measure "criterion" performance. For the most part, predictability is the primary objective of proficiency tests used as measures of aptitude. For this purpose, scores on these tests are reported in relative terms. Additional detail about tests used in selection and classification has been given in Chapter 7.

Placement.   After training begins, further performance assessment is usually required. For example, "job knowledge" tests may be used at the beginning of training to assess the extent to which the individual already can perform the job elements which are part of, or contribute to, the terminal performance desired at the end of training. When used for placement purposes, it is necessary that proficiency measures are criterion-referenced, since knowledge as to behavioral content is the information required.

Quality Control.   As training proceeds, tests may be given in order to determine how well each skill has been learned and to determine those aspects of performance where satisfactory and unsatisfactory attainment of proficiency is exhibited by the individual. As particular phases of training are completed and as the end of training is reached, proficiency is measured as a kind of quality control, in order to determine whether the individual has reached or surpassed performance standards that have been established. When used for this purpose, proficiency measures again must be criterion-referenced, since it is information as to the content of performance and not relative standing that is desired. End-of-training assessment can be based either upon minimal system requirements or the maximum contribution that can be made in terms of the capacity of the system. In most instances, the diploma, certificate, or license awarded at the end of a training program indicates that the individual has obtained some minimal standard of proficiency, but does not reflect how close he is to the maximum performance level which might contribute to system performance.

In the assessment of end-of-course proficiency, the desirability of identifying individuals performing far above the minimum levels required for system operation should not be overlooked. The test used should not necessarily have an arbitrary ceiling which precludes the evaluation of the indirect effects of training experiences, such as transfer of training and creativity.

System Performance.   Once the individual is on the job and functioning as a system component, periodic proficiency measurement is used to check performance adequacy and to assess whatever changes may have occurred as a result of field experience. Tests used for this purpose must have a wide range of coverage, since it should be possible to identify instances of enhancement in performance as well as instances of skill deterioration.

The use of proficiency measures for any of these purposes assumes that the test user has knowledge of the intent and objectives of training. If the stated objectives of the learning experience are unclear, it is impossible to decide what behaviors ought to be measured. Frequently, it is found that the objectives of training are either (1) defined in an overly general or ambiguous way, or (2) expressed in terms which are difficult to measure. If the former is the case, it is probably equally true that the objectives of the system are ambiguously defined, and an effort must be made to define them rigorously enough for performance measurement. If the latter is primarily the case, the proficiency tester must devise a measurement situation in which the required behaviors are elicited for assessment.

Assessing Group Differences

The use of proficiency measures are not limited to the evaluation of the present performance of an individual; they may also be used for evaluating the treatments or conditions which might be imposed to produced a given level of performance. These treatments can refer to any manipulation which may influence the proficiency of the human component, such as the training method, length of instruction, design of displays and controls, organization of the system, working conditions, and climate or environment. As noted above, when proficiency measures are used to distinguish between treatments by means of the differential performance of two or more groups, they should be maximally sensitive to the particular effects expected from the treatments being considered.

Group Comparisons.   Two or more treatments can be compared without reference to a criterion standard in order to determine which of the treatments yields the highest level of proficiency. Two designs for dials can be contrasted, for example, by observing the proficiency of groups of individuals as they perform using the dials. The results of such a study can then be used to evaluate the *relative* effectiveness of the two designs and to decide which of the dials might be most profitably incorporated into the system.

Several methods of training can be compared in this fashion; the methods can then be ranked as to their relative efficiency. In the conduct of these comparisons, no reference need be made to a criterion standard. Whether *any* of the treatments being investigated is adequate in terms of system requirements, however, cannot be determined without employing criterion-referenced measures of man-machine proficiency.

Group Attainment. Just as it is desirable to evaluate individual performance in terms of the requirements or capabilities of the system to which the individual is assigned, it is also desirable to assess the outcomes of specific treatments in terms of how successfully the human component attains system standards. The effectiveness of a treatment, when evaluated in terms of criterion-referenced measures, is based on the number of individuals in the group who achieve an established standard of performance. The training practices employed for a particular system, for instance, can be evaluated by determining the proportion of individuals completing training who perform up to standard. A training course which requires the rejection of, say, 90 percent of all trainees is probably not optimally meeting the needs of the system. Likewise, a control which has been designed in such a way as to be operable by only 10 percent of the individuals who otherwise might be qualified as system components, suggests the need for improved human engineering. Criterion-referenced group measures can also be used, of course, to compare the relative adequacy of several alternate treatments designed to achieve the same objective.

▣ DEFINITION OF THE BEHAVIOR TO BE MEASURED

Identifying the Performance to be Assessed

The first step in the development of a proficiency measure is the specification of the behavior to be observed and measured. The ease with which this step can be carried out is dependent upon several factors including (1) the complexity of the behavior involved and the explicitness with which the behavior has been defined, (2) the purpose for which the measurement of behavior has been undertaken, and (3) the accessibility of the behavior to observation.

Task Definition. With respect to the complexity and definition of the task, it is easy to see that many tasks actually involve several dimensions of performance. For purposes of proficiency measurement, the task of a radio operator in receiving code, for example, can be analyzed in terms of speed, accuracy, neatness of transcription, and other components. Specification of a similar set of defining behaviors for a production supervisor in a factory is obviously more difficult. In order to identify and describe the behavioral components of a particular job, and thereby accomplish the first step in the development of a proficiency test, it is essential to conduct some sort of task analysis yielding defined performance specifications which can be observed and measured. Techniques for carrying out the kind of systematic task analyses basic for accomplishing proficiency measurement are described in Chapter 6.

Purpose of Measurement. Once a task analysis is completed, a determination must be made of the specific samples of performance to be selected for evaluation. The sampling procedure employed depends, to a large extent, upon the use to which the evaluation is to be put. If proficiency tests are to be used as predictive instruments—that is, to predict future performance on the basis of the present behavioral repertory, then the content of the test should sample those tasks which have been found empirically to discriminate among levels of proficiency in terms of future performance. For selection purposes, the test content need not measure all aspects of present performance, but only those which are demonstrably useful for enhancing the prediction. Those aspects of proficiency which are necessary for adequate job performance, but which are performed reasonably well by all men tested, contribute little toward differentiating or predicting performance.

On the other hand, consider a proficiency test used to assess present performance for placement purposes. The objective of measuring performance in this instance is to assess skill level so that an individual may be entered into a training program at the proper point or assigned to a task which he is capable of completing satisfactorily. The behavior sampled on such a test must incorporate not only those aspects which reflect differential levels of competence, but also those aspects of performance which comprise the basic performance requirements necessary for all individuals to achieve the end products of training or assignment objectives.

A different use of proficiency measures, the diagnosis of training difficulties, requires still another definition of the behaviors to be sampled. In this case, it is necessary to obtain information about component behaviors which contribute to a later or final performance measure. The basis for sampling behavior for this purpose is to study the causes of inadequate performance so that these causes can be reflected in the test situation. For such diagnostic purposes, the content of the test must not only involve performance output, but must also reflect the component behaviors which contribute to the output.

Performance measures require still a different emphasis when they are used to assess the terminal behavior specified as the final training product. In this instance, the concern is less with diagnosis, and more with the determination of performance adequacy with respect to standards of proficiency. For tests of terminal performance, the behavior sampled must be selected in terms of the stated objectives of the training program and thus reflect the requirements of the human component in the over-all system. In general, a test of terminal behavior assesses performance with respect to minimal standards established to decide between passing and failing; in addition, such a test frequently samples situations other than those explicitly handled in training, in order to evaluate the degree to which specific behaviors have been generalized to a variety of potential job situations.

Accessibility of the Behavior. Measurement is only possible on the basis of specific, observable events. In attempting to evaluate supervisory behavior, for instance, both the supervisor's actions and the results of these actions on the performance of his subordinates can be measured. Much as it might be desirable to do so, the covert thinking and planning often assumed to precede overt actions cannot be investigated directly. A primary concern in the development of proficiency measures is the development of test instruments which elicit observable responses appropriate to the purposes of measurement.

In the assessment of proficiency, two kinds of performance can generally be observed. First, it is possible to examine the behavioral repertory of the individual being evaluated. His actions, both verbal and motor, can form the basis of a proficiency test. The performance of the supervisor can be assessed, for instance, by observing what he says to his subordinates, how he acts in their presence, how he prepares work schedules, and so forth. Secondly, it is possible to determine an individual's proficiency level by observing his effects on over-all system performance or output. Rather than measuring the movements of a pilot as he flies an aircraft, it is sometimes easier to look at the performance of the aircraft itself and infer the pilot's proficiency from these observations.

A further problem in the accessibility of behavior is the difficulty which sometimes occurs in producing situations which elicit the kinds of behavior to be evaluated. Several kinds of performance can be identified which, for one reason or another, cannot be assessed easily due to the difficulty in observing them. Classes of behaviors of this sort are those which are potentially dangerous to the participants, those which are themselves affected by the presence of an observer or measuring instrument, and those which are accessible only by indirect measurement. Proficiency in stressful situations, such as is involved in fire fighting aboard a Navy vessel, could be assessed realistically only with substantial risk to the safety of the seamen concerned. Performance at an isolated station, such as an arctic weather post, will be affected by the presence of observer personnel. Proficiency under the weightless conditions of space travel can only be assessed by the use of special instrumentation which permits the necessary observations to be made. The problem of accessibility of behavior for evaluation and the necessity for arranging situations which facilitate the occurrence of the behavior to be measured can frequently be solved by the use of simulation procedures such as those described later in this chapter.

Quantification of Performance

Measurement necessarily implies quantification. This means behavior which is to be assessed not only must be overt, but also must be amenable to having numbers assigned to it. The simplest instances, of course, are those in which the component behaviors which contribute to proficiency are either present or absent from the individual's or the system's performance. It is possible to count these events, such as the number of items produced per time period, the number of contacts a supervisor has with each subordinate, or the number of errors made during a battle exercise. In many other cases of proficiency measurement, it is possible to quantify observations by employing simple scale values, such as the time necessary to troubleshoot a radio receiver, or a marksman's score, where a given shot can be assigned a score of zero to ten depending on how far the shot was from the bull's-eye.

Measurement becomes more complex, however, when the important aspects of the behavior being assessed are qualitative rather than quantitative. For example, the skill of a pilot in reading an altimeter can be evaluated in terms of how many feet his readings are in error, but his skill in landing an aircraft cannot be effectively measured by a simple counting or measuring procedure. In cases such as these, it is necessary to translate observable performance into some numerical scale. The two most popular methods for quantifying judgments are by the use of rating scales and check lists.

Rating Scales. In applying rating-scale techniques to the evaluation of complex activities, major components of the task are first identified. Each of these job segments is then defined in terms of a skill dimension ranging from good to poor. One or more judges are then asked to observe an individual's performance and select a point on the scale which is most representative of the performance of the man being assessed. The most effective rating scales are those which define the extremes of the behavior being observed and, if possible, provide descriptions of intermediate points along the dimension. To a large extent, the adequacy of the measures obtained with rating-scale techniques depends heavily upon the experience of the raters and the thoroughness with which they have been trained. The "halo" effect—that is, the tendency for an observer's general impression of the man being rated to influence judgments about his specific behaviors—and other forms of contamination are frequently difficult to eliminate when rating scales are used.

Check Lists. Check-list techniques are another approach to the measurement of complex performance. A check list itemizes the specific behaviors which have been found to be "critical," in that they distinguish between effective and ineffective performance of the task (Flanagan, 1954). The observer then has the responsibility of detecting the presence or absence of these specified events rather than having the responsibility for judging the over-all proficiency level. The check list for a maintenance inspection task, for instance, would list the necessary inspections which must be made to complete the job satisfactorily; and a check list devised to assess the performance of a radar operator would list the adjustments, identifications, and so forth, which indicate an acceptable level of proficiency. While properly constructed check lists reduce the amount of contamination frequently encountered in the use of rating scales and frequently reduce the amount of training which must be given to the observers, it is often difficult to devise checklists that are sufficiently elaborate and comprehensive to fully reflect all aspects of job competence. Description of the techniques and procedures used to construct rating scales, check lists, and similar instruments, as well as the advantages or difficulties in their use, can be found in Guilford (1954), Ghiselli and Brown (1955), and other sources.

Infrequent Events as Proficiency Measures

Another problem encountered in proficiency measurement concerns the observation of infrequent events, such as accidents in the operation of a lathe, the location of unusual malfunctions during troubleshooting, or the ability to pilot a damaged aircraft. The decision as to whether or not such rare events should be included in a proficiency measurement instrument depends, for the most part, on the importance of correct performance during those occurrences for the over-all success of the system. Some events simply occur too infrequently, or their effects on system performance are too slight, to be included in a test. Rare events which are critical to the success of the system, however, deserve more careful attention. The use of data on infrequent occurrences for proficiency measurement purposes will often hinge upon records of performance systematically compiled over long periods of time. There is often a tendency, in the construction of proficiency tests, to exclude unique occurrences for the very reason that they are nonrepetitive. However, it is possible that a particular system may be characterized by a high rate or proportion of unique occurrences. Many of the larger guided-missile systems, for example, rarely have a given trouble or malfunction more than once during their development, since as soon as a trouble occurs, the malfunctioning part is redesigned. If every reparable trouble were to be recorded for one of these developmental systems, it might often be observed that the vast majority of these malfunctions actually consisted of single, relatively unrelated difficulties. If proficiency, in turn, consists of competence in handling these events, the proficiency measure must reflect the individual's ingenuity in making the system operative, rather than his performance at pre-selected tasks. In such cases, the evaluating instrument would sample skill in dealing with new problems which require generalization from previous knowledge of principles, and thus would not include items used as examples during training. The distinction being made here is between the assessment of proficiency in handling unique troubles and the assessment of proficiency in routine tasks. For purposes of measurement, unique or infrequent events must be considered as a class of occurrences, even though there may be little essential similarity among them.

Simulation for Proficiency Measurement

The behaviors which have been established as the product of training can be made available for observation and evaluation through the use of simulation techniques which utilize equipment designed to elicit joblike behaviors under controlled conditions, so they can be suitably measured. Simulation is widely used in conjunction with training, as has been noted in Chapter 10. However, simulators developed for use in proficiency measurement are not necessarily identical with those developed for use in instruction (Gagné, 1954). A proficiency-measurement simulator is designed primarily for the purpose of eliciting certain behaviors under conditions which facilitate their assessment; hence, it consists largely of the instrumentation necessary to obtain quantitative measures of performance. A simulator suitable for training, on the other hand, is designed primarily for the purpose of modifying behavior and therefore must incorporate guidance and feedback features which are unnecessary if only measurement is involved.

Whenever the behavior to be evaluated can be readily elicited for measurement without special equipment, a satisfactory proficiency measure can be developed without resorting to extensive simulation. When criterion performance is not readily accessible for measurement, however, a proficiency test must not only sample situations requiring the behavior, but must simulate these instances as well. Much of the ingenuity required during proficiency test development is directed at making otherwise inaccessible behaviors occur at the time and in the form which allows satisfactory observation and measurement. The use of simulation in assessing proficiency will be described further in a later section of this chapter.

▣ SAMPLING AND THE RELATIVE IMPORTANCE OF PERFORMANCE COMPONENTS

Sampling of Performance Objectives

The content of a proficiency test must accurately reflect the objectives of training or some other standard of performance. The adequacy of a proficiency test depends upon the extent to which it satisfactorily samples the universe of behaviors which constitute criterion performance. In this sense, a test instrument is said to have *content validity;* the greater the degree to which the test requires performance representative of the defined universe, the greater is its content validity. For many kinds of tasks, proficiency measurement can be carried out by observing an individual performing the entire job as many times as is necessary to obtain reliable results. Performance of highly repetitive operations, such as sorting or loading, need not be evaluated by means of sampling, since it is usually quite feasible to observe proficiency of several entire cycles of the activity during a single period.

At the other extreme, many jobs must be performed in a great range of situations and conditions, or may consist of a wide variety of component tasks involving behaviors of varying degrees of accessibility. Under circumstances such as these, when the over-all job is relatively complex, sampling must be used to select the content of the proficiency test. Consider the task of an electronics technician, for example. To assess the proficiency of an individual, one must expose him to a sample of problems which fully deflect those he will encounter during his career. There are several types of sampling errors which are to be avoided in preparing a proficiency test for a complex job.

First is the undue inclusion of test content selected because of ease of measurement—that is, items which are chosen principally on the basis of their simplicity of preparation, presentation, or scoring. Basic vocabulary, definitions, locations, and so forth, are often used in proficiency measurement while the evaluation of involved motor skills and the application of principles to actual system problems may be avoided. Several types of instruments have been described which are capable of assessing complex skills, as indicated by Fattu's compilation of troubleshooting tests (1956) and the Office of Strategic Services procedures to measure the proficiency of individuals in leadership, resourcefulness, and information gathering (OSS Assessment Staff, 1948).

Second is the error in sampling which occurs when the test instrument is derived from the content of the training course or developed from course materials rather than from the objectives of training. To the extent that the training program does not achieve its goals with respect to system requirements, a test of course content will not reflect the adequacy of end-of-training performance. Furthermore, it is sometimes necessary for effective training to use instructional situations which are simplified or modified so as to include guidance or motivational features not present in the job situation. For example, the training of navigators may be facilitated by specially designed classroom exercises, but the navigators' ability to determine the appropriate course for an aircraft should be evaluated under actual flight conditions where weather, load, pilot's skill, and other relevant factors are all present in their proper proportions. In this sense, the training program itself can only be assessed in terms of how successfully the course aims have been achieved when these aims have been defined independently of the training program.

Third is the error that results from sampling a universe of behaviors which fails to represent the behaviors required on the job. This type of error may result from the inclusion of skills which do not actually contribute to job success or from the exclusion of aspects of job performance not recognized as important in task proficiency. Perhaps the most common example of this type of error is the emphasis usually given to the measurement of job knowledge and theory in instances where this information may not be relevant to actual task performance. Also, it is often assumed that certain skills are not sufficiently important to proficiency to be included in a test, when actually they represent vital aspects of job success. A radar operator probably needs to know little about the electronic principles involved in the design of his equipment's circuitry; on the other hand, it may be important that he knows the proper way to clean the face of his display. The omission of pertinent job elements may be a function of selecting too few instances of the universe of job behaviors to adequately represent all important aspects of job performance. For purposes of a stable measure of proficiency, the sample must not only be large enough to be representative but, as will be discussed subsequently, must include a sufficient number of observations to result in a reliable score for a given individual.

Weighting Component Aspects of Performance

Closely related to the problem of sampling a universe of behaviors is the problem of appropriately weighting each of the observations to be used. Certain aspects of behavior, of course, are of greater importance in determining job success than others. For example, the success which a gunner achieves in hitting target aircraft is probably more significant than his ability to carry out detailed maintenance on his weapons. Improper weighting of various aspects of performance can produce serious distortions in the assignment of proficiency scores.

The determination of appropriate weights to be given to the behaviors being observed can be approached in several ways. Perhaps the most commonly employed method of weighting various aspects of proficiency is by the judgments of experts. This procedure is frequently employed in assessing performance when definitive measures of output are not available, as in academic performance, decision-making tasks, professional skills, and so forth. The quality of the weights assigned by judges depends heavily on the experience of the experts in observing the over-all performance being assessed, their knowledge of the system as a whole and of the influence exerted by the job being observed on the output of the system, and on the representativeness of the judges in terms of their own backgrounds, experience, and capabilities. The assignment of weights by judges should be based upon the opinions of a number of experts, which are combined and averaged to produce the weights used.

A second procedure that can be used for assigning weights depends on empirically identifying those specific aspects of performance which lead to system success or failure. The frequency with which some particular behaviors are noted as contributing to or detracting from system excellence can be used as the weighting factor. This approach again involves the use of "critical incidents," referred to previously. A large number of field observations are collected from system personnel as to which individual actions lead to the outstanding success or failure of a mission or assignment. It is then possible to use these critical incidents to define the important aspects of the job. The frequency with which any single kind of incident is reported can also serve as a basis for assigning weights to particular task components (Flanagan, 1956).

The frequency with which a given behavior occurs in the job situation is not by itself necessarily the best index of the importance of the behavior to job success. Weights are more properly assigned when the importance of the behavior to system output, operation, and cost is considered. Infrequent performance requirements—those with a very low probability of occurrence in the course of system operation—often deserve rather large weights because of their exceptional importance. While a fire aboard ship is quite rare, for example, the proficiency of the ship's crew in dealing with fires at sea might well be included in performance evaluation solely because of its importance. Many more common behaviors, on the other hand, may be omitted from a proficiency test because of their relative lack of influence on system performance.

In certain situations, weights for proficiency assessment measures can be determined in a third way, by investigating the correlation between skills to be observed and other measures of proficiency. This approach is especially useful in assessing end-of-course proficiency. Weights for the tests administered at the end of training can be established by ascertaining the degree to which any one measure predicts future performance on the job. The assumption here, of course, is that it is possible to obtain representative and stable measures of ultimate job success. The use of this procedure for establishing weights is probably most pertinent when the job requirements cannot be well simulated at the end of training; that is, when there is fairly little actual correspondence between end-of-training performance and that which occurs on the job.

A fourth approach that can be used to establish weights for proficiency measures results from the experimental investigation of the relationship between the variations in the specific job components being assessed and variations in total system performance. The degree to which individual competence at any one skill or task influences the output of the over-all system can be determined by systematically manipulating proficiency at that task and then measuring the effects produced on system performance. Success at surveying, for instance, may be far more a function of an individual's skill in making careful measurements than of his ability to rapidly solve equations involving trigonometric functions. The relative importance of each of these skills to the final product can be determined by an experimental comparison of the output of individuals differentially trained to maximize their skill at one or the other of these job elements. A special case of the use of system performance as the criterion for weighting proficiency measures occurs when it is possible to identify the cost to the system, in dollars, time, or other cost measure, of various components of proficiency in some particular task.

A fifth way in which several aspects of proficiency can be weighted is with reference to the variability in proficiency that can be observed for any job component. If the measures of several aspects of proficiency are combined by simple addition, the resulting score will be weighted in proportion to the variability associated with each of the submeasures. If the scores on measure A range from 15 to 25, for example, and the scores on measure B range from 0 to 40, a sum of the scores obtained by individuals on these two measures will far more heavily reflect the aspect of proficiency indicated by measure B than by measure A. It is reasonable to suppose that when the observed fluctuations in one job component are greater than the variations in the proficiency at another job component, the weighting that occurs as a function of adding scores from these two components is reasonably meaningful. Efforts should be made to independently evaluate the appropriateness of such weightings, however, since it may be that some of the tasks for which substantial variability in proficiency can be observed do not actually contribute to job success. Furthermore, variability in proficiency scores may be a function of the situation in which proficiency is assessed rather than a function of an individual's competence. Before permitting variability to determine weights, it is necessary to rule out that proportion of the observed variability which stems from bias in the measuring instrument. A considerable portion of the variability observable in bomber crew proficiency, for example, is probably due to conditions of weather and mission rather than to any factor relating to the performance of the crew members. While the variability due principally to the training and experience of crew members should contribute a major weighting, that portion of the variability which can be attributed to extraneous factors should be controlled or eliminated by the method of measurement and test administration or, if possible, by appropriate score corrections.

A sixth possible procedure which can be used to assign weights to various component skills involved in over-all job success is by establishing some equivalence relationship among the components. One very common weighting problem is that of deciding the relative importance of speed and errors in the performance of a task. In assessing proficiency at typing, for example, weights are often assigned arbitrarily, such as penalizing the individual five words of speed for each error. It is possible to actually determine the weight which should be given to each component, however, in terms of total output. If, as is usually the case, the material being typed must sooner or later be free of errors, an effective means of weighting could be in terms of the time required to correct each error satisfactorily. Proficiency in typing, then, would be measured by the amount of time required to turn out a perfect copy of the test material. Errors would be weighted in terms of the time spent by the particular individual being evaluated to correct each error, and a trainee who could rapidly correct an error would be penalized less than one who required much more time. Likewise, in assessing proficiency at aircraft gunnery where a "near-miss" is often no more effective than having not fired at all, a score based on some combination of firing rate and relative accuracy would probably not be as appropriate as one based solely on the number of test targets destroyed during a given period of time.

In summary, the first step in the construction of a proficiency measuring instrument is the selection of appropriate samples of behavior to be observed and the assigning of weights to these samples relative to their importance to the over-all job and thus to the output of the system. The degree to which the selection of samples and assignment of weights reflects the underlying universe of behaviors to be measured establishes the *content validity* of the test. Obviously, content validity is influenced by the adequacy with which the test stimuli elicit the behaviors to be observed, the conditions under which the test is administered, and the way in which the test is scored and interpreted. In examining sampling and weighting, emphasis has been given in this section to possible biases in the selection of behaviors to be observed. Biasing factors which are apt to influence the simulation of job conditions, the administration of the test, and the assignment and reporting of scores are discussed in the following sections of this chapter.

In general, bias introduced during the sampling of behavior to be included in the proficiency measure can be regarded as a special instance of assigning weights to specific job elements. As Brogden and Taylor (1950) point out, weighting is the determination of appropriate values for the contribution of each job element to total job performance. Whenever job elements are included in the proficiency-measurement instrument which are not relevant to task performance, nonzero weights have been assigned to elements which, in reality, should have had zero weighting. If relevant job elements are excluded through the sampling procedure, then the opposite is true; zero weights have been assigned to job elements which should have had nonzero weighting.

▣ PRECISION AND RELEVANCE IN PROFICIENCY MEASUREMENT

While the problems of sampling and weighting are concerned with potential bias in the selection of behaviors to be stressed during proficiency measurement, there are also potential biases which may arise in the course of making proficiency measurements. These biases may affect performance scores in some systematic or constant fashion, in which case they may be referred to as sources of contamination, or they may affect scores in some random fashion, in which case they are referred to as sources of unreliability.

In general, these two forms of bias affect the degree of confidence that can be placed in an obtained score as being representative of an individual's level of proficiency. Even when obtained scores have been precisely measured, there is a need to consider the relevance of the score with respect to the standards of reference being employed. This is the problem of the validity of a proficiency test. The degree of validity in a proficiency measure is a function of the difficulties which exist in identifying, quantifying, selecting, and weighting the behaviors to be assessed. Nevertheless, procedures are available for investigating the validity of proficiency measures and for increasing their relevance with respect to the requirements of a particular system.

Contamination and Systematic Measurement Bias

Several sources of bias which occur in the process of measurement and which tend to exert a *systematic* influence on estimates of proficiency can be identified. One of these is the error in measurement which results from assessing proficiency within an operating system. Since the observations to be made, or the scores to be obtained, are frequently determined to some extent by the performance of other components in the system, care should be taken to control the influence of such biasing influences during measurement. For example, Thorndike (1949) describes several biasing factors which might influence the evaluation of a bombardier during an airborne exercise. He points out that the accuracy of a particular bomb drop may be a function of the turbulence of the air, the condition and calibration of the bomb sight, the accuracy in construction of the bomb, its freedom from physical defects, the skill and conscientiousness with which the pilot flew the plane, circumstances of time of day, altitude, or length of bomb run under which the bomb was dropped, as well as the skill with which the bombardier performed his task (p. 129). Sources of bias such as these can be reduced by careful control of the test situation as, for instance, by effective simulation or careful administrative arrangements.

Further sources of contamination are sometimes found in the construction of the test instrument. An examination may differentially affect the scores of individuals because of factors unrelated to actual job performance. The test may lean heavily upon the individual's skill in understanding test directions, for example, or his speed in reading lengthy descriptive passages. In these instances, the influence verbal facility may have on the test score is to distort proficiency estimates in such a way that they systematically penalize individuals with poor vocabularies and reading skills, and thus fail to adequately reflect their proficiency in tasks which do not depend directly on verbal skills. A proficiency test may also be prepared in such a way as to differentially promote response sets in the individual being evaluated (Cronbach, 1946). A response set is a general tendency to respond consistently in one particular way. Depending on the way in which it is constructed, a test may encourage some of the individuals taking it to be overly cautious in their work, for example, and thus receive a higher or lower score than might otherwise have been the case.

Whenever individuals are used to evaluate proficiency on the basis of their observations of performance, as is the case when ratings or judgments are made, several kinds of judgmental errors can occur. Many of these sources of bias have been studied in detail (Guilford, 1954; Ghiselli and Brown, 1955). In general, this source of contamination stems from some previous knowledge or experiences on the part of the individuals used as judges. For example, the judge may have acquired a stereotyped belief that people with red hair are erratic and impetuous in their performance, or that pipe smokers are apt to be more thoughtful and intelligent than other people. A general tendency such as this causes the judge to rate certain individuals higher or lower than should be the case on specific tasks—a finding, as mentioned previously, usually referred to as the "halo" effect. Similarly, a particular judge may tend to be overly lenient or strict in his judgments and thus give too high or too low ratings to all individuals he observes. Then again, raters may tend to judge a disproportionate number of individuals as average. Prior knowledge by the raters about an individual's previous performance may also have a substantial effect on judgments made during proficiency assessment.

All in all, these judgmental biases are most pronounced when the judgments themselves are fairly general in scope or refer to poorly specified behaviors. Effective control over judgments sometimes may be obtained by carefully training the observers. Frequently, it is also possible to overcome these biases by more carefully focusing the rater's attention on specific behaviors, either their presence or absence, or differences in their quality. This can be accomplished by structuring the rating instrument in such a way as to add behavioral specificity to the observations, so that the judges can depend on check-list items or other detailed procedures rather than on general impressions.

Sources of contamination, or systematic bias in measurement, stem largely from characteristics of the test instrument or the way in which the instrument is administered. Careful analysis of the test and the test situation will frequently uncover such influences, and careful administrative control of the proficiency-measurement process will often provide adequate safeguards against systematic influences which may contaminate test scores. The effect of a general systematic error in measurement is quite crucial when criterion-referenced scores are being obtained, in that the proficiency level of all examinees will fall spuriously above or below established system standards. Norm-referenced measures, on the other hand, will be affected only when systematic biases differentially raise or lower the scores of particular examinees, as is the case with response sets.

Reliability and Random Measurement Errors

Aside from instances of systematic bias that may occur in the course of proficiency measurement, sources of unsystematic error may have an influence on the precision of the measures that are obtained. The effects of unsystematic error can be understood by considering an individual score as one instance of a large number of measurements. If all the measurements were perfectly stable—that is, if there were no unsystematic errors influencing the scores—an individual would receive exactly the same score each time his performance was measured. In actual practice, however, repeated measures of performance yield a distribution of scores rather than a single estimate of proficiency. The extent of the variability in scores is dependent on the proportion of the score attributable to unsystematic error. The greater the dispersion of obtained scores when a number of observations are made, the less the reliability of the measure. In effect, then, reliability refers to the precision of measurement; when the dispersion of scores all representing measures of a single individual on a particular task is large, the measure lacks reliability, and the test will be incapable of differentiating consistently among individuals who are at different skill levels. If the measure is precise—that is, if the scores are nearly identical—the measure is reliable in the sense that the range of values which can be expected for any one individual is small.

When an individual's proficiency is assessed, it is important to have some indication of the degree of reliability for the score that is obtained. For practical reasons, it is generally not feasible to repeat the measurement process often enough to obtain a large number of test scores. In practice, an estimate of the reliability of an obtained score can be made in two different ways, both of which involve the comparison of scores obtained from two sets of measurements on a single group of individuals. One procedure, called the *test-retest method,* involves correlating the scores obtained when the same test is given on two separate occasions. The second procedure, called the *alternate-form method,* involves correlating the scores obtained from two different but parallel forms of the same test, administered at the same time. A frequently employed variant of this second method is the "split-half" procedure, which considers the two halves of a test as separate forms, so that the scores obtained from the two halves may be correlated. It is also possible to combine the two procedures by evaluating performance using alternate test forms administered on two separate occasions. The correlation coefficient computed from the two sets of scores, whether the test-retest or alternate-form procedure is used, is called the *reliability coefficient.*

The two methods for arriving at reliability coefficients each require a slightly different interpretation (Cronbach, 1960; Thorndike, 1949). When test-retest procedures are used, the reliability coefficient indicates the stability of a score over a period of time. Hence, it is sensitive to sources of unsystematic error which are a function of day-to-day fluctuations in the individuals being tested and random fluctuations in environmental influences. When alternate-form procedures are used, the reliability coefficient indicates the equivalence of scores representing different samples of test items. This procedure is especially sensitive to sources of unsystematic error which are a function of the representativeness of the particular observations of behavior being made during proficiency assessment.

Sources of Unreliability.   One way to look at possible specific sources of unreliability is to consider the conditions which may produce differences in proficiency test scores when a single test is administered a second time or when an alternate form of a test is used to provide a second measure of an individual's performance level. Unequal scores from the two measures will result when, for one reason or another, the two measures are nonequivalent due to random fluctuations in the performance observed. One major source of unsystematic variability in a test situation is a function of variations in the environment in which proficiency is being assessed. The weather, for instance, may influence the performance of a pilot or radar operator in some unsystematic manner. In the same way, other situational factors such as noise, extreme temperatures, or distractions, and other environmental influences present during evaluation can randomly affect test scores.

A second source of unreliability is a function of fluctuations associated with the operation of the system in which an individual's performance is being measured. Variations in scores due to system instability may reflect random fluctuation either in the mechanical components or in other human components in the system. The performance of a crane operator, for example, may reflect not only his proficiency, but the condition of his equipment as well as the adequacy of directions from his helper on the ground.

The test materials or response-evaluating instruments used during proficiency assessment are a third possible source of unreliability. The equipment used during measurement must be carefully calibrated prior to testing. The evaluation of timed performance may reflect the random error attributable to a faulty stopwatch. In assessing troubleshooting, it is important to frequently examine the equipment being used for random malfunctions, so as to keep the test situation constant from one examinee to the next. Paper-and-pencil tests may incorporate similar sources of unreliability. Mark-sensing types of answer sheets, for instance, are sensitive to the heaviness of the pencil mark and the completeness with which erasures are made. The test instrument as a source of unreliability is especially critical when human judgment is used as part of the evaluation process. The rater or judge not only is apt to fluctuate randomly in his standards from day to day, but there may also be considerable unsystematic variability in the scores given by different judges.

A fourth source of unreliability is a function of the particular sample of items selected for inclusion in the test instrument. In general, the characteristics of test items which may vary from one sample of items to another in such a way as to produce random fluctuations in test scores are: the extent to which correct responses may be the result of guessing, the particular sequence of items, the difficulty of the items, the ambiguity in the questions, the degree to which examinees differentially may have been exposed to the item previously, and the degree of restriction on possible responses to the item as a result of test format. The determination of the equivalence of item samples used in alternate forms of a test, in terms of such statistical considerations as test means, score variability, and item characteristics, are discussed by Gulliksen (1950).

The complexity of the behavior being evaluated is a fifth type of influence on the reliability of a proficiency measure. If the behavior being measured involves many dimensions of performance, the items included in the test instrument will necessarily be relatively heterogeneous. Since it is possible that an individual's proficiency level may fluctuate considerably from one dimension to the next, each component element in one sense represents a somewhat different test. Thus, each of these dimensions is susceptible to all the sources of unreliability that have been described above. As the number of dimensions involved becomes larger, the number of items pertinent to any one element of over-all performance may be decreased in proportion to the total test. The effect of item-sampling fluctuations on score reliability is often assessed by procedures which measure the degree of homogeneity among items; that is, the extent to which performance on all test items is correlated. This internal consistency among test items is generally used to indicate the reliability of the test. The Kuder-Richardson procedure for assessing the reliability of a test was developed using this approach (see Gulliksen, 1950). It is important to recognize that the use of this procedure assumes that the test is measuring a unitary skill. This may be an unrealistic assumption in proficiency measurement, however, in that heterogeneity in a sample of items may be necessary to accurately reflect the nature of criterion performance.

A sixth source of unreliability is attributable to the characteristics of the human component itself. The performance of the individual being assessed fluctuates as a function of temporary variations in the state of the organism. Some of the factors frequently involved which may affect the stability of measurement are the individual's motivation, emotional state, susceptibility to fatigue and stress, and variations in the individual's speed of work and tendency to guess.

As can be surmised on the basis of these six sources of random error in measurement, some degree of unreliability is inherent in attempts to measure the proficiency of the human component in any complex system. One of the tasks of the test constructor is to minimize the degree to which random error influences the test score of an individual and thereby increase the precision of that score for assessment purposes.

Finally, reliable measurement is dependent, to a large degree, on careful control of the test situation. It is frequently possible to reduce the amount of instability in scores to some extent by manipulating one or more aspects of the measurement procedure. By clearly specifying the conditions under which the observations are to be made, it is possible to increase the standardization of the test situation and thereby reduce the amount of fluctuations in scores attributable to random error of measurement.

Estimating Test Reliability. In estimating test reliability by means of a correlation coefficient, the actual reliability of a particular test instrument will be underestimated if the range of talent being observed is small in relation to the actual range among individuals on which the test will be used. For this reason, statistical estimates of the reliability of a test instrument should be based on a reasonably representative sample of the population for which the test is designed. In some cases, apparent restrictions on the range of talent are largely a function of the characteristics of the test. The test may be too easy or too difficult for the population being tested, or the number of items on the test which actually differentiate among individuals may be too few. In general, factors which tend to decrease the observed variability or differentiation between individuals will tend to decrease the magnitude of the reliability coefficient.

An important consideration involved in applying the concept of reliability of test scores to proficiency measurement is the distinction between measures which are criterion-referenced and those which are norm-referenced. In psychological measurement in general, emphasis is given to the determination of reliability primarily as it relates to norm-referenced measures. When the human component in a man-machine system is being considered, however, the availability of a system standard may make it possible to estimate the precision of measurement using criterion-referenced measures. The concept of reliability as it pertains to criterion-referenced proficiency scores has a considerably different meaning pertaining to norm-referenced scores. Essentially, the reliability of criterion-referenced scores need not be estimated by correlating two sets of relative measures of proficiency; instead, it is possible to consider the stability of measurement with reference to its absolute value along a continuum based on system performance. For such measures, reliability is most meaningfully expressed in terms of some measure of the actual variability in performance, such as the standard deviation of scores assessing proficiency of the human component obtained on the basis of an adequate sample of observations of system performance. This is in contrast to the usual method of determining the reliability of norm-referenced scores, in which correlational techniques are used. In a sense, then, the reliability of a criterion-based score can be thought of as the *accuracy of measurement,* while the reliability of a norm-referenced measure can be thought of as the *consistency* of a score. This distinction is similar to the one made by Thorndike (1949), in which he points out the difference between absolute and relative consistency in estimating test reliability.

Validity

When test instruments are used for predictive purposes, the concept of validity is usually defined in terms of the relationship between test performance and subsequent criterion performance—that is, performance at the end of training or on the job. Proficiency measurement, as it has been considered in this chapter, is concerned with criterion performance itself. Thus, the concept of validity with respect to proficiency measurement has a somewhat limited meaning. The validity of a test used to assess proficiency is not established in the sense of how well it can predict any consequent or subsequent behavior. Instead, the validity of a proficiency measure is defined in terms of the content of the test. The validity of an arithmetic achievement test, for example, is not established by how well it may be able to predict future performance, but rather in terms of how adequately the content of the test reflects the kinds of behavior it is supposed to measure. Only in those cases when the achievement test is used as a predictor can the correlation of scores with future performance be used to establish some measure of validity.

A proficiency test, like all other tests, can be defined as a stimulus situation which has been constructed to evoke the particular kinds of behavior to be measured or assessed. In one sense, then, the validity of a test instrument is reflected in the degree to which the behaviors evoked provide a means for consistently differentiating among individuals according to their performance. In particular, a proficiency test can be considered valid if it discriminates among individuals presumed to range from no proficiency to high proficiency in a given skill. The validity of a proficiency test, then, is established by demonstrating that the test scores reflect differences in skill levels of the performance being assessed.

Establishing Proficiency Test Validity. The most common method employed to establish proficiency test validity is to employ the judgment of experts in the skill area under consideration. When judges are used, they typically participate in the development of the test instrument, so that the validity is established as the test is completed rather than afterward. In building a test to assess proficiency in supervisory skills, for instance, judges are used to specify in detail the kinds of behaviors to be observed and the skills to be measured. As the test items are prepared, the judges further evaluate the instrument in terms of the adequacy with which the items reflect the performance under consideration and encompass the range of skills involved.

While the use of judgmental methods for establishing the validity of a proficiency test is quite widespread, especially in the case of academic achievement examinations, several difficulties are often encountered. First, it is difficult to establish the expertness of a judge. It is possible that proficiency at a task does not qualify an individual as an expert in identifying the component skills which contribute to task proficiency. Second, different judges will have different definitions of skill levels, and it may be difficult to obtain satisfactory agreement among experts, especially when the behaviors under consideration are complex. Finally, and possibly most important, it is likely that the judgment of experts will be more adequate with respect to the coverage of the test than with respect to the quality of the items. Thus, the use of judges to assess test coverage in the preparation of item specifications is often more successful than the use of judges in evaluating the discriminability of the items.

In many respects, a preferable method for establishing the validity of a proficiency test employs the use of experimental techniques (DuBois, Teel, and Petersen, 1954). Using this approach, proficiency is viewed as the product of prior training and experience. Thus, the scores on a proficiency test should adequately reflect differences in performance levels attributable to these previous conditions. An individual who has completed a course in map reading, for example, should demonstrate a higher proficiency on a test prepared to measure this skill than an individual who has not been similarly exposed. It follows, then, that the validity of a proficiency test can be established by comparing the scores of two groups which have not been equally exposed or trained, to see if the test does reflect these differences. In using these experimental techniques, any treatment assumed to affect proficiency can be employed to demonstrate the effectiveness with which a test instrument can differentiate among individuals at different skill levels. In addition to training and experience, other variables such as the equipment used in accomplishing the task or the conditions under which the task is performed, could be used to establish proficiency test validity, providing there are reasonable grounds for assuming the treatment does indeed influence performance.

A number of experimental designs can be employed to demonstrate test differences in a given skill area. For example, the validity of a test designed to measure proficiency at troubleshooting a particular item of electronic equipment can be established in several ways. Perhaps the simplest demonstration would be to compare the performance of two groups, one of which had received troubleshooting training and the other of which had not. Another way would be to administer the test twice to the same group, once before the group had had a given amount of experience with the specific equipment and once afterward.

Under some circumstances it may not be possible to compare the performance of groups which differ in terms of the presence or absence of a treatment. Other possibilities which exist in these cases, and again using the troubleshooting example, would be to compare the performance of a group which had training on that specific equipment versus the proficiency of a group which had only generalized troubleshooting training; or to compare performance by the same individuals when they had or did not have access to well-designed test instruments and tools. Again, it must be assumed that the treatment differences will systematically affect performance.

An important consideration in establishing the validity of a proficiency measure is the relationship between the skills being assessed and ultimate job requirements. The proficiency test used at the completion of a training course, for instance, may establish the degree to which an individual has acquired knowledge about his job or has mastered the necessary skills. It does not demonstrate that the individual will perform effectively in the job situation. An individual with generally proficient skills may turn out to be an occupational failure because he spends a considerable amount of time on his job in a wasted manner. Whenever such a possibility exists, a valid proficiency-test instrument should sample job behaviors in such a way as to differentiate individuals who will perform a given task satisfactorily from those who are also able to perform it but will not.

Validity Relative to Reliability. A problem sometimes confronting the developers and users of proficiency measures is the evaluation of the relative merits of a test instrument which has satisfactory validity but low reliability versus one which has poor validity but high reliability. The validity of a proficiency test is primarily a function of the accuracy with which the task has been analyzed and the skill with which the items have been selected. Thus, the validity of a test is limited by psychological knowledge about the task and how this knowledge permits the task to be analyzed into component behaviors. The reliability of a measure, on the other hand, is influenced both by the degree to which psychological knowledge enables the precise determination of those factors which are apt to influence performance and by the control of factors in the test situation and test instrument which may influence test scores. Both the validity and reliability of a proficiency measure are limited by the extent to which psychological knowledge concerning the task is complete enough to specify the behaviors to be assessed, and the means by which accurate measures of performance can be obtained. Reliability is also a function of sources of error which can be controlled by careful design of the test instrument and careful administration practices. As a consequence, it is generally less difficult to improve the reliability of a test instrument than to raise its validity. For this reason, it is often more efficient to attempt to improve the reliability of a test with promising validity rather than to retain a highly reliable test which has lower validity.

In general, this section has dealt with several of the considerations involved in the construction of any psychological test. The problem of systematic measurement bias, random errors, and test validity are as important in proficiency assessment as they are in aptitude measurement. The role of these measurement problems in proficiency testing, where the criterion behavior itself, rather than a prediction of criterion behavior, is of primary concern, is somewhat different from aptitude testing. Contamination and random bias are especially critical in proficiency measurement, as a result of the field environment in which many of the tests are administered. Furthermore, the relatively frequent use of rating scales in proficiency measurement causes these measures to be highly dependent on observer judgments, and consequently, many proficiency tests lack the potential precision of more objective measures of performance. Establishing the validity of a proficiency measure is likewise different from the procedures used to determine the predictive validity of an aptitude test. In proficiency tests, validity is determined by demonstrating the effects of manipulations which are thought to influence proficiency levels.

▣ ELICITING BEHAVIOR FOR MEASUREMENT

A psychological test can be defined as a technique for evoking particular behaviors by means of specially designed stimulus situations. As has been pointed out previously, the degree to which the responses evoked by a particular situation are representative of the defined terminal behavior indicates the validity of a test developed to evaluate proficiency. Furthermore, the degree to which the responses evoked are recorded and evaluated in a consistent and unambiguous manner determines test reliability. These factors, in turn, are dependent on the characteristics of the stimulus situation and the means employed to score or assess responses.

Both of these characteristics of tests—that is, their stimulus properties and the type of response elicited—have been used as bases for categorizing proficiency measures. The stimulus dimension is reflected in categories such as "paper-and-pencil tests" or "situational-performance tests." The response dimension is reflected in the use of categories such as "recognition tests" or "free-response tests." These and other dimensions along which proficiency tests may vary will be examined before looking at some representative proficiency tests and testing techniques.

The Dimensions along which Proficiency Tests Differ

Process versus Product. In some instances, it is possible to measure some aspects of tangible products produced on the job as a means of assessing performance. The quality or quantity of a product is often assessed during proficiency measurement because it is the most definitive indication of the adequacy of performance in terms of the requirements of the system. In other instances, tangible products are inaccessible in the testing situation, and proficiency must be determined by assessing those responses which will ultimately contribute to a system product. In these cases, the process rather than the product is measured. Let us suppose the problem is to assess the proficiency of research scientists. It may be possible, in some cases, to obtain scores which reflect the product of their efforts—for example, the number of discoveries made or the importance of these discoveries. In many situations, however, it may be more practical to measure the proficiency of the scientists by observing behaviors which are likely to lead to important discoveries. By measuring the process, it may be possible to infer the product. The scientist's skill in identifying problems, collecting evidence, and analyzing data are some of the processes that can be measured.

When products are used as the basis of measurement, long-term as well as immediate products may be included in the sample. Long-term products frequently reflect aspects of proficiency which are difficult to measure in any other way. Supervisory behavior, for example, can be at least partially assessed in terms of employee turnover in a given department or division. Presumably, differences in the rate of turnover between two comparable departments reflects differences in employee morale and, in many cases, can be interpreted as indicating the kind of supervision the employees have received.

Categorizing proficiency tests as to whether they measure process or product depends primarily on where the observations, and hence the evaluation procedures, are focused. If primary attention is given to output, the test measures product; if attention is given to the means, the test measures process. Whether process or product is used as the basis for proficiency measurement often depends on which is most accessible and which is most likely to produce a reliable measure of performance.

Necessity for Observer Judgment. Proficiency tests can also be differentiated according to the degree to which a test score depends on observer intervention. Some test instruments involve only minimal observer judgments while others depend heavily on them. In general, the distinction between objectively scored and subjectively scored tests reflects the degree of reliability that can be attained in assessing performance. Proficiency tests which are scored primarily on the basis of the presence or absence of events require less observer judgment, and hence are more objective, than tests which depend on observations requiring extensive interpretation by a judge. In evaluating aircraft maneuvers, for instance, some aspects of the pilot's performance can be assessed by observing the aircraft's instruments. These observations are more objective than other aspects of each maneuver, which are evaluated by making judgments as to its tightness, its smoothness, and so forth. Frequently, it is possible to improve the reliability of a measure in which observers are used by reducing the extent to which judgments are required. For example, leadership or supervision generally can be assessed more reliably by means of check lists than by the use of rating scales. The role of observer judgment in proficiency measurement is especially clear in educational testing, where multiple-choice and other objectively scored tests are used mainly because they require considerably less human intervention than subjectively scored essay tests.

Component versus Global Measures. Some proficiency-measuring instruments attempt to assess performance of component tasks separately, while others attempt to evaluate job proficiency in a more global sense. Each of these approaches has its advantages. Whenever component skills are assessed, the results can be used for diagnostic purposes—that is, to indicate the particular tasks at which any given individual is highly or poorly qualified. A global test of proficiency, on the other hand, is more likely to sample virtually all interacting aspects of over-all job performance and weight each component skill in terms of its contribution to general job proficiency. As an illustration of this difference, a radio repairman's job performance can be evaluated by means of a series of tests based on components of his job such as theory, parts identification, troubleshooting, and repair procedures. His performance also can be assessed using a global approach, by basing the measurement on his over-all skill in identifying and repairing a selected group of troubles in which all the relevant component behaviors are required.

Observational Standardization. A fourth dimension along which proficiency tests may differ is related to the degree to which proficiency can be measured in a real-life situation. In many instances, it is necessary to modify the job situation in order to make precise measurement possible. For one reason or another, the job situation or the nature of the task being assessed may preclude the careful and controlled observation of performance or performance outcomes. One reason for modifying the situation is to provide a standardized test setting, one which will not vary from administration to administration. As noted earlier in this chapter, one of the difficulties in evaluating proficiency at complex tasks such as that of a navigator, is that each man may be tested under considerably different circumstances. In general, the degree to which performance in real-life situations may be a function of extraneous variables determines the degree to which the test situation must be made "artificial" for purposes of reproducibility and objectivity of observation. The task also may require modification before accurate measurement of performance is possible. In order to assess administrative skill, for example, it may be necessary to limit the responses permitted in the test situation to a discrete number rather than permitting the very large range of responses possible in the actual job.

In comparison with the real-life job situation, the test situation may only partially reproduce the stimulus conditions present in actual system operation, or it may evoke responses which do not correspond exactly to those required. These problems are similar to the simulation and response sampling problems discussed earlier. Modifications in test stimulus situations, as compared with real-life situations, can be fairly extensive without involving major modifications in the responses to be made by the individual being tested. The use of a jumping tower to evaluate the performance of parachutists, for example, requires that trainees make the appropriate responses, but it does not require that the responses be made under circumstances identical with those that exist when jumping from an aircraft. Similarly, the proficiency of student nurses in using a hypodermic syringe can be assessed by asking them to inject a grapefruit; while the responses the nurse must make are quite close to those which must be made on the job, the stimulus settings are substantially different.

There are other test modifications that can be made which will tend to influence the form of the response rather than the stimulus situation. Examples of changes of this kind are tests which require multiple-choice responses rather than composed answers to measure educational achievement, tests which measure ability to identify tools as an indication of tool usage on the job, or tests which require the recognition of safety hazards as an indication of an individual's proficiency in utilizing safety practices and observing precautions.

In general, the extent to which stimulus or response realism is modified for purposes of proficiency measurement depends on the degree to which satisfactory test validity and reliability can be achieved, by testing equipment and situations which are in keeping with the feasibility and cost considerations pertinent to the construction and administration of the test.

Types of Proficiency Measures

The tests available for specific proficiency-assessment purposes cannot be consistently categorized. Tests may vary according to their degree of remoteness from the job situation and the degree to which the behaviors that are elicited differ from terminal behaviors. Furthermore, tests can differ widely with respect to the cost of their administration, the degree of control exerted over extraneous factors and influences, the measurement procedure used, and the nature of the behavior contributing to adequate performance. It is not surprising, then, that the terminology traditionally employed in describing psychological tests, and proficiency tests in particular, tends to be inconsistent and reflects a variety of test characteristics. The term "performance test," for example, often means a test involving motor-manipulative as opposed to verbal skills; a term such as "procedural test" identifies a proficiency measure which assesses an individual's performance in relating and ordering job steps; and a term such as "group test" refers to a test instrument which can be administered to more than one individual at one time.

Despite this lack of consistency, proficiency tests may be grossly categorized on the basis of their remoteness from actual job performance. This remoteness may take the form of changes in the behavior elicited for measurement or in the eliciting stimuli themselves. In most instances, though, as the stimuli become more remote from those found in the actual job situation, the responses elicited are likewise less similar to those found in job performance. At one extreme along this continuum of remoteness is the measurement of proficiency during actual job performance. At the other extreme are measures which are not obviously similar to the criterion task, but instead assess performance at tasks which correlate with on-the-job behavior. Between these two extremes are test situations which attempt to simulate the job task while at the same time offering effective control of the factors which in "real" situations are likely to influence measurement. Although it is clearly a continuum of remoteness which is involved in categorizing proficiency measures in this way, it is possible to identify the three major segments of this continuum. These are on-the-job measures, simulated-performance measures, and correlated-behavior measures.

On-the-Job Measures. Ideally, the measurement of proficiency should be accomplished during typical performance of the system and under conditions generally present during day-to-day operations. As noted earlier, however, the degree of control which it is possible to achieve in a job situation is generally less than satisfactory for obtaining accurate measurements. Furthermore, attempts to standardize the situation for proficiency-measurement purposes, and even the observational or recording processes themselves, frequently introduce considerable artificiality into the situation. The feasibility of accurate measurement during typical system operation also may be a problem, in that work spaces are rarely designed to facilitate observation. Despite these difficulties, however, attempts to secure reliable and valid measures of on-the-job performance have been carried out successfully.

The techniques which have been employed for on-the-job proficiency assessment generally involve controlled observations of specified attributes of over-all performance or product. Gross judgments based on free observation of performance generally result in unstandardized and hence unreliable assessments, in that the behaviors attended to and the basis on which they are judged vary from observer to observer. On the other hand, procedures which specifically direct the attention of the observer toward critical aspects of task performance or product quality, and which include definitive standards to be used as the basis of judgment, can be employed satisfactorily in on-the-job situations. Since all aspects of the performance or product cannot be evaluated at one time, it is necessary to employ techniques such as time sampling, recording devices, observational instruments and other means to guide the observations being made. Many procedures have been devised for this purpose. For example, it is possible to measure product samples which have been selected so as to be representative of an individual's output. Check lists are used which indicate the procedural steps necessary to accomplish a given task or the presence or absence of certain desirable behaviors. Performance records can be developed which facilitate the recording of incidents of outstandingly effective or ineffective behavior over long periods of time. Finally, it is possible to use rating scales which have been carefully constructed and validated.

An interesting example of proficiency measurement in an on-the-job situation is described by Siegel, Richlin, and Federman (1958). Their aim was to assess the performance of parachute riggers some time after training was completed. In this case, attempts to evaluate product quality as an indicator of proficiency did not prove feasible and, instead, "Technical Behavior Check Lists," designed to assess individual task performance, were developed. On the basis of curriculum outlines, discussions with school personnel, and direct observation of students during training, a list of tasks was prepared and reviewed by field personnel. Items were then selected for inclusion in the final check list if they referred to tasks which occurred relatively frequently, were judged to be critical to over-all job performance, and reflected the existence of a range of proficency as indicated by the range of supervision required for individuals at different proficiency levels. The final version of the check list directed the observers' attention to such specific tasks involved in the parachute rigger's job as "inspecting and checking continuity of lines," "cutting material," "sewing pieces together," "testing quick release latch," and "fitting crash helmets" (see Figure 12.1).

An example of the use of tangible product measurement to assess proficiency is that reported by Mackie and High (1956). In this study, a typical Navy Machinist Repairman product, a valve stem and hex fitting, was manufactured in an on-the-job setting as the standardized proficiency-measurement task. The problem was presented in such a way as to be typical of actual

Job assignments (sample items)	Degree of supervision required when months in squadron was	
	1-3	4-9
A. Laying out measurements on material		
B. Sewing pieces together		
C. Rigging container and harness of seat–type parachutes		
D. Whipping and folding canopy		
E. Checking and installing barometric releases		
F. Attaching para–raft to parachute		
G. Lecturing on survival equipment and techniques to pilots, aircrewmen, and plane captains		

Figure 12.1.   An on-the-job checklist for the task of parachute rigging. Such check lists have been developed for many kinds of tasks in a variety of jobs. (After Siegel, Richlin, and Federman, 1958; courtesy Applied Psychological Services.)

product requirements. The component produced was evaluated by means of 33 separate inspections. Of these, 16 were objective scores based on measurements made with rulers and calipers. The remaining 17 measures were more subjective and consisted of judgments of fit, finish, and alignment of the valve stem and fitting. Correlation coefficients representing agreement among the judges were found to range between .70 and .98 for the objective measures and between .71 and .99 for the subjective measures.

When on-the-job proficiency measures are used, it is often important to collect pertinent information on the individual's performance over an extended period of time. Such a procedure tends to increase the stability of evaluations by decreasing the influence of day-to-day fluctuations in working conditions. An example of a proficiency measure prepared to facilitate such a longitudinal assessment of proficiency is the Clinical Experience Record for Nursing Students (Flanagan *et al.,* 1960). This performance record was developed on the basis of detailed information obtained on the effective and ineffective performance of nurses in on-the-job situations. A total of 2073 such incidents were collected from supervisors, nursing instructors, and patients. An analysis of these incidents defined a list of twelve categories under which observations could be recorded, such as "Meeting the patient's adjustment and emotional needs" and "Relations with co-workers, physicians, and visitors." These categories and their accompanying examples direct the attention of the observer to the kinds of behaviors most likely to differentiate between proficient and nonproficient nurses. A performance record form such as this one is designed for extended use, during which time records are made of behaviors to be encouraged, such as "Noted inconsistency in medication, treatment, or diet order," and those needing improvement, such as "Caused patient discomfort due to lack of skill or awkwardness." After each recording period, which might be several months, the compilation of specific instances serves as a basis for documenting evaluations of proficiency.

As these examples illustrate, on-the-job measures generally represent little alteration from the real job situation. Most of the efforts of the test constructor are devoted, not to the preparation of stimulus material, but to developing suitable procedures for making and recording the necessary observations. Perhaps an ideal approach to the evaluation of proficiency during system operation would be to design effective performance measurement and recording instrumentation to be incorporated into the system at the time it is constructed. This approach is similar to the one used during the developmental stages of missile design, where early models include sufficient telemetering equipment to provide accurate feedback as to the functioning of each important component during the launching and flight of the missile. The parallel use of telemetering devices to assess human performance would provide valuable information which could be used to strengthen training and human engineering efforts during system development.

Simulated Performance Measures. While on-the-job measures are frequently viewed as potentially the most valid for assessing proficiency, the conditions present in the job situation are such that the uncontrolled sources of error which may arise frequently tend to overshadow differences in proficiency among the individuals being evaluated. As a result, the job situation must be simulated in a controlled manner so as to effect a standardized environment in which performance can be readily and reliably assessed. The development of simulated job situations is often an expensive and inventive procedure. The essence of test simulation is the design of test stimuli which will evoke joblike behaviors that can be objectively measured.

The general category of simulated performance measures include a variety of proficiency-test techniques. Some of the most frequently used simulated measures are performance tests, in which an individual's proficiency is evaluated with respect to simulated system equipment and simulated environmental conditions. Another kind of simulated measure is the situational test, in which proficiency is assessed by having the individual attempt to act a realistic role in a "staged" situation. Finally, there are component-skill measures, where only a portion of over-all job performance is elicited by simulating the requirements of a specific subtask. This latter procedure is the case when a pilot is tested on emergency procedures, the electronic technician is tested on his ability to read schematic diagrams or use instruments, or a machinist is assigned the task of setting up his lathe in a particular way for evaluation purposes.

When the measurement procedure involves the operation of actual system equipment in a controlled test situation, only minimum simulation of actual job conditions may be required. Thus, evaluating the skill of a typist by having her prepare a copy of a letter, or evaluating the skill of a radar operator by measuring his ability to identify patterns projected onto his screen, involves only a limited amount of ingenuity on the part of the test constructor; and the more challenging aspects of the problem may be those of sampling appropriate job conditions and requirements for inclusion in the test. When actual system facilities are not available for assessment purposes, it is necessary to employ various methods to elicit the specific behaviors to be measured. In these cases, the more critical characteristics of the equipment and materials to be used must be suitably simulated in addition to the job environment.

An example of a proficiency test procedure developed to elicit administrative behavior is the In-basket Test for school administrators (Fredricksen, 1961). This test, which involves extensive simulation of representative aspects of the job environment, was an outgrowth of an earlier version prepared for military officers. One of the obvious difficulties encountered in trying to assess administrative proficiency of school personnel is the wide variations in influences attributable to the locale, population, and social conditions associated with particular schools. Thus, individual differences in administrative behavior is apt to be overshadowed by these factors. The In-basket Test program overcomes many of these difficulties by providing a standardized situation in which the examinee must perform. The situation is structured by means of a week-long, situational testing period, in which the examinees are introduced to an elementary school as they would be if they were assigned as principal. An extensive briefing based on filmstrips, motion pictures, written reports, and taped conference recordings provide the examinee with all the necessary background concerning the school, its faculty, and its students. At the end of the day and a half of orientation, examinees are presented with a variety of administrative problems similar to those which find their way into a typical principal's in-basket. The examinee is to handle these problems as well as he can; not by acting a role, but by actually doing what he feels ought to be done on the basis of his own training and experience. In the In-basket Test, the problems presented were developed so as to reflect an analysis of the school principal's job. The record of behavior produced by each examinee consists of memos, letters, working notes, and instructions to subordinates, which can then be scored on the basis of specified categories and standards.

Group discussion and role play are other examples of simulated job tests. A study involving the use of these and other simulated measures to evaluate supervisory proficiency has been reported by Glaser, Schwarz, and Flanagan (1958). In the group-discussion portion of the test, four supervisors were presented with a problem concerning plant management which they were to discuss as a committee in order to prepare a recommendation to their superiors. Observers recorded the performance of each of the four participants by means of both rating scales and a check list. These guides directed observer attention to specific details of the discussion, such as one member asking a noncontributing member for his ideas, or one member taking responsibility for summarizing the group's progress. In the role-play portion of the test, a supervisor was required to deal with a "staged" personnel problem as he would deal with it in an actual job situation. An actor took the part of a subordinate who interacted with the examinee in a standardized fashion as the two of them discussed a personnel problem. In this problem, the examinee's performance was recorded by means of a check list. A small-job management problem which involved the utilization of personnel and material in a miniature work situation was a third problem included in the test. The supervisor was required to train subordinates, organize the work flow, and monitor job activities. His performance was scored both by means of a check list and in terms of actual work output.

Another interesting example of a simulated situation, one which could be used both for training and proficiency-measurement purposes, has been described by Baker (1960), and discussed in Chapter 10. The problem was one of providing battlefield training for armor platoons, each consisting of five tanks. Because of administrative and logistic problems, the use of extensive field exercises to develop and assess tank-crew proficiency was not possible in many locations. Practice in tactical operations was possible, however, using a simulated battlefield consisting of a 76′ × 28′ terrain board. Five three-man trainee crews, located in booths above the board, operated radio-controlled scale-model tanks. The tanks were capable of moving and turning realistically and could fire a light beam to simulate the 90mm. tank gun. Each tank had photocells along its sides which were wired to "disable" the tank when struck with a light beam. Instructors operated up to five aggressor tanks and concealed antitank weapons, and they exploded harmless charges and smoke pellets located on the simulator. This equipment permitted the conduct and scoring of a variety of simulated tactical problems. The proficiency of the platoon leader and tank-crew commanders was assessed by a weighted check list completed by observers during the exercise. Items with unit weights included specific tactical maneuvers such as "sets up base of fire in *Woods X*." Greater weight was given to items representing particularly important maneuvers and over-all measures such as "completes problem with NO tank losses." (See Figure 12.2.)

One of the most frequently used approaches to proficiency measurement

Figure 12.2. A simulated situation for training and measuring the proficiency of tank crews. (From Baker, 1960.)

is to interrupt normal system operation so as to achieve a controlled test situation which nevertheless involves actual equipment. "War games" and battle exercises are examples of this type of procedure. The use of such vast amounts of equipment for proficiency measurement purposes is not always practical, however. As an alternative, it is frequently possible to develop simulated situations which not only facilitate measurement, but which involve relatively lower costs. For example, it is frequently possible to use training simulators for proficiency-assessment purposes, as was the case with the miniature tank battlefield. However, it is to be cautioned that training equipment often includes features to assist learning which are not included on the job, and these must be taken into account. The use of system simulation techniques in measurement is further elaborated in Chapter 13.

Correlated-Behavior Measures.   An extreme position along the dimension of correspondence between the conditions present on the job and in the proficiency test is represented by tests measuring correlated behaviors. Of the three types of proficiency measures that have been discussed in this section, correlated-behavior measures are the most remote from the actual job situation. In general, these tests represent a degree of abstraction from skill components required as part of proficient job performance. The most widespread type of correlated-behavior measure is the elicitation of verbal responses to assess skills which are substantially not verbal. Examples of this type of proficiency measure are the tests of job knowledge, vocabulary, and nomenclature used to evaluate performance at procedural and manipulative tasks. Other types of correlated-behavior measures are those which involve a deliberate modification in response topography so as to facilitate the recording and evaluation of responses. A common instance of this kind of construction is the use of multiple-choice tests to measure the ability to *produce* appropriate responses by measuring ability to *recognize* them. Another example of the use of correlated behavior measures is the measurement of related events, such as income or number of promotions, as a measure of skill level attained. The use of related events is somewhat analogous to the evaluation of product as a means of assessing on-the-job proficiency. However, the relationship between job performance and associated events is not always clear, and evidence of the correlation between them must be established prior to their use as proficiency measures.

An example of the use of correlated-behavior measures to assess proficiency when more direct procedures would be unnecessarily dangerous or expensive is the test of safety precautions for personnel aboard submarines developed by Wilson and Mackie (1952). Their test consisted of a series of 15 photographs which depicted men performing routine tasks aboard submarines. Examinees were required to indicate whether or not safety violations, such as the failure to wear goggles, were evident in the pictures and, if so, to list them. The validity of this test was demonstrated by data indicating a relationship between test scores and amount of training and experience. The use of correlated behavior in this instance proved satisfactory, especially considering the low frequency of safety violations and the difficulty which might have arisen in trying to observe them during job performance. It should be noted, however, that being able to respond verbally to safety violations does not insure that such practices will be carried over into actual performance, and some discrepancy between what a man knows and what he does can be expected. That caution must be exercised in interpreting the results of proficiency assessment based largely upon verbal descriptions can be illustrated by the example of the parachute rigger. One certainly would feel more secure after observing a rigger pack parachutes in a job situation than he would if he knew only the rigger's proficiency in describing verbally the procedure he would follow.

Because they are easily constructed, verbal or paper-and-pencil tests of job knowledge are frequently used to evaluate an individual's proficiency. When such measures are employed, it must be assumed that the job knowledge or theory being assessed is relevant to actual job performance. Tests measuring knowledge of technical information, tool nomenclature, technical vocabulary, or underlying theory do not measure actual performance. Instead, they measure verbal knowledge about the job and, hence, assess correlated behaviors especially in those cases where the job depends on motor and manipulative skills. The degree of correlation between tests of job knowledge and actual job performance is apparently related to the amount of perceptual and motor practice required for skilled performance, and the extent to which verbal practice has accompanied instruction in the motor task. An example of a test of job knowledge which was successful in differentiating among proficiency levels is reported by Hill, Buckley, and Older (1952). Their paper-and-pencil test, which included sections on job information, troubleshooting, and tool knowledge, correlated .63 with ratings on proficiency in a job sample involving representative tasks carried out with actual equipment. Thus, it is possible to construct tests which measure job proficiency indirectly by assessing the individual's knowledge *about* proper performance. These paper-and-pencil tests have the advantage of being easily constructed and economically administered, as compared with on-the-job or simulated-performance measures. It should be pointed out, however, that many more variables than job knowledge can affect actual performance, and before such tests are used for assessment, the degree of correlation must be assessed empirically.

The measures of correlated behavior discussed thus far have been concerned with aspects of an individual's performance which involve abstractions from behavior observable in job situations. The development of these measures is predicated on the correlations of various component behaviors in the performance of a given individual. Job performance is also correlated with environmental events, either directly in terms of job product, or indirectly in terms of events affected by an individual's output. Examples of this type of proficiency measure were investigated by Turner (1960), who compared a number of objective measures of supervisory effectiveness with ratings of job performance. The objective measures used were employee grievances, voluntary turnover, absences, suggestions, occupational injuries, disciplinary actions, amount of scrap, excesses in the use of tools and materials, and effectiveness as measured by time to complete a job compared with established time allowances. These correlated-event measures of proficiency were found to have low correlations with less objective ratings of job performance. Thus, Turner found little relationship between objective correlated-event measures and production-foreman ratings which assessed similar areas of job performance. Despite this lack of correspondence, the approach of using correlated-event measures deserves further study, since they may well be more representative of supervisory proficiency and effectiveness than are more subjective ratings.

An important characteristic of correlated-behavior measures is that they frequently include the modification of the topography or form of a response so that it may be objectively and easily observed, recorded, and scored. As has been indicated, the responses required on a test are frequently in multiple-choice form, even when the job involves recalling and constructing a response instead of recognizing the proper alternative. So long as the multiple-choice test and job-performance measures correlate reasonably well, however, the change in response topography is an acceptable measurement procedure, especially when the multiple-choice test has ben constructed in an ingenious way so as to involve more than simple recognition. Correlated-behavior measures, such as paper-and-pencil tests, are often useful in assessing those aspects of the task which involve "cognitive" skills such as reasoning and decision making, even though such tests may not evaluate proficiency at "simpler" but important components of over-all performance, such as manual dexterity. Thus, it is not surprising that tests measuring troubleshooting logic frequently have only a low correlation with actual job performance when proficiency on the job includes the location of troubles by simple techniques, such as looking for a broken connection or an obviously damaged component. Finally, it should be noted that not all tests involving verbal skills are necessarily measures of correlated rather than actual job behaviors. Assessing performance on a task such as the preparation of reports or records can be achieved with paper-and-pencil tests and yet involve little if any remoteness from actual job behavior.

Varieties of Proficiency Measures and Their Relation to Training

As noted in the beginning of this section, proficiency tests have been categorized in a variety of ways. The classification system used in this chapter is based on a continuum of remoteness between the situation represented by the proficiency measure and the behaviors elicited by it, and the corresponding situation and behaviors appearing in the actual job environment. In some instances, it is feasible to assess proficiency on the job; in most cases, however, some degree of simulation or change in response topography is necessary for measurement purposes. The degree of remoteness from the actual job situation employed in a proficiency measure is a function of the amount of standardization possible in the job situation, the cost of test administration, the feasibility of observation, the accessibility of the behavior, and the complexity and frequency of the task.

A final point to be made in considering types of proficiency measures is their relationship to stages of training. Early in training, when proficiency in large part represents familiarization with the job and with the verbal directions and nomenclature used, correlated-behavior measures of proficiency are probably the most useful. In support of this notion, research has shown that the intellectual and verbal components of a task are generally emphasized early in training (Fitts, 1961). Only after training has progressed does performance become more or less automatic. As the verbal components become increasingly covert, they not only are less amenable to measurement, but by that time, simulated or on-the-job performance measures are more apt to sample adequately the more integrative, complex, and relevant aspects of terminal behavior. As a result, simulated and on-the-job measures are frequently not efficient unless there have been substantial amounts of preceding training. In addition, the job situation may involve potential damage to equipment and trainees and thus preclude the possibility of proficiency testing on the job until training is relatively complete. In driver-training, for example, the goal may be to produce skilled and careful automobile drivers, but it would be difficult to assess behind-the-wheel behavior until after some of the basic principles and essential skills of driving have been learned. It is likely that the continuum along which proficiency tests vary from correlated measures through simulated measures to on-the-job measures parallels the level and kind of training then in progress.

▣ SOME APPLICATIONS OF PROFICIENCY MEASUREMENT

The approaches to proficiency measurement described thus far point to a number of the considerations involved in developing or using an instrument to assess human performance. In this section, the application of proficiency-measurement techniques to three representative man-machine tasks will be described. In each of these areas, some typical performance-evaluation studies will be used to illustrate methods employed for measuring proficiency in existing types of systems. The areas that will be examined reflect a broad picture of system types: equipment operation, equipment maintenance, and multiman systems.

Equipment Operation

Perhaps one of the most extensively investigated problems during World War II was the proficiency of aircraft pilots. A large number of approaches were evaluated and compared, in order to develop systematic and reliable tests with which to assess pilot performance. As described in a comprehensive report of these Army Air Forces efforts (Miller, 1947), the approaches could be categorized into five principal groupings. These were general subjective evaluation, subjectively rated work sample, objective observation, mechanical or photographic recording, and printed tests of flying information.

The use of general subjective evaluations of pilot performance was an attempt to evaluate proficiency by means of an over-all rating. Typically, a flight-school instructor flew with a student on a training mission and, at its completion, assigned the student a grade or rank with respect to his performance on the entire mission. Efforts to increase the reliability of these ratings by anchoring the high and low ends of the scale with behavioral descriptions yielded reliabilities or agreement among the judges which were not uniformly high, ranging from .35 to .89 in various studies. In many cases, the level of agreement was thought to be inflated as the result of halo effects, due to knowledge of previous evaluations and the classroom performance of trainees. When specific aspects or work samples of flying were rated instead of over-all performance, the intercorrelations among scores for various maneuvers were quite high, further suggesting that there was a rating halo affecting judgments of these specific samples due to the instructor's over-all impression of the trainee's performance. The difficulties encountered in using subjective ratings was further indicated by the low correlations obtained between judgments made at different levels of training. When the student advanced to a new instructor and a new training environment, his proficiency ratings at the new level correlated only between .20 and .35 with ratings made at the previous level.

While neither of these two approaches to subjective ratings proved very effective, observation techniques which were more objective tended to reduce the amount of variability attributable to the observer, and hence yielded more useful scores. A large number of objective check lists of pilot performance were prepared which were designed so as to be applicable both to complete missions and specific maneuvers. The check lists included items representing observations such as cruising speed, throttle setting, and degrees of turn, which could be scored on the basis of control settings and instrument readings rather than subjective judgments of pilot effectiveness.

Check-list observations were found to yield correlations as high as .88 between judges observing the *same flight,* indicating the levels of reliability that can be achieved with this technique. However, test-retest reliabilities when two sets of observations were made on the same day but not on the same flight were no higher than .32. When the observations were made by independent observers on different days and with the trainees using different airplanes, the highest reliability coefficient obtained was .04 (Miller, 1947, p. 143). The objective check-list approach, then, does reduce variability attributable to judges, but the variability in over-all performance from day to day or even from one part of the day to another suggests that fluctuations in weather, condition of the equipment, or condition of the pilot heavily influence the scores obtained. As a potential solution, it was suggested that ratings be gathered over a long enough period of time to reduce the effect of these fluctuations. It was also suggested that reliability could be improved by the use of weighted combinations of scores on selected maneuvers which were chosen in such a way as to maximize the stability of the total scores.

A further effort to reduce the influence of the human observer in pilot evaluation was the development of mechanical and photographic instruments to record data relevant in making judgments. Devices attached to aircraft controls or displays, for example, can permanently record pertinent pilot movements and deviations of instrument needles. One of the best known of these devices was the use of motion pictures to record target positions during fixed gunnery practice by fighter pilots. Complex recording equipment has not been widely adopted, however, inasmuch as it apparently contributes little to the reliability of judgments over and above that which can be obtained when judgments are guided by means of carefully constructed, objective check lists. Smith, Flexman, and Houston (1952), for instance, found that photographically recorded instrument readings correlated between .74 and .90 with observer recordings. Presumably, however, recording devices can add significantly to reliability when the observations to be made are so complex or must be continued over so long a period of time as to make it unlikely that human judges would produce reliable scores.

Printed tests of flying information used in the Air Forces studies were developed to measure kinds of knowledge correlated with flying skill, such as principles of aerodynamics, weather, instrument flying, and emergency procedures. As is typical of these kinds of proficiency measures, the reliabilities of scores on the printed tests were generally high, but the correlation between these measures and subjective ratings of flying skill were fairly low. Nevertheless, it was felt these measures did contribute to the assessment of total performance, and they were adopted to supplement flight checks and oral examinations.

Equipment Maintenance

For purposes of proficiency measurement, maintenance activities may be divided into two broad categories—preventive maintenance and corrective maintenance. Preventive maintenance tasks are those routinely performed to check out, inspect, adjust, lubricate, and calibrate an item of equipment. To a large extent, preventive maintenance is a procedural activity, carried out on a scheduled basis. Proficiency assessment of these procedural skills often is based on observing and recording actual job performance, since they involve relatively standardized routines and are part of normal job activities. Corrective maintenance is concerned with locating and repairing defective components in the equipment. Because these activities are not scheduled and are much less routine than preventive maintenance procedures, observation of on-the-job performance generally is not practical. The most elusive aspect of corrective maintenance are the skills involved in problem-solving—that is, diagnostic troubleshooting. Because of the complexity of troubleshooting behaviors and their importance to successful system operation, tests of troubleshooting skills have been extensively investigated.

In a comprehensive survey of troubleshooting measures, Fattu (1956) identifies four principal types of proficiency instruments that have been used by the military services to assess troubleshooting performance. These are on-the-job measures, performance tests, simulator tests, and paper-and-pencil or oral interview tests. A brief description of each of these types of tests will illustrate the variety of approaches which have been used to evaluate trouble-shooting proficiency.

As already noted, on-the-job assessment of troubleshooting skill is difficult because much of the behavior is covert and because the irregularity with which equipment failures occur makes it necessary to depend on the judgments and ratings of supervisors and peers rather than independent observers. Studies have been carried out on on-the-job proficiency in troubleshooting employing these measures, such as the one conducted by Demaree *et al.,* (1954, 1955). They collected supervisor's rankings on four aspects of job performance, supervisor's ratings on over-all job performance, and peer ratings of on-the-job proficiency. From their study, they concluded that ratings by peers more closely corresponded to estimates of proficiency based on a variety of other types of proficiency tests than did supervisor judgments. The over-all rating by supervisors was least satisfactory in this respect, because of differences between supervisors in their use of the rating scale.

A typical performance or work-sample measure of troubleshooting proficiency was developed by Rulon and his associates (1954). These investigators modified items of equipment with which trainees were familiar, so that the examiner could operate a switch in order to insert preselected malfunctions into the equipment. The malfunctions used in the test were selected from a large sample of possible troubles. Particular malfunctions were discarded from the sample if they were too difficult to insert, produced unreliable symptoms, or required testing time out of proportion to the information obtained. Each troubleshooting problem was divided into steps or segments, for convenience in scoring, and to allow the examiner to redirect the students at each step so that students who had made errors would not be overly penalized in later portions of the same problem. Detailed records of performance were made during the test, and these observations were later scored according to the amount of time spent on a problem and the number of times an examinee incorrectly selected defective components. The records obtained were also used to analyze troubleshooting approaches and the techniques that were used to locate a malfunction.

Unlike the performance measures just described, simulator tests attempt to assess troubleshooting skills without using actual equipment. A number of different simulators have been developed for this purpose. In general, the examinee is provided with a schematic diagram which identifies test points where he might obtain instrument readings or other information if he had access to the actual equipment. The student can then use the simulator to obtain whatever information he desires in order to locate the malfunction. One simulator of this type is the Tab Test (Glaser, Damrin, and Gardner, 1954). In using it, the examinee selects from a list of 30 or 40 checks those he might try in the job situation. When he selects a check, the examinee pulls up a tab revealing the information he would obtain had he actually performed that check on operating equipment which had the malfunction being simulated. A mechanical device developed for similar proficiency measurement purposes is the Automasts (Bryan *et al.*, 1954). This device also allows the student to select test points in the order in which he would investigate them, and permits him to choose the kind of information he would like about each test point, such as an ohm reading, volt reading, or oscilloscope pattern. Simulator tests of troubleshooting proficiency can be scored on a variety of performance aspects, such as the number of checks to solution, time to solution, redundancy of performance, or number of incorrect attempts at identifying the defective component.

Because of the sequential nature of the troubleshooting task and the interdependence of checks, the measurement of troubleshooting performance with familiar forms of paper-and-pencil tests imposes a high degree of artificiality. It is possible, however, to use multiple-choice and related test items to measure behaviors likely to be correlated with troubleshooting skills. Saupe (1955), for instance, developed a multiple-choice test of basic electronic knowledge consisting of 130 items. The test measured knowledge of terminology, procedures, schematic diagram interpretation, application of principles, and analysis of symptoms.

The correlations among the various types of troubleshooting measures mentioned in this section are of interest because they illustrate the relationships between proficiency tests having different degrees of remoteness from on-the-job performance. Several studies have been conducted in the area of troubleshooting performance to determine these relationships. Saupe (1955), for example, obtained a correlation coefficient of .55 when he compared scores on his paper-and-pencil test with a performance test measuring proficiency at troubleshooting actual equipment. Grings and his associates (1953) correlated performance, paper-and-pencil, and simulator measures, all measuring the troubleshooting skills necessary to perform corrective maintenance on the same item of equipment. They found a correlation coefficient of .56 between the performance measure and the simulator test, which was an earlier version of the Automasts Test described above. The paper-and-pencil troubleshooting measure, which consisted of troubleshooting items as well as items measuring general electronics knowledge, correlated .64 with the performance test and .46 with the simulator test. These investigators also obtained data on the relationship between the three tests and supervisor ratings of general troubleshooting performance on the job. The ratings by supervisors correlated .50 with the performance measure, .21 with the simulator measure, and .46 with a paper-and-pencil test. A specially modified version of the simulator test produced a correlation coefficient of .52 with supervisor ratings but did not materially affect the relationship between the simulator test and the other two measures.

Glaser and Phillips (1955) obtained correlation coefficients ranging from .74 to .88 between a paper-and-pencil test of troubleshooting proficiency and various scores derived from a version of the Tab Test. Scores on their simulator test correlated .54 to .70 with a paper-and-pencil test of general knowledge of the equipment. In a comprehensive study comparing various types of troubleshooting proficiency measures concerned with the same equipment, Demaree and his associates (1955) reported that paper-and-pencil, simulator, and performance measures had no strong relationship among themselves. They found that of these three measures, only the paper-and-pencil tests were very predictive of on-the-job performance, as measured by either supervisor rankings or peer ratings. It is difficult to generalize from the results of these studies, since it seems likely that the specific characteristics of the tests—such as the type of simulation, the form of paper-and-pencil items, the nature of the on-the-job measures, and the complexity of the equipment involved—all influence the correlation coefficients that were obtained.

Multiman Systems

In the complex man-machine systems of today, the human component is very likely to consist of a team of individuals. With respect to proficiency measurement, less work has been done in this area than has been carried out with individual performance, yet the importance of developing proficiency measures for multiman systems is being more frequently considered (compare Chapters 11 and 13). Several approaches for assessing group performance have been developed, both for small, face-to-face teams and large-scale, complex organizations, although the number of these studies is quite small when compared with the number of projects that have been carried out to develop tests to assess the proficiency of individuals.

A proficiency measure developed to evaluate shipboard Combat Information Center, Gunnery, and General Navy teams is described by Glaser, Glanzer, and Klaus (1956). Their instrument, the Team Performance Record, was designed to be used in diagnosing team performance during training exercises through records which identified performances needing improvement and performances to be encouraged. In using this measure, the observer's attention was directed to thirteen specific categories which previously had been found to be critical in differentiating high- and low-rated teams. The categories under which observers recorded effective and ineffective actions included such aspects of group performance as "composition of group and assignment of members," "communication procedures and coordination of information," and "interchangeability and assistance among team members." When used over a number of exercises, the Team Performance Record provided a series of measures which could be used both to evaluate teams and determine areas of weakness where additional training was required.

Another example of proficiency measurement applied to crew performance is described by Cook and Baker (1960). They employed several check lists, containing almost 500 specific items, to evaluate the actions of tank crew members, tank crews, and tank platoons consisting of five tank crews each. The observers watched the performance of the tank crews during 30-hour field exercises involving several kinds of tactical maneuvers, defensive and offensive actions, and special procedures. Observations were aided by allowing the judges to listen in during radio communications between crews. Each exercise was carefully standardized in terms of the terrain, aggressor action, and battle objectives assigned to the crews. The check-list items consisted of carefully described events, so that the observer only had to determine their occurrence or nonoccurrence and did not have to make elaborate, subjective judgments. During one exercise, when five observers independently scored crew performance, there was an average over-all agreement of 82 percent among scorers. In addition to the check list, a record was kept of the number of targets hit during range firing of live ammunition.

A different approach was employed by Chapman and Kennedy (1956). Their measures, which were developed for use in studying large experimental groups in laboratory settings, included scores which measured "effort expended" by the group and the group's ability to differentiate among items of information of varying degrees of relevance to the over-all task. "Effort expended" was defined in terms of the number of items of information utilized by the group in accomplishing a task. The group's ability to differentiate information input was defined in terms of how effective the group was in selecting the most relevant information from that made available to it. The results of these studies indicated that as the task load of the group was increased, "effort expended" did not show a proportionate increase; the group was able to maintain proficiency by more effectively selecting relevant information and by developing better procedures for handling each item of information.

The systematic measurement of proficiency in very large-scale systems is a relatively recent accomplishment. The most extensive of these efforts is the work on the North American Air Defense system (NORAD) reported by Carter (1961). During one NORAD exercise, exercise "Desk Top," the combined effectiveness of some 15,000 participants, representing more than 20 government agencies and military units, was assessed. The primary purpose of this study was to determine the processing and use of information of the kind that might be available during a large-scale attack. Data were collected to indicate flow of information; points at which information was impeded, lost, or misinterpreted; the use of information by decision-making units; time delays in initiating actions; the commitment and conservation of resources; the effects of simulated system damage; and other aspects of system performance. It should be pointed out that this effort is somewhat related to the recent interest in "business games," in which the operations of large-scale business enterprises are simulated for purposes of evaluating and training a team of "players."

In situations where it is possible to exert some control over team composition and environment, other measures of team proficiency may be possible. Glanzer and Glaser (1955), for example, have proposed two approaches which could be used to assess team performance by testing the limits of team behavior under stringent conditions. In one method—"overloading"—successively greater work loads are imposed to determine how long proficiency can be maintained before the team loses its effectiveness. Potentially, this method will distinguish between teams which are known to perform equally well under conditions of a uniformly low task load. In the second method—"subtraction"—the task load remains constant, but the personnel available to the team is varied. Like overloading, this method simulates conditions likely to be present during extreme periods of system operation. In one sense, these techniques measure team performance in a fashion analogous to that used in evaluating system hardware, where an item of equipment is operated to its "breakdown" limits.

Proficiency Measures and Their Applications

The examples of proficiency measures cited in this section illustrate the types of tests which have been developed for only a few kinds of performance. As is indicated by the measures applied to aircraft pilot skills, tests used to assess operator performance frequently are on-the-job measures. This is possible largely because operator performance is relatively easily measured during on-going training or during operational system exercises. Equipment operation often involves a large proportion of perceptual-motor components, and for such nonverbal skills, proficiency measures are generally adequate only when they sample behavioral components of this kind. Whenever symbolic skills, such as those which contribute to proficiency in troubleshooting, are being assessed, it is frequently possible to utilize proficiency measures which involve considerable abstraction from the real job situation. In addition, many other maintenance skills are difficult to assess during system operation in any standardized way, because of the unpredicability of scorable troubles, and because of the urgency of returning the system to full operational status.

In general, the appropriateness of any one type of proficiency measure is a function of the relative weight attributable to the behaviors which it measures in the job situation. Many maintenance tasks, such as the trouble-shooting of complex electronic equipment, involve a large proportion of symbolic and intellectual performance. On the other hand, there are a large number of maintenance activities, such as the repair of structural defects in an aircraft or missile, which are primarily manipulative in nature and cannot effectively be assessed without observing motor performance. Exclusive reliance on any one mode of testing may unduly emphasize those particular task components most readily elicited by that type of test.

The assessment of team proficiency has been investigated only in a limited way and much additional work needs to be carried out. It is frequently assumed that group performance can be readily measured by carefully investigating the proficiency of individual group members. The environmental effects attributable to communication and coordination among group members is an extremely important factor in group output, however, and is generally difficult to simulate. By and large, assessing the proficiency of multiman systems requires a careful analysis of all variables which may affect group output. It is conceivable that when considerably more is known about group performance than is known at present, it will be possible to simulate, for purposes of individual assessment, the type of group environment imposed by different organizational structures.

▣ CONCLUSION

This chapter has considered the problem of measuring the proficiency of the human component in a man-machine system. Proficiency is a consequence of many contributions; the performance of individuals and groups of individuals within the system is a function of their training, their capabilities, the design of their jobs and equipment, and their effective assignment within the system. The proficiency of the human component is ultimately a function of how skillfully the system was designed and developed. Thus, the careful assessment of human performance in the system can provide significant information concerning ways in which the system could be improved and maintained at desired standards of operation.

The methodology of performance measurement has advanced considerably since the early days of test development, but substantial research problems must still be considered. For example, relatively heavy emphasis has been given to tests based on norm-referenced, as opposed to criterion-referenced, measures. There is a substantial need for further development of proficiency instruments which will assess performance, not in terms of how an individual compares with other individuals, but with respect to how adequately he has attained the level of competence required for system operation. A weak link in the construction of proficiency tests is the definition of the behavior to be measured. Systematic techniques must be developed to more adequately identify and describe the components of proficient job performance and for determining the relative weighting of these components with respect to a given task. Advances must be made in techniques for appropriately sampling job performance, for establishing the reliability and validity of proficiency measures, and for specifying the kinds of test situations appropriate for eliciting various complex behaviors.

The degree of simulation required to elicit joblike behaviors, for example, cannot be determined in any systematic fashion, and there are no principles for deciding which features of the environment must be simulated for proficiency test purposes. Tests which are easily and inexpensively developed, administered, and scored may assess aspects of performance which are only remotely similar to on-the-job behaviors. On the other hand, extensive simulation is often employed, at considerable expense, to insure that the job environment has been adequately replicated in the test situation. It is likely that between these extremes some optimal degree of simulation exists which permits a valid evaluation of proficiency at reasonable cost. A basic psychological problem is the need for more detailed knowledge of the kinds of stimuli likely to elicit particular behaviors.

Further efforts also should be directed at the development of additional techniques for assessing the competence of performance. The most commonly used measures of proficiency are the degree of accuracy and speed of performance, and the occurrence of the desired response in a particular situation. Less emphasis has been given to other measures which may provide additional information about performance. Some examples of these are scores representing the characteristics of errors, the degree of retention of the response, the susceptibility of the response to decrement as a function of factors such as stress, and the likelihood of appropriate responses transferring to a new situation.

Finally, assessing the proficiency of the human component in a man-machine system requires the development of a precise terminology for describing behavior, in order to specify performance limits, job requirements, and existing performance levels. Knowledge of the relationships among these three descriptions of performance will facilitate the optimum utilization of the human component in system operation.

REFERENCES

Baker, R. A. 1960. *An evaluation of the effectiveness of the miniature armor battlefield for tank platoon leader training.* Fort Knox, Ky.: U. S. Army Armor Human Research Unit.

Brogden, H. E., and Taylor, E. K. 1950. The theory and classification of criterion bias. *Educ. psychol. Measmt., 10,* 159–186.

Bryan, G. L., et al. 1954. *The automasts: An automatically-recording test of electronics troubleshooting.* Los Angeles, Calif.: University of Southern California. Technical Report No. 11.

Carter, L. F. 1961. Training for decision-making in large-scale systems. In Glaser, R. (ed.), *Psychological research in training and education.* Pittsburgh, Pa.: University of Pittsburgh Press.

Chapman, R. L., and Kennedy, J. L. 1956. The background and implications of the Systems Research Laboratories studies. In Finch, G., and Cameron, F. (ed.), *Air Force human engineering, personnel, and training research.* Washington, D. C.: National Academy of Sciences.

Cook, J. G., and Baker, R. A. 1960. *The development and evaluation of the tank platoon combat readiness check.* Fort Knox, Ky.: U. S. Army Armor Human Research Unit.

Cronbach, L. J. 1946. Response sets and test validity. *Educ. psychol. Measmt., 6,* 475–495.

Cronbach, L. J. 1960. *Essentials of psychological testing* (2nd ed.). New York: Harper.

Demaree, R. G., *et al.* 1954. *Proficiency of Q–24 radar mechanics: I. Purposes, instruments, and sample of the study.* Lackland Air Force Base, Texas: Air Force Personnel and Training Research Center. Technical Report 54–50.

Demaree, R. G., *et al.* 1955. *Proficiency of Q–24 radar mechanics: Summary of findings.* Lowry AFB, Colo.: Armament Systems Personnel Research Laboratory. Technical Memo 55–6.

DuBois, P. H., Teel, K. S., and Petersen, R. L. 1954. On the validity of proficiency tests. *Educ. psychol. Measmt., 14,* 605–616.

Ebel, R. L. 1960. *Content standard test scores.* Paper presented at the APA Division 5 Symposium on Standard Scores for Aptitude and Achievement Tests, Chicago, Ill.

Fattu, N. A. 1956. *A catalog of troubleshooting tests.* Bloomington, Ind.: Indiana University.

Fitts, P. M. 1961. Factors in complex skill training. In Glaser, R. (ed.), *Psychological research in training and education.* Pittsburgh: University of Pittsburgh Press.

Flanagan, J. C. 1951. Units, scores, and norms. In Lindquist, E. F. (ed.), *Educational measurement.* Washington, D. C.: American Council on Education.

Flanagan, J. C. 1954. The critical incident technique. *Psychol. Bull., 51,* 327–358.

Flanagan, J. C. 1956. Evaluation of methods in applied psychology and the problem of criteria. *Occup. Psychol., 30,* 1–9.

Flanagan, J. C., *et al.* 1960. *The clinical experience record for nursing students: Instructor's manual.* Pittsburgh: Psychometric Techniques Associates.

Fredricksen, N. 1961. Proficiency tests for training evaluation. In Glaser, R. (ed.), *Psychological research in training and education.* Pittsburgh: University of Pittsburgh Press.

Gagné, R. M. 1954. Training devices and simulators: Some research issues. *Amer. Psychologist, 9,* 95–107.

Ghiselli, E. E., and Brown, C. W. 1955. *Personnel and industrial psychology* (2nd ed.). New York: McGraw-Hill.

Glanzer, M., and Glaser, R. 1955. *A review of team training problems.* Pittsburgh: American Institute for Research.

Glaser, R., Damrin, Dora E., and Gardner, F. M. 1954. The tab item: A technique for the measurement of proficiency in diagnostic problem solving tasks. *Educ. psychol. Measmt., 14,* 283–293.

Glaser, R., Glanzer, M., and Klaus, D. J. 1956. *The team performance record: An aid for team analysis and team training.* Pittsburgh, Pa.: American Institute for Research.

Glaser, R., and Phillips, J. C. 1955. *An analysis of tests of proficiency for guided missile personnel: II. The trouble-shooting board.* Pittsburgh, Pa.: American Institute for Research. BuNavPers Technical Bulletin 55–16.

Glaser, R., Schwarz, P. A., and Flanagan, J. C. 1958. The contribution of interview and situational performance procedures to the selection of supervisory personnel. *J. appl. Psychol., 42,* 69–73.

Grings, W. W., *et al.* 1953. *A methodological study of electronics troubleshooting skill: II. Intercomparisons of the MASTS test, a job sample test, and ten reference tests administered to fleet electronics technicians.* Los Angeles, Calif.: University of Southern California. Technical Report No. 10.

Guilford, J. P. 1954. *Psychometric methods* (2nd. ed.). New York: McGraw-Hill.

Gulliksen, H. 1950. *Theory of mental tests.* New York: Wiley.

Hammock, J. 1960. *Criterion measures: Instruction vs. selection research.* Paper presented at the meetings of the American Psychological Association, Chicago, Ill.

Hill, J. H., Buckley, E. P., and Older, H. J. 1952. *Post-training performance of aviation machinist's mates.* Washington, D. C.: Institute for Research in Human Relations. ONR Technical Report No. 5.

Mackie, R. R., and High, W. S. 1956. *Research on the development of shipboard performance measures: Supervisory ratings and practical performance tests as complementary criteria of shipboard performance.* Los Angeles: Human Factors Research. ONR Technical Report No. 9.

Miller, N. E. (ed.). 1957. *Psychological research on pilot training.* Washington, D. C.: U. S. Government Printing Office. AAF Aviation Psychology Program Research Report No. 8.

OSS Assessment Staff. 1948. *Assessment of men.* New York: Holt.

Rulon, P. J., *et al.* 1954. *Proficiency of Q–24 radar mechanics: II. The performance troubleshooting test.* Lackland Air Force Base, Texas: Air Force Personnel and Training Research Center. Technical Report 54–51.

Saupe, J. L. 1955. *An analysis of troubleshooting behavior of radio mechanic trainees.* Lackland Air Force Base, Texas: Air Force Personnel and Training Research Center. Technical Note 55–47.

Siegel, A. I., Richlin, M., and Federman, P. 1958. *Post-training performance criterion development and application. Development and application of TBCL criteria to the SESR program for the Air Controlman and the Parachute Rigger ratings.* Wayne, Pa.: Applied Psychological Services.

Smith, J. F., Flexman, R. E., and Houston, R. C. 1952. *Development of an objective method of recording flight performance.* Lackland Air Force Base, Texas: Human Resources Research Center. Technical Report 52–15.

Thorndike, R. L. 1949. *Personnel selection: Test and measurement techniques.* New York: Wiley.

Turner, W. W. 1960. Dimensions of foreman performance: A factor analysis of criterion measures. *J. appl. Psychol., 44,* 216–223.

Wilson, C. L., and Mackie, R. R. 1952. *The use of performance tests in the measurement of proficiency of enginemen and electrician's mates aboard submarines.* Los Angeles, Calif.: Management and Marketing Research Corp. ONR Technical Report No. 5.

WHEN A SYSTEM AND ITS COMPONENTS— equipment and human beings—have been designed and developed to the point at which actual operations seem both feasible and impending, questions about the employment of the system come to be of pressing importance. It is at this stage that specific procedures are planned and put into effect for the purpose of evaluating the system as a whole. Although earlier conceptions of the need for a "system test" tended to be described in terms of the proving of hardware characteristics, the development of modern systems has made the inadequacy of such ideas abundantly apparent. *System evaluation* is a phrase which implies the necessity for systematic observation and measurement of a system's capabilities in terms of its total functioning, including and even emphasizing the integrated operation of its subsystems with their human and equipment components.

The purposes of system evaluation, as seen in this chapter, are to make possible a prediction of the system's capability to perform its major and alternative missions, to compare these performances with those of other systems designed to accomplish a similar mission, and to develop the doctrines of system usage which will optimize its performance. Such purposes can best be achieved by broad-scale employment of simulation techniques, which make it possible to represent the inputs to the system, the conditions of its employment, the environment within which it is designed to function, and thus to permit the collection of data providing valid conclusions about system operations.

The approach to system evaluation described here has many close resemblances to scientific experimentation. The analysis of problems to be studied, the design of techniques of experimental control, the selection of performance criteria, and the formulation and testing of specific hypotheses, all display formal similarities to those occurring in the more familiar setting of the scientific laboratory. The design and control of studies for system evaluation pose some challenging methodological questions, particularly when one conceives of the entities of study as crews performing integrated system functions, rather than as mere collections of individuals.

EVALUATING SYSTEM PERFORMANCE IN SIMULATED ENVIRONMENTS

Robert H. Davis
and Richard A. Behan*

Although the interest in evaluating and improving systems is rooted in the remote past, the application of scientific techniques to this end is of relatively recent origin. From the beginning of written history, men appear to have been interested in assessing the adequacy of systems and improving them —particularly political, economic, and other social systems. Until recent years such efforts have been largely speculative and philosophical. But in the past few decades the emphasis has shifted from interest to necessity and from speculation to scientific experimentation.

This shift in emphasis probably began about the time of the industrial revolution and still continues. There are at least two reasons for relating the origin of the scientific interest in systems to the industrial revolution. First, there is an intimate relationship between the application by industry of scientific discovery and the stimulation of scientific enterprise by industry. The industrial and the scientific revolutions developed symbiotically and in parallel. Second, the man-machine system, which is in many ways a symbol of the

* Portions of this chapter were written while the authors were on the staff of the Data Systems Laboratory of the Thompson Ramo Wooldridge Corp., Denver, Colo.

industrial revolution, is—unlike political and economic systems—amenable to study by means of the experimental methods of science.

The characteristics of the industrial revolution embrace the development of the factory system, the application of power to industry, the mechanization of both industry and agriculture, and perhaps most important of all from our point of view, an amazing increase in the speed of communication and transportation. Fast, efficient and complex machines have become a part of our daily life, and because the size of machines influences their cost, speed of movement, and ease of handling, a premium has been placed on compressing them into smaller and smaller packages. As a result, machines have imposed greater and greater demands on the men who use them. Elementary system functions, previously performed by unskilled or semi-skilled workers, are now easily automated, and the remaining highly specialized functions which man performs in systems today frequently tax his physical, perceptual, and intellectual capacities.

As a result of this, the demands which today's machines place on the men who use them have reduced in many ways "the degrees of freedom" available to the system designer. There may, for example, be a dozen or more satisfactory ways of displaying visually the speed of a motor vehicle which does not exceed 90 mph, but there are only a very few satisfactory ways of displaying the speed of an aircraft traveling at 1200 mph. As the demands placed upon the human operator of a system increase, there are fewer and fewer "right" ways of presenting information to them to utilize their perceptual and motor capabilities. Taylor (1960) summarized these facts with the statement that "engineering psychology began with the intellectual discovery that man is not a perfectly adaptable organism."

But the man-machine system designer of today is faced with other sets of problems in addition to those commonly associated with human engineering. His systems require so long to develop that there is considerable danger of their being outmoded before they become operational. Modern weapon systems provide an excellent example of this. In contrast with the weapons of A.D. 1000, which had a useful life of 400 years, today's weapon systems have a useful life of only three to seven years and yet require about ten years to develop (Johnson, 1960). Today's systems are, in addition, so complex (and expensive) to operate that the designer is unable to use actual trial and error to solve basic design problems. Even in peacetime the efficient operation of modern weapon systems on the first trial may be a matter of life and death, and many countries depend upon information processing systems which, if inefficiently operated, could lead to a worldwide disaster. There is, in short, little room for error in most of today's weapon systems, and yet there is no opportunity for an orderly gradual evolution of their capability with a view toward improving them before they become operational.

The trend toward the integration of high-speed digital computers into man-machine systems in the last decade has greatly reinforced the need to evaluate and optimize systems prior to their utilization in real life. Systems which attempt to wed men, computers, and other equipments into an integrated whole are generally permeated with interactions which can virtually not be ferreted out without actually testing and evaluating them in some formal fashion.

Not only are computerized systems more complex in their interactions than others, but many of the functions and activities performed by these computerized systems are not readily accessible to system members or to system observers. Some of the system's activities are, in effect, "invisible" (Kepner and Tregoe, 1959) in the sense that the adequacy of a given action is not self-evident to system members or apparent to observers outside the system. The degree to which a given system activity or function is visible will depend on the provisions the system designer has made for displaying it. The activities and functions of all man-machine systems are spread along a visibility-invisibility continuum, but computerized systems have an extremely large number of invisible functions buried in the symbols and models of their computer programs, and consequently they are extremely difficult to design, evaluate, and optimize.

This chapter deals with the problem of evaluating and improving complex man-machine systems, particularly large-scale computerized data-processing systems. Before a system of this type can be evaluated in a controlled manner, the experimenter must have at his disposal a means of creating and manipulating the context within which the system operates. Simulation is a valuable and important tool for this purpose. In the following pages, therefore, we shall focus our attention on the problem of evaluating man-machine systems using simulation as a means of generating controlled system inputs.

Purposes of System Evaluation

Evaluation studies have as their primary purposes: (1) the prediction of a system's ability to accomplish its mission, (2) the comparison of a system with alternative systems, (3) the improvement of a system, or (4) some combination of these. Beyond these more immediate purposes, there are frequently others, particularly economic and political ones, in which there is a need to demonstrate the worth of a system.

Comparison of Alternative Systems. Although only one version of a system may be developed, more generally there are competitive versions. There are, for example, alternative ways of defending the country against air attack utilizing a centralized data-processing system. One such system uses high-speed digital computers to detect, track, and identify incoming aircraft. It has been argued that a man is a very light, economical, easily transported computer who excels in pattern discrimination and is easily programmed. On the other hand, he has only a very limited capacity for the storage and retrieval of data. Since a computer is difficult to program and has almost no capability to discriminate patterns, it can be argued by this analogy that such a system employs a computer in a less than optimal way; and that men should be used for the detection and tracking functions which involve figure-ground discriminations, whereas the computer should be used for the storage and correlation of flight paths. Clearly, arguments by analogy are not particularly scientific or convincing. But the possibilities suggested by this argument show that there are alternative systems for dealing with the air-defense problem, some of which do not even employ computers. It may be desirable to compare and evaluate them in a systematic manner.

In evaluating alternative systems, it is important to inspect the system design criteria very carefully. A system designed to process one type of data may show up very poorly when compared with a system designed to process another type of data. If tested against subsonic aircraft, one air-defense system may prove superior to another, but the previously superior system may fail completely when the test employs supersonic aircraft. In other words, there is frequently an interaction between criteria and systems, and the effectiveness of one system relative to another usually depends upon the evaluation criteria selected.

Improvement.   Evaluation is actually the first step toward the optimization of a system. In the course of evaluating a system, the experimenter begins to isolate problem areas which when corrected must be followed by another evaluation. As a matter of fact, system optimization is largely an iterative process of system evaluation $\longrightarrow$ system modification $\longrightarrow$ system evaluation $\longrightarrow$ system modification, and so on, until some satisfactory design specifications have been met.

Prediction of System Performance in Use.   Systems are sometimes evaluated solely for the purpose of estimating or predicting their effectiveness when in operational use. Frequently the cost of system evaluation is so great, however, that the evaluation is conducted for all three purposes simultaneously. It is also true that there are man-machine systems so extensive and costly that alternative systems will never be built and the only conceivable purposes of evaluation are the prediction of effectiveness and system improvement.

An Exemplar System

In order to have available referents to which the discussion of systems can be tied, a specific example will be developed in some detail. Air-defense direction centers are excellent systems to use for this purpose, because they have been studied extensively by psychologists and because their functions include many of those performed by other information-processing systems.

The mission of an air-defense direction center is to detect, identify, and track aircraft within a defined area of responsibility. When a detected aircraft cannot be identified with the information available at the direction center, an interceptor is assigned against the unknown aircraft for direct visual identification by a pilot. If visual inspection indicates that the aircraft is "hostile," it is either forced to land or shot down.

Direction centers use radar to collect raw data about aircraft in the vicinity of the site. This raw data is presented on radarscopes to human operators, who detect aircraft returns and track them. The operator "calls" tracks (via telephone lines) to men stationed behind a vertical plotting board (Figure 13.1). The plotting board is made of edge-lighted plexiglass, so that aircraft tracks drawn on it with special crayons will be visible throughout the direction center. Men stationed in the direction center use this display to perform their various functions.

One of the most important of these functions is the identification of tracks drawn on the vertical board. Flight plans are required of all aircraft flying at given speeds and altitudes within specified zones. The identification

Figure 13.1.   Photograph of an Air Defense Direction Center taken from an observation dais located in the back of the room. The large vertical, edge-lighted plotting board with its associated "tote" board is visible at the far end of the room.

is accomplished by correlating a track's position, its speed, direction of movement, and calculated altitude with flight plans forwarded to the site by the Federal Aviation Agency. When an aircraft cannot be identified, an interceptor must be assigned against it from the available inventory of weapons. Status information about the inventory of weapons, weather, and the like, is displayed throughout the direction center on "tote" boards placed alongside the large traffic display board.

Interceptors are guided to their targets by ground controllers. Consequently, weapons assignment includes not only the specification of the type of interceptor and its point of origin, but also the individual controller responsible for guiding it by radar to its destination. The various consoles within the direction center all have the same basic presentation; the controller uses the same radar display as that used by the scope operator initially detecting the aircraft. Since the unknown aircraft is within the zone of responsibility of the direction center and since the interceptor will also be within the same zone, the two tracks (unknown and interceptor) can be merged. All the tasks described require considerable skill, but the merging of the two aircraft is perhaps the most difficult of all. If the tracks are to merge, the officer controlling the interceptor must take dozens of factors into account, such as direction of wind, relative speed, and altitude.

A direction center is imbedded within a larger community called the air defense division, which normally consists of about ten individual radar sites. Any given radar has a limited range, and therefore many radars are needed to defend a particular area. Hundreds of radars are required to defend a large land mass such as the North American continent; consequently, air divisions must be tied together into still larger units. Furthermore, radars overlap in coverage, and it is necessary for these various systems to be interconnected with one another and to pass information back and forth. Communication of this kind between sites is called "cross-telling." The need to do this rapidly and accurately greatly complicates the over-all problem of air defense.

▣ SIMULATION AS A TOOL FOR SYSTEM EVALUATION

Simulation techniques, conceived in their broadest sense, have been used by psychologists for many years. As the term simulation is used in this chapter, it means reproducing or representing a specific set of environmental conditions. The difference between the use of simulation in the standard psychological experiment and in what is here called the "system evaluation experiment" is largely a matter of degree. In the standard psychological experiment, the experimenter abstracts and simplifies large chunks of the environment; in the system evaluation experiment, he attempts to include to a greater degree the complexity and richness of the environment. Experiments in these two areas tend to be distributed along a continuum of abstraction.

Many psychological experiments, such as those involving a Skinner box, T-Maze, or memory drum, have very little direct relationship to the natural habitat or environmental conditions of the animals being studied. Such experiments tend to be at one end of the continuum. At the other extreme are such studies as those reported by Chapman and his associates (1959). During these latter studies all relevant aspects of an air-defense direction center and its environment were simulated, and the behavior of four air-defense crews studied in relation to a variety of input conditions. In between these two extremes of abstraction and concreteness, there are numerous psychological experiments from various specific disciplines involving different degrees of environmental simulation.

Although simulation is not essential to the scientific evaluation of systems, it is widely employed for this purpose, and when properly used, it is an extremely powerful tool. Simulation is used in the evaluation of systems in two quite different ways. Sometimes it provides only the inputs to an operational system or system mock-up, in which case the responses of the system to these simulated inputs are studied and analyzed. Simulation is also arranged to represent the internal functioning of the system itself and not merely system inputs. When this technique is used for system evaluation, the entire process is commonly accomplished on a high-speed digital computer. In recent years, a number of psychological studies have been reported in which the internal functioning of the organism as well as the inputs was simulated (Ashby, 1952; Newell, Shaw, and Simon, 1958; Rosenblatt, 1958; Hovland, 1960).

Simulating System Inputs

When simulation is used to generate system inputs, the integrity of the organization of men and machines is maintained. Insofar as possible, the men and the machines are kept as they are in real life; although the inputs may be simulated in a laboratory setting or in the field, the illusion of reality is maintained. Simulation is used in this way to study a system in an operational configuration, and the simulated inputs are, of course, artificial only in the sense that they have been deliberately prepared by the experimenter.

A distinction should be drawn between the terms "real" and "actual" as they apply to evaluation experiments. Realism is a characteristic of simulated as well as of actual operations, and it frequently happens that simulated exercises are more "realistic" with respect to the stated mission of an organization than actual ongoing operations. Military organizations, in particular, often state their missions in terms having very little to do with the everyday activities of the group. An Air Force command, for example, may state that its mission is to seek, attack, and destroy invading enemy aircraft, whereas in fact such a mission is peculiar only to the combat situation. During times of peace, the organization's mission might be more realistically stated as training and preparing for combat. In such situations, the actual daily operations may have very little to do with realistic preparation for the ultimate mission of the group, and simulation may be the only way to achieve realism.

The conventional psychological approach to experimentation is one of abstraction. The intent of the psychologist is to construct a highly distilled experimental situation which will permit the study of selected independent variables. The richness and variety of the real-life environment is deliberately omitted in favor of the creation of a completely controlled habitat; the experimental situation is chosen with care, to guarantee that subjects will have very little freedom of response selection; and subjects are selected for the particular skills which they bring (or do not bring) to the experimental situation.

The most important characteristic of the conventional experimental approach is that it provides the scientist with an abstract environment—that is, isolated independent variables can be studied carefully, their relationship to behavior analyzed, and their interactions determined. Although the experimental psychologist is concerned with the realities of the subject's environment in the selection of independent variables and the performance measures to be taken, he has very little concern with replicating precisely the typical behavioral environment of subjects. Unfortunately, the frequency of interactions between psychological variables is so great as to place a limit of usefulness on this process of isolating independent variables for study. Indeed, in psychological experimentation, it is frequently the interactions which are of greatest interest.

In the simulation approach to the evaluation experiment, the emphasis is placed on providing subjects with a more complete experimental situation— that is, one closely resembling the real-life environment of the subject. The intent of the experimenter is to construct an experimental situation which corresponds as closely to the normal operating environment as possible. To this end, subjects are placed in an environment of machines which duplicate, wherever possible, the operational situation; insofar as it is practical, the properties of the inputs to the experimental situation duplicate those of the operational situation; subjects are chosen from the same population as operators in the operational situation, and the culture of the population is preserved.

Three of the consequences of these efforts are similar to those achieved using the abstracted experimental situation: (1) although the variety of responses possible is much greater, experimental subjects still respond in a clearly defined and specified manner, and thus one may plan for and collect specific data on their behavior; (2) controls can be implemented and experimental manipulations arranged, to guarantee the operational validity of the independent variables chosen for study—that is, to insure that causal relationships can be determined; and (3) subjects are chosen for those skills which they bring (or do not bring) to the experiment. Thus, the main difference between the conventional approach to psychological experimentation and the simulation approach to system evaluation is the emphasis which the latter places on the preservation of a more complete experimental environment, as opposed to a more abstracted experimental environment, and the consequent possibility of making highly specific predictions about a particular system, rather than the more generalized predictions of conventional psychology. (For a more extended discussion of these points, see Chapter 14.)

There are a number of advantages in the use of simulated inputs to evaluate a system, as opposed to the use of so-called live inputs. First, simulated inputs are precisely controllable. They permit the experimenter to maintain what has sometimes been called "stimulus control." If, for example, one is interested in evaluating the ability of a new data-processing system to route and control civil air traffic in the United States, it is conceivable that "live" inputs or actual aircraft could be used to test the system. The probability of precisely controlling live inputs in order to provide a base against which to evaluate system performance is, however, quite remote. Second, simulated inputs permit the experimenter to replicate precisely his stimulus conditions so as to draw accurate comparisons between alternative system configurations. Third, although simulation is often quite expensive, other things being equal it is generally more economical than using live inputs. Fourth, once techniques for simulating system inputs have been developed, they are available on demand. Unlike live inputs, they are not subject to extensive coordination and clearance and the vagaries of politics or the weather. Although simulation has other advantages, these are the more important ones and will serve to illustrate the point.

Simulating the Entire System

When the entire system is simulated, no effort is made to achieve the illusion of reality. Indeed, such simulation is commonly accomplished on a digital computer in an environment totally unlike that of the real system. Simulation of this type involves the fabrication of a mathematical model with appropriate parameters, so that the effects of changing the values of these parameters can be evaluated. There are a number of mathematical techniques for the simulation of systems and the evaluation of alternative system configurations and parameter values. The values to be attached to the parameters in such simulation often provide the mathematician with considerable trouble, particularly where these parameters represent psychological or sociopsychological variables. The result of this has been a tendency to circumvent the problem of establishing true values for these parameters by sets of simplifying assumptions about human behavior. Where accurate estimates of these parameters can be empirically obtained, simulation of this type can be a powerful technique for system evaluation. The role of the psychologist in this type of system evaluation is generally limited to the estimation of parameter values. For this reason, we are concerned in this chapter primarily with the use of simulation as a tool for creating controlled inputs to *operational systems,* and not as a technique for simulating the entire system.

Some Considerations in the Development of a Simulation Vehicle

One of the most important advantages of simulation is that it allows the experimenter to maintain "stimulus control." The term *stimulus control* means that the simulation vehicle is designed to insure the experimenter knowledge of—and control over—all information entering the system.

In many respects, the development of a simulation vehicle adequate for the purpose of system evaluation can be the most complex aspect of the entire evaluation task. For this reason, some of the considerations entering into the development of the simulation program deserve special consideration. One of the most important of these considerations is the isolation of relevant inputs into the system and the decision as to which of these inputs will be simulated, that is, the extent to which realism will be preserved.

The psychologist confronted with the task of creating simulated inputs to preserve "control of the stimulus" must decide which of the many inputs to a system he wishes to simulate and the extent to which he can deviate from "real life" without compromising the kind of experimental predictions he wishes to make. Obviously, this kind of problem cannot be solved solely on the basis of experimental considerations. Economic and other factors, particularly time, force the psychologist to compromise, but he must understand the system and his objectives if he is to decide simulation questions intelligently.

Let us consider an air-defense system. Radar impulses are propagated into the space surrounding a given site. Certain of these impulses strike an aircraft or other flying object and are reflected back to the receiver of the radar set. These appear on the radarscope as small blips of light. These blips constitute the information to be processed, and the entire system is designed for this purpose. However, other influences will also be reflected in the visual display on the radarscope face. Some of these influences have been predicted, and the system equipments are designed to deal with them. For example, there is a certain amount of residual energy in the receiver itself, which results in a random visual effect on the scope face (noise). Radar equipments, however, are designed in such a way that the effects of the energy reflected from aircraft are augmented so as to minimize the random noise in the system. But how much, if any, of this noise should be simulated?

In addition to system inputs appearing on the face of a radarscope, numerous other sources of information can be isolated. Flight plans from civil and military agencies flow into the direction center; other radar sites "cross-tell" information about radar tracks and flight plans; pilots of interceptors talk to aircraft controllers in the radar site; weather reports arrive from division headquarters; and the like. To what extent can the simulation program deviate from, or omit, these?

Besides planned inputs to the system, others may be unwanted. These other kinds of information are often called noise. The manner of dealing with these sources of noise will depend on the needs of the system for the kind of information represented by the noise. For example, clouds and heavy weather are reflected as areas of intense textured brightness on a radarscope. These displays can be valuable adjuncts to weather prediction, and in such cases, the system may be modified so that certain radar consoles display this information for purposes of weather prediction. From the point of view of an operator controlling aircraft, the weather on a scope may represent "noise," whereas from the point of view of a weatherman it will represent information.

Which of these many inputs coming into a system should be simulated? Generally speaking, when used for evaluation purposes, the simulation vehicle must be designed so as to consider all relevant inputs into the system, and equally important, it must also consider all the demands for outputs. If the purpose of simulation is purely the evaluation of a given set of components and subsystems, the outputs to be considered may be relatively constricted, and the boundaries of the system to be considered may likewise be narrowed to those information-processing tasks to be considered. If, on the other hand, one of the purposes of simulation is to determine the nature of the contributions which the system *might* make to the wider information-processing community, the boundaries of the system must be enlarged to include additional portions of this community.

Once the decision to enlarge the system has been made, these additional portions of the information-processing community may be dealt with in one of two ways. In the first case, they may actually be included in the information-processing system being studied. Under these circumstances, all their inputs, tasks, and functions must be accounted for in the simulation vehicle. This course was taken by the System Development Corporation in the preparation of an adequate training program for the air-defense system (Goodwin, 1957). The training program as it was originally developed included only units as large as an air defense division, consisting of an average of about 10 radar sites. However, it was soon determined that the training exercises should encompass larger command units than the division, and the decision was made to proceed in this direction. A much more extensive simulation program was developed, and this ultimately permitted exercises which simultaneously included all radar sites in the United States.

A second manner of dealing with the wider information-processing community is to simulate the activities of those portions of the larger community which contribute to the inputs, or utilize the outputs, of the system being studied. In this approach, those agencies adjacent to the system in question do not actually participate as subjects in the exercise or test, but their activities and inputs are simulated by members of the experimental (training) team using scripts or other aids. The generic term "imbedding organizations" is used to describe agencies surrounding the system under study and simulated by the experimental team.

Given the air-defense system which has been described and the considerations just discussed, how do these get combined to form a total experimental environment in which controlled tests can be conducted? First, let us consider the kinds of simulated inputs required to test experimental hypotheses about such a system. As a minimum, these inputs in the case of the air-defense direction center would probably include: (1) a means of generating the radar displays—that is, moving targets on the scopes; (2) a set of flight plans in an appropriate format to be correlated with the display; (3) status information for the tote boards, describing the available weapons, weather, personnel, and the like; (4) information about traffic being handled by adjacent direction centers; and (5) normal information from higher echelons of command.

If it is assumed that organizations external to the direction center are simulated by the experimental team (imbedded), the entire experimental environment can be illustrated as in Figure 13.2. The air-defense direction center (the system being studied) is shown in white. The experimental team shown in the light-gray area (right and left of center) generates controlled inputs into the direction center, observes the crew in action, collects performance data, and simulates the activities and inputs of the various "real-life" organizations shown in the adjacent dark-gray areas.

▣ THE SCIENTIFIC APPROACH TO SYSTEMS RESEARCH

Faced with the problem of evaluating a large-scale system, a psychologist typically turns to his background and training in search of a solution. While this is undoubtedly a desirable course of action, there are two important points to keep in mind in this connection. First, the area of systems research is relatively new and consequently has a number of special problems which are peculiar to it and which must be thoroughly understood. Second, while the scientist's background and training often provides him with valuable insights, they can also blind him to possible solutions. In this connection, inexperienced experimental psychologists are sometimes inclined to believe that well-designed experiments are *per se* a panacea; and when confronted with evaluation problems such as those under discussion, the researchers' first inclination is to devise a controlled experiment.

Unfortunately, carefully controlled experiments to evaluate large-scale systems are extremely costly and require essential ingredients such as methods for generating controlled inputs, meaningful hypotheses about the system being studied, methods of monitoring the system's performance, and definitions of the boundaries of the system. In many cases the system being studied has never been "turned over" in an operational sense, and it is little short of ridiculous to attempt to generate controlled experiments without developing a program of research. It is necessary to begin by recognizing that all scientific experimentation proceeds in steps and that these steps are essential to the conduct of controlled experiments.

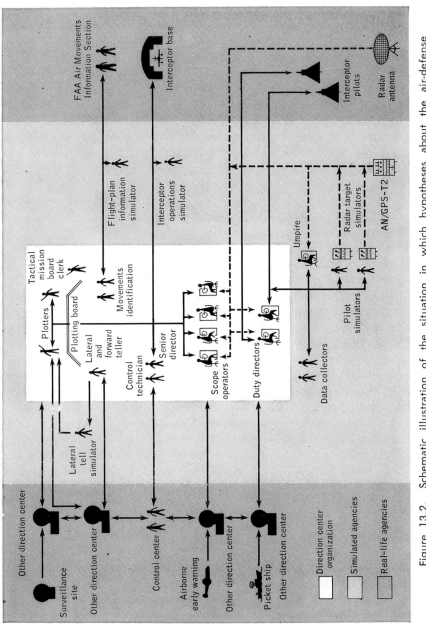

Figure 13.2. Schematic illustration of the situation in which hypotheses about the air-defense direction center are tested (From Goodwin, 1957.)

In this section we shall discuss some of the major steps in the conduct of a meaningful scientific experiment, and their importance to system research in general and system evaluation in particular. First, it is necessary to arrive at some clearcut understanding of the phenomena (system) to be investigated. This understanding will include a definition of problem areas and the development of testable experimental hypotheses. Second, a methodology or methodologies must be developed for experimentally investigating proposed hypotheses. Finally, experiments and studies must be designed and conducted to test hypotheses. The evaluation of a complex system involves welding these three elements into a total evaluation strategy or program. Only the first two of these three aspects of scientific experimentation will be discussed in the present section; problems associated with the design and conduct of the system evaluation experiment will be taken up in the next section.

Understanding the System

In all scientific experimentation, the investigator's first task is to acquire some familiarity with the literature in the area he proposes to study. One of the most important reasons for doing so is to isolate problem areas and to begin to construct explanations for data in the area under investigation. The scientist may wish to describe a phenomenon, he may wish to explain it, or both. In any case, he begins by collecting facts about it and by seeking to arrive at as comprehensive an understanding of it as possible. Scientists have, of course, been working in this manner for many years, and the scientific neophyte seldom appreciates fully the immense supporting structure provided to him by his professional community. In conducting a scientific experiment, the scientist seldom starts at the very beginning; usually he has available to him scores of published reports in his area of specialization. Perhaps equally important is the fact that these reports have been abstracted and indexed for easy review and access. Also, in most cases the research methodology in the particular area of interest is highly developed: special experimental apparatus has been designed; performance measures and performance criteria have been specified. Indeed, the research tools available for use by the basic scientist are as extensive as the range and development of his science.

Few of these methodologies are ever directly available to the system scientist about to evaluate a large-scale system. Nevertheless, and despite these difficulties, the basic approach is the same in both conventional and system research. The system psychologist begins by obtaining as complete a description of the system as possible. In large-scale systems, obtaining such a description is usually a complex task, and in point of fact, the truly complete description often flows from the evaluation experiments.

Because complex systems are often divided arbitrarily into personnel subsystems, communication subsystems, equipment subsystems, and the like, total system descriptions are generally not obtained by inspecting any single set of design specifications. Each of these so-called subsystems has associated with it a set of specifications. The Qualitative Personnel Requirements Information (QPRI), for example, is a required Air Force document which describes in detail the personnel subsystem. Most large-scale systems require similar documents defining system tasks, the specialized training most appropriate to the accomplishment of these tasks, and the organization of the group manning the system. In addition, procedures for the operation of each item of equipment in the system are generally developed and documented separately. In the case of computerized systems, computer programs must be written. Computerized systems also often require the development of special languages by which the man communicates with the computer and vice versa.

If the system has actually operated prior to experimentation, link analyses may have been conducted to study the communication channels and establish the frequency with which they are used. If information-flow diagrams have been developed and information-delay times established, these can be extremely valuable aids in the understanding of system operation. Moreover, developing information-flow diagrams is an excellent way of coming to understand a system. Variants of a number of established methods can be used to accomplish link analyses and information- and process-flow diagrams. Numerous references contain discussions of these techniques (Chapanis, 1959; Chapanis, Garner, and Morgan, 1949). From such sources as these, the psychologist begins to construct a description of the system which is adequate for the determination of problem areas and the definition of experimental hypotheses. To a large extent, information of this sort can be obtained from other professional people studying the system. With respect to one aspect of this problem, however, the system psychologist must depend largely on his own ingenuity and understanding of the system. This aspect is concerned with the establishment of the bounds of the system and its subdivisions for the purposes of experimentation—that is, the levels at which evaluation experiments will be conducted.

Levels of Evaluation

Generally speaking, evaluation experiments may be conducted at one or all of three levels of complexity. These are the component, subsystem, and system levels. Components and subsystems are abstracted out of the system context by a consideration of the inputs for processing and the tasks to be accomplished. A component of the system is not necessarily an individual piece of equipment, or even a single piece of equipment and the man who operates that equipment. A component may be conceived as the complex of machines required by a man to utilize a given input in the preparation of a specific output through the performance of a given task. The preparation of the outputs, through the use of the machine complex and the given input, constitutes the performance of the task. A very simple example of such a component is the complex of a telephone switchboard and its operator. The input to the situation is a vocal request to speak to some individual. The operational procedures involve establishing the correct line and "flipping" a switch to ring the individual called. The output is the completed connection or the discovery that there is no answer.

A subsystem is either (1) a sequence of components such that the output of one component serves as the input for a second, or (2) a parallel sequence of components such that each contributes to a common output. In the sense that subsystems integrate component outputs, they perform a higher order of unifying function than components. On the other hand, subsystems perform a subordinate system function, in that their outputs are integrated by the system.

An example of the first of these two types of subsystems would be the sequence of components in the air-defense system transmitting information about aircraft from a radar site to a higher echelon of control. The first component in the series is the radar operator who reads the positions of aircraft on a radarscope and calls these over the telephone line to the plotter. A third individual at the site reads the plotted positions of the aircraft and cross-tells these to a plotter at the next echelon of command, often many hundreds of miles away. The plotter at the higher echelon prepares a second display of the positions of the aircraft.

An example of the second kind of subsystem is the identification subsystem of the air-defense direction center. Two different types of inputs are involved in the identification function. The first is the display of aircraft tracks on the plexiglass plotting board described above. The second is the flight plan to the air-movements identification section of the radar site. These two parallel inputs are correlated, and the output is an identification of the track as either being "known," "unknown," or "hostile."

The reader, by now, must be aware that either of the so-called subsystems used as examples could also be called systems. The distinction is made between a subsystem and a system to the effect that a given sequence of components is called a subsystem if it is contained in a larger information-processing context. The larger context, containing both our examples, is the air-defense system, and our two examples are replicated many times over in this larger system.

The value of a distinction between these three levels for system study is twofold. First, the excellence of performance at any level is a function of the excellence of performance at the next lower level. Thus, if the component tasks are not adequately performed, the subsystem tasks will not be adequately performed, and so on. Second, because of the large number of potential measures of performance available and the time required to analyze large masses of data, a selection of performance measures must be made, and some criteria for selection must be decided upon. As research is done with one level of the system, potential areas of difficulty at the next higher level are discovered, and thus some preliminary hints are obtained of what performance measure will be required at the next higher level. Since the performance of the components often changes in the context of the subsystem and system, however, this procedure does not eliminate the necessity for designing special measures to be used at the component level at the time the subsystem or system is being studied.

Performance Measures and Criteria

When a large-scale man-machine information-processing system is functioning, its behavior is extremely complex. The untutored observer, watching a well-trained system of this type in operation, seldom realizes that he is observing a highly coordinated and smoothly functioning team. Instead, the activities of the system seem confused and uncoordinated. Consider a stock exchange: men answer telephones, move from one desk to another, tote information on vertical boards visible to other system members, shout to one another over the general noise level of the system, and observe a variety of displays on which coded information appears. The completely naive observer of such a system is in the position of a spectator at a football game who knows nothing of the intricate planning and rules governing the performance of the players. In some ways, the hypothetical spectator of the football game has the advantage; a football stadium is designed to allow the observer to see all the important action, and the rules of the game effectively circumscribe the play to a limited field of purview. Nevertheless, unless the hypothetical spectator has had some assistance, he will see little more than one group of men attempting to ram a ball through to the goal of another. In reality, of course, virtually every move of every player is planned before the ball is set in motion, and an intricate set of rules governs the entire game from beginning to end. The trained observer, who knows precisely what to look for, can quickly evaluate the performance of both sides, isolate points of strength and weakness, account for the behavior of umpires as well as players, and even predict future performance to some extent.

Before any system can be studied intelligently, the experimenter must know "what to look for." He must know what aspects of the system's behavior are important to the kinds of predictions he wants to make. There are those who will contend that all behavior is important, and it is difficult to disagree with this assertion when one realizes the importance of subtle cues for predicting a response. On the other hand, in the interest of economy, if for no other reason, it is necessary to select from among the thousands of responses which occur in a system of any appreciable size in a 24-hour period. While selection of the responses to be measured is sometimes a matter of convenience—that is, determined by what is possible, not what is desirable—such re-

sponses are usually selected on an entirely different basis. The experimenter
has reason to believe that the responses he has decided to measure are correlated in some way with the variables he is manipulating, and that information about this relationship will enable him to make intelligent and useful
predictions about the system's future performance. During the course of the
experiment, he may observe instances of behavior which he believes to be
meaningfully related to the phenomena under study, and he may, as a result
of such observations, expand the measures he takes in future experimentation.

One of the key problems in system evaluation is the determination of
performance criteria. Only after performance criteria have been established
is it possible to select intelligent and useful performance measures. Performance measures are the standards against which the performance of a system
is evaluated. In some cases, these standards are defined points along scales
of measurement. In other cases, they are implicit in the statement of performance criteria. Performance criteria for a single system may differ greatly,
depending on the evaluator and his objectives; and because one performance
criterion frequently conflicts with another, it is always necessary to select
and choose from those available. An example may help to clarify these points.

Let us assume that one is interested in evaluating this year's automobiles.
Before such a task can be undertaken, it will be necessary to define for what,
and perhaps for whom, the evaluation is being undertaken. If the automobiles
are being evaluated for the commissioner of roads, or for the smog-control
district, the criterion of performance may be quite different from that acceptable to a potential buyer. The commissioner of roads may be interested in the
weight of the car and the damage which it is apt to produce on roads. The
smog-control director may be interested in the efficiency of the engine and
the quantity of unburned gases which the car releases into the atmosphere.
A potential buyer may evaluate the car against any one or a combination of
criteria, including: (1) economy of operation; (2) ease of handling; (3) riding comfort; (4) seating capacity; (5) luggage space; (6) cost of maintenance; and (7) style. Furthermore, individual buyers will differ greatly in
particular requirements. A salesman, traveling at company expense, may care
very little about economy of operation but will instead want comfort, ease of
handling, luggage space, and style. If his company is buying the car, on the
other hand, it may be quite concerned with economy of operation and cost
of maintenance.

The number of possible criteria against which a system can be evaluated
is usually very large, and the evaluator must always select from the ones
available. Such a selection can only be made when the user's requirements
are fully understood. This understanding should include not only the important criteria and their relative weightings, but a clear notion as to which of
the criteria can be "traded off" for others. The need to "trade off" arises
because individual criteria often conflict with one another. It may not be
possible, for example, to get economy of operation *and* riding comfort *and*

luggage space. One may have to be traded off for the other. Similarly, in information-processing systems, time and quality may be seen to come into conflict. It may be extremely important to process given items of information in the shortest possible time, but it is usually necessary to sacrifice some quality in order to do so.

Generally speaking, the measures taken of system performance involve some clear-cut base against which to evaluate performance. A criterion frequently used is *perfect performance*. Perfect performance may have some absolute meaning, or it may have a relative meaning. One measure of system performance might, for example, be the time required to accomplish a particular task, such as the detection of a penetrating aircraft. Perfect performance in the absolute sense might in this case mean the detection of aircraft with zero delay or the detection of all penetrating aircraft. Let us cite another example, contained in a system designed to process photographic intelligence extracted from photographs. If the pictures were first viewed by the experimenter under extremely favorable conditions, with images enhanced and with improved ground resolution, a relative basis against which to evaluate future performance of the system could be established. Measures such as these— either absolute or relative—involve calculating the discrepancy between a criterion measure and the performance of a crew.

Once the question of performance criteria has been settled, it is possible to decide upon the performance measures which will be taken to evaluate the system against the criteria. These measures will vary greatly from one system to another. In the case of our example of the automobile-evaluation study, the performance measures may include miles per gallon of gasoline, answers to questionnaires, cubic feet of luggage space available, cost of repairs per mile driven, and the like. Performance measures employed in information-processing systems are commonly latency, error rates, and information-flow rates.

The Development of Monitoring Techniques

Establishing the measures of performance one wishes to collect is only one aspect of the task; actually getting them is another. The development of aids and techniques for monitoring system performance is a major task in itself. Aids for this purpose are generally of the pencil-and-paper variety, although in some cases it is most economical to produce them by using a computer. It is always necessary to plan their production along with simulated inputs. If, for example, a simulation program has been developed for presenting to operators information on radarscopes, and if performance is to be evaluated using the kinds of techniques described in the previous section, it will be necessary to develop special experimental aids which, in effect, provide the experimenters with a running description of what is actually appearing on the scopes.

An experimental aid of this kind is shown in Figure 13.3. This particular

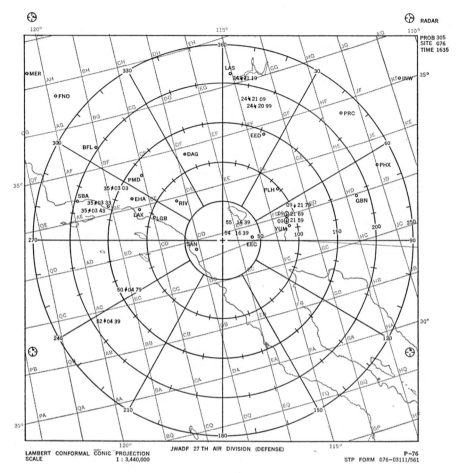

Figure 13.3. An example of a computer-generated aid used to follow the course of a problem presented to air defense crews.

aid is called a radar map. It is used in conjunction with the System Training Program (Goodwin, 1957)—a program developed to train air-defense command crews—and is used by psychologists monitoring the system's performance. This example indicates all tracks appearing on the scope for the particular sweep of the radar's antenna occurring at 1635 (4:35 P.M.). In addition, certain amplifying information about each of these tracks is printed on the map itself and in the margin. Each arrow, for example, represents a particular aircraft position and its direction of flight. Numerical information on each side of the arrows is codified to indicate altitude, aircraft serial number, and other information about the flight. Using such aids as the radar map, the system psychologist can compare and evaluate crew performance against the controlled stimulus input. Such aids as these are, in effect, "ponies," and they are essential tools for the study of systems.

In addition to such special aids as these, decisions have to be made with respect to the amount of data to be collected and the way in which it will be collected. There is a good deal of difference of opinion as to the amount of data which ought to be collected during system runs. Some system psychologists believe that good experimental practice dictates the advance specification of an experimental design, the performance measures to be taken, and the statistical tests to be applied. At the other extreme, there are those who believe that every possible scrap of data should be collected and subsequently culled for relevance. Psychologists at both extremes justify their respective positions on the grounds of economy.

In an absolute sense, it is, of course, extremely expensive to collect all possible performance data during system runs, but in a relative sense, this is not necessarily true. There is very little chance of repeating a system run because of the costs involved—and those who advocate collecting all possible data during a run view the relatively small added expense as a kind of insurance. There is no one answer to this question. Early in the study of a particular system, arguments favoring the collection of vast amounts of data are somewhat more potent than later in the history of the system, when its operation is relatively well understood and the chances of an experimenter oversight are remote.

The number and type of component or system measures selected will also depend upon one's knowledge of the manner in which a given independent variable influences performance, and upon the purpose of the experiment—for example, whether one is interested in the system *per se* or in the effects of particular independent variables. If the interest is in subsystems of a system, or the system as a whole, the practice is usually to collect as many measures as can be shown to vary with the independent variables used. This is a wasteful procedure, but not an entirely unreasonable one. Systems research is a new area of research, and the development of research procedures including valid and reliable measures of performances has only just begun. The constraints to reduce the number of measures taken are in terms of the time available for preparing reports of research and the amount of knowledge available about the system.

If the effect of one or more independent variables on a fixed system is the object of the study, a knowledge of the functions of the subsystems and interrelations between subsystems and of the points of effect of the independent variables in question will allow the experimenter to make a selection of measures which will reflect the nature of the relationship between the independent variables in question and the performance of the system. It should be obvious from the above that this latter type of research—study of the effects of independent variables—assumes a good deal of knowledge about the system in question. In addition, this type of research usually comes at a somewhat later stage in the evaluation of a system.

There is a wide range of techniques for collecting experimental data about a system's performance. Direct observation is one of the commonest and most widely used methods, and in recent years closed-circuit TV has extended the visual range of the experimenter to formerly inaccessible areas. Various techniques have also been developed for the remote monitoring and recording of auditory information, and these are, of course, also widely used. Whether one uses visual or auditory monitoring techniques, closed-circuit TV, or magnetic recordings, one of the principal problems is to keep from contaminating the experimental environment. The methodological problems in this area are virtually identical with those of the conventional psychological experiment, and consequently will not be elaborated.

Experimental Hypotheses about Systems

It is generally agreed that hypotheses are propositions about the world, stated in the form of empirically testable predictions. There are two key words or phrases in this definition. The first of these is the word "proposition." A proposition is something set forth or proposed. A hypothesis is a proposed solution to a problem or explanation for a fact; it is not formulated as a problem or question, but as a solution or explanation. Although hypotheses stem from an understanding of the system and a recognition of problem areas, they are not statements of problems. The second key phrase in our definition of the word hypothesis is the phrase "empirically testable." By this we mean the hypothesis must be stated in such a way that it can be subjected to empirical, experimental test, and either accepted or refuted. For this to be possible, terms in hypotheses must be defined operationally, and the hypotheses must be stated in such a way that they can be refuted—that is, possible outcomes of the experiment must permit the refutation as well as the acceptance of the hypothesis. The hypothesis is stated, therefore, as a prediction about the world, having possible outcomes in support of or in refutation of it.

We have stated that hypotheses spring from problem areas. What are some examples of these problem areas in system research, and what kinds of hypotheses result? System problems tend to arise in five or six major areas, having to do with the *equipment* of the system, the *personnel* manning the system, the nature of the *inputs* to the system, the *environment* within which the system is imbedded, the *operating procedures* defining how the system will be run, and, if a computer is part of the system, the *computer programs*.

There are two types of variables with which an experimenter is concerned: independent and dependent variables. The problem areas just described represent broad classes of independent variables which may be manipulated for the purpose of system evaluation, and each of these classes can be broken down into subclasses (Figure 13.4).

Experimental problems, for example, may concern the allocation of functions to men and machines, the format of displays to be used in the system, the number of items of equipment required, or the optimum arrangement of men and machines. These problems as a class are sometimes thought of as human-engineering problems. In the case of the air-defense direction center,

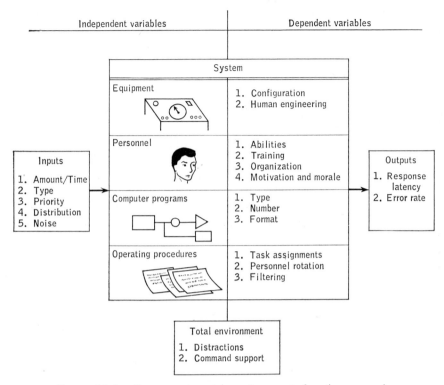

Figure 13.4. The experimental environment for the general case, illustrating typical areas within which evaluation hypotheses are generated.

specific examples of problems in this area might include the following: men note that the vertical plotting board is found to be too small, and tracks drawn on it tend to become confused during heavy raids; a change of format for the "tote" boards is suggested; a new item of equipment is proposed, to help duty directors vector interceptor aircraft to their targets; and it is suggested that covering the scope face with transparent plastic of an amber hue will improve performance. How these suggestions are evaluated will depend on many things, not the least of which is money, and it should be clearly understood that they are merely illustrations of equipment problem areas, some of which might be tested in a component setting, tested in a subsystem or system context, or perhaps not formally tested at all. Similar kinds of examples could be cited for each of the other classes of variables of Figure 13.4, but for the purpose of the present discussion it will be more profitable to trace a single air-defense problem through a complex experimental evaluation.

An Example of an Evaluation Problem

Our example comes from the area of operating procedures. In real-life operations, the men of a particular crew change from week to week and even from day to day. For a variety of reasons, different men work at the same position within a given crew. Often these changes in crew composition are temporary and occur because of illness or because other duties interfere. Sometimes the changes are more permanent and occur because a man finds or is promoted to another job. Whatever the reason, such changes can degrade the performance of the system, and it may be desirable to determine the extent to which performance is degraded by such changes in crew composition.

All we have done thus far is define in very broad terms a system problem. Obviously, some of the notions introduced will have to be sharpened a great deal before the problem can be subjected to a controlled test. To begin with, what precisely do we mean by changes in crew composition? How do we want to go about testing the effect of such changes? There are two general approaches which might be adopted. First, if the experiment is to take place over a reasonable period of time, it would be possible to hold the composition of some crews constant and compare their performance with control crews—that is, crews which are allowed to vary in an uncontrolled way, as in real life. Second, it would be possible to vary the composition of crews in some systematic manner and compare the performance of these crews with one another. Crew composition might be systematically varied by position or experience level, for example. Varying a crew by position might mean that we would limit our evaluation to the effect of changing senior directors or scope operators or some other class of system members. To vary by experience might mean to rotate more experienced men among crews and compare their performances with the performances of junior men who are rotated among crews. Since it would be impossible to test all these permutations in a single experiment, let us assume that it has been decided to adopt the first of the two approaches—that is, to hold some crews constant and compare their performances with crews allowed to vary in composition, as in real life (uncontrolled).

It is unlikely that differences between the two types of crews will be significant regardless of inputs. Common sense tells us that the more difficult the problem, the greater the likelihood of crew rotation having an adverse effect on performance. Difficulty presumably is defined in terms of the inputs to the system. It is therefore necessary for us to specify precisely the input conditions under which we propose to evaluate the crew's performance. Assuming that it has been decided to determine difficulty by varying the number of penetrating aircraft per unit of time, what does this imply? Are the penetrating aircraft to be friendly or hostile or both; and if both, what is the ratio of one to the other? How is the phrase "per unit of time" related to difficulty? For example, 100 penetrating aircraft may be distributed within any given time period in a variety of ways, and presumably distribution would have a great deal to do with "difficulty." How is input distribution to be controlled? One way of dealing with this problem would be to specify the number of tracks appearing during any given unit of problem time, as in Table 13.1, but even the "definitions" given in this table are not entirely adequate since they do not specify input characteristics which may have a significant effect on the performance measures taken unless controlled—for example, duration of tracks on scopes, aircraft altitude, or crossing and merging of tracks. Furthermore, no rationale has been developed for the values used.

The air-defense problem we are examining has one other key concept—namely, degradation. What does it mean to say that the performance of a system has been degraded? It means, for one thing, that the measures which are used to evaluate system performance have changed significantly. The number of cities bombed increases; the number of hostiles detected and destroyed decreases; and so on. Some examples of operational definitions for these measures appear in Table 13.1.

There is an important point to be observed in connection with all these examples: they differ greatly with respect to adequacy of definition. Both the dependent and the independent variables of an experiment should be operationally defined—that is, they should be defined in terms of the operations an experimenter must go through in order to demonstrate their meaning. The term latency of detection, for example, can operationally be defined as the difference in real time between the initial appearance of a target on a radarscope (t_i) and its detection by an operator as indicated by his reporting the presence of that target to a plotter (t_o); thus, latency $= t_o - t_i$. To be meaningful, every dependent and every independent variable must be defined in this manner.

The term "problem difficulty," for example, can have a number of meanings, but to be meaningfully manipulated in a system evaluation experiment, it must be operationally defined. In the example of air defense, difficulty might mean the amount of air traffic to be handled in a given period of time, or the amount of noise in the system, or some similar "burden" placed on the system. But even these definitions are far from adequate. Noise varies in type and amount, and increasing the number of aircraft alone does not necessarily increase the "difficulty." To adequately define these—and similar—variables the experimenter must be prepared to specify the operations which demonstrate their meaning.

Once an adequate definition of the independent variables to be manipulated has been arrived at, a question arises as to the range over which these variables will be presented to the system. Obviously, they fall into two major categories: (1) those which are continuous in nature, such as problem load; and (2) those which are essentially discrete, such as crew procedure or equipment configurations. The range of presentation will depend on whether the variable in question is continuous or discrete, and it will depend upon the purpose of the study. There is actually very little by way of guidance which can be provided here. One fact, however, is clear. The expense of sys-

Table 13.1

Operational Characteristics of the Independent and Dependent Variables of the Air Defense Study Discussed in Text

Experimental Variables			Operational Characteristics
Independent	Crew composition	Experimental	Crew Size = 30 Men Crew Composition = No variation in number or individuals from exercise to exercise.
		Control	Crew Size = 30 Men Crew Composition = No variation in number; individuals selected from those available for duty each test day.
	Problem difficulty	High	Number of penetrating aircraft appearing on scopes by type, hostile and friendly, for each 10 minutes of problem time. (Total problem time = 120 minutes.)
		Low	One half the number of penetrating aircraft appearing on scopes by type and problem time in high difficulty problem.
Dependent	Performance measures of degradation	Directly correlated with degradation	Targets bombed/penetrating hostile aircraft Median latency of initial detection of aircraft Percentage of friendly aircraft identified as hostile
		Indirectly correlated with degradation	Percentage of bombers detected Percentage of bombers destroyed Percentage of hostiles identified as hostiles

tem experiments precludes the testing of systems in a controlled fashion using a large number of treatments or values of a particular independent variable. The practice, therefore, is to select independent variables only after completing limited-control pilot studies at the component and system levels.

With all these facts in mind, it is now possible to specify an initial experimental hypothesis for this problem. If all contingencies are to be met, there will still be much planning, definition, and scheduling to be done; but the elements of a testable hypothesis have taken shape: *it is hypothesized that the system performance of air-defense direction centers is significantly degraded by day-to-day changes in crew composition.* This hypothesis is stated positively—that is, it is predicted that degradation will occur. To state the present hypothesis as a null hypothesis, it is only necessary to insert the word "not" before the phrase "significantly degraded by day-to-day changes . . . composition."

▣ DESIGN AND CONTROL OF
SYSTEM EVALUATION EXPERIMENTS

The Research Program

It should now be obvious that a large number of hypotheses can be generated about a system. Not all these hypotheses will be formulated at the same level of sophistication, and they will differ in their relevance to the evaluation mission at hand. The present section describes some of the conditions which influence the development of an experimental program to test such a set of hypotheses. An experimental program provides direction for the experimental effort; it determines the manner in which particular hypotheses will be tested; it establishes the order in which hypotheses will be tested; and, finally, it helps to determine the type of study which will be used to test each of the various hypotheses. In many respects the adequacy of the experimental program will determine the adequacy of the evaluation effort.

A number of considerations enter into the formulation of such an experimental program. While many of these considerations are of a strictly practical nature—for example, time, money, and personnel—others concern the content of the hypotheses and the hierarchical relations which exist among them. The nature of the studies to be undertaken in order to evaluate the system will be determined largely by the content of the hypotheses. Decisions about the order in which particular hypotheses will be tested are generally determined by the hierarchical relationships among hypotheses.

There are at least five ways in which system-evaluation questions may be studied and answered. These include: (1) using common sense; (2) consulting previous research; (3) employing a descriptive analysis; (4) conducting pilot studies; and (5) conducting definitive experiments.

Common Sense. At the common-sense level of inquiry, the types of problems considered are simple; their scope is relatively limited; and no elaborate experimental methodology is needed to arrive at adequate solutions. Such problems frequently arise in the design of equipment or the utilization of system equipment. Let us consider, for example, a device controlled by a movable foot pedal. The foot pedal as it comes from the factory lies with the smooth side down against the floor. When the operator uses the foot pedal to control the output of the device, the foot pedal slips. Eventually, the foot pedal slips so far that the operator must stop, feel around for the foot pedal, and bring it back to a comfortable working position. The problem is a simple one. No elaborate experimentation is required for its solution, and there is sufficient knowledge already at hand to arrive at a solution once the problem is isolated. One could, for example, place an abrasive substance on the back of the foot pedal, or one could determine an adequate position for the foot pedal and fasten it to the floor.

Previous Research.   Unfortunately, all the problems arising in the evaluation of a system cannot be solved by the application of common sense. However, the information necessary for the solution of a problem is frequently available, though not on a wide enough basis to be considered a matter of common sense. Such a state of affairs gives rise to our second level or way of inquiry—that is, the utilization of previous research. Problems soluble by this approach are usually those which have been encountered in the past and, as a consequence, have already been experimentally studied and reported in the literature. Generally speaking, the precise problem facing the system evaluator has *not* been encountered before, but problems sufficiently similar to it may have been studied, so that extrapolations can be made from the results of the previous research. Let us consider the individual who wishes to design a console at which a human being will sit to perform a particular task. How high should the console be from the floor? What sort of a work space should be provided for the individual who will operate the console? How much knee room should be provided? Such questions could be asked almost indefinitely. Many of these questions have already been encountered by human engineers in the past, and many of them have been extensively studied. As a consequence of such research, there is a good deal of anthropometric data available for use in console design.

Descriptive Analysis.   At the two levels of inquiry previously discussed, the information necessary for the solution of the problem was available to the system psychologist. In this and in the next two cases, the information the system evaluator needs is not available and becomes so only through experimentation. When the methodology of descriptive analysis is employed, a minimum of experimental controls are required; the fundamental objective is an empirical description of the system, its data flow, and its response times.

Three types of information are commonly collected for a descriptive analysis: (1) through-put times for man-machine operations, including those applicable to (a) individual components, and (b) sequences of components where the output of one component serves as an input to the next; (2) failure rates in machine operations; and (3) frequency and content analyses of system communication links. Since the collection and utilization in system evaluation of the first two of these types of information is relatively obvious, further discussion of them is not required. This is not true, however, of the third type of information collected for descriptive analysis, frequency and content analyses of communication links. Such analyses of communication links are commonly conducted on the communication channels linking men with one another, or linking men with machines. The technique most commonly employed for this purpose consists of making an exhaustive listing of all possible man-to-man communications and all possible man-to-machine communications and then observing the system in operation, tabulating the frequency with which the different types of communications occur. An illustration of such a tabulation is shown in Table 13.2. Once such a tabulation

Table 13.2

An Illustration of a Link Analysis[a]

		Men					
		Com. Off.	Eval.	Asst. Eval.	GLO	Fight. Dir.	VF Oper.
Men	Communications Officer (Com. Off.)		6			6	
	Evaluator (Eval.)	6		5		7	
	Assistant Evaluator (Asst. Eval.)		5				
	Gunnery Liaison Officer (GLO)						
	Fighter Director (Fight. Dir.)	6	7				
	VF Radar Operator (VF Oper.)						
Machines	VC Radar					8	
	Air Plot	1	9				
	Radio Desk	1					
	PD Panel				2		1
	VG Radar No. 1		9				
	VG Radar No. 2			8	7	4	
	VF Radar				3		9
	Director Repeaters				7		

[a] Linkages between men and men and between men and machines in the CIC of the USS *Louisville* during air attacks. Data is fictitious. Men and machines are genuine.
Table and note from Chapanis (1959), by permission of the author and the publisher.

has been accomplished, it can provide considerable insight into the scope of the communication of one man or one machine with other men and machines in the system; it also provides clues regarding the communication demands being placed upon particular links. Such results can be used to plan the arrangement of men and machines, determine the number of communication channels required to handle various communication loads, and help to plan ways and means of accomplishing load-sharing between individual system members.

Pilot Studies.   The pilot study is an almost indispensable tool for any developmental activity; it is generally used as a device to help collect information in those situations where very little or no information about a system is available. Typically, pilot studies are used to obtain some initial indications of the kinds of measures which should be taken, to discover where specific types of experimental controls should be applied, and to help establish the important independent variables for further study.

One way to characterize the pilot study is to assert that it is an experiment in which the experimenter is more concerned about making a so-called Type II error than making a Type I error. Technically speaking, a Type II error is made when the null hypothesis is erroneously accepted. The experimenter, in other words, accepts the hypothesis that a variable is not significant when it actually is. In the pilot study, one is interested in accepting as many potential variables as possible in order to be sure that all pertinent variables are, in fact, considered; consequently, the aim is to minimize the likelihood of committing a Type II error. At this stage, the experimenters are concerned with excluding those variables which obviously have no effect on the phenomena being studied.

The methodology of the pilot study is somewhat different from the methodology of the conventional experiment. The difference lies primarily in the amount of information which one expects to get from the experiment and in the fact that one will reject the null hypothesis more readily in order to keep from committing a Type II error. In the context of the system study, this usually means a willingness to consider designs employing smaller numbers of subjects and an acceptance, at the outside, of a 5 percent level of confidence, and frequently, results which are significant at between the 5 percent and the 10 percent level of confidence. If the requirement for the acceptance of the null hypothesis is less stringent than 10 percent, however, there is considerable danger that the experimenter will pursue false leads in subsequent controlled experimentation and will consequently waste valuable research time. In general, it should be remembered that a pilot study is exploratory in nature; it is an instrument used to search for valid measures, to explore potential independent variables, and to establish the experimental controls to be exerted.

Definitive Experiments. The nature of the problem in this case is somewhat different from that which we have just considered. When definitive experiments are used, it is assumed that the important variables in a particular situation are known and that something is known about the controls which must be exerted and about what measures must be employed in the situation. The purpose of definitive experimentation in system evaluation is, first, to check the results of pilot studies in order to be sure that the kinds of variables which have been selected as a consequence of conducting these studies are, in fact, those which do operate in the particular context. A second purpose of the definitive experiment is to determine the nature of the relationship which holds between important independent variables and measures of system performance. A third purpose of the definitive experiment is to determine the limits of a relationship which may hold between the chosen measures and given independent variables. It is seldom the case that a relationship between a given independent variable and a given measure holds over all ranges of the values of these measures and variables. It is more often the case that a given relationship will hold only within certain limits. Finally, the definitive experiment is conducted to determine the nature of the interactions which occur between the various independent variables operating in the system.

In the definitive experimental situation, the experimenter is much more concerned with the commission of a Type I error than a Type II error. A Type I error involves the rejection of the null hypothesis when it is true—that is, the experimenter asserts that a difference probably exists, when this is not the case. As a consequence of this fact, the levels of confidence which are accepted for significance are considerably more stringent. In addition, the usual context of a definitive experiment is one in which there is more and more concern with the reliability of the results. More time, more effort, more subjects, and more money are invested in a definitive experiment than in a pilot study. The definitive experiment is a reasonable extension of the pilot study. The relative concern with the Type II error in the pilot study must be compensated for by a concern for a Type I error in the definitive experiment. The acceptance of a lower level of significance under the relatively limited conditions of a pilot study must be checked in a more carefully controlled experimental situation. For a more thorough treatment of the topic of Type I and Type II errors and their relationships to levels of significance, the reader is referred to Lindquist (1953).

Experimentation with Systems

The experimental methodology used in the conduct of controlled system evaluation experiments reflects the kinds of constraints which almost inevitably accompany this type of experimentation. In the present section, three of the most important of these constraints will be discussed. The first of these has to do with the kinds of experimental control exercised in systems research; the second concerns the collection of experimental data; and the third concerns problems in the area of experimental design.

Experimental Control. Two characteristics of a conventional experiment are worth noting, both having to do with the reliability of experimental results. One concern for reliability arises as a consequence of random variations among subjects when a large number of subjects is being utilized. The university psychologist studying a problem in learning in human beings, for example, generally has at his disposal a large number of potential subjects from introductory classes in psychology. When large numbers of subjects are used, it is unlikely that the effects of individual differences will materially influence the results of an experiment. There is, however, a difference between this type of situation and the one in which system evaluation experiments are typically conducted. Subjects in system experiments are the groups of people operating the system, and it is usually very difficult to get a large number of such groups or crews. The time-honored technique of randomizing individual differences, therefore, does not generally apply in the evaluation of large systems.

A second characteristic of the conventional experimental problems concerns the range of external variables which must be controlled and the techniques which are used to control them. Let us consider the problem of human interactions. If the experimenter in a university setting is concerned with the interactions of human beings during an experiment, the experiment can be conducted so that only one subject is tested at a time. The very nature of the phenomena studied in the typical system experiment requires that human beings interact with each other. As a consequence, human interactions will always occur. The control of the environment in which the human being performs in a system experiment is complicated by a second problem. Individual system members are almost always involved with a machine; the machine contributes to what the man does, and the man contributes to what the machine does. Thus, in any man-machine system, there is a large number of interactions between men and machines. These two sources of variations in performance are not necessarily objectionable in and of themselves. They are characteristic of all systems and should be included in system studies. Problems arise, however, when human beings become involved in tasks not directly related to their system performance, or when machines malfunction. Such difficulties translate themselves into problems of attention span, motivation, and morale in the case of a human being, and into problems of reliability and failure in the case of the machine. The fundamental problem is to keep the human being (or the machine) task-oriented.

The environment of the system experiment is complicated in another sense—that is, there is considerable interaction between related information-processing tasks. This gives rise to the problem of description of the stimulus. The input to a system can be described in considerable detail and with considerable accuracy. As soon as this input information has gone through the first of a series of processes, however, the experimenter loses the opportunity to describe and specify precisely what the input to subsequent processing tasks actually is.

A third characteristic of the system context which creates control difficulties is the existence of a number of alternative responses in the system context. In the typical psychological experiment, the experimenter is concerned with one, or at most a few, of the responses of his subjects. Furthermore, the experimenter often constrains the experimental situation in such a way that the responses of the subject are directed toward the particular aspects of behavior of interest. In reaction-time experiments, for example, the task of the subject is specifically oriented toward a particular form of behavior. Other examples of the same sort of attitude are to be found in nonsense-syllable learning, in experiments involving anagrams, and in maze learning in human beings. It is characteristic, then, of the usual experimental situation employed in psychology for the experimenter to be concerned with a particular aspect of a subject's behavior. This is not the case in a system context. There is, of course, a preferred mode of behavior, and appropriate modes for interaction are provided for the members of a crew. But there is no guarantee that crew members will utilize these preferred modes of interaction. In most systems situations, modes of communication are provided for those channels the system designer wishes to have employed. It is not always possible, however, to restrict the behavior of crew members to such modes of communication or to restrict communication to specific individuals. Typically, when an individual wishes to talk to someone with whom he has no official connection, he simply raises his voice and completes the communication. These "extracurricular" modes of communication serve two purposes. On the one hand, they contribute to the lack of precise control in the experimental situation, and in this respect they are an unfortunate occurrence. On the other hand, in the development of a system, it is just exactly this sort of occurrence that the experimenter often wishes to observe. Frequently, such "extracurricular" communications (particularly if they occur with any great frequency) are a source of information about inadequate communication facilities within the systems context. If one is in the developmental phase and one is concerned with the development of measures or techniques for experimental control, or with the isolation of important independent variables, he may welcome such occurrences. On the other hand, if the experiment is relatively precisely controlled and such acts occur, they will be anything but welcome.

A final consideration with respect to control concerns the problem of variability of performance among human beings. Given a crew of individuals to man a particular system, individual abilities differ over a relatively wide range. In itself, this is not a particularly surprising observation. When considered in conjunction with the fact that information-processing systems frequently involve a sequence of processing events, however, it can be seen to lead to considerable variation in system performance, as well as lack of control in the experimental situation. One person may be assigned to do a particular job and he may do his job very well; another individual—presumably possessing similar skills—may perform the same task very poorly. Thus, the output of the component in the two different situations is quite different, and the input to a subsequent component is not the same. As a consequence, there is a real problem in the selection of individuals to fill particular positions on an experimental crew. One method of dealing with this problem is to attempt to match individuals from one crew to individuals from the next on the basis of skill. However, this is only practical in those instances in which there is a large number of individuals to choose from and the crews are relatively small. Another solution to the problem is training; and indeed, it frequently happens in the system context that one spends as much time preparing individuals to serve as subjects as one spends utilizing them in evaluation experiments.

These considerations imply that the problem of control in a systems experiment is considerably greater than the problem of control in the more conventional psychological experimental situation. This difficulty has led to two attempts to solve the problem of control. One has been the search for "system measures" which would transcend the difficulties mentioned, and the second has been the attempt to break systems up into subsystems, to study the subsystem independently and then to put the subsytems together in a selective fashion. Both these techniques are useful and both are currently used in present-day systems evaluation.

Data-Collection Problems.   As we have pointed out, the system evaluation experiment may involve as many as 15 or 20 different types of response measures. There are three consequences of this state of affairs worth discussing. The first and most obvious of these is that a relatively large number of monitors of system performance are generally required to collect the necessary data. This means that a considerable amount of staff training is required. It also means that the data collection and reduction task creates a second-higher-level system. A set of individuals who are concerned with the collection of data on system behavior, together with their various aids for data collection, constitute another kind of system—in effect, a metasystem. The same variables which influence the behavior of the data-processing system of interest also influence the behavior of the data-collection system which monitors the system of interest. Since one of the most pervasive variables affecting all system performance is input load, the experimenter must always be sure that the individuals collecting data are trained to recognize and collect the data required, and that in the process of collecting this data they do not become overloaded. When data collectors become overloaded, there is an interaction between the system that is being observed and the system doing the monitoring. In such a situation, the response measures being collected are no longer related solely to the system under observation, but reflect instead the behavior patterns of both systems.

Experimental Design Problems. There are two considerations in the selection of an experimental design for system experimentation. The first of these has to do with the problem of replication, and the second has to do with the independence of measures. These two problems are, of course, inter-related; but, for the purpose of the present discussion, they may be considered separately.

The conventional experimental design generally utilizes different subjects to counter the problem of variability. As indicated previously, in a system context individual human beings are rarely if ever subjects; crews are the subjects for experimentation. Since crews consist of relatively large numbers of human beings, there are problems in obtaining a satisfactory number of crews. A second consideration which enters here, and one which frequently serves as a basis for the relationship between our two points of discussion, is that the difficulty of obtaining crews makes it necessary to use a particular crew over a series of experimental trials. In consequence, it is seldom possible to deal with independent measures in a typical system experiment. The problem of replications is handled by utilizing a crew on more than one occasion, and assumptions about independence of measures cannot be met.

A cursory examination of the considerations described in the above paragraphs will convince the reader that the system experiment requires the more sophisticated types of experimental design. Only a few subjects (crews) are available, and hence very little use of between-subject variance can be made as a source of the effect of independent variables. Since we deal with small numbers of subjects and are very seldom able to utilize the between-subject variance as the source of the effects of an experimental variable, the conventional experimental designs as they appear in the literature of statistics are not particularly useful. The most useful experimental design is the mixed factorial design in which the effects of the experimental variables are taken out of within-subject variance, and in which the interaction terms are frequently split between the between-subject variance and the within-subject variance (Lindquist, 1953).

Crew Preparation and Motivation

Most experimentation in the area of psychology assumes some subject preparation. Such preparation may include extensive preliminary training or it may only involve presenting to the subjects a set of prepared instructions.

The degree of preparation will depend on the design of the experiment. Such preparation is aimed at establishing appropriate sets and attitudes and insuring that subjects have achieved a level of proficiency appropriate to the experiment. In the case of system research, this problem is compounded many times. Each individual in the system must either be trained to the level of skill required after arrival at the experimental site, or he must bring such proficiency to the experimental situation. In either case, the experimenter is faced with a problem. If it can be assumed that the subject can bring the requisite skills to the experimental situation, then the problem is one of selection. If the subjects cannot acquire the skills prior to experimentation, the problem involves setting up appropriate training procedures after arrival.

As we have emphasized, the term "subject" in system research implies a crew, and crews consist of many individuals. When such is the case, the treatment of these individuals becomes an extremely complex problem. Since crew members will live in the experimental area for many days, there are a number of important questions which have to be dealt with. What kind of contact should crew members have with the experimenters? What should they be told about the objectives of the experiment? How much information should they be given about the techniques for generating controlled inputs? What provisions must be made for sickness, accidents, and unexpected shifts in crew composition? What level of motivation should be maintained, and how?

The results of an experiment can be seriously affected by the motivation and morale of the crews manning the system. Despite the effort which psychologists have expended on the study of motivation, there is little in the literature to aid the system psychologist.

Some very tenuous generalizations can be drawn from the experience of the authors in the area of system research (Behan, Davis, and Pelta, 1959). In general, the longer a given crew must participate in an experiment, the greater the drop in motivation. Similarly, if some unusual circumstances surround a crew's participation in an experiment, there is a greater likelihood that motivation can be maintained. Bringing crews to a special laboratory for system studies essential to the national welfare, and introducing special incentives such as competition between crews, have been used to maintain motivation. Some experimenters have, in fact, systematically cultivated an "aura of mystery" in order to stimulate crew motivation.

Many such techniques used to enhance performance are variants of the so-called Hawthorne effect. For discussion of this effect, the reader is referred to Brown (1958) and Chapanis (1959). The advisability of exploiting the Hawthorne effect depends on the generalizations one wishes to draw from the experiment. Where motivation has been artificially increased by manipulating the social (laboratory) climate, it becomes extremely difficult to generalize experimental results to everyday field operations. On the other hand, if one wishes to know what kind of performance can be expected with optimum motivation, such procedures may be justified.

Changes in System Behavior as a Function of Practice

Change of behavior as a function of practice is a characteristic of systems as well as of individuals. The conventional response of the psychologist to evidence of improvement in performance with repeated trials is to assert that learning has occurred, and many psychologists have accepted learning as a valid explanation of this finding. However, it is unlikely that all instances of a change in system performance as a function of practice can be explained by learning in the conventional sense of the word. While it is probable that a certain amount of learning, and consequent improvement in system performance, does occur among the men who work in information-processing systems, it is also quite probable that a large share of the change in system performance is due to the adoption of more fortunate operational procedures by men working in the system (see Chapter 11). Evidence for this latter assumption comes from the fact that: (1) such changes in performance are observable in systems which have been operational for long periods of time, in which, presumably, the task proficiency of the men working in these systems should have reached a maximum; and (2) one can often find decreases in activities which correlate with observed increases in other measures of system performance. For example, in one set of studies (Chapman et al., 1959) it was observed that the experimental crews displayed a consistent increase in the number of hostile aircraft which were detected and intercepted. This improved performance was, however, accompanied by a decrease in the number of friendly aircraft which were processed by the crews. Crews were not processing more aircraft; they were merely being more selective in aircraft processing.

The use of certain procedures may have a detrimental rather than a beneficial effect on system performance. System input and information-processing procedures are almost invariably designed to deal with a clean input, but a not infrequent occurrence is for an information-processing system to experience noise in the input to the system. When a system experiences noise in the input, supervisory personnel frequently want rather extensive—and often unnecessary—information about the noise itself. The use of such procedures on the part of supervisory personnel increases the information-processing load on the system and thus results in a decrease in system performance with respect to that information which the system was designed to process. It sometimes happens that crews establish priorities with respect to information to be processed, and the establishment of such priorities often results in significant improvement in system performance.

Thus, the term "system learning" has come to have many meanings. It obviously refers to the fact that some system-performance measures show improvement as a result of repeated trials (experience). The source of this improvement, however, is not always obvious. It may result from the component-skills training which accompanies practice in a system context; it may also result from the adoption of special procedures; or it may reflect the establishment of priorities by the system.

In the final analysis, all so-called system learning must reflect changes in the behavior of individual system members. On the other hand, it may be valid to continue to draw the distinction between system learning and individual learning, because the former can only be learned in the context of the system. One may, for example, train a man outside the systems context to read a radarscope and report his observations to another individual who plots them on a vertical board. But there is a great deal of procedure learning which takes place between these two individuals which cannot be taught in isolation from the system. The radarscope operator will learn, as a result of his system experience with the plotter, something about the speed with which the plotter can handle the traffic which he calls to him. He will learn something about his idiosyncrasies and weaknesses, and as a result of knowing these, he may be able to adjust his reporting speed and format to insure the accurate and timely transmission of the information. Thus, the distinction between systems and individual learning can be a useful one, even though its bases have not yet been fully explored.

REFERENCES

Ashby, W. R. 1952. *Design for a brain.* New York: Wiley.

Behan, R. A., Davis, R. H., and Pelta, E. 1959. *Radar operator and ACW system behavior in an ECM environment.* Santa Monica, Calif.: System Development Corp. (Contents SECRET). Report TM–383.

Brown, J. A. C. 1958. *The social psychology of industry.* Baltimore: Penguin Books.

Chapanis, A. 1959. *Research techniques in human engineering.* Baltimore: Johns Hopkins Press.

Chapanis, A., Garner, W. A., and Morgan, C. T. 1949. *Applied experimental psychology.* New York: Wiley.

Chapman, R., Kennedy, J., Newell, A., and Biel, W. 1959. The system research laboratory's air defense experiments. *Mgmt. Sci., 5,* 250–269.

Goodwin, W. R. 1957. The System Development Corporation and system training. *Amer. Psychologist, 12,* 524–528.

Hovland, C. I. 1960. Computer simulation of thinking. *Amer. Psychologist, 15,* 687–693.

Johnson, E. 1960. Operations research in the world crisis in science and technology. In Flagle, F. L., Huggins, W. H., and Roy, R. H. (ed.), *Operations research and systems engineering.* Baltimore: Johns Hopkins Press.

Kepner, C. H., and Tregoe, B. B. 1959. *On the concept of visible and invisible functioning.* Santa Monica, Calif.: System Development Corp. Report TM–409.

Lindquist, E. F. 1953. *Design and analysis of experiments in psychology and education.* Boston: Houghton Mifflin.

Newell, A., Shaw, J. C., and Simon, H. A. 1958. Elements of a theory of human problem solving. *Psychol. Rev., 65,* 151–166.

Rosenblatt, F. 1958. The perceptron: A probabalistic model for information storage. *Psychol. Rev., 65,* 386–408.

Taylor, F. V. 1960. Four basic ideas in engineering psychology. *Amer. Psychologist, 15,* 643–649.

14

DURING THE COURSE OF HIS WORK IN SYS-
tem development, the psychologist may be called upon
to participate in activities extending from the original
conception of a system to its testing and use, as previous chapters have shown. As a scientist, he is called
upon to make many decisions throughout this process,
some of the most important of which are decisions
about methods to be employed in answering system questions.

In general, because of his scientific training, the psychologist tends to be
well acquainted with the methodology of obtaining behavioral evidences
which support hypotheses derived from theory. He is likely to be less well
acquainted with the requirements of "psychological engineering" that are
frequently generated by systems problems. For this reason he may find himself in a situation of conflict when it comes to a choice of methodology, or
may even be unaware that he faces an option. Such conflict need not exist
when there is adequate understanding of the methods appropriate to engineering, and their specific relationship to those used by the scientist in
answering questions of a theoretical nature.

The discussion of this chapter is one which compares and contrasts the
methodologies appropriate to two kinds of "system"—the conceptual system
of the scientist, and the empirical system of the engineer. The primary purpose of the former is seen to be understanding, and of the latter, control.
When the implications of this distinction are traced, it becomes evident that
the system psychologist needs to recognize a number of methodological
options in the planning and conduct of his work. These range all the way
from the initial formulation of the problem through the stage of analysis to
the drawing of conclusions and the utilization of research findings. The
varieties of these options, and how they influence the research activities of the
investigator, are explored and illustrated by means of examples.

There is provided here a most important philosophy and point of view
toward the entire process of system development, and toward the role of the
psychologist in the enterprises described in previous chapters of this book.
In particular, the present chapter may be conceived as laying the foundation
for some truly systematic methodologies for psychotechnology, which will
hopefully be developed extensively in years to come.

THE SYSTEM CONCEPT

AS A PRINCIPLE OF

METHODOLOGICAL DECISION

John L. Finan

Most of the systems with which the preceding chapters of this book have been concerned are examples of directly observable, "natural" groupings. It will be useful here to consider such systems as special cases that fall under a concept of broader scope. A system is essentially a way of conceptualizing experience, according to which the components of an organized grouping interact to achieve a designated purpose. The objective of the present chapter is to examine some of the ways in which the system orientation, particularly as it reflects the pragmatic principle, provides explicit criteria to which decisions of research design may be referred.

A fundamental distinction first needs to be made between empirical and conceptual systems. The theoretical scientist who sets understanding of phenomena as his immediate goal is mainly concerned with conceptual systems. By contrast, the engineering scientist whose immediate interest is in controlling "nature" deals with systems of an empirical type. Whether research is thus *problem-oriented* or *product-oriented* will govern the decisions made at various critical stages of inquiry. The discussion which follows is organized around eight design options that are considered applicable to these two kinds of research.

An initial option is taken at the stage of selecting and formulating the research problem. In theoretical research, the problem is transposed into a more controllable context, and the variables involved are translated into conceptualized dimensions. In contrast, the prime requirement for the results of engineering research to be relevant to practical goals restricts this latter type of study to situations and variables that closely simulate the complex of operational conditions.

A second option concerns the use of analogies in research. The explanatory model of theoretical inquiry is essentially a symbolic idealization of observations, while the forecast formula of engineering psychology can be considered an empirical summary of results. A related distinction is made between *validity* of theoretical research—the correspondence between a concept and germane phenomena—and *fidelity* of engineering research—the degree of relationship between forecaster and criterial terms required for a specified practical purpose.

A third option is taken with respect to the differential role of hypothesis. In theoretical research, hypotheses are explicitly linked to a model, and if experimentally corroborated, make possible attribution of effect to cause. When employed in engineering psychology, hypotheses may serve to suggest the content of forecaster and criterial terms, and may, *post hoc,* be used to interpret the observed relationship between them. The hypothesis-testing and demonstration types of experiment exemplify this contrast.

A fourth option is taken in dealing with the problem of the variability of observations. Causal attribution depends, in the ideal, on the possibility of rigorously controlling all relevant experimental conditions other than the one manipulated. Forecasting, however, depends on representing with maximum fidelity *whatever* sources of variability may operate within the criterial situation. This is the important difference between systematic and representative design.

A fifth option is taken in order to define units of analysis. In theoretical research, units are selected for the purpose of demonstrating behavioral uniformities; in engineering research, the requirement is to define a unit that proves manageable for producing or forecasting a particular operational system.

A sixth option is taken with reference to the criteria of acceptable inference. Statistical hypothesis-testing is considered more appropriate to the demonstration of model relationships, while statistical estimation techniques are deemed more suitable for forecasting to a criterion. The appropriateness for engineering studies of the conventional .05 probability level for acceptance of findings will subsequently be questioned.

A seventh option is taken when conclusions of research study are extended to new situations. In theoretical research, generalization proceeds by demonstrating the extensibility of the model dimensions to the new conditions. Limited engineering generalizations can be based on inference from populations and guessed interclass relationships.

A final option is taken in connection with utilization of research outcomes in practical situations. Results obtained under the *pure* conditions of the laboratory yield *abstract predictions* which may have implications that are adaptable to operational systems. Engineering studies yield *forecasts,* which constitute a direct and immediate basis for action.

▣ SOME IMPLICATIONS OF THE SYSTEM CONCEPT

The term *system* refers to a set of components organized in a way that tends to constrain action toward a specified end. The particular value of an input-output relationship which the system is designed to produce defines the purpose of the system. The purpose is what gives integrity to the system. A purely conceptual system—for example, a non-Euclidean geometry—is organized under the theoretical goal of explicating the logical consistencies obtaining within the postulate structure. Or, to consider another kind of example, a particular man-machine system is designed and developed in relation to the goal of defeating an enemy under a specified set of conditions. It is important to note that *the concept of system poses explicitly, and as its central problem, the role of purpose or value* in relation to the design and methods of inquiry. The pragmatic principle, according to which purpose or value is regarded as a criterion of valid knowledge, lies at the root of the system concept.

Organizations may consist of concepts or of observed events. A distinction has already been made between conceptual systems, to which the question of homology with observed nature is irrelevant, and veridical systems, which are accorded the status of observed events. Characteristically, in theoretical science, a set of concepts is employed in an analogical relationship with a set of observed events, and the degree of correspondence is noted. Abstractions of this theoretical sort are, within the logic of systems, explicitly recognized as tools *invented* to further the purpose of understanding, rather than as "ultimate principles" which are "discovered" to exist in nature.

Integrating what has been said up to now about purpose with the conceptual-empirical dichotomy puts us in a position to grasp the main point of the present discussion. Research decisions will differ in fundamental ways, depending on whether the primary purpose of a given research inquiry is to build a conceptual system that represents the logical relationships obtaining within a given range of phenomena, or whether it is to produce or forecast an efficient natural system.

Within science broadly understood, two purposes are distinguishable: the theoretical, which seeks to understand, and the engineering, which seeks to control. "On what principle does the system work?" is the question to which the scientific theorist seeks an answer; "How can a system which is intended to meet a specified objective be produced or improved?" is the engineer's question. To formulate laws of a highly abstract type which subsume broad areas of phenomena beyond those brought under immediate observation is the goal of theoretical science. To develop or to improve a machine, or other natural function, in accordance with some practical end is the goal of engineering science. Stated in another way, theoretical research is concerned with the entire range of output variation in relation to changes in input; engineering research restricts interest to those input factors that yield a particular output judged to be of practical value. Within the area of human behavior, theoretical psychology is concerned, for example, with laws of learning, motivation, and attitude change, while psychological engineering deals with such matters as man-machine interactions, intelligence and aptitude testing, clinical diagnosis and therapy, control of attitudes and beliefs, and the improvement of educational programs.

In order to make the distinction between these two approaches to research more concrete, two experimental studies—Miller's investigations of conflict behavior (1959) and MacCaslin, Woodruff, and Baker's work (1959) in developing a course of training for Armor trainees (SHOCK-ACTION VI)—will be followed as paradigms throughout the discussion. The summary accounts of these studies given below are intended to emphasize those features that will become relevant to points discussed subsequently in the chapter.

A Paradigm of Theoretical Research

A closely integrated program of investigation of approach-avoidance behavior conducted by N. E. Miller serves as the reference study for the theoretical approach to psychology (Miller, 1959). The stated goal of this research is to formulate the laws of conflict-behavior.

As a first step, a limited postulate system, based in large part on principles borrowed from Hull's learning theory, is set forth. Hull's principle of the goal gradient is, for example, the source of the assumption that the nearer the subject is to a goal, the stronger is the tendency to approach it. A parallel postulate assumes that the closer the subject approaches a frightening stimulus, the stronger is the tendency to avoid it. Next, deductions rigorously derived from the set of postulates are explicitly stated. Miller hypothesizes that under certain conditions the subject should approach the goal and stop at the point where the strength of the approach and avoidance gradients are equal. Or, to cite a second example, it follows deductively from the postulates that when the strength of hunger is increased, the subjects will approach more closely to the goal.

As Miller points out, in many studies of the present type it is strategic to employ lower species in simple situations, which can then be rigorously controlled, for first roughing out the approximate lawful relationships. Accordingly, he employs hungry albino rats trained to run down a short straight alley to obtain food. In a later phase of the study the animals are given electric shock at the goal position. The independent variables manipulated are selected on the basis of their unitary and readily specifiable character—

as, for example, hours of food privation and distance from the point of rein- forcement. Dependent variables, such as an animal's strength of pull on a string harness, and its speed of running, are also chosen to meet requirements of objectivity and unidimensionality. Between these two terms, and explicitly related to each one, stand the intervening variables. In order to gain generality, the empirical variables are translated by means of operational definitions into assumed dimensions of the intervening variables. Although admittedly limited, Miller's operational definitions attempt to perform the crucial job of relating the systematic variables (parameters) posited in the conflict model to specific experimental conditions. Examples are the assumed positive relationship be- tween the strength of the animal's response tendency and the strength of pull when temporarily restrained, or that between greater strength of electric shock and greater strength of the fear drive. Sources of variation presumed to be of minor importance—such as duration of shock, or amount of food—are either held constant or randomized.

The results of Miller's preliminary experimentation (see Figure 14.1)

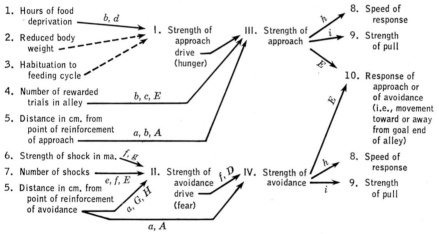

Figure 14.1. The diagram presents an abbreviated formulation to account for results obtained by Miller and his associates working with white rats in the simple conflict alley. Listed on the left side are the independent (1-7) and on the right, the dependent variables (8-10). Although these variables are closely anchored to specific experimental operations, it will be noted that they are stated in general (conceptualized) terms. Variables I-IV shown in the center of the diagram are the intervening variables, or model parameters. The arrows representing functional relationships between the terms are labeled with letters which indicate the definitions (small let- ters) or postulates (capital letters) to which they refer in Miller's system. These relationships illustrate the operationally defined nature of the concepts included in the model. Variables represented by dotted lines, reduced body weight and habituation to the feeding cycle, and others omitted from the diagram—for example, amount of food and size of bars on grid—were con- trolled by holding them at a constant value, or by randomization, in the series of experiments. (Adapted from Miller, 1959.)

tend to corroborate his model of conflict behavior. To consider one of the simpler instances, the data confirm the hypothesis that animals placed nearer the end of the alley where they had received shocks would start to run faster than those placed farther from the shock position. A more complex deduction, also confirmed, required that the animals move closer to or farther from the goal, depending jointly on strength of shock and degree of hunger. In a preliminary series of experiments, 10 out of 11 deductions were confirmed on small groups of animals at the conventional level of significance. The fact that these experiments were specifically designed to validate deductions rigorously drawn from the system of postulates is important. Further, the fact that the outcomes were predicted from six postulates (in addition to coordinating definitions) is impressive evidence in favor of the functional unity of the hypothetical constructs posited by the model.

The generality of Miller's theory of conflict may be seen in his successful extension of the simple model to a wide variety of conflict phenomena beyond those initially investigated. The original assumptions, for example, have application to avoidance-avoidance and double approach-avoidance conflict. Further extension of the scope of the postulate system to cover aspects of the phenomenon of displacement, projective tests, psychotherapy, combat, economic competition, and even international relations, remains to be demonstrated.

A Paradigm of Engineering Research

An experimental study in curriculum development entitled SHOCK-ACTION VI offers a representative example of the engineering approach to psychological problems (MacCaslin, Woodruff, and Baker, 1959). This research has been previously described (Chapter 9), but will be reviewed briefly here to emphasize its methodology.

The problem situation for which a solution was sought arose out of performance deficiencies of armor crewmen. The objective of the task was to develop by experimental means an improved program of training for tank gunners, drivers, and loaders, as judged in terms of the proficiency level of their skills and knowledges.

The ultimate criterion for this task, as with most military research, is successful performance in combat, which constitutes the set of conditions to which a forecast based on the outcome of the study must apply. Presumably, training objectives established by armor experts and detailed task descriptions drawn up by researchers reflect the requirements of combat closely enough to provide a basis for developing the curriculum, as well as for constructing proficiency tests to determine its effectiveness.

The experimental treatment carefully limited the content of the course to materials judged directly relevant to the essential functions of the crewmen, emphasizing training objectives and combat realism. To maximize the effectiveness of training, several empirically founded rules of learning were incorporated into the developed program: (1) making explicit the relationship of tasks to one another and to the program as a whole; (2) insuring understanding by simplification of materials; (3) emphasizing learning by doing; (4) giving knowledge of progress to the student; (5) increasing motivation by means of demonstrations, orientation sessions, and compulsory make-up of deficiencies.

In addition to differences in content and training procedures already mentioned, the experimental program included several departures from the standard administrative procedures employed by the Armor Training Center: (1) schedule of training by platoons rather than by companies; (2) formalization of make-up and remedial training; (3) changes in the manner of utilizing instructors; and (4) provision of additional equipment and materiel, including illustrated manuals, tank instruments used as training devices, and modified firing and driving ranges. The altered administrative procedures were deemed to fall within the limits of feasibility and efficient utilization of manpower and materiel resources available under actual conditions of training.

The experimental training program was administered over a period of six weeks to an available company (N = 160) that had been constituted by routine administrative procedures. At the end of this period, performance tests were administered to the experimental company, as well as to an equivalent company that had simultaneously completed the conventional eight-week training course. Variables other than those comprising the treatment were equated or otherwise controlled. Performance of the two companies was compared by means of a specially constructed test battery consisting of some 400 items, grouped into 21 categories of subject matter. Each subject-matter test was judged to sample an aspect of performance considered essential to efficient performance of a tank crewman because of its frequency or importance.

The results demonstrated that the over-all proficiency of armor graduates trained in the six-week program was slightly higher than that of graduates of the eight-week program in the essential skills of tank gunner, driver, and loader (see Figure 14.2). The principal gains of the experimental program were, first, a somewhat higher level of trainee proficiency; and second, a saving of 25 percent of the eight-week training time consumed by the standard program. An appreciable reduction in gasoline and ammunition requirements also resulted. The principal costs were (1) an increased requirement for training aids and literature, as well as for tank instruments; and (2) an increased requirement for holdover students to serve as assistant instructors. A comparison of the two programs in terms of gains and costs was considered to justify the recommendations that the experimental program be adopted for operational use in the Armor Training Center where the study was conducted. The developed program was also recommended for use in other, similar Army programs. As a final point in connection with this study, it is noteworthy that a precautionary statement is included warning the user of the program against assuming that departures from the recommended procedures would be effective if isolated from the context of the total program.

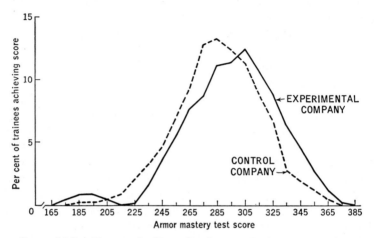

Figure 14.2.   The graph shows the degree of superiority of the group trained under the developed program of Armor Individual Advanced Training in terms of combined scores obtained by 160 trainees on the 21 subtests comprising the Armor Mastery Test. Subanalysis of results indicated that the experimental company exceeded the control reliably on 11 of the 14 subtests on which differences were observed. It is noteworthy that this superiority was demonstrated despite the fact that the experimental program required two weeks less than the standard program of training for tank crewmen. The program engineered by the Human Resources Research Office was recommended to the Army for adoption in lieu of the one in standard use on the basis of reduced time, dollar cost, and higher level of proficiency. (From MacCaslin, Woodruff, & Baker, 1959.)

▣ COMPLEMENTARY NATURE OF THEORETICAL AND ENGINEERING SCIENCE

The two experimental examples have been presented in detail mainly in order to emphasize *differences* between the theoretical and engineering approaches. There is a risk, however, in regarding the two positions as more than conceptual extremes, for although in some ways they reflect marked differences in purpose and procedures, in others they are complementary; the processes and products of both kinds of activity contribute to the ultimate goal of science as man's systematic efforts to master his environment. Viewed in more than an instantaneous time frame, the more immediate goal of each approach becomes the longer-term goal of the other; the abstract laws of pure science find eventual application to particular situations of practical consequence, and the specific productions of engineering at length take their place within the ordered structure of theoretical knowledge. The reciprocal relationship between theoretical and engineering science is a fact to which the whole history of scientific endeavor attests.

Another important aspect of mutual support is seen in the dependence of theoretical science on engineering developments for improvements in methods and technique. Production of stable behavior functions, such as the lever-pressing behavior of white rats, or the production of experimental neurosis in animals, provides base lines to which systematic behavioral variations can be meaningfully referred.

Technology is jointly supported by both approaches to science. Within the psychological sciences, for instance, *applied psychology*—the application of scientific laws to particular behavioral situations of practical interest— forms one base. The fact that the laws of behavior *are* largely unknown in no way alters the relationship they would bear to a mature psychotechnology. The second base is built from the systematized and generalized findings of the behavioral engineer. Again, the fact that the contributions of engineering psychology are relatively scant merely serves to emphasize the need to open up this channel of psychotechnological knowledge.

Although it is a fact of vital importance that applications of abstract relationships do emerge as by-products from studies whose immediate purpose is to understand, it is nonetheless true that theoretical science is itself *application-neutral*. In the same way, it must not be overlooked that invaluable suggestions for theoretical relationships that "peel off" as bonuses from engineering efforts are, from a methodological point of view, incidental to the primary purpose of control.

Most important of all, both research approaches have a common forebear in exploratory studies whose purpose is the very general one of identifying and estimating the range of variation of empirical variables. In their present stage of advancement, the great bulk of effort in the behavioral sciences would appear to fall under the category of variable plotting, which is the indispensable precursor of any methodologically designed research. The surprising robustness of exploratory research under the stress of informal and intuitive procedures is a fact of greater importance to the psychology of invention than to the formal methodology of corroboration. Use of the incompletely controlled "quasi-experiment" as an expedient means of teasing out an effect from a tangle of factors often yields invaluable insights into fundamental parameters. Likewise, when supplemented with passive statistical control techniques, procedures which are primarily those of the engineer, such as those of partial correlation or of conventional factor analysis, may be usefully adapted to the derived purpose of elucidating relationships. However, the extent to which the methods of either approach are interchangeable with the other may not be merely assumed. The fact that, in practice, scientists commonly "get away with" ignoring and violating methodological canons without prejudicing the usefulness of results must be interpreted with great caution.

It is still true that the researcher who uses theory implicitly and as an after-thought, to "verify" his findings, assumes a grave risk. To regard the two views as end points on a continuum between theoretical and engineering re-search may suffice at some stages of investigation—particularly, as already noted, for the informal and approximate purposes of exploratory research. However, at other stages, it is difficult to see how either approach can tolerate much of any compromise by the other. Indeed, it is the burden of the discus-sion that follows to show that certain design options cannot be confused without risking serious inefficiency or error. The proper question to be con-sidered, then, relates less to the abstract issue of whether theoretical science and engineering are complementary or antithetical, than to the extent of fungibility of a particular methodological procedure across the two areas, for a given research purpose.

In outline, problems in research design are viewed under the system approach as methodological decisions to be determined essentially by the broad purpose of the inquiry. Depending on whether the purpose of research is that of theoretical or engineering psychology, decisions will differ with respect to the choice and formulation of a problem, use of models and hypoth-eses, kind of criterion, handling of variability of data, units of analysis, criteria of inference, method of generalization, and kinds of emergent action.

▣ CHOICE AND DEFINITION OF THE PROBLEM

Psychological research problems are uncertainties in our efforts to under-stand or control behavior. The question to be investigated may arise from an interest in testing or extending a conceptual model; or from a requirement to control—that is, to forecast events for some practical end. Problems in theoretical research are generated from a model as implications for testing. Since generality of result is the major consideration in this type of inquiry, a parameter or limited group of parameters that promises to have relevance to many different situations is characteristically chosen for study. The choice of situations in which the problem is to be investigated will be governed by those factors that are implied by some theory as being central to the problem. Characteristically, the problem is transposed into a simplified context in the interest of controlling irrelevant variation attributable to the particular cir-cumstances of the experiment. In discussing Miller's investigations of conflict, we noted that although the hypotheses investigated are limited to a few aspects of conflict behavior, they are believed applicable to a wide variety of complex situations. On the assumption that human behavior is similar to that of lower mammalian forms, albino rats are used as subjects to gain simplification and control of experimental conditions.

Problems of engineering psychology are basically different from those of theoretical psychology. The question asked will be of a practical sort, on which action within a concrete operational system can be based. How to develop a course of training in armor skills which is acceptably better than the conventional program, such as that developed by SHOCKACTION VI, is a representative problem. In principle, the range of problems is limited only to that class of situations in which a barrier to some action objective is encountered. No assumption is made that the problem has a "unique answer," or that it is soluble in closed form. Instead, formulation of a problem of the present type requires an exhaustive identification of the facts or variables that enter the particular problematic situation. To approximate a reasonably adequate definition requires that consideration be given to the total operational context within which the problem has been generated. If, for example, the difficulty is that the performance of the man-tank system fails to achieve a required level of performance, and it can further be demonstrated that the deficiency cannot be attributed to machine components, the human component would appear to be at fault. Further delineation of the problem within the general area of human factors is then required. Selection and placement of personnel, interaction of the machine components with operator and maintenance personnel, training, management factors (including job structure and morale), might all be probed to determine the contribution of each of these subsystems, or some linkage thereof, to degradation of the system output. A high degree of generality of the solution is subordinated to the specific needs of the agent; in fact, the particular situation in all its uniqueness is precisely what the practitioner usually seeks to manage. It follows that the conditions under which the study is to be conducted should, ideally, be precisely representative of those which will also obtain under the actual operation of the system involved. In SHOCKACTION VI the skills taught were limited to those that a task analysis had revealed to be important; and the conditions, to those that would be likely to obtain under future training environments.

The Krogh principle in biology—according to which there is an optimum species for the solution of any problem—however useful to theoretical research, obviously has little application to the problems of the engineering psychologist. If the risk of immediate applicability of his research is to be minimized, he will enjoy far fewer degrees of freedom in formulating his problem. By the nature of his objective, he is constrained to employ something very close to the actual tasks of the military operational system—for example, using the tank rangefinder, firing the tank gun, or any of numerous other tasks essential to the armor soldier's performance of his job. His subject population will be limited to men assigned for armor training, to which his findings will be reapplied when integrated into the operational system. However, the sharp limit on the generality of his results will not, within the values of the study, be considered a penalty. In fact, to frame studies of the present sort in terms of a range of factors that attempts to include the goal of generality along with that of specific applicability would risk a compromised result of little value to either the theoretical scientist or to the engineer. There would appear to be no obvious basis for the commonly held assumption that an intermediate range of problems combining both theoretical and practical importance can be formulated.

A methodologically adequate formulation of a research problem of either type requires, before undertaking a study, specification of the set of alternatives that will be evaluated by the outcome, together with a rational basis for acceptance or rejection of each one. Unless the possible actions can be explicitly anticipated and evaluated, a rational basis for making design decisions is lacking. Advance specification of the values that will determine acceptance or rejection of the outcome is, within the meaning of methodologically designed research, an essential part of defining the problem, and to the extent that the basis for such a decision fails to antedate the actual collection of data, the research problem, whether theoretical or practical, remains only partially formulated.

▣ THE USE OF ANALOGY

The explicit role of analogy in scientific procedure is an important characteristic of the system approach. The question of whether a concept is "true" is transposed to mean under what conditions and with what degree of accuracy an analogy can be usefully employed for a given purpose. The main point about analogies is that they provide ways of representation which imply relationships among observations.

A fundamental distinction between types of analogies is made according to whether they are to serve the purpose of subsuming a matrix of observed events under an explicitly stated set of conceptual principles, or to provide a basis for controlling the operation of a natural system. The much misused term "model" is reserved to denote a set of conceptual relationships whose degree of correspondence with relevant observations is demonstrable. The methodological status of a model is that of a corroborative or "verificatory" instrument. Miller's model of conflict behavior is a case in point. His formulation hinges, not on the assumption that the intervening variables describe the actual nature of the organism, but rather on the assumption that their input-output relationships are isomorphic with what is observed. It can thus be considered that the organism behaves *as if* it were constructed according to the principles of the model. In general, providing a model satisfies the condition of logical consistency, its validity will be decided by the consequences of the directed research action which it prescribes.

The engineering counterpart of the model of theoretical science we shall here designate as a *schema*. The methodological status of schemata is more that of a pedagogical device, since they function *not to corroborate* but to *suggest* a basis for constructing a recipe or formula for effecting, or for forecasting, a given end. The engineer's requirement is met if a criterial state of affairs can be generated—that is, produced (material) or forecast (information)—from another set of variables. *Formulas,* as here defined, specify in the basic equation, Output = (*f*) Input, what the degree of relationship is. Such restriction of the formula to a summarizing statement of the relation between input and output is recognized as the engineer's "black box," which translates directly into the engineering psychologist's "empty organism."

The Model of Theoretical Research

The model of basic research, which is essentially a symbolic idealization of observations, subserves a number of closely related functions.

First, the model guides abstraction from a complex matrix of observations. Without some constraints, observations would be illimitable and haphazard. It is a paradox of theoretical science that "in order to look, the scientist must know what he is looking for." Miller's formulation of conflict behavior is, consciously, highly selective and limited to a very few aspects of a virtual infinitude of events and possible relationships. On the basis of an explicitly formulated model, the problem of what to observe is reduced to manageable terms.

A second function of the model is to translate observed variables that are guessed to be germane, from empirical (phenotypic) to conceptual (genotypic) dimensions. These model dimensions, or parameters, represent further guesses about variables that can be grouped together on the basis of their functional unity, and not merely on the basis of superficial similarity in content. The present point is made plain in Miller's studies in the distinction between *systematic* and empirical variables. For example, hours of food deprivation as a generic term includes many empirically different variables, such as the feeding schedule, differences in body weight, and the proportion of various elements in the animals' diet. Unless we risk the assumption that the diverse factors can be consolidated under a single parameter, their meaning becomes trivial.

Third, to qualify as a useful model, the parameters must be in some degree articulated. Ideally, the complete set of functional relationships between the several dimensions of the model are explicitly specified. Relatively few models that are complete in the present sense can be found in contemporary psychology. In Miller's model of conflict behavior, a number of functional relationships between the terms of the model are approximated, although, as he is careful to note, partially and qualitatively. For heuristic purposes, Hull (1943) pushed his model of habit-strength farther in the direction of quantitative articulation, though at the cost of premature precision.

Fourth, the model must, for certain purposes, permit of being treated as a closed system of parameters. The serious difficulties entailed in specifying an exhaustive set of behavioral parameters, even for a limited range of phenomena, are well known. As a matter of expediency, it is usually necessary to close the system by invoking the *ceteris paribus* disclaimer, which assumes that other factors are known and, within broad limits, evaluated. The conditions required for the use of this assumption in psychological research are in large part not met, with the consequence that the extent to which error may be introduced cannot be formally estimated. Nonetheless, the principle of rigorous deduction of hypotheses as implications from a model must remain uncompromised. Miller lists a number of such rigorously derived deductions, given in simple graphic form. A typical example is that increasing the strength of hunger should cause subjects to approach nearer to the goal.

Finally, in our present consideration of the functions of the model, it should supply guidance for inference from its conceptualized dimensions to the measures of behavior that are actually observed. A model must have implications for the kinds and properties of measures essential to its corroboration. In testing his deductions, Miller formulates a number of partial definitions relating the terms of his model to specific experimental conditions. For example, it is assumed that greater strengths of electric shock produce greater strength of fear drive, and that strength of response is positively related to initial speed of running. He is careful to qualify his definitions by calling them partial, because their theoretical linkage is not completely worked out. To the degree that behavioral indicants remain intuitive, and hence not explicitly related to their model, they fall short of qualifying as completely valid criteria for corroborating it.

The Forecast Formula in Engineering Research

In line with its difference in purpose, the forecast formula of the engineering psychologist differs from the theoretical psychologist's model in several ways. Primarily, the symmetrical relationship between prediction and explanation which is characteristic of an established model has no parallel in a forecast formula. *Prediction* refers to the successful deduction of a relationship between independent and dependent variables in advance of observation. The correlative term *explanation* means understanding a relationship after it has been observed, by subsuming it under a principle given by the model. *Forecasting* is here defined as indicating in advance the extent to which a state of affairs can be anticipated by means of some set of independently selected variables. The associated term *interpretation* means the specification of a relationship under which an already observed effect *may* be subsumable. Forecasting *requires* no statement of the logical principle in terms of which the forecast is warranted; no rigorous basis for including the ingredients that enter the forecaster term need be given. In SHOCKACTION VI, the factors comprising the treatment include elements of empirical generalization, common sense, and hunch. The criterial variable is also limited only by the requirements of the practical problem, or, more accurately, by the researchers' guesses about what constitutes an acceptable representation of the state of affairs to be forecast. Again, the proficiency tests which serve as the immediate criterion are judged relevant to the combat criterion on the basis of expert *judgment* of researchers and armor officers. The model of theoretical research performs the functions of generating highly explicit hypotheses about the properties of independent and dependent variables as well as about their form of relationship. But, for the purpose of forecasting, there is no requirement to give explicit statement of the basis that may underlie the forecaster and criterial terms, or the relationship between them.

Use of Schemata in Engineering Research

By contrast with the model of theoretical research, the forecast formula offers no rigorous basis for abstracting from the flux of events certain ones that "count" as observations. The criterial situation we seek to forecast is, in concept, a total interaction of all the variables that comprise it. In SHOCK-ACTION VI, the proficiency tests, if they are to reflect the criterion of combat efficiency, require in principle no less than a complete photographic representation of everything that armor troops do that contributes to successful and unsuccessful combat. Because of the impracticability of meeting such an extravagant requirement in practice, approximations must be resorted to in order to simplify the criterial complex and render it manageable.

The indispensable role of schemata in criterion construction is perhaps most readily apparent in research studies which are dependent on some type of representation of the criterial state of affairs because of its cost, inaccessibility, or nonavailability. Use of simulators as surrogates for actual performance of systems is essential, for example in complex air-defense systems, where evaluation would otherwise become possible only under actual attack (see, for example, Chapter 13). In certain military man-missile systems, schemata serve the invaluable role of making it possible to evaluate performance prior to the systems' coming into actual being. The mock-up of the design engineer, the wind tunnel of the aeronautical engineer, or the war gaming of the military forces provide further instances of the usefulness of schemata in the construction of criteria.

The variables of engineering research are held close to the level of everyday observation in contrast to the highly conceptualized dimensions of theoretical research. In SHOCKACTION VI, it would be pointless to render into theoretical terms the specific skills and knowledges required to perform the armor soldier's task. This is so because behavior as observed directly and described in the categories of "common sense" has more relevance to the practical problem in hand than would a higher order of abstractions.

A further difference between the engineering and theoretical approaches relates to the absence of any formal requirement to specify causal relationships, or mechanisms, between the forecaster and criterial terms of the forecast formula. Once more, it is not a primary function of the forecast formula to make possible attribution of a dependent variation to a particular manipulation of an independent factor. Rather, the requirements are those of any efficient psychometric instrument—unambiguous identification of predictor and criterial variables, together with a demonstrated degree of association, under specifiable conditions, between the two terms. To the extent that schemata aid the engineering psychologist in building his formula to meet these three specifications, and not because they provide any formal basis for inference, they may be usefully employed.

Lack of a *requirement* for rigorous grounds of inference does not offer a complete basis for distinguishing between schemata and models. Forecasts are often *aided* by schemata which are both explicit and highly rigorous. Both function as analogies to represent specified sets of observations, but beyond this similarity, they are fundamentally different: unlike the model, the forecast formula is *not* corroborated, in any formal sense, by generated outcomes. Only by the gross evidence lent by the success or lack of success of the global product of the particular study is a schema "checked" for its correspondence with relevant observations.

▣ VALIDITY VERSUS FIDELITY

The term *validity* refers to the degree of correspondence of a model to germane observations. To the extent that it can be demonstrated to be homologous with observation, a model is valid for the purpose of establishing scientific laws. To illustrate the point, we turn again to Miller's theory of conflict behavior, which he attempts to validate by checking the extent to which the logical implications from the model are borne out by a program of carefully arranged experimental observations.

To distinguish validity as a concept appropriately applied only to theoretical research from its counterpart in engineering, we have somewhat arbitrarily labeled the latter *fidelity*. The sufficient condition which defines fidelity is that a given variable permit us to forecast a second, criterial variable to the extent required by the problem in hand. In SHOCKACTION VI, the developed program was judged sufficiently likely to forecast performance under future operational conditions to warrant its adoption by the Army.

It is relevant in the context of the present discussion to make a further distinction between an *indicant,* as employed in theoretical research, and a *criterion,* which is its engineering-research counterpart. Although the two concepts are often interchanged in practice, their defining functions are by no means identical. The term indicant focuses attention on the role of the dependent variable as a basis for inferring the values of the model parameters. Selection of the indicant is prescribed by the theoretical model to reflect changes resulting from a given independent variation in experimental conditions. Variation of indicants is determined by the values assigned to the independent variables, without restriction of range. A criterion is the wanted output which a to-be-developed input will yield; its value will be assigned by the set of practical considerations that have generated the problem. Both in respect to the logic and sequence of research, the criterion is prior to the forecaster term which it governs. In our reference study, SHOCKACTION VI, it is seen that the components of the engineered course of training must, above all, meet the standard of judged combat relevance. In brief, the engineer reverses the direction of the cause-to-effect reasoning of the theoretical scientist by "working back" from a specified output to a set of generating conditions.

The Operational Definition

Operational definition is the term Bridgman (1927) has given to linkages between the antecedent conditions and deduced consequences of a model and relevant observations. As he is careful to point out, definitions of the present type can be formulated only for highly idealized situations, to embrace a set of phenomena whose interrelationships are already known or accurately surmised. Miller's partial definitions of strength of fear drive and response strength, previously considered, are probably as good approximations to operational definitions as the present state of psychological theorizing affords.

Two serious misconceptions about the nature and purpose of operational definitions have plagued much psychological research. The first is the untenable position that a concept of the present sort can be defined as the sum of empirical operations required for its demonstration. A familiar example is the attempt to define hunger motivation exclusively in terms of the laboratory operations involved in withholding food from an animal for a specified interval of time. Or, to take another instance, unit morale in the Army is often defined "operationally" as the frequency with which members of a military organization go AWOL, "ride the sick-book," or otherwise demonstrate behavior that is regarded as undesirable. Without question, the property of objectivity which these definitions emphasize is an essential requirement of any scientific research. However, more than a lack of ambiguity of terms is required to perform the function of bridging model and observation. To satisfy the additional requirement, the objectively defined measures must be explicitly related to the model to which they stand as indicants. Operational definitions, properly understood, are a tool of theoretical research. Their purpose is to make concepts unambiguous, not to make it possible to theorize without concepts. Restriction of definition of psychological concepts to empirical variables is a common confusion that misses the essential point of the theoretical approach to science.

A second error, the converse of the one just considered, is committed when a requirement for an operationally defined concept is imposed on an engineering problem. The current advocacy of "construct validity" appears to offer a case in point (Cronbach and Meehl, 1955). Interposition of a construct between the forecaster and criterial terms in an engineering investigation is not merely superfluous, but can scarcely avoid resulting in inefficiency through sacrificing direct relevance of the forecaster term to the criterion. For the purpose of forecasting, empirically defined terms are sufficient. If the goal of avoiding the limited generality of a particular testing instrument is sought, a theoretical reorientation to the problem is called for. Only by means of hypothesis-testing research can the parameters that underlie empirical relationships and the conditions of their variation be rigorously demonstrated.

▣ THE USE OF HYPOTHESIS

In theoretical research investigations, hypotheses are generated from a model as logical implications to be tested by experiment. In form, the hypothesis specifies a relationship between a dependent and an independent variable. Testing of such a relationship consists in demonstrating its tenability under appropriate rules of inference. The controlled experiment, which is essentially a hypothesis test, permits the attribution of variation in a dependent variable to an introduced manipulation of an independent variable. The goal of hypothesis testing is causal analysis. The characteristics of the hypothesis in the present sense are readily observable in the reference experiment by Miller.

The "hypotheses" of engineering psychology contrast with those of theoretical research in origin, in form, and in purpose. No *a priori* constraints are placed on the selection of schematic relationships that may be employed in connection with the forecast formula; they may be entirely unsupported by structural knowledge. The alternative to be tested consists of two possible courses of action, and the question to be answered is which one better forecasts the designated criterion. The purpose of the engineering study, as we have already noted, is not that of attributing a dependent variation to a particular independent variation, but rather of demonstrating that a desired output can be achieved by a specifiable set of input conditions.

SHOCKACTION VI, which was designed to produce an improved training program, employed a complex treatment, the components of which were drawn from various sources, including psychological theory, rules of thumb, and training lore. It was not important for the objectives of the study to state the basis on which it was assumed that such ingredients as inclusion of knowledge of results, trainee participation, or whole-to-part learning might improve proficiency. Further, it is apparent that the aggregation of variables in the design of the experiment does not permit any single factor or group of factors comprising the treatment to be isolated as causal. The degree of aggregation of variables is determined by the requirement for their manageability within the operational system concerned. For the purpose of studies of the present type, it would be inefficient to insist on conformity with the ideal of the analytic experiment in maintaining identity, except for a unitary independent variation, between the experimental and control groups. What is demonstrated by the outcome is an association between the global interaction represented by the treatment, and the total effect. Nor is any further interpretation needed to decide between the developed and standard programs of training. In general, the engineering study provides a basis for choosing between the two courses of action by successfully demonstrating that certain values of one total set of conditions yield an output greater than that yielded by different values, or factors. The distinctions noted between the two kinds of experiments might be better served if that of theoretical research were consistently designated as a *hypothesis-testing* experiment, in contrast to the *demonstration-experiment* of engineering psychology.

Control versus Representation of Variability

The different purposes of the theoretical scientist and the engineer are sharply reflected in their different approaches to the problem of variability of observations. To the "pure" researcher, error means *error of observation*—that is, failure to control factors not included within the parameters of the model. It follows that unless observations can be related to a model, a basis for determining factors to be controlled is lacking. Because determination of laws of behavior depends on elimination of error introduced by accidents of observation, simplification of conditions is necessary. In the interest of controllability, Miller, as we have noted, limited his experimental conditions to those of a very simple kind. For the purpose of theoretical research, the sophomore often suffices as a subject, the unnaturally restricted atmosphere of the laboratory as a setting, the tachistoscopically presented nonsense syllables as the independent variation, or the manual pressing of a key as the isolated measure of response.

To the engineering researcher, error refers mainly to a failure to completely represent essential criterial variables among the factors included in the forcaster term. For the purpose of forecasting, the particular variabilities of observations in the criterial situation must be accepted as given. If, in SHOCKACTION VI, men of low aptitude will actually be included among the population who will undergo training under conditions of operation, such subjects cannot be excluded from the experiment; if the tank nomenclature to be mastered consists of complex, meaningful verbal symbols, a study that employed nonsense syllables would not be efficiently designed to maximize successful prediction; if driving skills must be performed under the noise and stress of battle, these factors may not be omitted from the developed training without loss of efficiency. The general requirement for this type of study is that the populations of subjects, treatments, environmental factors, and performances which comprise the complex system of interest to the practitioner be represented as closely as possible in the forecaster term.

Allowing for the important exception of varying several model parameters simultaneously to determine their interactions, classical design attempts to eliminate or hold at a constant value all variables other than the experimental variable. In principle, the "rule of one variable" obtains in research designed to make attribution of effect to cause possible. Thus, the quest for uncontaminated, unidimensional factors which theoretical research demands would appear to be best met by univariate research designs.

Univariate versus Multivariate Design

Confusion between the two ways of dealing with variability has led to the erroneous view that the use of experimental controls in an observation necessarily decreases the generality of the obtained findings—an argument frequently adduced in favor of multivariate design. R. A. Fisher (1951) makes the point that the exact standardization of experimental conditions always entails the disadvantage of yielding information that is restricted to the narrow set of conditions permitted by the standardization. He argues further that standardization weakens rather than strengthens the grounds for inferring a like result since, in practice, conditions are never invariant. From the point of view of the agricultural engineer, which Fisher represents, the statement is valid. However, a wide inductive basis for application of results is of less interest to the theoretical scientist than their precision under highly restricted conditions. Systematic variation of conditions for the theorist serves the purpose of delineating the scope of a model, rather than that of demonstrating its applicability over the broadest possible range of conditions. Combining several conditions within a study of multivariate design more often than not denies a basis for inferring that a model holds under any one of the particular conditions.

Representative Design

Brunswik (1956) carries the case for representation of variability to its logical extreme, arguing for abandonment of systematic control in favor of registration of the totality of variables by passive observational procedures. His position is prescribed by a fundamental interest in biological adaptation— that is, in the functioning of organic systems with reference to their goal of achieving behavior states which are adapted to "representative" environments. So stated, the problem that interests Brunswik is seen to be cast in the form of an engineering task of a special kind: how have the processes of natural selection designed and developed organic systems to accomplish the goal of survival under the complex ecological conditions to which they must adapt?

This problem, although essentially one in engineering, differs from those of a more conventional type in two ways: first, in the respect that natural process stands in surrogate for the engineer, who commonly controls the development of the system himself; and, second, in the respect that a methodology primarily designed for the purpose of control is being employed to facilitate understanding. Approaching problems of behavior from the standpoint of their adaptive function has proved its great utility to theoretical science, without, however, answering the fundamental question of the laws under which behavioral processes mediate adaptation. Our consideration of the issue makes it clear that representative and systematic design are not to be viewed as completely antithetical, but in certain ways as complementary procedures for dealing with the problem of variability of data.

A rule for determining the extent to which a "realistic" environment may be required in a particular research investigation emerges from the methodological distinction between representative and systematic design. It is inherent in controlled situations that they are artificial; no demand is imposed on theoretical research investigations that they be otherwise. The special arrangements of the laboratory are wholly intended to reduce the accidental variation of "real-life" situations in order to permit observation of an uncontaminated relationship · between independent and dependent variable. Conditions of observation that permit a welter of unidentified variables having unknown consequences to play without restraint seldom illuminate model relationships. Equally, it is essential in the approach of the behavior engineer that the inductive leap which generalizes from the forecaster term to the criterial situation be held at a minimum. Since the criterion is a particular value of a state of affairs in the world of operations, a good deal of realism is called for. Inevitably, the cost for such close relevance to the complex circumstances of practical life is paid in the limited generality of results obtained under naturalistic conditions of observation. The extent to which realism may be effectively traded for control can be seen to depend on the nature and purpose of the particular research.

Large versus Small Numbers of Observations

A further design option closely related to the representation-control dichotomy raises the question of the number of observations on which a particular research can be appropriately based. Although a definitive answer to this problem is obviously a matter of considerable complexity, the principles outlined above provide some general guidance. In studies whose purpose requires that the total variation of the population be represented, use of small samples entails a disproportionate risk of introducing error which can result in erroneous generalization of an extreme value to the underlying population. If, on the other hand, the purpose of the research defines an interest in some few factors that are known, or guessed to be the essential determinants of the variation, then, even in the face of the risk, the greatest likelihood is that effects of the primary determinants rather than those of secondary factors will be observed (Sidman, 1960). Multiplication of instances, as an alternative to increasing experimental control, would, under the circumstances, tend to increase the heterogeneity of data without yielding a basis for assigning the additional variation to particular determinants. In brief, it can be seen that reliance on large numbers of observations generally belongs with the representative designs of engineering psychology, and that use of small samples is associated with the systematic designs of theoretical research.

▣ DEFINITION OF UNITS AND LEVEL OF ANALYSIS

An important set of methodological options that arises in any research effort is concerned with the delimitation of units which are isolable from the complex interplay of observed events. Classically, this problem has been handled by the assumption of ultimate and "irreducible" units, as for example, the sensation of Titchener's Structuralism, or the reflex of Watsonian Behaviorism. More recent theorists have tended to make some increased concession to a relative concept which assumes a hierarchy of levels of analysis, as Tolman (1932) and Hull (1943) do in their concept of molar behavior. Miller, who works largely, though not exclusively, at the behavioral level, recognizes that the most profitable level of analysis within an area of investigation depends on the phenomena of interest, and on the stage of development of the relevant disciplines. The system orientation goes a step farther in the degree of explicitness with which it assumes that constituent elements are not "given in nature" but are to be defined under the objective of an inquiry.

For the purpose of theoretical research, definition of units is constrained and guided by the research model. When a given unit has proved successful in demonstrating generalizable behavior uniformities, under specified conditions, it may be considered valid for its purpose. As Skinner (1938) has noted, behavioral units are defined at levels of specification marked by the orderliness of dynamic changes. Operant behavior offers an almost unique example of a behavioral unit that has been demonstrated to enter into a large variety of lawful relationships.

If, on the other hand, the objective of a research task is to demonstrate that a given treatment will improve the efficiency of an operational system, no formal requirement for analysis of the treatment, or of its effects, is imposed. An attempt to break the complex into component factors would be inefficient, since it is the totality of their interaction that is of inerest. Thus, in SHOCK-ACTION VI, the individual contribution to the several aspects of performance made by content, methods of teaching, and motivational devices are of less importance than that of the total interaction of these factors operating jointly on gross performance. In the present connection, Brunswik's concept of the "ecological package" provides a cogent argument for the need to define the unit as the total situation to which the organism must adapt. Aggregation of factors is an invaluable engineering tool; if the total complex of factors can be feasibly identified and administered with a gain in efficiency in the system involved, it is a valid unit for the engineer's purpose.

◙ STATISTICAL INFERENCE

The problem of statistical inference is concerned with the acceptability of the results of observation for a designated purpose in face of an estimated likelihood of error. Criteria of inference will differ depending on the purpose of the investigator: whether to justify inclusion of the outcome of a hypothesis test within a comprehensive postulate structure, or to demonstrate that one course of action offers a more efficient solution to an administrative problem than another.

In theoretical research, our chief concern is with the acceptability of a set of observations for testing an implication derived from a model. With certain exceptions that fall beyond the scope of the present discussion, model relationships are, by virtue of their conceptual status, deterministic rather than probabilistic in nature. Therefore, the probabilities assigned to a hypothesis are restricted to the two values, one or zero; the hypothesized relationship is accepted as "true" or rejected as "not true." The corroboration of a hypothesis is thus an all-or-none affair based on the decision that its acceptance is more useful than its negation, for the purpose of building a conceptual system. Because the decision to accept or to reject does not admit of gradations, the salient question becomes one of whether or not it will be considered that an observed change is attributable to a specified independent variation, rather than the question of the likelihood of its occurrence or of the magnitude of its effect. The question to which an answer is sought is whether the conceptual relationship holds under a specified set of conditions. Apart from the matter of the degree of replicability of findings which the theoretical scientist finds essential to experimental study, it would be difficult to assign a meaning to such a statement as, for example, "the probability that this relationship implied by Miller's model of conflict is true is .95." As already noted, 10 deduced implications were accepted by his series of experiments, and 1 rejected. This impressive record has an important bearing on the validity of the model, although the question of precise statistical significance poses a problem that has received no completely acceptable answer.

Conventionally, a finding is considered significant when it can be subsumed under a rule that would minimize the risk of accepting, within the scientific structure, relationships that might more usefully be considered to result from random factors. To accomplish this objective, the researcher sets up a statistical counterhypothesis (null hypothesis) which assumes that an observed variation in the dependent variable is *not* the result of the experimental manipulation, but rather that of chance variations in the experimental conditions. If the counterhypothesis is then rejected, one possible set of determinants of the result—chance factors—is considered to be negated, and the alternate hypothesis, as one among the remaining set of possibilities, is regarded as corroborated. In much theoretical scientific practice an extreme convention is followed in determining the acceptability of the alternate hypothesis—the requirement that the null hypothesis be rejected at the .05 (.01) level. Insistence on what is, in effect, an absolute criterion of significance is usually rationalized on the grounds of the serious consequences resulting from acceptance of erroneous findings into the superstructure of scientific knowledge. Although application of the concept of probability to theoretical relationships appears to have no clear bearing on their correspondence to a given set of observed data, statistical inference procedures are essential to the technical purpose of insuring sufficient stability of an observation to make its investigation possible.

The criteria of acceptability of findings appropriate for the purpose of the engineer differ in several important respects from those outlined immediately above. The alternatives tested by the demonstration experiment are not model relationships, but are, instead, possible courses of action in the world of operations. The universes of observations on which inductive inferences of the present type rest can never be exhaustively sampled. Therefore, the probability values which outcomes may assume will vary continuously between the limits of zero and one, without attaining either value. Moreover, it seldom makes sense to employ the value of chance as the baseline from which a practical outcome must differ in order to achieve significance. The alternative to be compared with the experimental treatment is virtually never based on complete ignorance. The basis of comparison will, hence, be some alternative procedure that meets the requirement of action with some finite degree of efficiency. A standard often employed for this purpose is the existing action procedure; for example, SHOCKACTION VI used the conventional course of armor training. In general, the question of acceptability of findings in engineering studies takes the following form: at a specified level of risk, should action alternative A, which has been demonstrated to yield a criterion score higher by a given increment, be adopted over action alternative B, for situations that fall within the class of the one investigated?

The practical issue is usually whether the degree of likelihood of reproducibility under operational conditions, taken together with the increment of improvement in terms of gains and costs, are sufficient to justify one line of administrative action over another. In making such judgments, Type II statistical errors, which weigh the cost of erroneously rejecting useful courses of action, are appropriately given more consideration than they are in theoretical research. It is apparent, for example, in the case of the mentally incurable, that a small increment of improvement observed in response to administration of a new drug would often be sufficient basis for more extended use— even when the risk that its effects would not be duplicated in actual practice may be considerable. On the contrary, rejection of the treatment under such conditions should be based on the most cogent counterevidence—damaging side effects, death of the patient, or other equally undesirable consequences. Particularly in the case of military decisions, the need for improved courses of action may often be great enough to warrant acceptance of a small advantage together with grave risk of failure. Saving two weeks' time through the use of the training program developed by SHOCKACTION VI could, almost regardless of other costs, represent a critical gain under the necessity for rapid military mobilization. Criteria of acceptable inference that minimize the likelihood of Type II errors are seldom appropriate for practical problems. Indeed, the methods of statistical hypothesis-testing generally appear to be better suited to the requirements of the theoretical researcher. The methods of statistical estimation, which permit statement of the limits within which a difference may range, are more directly applicable to the problems of the engineering psychologist. The practitioner is usually more interested in the estimation question of how much difference, than in the hypothesis-testing question of whether there is any difference.

Confusion between *statistical* and *practical* significance in the research literature takes a variety of forms. One of the most common errors of the present type is the view, usually adamantly held, that the stringent statistical criterion of theoretical research alone defines "real" significance as contrasted with some second-class or makeshift variety. Scarcely less incongruous is the growing practice of assigning two significance values, one *statistical,* the other *practical,* to the same research outcome. Not uncommonly, small differences measured between groups, when statistical significance is mainly accountable in terms of a large number of observations, are of trivial consequence to the administrator for whose purposes significance must be measured in dollars or in other comparable gains and costs. Under other circumstances, a small difference that falls considerably below the criterion of conventional statistical significance may represent a finding of extreme practical value.

▣ PRINCIPLE VERSUS POPULATION GENERALITY

Up to now our consideration of generality has been limited to the question of reliability—that is, whether the quantitative incidence of certain characteristics noted in a sample of observations will also hold of its parent population. Another meaning of generality, however, deals with the extensibility of findings beyond the set of conditions under which they have been demonstrated to hold. The following are examples of the present kind of question: can Miller's preliminary model of conflict behavior be extended to subsume the complex phenomena of displaced aggression; or, will the SHOCKACTION VI training, which has been developed on a sample of trainees limited in range of age and geographic origin, continue to yield superior scores when applied to a new batch of trainees who differ in these characteristics? The questions suggest two distinguishable bases of generalization. One is of theoretical importance, and rests on the assumption that an invariable relationship applies in a particular case. The other, of practical importance, is based on the premise that a given sample is representative of its universe.

Population inferences are grounded in the logic of classification. Sharp limitations are imposed on generalization of the present type by difficulties encountered in specifying relationships between classes. An important example of this weakness is seen in the field of psychometric testing, where the relationships among a large number of "blind," *ad hoc,* testing instruments have long continued to remain unknown. The same kind of limitation holds of studies like SHOCKACTION VI, which yield no formal basis for inferring that the improvement in efficiency observed in the experimental situation would continue to hold if conditions were changed in any way. Some increment of generality may, of course, be attained by empirically demonstrating that results are not impaired by a particular alteration in the attributes that define the class of such studies. But the number of possible attributes to be eliminated in this way is, in any practical situation, usually so formidable as to preclude any high degree of generality based on content. As a matter of practice, informal guidance is often provided by common sense, or by accumulated empirical findings with respect to particular variables or their magnitudes, that can be altered without compromising the result. As a consequence of the difficulties inherent in systematizing the accumulated findings of individual engineering studies, a science of *psychotechnology,* which relies heavily on the integration of such outcomes, exists mainly as a program for future effort. Engineering studies are neither designed nor undertaken primarily to yield an integrated body of principles. Systematization of findings derived from studies undertaken essentially to cope with practical problems, in which many different unanalyzed complexes have been permitted to vary in unknown ways, poses a task which yields to attack only grudgingly.

Principle generality bases its inferences on the logic of relations. Groupings of observations into classes according to their attributes are replaced by dimensions that permit observations, within defined limits, to assume continuous values, and that can be related to other dimensions prescribed by a particular model. In the reference study of conflict behavior, Miller's model, for example, relates the dimensions of approach, avoidance, motivation, and reinforcement, within defined limits. Generalization becomes a matter of extending the scope of a limited model to a more complex set of phenomena. An effort is made to determine whether the new conditions are of the sort to which the model has application. If these antecedent conditions have been demonstrated, by means of independent criteria, to obtain, the consequence specified by the model *must* follow. With the preliminary establishment of a model relationship, further research efforts will be directed at determining, systematically, results yielded by other combinations of the parametric values. Miller's subsequent extension of the preliminary conflict model to certain phenomena of projective testing illustrates, in a very primitive way, use of generalization procedures of the kind under consideration.

⊡ ABSTRACT PREDICTIONS VERSUS FORECASTING

The outcome of a controlled laboratory investigation yields a basis for *abstract prediction*. When the specified conditions under which a generalization has been demonstrated obtain, the result of a change in the independent factors can be predicted with precision. Thus, it can be asserted with a high degree of confidence that under the *pure* conditions of the chemical laboratory, water vapor, when contained within a confined volume of air at a given temperature and pressure, will be precipitated. Similarly, in the area of human factors, numerous studies have demonstrated that, *ceteris paribus,* acquisition of a habit is facilitated by letting the learner know how effective his performance has been. For the purpose of theoretical science, the goal of an investigation is achieved with the statement of a general relationship of the present type—that is, a conclusion. For application to a *real life* problem, however, the closed system of parameters must be opened up to the influences introduced by the complex environment of a particular operationa! system. Thus, to apply the gas laws to a set of actual meteorological conditions requires, in addition to an understanding of the basic relationships involved, evaluation of the conditions that obtain within the air masses involved. Likewise, in an actual training situation, to assert with confidence that feedback of results will improve learning hinges on the possibility of identifying and evaluating the relevant empirical factors included in the complex of events. Knowledge of such factors as the amount and kind of content to be mastered, length of practice sessions, incentives, and rewards and punishments, would be required to provide a sound basis for forecasting successful articulation of the principle of feedback into the system of training involved. Thus an abstract relationship may yield an *implication* for action, but without a formal estimate of the likelihood of its applicability to a particular set of operational conditions it fails to lend a complete basis for *recommending* that a particular course of action be taken. The field test plays a crucial role in bridging the gap between abstract predictions based on theoretical relationships, and the concrete variable interactions of actual environments.

In contrast to the indeterminate degree to which abstract predictions may apply to a particular set of operational conditions, the relevance of engineering forecasts is direct and immediate. This important difference stems from the fact that the behavioral engineer builds the higher order interactions among the situational variables into the forecaster terms of his formula. Thus, in SHOCKACTION VI, the developed training program was tested in the context of actual Army operations. The closer the degree of similarity between the experimental conditions and those that might be presumed to hold later in the criterial situation, the greater the likelihood that the developed program would work when plugged into the operational system of armor training. *An engineering forecast, then, provides a direct basis for recommended action* because the degree of replicability of the effect of the developed conditions within the total system environment can be estimated. As a practical matter, operational environments are often unstable, and the effects of extraneous factors that are unrepresented in the forecaster term cannot be taken into account. To cope with such unforeseeable intrusions, the engineering psychologist finds it necessary, as a matter of practice, to hedge his recommendations by means of ample safety factors.

Finally, to assert that the outcomes of theoretical research studies are stated as conclusions, while those of engineering research are framed as recommendations, is true only in a relative sense. The results of either approach to research may have implications for both the systems of knowledge and action. Both are subject to the reign of the pragmatic principle, but under value structures which are different. The engineer's action must be immediately tested against those values that inhere in the world of affairs, while the action taken by the theoretical scientist must meet that criterion of value that is appropriate to building a system of knowledge.

Whether a stated outcome is a recommendation or a conclusion can only be defined relatively to the purposes of action. Viewed from within the limited system of science, the conclusions of theoretical research are, in fact, implicit recommendations for that special kind of action that seeks primarily to extend our understanding of nature. From the same perspective, the engineer's recommendations are accorded the status of information, since they have not yet been transformed into principles of action of the type useful for theoretical purposes. From the more inclusive viewpoint of the world of affairs, the engineer's recommendations serve as formulas for immediate action directed toward controlling the environment; the conclusions of the theoretical scientist now serve the purpose of information to be adapted to the practical requirements of action.

REFERENCES

Anastasi, A. 1950. The concept of validity in the interpretation of test scores. *Educ. psychol. Measmt., 10,* 67–78.

Bechtoldt, H. P. 1959. Construct validity: A critique. *Amer. Psychologist, 14,* 619–628.

Boldyreff, A. W. 1954. *Systems engineering.* Santa Monica: The RAND Corporation. Report P–537.

Bridgman, P. 1927. *The logic of modern physics.* New York: Macmillan.

Bross, I. D. 1953. *Design for decision.* New York: Macmillan.

Brunswik, E. 1956. *Perception and the representative design of psychological experiments.* Berkeley: University of California Press.

Cartwright, D. 1959. Lewinian theory as a contemporary systematic framework. In Koch, S. (ed.), *Psychology: a study of a science,* Vol. 2. New York: McGraw-Hill, 7–91.

Cartwright, D. 1949. Basic and applied social psychology. *Phil. Sci., 16,* 198–208.

Cassirer, E. 1953. *Substance and function.* New York: Dover.

Cochran, W. G. 1960. The design of experiments. In Flagle, C. C., Huggins, W. H., and Roy, R. H. (ed.), *Operations research and systems engineering.* Baltimore: Johns Hopkins Press, 508–533.

Cronbach, L. J. 1957. The two disciplines of scientific psychology. *Amer. Psychologist, 12,* 671–684.

Cronbach, L. J., and Meehl, P. E. 1955. Construct validity in psychological tests. *Psychol. Bull., 52,* 281–302.

Festinger, L., and Katz, D. (ed.). 1953. *Research methods in the behavioral sciences.* New York: Holt.

Festinger, L. 1953. Laboratory experiments. In Festinger, L., and Katz, D. (eds.), *Research methods in the behavioral sciences.* New York: Holt.

Fisher, R. A. 1951. *The design of experiments* (6th ed.). Edinburgh: Oliver & Boyd.

Flagle, C. C., Huggins, W. H., and Roy, R. H. (ed.). 1960. *Operations research and systems engineering.* Baltimore: Johns Hopkins Press.

French, J. R. 1953. Experiments in field settings. In Festinger, L., and Katz, D. (ed.), *Research methods in the behavioral sciences.* New York: Holt, 98–135.

Garner, W. R., Hake, H. W., and Eriksen, C. W. 1956. Operationism and the concept of perception. *Psychol. Rev., 63,* 149–159.

George, F. H. 1953. Logical constructs and psychological theory. *Psychol. Rev., 60,* 1–6.

Gibson, R. E. 1960. The recognition of systems engineering. In Flagle, C. C., Huggins, W. H., and Roy, R. H. (ed.), *Operations research and systems engineering.* Baltimore: Johns Hopkins Press, 58–81.

Hauser, P. M. 1949. Social science and social engineering. *Phil. Sci., 16,* 209–218.

Helmer, O., and Rescher, O. 1960. *On the epistomology of the inexact sciences.* Santa Monica: The RAND Corporation. Report R–353.

Hilgard, E. R. 1958. Intervening variables, hypothetical constructs, parameters and constants. *Amer. J. Psychol., 71,* 238–246.

Hull, C. L. 1943. *Principles of behavior.* New York: Appleton.

Koch, S. (ed.) 1959. *Psychology: a study of a science,* Vol. 2. New York: McGraw-Hill.

Lachman, R. 1960. The model in theory construction. *Psychol. Rev., 67,* 113–129.

Lewin, K. 1951. *Field theory in social science.* New York: Harper.

Loevinger, J. 1957. Objective tests as instruments of psychological theory. *Psychol. Rep., 3,* 635–694.

MacCaslin, E. F., Woodruff, A. B., and Baker, R. A. 1959. *Shockaction VI: An improved advanced individual training program for armor.* Washington, D. C.: The George Washington University, Human Resources Research Office.

McFann, H. H., Hammes, J. A., and Taylor, J. E. 1955. *Trainfire I: A new course in basic rifle marksmanship.* Washington, D. C.: The George Washington University, Human Resources Research Office.

McGrath, J. E., Nordlie, P. G., and Vaughan, W. S. 1959. *A systematic framework for comparison of system research methods.* Arlington, Va.: Human Sciences Research, Inc., November. Report No. 1.

Meadows, P. 1957. Models, systems, and science. *Amer. sociol. Rev., 22,* 3–9.

Melton, A. W. 1952. Military requirements for the systematic study of psychological variables. In J. C. Flanagan *et al., Current trends in psychology in the world emergency.* Pittsburgh: Univ. of Pittsburgh Press.

Merton, R. K. 1949. The role of applied social science in the formation of policy: A research memorandum. *Phil. Sci., 16,* 161–181.

Miller, J. G. 1955. Toward a general theory for the behavioral sciences. *Amer. Psychologist, 10,* 523.

Miller, N. 1951. Comments on theoretical models. *J. Pers., 20,* 82–100.

Miller, N. E. 1959. Liberalization of basic S-R concepts: extensions to conflict behavior, motivation, and social learning. In Koch, S. (ed.), *Psychology: a study of a science,* Vol. 2. New York: McGraw-Hill, 196–292.

Peak, H. 1953. Problems of objective observation. In Festinger, L., and Katz, D. (ed.), *Research methods in the behavioral sciences.* New York: Holt, 243–299.

Rommetveit, R. 1955. Model construction in psychology: A defense of "surplus meaning" of psychological constructs. *Acta Psychol., 11,* 335–345.

Rosenblueth, A., and Weiner, N. 1945. The role of models in science. *Phil. Sci., 12,* 316–321.

Selltiz, C., and Cook, S. W. 1948. Can research in social science be both socially useful and scientificially meaningful? *Amer. Sociol. Rev., 13,* 454–459.

Shils, E. A. 1949. Social science and social policy. *Phil. Sci., 16,* 219–242.

Sidman, M. 1960. *The tactics of scientific research.* New York: Basic Books.

Skinner, B. F. 1938. *The behavior of organisms.* New York: Appleton.

Tolman, E. C. 1932. *Purposive behavior in animals and men.* New York: Appleton.

Von Bertalanffy, L. 1950. An outline of general systems theory. *British J. Phil. Sci., 1,* 156–157.

Von Bertalanffy, L. 1955. General system theory. *Main Currents in Modern Thought, 11,* 77.

Zubin, J. 1952. On the powers of models. *J. Pers., 20,* 430–439.

INDEX